"Dr. Barrett has gathered a full stable of blue-ribbon theologians for this winning volume. All the essays are carefully contextualized, the Reformers judiciously selected, and the bibliographies thoughtfully assembled. Some chapters are especially notable for the breadth and depth of the author's research, others for their adroit summaries of complex themes. There is little doubt that *Reformation Theology* will ably serve the church and academy as a textbook for students and a reference work for scholars. It is already reshaping my own teaching on late-medieval and early-modern theology, and I commend it heartily."

Chad Van Dixhoorn, Chancellor's Professor of Historical Theology, Reformed Theological Seminary–Washington, DC

"This delightful volume is a breath of fresh air in Reformation studies, putting theology back at the center. It shows with crystal clarity how the Reformers expounded the heart of the Christian faith, and why these evangelical doctrines still matter so much."

Andrew Atherstone, Latimer Research Fellow, Wycliffe Hall, University of Oxford

"This rich book takes up the challenge to think beyond 2017 and does so in a very stimulating manner. Each of the contributors is an expert in his field and knows that the Reformation is a highly relevant treasure for both the church and theology. They convincingly encourage the readers to think through this treasure and adopt it. Everyone eager not just to look back at five hundred years of reformation but also to look forward finds here the perfect material."

Herman Selderhuis, Director, Refo500; Professor and Director of the Institute for Reformation Research, Theological University Apeldoorn, the Netherlands; author, *Calvin's Theology of the Psalms*

"Dr. Matthew Barrett has assembled a first-rate team of pastors and scholars to write an anniversary volume of the Reformation that promises to receive a welcoming readership across a wide spectrum of the evangelical community. At a time when some are suggesting that for all practical purposes the Reformation is 'over,' Barrett's *Reformation Theology* offers a needed corrective by showing the relevance of the Reformation for healthy church ministry and the Christian life today."

Philip Graham Ryken, President, Wheaton College; author, *Loving the Way Jesus Loves*

"This collection of essays is both necessary and appropriate. It's necessary because the issues addressed mattered then and matter now. It's appropriate because this is how we best remember our past and honor the Reformers. The Reformation is our pivot point in the past, and the issues it addressed remain the pivot point for church life and discipleship."

Stephen J. Nichols, President, Reformation Bible College; Chief Academic Officer, Ligonier Ministries; author, *Martin Luther: A Guided Tour of His Life and Thought* and *The Reformation: How a Monk and a Mallet Changed the World*

"A superb collection of first-rate essays on Reformation theology—one of the best I have seen. A welcome addition to the swell of literature in this year of Reformation remembrance."

Timothy George, Founding Dean, Beeson Divinity School; General Editor, Reformation Commentary on Scripture

"An anniversary is a great moment to do a book like *Reformation Theology*. And with the passing of time, Reformation truths and the importance of the Reformation as a milestone in church history get forgotten—incredible as that sounds. But it is true. Perhaps we should not be surprised. How many times in the Old Testament do we read that the Israelites 'forgot'? So I am enthusiastic about *Reformation Theology*."

David F. Wells, Distinguished Senior Research Professor, Gordon-Conwell Theological Seminary; author, *The Courage to Be Protestant: Truth-Lovers, Marketers and Emergents in the Postmodern World*

"Matthew Barrett is certainly to be congratulated on bringing together this outstanding group of top-tier theologians and Reformation scholars to produce this wonderful resource. Not only are readers given a masterful survey of historical theology illuminating the key reformational themes of the sixteenth century, but also we are provided thoughtful and insightful guidance to wrestle with the important theological issues facing the church in the twenty-first century. I am delighted to recommend this comprehensive work."

David S. Dockery, President, Trinity International University

"*Reformation Theology* promises to be an influential book indeed. Written by recognized historians and theologians, this volume aims to clearly articulate the teaching of the Reformers according to traditional theological categories. It is a genuine contribution and a great read besides."

Fred G. Zaspel, Pastor, Reformed Baptist Church, Franconia, Pennsylvania; author, *The Theology of B. B. Warfield: A Systematic Summary* and *Warfield on the Christian Life: Living in Light of the Gospel*

"Nothing would benefit American evangelicals more than a real rediscovery of the Reformation—not a superficial regurgitation of the familiar talking points but a powerful, experiential encounter with the learned depth, wisdom, humility, piety, and practical know-how of our Reformation forefathers. A volume like the one Dr. Matthew Barrett has put together is a big step in the right direction."

Greg Forster, Director, Oikonomia Network at the Center for Transformational Churches, Trinity International University; author, *The Joy of Calvinism*

"The lineup of authors in *Reformation Theology* and their respective topics reflect the very best in Reformed evangelical scholarship. The book should be of widespread interest. Not only would seminary and college students find the volume profitable in their studies, but all informed Christians would benefit from the essays."

W. Andrew Hoffecker, Professor of Church History Emeritus, Reformed Theological Seminary–Jackson; author, *Charles Hodge: The Pride of Princeton*

"A clear articulation of one's Reformed faith requires familiarity with the ideas and events in which that faith is rooted. Unfortunately, there are few books on the subject currently in print that are both learned and accessible. Thankfully, this volume offers an outstanding solution to this problem."

Chris Castaldo, Pastor, New Covenant Church, Naperville, Illinois; author, *Talking with Catholics about the Gospel*; coauthor, *The Unfinished Reformation: What Unites and Divides Catholics and Protestants after 500 Years*

Reformation Theology

A Systematic Summary

Edited by Matthew Barrett

Prologue by Michael Horton

∷ CROSSWAY®

WHEATON, ILLINOIS

Reformation Theology: A Systematic Summary

Copyright © 2017 by Matthew Barrett

Published by Crossway
       1300 Crescent Street
       Wheaton, Illinois 60187

Cover design: Tim Green, Faceout Studio

Cover image: Martin Luther before the Diet of Worms, 1965 (color litho), Taubert, Wolfgang / Deutsches Historiches Museum, Berlin, Germany / © DHM Bridgeman Images

First printing 2017

Printed in the United States of America

Hardcover ISBN: 978-1-4335-4328-9
ePub ISBN: 978-1-4335-4331-9
PDF ISBN: 978-1-4335-4329-6
Mobipocket ISBN: 978-1-4335-4330-2

Library of Congress Cataloging-in-Publication Data

Names: Barrett, Matthew, 1982– editor. | Horton, Michael Scott, writer of prologue.
Title: Reformation theology : a systematic summary / edited by Matthew Barrett ; prologue by Michael Horton.
Description: Wheaton, Illinois : Crossway, 2017. | Includes bibliographical references and index.
Identifiers: LCCN 2016022741 (print) | LCCN 2016025534 (ebook) | ISBN 9781433543289 (hc) | ISBN
    9781433543296 (pdf) | ISBN 9781433543302 (mobi) | ISBN 9781433543319 (epub)
Subjects: LCSH: Reformation. | Theology, Doctrinal—History—16th century.
Classification: LCC BR305.3 .R425 2017 (print) | LCC BR305.3 (ebook) | DDC 230/.4—dc23
LC record available at https://lccn.loc.gov/2016022741

Crossway is a publishing ministry of Good News Publishers.

SH   28   27   26   25   24   23   22   21   20   19   18   17
16   15   14   13   12   11   10   9   8   7   6   5   4   3   2   1

This book is dedicated to my father, Michael Barrett. You are always so very proud of me for becoming a theologian. I hope this book makes you all the more proud. Thank you for your love and encouragement from beginning to end.

Contents

Prologue..13
    What Are We Celebrating? Taking Stock after Five Centuries
    Michael Horton

Abbreviations..37

INTRODUCTION

1   The Crux of Genuine Reform 43
    Matthew Barrett

PART 1: HISTORICAL BACKGROUND
TO THE REFORMATION

2   Late-Medieval Theology..67
    Gerald Bray

3   The Reformers and Their Reformations 111
    Carl R. Trueman and Eunjin Kim

PART 2: REFORMATION THEOLOGY

4   *Sola Scriptura*...145
    Mark D. Thompson

5   The Holy Trinity 189
    Michael Reeves

6   The Being and Attributes of God................................217
    Scott R. Swain

7   Predestination and Election..241
    Cornelis P. Venema

8   Creation, Mankind, and the Image of God........................283
    Douglas F. Kelly

9   The Person of Christ..313
    Robert Letham

10 The Work of Christ...347
    Donald Macleod

11 The Holy Spirit...393
    Graham A. Cole

12 Union with Christ..423
    J. V. Fesko

13 The Bondage and Liberation of the Will..........................451
    Matthew Barrett

14 Justification by Faith Alone.......................................511
    Korey D. Maas

15 Sanctification, Perseverance, and Assurance.....................549
    Michael Allen

16 The Church..577
    Robert Kolb

17 Baptism..609
    Aaron Clay Denlinger

18 The Lord's Supper..643
    Keith A. Mathison

19 The Relationship of Church and State............................675
    Peter A. Lillback

20 Eschatology...721
    Kim Riddlebarger

Contributors 757

Name Index. 762

Subject Index. 769

Scripture Index. 780

Prologue

What Are We Celebrating?

Taking Stock after Five Centuries

Launching the festivities for the celebration of the Reformation's five hundredth anniversary, a joint service is planned for Lund, Sweden, on October 31, 2016, led by Pope Francis and Lutheran World Federation president Bishop Munib Younan. In the run-up to an official commemoration in Wittenberg exactly one year later, an international and ecumenical church convention is scheduled for May, according to a World Council of Churches report, with one hundred thousand attendees expected for the Berlin event. "Reformation means courageously seeking what is new and turning away from old, familiar customs," according to the convention's president, Christina Aus der Au of Switzerland.[1]

Comments like this one, already replete in the mainline Protestant world, illustrate the wide variations in interpreting the Reformation and its ongoing significance. Many of these erstwhile heirs of the Reformation have long since moved the creeds and confessions to the "Historical Documents" section of the hymnal. As the mighty river

---

1. Quoted in Stephen Brown, "Reformation celebrations will be ecumenical and international, says German Protestant leader," World Council of Churches, May 12, 2016, https:// www.oikoumene.org/en/press-centre/news/reformation-celebrations-will-be-ecumenical-and -international-says-german-protestant-leader.

has become a virtually dry riverbed, one wonders how such crowds can be mustered to celebrate a movement whose teachings are today less significant to inhabitants of Wittenberg and Geneva than they are to many in Indonesia, Nigeria, and Seoul.

But what of the historical evangelical witness? Arising out of various Protestant revival movements in the eighteenth century, evangelical mission societies were formed in the old Reformation capitols and for a time breathed new life into churches and institutions that, to a large extent, had succumbed to Enlightenment rationalism and doctrinal indifference. In many instances, Lutheran and Reformed theology combined with Pietism to form a creative if sometimes combustible mixture. Although a relatively small but vigorous evangelical party thrives today in the Church of England (and smaller ones in the Episcopal churches of the United States and Canada), the strength of evangelical Anglicanism has shifted to the Global South.

To be sure, there is a substantial presence of continuing churches of the Reformation in the United States, including, for example, over 2 million Missouri Synod Lutherans, 350,000 Wisconsin Evangelical Lutheran Church members, and about the same number who belong to the Presbyterian Church in America. However, these tallies are dwarfed by their Global South partners. To offer only a few examples, the Presbyterian Church in Nigeria numbers 4 million, and the Evangelical Reformed Churches of Christ, centered in the Plateau region, boasts around 1.5 million communicant members. The National Presbyterian Church of Mexico reports 2.8 million members, and there are 10 million Presbyterians in South Korea, most of whom are much more conservative than the mainline Presbyterian Church (USA). It is a similar story throughout the majority world. In many if not most of these instances, the growth has been due to the mixture of confessionalism and pietism that was brought by missionaries and now thrives in the seminaries and churches.

Doctrine: From Minimalism to Indifference[2]

British and North American evangelicalism has always been a coat of many colors in terms of doctrine and practice. In addition to the

2. This and the following section borrow and adapt material from Michael S. Horton, "To Be or Not to Be: The Uneasy Relationship between Reformed Christianity and American Evangelicalism," *Modern Reformation* 17, no. 6 (2008): 18–21. Used by permission of *Modern Reformation*.

older traditions of the Reformation and Pietism, it has been shaped by revivalism and the massive upheaval in mainline Protestantism that eventually split into modernist and fundamentalist camps. Many confessional Lutherans as well as Presbyterian, Reformed, and Anglican churches found themselves divided from one another. On the one hand, they found allies among those who were willing to take unambiguous stands on the authority of Scripture and salvation by grace alone in Christ alone through faith alone. They stood shoulder to shoulder in their defense and proclamation of Christ's deity, vicarious death for sinners, resurrection, and bodily return. On the other hand, confessional churches found themselves somewhat alienated by fundamentalist obscurantism, legalism, and end-time scenarios. When a united evangelical stand was to be taken, it always seemed that it was the confessional churches rather than those of the more revivalistic orientation that had to suppress confessional distinctives that were for them hardly peripheral matters.

And yet, it seems to be in these broader evangelical circles where renewed interest in the Reformation erupts periodically. The most recent example, at least in the United States, is the enormously successful effort of the Gospel Coalition, founded by Tim Keller and D. A. Carson. Though far from alone, the Gospel Coalition has awakened widespread interest globally in the authority of Scripture, Christ-centered proclamation, and God's grace in justifying and sanctifying sinners. Yet even this promising movement exhibits some of the weaknesses as well as strengths of American evangelicalism. Reading through the Book of Concord, the Three Forms of Unity, the Westminster Standards, and the Thirty-Nine Articles, one appreciates the concern to confess the fullness of the ecumenical, catholic, and evangelical faith rather than to reduce the essentials to a few propositions.

The *strength* of evangelicalism is its minimalism. While sometimes moving peripheral matters to the center and more central convictions to the realm of nonessentials, the focus on Scripture, Christ's person and work, the necessity of the new birth, and Christ's return has afforded not only a wide berth for cooperation but also a laser focus on contested points. The *weakness* of evangelicalism is also its minimalism. Doctrinal minimalism in one generation can be a way of focusing the fight; in another, the path to doctrinal indifference.

In 1920, a "plan of union for evangelical churches" was put forward. The Princeton theologian B. B. Warfield evaluated the "creed" of this plan as it was being studied by Presbyterians. Warfield observed that the new confession being proposed "contains nothing which is not believed by Evangelicals," and yet "nothing which is not believed . . . by the adherents of the Church of Rome, for example." As he summed it up,

> There is nothing about justification by faith in this creed. And that means that all the gains obtained in that great religious movement which we call the Reformation are cast out of the window. . . . There is nothing about the atonement in the blood of Christ in this creed. And that means that the whole gain of the long mediaeval search after truth is thrown summarily aside. . . . There is nothing about sin and grace in this creed. . . . We need not confess our sins anymore; we need not recognize the existence of such a thing. We need believe in the Holy Spirit only "as guide and comforter"—do not the Rationalists do the same? And this means that all the gain the whole world has reaped from the great Augustinian conflict goes out of the window with the rest. . . . It is just as true that the gains of the still earlier debates which occupied the first age of the Church's life, through which we attained to the understanding of the fundamental truths of the Trinity and the Deity of Christ are discarded by this creed also. There is no Trinity in this creed; no Deity of Christ—or of the Holy Spirit.[3]

Where justification through faith is the heart of the evangel, how can "evangelicals" omit it from their common confession? "Is this the kind of creed," Warfield continued, "which twentieth-century Presbyterianism will find sufficient as a basis for co-operation in evangelistic activities? Then it can get along in its evangelistic activities without the gospel. For it is precisely the gospel that this creed neglects altogether." Warfield concluded, "Fellowship is a good word, and a great duty. But

---

3. B. B. Warfield, "In Behalf of Evangelical Religion," in *Selected Shorter Writings of Benjamin B. Warfield* (Nutley, NJ: Presbyterian and Reformed, 1970), 1:386.

our fellowship, according to Paul, must be in 'the furtherance of the gospel.'"[4]

The current doctrinal statement of the National Association of Evangelicals (NAE) at least improves on the "creed" that Warfield criticized. Yet, like that 1921 statement, the NAE basis includes nothing to which a Roman Catholic could not yield assent in good conscience:

> We believe the Bible to be the inspired, the only infallible, authoritative Word of God.
>
> We believe that there is one God, eternally existent in three persons: Father, Son and Holy Spirit.
>
> We believe in the deity of our Lord Jesus Christ, in His virgin birth, in His sinless life, in His miracles, in His vicarious and atoning death through His shed blood, in His bodily resurrection, in His ascension to the right hand of the Father, and in His personal return in power and glory.
>
> We believe that for the salvation of lost and sinful people, regeneration by the Holy Spirit is absolutely essential.
>
> We believe in the present ministry of the Holy Spirit by whose indwelling the Christian is enabled to live a godly life.
>
> We believe in the resurrection of both the saved and the lost; they that are saved unto the resurrection of life and they that are lost unto the resurrection of damnation.
>
> We believe in the spiritual unity of believers in our Lord Jesus Christ.[5]

There is nothing about the sacraments, of course. We may lament the failure of the Reformers to find unity on the scriptural doctrine, but as J. Gresham Machen observed, all the parties at least thought that the Eucharist was central enough to provoke debate. But the tendency in evangelicalism has been to conclude that whatever is not included in its "statements of faith" is of secondary importance and is "not a gospel issue."

In contrast with the confessions and catechisms produced by the magisterial Reformation, this NAE statement not only leaves out

---

4. Ibid., 1:387.
5. "Statement of Faith," National Association of Evangelicals, accessed June 2, 2016, http://nae.net/statement-of-faith/.

entirely the central article of justification (while including the new birth) but fails even to express the *catholic* heart of evangelical faith. It bears the marks of a doctrinal minimalism that has increasingly accommodated a doctrinal indifference in evangelical circles.

For some reason, we acquired the assumption that if we surrendered the confession, we could keep the creed; then, if we surrendered the creed, we could keep a few fundamentals. At the end of the line arrives a generation that does not even know enough of its legacy to be aware when it is straying from or rejecting it. Fundamentalism devolved into a spirit of controversy without its proper coordinates; evangelicalism sought to correct the imbalance but did so by further downplaying the richness of the Reformation confessions—even in their differences.

"Protestantism without the Reformation"

Winding up his lecture tour in the United States before returning to Europe, where he would meet his death in a Nazi concentration camp, Dietrich Bonhoeffer (1906–1945) described America as "Protestantism without the Reformation."[6] Although the influence of the Reformation in America's religious history has been profound (especially prior to the mid-nineteenth century), and remains a counterweight to the dominance of the revivalist heritage, Bonhoeffer's diagnosis seems justified:

> God has granted American Christianity no Reformation. He has given it strong revivalist preachers, churchmen and theologians, but no Reformation of the church of Jesus Christ by the Word of God. . . . American theology and the American church as a whole have never been able to understand the meaning of "criticism" by the Word of God and all that signifies. Right to the last they do not understand that God's "criticism" touches even religion, the Christianity of the church and the sanctification of Christians, and that God has founded his church beyond religion and beyond ethics. . . . In American theology, Christianity is still essentially religion and ethics. . . . Because of this the person and work of Christ must,

---

6. Dietrich Bonhoeffer, "Protestantism without the Reformation," in *The Collected Works of Dietrich Bonhoeffer*, vol. 1, *No Rusty Swords: Letters, Lectures and Notes, 1928–1936*, ed. Edwin H. Robertson, trans. Edwin H. Robertson and John Bowden (London: Collins, 1965), 92–118.

for theology, sink into the background and in the long run remain misunderstood, because it is not recognized as the sole ground of radical judgment and radical forgiveness.[7]

The career of Charles G. Finney (1792–1875) illustrates the extent to which evangelical revivalism can stray from the evangelical convictions of the Reformation. Setting aside the sufficiency of Scripture for the message and methods of outreach, Finney devised new methods based on his conviction that the new birth was as natural as any conversion from one form of behavior to another. Rejecting the doctrines of Christ's substitutionary atonement as contrary to reason and morality, he called the doctrine of justification by Christ's imputed righteousness "another gospel." Referring to the Westminster Confession's statement on justification, Finney declared, "If this is not antinomianism, I know not what is." Justification by Christ's imputed righteousness not only is "absurd" but also undermines all motivation for personal and social holiness. In fact, "full present obedience is a condition of justification." No one can be justified "while sin, any degree of sin, remains in him." The teaching that believers are "simultaneously justified and sinful," he judged, "has slain more souls, I fear, than all the universalism that ever cursed the world." "Representing the atonement as the ground of the sinner's justification has been a sad occasion of stumbling to many."[8] Finney's system, with its Pelagian tendencies, went well beyond anything that the Reformers faced from the Council of Trent. If Pelagianism is the natural religion of the fallen heart, it is especially evident in the religious history of a nation devoted to the self-made individual.

American Christianity has not been without its heroic defenders of the faith. In fact, British and American evangelicals have contributed the most energetic efforts on behalf of, as well as detractions from, the *evangel* in the modern age. In the majority world, the torch is carried by Archbishop Henry Luke Orombi of Uganda, Stephen Tong in Indonesia, Nam-Joon Kim in Seoul, Paul Swarup in Delhi, and countless others who—without fanfare and prestige—proclaim Christ as the

---

7. Ibid., 117–18.
8. All references from Charles G. Finney, *Systematic Theology* (1846; repr., Minneapolis: Bethany Fellowship, 1976), 46, 57, 321–22.

only hope of sinners to the nations. Not all "evangelical creeds" are minimalistic like the one evaluated by Warfield.

Yet as we survey the landscape of global Christianity, it would appear that diverse and even contradictory streams weave in and out of each other under the name *evangelical*. I am haunted by John Stott's warning to me years ago that evangelicalism is "growing, but superficial." All that I have said in favor of the growth of evangelical Christianity in the Global South must be qualified by Stott's observation, informed by a long ministry that has contributed in no small part to that success. As the 2010 Lausanne event in Cape Town highlighted, one of the greatest threats to Christianity, especially (but by no means exclusively) in Africa, is the prosperity gospel. In addition, wherever the North Atlantic academies (including some evangelical seminaries) continue their influence, the Global South will be increasingly infected by the trends that have corrupted our own schools and churches.

Sola: Should We Still Protest?

Stirring up dissension, a false teacher has "an unhealthy craving for controversy and for quarrels about words," Paul warns (1 Tim. 6:4). But sometimes a word makes all the difference; in fact, as Cardinal Newman observed, the Rubicon between heresy and orthodoxy with respect to the *homoousion* debate was as thin as a single vowel. Similarly, the entire Reformation controversy turned on the qualifier *sola*— "only."

This too would be just another form of minimalism if the Reformation had reduced its confession to "the five solas." However, this it did not do. After all, it was not just a movement; it was a continuing Christian tradition—a reformed catholic church, in spite of its own quarrels and dissensions. The evangelical confessions and catechisms that came out of that era incorporated all the great achievements of the patristic consensus, carefully and discerningly included sound insights of medieval theology, and encompassed the essential truths of Scripture reaching from creation to consummation. Thus, the churches of the Reformation were defined not merely by what distinguished them from other professing churches but also by what they shared as a common treasury.

Having said that, *sola* was—and remains—an important word. Of course, all parties at that time agreed that Scripture is God's infallible revelation. Yet in addition to the scriptural letter, there was the "living voice" of the magisterium that could establish new articles of faith and practice. Of course, everyone believed in the necessity of grace, faith, and Christ. But free will must cooperate with grace, and faith must become love, expressed through good works, in order to be justifying, and to the merits of Christ one must add his or her own merits as well as those of Mary and the saints. To be sure, God receives the glory for making all this possible, but he does not receive *all* the glory because salvation comes "to those who do what lies within them," as the Counter-Reformation taught.

Solo Christo, Sola Fide[9]

Although it had been said in various other ways by the Reformers, it was the early seventeenth-century Reformed theologian Johann Heinrich Alsted (1588–1638) who identified the doctrine of justification as "the article of a standing or falling church."[10] Many respond today, as they did at the time of the Reformation, by saying that a doctrine that is as widely disputed within Christendom can hardly hold that kind of status. However, the issue can only be settled on the basis of Scripture. After all, the doctrine was already challenged within the churches planted by the apostles, including Paul.

Since the Second Vatican Council, Protestant–Roman Catholic dialogue on justification has opened the door to greater understanding, and this process itself remains vital. It is repeatedly asserted that the Joint Declaration on the Doctrine of Justification (2000) resolved the central debate of the Reformation.[11] Signed by representatives of the Vatican and the Lutheran World Federation, the Joint Declaration announced that Trent's anathemas were no longer binding

---

9. Brief portions of this section are drawn and adapted from Michael S. Horton, "Does Justification Still Matter?," *Modern Reformation* 16, no. 5 (2007): 11–17. Used by permission of *Modern Reformation*.

10. Johann Heinrich Alsted, *Theologia scholastica didactica* (Hanover: Conradi Eifridi, 1618), 711, cited in Alister E. McGrath, *Iustitia Dei: A History of the Christian Doctrine of Justification* (Cambridge: Cambridge University Press, 1986), 2:193n3.

11. The Lutheran World Federation and the Roman Catholic Church, *Joint Declaration on the Doctrine of Justification* (Grand Rapids, MI: Eerdmans, 2000).

because they no longer referred to the views held by today's mainline Lutheran partner.

Other initiatives, including (in the United States) the statement "Evangelicals and Catholics Together" (ECT), followed by "The Gift of Salvation," have been regarded by many as significant advances not only in understanding but in agreement on the basic message of the gospel.[12] In these common statements, divine acceptance is said to be by God's grace rather than human merit,[13] although "Evangelicals and Catholics Together" placed this question on the list of continuing disagreement while nevertheless expressing agreement on the gospel.

Perhaps the clearest statement of caution against impatient announcements of success on this point has been offered by the principal theologian on the Roman Catholic side of ECT, Avery Cardinal Dulles. He begins by acknowledging the importance of the doctrine of justification as "a matter of eternal life or death." "If it is not important," he says, "nothing is."[14] Yet the following are differences yet to be resolved:

> 1) Is justification the action of God alone, or do we who receive it cooperate by our response to God's offer of grace? 2) Does God, when He justifies us, simply impute to us the merits of Christ, or does He transform us and make us intrinsically righteous? 3) Do we receive justification by faith alone, or only by a faith enlivened by love and fruitful in good works? 4) Is the reward of heavenly life a free gift of God to believers, or do they merit it by their faithfulness and good works?[15]

For all the progress in mutual understanding represented by the Joint Declaration, says Dulles, at least for its part, Rome continues to affirm over against the Reformers the second answer to each of these questions. Dulles observes first that, according to the Council of Trent's "Decree on Justification" (1547), "human cooperation is involved" in justification. "Secondly, it taught that justification consists in an inner renewal brought about by divine grace; thirdly, that justification does

---

12. These two statements appeared in *First Things*.
13. *Joint Declaration*, par. 15.
14. Avery Cardinal Dulles, "Two Languages of Salvation: The Lutheran-Catholic Joint Declaration," *First Things* 98 (December 1999): 25.
15. Ibid.

not take place by faith without hope, charity, and good works; and finally, that the justified, by performing good works, merit the reward of eternal life."[16]

Nothing in the Joint Declaration may be interpreted as contradicting Trent or any subsequent magisterial teaching. Furthermore, Dulles continues, "Because the Holy See had been heavily involved in the composition" of the Joint Declaration in 1994, "its acceptance was taken for granted." "But to the surprise of many observers," Dulles relates, "the Council for Promoting Christian Unity on June 25, 1998, released an 'Official Response' expressing a number of severe criticisms and apparently calling into question the consensus expressed by the Joint Declaration."[17]

After acknowledging the more tenable statements of consensus, Dulles points to the reason for the Vatican's initial disapproval. Among other things, the "Official Response" challenged "its lack of attention to the sacrament of penance, in which justification is restored to those who have lost it." Dulles continues,

> In addition, it contests the Lutheran view that the doctrine of justification is the supreme touchstone of right doctrine. . . . Most importantly for our purposes, the Catholic Response raises the question whether the Lutheran positions as explained in the Joint Declaration really escape the anathemas of the Council of Trent.

Trent clearly denies that we are justified solely on the basis of Christ's righteousness imputed, Dulles observes. Roman Catholics are thus bound to affirm that believers truly merit everlasting life. Dulles concludes that on these and related issues, "no agreement has been reached."[18]

It is difficult to resist the conclusion, therefore, that the ecumenical conversations that reached their apogee in the Joint Declaration are nothing more than pious advice from the Roman Catholic point of view. For the mainline Lutherans (and the other mainline Protestant bodies that endorsed it), it was quite a different matter. They had in fact

---

16. Ibid.
17. Ibid., 26.
18. Ibid., 27–28.

altered their view of justification. According to the Joint Declaration, faith in its reception of justification is the same as love.[19] However, this was the heart of the difference between the Reformers and Rome. It is difficult to know how an evangelical doctrine of justification can be salvaged from such a concession. While *the faith that justifies* is active in love, crucial to the evangelical argument has been the insistence that faith *in the act of justification* is merely a passive receiving. Since love is the fulfillment of the law, justification by love is equivalent to justification by law.

For many across the ecclesiastical spectrum, whether Roman Catholic or Protestant, liberal or evangelical, there is a temptation to want to conserve the cultural clout that Christianity has exercised at least nominally in the West. Like an abandoned spouse, churches often go to enormous lengths in order to demonstrate that Christianity is still relevant for our moral, social, economic, and political crises. Thus, the real divide, we are told, is between secularism and faith, immanence and transcendence. At least in the classical Reformation perspective, however, it is unclear what kind of transcendence would be worth believing in if God does not justify the wicked by free grace alone. Even here we recognize the cleavage between synergistic and monergistic theologies, regardless of whether the former is Roman Catholic or Protestant in character. The real divide is therefore not between secularism and spirituality or even between those inside and outside the church but between the gospel of Christ and other gospels. While substantial differences remain in our definition of that gospel, those issues remain, tragically, church dividing.

Justification is not just one doctrine among many. Nor is it an isolated *sola*—one of the "five points" of Protestants. The judgment of Roman Catholic theologian Paul Molnar is exactly right: "For all the supposed agreement of the Joint Declaration, the fact remains that Roman Catholic and Reformed theology are still separated in practice by this most basic way of thinking about our relationship with God."[20] At stake is *solo Christo*—whether we are saved solely by the

---

19. *Joint Declaration*, par. 25.
20. Paul Molnar, "The Theology of Justification in Dogmatic Context" in *Justification: What's at Stake in the Current Debates*, ed. Mark A. Husbands and Daniel J. Treier (Downers Grove, IL: InterVarsity Press, 2004), 238.

merits of Christ or whether, by our grace-empowered cooperation, we can truly merit everlasting life. It is a question about whether God is just and merciful; whether fallen human beings are spiritually dead or only morally weak; whether Christ's obedient life, sacrificial death, and victorious resurrection are sufficient for the redemption of sinners; and whether the triune God should therefore receive all the praise and thanksgiving for salvation from beginning to end. It is therefore a question, too, about whether the church is the mother of Scripture, able to promulgate new doctrines and forms of worship, or whether the church is the daughter of the Word, rescued and ruled by a Word that it does not and cannot speak to itself.

Yet, as I have proposed above, matters are not so settled in Protestantism either. Yale theologian George Lindbeck has persuasively argued that the disconnect in many minds with respect to justification is more fundamentally an inability to comprehend the meaning of the atonement itself. Referring to the eleventh-century debate between Abelard and Anselm, Lindbeck says that at least in practice, Abelard's view of salvation by following Christ's example (and the cross as the demonstration of God's love that motivates our repentance) now seems to have a clear edge over Anselm's satisfaction theory of the atonement. "The atonement is not high on the contemporary agendas of either Catholics or Protestants," Lindbeck surmises. "More specifically, the penal-substitutionary versions (and distortions) of Anselm's satisfaction theory that have been dominant on the popular level for hundreds of years are disappearing."[21]

This situation is as true for evangelicals as for liberal Protestants, Lindbeck observes. This is because justification through faith alone (*sola fide*) makes little sense in a system that makes central our subjective conversion (understood in synergistic terms as cooperation with grace), rather than the objective work of Christ:[22]

> Those who continued to use the *sola fide* language assumed that they agreed with the reformers no matter how much, under the

21. George Lindbeck, "Justification and Atonement: An Ecumenical Trajectory," in *By Faith Alone: Essays on Justification in Honor of Gerhard O. Forde*, ed. Joseph A. Burgess and Marc Kolden (Grand Rapids, MI: Eerdmans, 2004), 205.
22. Ibid., 205–6.

influence of conversionist pietism and revivalism, they turned the faith that saves into a meritorious good work of the free will, a voluntaristic decision to believe that Christ bore the punishment of sins on the cross *pro me*, for each person individually. Improbable as it might seem given the metaphor (and the Johannine passage from which it comes), everyone is thus capable of being "born again" if only he or she tries hard enough. Thus with the loss of the Reformation understanding of the faith that justifies as itself God's gift, Anselmic atonement theory became culturally associated with a self-righteousness that was both moral and religious and therefore rather nastier, its critics thought, than the primarily moral self-righteousness of the liberal Abelardians. In time, to move on in our story, the liberals increasingly ceased to be even Abelardian.[23]

"Our increasingly feel-good therapeutic culture is antithetical to talk of the cross," and our "consumerist society" has made the doctrine a pariah.[24] "A more puzzling feature of this development as it has affected professedly confessional churches," Lindbeck adds, "is the silence that has surrounded it. There have been few audible protests."[25] Even most contemporary theologies of the cross fit the pattern of Jesus-as-model, but justification itself is rarely described in accordance with the Reformation pattern even by conservative evangelicals, Lindbeck suggests. Most of them, as has already been indicated, are conversionists holding to Arminian versions of the *ordo salutis*, which are further removed from Reformation theology than was the Council of Trent.[26] "Where the cross once stood is now a vacuum."[27]

All this is significant for ecumenical discussions, says Lindbeck, who has been a leader in mainline Lutheran and Vatican ecumenism. After all, he concludes, even if we might reach some agreement on justification, it seems like a hollow victory if the atonement has slipped from view across the ecclesial divide. "It seems that the withdrawal of the condemnations under these circumstances is not wrong, but vacuous."[28]

---

23. Ibid., 207.
24. Ibid.
25. Ibid., 208.
26. Ibid., 209.
27. Ibid., 211.
28. Ibid., 216.

If the foregoing arguments are close to the truth, it would be premature to conclude that the Reformation is over. On the contrary, its rich and saving truths are as desperately needed today in Protestant as in Roman Catholic and Orthodox circles. It may well be that Protestantism is in its death throes as an identifiable tradition within Christianity. And it would be churlish to preserve a name that means nothing more than "courageously seeking what is new and turning away from old, familiar customs." If "Protestant" does not refer to a specific set of convictions grounded in God's revelation, then it is merely an attitude—and not a particularly healthy one—looking for occasions to protest. If this is what Protestantism now means, then it is no more than another schismatic sect, cultural rallying point, self-help group, or political action committee.

SOLA SCRIPTURA[29]

John Calvin complained of being assailed by "two sects"—"the Pope and the Anabaptists." Obviously quite different from each other, both nevertheless "boast extravagantly of the Spirit" and in so doing "bury the Word of God under their own falsehoods."[30] Both separate the Spirit from the Word by advocating the living voice of God with the inner speech of the church or of the pious individual. Of course, the Bible has its important place, but it is the "letter" that must be made relevant and effective in the world today by Spirit-led popes and prophets.

Radical Anabaptist leader Thomas Müntzer taunted Martin Luther with his claim to superiority through a higher word than that which "merely beats the air." The Reformers called this "enthusiasm" (lit., "God-within-ism"), because it made the external Word of Scripture subservient to the inner word supposedly spoken by the Spirit today within the individual or the church. In 2 Corinthians 3, Paul's letter-Spirit contrast refers to the law apart from the gospel as a "ministry of

---

29. This section is adapted from Michael S. Horton, "The Gospel and the Sufficiency of Scripture: Church of the Word or Word of the Church?," *Modern Reformation* 19, no. 6 (2010): 25–32. Used by permission of *Modern Reformation*.

30. John Calvin, *Reply by Calvin to Cardinal Sadolet's Letter*, in *Tracts and Treatises*, vol. 1, *On the Reformation of the Church*, trans. Henry Beveridge, ed. Thomas F. Torrance (1844; repr. Grand Rapids, MI: Eerdmans, 1958), 36.

death" and the gospel as the Spirit's means of justifying and regenerating sinners. However, Gnostics, enthusiasts, and mystics throughout the ages have interpreted the apostle's terms as a contrast between the text of Scripture ("letter") and inner spiritual knowledge ("spirit").

Modern "Enthusiasm"

If only it were that easy to identify the "two sects" in our day. Tragically, "enthusiasm" has become one of the dominant ways of undermining the sufficiency of Scripture, and it is evident across the spectrum. Rome has consistently insisted that the letter of Scripture requires the living presence of the Spirit speaking through the magisterium. Radical Protestants have emphasized a supposedly immediate, direct, and spontaneous work of the Spirit in our hearts apart from creaturely means. Enlightenment philosophers and liberal theologians—almost all of whom were reared in Pietism—resurrected the radical Anabaptist interpretation of "letter" versus "spirit." "Letter" came to mean the Bible (or any external authority), while "spirit" was equivalent not to the Holy Spirit but to our own inner spirit, reason, or experience.

By the mid-twentieth century, the synods and general assemblies even of denominations historically tied to the Reformation began to speak of the Scriptures as an indispensable record of the pious experiences, reflections, rituals, beliefs, and lives of saints in the past, while what we really need in this hour is to "follow the Spirit" wherever he, she, or it may lead us. And we now know where this spirit has led these erstwhile churches, but it is the spirit of the age, not the Spirit of Christ, that has taken them there.

This broad tendency in modern faith and practice has been finely described by William Placher as the "domestication of transcendence."[31] In other words, it is not that revelation, inspiration, and authority are denied but that the surprising, disorienting, and external voice of God is finally transformed into the "relevant," uplifting, and empowering inner voice of our own reason, morality, and experience.

Such domestication of transcendence means that the self—or the "community" (whatever name it goes by)—is protected from the sur-

---

31. William C. Placher, *The Domestication of Transcendence: How Modern Thinking about God Went Wrong* (Louisville: Westminster John Knox, 1996).

prising, disorienting, and judging speech of our Creator. Yet this also means that we cannot be saved, since faith comes by hearing God speak his word of salvation in his Son (Rom. 10:17). This is not something that bubbles up within us, either as pious individuals or as the holy church, but a Word that comes to us. It is not a familiar Word but a strange and unsettling speech that strips us of our moral pretenses, overturns our most intuitive assumptions, disturbs our activistic programs. Basically, we are told to stop talking to ourselves as if we were hearing the voice of God. Through the lips of other sinful messengers, we are put on the receiving end of our identity. We do not discover our "higher selves" but are told who we really are: treacherous image bearers of God. We do not find our bearings "in Adam" toward a fuller sense of inner peace and security but are driven out of ourselves to Christ, who clothes us in his righteousness.

"Enthusiasm"—the tendency to assimilate God's external Word to the inner word—is inseparable from the Pelagian tendency to assimilate God's saving gospel to our own efforts. Conversely, *sola Scriptura* (the sufficiency of Scripture as the final authority for faith and practice) is inseparably bound to *solo Christo*, *sola gratia*, and *sola fide* (the gospel of Christ alone by grace alone received through faith alone).

There is a "fundamentalist" approach to *sola Scriptura* that can be reduced to the bumper sticker, "God said it. I believe it. That settles it." In this expression, there is no sense that the *content* of what God said in any way constitutes its authority. A Muslim might use the same phrase in speaking of the Qur'an or a Mormon of the Book of Mormon.

However, a genuinely evangelical approach maintains that Scripture is sufficient not just because it alone is divinely inspired (though that is true) but also because these sixty-six books that form our Christian canon provide everything that God has deemed sufficient for revealing his law and his gospel. Speculation will not help us find God but will only lead us to some idol that we have created in our own image. We may feel more secure in our autonomy when we pretend that our own inner voice of reason, spirituality, or experience is the voice of the Spirit. We may be excited about a new program for updating our churches and transforming our nation, our families, and our lives, but there is no power of God unto salvation in our own agendas and efforts. We can find all sorts of practical advice for our daily lives out-side the Bible.

As with justification, the church today has never been in greater need of recovering the Reformers' sense of being gripped by an external Word "above all earthly pow'rs." And, as with justification, Protestantism generally displays a weaker confidence in the authority of Scripture than the Reformers faced in the medieval church.

In the best-selling *Habits of the Heart*, Robert Bellah and fellow sociologists surveyed religion in the United States. They concluded that it is best described as "Sheilaism," named after one person they interviewed who said that she follows her own little voice. Every American is the founder of his or her own religion, following the dictates of his or her own heart.[32]

But two centuries ago Immanuel Kant had already told us that the most certain tenet he knew was "the moral law within." External religions may have different ways of expressing it, each with its own sacred texts and miraculous claims to vindicate its authority, its own forms of worship, and its own creeds. The externals he called "ecclesiastical faiths," contrasted with the "pure religion" of practical morality. The latter needed no external authority or confirmation. We look within ourselves, not only for the law inscribed on our conscience but also for the power to save ourselves—and our world—from whatever evils vie for our allegiance. Kant insisted that we do not need an external gospel because we are not born in original sin, helpless to save ourselves. We do not need to hear the good news of God's rescue operation because we already have everything we need within ourselves to handle the situation just fine.[33]

This "enthusiast" legacy has found fertile soil in American religious experience, particularly in the history of revivalism. Writing in the nineteenth century, Alexis de Tocqueville observed that Americans wished "to escape from imposed systems" of any kind, "to seek by themselves and in themselves for the only reason for things, looking to results with-

32. Robert Bellah, Richard Madsen, William M. Sullivan, Ann Swidler, and Steven M. Tipton, *Habits of the Heart: Individualism and Commitment in American Life*, updated ed. (Berkley, CA: University of California Press, 2008).

33. For citations and interaction with Kant on these points, see Michael Horton, *The Christian Faith: A Systematic Theology for Pilgrims on the Way* (Grand Rapids, MI: Zondervan, 2011), 62–67.

out getting entangled in the means toward them." They do not need external guidance to discover truth, "having found it in themselves."[34]

Placing human experience at the center was a more general trend in European Romanticism, notes Bernard Reardon, with its "intense egoism and emotionalism."[35] The effect of Pietism (especially culminating in the Great Awakening), as William McLoughlin observes, was to shift the emphasis away from "collective belief, adherence to creedal standards and proper observance of traditional forms, to the emphasis on individual religious experience."[36] At the same time, the effect of the Enlightenment was to shift "the ultimate authority in religion" from the church to "the mind of the individual."[37] Romanticism then simply changed the faculty (from mind to heart), while retaining the subject (the self, not an external authority). Even evangelical hymnody was drawn into this Romantic tide, as seen in the familiar line from the Easter song, "You ask me how I know he lives? He lives within my heart." Yet this inner spark, inner light, inner experience, and inner reason that guides mysticism, rationalism, idealism, and pragmatism in all ages is precisely that autonomous self that, according to the New Testament, must be crucified and buried with Christ in baptism, so that one can be raised with Christ as a denizen of the new age.

The gospel is not something that wells up within us. It is not a dictate of moral conscience or a universal doctrine of reason. As a surprising announcement that in Christ we have passed from death to life and from wrath to grace, however, the gospel is counterintuitive. So if we allow reason and experience—that which is inherent, familiar, and inwardly certain—not only to guide our access to but also to determine reality, we will be left with Kant to "the moral law within." The good news has to be *told*, and to the extent that it is assimilated to what we think we already know and experience, it will not be good news at all: perhaps pious advice, good instruction, and practical suggestions, but not good news.

34. Alexis de Tocqueville, *Democracy in America*, ed. J. P. Mayer and Max Lerner, trans. George Lawrence (New York: Harper and Row, 1966), 429.

35. Bernard M. G. Reardon, *Religion in the Age of Romanticism: Studies in Early Nineteenth-Century Thought* (Cambridge: Cambridge University Press, 1985), 9.

36. William McLoughlin, *Revivals, Awakenings, and Reform: An Essay on Religion and Social Change in America, 1607–1977*, Chicago History of American Religion (Chicago: University of Chicago Press, 1980), 25.

37. Ned Landsman, *From Colonials to Provincials: American Thought and Culture, 1680–1760* (Ithaca, NY: Cornell University Press, 2000), 66.

Does salvation come to us from outside ourselves, from above, from heaven, as the triune God acts in history for us? Or does salvation come from our own inner resources, enlightenment, and experience? Does God's Word declare into being a new creation, or give us helpful principles and motivations for our own self-transforming and world-transforming activities? How we answer these questions determines our view not only of the sufficiency of Scripture but also of the nature of the gospel itself.

The root of all "enthusiasm" is hostility to a God outside us, in whose hands the judgment and redemption of our lives are placed. To barricade ourselves from this assault, we try to make the "divine" an echo of ourselves and our communities. The idea of being founded by someone else has been treated in modernity as a legacy of a primitive era. We have come to think that what we experience directly within ourselves is more reliable than what we are told by someone else. Thus, we are always ready for new awareness or new advice but not for new news that can come to us only as a report that is not only told by someone else but is also entirely concerned with the achievement of someone else for us.

New Visions for Evangelical Theology

In evangelical circles today, these "two sects" converge. This is explicit, for example, in the work of Stanley Grenz, who combined his Anabaptist-Pietist heritage with "high church" arguments. Essentially, spirituality takes precedence over doctrine, personal and communal experience over external authority, and inspiration is extended beyond Scripture to include the Spirit's speaking through believers and the community—indeed, even culture today. Reason, tradition, and experience serve alongside Scripture as the four legs of the stool. Nowhere in this account does Grenz locate the origin of faith in an external gospel; rather, faith arises from an inner experience. "Because spirituality is generated from within the individual, inner motivation is crucial"— more important, in fact, than "grand theological statements."[38] The Christian life is not defined by God's action through Word and sacra-

---

38. Stanley J. Grenz, *Revisioning Evangelical Theology: A Fresh Agenda for the 21st Century* (Downers Grove, IL: InterVarsity Press, 1993), 46.

ment. In fact, "The spiritual life is above all the imitation of Christ."[39] We go to church, he says, not in order to receive "means of grace" but merely for fellowship and "instruction and encouragement."[40] Grenz does acknowledge that his interpretation calls into question the confessional Protestant emphasis on "a material and a formal principle"—in other words, *solo Christo* and *sola Scriptura*.[41]

This convergence of Pietism and community-romanticism could already be seen in the work of Friedrich Schleiermacher (1768–1834), father of modern liberal theology. The individual and the community seem to converge in Grenz's account (similar to Schleiermacher's) at the level of common experience. Consequently, a revisioning of evangelical theology entails viewing "theology as the faith community's reflecting on the faith experience of those who have encountered God through the divine activity in history and therefore now seek to live as the people of God in the contemporary world."[42] Scripture is essentially the church's record of its religious experience.[43] "Faith is by nature immediate," Grenz astonishingly asserts, and Scripture is the record of the faith-community's encounter with God.[44]

Grenz therefore reverses the Word-faith relationship. Rather than faith being created by the Word of God, the word itself is created by the experiences of the community. Obviously, this requires "a revisioned understanding of the *nature* of the Bible's authority."[45] *Sola Scriptura* has a venerable history in evangelicalism, he acknowledges; "the commitment to contextualization, however, entails an implicit rejection of the older evangelical conception of theology as the construction of truth on the basis of the Bible alone."[46] Besides Paul Tillich's "method of correlation," Grenz appreciates the growing popularity within evangelical circles of the "Wesleyan quadrangle"—Scripture, reason, experience, and tradition—as shared norms.[47] The Bible, our heritage, and the contemporary cultural context should be reciprocally rather than hierarchi-

---

39. Ibid., 48.
40. Ibid., 54.
41. Ibid., 62.
42. Ibid., 76.
43. Ibid., 77.
44. Ibid., 80.
45. Ibid., 88.
46. Ibid., 90.
47. Ibid., 91.

cally related—and even here, he adds, "the Bible *as canonized by the church*," as if the church authorized rather than received the canon.[48] "In contrast to the understanding evangelicals often espouse, our Bible is the product of the community of faith that cradled it. . . . This means that our confession of the moving of the Spirit in the Scripture-forming process, commonly known as inspiration, must be extended."[49]

Not surprisingly, Grenz suggests that this will yield greater convergence between Protestants and Roman Catholics on the relation of Scripture and tradition.[50] Yet it also incorporates an important charismatic and Pentecostal perspective on continuing revelation: "In this way, paradigmatic events become a continual source of revelation, as each succeeding generation sees itself in terms of the events of the past history of the community." Such conclusions "chart the way beyond the evangelical tendency to equate in a simple fashion the revelation of God with the Bible—that is, to make a one-to-one correspondence between the words of the Bible and the very Word of God."[51]

I have focused on the formal (*sola Scriptura*) and material (*solo Christo*) principles of the Reformation because both are mutually interdependent and both are under tremendous stress today, as they have always been. Scripture and the gospel stand or fall together.

What's Next?

Frankly, I'm a bit ambivalent about this anniversary. If it is another occasion for liberals to hail Luther's "Here I stand!" as the harbinger of modern autonomy, or for conservatives to celebrate Protestant values, or for confessionalists to rewatch the Luther movie and dredge up polemical grudges, then it will be at best a colossal waste of time. If, on the other hand, it is an occasion to allow God's Word once again to break into our self-enclosed circles with a word of radical judgment and radical grace, then it will be a happy anniversary indeed.

This is a time neither for vague celebration nor for hand wringing but for sober examination, critique, and fresh ways of engaging our own time and place with God's strange speech. There is too much

48. Ibid., 93. Italics added.
49. Ibid., 121–22.
50. Ibid., 123.
51. Ibid., 130.

evidence of God's faithfulness to his church. With renewed interest in the truths of the Reformation among younger generations not only in the North Atlantic world but also in the global church, there is much to celebrate. But the real reformation of our day is going to happen, as it always has, in the *churches*. And at some point the "young, restless, and Reformed" are going to have to study for themselves to see the greater wisdom of the confessions and catechisms of the churches that have struggled, against mighty odds, not only to "stay alive" but also to reach their neighbors who are increasingly oblivious to the most basic story line, beliefs, and practices of Christianity. We may be entering a new dark ages in the West. But Jesus told disciples on the verge of persecution, "Fear not, little flock, for it is your Father's good pleasure to give you the kingdom" (Luke 12:32). He still delivers the kingdom to us, as a gift, not through our anxious activism but through his Word and Spirit: "I have said these things to you, that in me you may have peace. In the world you will have tribulation. But take heart; I have overcome the world" (John 16:33). Only confidence in what he has accomplished for us can cheer us for our daunting task: "I will build my church, and the gates of hell shall not prevail against it" (Matt. 16:18).

With all these hopes and dreams in mind, I join the reader in exploring the richness of the chapters that unfold in this terrific collection of truly important essays. Many of them stand alone as passionate manifestos for the way forward. Regardless of your own tradition or church experience, give them a willing ear. They are, in the best sense, catholic and evangelical. Go deeper into a tradition that is definitely "not over," as some suggest, even if the evangelical movement itself may ebb and flow. Regardless, any church that seeks to thrive and become part of the kingdom that Christ is building through his Word and Spirit will sing with Martin Luther,

> Let goods and kindred go,
> This mortal life also.
> The body they may kill,
> God's truth abideth still.
> God's kingdom is forever!

Pentecost Sunday, 2016
Michael Horton

Abbreviations

AHR   *American Historical Review*

APSR   *American Political Science Review*

BSELK   *Die Bekenntnisschriften der Evangelisch-Lutherischen Kirche*. Edited by Irene Dingel. Göttingen: Vandenhoeck & Ruprecht, 2014.

BSHPF   *Bulletin de la Société de l'histoire du Protestantisme français*

BSRK   *Die Bekenntnisschriften der reformierten Kirche*. Edited by E. F. K. Müller. Leipzig: Deichert, 1903.

CCFCT   *Creeds and Confessions of Faith in the Christian Tradition*. Edited by Jaroslav Pelikan and Valerie Hotchkiss. 4 vols. New Haven, CT: Yale University Press, 2003.

CH   *Church History*

CHR   *Catholic Historical Review*

CNTC   *Calvin's New Testament Commentaries*. Edited by David W. Torrance and Thomas F. Torrance. 12 vols. Grand Rapids, MI: Eerdmans, 1959–1972.

CO   *Joannis Calvini Opera Quae Supersunt Omnia*. Edited by Guilielmus Baum, Eduardus Cunitz, and Eduardus Reuss. 59 vols. *Corpus Reformatorum* 29–88. Brunswich and Berlin: Schwetschke, 1863–1900.

CR   *Corpus Reformatorum*. Edited by C. G. Brettschneider. Halle: Schwetschke, 1834–1860.

CSEL   *Corpus Scriptorum Ecclesiasticorum Latinorum*. Edited by Johannes Vahlen et al. Currently housed at the University of Salzburg and published by De Gruyter, Berlin. 1864–.

CTJ   *Calvin Theological Journal*

CTM   *Concordia Theological Monthly*

CTQ   *Concordia Theological Quarterly*

DH   Denzinger, Heinrich. *Compendium of Creeds, Definitions, and Declarations on Matters of Faith and Morals*. Revised and enlarged by Helmut Hoping. Edited by Peter Hünermann (original bilingual ed.) and by Robert Fastiggi and Anne Englund Nash (American ed.). 43rd ed. San Francisco: Ignatius, 2012.

EILR   *Emory International Law Review*

EvQ   *Evangelical Quarterly*

HTR   *Harvard Theological Review*

Institutes   Calvin, John. *Institutes of the Christian Religion*. Edited by John T. McNeill. Translated by Ford Lewis Battles. 2 vols. Library of Christian Classics 20–21. 1559 edition. Philadelphia: Westminster, 1960. References to *Institutes* refer to this edition unless otherwise noted.

Int   *Interpretation*

JChSt   *Journal of Church and State*

JEH   *Journal of Ecclesiastical History*

JETS   *Journal of the Evangelical Theological Society*

JR   *Journal of Religion*

LCC   Library of Christian Classics. Edited by John Baillie, John T. McNeill, and Henry P. Van Dusen. 26 vols. Philadelphia: Westminster, 1953–1966.

LQ   *Lutheran Quarterly*

LW   *Luther's Works*. Edited by Jaroslav Pelikan and Helmut T. Lehmann. American ed. 82 vols. (projected). Philadelphia: Fortress; St. Louis, MO: Concordia, 1955–.

MAJT   *Mid-America Journal of Theology*

MQR   *Mennonite Quarterly Review*

MS   *Mediaeval Studies*

NPNF   Nicene and Post-Nicene Fathers

OER   *Oxford Encyclopedia of the Reformation*. Edited by Hans J. Hillerbrand. 4 vols. New York: Oxford University Press, 1996.

PG   J-P Migne, ed. *Patrologiae cursus completus: Series Graeca*. 161 vols. Paris: Migne, 1857–1886.

PL   J-P Migne, ed. *Patrologiae cursus completus: Series Latina*. 221 vols. Paris: Migne, 1841–1864.

ProEccl   *Pro Ecclesia*

R&R   *Reformation and Revival*

RRR   *Reformation & Renaissance Review*

SBET   *Scottish Bulletin of Evangelical Theology*

SCJ   *The Sixteenth Century Journal*

SJT   *Scottish Journal of Theology*

WA   *D. Martin Luthers Werke, Kritische Gesamtausgabe.* 73 vols. Weimar: Hermann Böhlaus Nachfolger, 1883–2009.

WABr   *D. Martin Luthers Werke, Kritische Gesamtausgabe: Briefwechsel.* 18 vols. Weimar: Hermann Böhlaus Nachfolger, 1930–1983.

WADB   *D. Martin Luthers Werke, Kritische Gesamtausgabe: Deutsches Bibel.* 12 vols. Weimar: Hermann Böhlaus Nachfolger, 1906–1961.

WATr   *D. Martin Luthers Werke, Kritische Gesamtausgabe: Tischreden.* 6 vols. Weimar: Hermann Böhlaus Nachfolger, 1912–1921.

WCF   Westminster Confession of Faith

WTJ   *Westminster Theological Journal*

ZSW   *Huldreich Zwinglis Sämtliche Werke.* Edited by Emil Egli, George Finsler, et al. *Corpus Reformatorum* 88–101. Berlin-Leipzig-Zurich, 1905–1956.

INTRODUCTION

1

The Crux of Genuine Reform

Matthew Barrett

Here, then, is the sovereign power with which the pastors of the church, by whatever name they be called, ought to be endowed. That is that they may dare boldly to do all things by God's Word; may compel all worldly power, glory, wisdom, and exaltation to yield to and obey his majesty; supported by his power, may command all from the highest even to the last; may build up Christ's household and cast down Satan's; may feed the sheep and drive away the wolves; may instruct and exhort the teachable; may accuse, rebuke, and subdue the rebellious and stubborn; may bind and loose; finally, if need be, may launch thunderbolts and lightnings; but do all things in God's Word.

JOHN CALVIN[1]

No other movement of religious protest or reform since antiquity has been so widespread or lasting in its effects, so deep and searching in its criticism of received wisdom, so destructive in what it abolished or so fertile in what it created.

EUAN CAMERON[2]

---

1. Calvin, *Institutes*, 4.8.9.
2. Euan Cameron, *The European Reformation* (Oxford: Oxford University Press, 1991), 1.

Reformation as Rediscovery of the Gospel

Countless historians have gone to great lengths to explain the Reformation through social, political, and economic causes.[3] No doubt each of these played a role during the Reformation, and at times a significant role.[4] Yet most fundamentally, the Reformation was a theological movement, caused by doctrinal concerns.[5] Though political, social, and economic factors were important, observes Timothy George, "we

---

3. I have chosen to use the singular *Reformation*. However, others (even in this volume) have used the plural *Reformations* to refer to the diversity and plurality that existed during the sixteenth century and the multiple Reformations that took place throughout Europe. See, e.g., Carter Lindberg, *The European Reformations* (Oxford: Blackwell, 1996). I agree with this observation; we can speak of a plurality of Reformations, each of which differed from one another. Nevertheless, I stick with the traditional language, using the singular, because, as this introduction reveals, a shared theological center characterized all the Reformers. It is not without justification to speak of *the* Reformation as a whole. While there is diversity among the Reformers, there is also unity when it comes to their common cause in restoring the gospel of grace, which is all too apparent in their united attack against Rome.

Additionally, sometimes the motive behind emphasizing a plurality of Reformations is to include the Catholic Reformation. However, from a Protestant perspective of history, it is more appropriate to label Trent a *Counter-Reformation*. It is no surprise that some Catholic scholars want to even get rid of the term *Reformation* since it "goes along too easily with the notion that a bad form of Christianity was being replaced by a good one." John Bossy, *Christianity in the West, 1400–1700* (Oxford: Oxford University Press, 1985), 91. But this is exactly what the Reformers believed to be the case—hence the need they saw for reformation. McGrath makes this point by noting Luther's interpretation of certain forerunners of the Reformation: "For Luther, the reformation of morals and the renewal of spirituality, although of importance in themselves, were of secondary significance in relation to the *reformation of Christian doctrine*. Well aware of the frailty of human nature, Luther criticized both Wycliffe and Huss for confining their attacks on the papacy to its moral shortcomings, where they should have attacked the theology on which the papacy was ultimately based. For Luther, a reformation of morals was secondary to a reformation of doctrine." Alister E. McGrath, *Luther's Theology of the Cross: Martin Luther's Theological Breakthrough*, 2nd ed. (Oxford: Wiley-Blackwell, 2011), 26.

4. For example, reading through some of the most recent biographies and treatments of Reformation figures will give one a sense for how such factors coincided with the success or failure of reform. See, e.g., Scott H. Hendrix, *Martin Luther: Visionary Reformer* (New Haven, CT: Yale University Press, 2015); Jane Dawson, *John Knox* (New Haven, CT: Yale University Press, 2015); Scott M. Manetsch, *Calvin's Company of Pastors: Pastoral Care and the Emerging Reformed Church, 1536–1609*, Oxford Studies in Historical Theology (Oxford: Oxford University Press, 2013).

5. We must be careful not to swing the pendulum too far to the other side as well. Whitford reminds us that in the sixteenth century, theological beliefs heavily influenced social and political beliefs: "Because the early-modern world was not yet a secular world, the theological affected the social and political just as much and sometimes more than the narrowly defined ecclesiastical." At the same time, Whitford recognizes that the European Reformation "was primarily a religious event driven by theological concerns." David M. Whitford, "Studying and Writing about the Reformation," in *T&T Clark Companion to Reformation Theology*, ed. David M. Whitford (London: T&T Clark, 2012), 3. Also, McGrath observes that the new trend in social history is to define and interpret the Reformation in economic and social categories, and he notes how such an approach has led some to misinterpret the Reformation, resulting in "embarrassing" conclusions. Nevertheless, he argues, "While such nonsense can now be safely disregarded, it is now beyond dispute that any attempt to make sense of the origins, the popular appeal, and the transmission of Protestantism demands careful study of the structures and institutions of contemporary society." Alister McGrath, *Christianity's Dangerous Idea: The Protestant Reformation—A History from the Sixteenth Century to the Twenty-First* (New York: HarperOne, 2007), 8.

must recognize that the Reformation was essentially a religious event; its deepest concerns, theological."[6] What this means, then, is that we must be "concerned with the theological self-understanding" of the Reformers.[7]

But more can be said. Yes, the Reformation was a "religious event," and its deepest concern was "theological." But history is filled with religious and ethical reform movements that considered themselves theological in orientation. What distinguishes the Reformation, however, is that its deepest theological concern was the gospel itself. In other words, the Reformation was a renewed emphasis on right doctrine, and the doctrine that stood center stage was a proper understanding of the grace of God in the gospel of his Son, Christ Jesus. In part, this is what distinguished Luther from the forerunners of the Reformation. As Lindberg notes, referring to one of Luther's early sermons, the "crux of genuine reform . . . is the proclamation of the gospel of grace alone. This requires the reform of theology and preaching but is ultimately the work of God alone."[8] For Luther, explains McGrath, a "reformation of morals was secondary to a reformation of doctrine."[9] While forerunners stressed the need for ethical reform in the papacy, Luther recognized that the real problem was a dogmatic one. The great need was theological; the "crux of genuine reform" had to do with the recovery of the gospel itself.

The Reformers believed that this gospel had been lost (or at least corrupted). Luther was convinced that Pelagianism and semi-Pelagianism had spread like the plague, at least at a popular level, thanks to the influence of certain strands of medieval Catholicism.[10] As

---

6. Timothy George, *Theology of the Reformers* (Nashville: Broadman, 1998), 18. McGrath likewise warns against the temptation of treating the ideas of the Reformation as a "purely social phenomenon." Alister E. McGrath, *Reformation Thought: An Introduction*, 4th ed. (Oxford: Wiley-Blackwell, 2012), xv, xvi, 1.

7. George, *Theology of the Reformers*, 18.

8. Lindberg, *The European Reformations*, 10.

9. McGrath, *Luther's Theology of the Cross*, 27.

10. The "essential factor which led to this schism in the first place" was "Luther's fundamental conviction that the church of his day had lapsed into some form of Pelagianism, thus compromising the gospel, and that the church itself was not prepared to extricate itself from this situation." Ibid. Some today will contest such a traditional view, believing Luther and Calvin to have been seriously mistaken in their understanding both of the late-medieval period and of the state of Rome in the sixteenth century as theologically and morally corrupt. Furthermore, the argument goes, the Catholic reform responded not to the Protestant Reformers but rather to pre-Reformation criticisms within the Catholic Church. In response, to label as erroneous the view that the late-medieval church was theologically mistaken is itself a theological evaluation, one that goes directly against

Luther's conflict with Rome heated up, eventually erupting like a volcano, it became increasingly clear to Luther that the corruption of the gospel in his own day had resulted in the abandonment of justification *sola gratia* and *sola fide*, and vice versa. The consequences were grave. Luther warned at the start of his 1535 Galatians commentary that "if the doctrine of justification is lost, the whole of Christian doctrine is lost."[11] And again, "If it is lost and perishes, the whole knowledge of truth, life, and salvation is lost and perishes at the same time."[12] Nothing less was at stake. Therefore, apart from a rediscovery of doctrines like *sola fide* and the imputation of the righteousness of Christ, lasting reform would never take root. That being the case, it was undeniably obvious to Luther that his teaching, preaching, and writing had to revolve around the gospel, specifically its ramifications for justification by faith alone. As Luther wrote to Staupitz, "I teach that people should put their trust in nothing but Jesus Christ alone, not in their prayers, merits, or their own good deeds."[13] This one sentence, says Scott Hendrix, summarizes "the essence" of Luther's "reforming agenda."[14]

Of course, Luther's rediscovery of the gospel—which he called the "treasure of the Church"—was an experience Luther knew firsthand. Recounting his own personal *durchbruch*, or "breakthrough," Luther's testimony is powerful:

> Though I lived as a monk without reproach, I felt that I was a sinner before God with an extremely disturbed conscience. I could not believe that he was placated by my satisfaction. I did not love, yes, I hated the righteous God who punishes sinners, and secretly, if not blasphemously, certainly murmuring greatly, I was angry with God, and said, "As if, indeed, it is not enough that miserable sinners, eternally lost through original sin, are crushed by every kind of calamity by the law of the Decalogue, without having God add

---

the evaluation of the Reformers. Additionally, while we do not want to ignore the significance of dissenting voices within the Catholic Church even prior to Luther's protest, to say that Rome was not responding to the attacks of the Protestant Reformers is off the mark, as the Council of Trent's explicit and direct anathemas of Reformation doctrine demonstrate.

11. Martin Luther, *Lectures on Galatians* (1535), *LW* 26:9.

12. On the other hand, he said, "if it flourishes, everything good flourishes—religion, true worship, the glory of God, and the right knowledge of all things and of all social conditions." Ibid., *LW* 26:3.

13. Martin Luther, "Letter to Johann von Staupitz" (March 31, 1518), WABr 1:160.

14. Hendrix, *Martin Luther*, 68.

pain to pain by the gospel and also by the gospel threatening us with his righteousness and wrath!" Thus I raged with a fierce and troubled conscience. Nevertheless, I beat importunately upon Paul at that place, most ardently desiring to know what St. Paul wanted.

At last, by the mercy of God, meditating day and night, I gave heed to the context of the words, namely, "In it the righteousness of God is revealed as it is written, 'He who through faith is righteous shall live.'" There I began to understand that the righteousness of God is that by which the righteous lives by a gift of God, namely by faith. And this is the meaning: the righteousness of God is revealed by the gospel, namely, the passive righteousness with which merciful God justifies us by faith, as it is written, "He who through faith is righteous shall live." Here I felt that I was altogether born again and had entered paradise itself through open gates.[15]

In light of Luther's *durchbruch*, if we were to use but one word to characterize the Reformation, it might be *rediscovery*, that is, a rediscovery of the *evangel*, the gospel. It is right to conclude, then, that the Reformation was an *evangelical* reform at its root.

Nevertheless, even the word *rediscovery* assumes that the Reformers did not think they were inventing something new (contra Rome's accusation of novelty). Indeed, they were renewing, retrieving, and reviving what they believed had been lost. This lost gospel had been taught by the biblical authors, as well as by the apostles and church fathers.[16] And since they insisted on reform not just in externals but also in doctrine, the Reformers became characterized by the theology behind that slogan *Ecclesia reformata, semper reformanda*—"The church reformed, always reforming," even if the slogan itself was a much later development.[17]

---

15. Martin Luther, "Preface to the Complete Edition of Luther's Latin Writings," *LW* 34:336–37.

16. Such a principle also applies to other Reformation doctrines, such as *sola scriptura*. Lindberg gives an excellent example from Luther: "Thus in the Leipzig debate (1519) over papal authority, Luther stated that papal claims to superiority are relatively recent. 'Against them stand the history of eleven hundred years, the text of divine Scripture, and the decree of the Council of Nicea [325], the most sacred of all councils' (*LW* 31:318)." Lindberg, *The European Reformations*, 5.

17. From the humanist side of things, this emphasis can be seen in the motto of the Renaissance, *ad fontes*, "to the sources." Many of the Reformers were influenced by humanism and thus applied this motto to the Scriptures, as well as to the early church fathers. For example, Philipp Melanchthon believed that God, in the days of the Reformation, "recalled the church to its origins." See Lindberg, *The European Reformations*, 6.

The Life of the Bible in the Soul of the Church

Ecclesia reformata, semper reformanda, however, did not address only soteriological matters (i.e., *sola fide, sola gratia, solus Christus*). Rather, beneath this Reformation motto was the foundation itself, the formal principle of the Reformation, *sola Scriptura*—the belief that *only Scripture, because it is God's inspired Word, is the inerrant, sufficient, and final authority for the church*.[18] Nowhere was this formal principle more visible for the common person than in the reorientation of the church around the preached and proclaimed Word.

One of the most shocking statements the Reformers ever made in response to Rome involved the rearranging of furniture in the church. Upon walking into a sanctuary, one could immediately tell the difference between a church still in the clutches of Rome and a church under the influence of the Reformation program. For Rome, the service revolved around the altar, but for the Reformers, the pulpit was given the position of priority.[19] For Rome, the Latin Mass was the central event, but for the Reformers, it was the Word of the living God preached and proclaimed in the vernacular for the salvation and edification of the saints.[20] Scott Manetsch provides insight:

> Martin Luther's message that sinners were righteous before God through faith in Christ alone (*sola fide*) not only undermined the Catholic penitential system, but also cut at the root of the medieval priest's sacral role as a dispenser of salvific grace through the sacraments of the church. The Protestant reformers elevated instead the biblical office of the Christian minister or pastor, whose primary responsibility was to preach the Word of God and supervise the behavior of the spiritual community. . . . That is not to say that late medieval Catholics ignored the ministry of preaching, nor that Protestant life and worship was empty of religious ritual. Historians now recognize a significant revival of preaching the century before the Reformation, most evident in the work of mendicant friars and the creation of municipal preacherships. At the same time, despite

---

18. For a defense of the formal principle, see Matthew Barrett, *God's Word Alone: The Authority of Scripture* (Grand Rapids, MI: Zondervan, 2016).
19. To see this point demonstrated in Calvin's preaching ministry, see T. H. L. Parker's *The Oracles of God: An Introduction to the Preaching of John Calvin* (Cambridge: Lutterworth, 1947).
20. Manetsch, *Calvin's Company of Pastors*, 5.

Protestant criticisms of Catholic "ceremonies" and "superstitions," and despite explosive acts of iconoclasm against Catholic images, the evangelical reformers preserved in modified form traditional rites surrounding the Eucharist, baptism, and reconciliation. Nevertheless, the general pattern still holds true: *for Catholics, the primary role of the clergy remained sacramental and liturgical; for the Protestant reformers, it was to preach the Word of God.*[21]

Two very different theologies were pictured visibly. And they were so apparent that churchgoers no longer asked each other if they had been to Mass but whether they had been to the *prêche* ("the preaching").[22]

In the late-medieval period, the sermon was not typically the focal point of the worship service, though this is not to deny the practice of preaching in the medieval church altogether.[23] Instead, sermons were usually preached at specific points in the liturgical calendar, such as Easter or Christmas, or at specific locations, such as pilgrimage sites dedicated to the veneration of Mary and the saints.[24] But normally, one would attend church expecting to listen to Mass being said, not Scripture being proclaimed. To hear a sermon in the late-medieval period sometimes meant leaving the walls of the church and instead traveling to the open field where one might hear a preacher (perhaps in secret). Such was the case with the Franciscan preacher Bernardino of Siena (1380–1444) and the Dominican friar Girolamo Savonarola (1452–1498), the latter of whom was excommunicated and then executed in 1498, just on the eve of the Reformation.[25] The awful fates of forerunners and martyrs like Savonarola were vivid in Luther's mind as he traveled to Worms, wondering if he would come back alive or not.[26]

Such a downgrade, however, was not limited to Luther's Germany;

---

21. Ibid, italics added.

22. Here I have in mind the French Huguenots specifically. See Timothy George, *Reading Scripture with the Reformers* (Downers Grove, IL: IVP Academic, 2011), 238.

23. On preaching in the late-medieval period, see Hughes Oliphant Old, *The Reading and Preaching of the Scriptures in the Worship of the Christian Church*, vol. 3, *The Medieval Church* (Grand Rapids, MI: Eerdmans, 1999).

24. In what follows I will be using George and Manetsch as dialogue partners. I am indebted to their insights. See George, *Reading Scripture with the Reformers*, 229–59; Manetsch, *Calvin's Company of Pastors*, 5–10.

25. George, *Reading Scripture with the Reformers*, 230.

26. Luther even carried a picture of Savonarola with him on his way to Worms. See Martin Brecht, *Martin Luther*, trans. James L. Schaaf, vol. 1, *His Road to Reformation, 1483–1521* (Philadelphia: Fortress, 1985), 448.

England suffered an expository drought as well. Describing life in the church prior to the Reformation, English Reformation historian Philip Hughes explains how "preaching had fallen into such neglect that it had virtually ceased to be a function of the Church."[27] Hughes goes on to explain just how bad the situation had become. Clergy did not show up at their parishes, nor could one assume that a bishop would be personally involved with his diocese. Titles and offices could simply be purchased. Showing up in the flesh to feed the gospel to spiritually hungry churchgoers was unnecessary. Is it any surprise, then, that when real reform took root, the authoritative Word and the expository sermon became inseparable? It was inevitable that "the rediscovery of the Word of God involved the rediscovery of the necessity of preaching."[28] Given the "decay of preaching" in England, Thomas Cranmer led the way by publishing the Books of Homilies, which were "to be read regularly in church by those clergy who were incompetent to preach sermons."[29] Never designed to replace sermons, these homilies, explains Hughes, were a "temporary expedient to tide the Church over until such time as there should be an instructed and spiritual ministry."[30]

What was so radical, then, about the Reformation was how the Reformers recovered the sermon by taking it from the obscurity and secrecy of the fields back into the service and liturgy of the church. Such a move was not done in secret but was conspicuous, visibly manifested in the literal elevation of a pulpit in the air, above the people.

For example, consider the well-known painting of a French Protestant church in Lyon by the name of Temple de Paradis.[31] What catches one's eye in this painting is the pulpit, which is front and center, lifted

---

27. "This was due to the widespread ignorance, indolence, and general dissoluteness of the clergy, encouraged by the all too common failure of the bishops to exercise due oversight in the dioceses for which they had accepted responsibility." Philip E. Hughes, *Theology of the English Reformers* (Grand Rapids, MI: Eerdmans, 1965), 121. On the absence of sermons in local parish church life, also see Kevin Madigan, *Medieval Christianity: A New History* (New Haven, CT: Yale University Press, 2015), 87–88, 308–9.
28. Hughes, *Theology of the English Reformers*, 121.
29. Ibid., 122.
30. Ibid., 122–23.
31. "The Protestant Church in Lyon, called 'The Paradise,'" is located at Bibliotheque Publique et Universitaire, Geneva, Switzerland. Erich Lessing/Art Resource, NY. Available online: http://www.artres.com/C.aspx?VP3=ViewBox_VPage&VBID=2UN365C1DI1XO&IT=ZoomImageTemplate01_VForm&IID=2UNTWAEU1CNQ&PN=1&CT=Search&SF=0.

up so that the preacher is seen and heard by all. The people not only
are seated below but are seated throughout in the shape of a circle (or
at least a half circle) around the preacher. The pulpit is the centerpiece.
Children are also pictured sitting and listening, following along and
ready to learn with their catechism books in their laps. The artist even
places a dog (!) in the service, sitting as if he too is listening, his head
fixed on the preacher. In front of the pulpit is a couple ready to be married, and to the left of the pulpit, "preparations are being made for the
baptism of an infant." The point in these details is that all these people
and all these activities centered on and revolved around the proclamation of God's Word.[32] They believed the Bible was God's message for
them and to them, sufficient not only to save but also to guide one in
a life of godliness. As the Word from God, therefore, it had to be proclaimed, heard, and obeyed. Indeed, it had to have the final say.

Or consider Saint Pierre's in Geneva, the church where Calvin
preached and ministered, as well as the surrounding churches in that
area. Calvin initiated a program that cleansed the church building
from Roman distraction and idolatry, seeking to wash clean this sacred
space. Statues of saints, relics considered holy, crucifixes, the tabernacle
that housed the consecrated host, and the altar where the Mass was
conducted were discarded and destroyed.[33] The cleansing of anything
that could lead to idolatry was so thorough that even the walls and
pillars were whitewashed, hiding iconography that pictured Rome's
unbiblical theology.[34] With the church stripped bare, the sacred space

---

32. This painting is also described by George, *Reading Scripture with the Reformers*, 231.
33. Manetsch, *Calvin's Company of Pastors*, 33. One crucifix did remain: the cross on the top
of Saint Pierre's. However, when it was struck by lightning, the church did not act to replace it.
Manetsch also notes how the stained-glass windows were not destroyed but were left in disrepair.
Also, the organ was melted down in 1562 and used to make tin plates for the city hospital and Communion vessels for the temples. In other words, nothing was left untouched. One might be tempted
to think that Calvin had an aversion to the physical. However, Manetsch corrects such a misconcep-
tion by drawing our attention to the centrality of the Word in preaching and Calvin's concern for
pure worship: "Calvin's insistence that the liturgical content and physical space of true worship be
'bare and simple' was thus not primarily the result of his personal austerity or an aversion to the
material world. Rather, it reflected his conviction that only through pure and simple worship might
the beauty of the gospel shine forth resplendent." And again, "In their aesthetic of worship, Calvin
and his pastoral colleagues in Geneva gave priority to the virtues of simplicity, modesty, and gravity
so that the Word of God and the message of salvation in Jesus Christ might sound forth in all its
clarity and beauty. This was an aesthetic discerned by the sense of hearing rather than of sight."
Calvin's Company of Pastors, 36. For a fuller portrait of how these "cleansings" took place across
the Reformation, see Carlos M. N. Eire, *War against the Idols: The Reformation of Worship from
Erasmus to Calvin* (New York: Cambridge University Press, 1986).
34. Manetsch, *Calvin's Company of Pastors*, 33.

could finally give priority to the preaching of God's Word. A wooden pulpit was crafted and fixed against a pillar at the front of the sacred space. The seats—for men, women, and children—were then situated around it, in front of it, and even behind it.

While the pulpit's centralized position was certainly practical, allowing large crowds to hear, its location was blatantly theological. "The proclamation of Scripture in the middle of the congregation," says Manetsch, "was a potent symbol that Christ, the living Word, continued to speak and dwell among his people."[35] For Rome, the service was most fundamentally a visual experience. In contrast, while the Reformers believed that the Eucharist played an essential role in the service as a means of grace (all the while affirming a very different sacramental theology than Rome), nevertheless, the focal point was the gospel inscripturated, and its pages they read, prayed, sung, and exposited. Not only was the Word sung by the congregation via the Psalms, but the Word was also exposited for all to hear, typically by means of the *lectio continua* method. When the congregation gathered in Saint Pierre's, Calvin was convinced that it was through the Word that the Spirit created worship—in spirit and in truth—within the hearts of the listeners (John 4:24): "Through the ministry of the written and proclaimed Word," says Manetsch, "the Spirit solidifies the faith of God's people, calls forth their prayers and praise, purifies their consciences, intensifies their gratitude—in a word, guides them into spiritual worship."[36] As Calvin said, "God is only worshiped properly in the certainty of faith, which is necessarily born of the Word of God; and hence it follows that all who forsake the Word fall into idolatry."[37] For Calvin, preaching God's Word was a means to true worship and a safeguard against idolatry, specifically the idolatry previously performed under Rome.[38]

In all this we cannot miss the critical point: preaching was a means of grace, a sacrament, in fact.[39] For the medieval church, George ex-

---

35. Ibid., 33.
36. Ibid., 34–35.
37. John Calvin on John 4:23, in *CNTC* 4:99.
38. "The sine qua non of true Christian worship is the preaching of the Word of God and the congregation's heartfelt response to the divine message. Consequently, the chief adornment of public worship must always be the precious Word of God and the beautiful message of the gospel of Jesus Christ, proclaimed in both sermon and sacraments." Manetsch, *Calvin's Company of Pastors*, 36.
39. On Scripture as a means of grace, see J. Todd Billings, *The Word of God for the People of God* (Grand Rapids, MI: Eerdmans, 2010); George, *Reading Scripture with the Reformers*, 28.

plains, preaching "was attached to the sacrament of penance," and therefore, preaching "itself was not considered a sacrament, but it was, we might say, a vestibule to the sacrament of penance."[40] The job of the preacher was to move his listeners to contrition, confession, absolution, and then to works of satisfaction.[41] As Luther saw in Tetzel's fiery sermons on purgatory, at a popular level the oral word was meant to create unbelievable anxiety so that penance would follow.[42] "Why are you standing there?" asked Tetzel. "Run for the salvation of your souls! . . . Don't you hear the voice of your wailing dead parents and others who say, 'Have mercy upon me, have mercy upon me, because we are in severe punishment and pain. From this you could redeem us with small alms and yet you do not want to do so.'"[43] Hearing sermons like this one impelled listeners to quickly and fearfully throw their money into the coffer.

This was the type of anxiety Luther knew all too well prior to his eyes being opened to a God of grace. What was so different in the Reformers' sermons was not that anxiety in the listener was absent—the Reformers believed in the wrath and judgment of God and the sinner's need to repent. Rather, what was so different was how the Reformers proclaimed from the pulpit a *gracious* God, one who justifies the ungodly by grace alone (*sola gratia*) through faith alone (*sola fide*). Proclaimed from the pulpit was not only the righteousness *of* God but also the righteousness *from* God. The Reformers did not leave anxious souls to their own merits (or money bags) but turned their eyes from themselves to the cross and empty tomb. The answer was not penance but a crucified and risen Savior—a Savior, we should remember, whose righteousness was imputed to anyone who trusted in him alone for salvation (*solus Christus*). In contrast to a theology of glory, the Reformers heralded a theology of the cross.

Luther's stance was perspicuous in his 1519 "Sermon on the Sacrament of Penance." He was opposed to those who "try to frighten people into going frequently to confession," and he warned against

40. George, *Reading Scripture with the Reformers*, 231.
41. Ibid.
42. Steven E. Ozment, *The Reformation in the Cities: The Appeal of Protestantism to Sixteenth-Century Germany and Switzerland* (New Haven, CT: Yale University Press, 1975), 24.
43. "John Tetzel: *A Sermon* [1517]," in *The Protestant Reformation*, ed. Hans J. Hillerbrand, rev. ed. (New York: Harper Perennial, 2009), 20–21.

questioning, as he once did, whether one's contrition was sufficient: "Rather you should be assured that after all your efforts your contrition is not sufficient. This is why you must cast yourself upon the grace of God, hear his sufficiently sure word in the sacrament, accepted in free and joyful faith, and never doubt that you have come to grace."[44] This is the message the preacher proclaimed, and it was a message that came from the very lips of God, written down in the Scriptures. With this message of good news from God himself, how could the sermon not stand at the center of worship? To put the sermon at the center was to put Scripture at the center, and to put Scripture at the center was to put God at the center with his gospel of free grace for all who come to his Son in faith. The Reformers preached thousands of sermons because they were convinced that the Word proclaimed was "indispensable" as a "means of grace."[45]

The Scriptures were, as Calvin called them, "spectacles" that the Spirit used to open blind eyes to the gospel.[46] Bullinger could even say in the Second Helvetic Confession of 1566 that the "preaching of the Word of God *is* the Word of God."[47] Bullinger did not mean that the preacher's words and thoughts were revelatory, as if the canon was open and ongoing. By this expression Bullinger instead meant to communicate that when the preacher proclaims the true meaning of Scripture, the people of God are fed the Word of God. God is present, talking to his people. Though the preacher is fallible, weak, and unworthy, God's Word is not; it is true, objective, powerful, and sufficient. Transcending the preacher, the Word brings God himself into the room with the good news of his Son to troubled, hell-bound souls held captive by the law.[48] Calvin contended that the Spirit utilizes the

---

44. Martin Luther, "Sermon on the Sacrament of Penance," in *LW* 35:9–22. Cf. George, *Reading Scripture with the Reformers*, 233.

45. George, *Reading Scripture with the Reformers*, 234.

46. See Randall C. Zachman, *Image and Word in the Theology of John Calvin* (Notre Dame, IN: University of Notre Dame Press, 2007); J. Todd Billings, *Calvin, Participation, and the Gift: The Activity of Believers in Union with Christ* (Oxford: Oxford University Press, 2007); Heiko A. Oberman, "Preaching and the Word in the Reformation," *Theology Today* 18, no. 1 (1961): 16–29.

47. "The Second Helvetic Confession," chap. 1, in James T. Dennison Jr., ed., *Reformed Confessions of the 16th and 17th Centuries in English Translation*, vol. 2, *1552–1566*, (Grand Rapids, MI: Reformation Heritage Books, 2010), 811.

48. "The event of preaching, not unlike the Eucharist in medieval Catholic theology, has an utterly objective character that transcends even the weak and sinful status of the preacher. God truly speaks and is truly present in judgment and grace whenever his Word is proclaimed. Despite the deep and divisive differences between Lutheran and Reformed theologies over the Lord's Supper

preached Word (along with the Lord's Supper) to elevate the church into the heavens where Christ sits so that she might enjoy all his saving benefits.[49] The believer's union with Christ, therefore, is not at all unrelated to the proclamation of God's Word.[50]

A Sacred Trust

Luther would be disturbed (to put it mildly) to see pastors today enter the pulpit nonchalantly. For Luther, the office of preacher was a "sacred trust."[51] "Whoever does not preach the Word," Luther warned emphatically in *The Babylonian Captivity of the Church*, "is no priest at all."[52] Preaching carried a weightiness—indeed, an authority. To preach Scripture was to preach the very Word of God. The preacher's authority was derivative, springing from the church's supreme authority, the God-breathed Scriptures. *Sola Scriptura*, in other words, was the engine that drove the Reformers' theology of preaching. As Manetsch observes,

> The Protestant doctrine of *sola scriptura*—the conviction that Holy Scripture was the unique, final authority for the Christian community—had important consequences for pastoral ministry. *The scripture principle gave gravitas to the office of preacher* [italics added]. It also made the educational formation of Protestant clergy an urgent priority, especially in those academic disciplines most necessary for biblical exposition such as classic rhetoric, theology, and biblical exegesis. By transferring the locus of authority from the Catholic magisterium to the written Word of God, the reformers enhanced the personal authority of the minister, who was now entrusted with special responsibility to interpret and proclaim the sacred text.[53]

The authoritative Word, which necessitated proclamation, brought with it not only law but also gospel. *Sola Scriptura* bestowed gifts on

---

in the sixteenth century, they found common ground in 'the *ex opere operato* presence of God's Word in the preached Word.'" Oberman, "Preaching and the Word in the Reformation," 26, cited in George, *Reading Scripture with the Reformers*, 252.

49. John Calvin, *Tracts and Treatises*, vol. 1, *On the Reformation of the Church*, trans. Henry Beveridge, ed. Thomas F. Torrance (1844; repr., Grand Rapids, MI: Eerdmans, 1958), 186.

50. E.g., Martin Luther, "Sermons on John 4" (1537), *LW* 22:526; Luther, "Sermons on John 15" (1537), *LW* 24:218.

51. Martin Luther, *Commentary on the Sermon on the Mount*, *LW* 21:9.

52. Martin Luther, *The Babylonian Captivity of the Church*, *LW* 36:113.

53. Manetsch, *Calvin's Company of Pastors*, 6.

the people, gifts called *sola gratia*, *sola fide*, and *solus Christus*. Once God's Word was at the center, supreme in its authority and infallibility, it gave birth to the gospel. In the Word one received *the* Word, Jesus the Christ (John 1:1). As Luther memorably said, the Scriptures are the "swaddling clothes in which Christ lies."[54]

It was not enough, therefore, for Scripture to be merely read; it had to be proclaimed. "The ears alone," Luther said, "are the organs of the Christian."[55] And the "lips are the public reservoirs of the church":

> In them alone is kept the Word of God. You see, unless the word is preached publicly, it slips away. The more it is preached, the more firmly it is retained. Reading is not as profitable as hearing it, for the live voice teaches, exhorts, defends, and resists the spirit of error.[56]

Luther concluded this thought with a startling statement: "Satan does not care a hoot for the written Word of God, but he flees at the speaking of the Word."[57] Satan does not worry about Bibles sitting around on shelves. He begins to worry when those Bibles are picked up and taken into pulpits. He knows that when the Word is proclaimed, the Holy Spirit comes alongside it and penetrates "hearts and leads back those who stray," for "the Word," said Luther, "is the channel through which the Holy Spirit is given."[58] And when the Holy Spirit is given, souls are made alive, justified, and set on the pathway to glorification.

We see this biblical principle dramatically exemplified in the return of Marian exiles. With the Elizabethan era underway, the Word of God—and with it the true gospel—entered pulpits once more, leaving many Christians overjoyed. Thomas Lever, for example, wrote to Henry Bullinger on August 8, 1559, and reported that they "preached the Gospel in certain parish churches, to which a numerous audience eagerly flocked together." When they "solemnly treated of conversion to Christ by true repentance, many tears from many persons bore witness that the preaching of the Gospel is more effectual to true repentance and wholesome reformation than anything that the whole world

---

54. Martin Luther, "Prefaces to the Old Testament," *LW* 35:236.
55. Martin Luther, *Lectures on the Epistle to the Hebrews* (1517–1518), *LW* 29:224.
56. Martin Luther, *Lectures on Malachi*, *LW* 18:401.
57. Ibid., *LW* 18:401.
58. Ibid., *LW* 18:401.

can either imagine or approve."[59] It is fitting that Hugh Latimer, one of the martyrs under "Bloody Mary" (i.e., Queen Mary I of England), could label preaching "God's instrument of salvation" and conclude that to "take away preaching" is to "take away salvation."[60] Given the authority of the Word, as well as its gospel-saving power, the Reformers not only made the pulpit the center but also prescribed and exemplified a certain method of proclamation: expositional preaching. The Reformers expounded the meaning of the biblical text, explaining the biblical author's intent, only to apply the text to their listeners. The point of the passage became the point of the sermon. However, the Reformers did not necessarily pick texts at random; they preached through books of the Bible, often chapter by chapter and verse by verse.

Calvin, for example, expounded his way through entire books of the Bible. Typically, Sundays were occupied with the New Testament (though he did preach a series on the Psalms on Sunday afternoons), and weekdays were devoted to the Old Testament.[61] Notice the pattern:

1554–1555: 159 sermons on Job
1555–1556: 200 sermons on Deuteronomy
1558–1559: 48 sermons on Ephesians
1560: 65 sermons on the Synoptic Gospels
1561–1563: 194 sermons on 1–2 Samuel[62]

So important was the *lectio continua* method that when Calvin returned to the pulpit in Geneva in 1541, after years of exile, he started preaching at the exact verse he had left off with before he had been kicked out of town! Why exactly? Because the Reformation was first and foremost about the Word of God, which the people of God needed more than anything else. As George astutely notes,

The Reformation was not about Calvin or any other personality. Much less was it about the ups and downs of church politics by

---

59. *The Zurich Letters*, 2nd Series, 30; as quoted in Hughes, *Theology of the English Reformers*, 141.
60. Hugh Latimer, *Works*, 1:178, 155, as quoted in Hughes, *Theology of the English Reformers*, 130.
61. Calvin preached without notes, having only his Greek or Hebrew text with him. He spent countless hours studying the text of Scripture in preparation each week.
62. George, *Reading Scripture with the Reformers*, 241.

which the church is ever beset. No, the Reformation was about the Word of God, which was to be proclaimed faithfully and conscientiously to the people of God. Calvin held himself to a high standard and demanded no less of others called to the office of preaching. The true pastor, he said, must be marked by "ruthless persistence" (*importunitas*). Pastors are not granted the luxury of choosing their own times of service, or suiting their ministry to their own convenience or preaching "sugar stick" sermons removed from their biblical context.[63]

"Sugar stick" sermons, said Calvin, were those sermons that took Scripture up "at random," paying no attention to the context; in such cases, it is "no wonder that mistakes arise all over the place."[64] Instead, said Calvin, "I have endeavored, both in my sermons and also in my writings and commentaries, to preach the word purely and chastely, and faithfully to interpret His sacred Scriptures."[65]

The *lectio continua* approach assumed *sola Scriptura* at every turn. Because the Bible was inspired by God, inerrant, clear, and sufficient, every book, every chapter, and every verse mattered. This was God speaking after all. And if his people were to be nurtured, then they had to have the authoritative words of life; nothing else would do.[66]

But it wasn't just the pulpit that placed Scripture at the center of worship; the entire Protestant service was immersed in Scripture, from beginning to end. The Bible, in other words, became the DNA of the worship time, infiltrating everything from the opening call to worship to the singing of psalms to the closing benediction. For example, consider this sample Sunday morning service that Calvin followed:

---

63. Ibid., 243.

64. CO 36:277; John Calvin, *Calvin's Commentaries* (Grand Rapids, MI: Baker, 2003), 7:442.

65. John Calvin, "Calvin's Will and Addresses to the Magistrates and Ministers" (1564), in *John Calvin: Selections from His Writings*, ed. John Dillenberger, American Academy of Religion Aids for the Study of Religion 2 (Atlanta: Scholars Press, 1975), 35. Zwingli felt the same, having little patience for those preachers who used "pious chatter" that left people confused and empty. Palmer Wandel, "Switzerland," in *Preachers and People in the Reformations and Early Modern Period*, ed. Larissa Taylor, New History of the Sermon 2 (Leiden: Brill, 2001), 229.

66. Hughes Oliphant Old, *The Reading and Preaching of the Scriptures in the Worship of the Christian Church*, vol. 4, *The Age of the Reformation* (Grand Rapids, MI: Eerdmans, 2002), 130. Cf. George, *Reading Scripture with the Reformers*, 238.

Liturgy of the Word
Call to worship: Psalm 124:8
Confession of sins
Prayer for pardon
Singing of a psalm
Prayer for illumination
Scripture reading
Sermon

Liturgy of the Upper Room
Collection of offerings
Prayers of intercession and a long paraphrase of the Lord's Prayer
Singing of the Apostles' Creed (while elements of the Lord's Supper
    are prepared)
Words of institution
Instruction and exhortation
Communion (while a psalm is sung or Scripture is read)
Prayer of thanksgiving
Benediction: Numbers 6:24–26[67]

For Calvin, it was crucial that the Word be the controlling principle, for it is in the Word that God meets his people and his people meet him. As Calvin said, "Wherever the faithful, who worship him purely and in due form, according to the appointment of his word, are assembled together to engage in the solemn acts of religious worship, he is graciously present, and presides in the midst of them."[68] In what would become known as "the regulative principle of worship," Calvin

---

67. William D. Maxwell, *An Outline of Christian Worship* (London: Oxford University Press, 1958), 114. Cf. W. Robert Godfrey, *John Calvin: Pilgrim and Pastor* (Wheaton, IL: Crossway, 2009), 71. Calvin talks about the intention of this order in his *Institutes* (4.17.43). Luther and his followers also saw the Word as central to the liturgy as they followed the practices of the earliest worship services in the Jewish synagogues, which placed Scripture reading at the center of their gatherings. See Robert Kolb and Charles P. Arand, *The Genius of Luther's Theology: A Wittenberg Way of Thinking for the Contemporary Church* (Grand Rapids, MI: Baker Academic, 2008), 172. George adds, "As part of their protest against clerical domination of the church, the reformers aimed at full participation in worship. Their reintroduction of the vernacular was jarring to some since it required that divine worship be offered to God in the same language used by businessmen in the marketplace and by husbands and wives in the privacy of their bedchambers. However, the intent of the reformers was not so much to secularize worship as to sanctify common life. For them, the Bible was not merely an object for academic scrutiny in the study or the library; it was meant to be practiced, enacted and embodied as the people of God came together for prayer and praise and proclamation." George, *Theology of the Reformers*, 387.

68. John Calvin, *Commentary on the Book of Psalms* (Grand Rapids, MI: Baker, 1979), 1:122.

taught that God's Word must regulate the service, so that whatever is not explicitly commanded by the Word must not be incorporated into the worship service.[69]

Calvin would have been horrified by the church's obsession today with "putting on a show," driven first and foremost by pragmatic, consumeristic motivations. "For Calvin," says W. Robert Godfrey,

> worship was not a means to an end. Worship was not a means to evangelize or entertain or even educate. Worship was an end in itself. Worship was not to be arranged by pragmatic considerations but was rather to be determined by theological principles derived from the Scriptures. The most basic realities of the Christian life were involved. In worship God meets with his people.[70]

The Word, for Calvin, was not merely at the center of worship; it was the very content of worship, as seen in the liturgy above, for in it Christ himself stoops down to hear the praises of his bride, only to then bring them back up to heaven in the Lord's Supper.[71] Unlike so many worship services today, Calvin's were characterized by a noticeable simplicity—no symbols, ceremonies, and rituals, just the preaching, singing, and presence of Word and sacrament. Through the Word, the people had communion with God.

Reformation Today

This lengthy introduction thus far is meant to make one pivotal point: at the center of the Reformation was a return to a gospel-centered, Word-centered church. No question about it, this was the great need in the sixteenth-century church.

In the twenty-first century, the church's need has not changed. The words of James Montgomery Boice still ring true: while the Puritans sought to carry on the Reformation, today "we barely have one to carry on, and many have even forgotten what that great spiritual revo-

---

69. The regulative principle, therefore, is no invention of the Puritans, but its seed can be found in Calvin himself. This is not to say, however, that there is total continuity between the two. See Calvin's "On the Necessity of Reforming the Church," in *Selected Works of John Calvin*, ed. Henry Beveridge and Jules Bonnet (Grand Rapids, MI: Baker, 1983), 1:128–29; Godfrey, *John Calvin*, 78n24.

70. Godfrey, *John Calvin*, 80.

71. Ibid., 82–83.

lution was all about." We "need to go back and start again at the very beginning. We need another Reformation."[72]

If Boice is right, and we believe he is, then the Reformation is far from over. In the twenty-first century, not only do important and significant differences remain between Protestants and Catholics, but also a host of doctrinal and ecclesiastical issues challenge a modern reformation. Unlike the sixteenth century, in other words, the issues Protestant evangelicals must address are not limited to the Protestant-Catholic conversation but also include challenges from within evangelicalism itself.[73] As a result, not only is the Reformation not over, but also its scope and breadth today may need to be far more extensive than that in the sixteenth century, as we seek to answer objections not only from those outside Protestantism but also from those within. Unfortunately, in our churches, universities, and seminaries, many have never been taught Reformation theology, nor do they have a thorough understanding of who the Reformers were and what their historical context looked like, let alone the lasting legacy they left behind. That is where this book comes into play. This volume brings together outstanding evangelical theologians and historians in order to present to readers a systematic summary of Reformation theology. Our hope is that readers will then apply this theological heritage to issues in our own day.

About This Book

At the start of any book, it is always helpful to know something about the author (or authors), the drive behind the book, and its scope and intention. *Reformation Theology* is written by a group of theologians and historians who are committed to Reformation theology. And that, in and of itself, is quite unique.[74] Of course, this does not mean that the authors agree with every jot and tittle of what the Reformers taught.

---

72. James Montgomery Boice, "Preface," in *Here We Stand: A Call from Confessing Evangelicals*, ed. James Montgomery Boice and Benjamin E. Sasse (Grand Rapids, MI: Baker, 1996), 12.

73. As to what some of these challenges may be, see my review of *Four Views on the Spectrum of Evangelicalism*, ed. Andrew David Naselli and Collin Hansen, The Gospel Coalition, November 30, 2011, https://www.thegospelcoalition.org/article/four_views_on_the_spectrum_of_evangelicalism.

74. Writing history is never a neutral endeavor—and to believe so would be to buy into Enlightenment thinking. As many have pointed out, writing history, even if one seeks to be purely descriptive, is an interpretive task. For several excellent histories of the Reformation, see Euan Cameron, *The European Reformation*, 2nd ed. (Oxford: Oxford University Press, 2012); Lindberg, *The European Reformations*; Diarmaid MacCulloch, *Reformation: Europe's House Divided, 1490–1700* (London: Allen Lane, 2003).

Indeed, even the Reformers disagreed among themselves (as attested by their heated debates over the Lord's Supper). But it does mean that the authors of this book are committed to the essence of Reformation theology as that which is faithful to the biblical witness.

The advantage of such an approach is that each author writes with conviction. Rather than studying and observing these old truths as one would an antique artifact in a museum, these authors know these truths firsthand, having not only studied the theology of the Reformers but also applied it in their teaching and pastoral contexts. While many books have been written by historians who do not profess the truths they are analyzing, this book is written by historians and theologians who actually believe these great doctrines and consider themselves heirs of the Reformers. Like the Reformers, the authors you will read are rearticulating the theology of the Reformation because they desire to see reformation in our own day and age.

Additionally, *Reformation Theology* provides a systematic summary of Reformation thought. While not every subject or Reformer can be tackled in great depth in this volume, the book nonetheless covers the major loci of systematic theology.[75] In short, this volume serves as an introduction to the theology of the Reformers. Also, while approaching the subject biographically has many advantages, taking a systematic approach allows the reader to see what the major Reformers taught about any single doctrine.[76] Such an approach is advantageous since it allows the reader to see areas of continuity and discontinuity between the Reformers on any particular doctrine.

Moreover, this book is written in such a way that the specialist and

---

75. It should be acknowledged, of course, that the Reformers did not write systematic theologies as we do today. Melanchthon's *Loci Communes* and Calvin's *Institutes of the Christian Religion* are perhaps the closest thing one will find to a systematic theology, and even these are not really systematic theologies in the modern sense. Many of the Reformers' writings were occasional, motivated by the polemics of their day, or they arose out of their sermons, since the pulpit was often at the center of the Reformation movement.

76. For works that take a biographical approach, more or less, see George, *Theology of the Reformers*; David Bagchi and David C. Steinmetz, eds., *The Cambridge Companion to Reformation Theology* (Cambridge: Cambridge University Press, 2004); Carter Lindberg, ed., *The Reformation Theologians: An Introduction to Theology in the Early Modern Period* (Oxford: Blackwell, 2002). Some works do take a theological approach, as we will see in this book. Nonetheless, as impressive as they are, they do not necessarily cover the entire scope of theological topics—e.g., Jaroslav Pelikan, *Reformation of Church and Dogma (1300–1700)*, vol. 4 of *The Christian Tradition: A History of the Development of Doctrine* (Chicago: University of Chicago Press, 1984); McGrath, *Reformation Thought*. This book is not intended to replace these fine studies but rather to provide students of the Reformation with an additional angle.

the nonspecialist alike will enjoy it. Academic specialists will find the book helpful because it provides a fresh perspective by approaching Reformation thought within the framework of systematic theology, and it also addresses areas of Reformation thought that have received little attention in the past (e.g., the Trinity, the attributes of God, the image of God, eschatology). Nonspecialists, however, will benefit the most. Each chapter serves as an introduction to the doctrine at hand, explaining what the major Reformers believed, why they believed it, and what impact their beliefs had. At the same time, no chapter is limited to the basics, but rather, they penetrate into the doctrinal details, controversies, and theological distinctions that characterized the Reformers. Naturally, the book has a textbook feel, though we like to think, especially given the topic, that it is without the dryness that too often accompanies such books.

A brief word of qualification is also necessary. A book on Reformation theology could easily have been at least five times the size of this one. But we felt that a massive book would impede its accessibility to nonspecialists and students. So each chapter tries to be as concise as possible. Unfortunately, this means that not every Reformer or reform movement could be discussed. In order to prize accessibility, most chapters limit themselves to the major Reformers known to us today and the major reform hot spots of the sixteenth century, though this is not to say that the book never interacts with lesser-known Reformers. Nevertheless, each author of each chapter has recommended some of the key resources, primary and secondary, to which students of the Reformation can turn for further study. Our hope is that readers will find each chapter to be an entryway into the world of Reformation theology.

May this primer serve to highlight the importance, relevance, and indispensability of Reformation theology, both for understanding the sixteenth century and for thinking through its significance for the twenty-first century.

Part 1

HISTORICAL BACKGROUND TO THE REFORMATION

2

Late-Medieval Theology

Gerald Bray

ABSTRACT

Late-medieval theology was characterized by two major areas of
discussion that were to influence the Protestant Reformation. The
first of these was the debate about the nature and reception of divine grace. Peter Lombard had developed the scheme of seven sacraments, through which saving grace was mediated by the church
to its members. Of these, two (penance and the Eucharist) were
meant to be repeated frequently, but even so, most people died
with a burden of unforgiven sins that they then had to work off
in purgatory. It was possible to lessen this punishment by obtaining indulgences, which the church even offered for sale. Christians
could obtain grace by their own merit, and receiving the sacraments
that imparted this grace was the closest a believer could come to
being assured of his salvation. Behind this sacramental scheme lay a
hierarchy of authority, the second major late-medieval debate. The
church claimed that this authority was derived from God and had
been given to the church. In practice, this authority was exercised
by the pope and the bishops, but it was disputed whether the pope
could act on his own or whether he had to follow the dictates of
church councils. Secular rulers also played a part in this, because

only those church pronouncements that they agreed to implement actually took effect. The Bible was a source of authority, but it was interpreted by the church's hierarchy and supplemented by additional canons and decrees that formed an extrabiblical "tradition." A few commentators noticed how the church had been corrupted by the use and abuse of this system, and they advocated the principle of *sola Scriptura* ("Scripture alone") as the foundation of the church's authority. The Protestant Reformers picked up on this thinking, often subconsciously, and by rejecting the claims of nonbiblical tradition, sought to establish the church on what they regarded as its ancient base of Scripture alone.

The Medieval View of Salvation[1]

The Protestant Reformation began as a theological dispute over the nature and reception of divine grace. To understand how this occurred and why its effects were so dramatic, we have to go back to the origins of the sacramental practice of the late-medieval church, which drew its primary inspiration from the *Sentences* of Peter Lombard (ca. 1090–1160).[2]

Peter Lombard and the Seven Sacraments

As Lombard saw it, there were seven sacraments. Five were meant for every Christian—baptism, confirmation, Holy Communion, penance, and extreme unction. Two were not meant for everyone and came to be seen as mutually exclusive—ordination and matrimony. As far as anyone knows, Lombard invented this number. Seven was often used for holy things, and it represented the perfection of God's gifts, just as the seven-day week represented the perfection of his creation.

---

1. This section is adapted from *God Has Spoken: A History of Christian Thought*, by Gerald Bray, © 2014, pp. 469–70, 476–508, 513–23. Used by permission of Crossway, a publishing ministry of Good News Publishers, Wheaton, IL 60187, www.crossway.org.

2. Peter Lombard, *Sententiae in IV libris distinctae*, ed. Ignatius Brady, 2 vols. (Grottaferrata: Editiones Collegii Sancti Bonaventurae ad Claras Aquas, 1971–1981); Lombard, *The Sentences*, trans. Giulio Silano, 4 vols., Mediaeval Sources in Translation 42–43, 45, 48 (Toronto: Pontifical Institute of Mediaeval Studies, 2007–2010). For an analysis and introduction, see Philipp W. Rosemann, *Peter Lombard* (Oxford: Oxford University Press, 2004), and Marcia L. Colish, *Peter Lombard*, 2 vols., Brill's Studies in Intellectual History 41 (Leiden: Brill, 1994). See also *Medieval Commentaries on the "Sentences" of Peter Lombard*, vol. 1, *Current Research*, ed. G. R. Evans (Leiden: Brill, 2002), and vol. 2, ed. Philipp W. Rosemann (Leiden: Brill, 2009).

Baptism needed no special justification since it was clearly enjoined in the New Testament. By Lombard's time, confirmation had become a rite in which those who had been baptized in infancy made a personal profession of faith, after which they were admitted to Holy Communion. Holy Communion, for Lombard, was the centerpiece of the sacramental system, the rite that made sense of all the others and that bound the church together in a way that nothing else could. As he put it,

> Baptism puts out the fire of [our] vices, but the Eucharist restores [us] spiritually. That is why it is so well called the Eucharist, meaning "good grace," because in this sacrament not only is there an increase of virtue and grace, but he who is the source and origin of all grace is received entire.[3]

We do not know who was the first to describe the Eucharist in terms of substance and invent the term *transubstantiation* to describe what happened to the elements of bread and wine. A number of textbooks claim that it was Hildebert of Tours (ca. 1055–1133) but without citing any text in support. A more likely candidate would be Hugh of St. Victor (ca. 1096–1141), who is now thought to have written the *Tractatus theologicus*, traditionally ascribed to Hildebert. Although Hugh most certainly held the doctrine, he avoided using the word itself in his great treatise *On the Sacraments*. For his part, Peter Lombard rejected the crude idea that the Eucharistic elements became the body and blood of Christ, but he was forced to admit that his sources said different things.[4] In the next generation, Baldwin of Forde (ca. 1125–1190) wrote that "although there is a considerable variety of expression in this confession of faith, there is only one devout belief and an undivided unity of confession."[5] To this he added,

> Therefore we hold, believe and confess simply and with confidence, firmly and constantly, that the substance of bread is changed into the substance of the flesh of Christ—though the appearance of

---

3. Lombard, *Sententiae* 4.8.1.1.
4. In particular, he juxtaposed Ambrose and Augustine, pointing out how they differed from one another.
5. Baldwin of Forde, *Liber de sacramento altaris*, in *PL* 204:662.

bread remains—and that this takes place in a way that is miraculous and beyond description or comprehension.[6]

Transubstantiation became official church teaching at the Fourth Lateran Council in 1215, the first canon of which declared,

> There is only one universal church of the faithful, outside which absolutely no one is saved and in which Christ himself is both priest and sacrifice. In the sacrament of the altar, his body and blood are truly contained in the species of bread and wine, the bread being transubstantiated into the body and the wine into the blood by divine power, so that, in order to perfect the mystery of unity, we receive from him what he received from us. Moreover, no one can confect this sacrament except a priest who has been legitimately ordained according to the keys of the church, which Jesus Christ himself gave to his apostles and their successors.[7]

Extreme unction was originally the anointing of the sick mentioned in James 5:14–15, which came to be seen as a preparation for death, probably because relatively few people recovered from their illnesses, but Lombard said little about it. What he was most interested in was penance, to which he devoted more space than to baptism, confirmation, and Holy Communion *combined*. Consider the following:

> Penance is necessary for those who are far away [from God], to enable them to draw near to him. As Jerome says: "it is the second plank after the shipwreck," because if someone has stained the robe of innocence he received in baptism by sinning again, he can clean it by recourse to penance. . . . Those who have fallen after baptism can be restored by penance, but not by baptism, because it is all right to do penance frequently, whereas rebaptism is forbidden. Baptism is a sacrament only, but penance is both a sacrament and a virtue of the mind. There is an outer penance which is a sacrament, and an inner penance which is a virtue of the mind, but both bring about justification and salvation.[8]

---

6. Ibid., *PL* 204:679–80.
7. Giuseppe Alberigo, ed., *Conciliorum oecumenicorum decreta* (Bologna: Istituto per le scienze religiose, 1973), 230; DH §802. The DH edition features the original (usually Latin) texts with an English translation on facing pages.
8. Lombard, *Sententiae* 4.14.1.1–2. The Jerome quotation is from *Epistula* 130.9.

Outer penance was required because it testified to the inner change of heart, which in turn was the basis of one's justification before God. But what if a person was inwardly sorry yet had not demonstrated that sorrow outwardly? Lombard accepted that possibility but only reluctantly:

> Just as inner penance is enjoined on us, so too are both the confession of the mouth and outer satisfaction, if the opportunity for them exists. Someone who does not have any desire to confess is not truly penitent. Just as the forgiveness of sins is a gift from God, so the [outer] penance and confession by which sin is erased must also be from God. . . . The penitent must therefore confess if he has the time to do so, but forgiveness is granted to him before his oral confession if the desire is present in his heart.[9]

Lombard preferred oral confession, using as his pretext the authority of the apostle James, who said, "Confess your sins to one another" (James 5:16). He took it for granted that it should be made to a priest: "It is necessary to make confession to God first, and then to a priest. It is not possible to get to heaven otherwise, if the opportunity [for making such a confession] exists."[10] But he conceded that "if a priest is not available, confession should be made to a neighbor or to a friend."[11]

Lombard was aware, however, that forgiveness is a gift of God. Jesus had given the apostle Peter the keys of the kingdom of heaven (Matt. 16:19), but Lombard explained this power as follows:

> We can rightly say and teach that God alone forgives or does not forgive sins, even though he has granted the church the power of binding and loosing. He binds and looses in one way, and the church in another. He forgives sin in a way that cleanses the soul from its inner stain and frees it from the punishment of eternal death. But he has not granted this power to priests. On the contrary, he has given them the power of binding and loosing, which means the power of telling people whether they have been bound or loosed.[12]

---

9. Lombard, *Sententiae* 4.17.1.13.
10. Ibid., 4.17.3.1, 4.17.3.8.
11. Ibid., 4.17.4.2.
12. Ibid., 4.18.5.5–6.1.

The theory of penance was one thing, but Lombard knew that it was hindered, not only by a certain unwillingness (or inability) on the part of church members to confess their sins but also by the lack of pastoral skills required in those whose duty it was to administer the sacrament.[13] What was supposed to be an act of overflowing love too often turned into a ritual that followed on from confessing sin to a priest who had little or no idea of how to respond, and this defect stored up trouble for the future.

Alongside the five sacraments mentioned above were ordination and matrimony. By the time Lombard was writing, only celibates could be ordained to the ministry of the church, and those who were already married could not enter holy orders. Lombard said nothing about compulsory celibacy, possibly because he disagreed with it, but only those who entered the priesthood were required to be celibate. Lombard saw the office of bishop as sacramentally part of the priestly order. As for the pope, he said,

> The pope is the prince of priests. . . . He is called the highest priest because he is the one who makes priests and deacons; he dispenses all ecclesiastical orders.[14]

Lombard then turned to the institution of matrimony. Unlike the other sacraments, matrimony was not of Christian origin but went back to the beginning of the creation (Gen. 1:28). Lombard had to face the difficulty that the apostle Paul spoke of marriage as second best for those who could not remain celibate (1 Cor. 7:1–2, 6), but he succeeded in demonstrating that, properly understood, it was indeed a sacrament and that Paul had said as much elsewhere (Eph. 5:31–32)![15]

Penance and the Eucharist

Of the seven sacraments, only penance and the Eucharist were meant to be repeated on a regular basis, and the two became closely interconnected. A person who wanted to receive Holy Communion was supposed to be in a "state of grace," which implied that he had repented

---

13. Ibid., 4.19.1.3.
14. Ibid., 4.24.16.1.
15. Note that Lombard interpreted the Greek word *mystērion* in the text not as "mystery" but as "sacrament."

of his sins and made his peace with God and his neighbors by doing the appropriate penance. Over time this led to a whole sin industry, with theologians compiling lists of "mortal" and "venial" (forgivable) sins, each of which came with a specific act of penance attached. The whole thing became a vast calculation, with sins and penances being ticked off against one another just like crimes and punishments. The sinner who had performed his penance satisfactorily would then return to the priest to seek absolution from him and proceed to receive Holy Communion.

The sacramental system was developed on the principle that the seven sacraments were the means by which the Spirit applied the work of Christ to the life of the believer, who was expected to grow in grace and be progressively transformed into a true child of God. The sacraments were a progression through life, from baptism at the beginning to extreme unction at the end, with the option of holy orders or matrimony at some point in the middle. Even Eucharistic devotion, which was essentially corporate, was increasingly privatized as time went on. Private masses became increasingly common, and some priests even made their living by saying them with specific "intentions" for healing, for the departed, or for anything that those willing to pay for them wanted.[16] One recent study of the phenomenon puts it this way:

> The "fruits" of the mass—the benefits that it brought—were commonly understood in a quantitative sense, so that two masses were believed to bring twice as many benefits as one mass, and this led to a dramatic increase in the number of celebrations. Paying a stipend to a priest to celebrate one or more masses on one's behalf became one of the accepted ways in which a sinner might seek to expiate his or her fault, and doing the same on behalf of a deceased person in order to purge their sins and secure their salvation also became widespread. The very wealthy would leave money in their wills so that the same might be done for them after their demise. Offering the sacrifice for particular purposes—the "votive" mass—was what the Eucharist came to be thought of as being all about.[17]

---

16. See Gary Macy, *The Banquet's Wisdom: A Short History of the Theologies of the Lord's Supper*, 2nd ed. (Akron, OH: OSL Publications, 2005), 144–51.
17. Paul F. Bradshaw and Maxwell E. Johnson, *The Eucharistic Liturgies: Their Evolution and Interpretation* (London: SPCK, 2012), 219. See also Macy, *Banquet's Wisdom*, 114–20; David N. Power, *The Eucharistic Mystery: Revitalizing the Tradition* (New York: Crossroad, 1994), 226–30, 248–49.

Doing the same on behalf of a dead person in order to purge his or her sins? It was one thing for the living to ask for masses to be said on their behalf, but could they reach out to the dead and pray for them? The belief that the dead still needed the prayers of the living was the catalyst for the next important theological development, which would transform the sacramental system into a way of salvation in its own right.

What happened to people when they died was always a major concern of the church. The Christian gospel promised a heavenly reward to all believers, irrespective of any merit on their part, but this message proved to be extremely difficult to accept. There was a feeling that only the good went to heaven and that the church's purpose was to give people the goodness they needed in order to get there. Baptism removed the taint of original sin, which took care of babies who died before reaching the age of accountability. Those who sinned after baptism had recourse to the sacraments, and it was here that penance acquired its importance. Only the truly penitent could be admitted to Communion, which was the foretaste of the heavenly banquet. It could therefore be assumed that those who did not make it that far did not get into heaven either, but where did they go instead? Quite a number of people died before having the opportunity to repent and do the necessary penance, but would they be excluded from God's presence merely because of that? Surely there had to be a second chance, an option for those with basically good intentions but who, for one reason or another, were not ready for the Bridegroom when he came for them (Matt. 25:1–13).

A few really dedicated individuals might succeed in becoming perfect, and it was generally accepted that those who were martyred for their faith had passed through the baptism of suffering mentioned by Jesus and been cleansed of their remaining sinfulness in the process (Mark 10:38–40). These were the saints who were fit to go to heaven when they died. Proof of such sainthood was not always easy to come by, but if it could be demonstrated that prayers to one of them or the bones (or other relics) they left behind on earth had produced a miracle or two, the likelihood that they had made the grade was greatly increased. The church would thus set its seal of approval on them by "canonizing" them and allowing people to pray to them for assistance. Over time, it came to be thought that some of these saints had particular interests—Christopher was the patron saint of travelers, for example, and Jude, of lost causes.

THE FLAMES OF PURGATORY

Unfortunately, the majority of people were not as successful in this life as the small band of "saints"—real or imaginary. What happened to them when they died if they were not good enough to go straight to heaven? At first, the church was tempted to say that all would go to hell. It had a very pessimistic view of human nature and did not find this particularly shocking, but it was soon felt that such a conclusion was too extreme. Many people did their best and were not particularly evil, and it seemed unfair to exclude them from heaven merely because of a few sins that could have been but for some reason had not been paid for in this life. Did not the Bible hold out at least some hope for the eventual salvation of such people? Eventually, theologians came up with the idea that there was a place of the dead where those who had not confessed or paid for their sins in this life could do so and could thus prepare themselves for eventual entry into heaven. This place came to be called purgatory, a medieval invention that stretched biblical interpretation to its limits even as it brought a new sense of order and purpose to previously vague notions of what life after death really entailed.

Finding biblical sources for the existence of purgatory was not easy. The passage most often cited was in 1 Corinthians, where the apostle Paul talks about believers building their spiritual lives on the foundation laid by Christ. He says that if the resulting building turns out to be unsuitable, it will be destroyed by fire, but the believer himself will be saved (1 Cor. 3:11–15). Augustine (354–430) expounded this passage in a way that would sound familiar to later generations:

> As for the interval between the death of this present body and the coming of the day of judgment and reward at the general resurrection, it may be claimed that it is then that the spirits of the departed suffer this kind of fire. . . . I am not concerned to refute this

suggestion, because it may well be true. It is even possible that the death of the body is part of this tribulation.[18]

Augustine was the first person to call this fire "purgatorial," though what he meant by that is unclear. That he believed there were two kinds of fire, one that tormented and one that cleansed, seems clear enough, but it is virtually certain that in his mind the purifying fire was part of the last judgment, not a process leading up to that event. Even so, he taught that there was room for praying for the departed, especially if their manner of life on earth justified it:

> Between death and the final resurrection, men's souls are kept in secret storehouses, where they are either at rest or suffering, according to their deserts. . . . They obtain relief by the dutiful service of friends who are still alive, when the Mediator's sacrifice is offered on their behalf or alms are given to the church. But these acts are only of use to those who during their lives had shown themselves deserving of them. Some people live in a way that is not good enough to be able to dispense with such assistance after their deaths, but not bad enough to make it pointless either. . . . The advantage these acts obtain [for the dead] is complete forgiveness of their sin, or at least a mitigation of their punishment.[19]

Without a clear lead from either Scripture or tradition, early medieval theologians drifted along in uncertainty, occasionally borrowing ideas from pre-Christian cults of the dead in the newly converted Celtic or Germanic countries of northern Europe but mainly just repeating what they could glean from Augustine and other great theologians of the past.[20] It was not until the twelfth century that the thorny subject of the intermediate state was finally grasped and some attempt was made to bring conceptual order out of the chaos that until then had prevailed. Gratian quoted Augustine as his authority and added a letter sent by Pope Gregory II (r. 669–731) to St. Boniface (ca. 672–754)

---

18. Augustine of Hippo, *De civitate Dei* 21.26.
19. Augustine of Hippo, *Enchiridion* 109–10. The text acquired great authority in the Middle Ages because it was included in Gratian's *Decretum* (C. 13, q. 2, c. 23).
20. See Jacques Le Goff, *The Birth of Purgatory* (Chicago: University of Chicago Press, 1984), 96–127.

sometime around 730, in which he explained that the souls of the dead are delivered from punishment in four different ways: by the sacrifices of the priests, by the prayers of the saints, by the alms of close friends, and by the fasting of relatives.[21]

Like his sources, Gratian said nothing about purgatory as a place, but greater clarity on this subject can be found in the writings of his contemporary, Hugh of St. Victor. Hugh explained it as follows:

> There is a punishment after death that is called purgatorial. Those who depart this life with certain sins may be righteous and destined for eternal life, but they are tortured there for a while in order to be cleansed. The place where this happens is not definitely fixed, although many instances in which afflicted souls have appeared [as ghosts] suggest that the pain is endured in this world, and probably where the sin was committed. . . . It is hard to know whether such pains are inflicted anywhere else.[22]

Bernard of Clairvaux (1090–1153) concurred with this view but added a more personal and pastoral note:

> We sympathize with the dead and pray for them, wishing them the joy of hope. We have to feel sorry for their suffering in purgatorial places but must also rejoice at the approach of the moment when "God will wipe away every tear from their eyes, and death shall be no more, neither shall there be mourning, nor crying, nor pain anymore, for the former things have passed away."[23]

Like his contemporaries, Peter Lombard knew nothing of purgatory as a particular place, though he accepted the possibility of penance after this life and made provision for it in the *Sentences*.[24] The importance of his comments lies not so much in what he himself said, which was very little, but in the way in which later commentators used his remarks as the basis on which to build their own far more elaborate theories.

According to Jacques Le Goff, purgatory as a place was first

21. Gratian, *Decretum*, C. 13, q. 2, c. 22.
22. Hugh of St. Victor, *De sacramentis* 2.16.4.
23. Bernard of Clairvaux, *Sermo de diversis* 16. The biblical quotation is from Rev. 21:4.
24. Lombard, *Sententiae* 4.21, 4.45.

identified by Peter Comestor (ca. 1100–ca. 1178), writing sometime in or shortly after 1170.[25] The transition from *ignis purgatorius* ("purgatorial fire") or *locus purgatorius* ("purgatorial place") to *purgatorium* ("purgatory") was so easy and natural that it is hard to tell whether those who first made it did so deliberately. In the oblique cases in Latin, the masculine *purgatorius* and the neuter *purgatorium* fall together, and there is evidence that later copyists omitted the accusative forms *ignem* and *locum* that seemed to them unnecessary when accompanied by the qualifying adjective-cum-noun *purgatorium*. This omission thereby gave the false impression that purgatory had been identified as a particular place some years earlier.[26] Be that as it may, there is no doubt that by 1200, purgatory was established in people's minds as a definite location, though whether it was nearer to heaven or to hell remained uncertain. Those who emphasized that it was a preparation for entry to heaven naturally leaned toward the former view, while those who thought in terms of fiery punishment preferred the latter.

It was around the time of the Fourth Lateran Council in 1215 that purgatory became an established part of the church's spiritual universe, as can be seen from the important guidebook for priests who were called to hear the confessions of penitent sinners, written in the wake of the council by Thomas of Chobham (ca. 1160–ca. 1236). Thomas explained that "mass is celebrated for the living and for the dead, but doubly for the dead, because the sacraments of the altar are petitions for the living, thanksgivings for the saints [in heaven], and propitiations for those in purgatory, that result in remission of their punishment."[27] As far as he was concerned, no one could do anything for those in hell, so the Mass as a propitiation could apply only to souls in purgatory, which therefore had to exist!

About the same time, William of Auvergne (ca. 1180–1249) was also making a case for the necessity of purgatory, based on the need for penance.[28] To him it was obvious that most people died with unconfessed sins that had to be dealt with before the departed soul could

---

25. Le Goff, *Birth of Purgatory*, 155–58, 362–66. Peter was given the name Comestor, or Manducator, which means "the Eater," because he devoured books!
26. Ibid., 364–65.
27. Thomas of Chobham, *Summa Confessorum*, ed. F. Broomfield, Analecta Mediaevalia Namurcensia 25 (Louvain: Editions Nauwelaerts, 1968), 125–26.
28. See Le Goff, *Birth of Purgatory*, 241–45, for more details.

enter heaven. It was equally obvious to William that some sins were more serious than others—murder, for example, had to be punished, but gluttony or frivolity could be expiated by penance. This was the penitential practice of the church in this world, and there seemed to William to be no reason why it should not be carried on in the next life. He did not believe, however, that this continuation of penance could be used as an excuse for deferring penance in this life. On the contrary, the more sins expiated now, the fewer there would be to take care of after death, and the soul's time in purgatory would be correspondingly shortened. As an extension of justice on earth, purgatory appealed to William as the supreme example of God's fairness, but it was also an assurance that this life was closely bound up with the next. In fact, William seems to have located purgatory on earth, rather than somewhere nearer to heaven or hell, which naturally increased his feeling that it was little more than an extension of the church's ministry to the living.

Moving things a step further was Alexander of Hales (ca. 1185–1245), the first man to write a commentary on Peter Lombard's *Sentences* and the first teacher to use the *Sentences* as his main theological text. In his gloss on *Sentences* 4.21, he expounded Lombard's theory of penance in the context of purgatory, making the following points:

1. Purgatory is a fire that burns up venial sins.
2. Purgatory wipes out penalties for mortal sins that have not been sufficiently paid for.
3. Purgatory is more severe than any earthly punishment.
4. Purgatory is not an unjust or disproportionate punishment.
5. Purgatory is a place of faith and hope but without the heavenly vision of God.
6. Hardly anybody is good enough to escape the need to pass through purgatory.

Having established these six points, Alexander went on to examine the relationship between purgatory and the church in greater detail. Up to this time, it was generally assumed that the church could forgive sins in this life but that its jurisdiction ended at death. But if purgatorial penance merely continued what had already started on earth, it seemed logical to assume that the church's jurisdiction over it would

extend beyond the grave. Alexander did not intend to rule God out of
the picture altogether, since his grace was still regarded as essential for
the assurance that penance was effective, but it was also self-evident to
him that the church had an important role to play in purgatory:

> Just as specific pain brings satisfaction for a particular sin, so the
> common pain of the universal church, which cries out on behalf
> of the sins of dead believers . . . , is an aid to satisfaction. It does
> not create satisfaction in itself, but contributes to it along with the
> pain suffered by the penitent. This is what intercession is all about.
> Intercession is the merit of the church which is able to lessen the
> pain of one of its members.[29]

INDULGENCES AND SUFFERING IN PURGATORY

Here we catch a first glimpse of the system of "indulgences" by which
the church would claim to remit the sins of the dead and lessen their
suffering in purgatory. In the late eleventh century, Ivo of Chartres
(ca. 1040–1115) had worked out a theory of dispensation, that is, not
applying the rules of ecclesiastical law in certain circumstances.[30] According to him, a distinction had to be made between different kinds
of legal principles, as follows:

Praecepta (precepts): absolute, binding rules
Consilia (counsels): suggestions as to how to apply the rules
Indulgentiae (indulgences): permitted exceptions to the rules

Justice demanded obedience to the rules, though of course those
rules had to be applied in the right way. The *praecepta* and the *consilia*
were therefore essential and interdependent. But human life is seldom
as straightforward as the rules would like it to be, and recognizing that
variety in life experience engendered a certain tolerance of weakness
and failure. It was not easy to determine how much leeway should be
granted, but this could be decided only on a case-by-case basis, which
is what canon lawyers were employed to do. Indulgences would not be
granted without good reason though, because somehow the rules had

---

29. Alexander of Hales, *Glossa in quatuor libros Sententiarum Petri Lombardi* 4.21.
30. Ivo of Chartres, *Prologus in Decretum*, in *PL* 161:47–60.

to be kept if justice was to be done. The answer was found in penance, which offered payment and restitution for the offenses that had been committed. In the early days, a full indulgence was granted only to those who went on crusade, as a reward for their sacrifice, but in time this practice was extended and indulgences made readily available to almost anyone who was prepared to pay for them. In special circumstances, they might even be granted *without* such payment, though for obvious reasons, such generosity was rare.

To control all of this, it was necessary to establish a form of penance that would be fair and applicable to all. In 1215, the Fourth Lateran Council issued a canon obliging every Christian, male and female, to confess his or her sins to a priest at least once a year and to receive from him an appropriate penance.[31] This canon made it necessary to define what sins could be forgiven and what sins could not—the distinction between "venial" and "mortal" sins mentioned earlier. In this respect, Thomas of Chobham was the right man at the right time, and his little manual on the subject became one of the most popular sources for clerical guidance in this area. The potential for intellectual madness, however, was enormous, as Jacques Le Goff has pointed out:

> Purgatory was dragged down into a whirlpool of delirious scholastic ratiocination, which raised the most otiose questions, refined the most sophisticated distinctions, and took delight in the most elaborate solutions. Can a venial sin become mortal? Does an accumulation of several venial sins equal a mortal sin? What is the fate of a person who dies with both a mortal sin and a venial sin on his head (assuming that it is possible for this to occur, which some authorities doubted)? And so on.[32]

By about 1250, the outlines of purgatory were clear, and it remained only to define some of the more obscure details. Theologians continued to discuss where exactly purgatory was located, what purgatorial fire consisted of (i.e., was it purely spiritual or partly material as well?), and whether a soul was set free to go to heaven as soon as its penance was complete or whether it had to wait until the last judgment to be

---

31. Alberigo, *Conciliorum oecumenicorum decreta*, 245 (canon 21).
32. Le Goff, *Birth of Purgatory*, 217.

finally acquitted. The great Franciscan friar and teacher Bonaventure (1221–1274) dealt with each of these, concluding, for example, that purgatory had become a distinct place only after the incarnation of Christ. Before that time, souls had gone to a place called "limbo" or "the bosom of Abraham," which offered no opportunity for active penance but only a place of waiting for judgment.[33] He thought that purgatorial fire was both spiritual and material—the spiritual fire was redemptive, whereas the material fire was merely punitive.[34] He was also vehemently opposed to any suggestion that a cleansed soul might have to delay its heavenly bliss to the last judgment—once its time in purgatory was done, it was free to go, and so away it went![35]

Very similar views were expressed by Bonaventure's contemporary Albert the Great (ca. 1206–1280), a German who joined the Dominican order and lectured in Paris (1242–1248), where he was a major influence on the young Thomas Aquinas (1225–1274). Thomas, despite his immense theological output, had relatively little to say about purgatory and seems to have been uninterested in the subject.[36] He died before getting to it in the course of his *Summa Theologiae*, and most of what we have from him was put together later by his students and attached to the *Summa* as a supplement. Essentially, he repeated what earlier doctors (and especially Albert the Great) had said, adapting it to the needs of the subject's controversies in which he was periodically engaged.

Thomas Aquinas reminds us that purgatory was not only far from being universally popular but was actually rejected by a large number of people—indeed, by virtually everyone who had reason to quarrel with the authority of the papacy. This was something new in the history of doctrine. Earlier disputes had been much more "objective" in the sense that nobody of any stature had opposed a doctrine merely because it was held by Rome or by some other episcopal see. But purgatory was so closely linked to the power claimed by the papacy that it was very difficult, if not impossible, to keep the two apart. If the pope lacked the power to forgive sins on earth, he could hardly have

---

33. Bonaventure, *Commentarium in IV libros Sententiarum* 4.20.
34. Bonaventure, *Breviloquium* 7.2.
35. Bonaventure, *Commentarium in IV libros Sententiarum* 4.21.3.
36. See Le Goff, *Birth of Purgatory*, 266–78.

done so after a sinner's death, and if that were true, the question of the church's involvement with purgatory would not have arisen. If, on the other hand, the pope did have the power to forgive sins, rejecting his authority would be a dangerous move in this life—never mind what might happen after death. So either way, purgatory and the papacy were bound up together, and to reject the one was to reject the other.

We should therefore not be surprised to discover that, by and large, heretical sects that objected to the papacy, such as the Waldensians, also rejected purgatory.[37] It is hard to know what to make of the evidence for this, though, because almost all of it comes from hostile sources who may have been poorly informed.[38] Nevertheless, the connection was there and can be seen in Martin Luther's (1483–1546) *Ninety-Five Theses* (1517), which repeatedly insinuates that the pope has no jurisdiction over purgatory, although Luther was careful not to say so explicitly.[39]

Purgatory caught on in the medieval church because it gave people hope for eternity even if they were not perfect in this life.[40] It provided a means by which they could continue to pray for their loved ones after they had died and help them on their way to heaven. It was also possible for them to perform extra acts of penance in this life—or works of supererogation, as they were called—and thereby reduce the time that they would have to spend in purgatory themselves.

In time, this structure of penance and works of supererogation became a burden both for the church and for the penitents. Telling people to stand barefoot in the snow while holding a lighted candle for hours on end, for example, soon came to be seen as a pointless exercise. It did nothing for the church, and the people so burdened were merely

---

37. Ibid., 278–80.

38. See Walter L. Wakefield and Austin P. Evans, *Heresies of the High Middle Ages*, Records of Civilization, Sources and Studies 81 (New York: Columbia University Press, 1969), 346–51, 371–73, where we find evidence for early Waldensian beliefs to this effect. See also Gabriel Audisio, *The Waldensian Dissent: Persecution and Survival, c. 1170–c. 1570* (Cambridge: Cambridge University Press, 1999), and for a different group, see Robert Lerner, *The Heresy of the Free Spirit in the Later Middle Ages* (Notre Dame, IN: University of Notre Dame Press, 2007).

39. See theses 5, 6, 8, 10, 13, 15, 20–22, 25–27, 82. An English translation of the original Latin text is available in *Martin Luther's Basic Theological Writings*, ed. Timothy F. Lull, 2nd ed. (Minneapolis: Fortress, 2005), 40–46.

40. This aspect of it still appeals to some people, including those who ought to know better. For example, see Jerry L. Walls, *Purgatory: The Logic of Total Transformation* (Oxford: Oxford University Press, 2012), written by someone who claims to be an evangelical Protestant!

humiliated, which could be almost intolerable if they were prominent members of their local community. The problem was that if such leading citizens lost the respect of others, they could also lose their authority, and social order might break down. For these and similar reasons, a way out was eagerly sought and over time was hard to resist, despite the anguished protests of reformers who thought that public penance was good for the soul and ought to be continued.

Perhaps the best way for us to understand this thinking is to compare it with how authorities today handle people who break the law in minor ways. In theory, lawbreakers should be put in prison, but prisons are often full and seem to do little good for their inmates. To lock someone up merely for speeding, for instance, seems excessive. So the state has devised another means of punishing this sort of infraction. Instead of doing time behind bars, the guilty are fined. The state gets additional revenue, the offender does not have to suffer major inconvenience or unwanted publicity, and everyone is more or less happy with the result. It was this way of thinking that drove the church to commute penance to a fine. Those who paid up were given a certificate of "indulgence," which effectively wrote off their need to do penance. Once it became clear that people could buy indulgences, both for their loved ones and for themselves, why would they want to go to the trouble of doing works of supererogation when they could pay for a certificate instead? And so, gradually the sale of indulgences became an established practice of the church. The ecclesiastical coffers were filled with donations, and the individuals who bought them had the satisfaction of knowing that their time in purgatory had been reduced.

What this system did not say was whether or not the people who were thus excused became holier as a result. Paying off a debt was one thing, but did it make one a better person? How do sinful human beings receive God's righteousness, and what difference does that make to them? To describe how sinners are transformed, Augustine chose the word *iustificare* and its derivatives, and his usage passed into the Western tradition. He himself believed that the word meant "to make righteous," since it was composed of the two Latin words *iustum* ("righteous") and *facere* ("make"). However, it was unclear what in practice that entailed. To the extent that *iustificare* was a translation of the Greek verb *dikaioō*, it meant "pass judgment on," which was usually taken in a negative sense but in this case was understood positively, meaning "acquit." Yet Augustine also used *iustificare* to convey the idea of "transforming someone into a righteous person," which *dikaioō* does not (and cannot) mean. This is important, because this additional implication caused much trouble and misunderstanding later on.

Made Righteous by Infused Grace

Augustine believed that a person was made righteous by a process of inner transformation that governed not only his actions but also the motivation that lay behind them.[41] In practice, this made motivation more important than action, because if a particular action failed to achieve its purpose, it would still count as righteous in the sight of God if it had been done with the right intention. As Augustine understood it, righteousness was a divine attribute in which Christians participated directly and not merely a word used to express a sinful believer's relationship with (and total dependence on) a righteous God. It could only be obtained by God's free gift ("grace"), but obtained it was, and the person who was made righteous by Christ became a better human being than he or she had been before. This was possible because for Augustine, grace was not an abstract gift of righteousness but the presence of the Holy Spirit in a person's life. The Spirit is the love of God that makes it possible for those who receive that gift to love God with all their hearts and their neighbors as themselves, which is what God demands of us.[42]

Faith was the fruit of love, and so for Augustine, "justification by faith" really meant "justification by love," which expresses itself in and through faith (Gal. 5:6). Working in a person's life by the power of God, faith gradually overcomes the desires of the flesh (*concupiscentia*) in the way that a medicine overcomes disease. To be effective, the grace of faith in love has to be periodically refreshed and strengthened so it can pursue and eventually complete its work. How this was meant to happen Augustine did not specify, but any doubts

---

41. Augustine of Hippo, *De spiritu et littera* 26.45.
42. Augustine of Hippo, *De Trinitate* 15.17.31.

on that score were laid to rest by Haimo of Auxerre (d. ca. 855): "We are redeemed and justified by the passion of Christ, which justifies mankind in baptism through faith, and subsequently by penance. The two are so closely linked that it is impossible to be justified by one without the other."[43]

Much the same thing was said more than two centuries later by Bruno of Cologne (ca. 1030–1101), who made a point of adding that penance was the divinely appointed means of cleansing the soul from sins committed after baptism.[44] The explanation of this process given by the French monk Hervé de Bourg-Dieu (ca. 1080–1150) may be regarded as typical:

> Through the law there comes a recognition of sin, through faith there comes the infusion of grace in opposition to sin, through grace comes the cleansing of the soul from sin's guilt, through the cleansing of the soul comes freedom of the will [*libertas arbitrii*], through the freedom of the will [*liberum arbitrium*] comes the love of righteousness, and through the love of righteousness comes the implementation of the law.[45]

Note the way the process unfolds: the law points out the need for faith, and faith leads to grace, which sets the ball rolling—purification, freedom, love, and righteousness follow in quick succession, leading in the end to the fulfilling of the law, which takes us back to where we started but now in a way that actually works. Peter Comestor condensed this into a neat scheme describing the stages of justification that, with minor variations, was repeated by most medieval writers:

1. The infusion of grace, given to beginners
2. The cooperation of free will (*liberum arbitrium*), given to those making progress
3. The consummation (i.e., remission of sins), given to those who have arrived[46]

43. Haimo of Auxerre, *Expositio in epistulas Sancti Pauli*, in *PL* 117:391C. The text being commented on is Rom. 3:24: "Justified by his grace as a gift."
44. Bruno of Cologne, *Expositio in omnes epistulas Pauli*, in *PL* 153:55B–C. The text being commented on is Rom. 5:20: "The law came in to increase the trespass."
45. Hervé de Bourg-Dieu, *Expositio in epistulas Pauli*, in *PL* 181:642D. This comment relates to Rom. 3:31. Note that Hervé did not distinguish *libertas* from *liberum arbitrium*.
46. Peter Comestor, *Sermo*, 17.

This scheme was subsequently modified into a fourfold pattern, with the second element divided into two. The classic statement of it was worked out by William of Auxerre (ca. 1160–1231), who expressed it like this:[47]

1. The infusion of grace
2. The movement of the free will (*liberum arbitrium*)
3. Contrition
4. Remission of sins

The inclusion of contrition made it easy to tie this fourfold scheme into the sacrament of penance, thus encouraging the integration of justification with the sacramental system, which took place in the thirteenth century. But those who moved in that direction insisted that penance by itself had no power to justify anyone. Justification was from beginning to end a work of divine grace in which penance was only the necessary condition for that grace to be given.[48] This was the pattern adopted by Alexander of Hales, Albert the Great, Bonaventure, and Thomas Aquinas, as we can see from their respective commentaries on the *Sentences* of Peter Lombard.[49] Thomas modified the scheme somewhat by making a clearer distinction between the second and third stages:[50]

1. The infusion of grace
2. The movement of the free will directed toward God through faith (i.e., love)
3. The movement of the free will directed against sin (i.e., contrition)
4. The remission of sin

To understand what effect this had, we must appreciate that for Thomas and his contemporaries, who had been trained in Aristotelian physics and reflected that in their approach, progress from the first to the last item on the list was a process set in motion by the initial

---

47. William of Auxerre, *Summa aurea* 3.2.1 (fol. 121v).
48. Alan of Lille, *Contra haereticos* 1.51.
49. Alexander of Hales, *Glossa in quatuor libros Sententiarum Petri Lombardi* 4.17.7; Albert the Great, *Commentary on the Sentences of the Lombard* 4.17a.10; Bonaventure, *Commentarium in IV libros Sententiarum* 2.16.1.3; Thomas Aquinas, *Super Primo Libro Sententiarum* 4.17.1.4; Thomas Aquinas, *Summa Theologiae* 1a2ae.113.6.
50. *Summa Theologiae* 1.2.113.8.

infusion of grace that led inexorably to the forgiveness of sins. Turning toward God in love and against sin in sorrow were integral parts of this process, which could be distinguished in theoretical terms within a chain of cause and effect but which normally occurred more or less simultaneously.

For Thomas, justification before God was identified with the second stage. The infusion of grace involved a real change in the recipient, who was set free from the constraints of his sinful nature and given the ability to subordinate his mind and will to God. When he did so, he was justified in God's eyes because he had demonstrated his desire to do what was right. The infused grace that made this possible was not an extension of God's nature but a created equivalent of it that God implanted in the soul of the believer, giving him an inbuilt disposition (*habitus*) toward righteousness. This made it possible for him to avoid mortal sin, but as he was not yet perfect, he would still fall into venial sin and stand in need of penance. It was at this point that the penitential system described above kicked in. Even justified believers needed to be purified further because they continued to struggle against the effects of their "lower nature"—what the Bible calls the war of the spirit against the flesh. Very few people would succeed in winning that battle in this life, but the chance to carry on in purgatory ensured that they would triumph in the end.

Meriting the Grace of Justification

It was generally agreed that God responded to the movement of a man's free will toward him because he regarded such a movement as meritorious—it was a good thing for the man to do, and it deserved an appropriate response from God. The question then arose as to how meritorious it actually was. Could a human being do anything that would really please God? In the strict sense, the answer to this had to be no, because human beings are both finite and sinful and therefore incapable of dealing with God on his level. But like little children who want to do something good but cannot because they lack the strength and knowledge required for success, sinful people who try their best and have the right intentions ought to be applauded for making the attempt, not rejected as failures because they have not managed to do something they are incapable of doing. This, said the theologians of the time, was what happened when souls infused with created grace turned to God. They were justified, not because they had managed to become righteous by their own efforts but because it was the right response on God's part to those who were doing the best they could. What God honored in them was merit *de congruo* ("appropriate")—they wanted the right thing, and thus God gave it to them even though they had not really earned it.

Had sinful souls been able to make the grade on their own, God would have acknowledged their merit as being *de condigno* ("deserved"), but that was impossible. Instead, God promised that if sinners acted in a certain way, he would respond to them accordingly by giving infused grace. And once a sinner received infused grace, he or she could achieve what God had laid down in his covenant with mankind.[51] This made merit *de condigno* a real possibility, because the promised reward was proportionate to its efforts. A divine reward for human achievement was therefore expected as the just outworking of God's righteousness.[52]

ATTRITION AND CONTRITION

Criticism of this scheme of things began with John Duns Scotus (ca. 1266–1308) in the generation after Aquinas and Bonaventure. Scotus pointed out that if contrition were necessary before a sinner could receive the sacrament of penance, the sacrament would be effective not in and of itself (*ex opere operato*) but only if the person receiving it was in the right spiritual mood (*ex opere operantis*). In that case, penance would hardly be necessary, since the penitent would already have reached the point to which the sacrament was meant to bring him.[53] Scotus tried to resolve this problem by saying that contrition was not a necessary precondition for receiving the sacrament. All that was needed was repentance based on fear of punishment. If that was sincere, it might merit the grace of justification *de congruo*, but if not, it could still be enough to allow the sinner to do penance. Scotus called

---

51. See William of Auvergne, *Opera omnia* 1.310.aF, where he defines this principle.
52. Aquinas, *Summa Theologiae* 1.2.114.1.
53. John Duns Scotus, *Opus Oxoniense* 4.1.6.10–11.

this "attrition." To his mind, a sinner who started out at the lowest level of attrition would gradually be strengthened by sacramental grace to the point where he would be genuinely contrite.

Scotus even allowed for the possibility that a sinner could be justified without having to do penance at all, but this was more theoretical than real. Nobody could know for sure whether he had done enough to merit anything, and so in practice the sacrament became more necessary than ever, because it gave penitents the *assurance* that they were in a state of grace.[54]

Scotus's views were taken over by William of Ockham (ca. 1287– ca. 1347), who moved the discussion on to another level of philosophical analysis. He believed that God's acceptance of moral acts was what gave them their meritorious value and that this acceptance was a matter of course in the case of believers.[55] Ockham's followers went further and denied that there could be such a thing as merit *de condigno*; any merit must by definition be *de congruo*, and even that depended entirely on grace.[56] However, the general drift of their thinking was away from merit altogether, making everything depend entirely on God's grace, which was essentially the position taken by John Wyclif (ca. 1328–1384) and Jan Hus (ca. 1369–1415).[57]

The full effect of Ockham's ideas can be seen in the work of Gabriel Biel (ca. 1420–1495), which in many ways represents the culmination of medieval theological developments.[58] Unlike Ockham, Biel was not an uncritical admirer of Duns Scotus, and he firmly rejected any notion of attrition as a prelude to penance. For Biel, only contrition would do, and he believed, along (as he thought) with Peter Lombard, that in the sacrament of penance all the priest could do was to declare that the sinner had already been justified on that basis.[59] Biel did not rule out the possibility of presacramental justification, but even if that happened

---

54. Ibid., 4.14.4.14.
55. See Gordon Leff, *William of Ockham: The Metamorphosis of Scholastic Discourse* (Manchester: Manchester University Press, 1975).
56. See, for example, Manuel Santos-Noya, *Die Sünden- und Gnadenlehre des Gregor von Rimini*, Europäische Hochschulschriften, ser. 23, Theologie 388 (Frankfurt-am-Main: Peter Lang, 1990).
57. John Wyclif, *De scientia Dei*, fol. 61v.; Jan Hus, *Super IV. Sententiarum* 2.27.5.
58. See Heiko A. Oberman, *The Harvest of Medieval Theology: Gabriel Biel and Late Medieval Nominalism*, 3rd ed. (Durham, NC: Labyrinth, 1983). The process of justification is discussed on 146–84.
59. Gabriel Biel, *Collectorium* 4.14.2.1, n. 2D.

in a few cases, it could not be understood apart from the sacrament because the latter was always implied. The reason for this was that contrition, with or without the sacrament, only offered remission of the *guilt* for sin. The *punishment* for it was accordingly downgraded from the eternal to the temporal realm, but that, of course, was the sphere of penance, which therefore still had an important part to play.

Biel believed that human beings could love God in their natural strength without the infusion of divine grace, but he also recognized that God intended for them to accomplish his will in such a state of grace, which was obviously beyond their natural abilities.[60] He was also deeply concerned with the need to demonstrate moral integrity. Sacramental merit was not meant to be a substitute for that, and Biel often warned his hearers not to think that they could remove their sins by good works if they were not inwardly repentant (i.e., contrite).[61] As he saw the matter, his proposal was a way of avoiding the easygoing pattern of attrition, which many people besides himself thought was a lazy way out of sincere repentance, without demanding the kind of superhuman self-sacrifice that only a spiritual athlete could achieve.

As for the disposition (*habitus*) needed for sacramental justification, Biel insisted that a believer should love God for his own sake and not for what he could get out of him.[62] The external penance performed in the sacrament had to be matched by a corresponding internal repentance, without which it would have no effect. Biel did not deny the power of divine grace in a person's life, but he did not think that it was essential in every case. As he saw it, human beings could often act rightly, according to the light of reason given to them, whether they were aided in this by divine grace or not. It was ignorance, not the lack of grace, that prevented people from doing the right thing.[63] The church's primary duty, therefore, was not to infuse grace into sinners but to enlighten them with the correct understanding, so that they could act properly of their own accord. Apparently Biel thought that if people knew what was right, they would do it automatically![64]

---

60. Ibid., 4.14.2.2.
61. Ibid., 4.4.1.2, concl. 5O.
62. Gabriel Biel, *Sermones* 1.102E.
63. Ibid., 1.101D.
64. Oberman, *Harvest of Medieval Theology*, 165.

None of this suggested to Biel that the inner disposition (*habitus*) of created grace was superfluous. On the contrary, it was essential, not because of any metaphysical necessity but because that was the way that God had ordained his plan of salvation. This was the covenant (*pactum*) that set out his requirements of us and his response to our attempts to meet those requirements. Created grace by itself could never determine God's actions for the simple reason that it was a created thing and not part of his nature.[65] But within the covenant order of things, God has accepted sinners and given them the grace they need to perform acts of meritorious value, and it is for that reason that they are justified. In Heiko Oberman's words:

> The gratuitous character of God's remuneration is therefore not based on the *activity* of the habit of grace nor on the *presence* of the habit of grace, but on God's eternal decree according to which he has decided to accept every act which is performed in a state of grace as a *meritum de condigno*.[66]

As far as merit *de congruo* was concerned, Biel thought of that as the supreme achievement of a man unaided by the infusion of grace. God may accept this act as meritorious and bestow his grace on the penitent sinner, but he is not obliged to, and if he does so, it is an act of generosity on his part, not of justice.[67] Just as God's acceptance of the repentant sinner follows from and is necessitated by his covenant promise, so the same must be said of infused grace, because no outside power can force God to do anything.[68] Indeed, it is precisely because God is free (*liber*) and does not operate under any form of external constraint, that he can show his generosity (*liberalitas*) by ignoring any sense of due proportion between an act and its reward, revealing his superabundant mercy instead.[69]

The result of Biel's doctrine was that the sinner was unwittingly placed under an extraordinary burden to produce good works deserving of grace. God's righteousness brought only judgment and punish-

---

65. Biel, *Collectorium* 1.17.3.3, dub. 2G.
66. Oberman, *Harvest of Medieval Theology*, 170.
67. Biel, *Collectorium* 2.27.1.1, n. 3.
68. Ibid., 2.27.1.3., dub. 4O.
69. Ibid., 2.27.1.2., concl. 4K.

ment in its wake, and by doing good works, the sinner had to hope that the divine wrath could be deflected. As Biel put it, "Man does not know whether he is worthy of [God's] hatred or love."[70] Without that assurance, the sinner could face the prospect of hearing about God's covenant and the justification it promised only with fear and trepidation, because he had no way of knowing whether he would ever be worthy enough to receive it.

THE CRISIS OF ASSURANCE

The system outlined by William of Ockham and his followers was seldom seriously questioned in its fundamentals. As the young Martin Luther put it,

> The doctors are right to say that when people do their best, God inevitably gives them grace. This cannot mean that this preparation for grace is [based on merit] *de condigno*, because they are incompatible, but it can be regarded as *de congruo* because of God's promise and the covenant (*pactum*) of mercy.[71]

It took a spiritual crisis in his own life to shake Luther out of this way of thinking. He did his best but discovered that it was not good enough. Whatever grace he may have received *de congruo*, it did not bring him peace with God. After much searching, he found the answer in the words of the prophet Habakkuk, quoted by the apostle Paul in his letter to the Romans: "The righteous shall live by faith" (Rom. 1:17; cf. Hab. 2:4). The scales dropped from his eyes as he realized that it is by grace that we are saved through faith and not by our works, however meritorious they are in themselves. The foundations of the old system were shaken to the root, and the result was the Protestant Reformation.

The Medieval View of Authority

THE EARLY CHURCH

Almost as important for the Reformers as the doctrine of salvation was the question of authority in the church, which had become a key issue

---

70. Biel, *Sermones* 1.70F.
71. Martin Luther, *Dictata super Psalterium* 114:1 (Vulgate: 113:1), *LW* 4:257.

of debate in the fourteenth and fifteenth centuries. In some respects this debate went back to the earliest days of Christianity, and it was on the witness of the New Testament that the arguments increasingly focused. In premodern times, most people thought of *authority* as something primarily personal. The Word was connected to its *author*, and the ultimate author was God himself, from whom all authority derived. God the Father gave his authority to the Son, and the Son sent the Holy Spirit to bring the church into being and to preserve it until he returns in judgment (1 Cor. 15:25–28).

The theological question was how the Holy Spirit performed the task assigned to him. In the New Testament church, the answer was clear enough. Jesus chose disciples who became the apostles. They governed the early church and gave it the New Testament Scriptures, which contained the teaching they had received from Jesus himself. The transition from disciples to apostles was not automatic—Judas was excluded from the apostleship, and Paul was added by an exceptional divine intervention. But the principle was clear enough: an apostle had to be a witness of the resurrected Christ and to have been specially commissioned by him for his task. Initially, the apostles worked together from their base in Jerusalem, but gradually they spread out and developed their own ministries. Peter became the apostle to the Jews, while Paul was recognized as the apostle to the Gentiles. Disagreements between Jews and Gentiles were resolved by consensus, which church leaders arrived at by open debate in a church council (Acts 15).

What happened after the apostles died was (and still is) unclear. Some of them may have appointed successors in the way that Paul entrusted his ministry to Timothy and Titus. Or perhaps local churches elected one of their number to become their overseer, or bishop, on the understanding that he would be responsible for maintaining the apostolic deposit of truth. What is certain is that a hundred years after the ascension of Christ, his churches were almost all being led by elected bishops, and that congregations founded by the apostles had a special responsibility to preserve and defend their legacy. This duty was necessary because of the growth of heretical movements that these churches had no power to suppress and could combat only by appealing to their own traditions, which they claimed had come from the apostles. The fact that different apostolically rooted churches agreed with each other was evidence that their claims were true, and it was in this way that the New Testament came to be accepted as Scripture on a par with the Hebrew Bible.

It is a remarkable fact that when the church was legalized in the early fourth century, it emerged as a single worldwide body. There were certainly disputes and incipient divisions—Donatism in North Africa, for example, and Arianism in much of the East. But there was also a widespread consensus, revealed in church councils that the emperor now convened. The councils counteracted these dissident movements and established a common orthodoxy that every local church was obliged to accept. The crowning achievement of the conciliar era was a creed that was accepted as the touchstone of Christian belief virtually everywhere.[72]

Church councils were not always summoned by imperial authority, but unless their decisions were ratified by the emperor, they did not become law and could not be enforced. Most councils met on a provincial basis and legislated only for the needs of their province, though in some cases (North Africa and Spain in particular), they exerted a much wider influence. Imperial councils met less frequently, but they were more important, and their decisions applied universally.[73] Only bishops could go to councils and vote on behalf of their congregations, but although attendance was sometimes fairly high, it was never universal. In particular, the bishops of Rome never summoned or attended any of them, though they usually sent representatives and later ratified the councils' decisions.

The system of provincial and imperial councils was not perfect, but it functioned reasonably well for a time. It began to break down when many of the Eastern churches refused to accept the decisions of the Council of Chalcedon (451). This led to schisms in Egypt and Syria that the imperial government was unable to suppress, despite many attempts to do so. In the course of the sixth century the schisms

---

72. This creed was probably written at (or shortly after) the First Council of Constantinople in 381, though we know it today as the Nicene Creed because of a mistaken belief that it was produced by the First Council of Nicaea in 325. It quickly became, and has remained, the most widespread statement of faith in the Christian world.

73. These councils are called *ecumenical* from the Greek word *oikoumenē*, which was the term used to describe the Roman Empire (see Luke 2:1).

hardened, and when the Muslim Arabs invaded in the decade after Muhammad's death in 632, the Roman Empire lost these regions. This geopolitical break made it impossible for the emperor to compel the dissidents to return to the imperial fold, but it also took the theological questions involved out of the realm of practical politics in what remained of the Christian world.

The Emergence of the Papacy

Just as significant for the future of the church as the rise of Islam was the collapse of the Roman Empire in the West. In 476, Rome sent the imperial insignia to Constantinople, signaling that the West would henceforth recognize the authority of the Eastern (Byzantine) emperor, but in reality the barbarian kingdoms that had set themselves up in Western Europe went their own way. The Eastern Empire attempted to regain the lost provinces and managed to hold onto Rome for more than two centuries (536–751), but the reconquest was only partial. To buttress their authority over the West, the emperors needed the support of the bishop of Rome, whom they recognized as their chief representative there. This status could be traced back to the First Council of Constantinople in 381, when the world had been divided into five regions and the bishop of the most important city in each region was appointed as the *patriarch* of that area. The hierarchy of patriarchates was Rome, Constantinople, Alexandria, Antioch, and Jerusalem, in that order. By 700, the last three of these had fallen under Muslim rule and no longer counted for much, so for practical purposes, Rome vied with Constantinople for supremacy. Rome had an advantage because its church was of apostolic origin, or so it was thought. The claim that Peter had been its first bishop and that he was martyred there (along with Paul) was generally accepted, but in fact, Rome's spiritual authority rested more on its position as the ancient imperial capital than on anything else. For that reason, Constantinople was a genuine rival, because although it lacked Rome's apostolic pedigree, it was where the emperor lived and where imperial church councils continued to meet.[74]

---

74. Councils were held there in 553, 680–681, 692, 870, and 880. The one exception was the Second Council of Nicaea (787), but Nicaea is only a day's journey from Constantinople, so it was easily accessible from the capital.

As long as the bishops of Rome remained subject to the emperor at Constantinople, they could not establish an independent spiritual authority, nor did they want to. The situation changed, however, when the pagan Lombards extinguished the imperial province (or "exarchate," as it was known) in central Italy and threatened Rome in 751. In desperation, its bishop appealed to the king of the Franks, who subsequently crossed the Alps, annihilated the Lombards, and established the Roman bishop as the secular ruler of the old exarchate in 754. This was the beginning of the Papal States, a political entity that would survive until 1870. It also marked the rise of Frankish power, which in 800 led to the creation of the Holy Roman Empire in Western Europe. The Frankish king Charlemagne became the new Western emperor, and Rome repudiated its residual allegiance to Constantinople. The Holy Roman Empire was to endure until 1806, and its rulers frequently found themselves in conflict with the bishop of Rome, who could then appropriately be called the pope, even though it was he who crowned them and legitimated their rule.

In theory, the two halves of the ancient Roman Empire had been restored, but they were very different from one another. In the East, the emperor and the patriarch lived in the same city and worked closely together, but this was never true in the West. The pope remained in Rome, but the emperor hardly ever went there and did not stay long when he did. Furthermore, the empire in the West never covered the whole of Western Christendom, and in 843, it was subdivided among Charlemagne's grandsons. While an emperor was still elected from among the corulers, he had restricted powers, and the Holy Roman Empire was never to become a powerful European state. At the same time, the papacy declined as it became the plaything of the Roman aristocracy, the members of which vied with each other to appoint relatives to the office. For two hundred years, Western Europe was devoid of any real authority, a situation that many people found increasingly intolerable.

Reform began under the impulse of the monks of Cluny in Burgundy (now part of France), who believed that only a strong papacy could rescue the church and Western society from its chaos. To achieve this, they maneuvered their own candidate into the office. Leo IX (r. 1049–

1054) reasserted the ancient claims of Rome to supreme jurisdiction over the church at large, though the only immediate effect of this was to alienate the East, which refused to knuckle under to his authority. This led to a schism in 1054, which later came to be recognized as the moment when East and West went their separate ways.[75] In 1059, the Cluniac reformers were able to establish the college of cardinals in Rome, a group of senior clerics whose responsibility it would be to elect the pope. This development was of immense importance because it took papal elections out of the hands of the lay aristocracy in Rome and made it possible to choose men who would advance the interests of the church, not those of their own families. The most famous of the reforming popes was Gregory VII (r. 1073–1085), often known by his secular name, Hildebrand. He tackled the emperor over the appointment of bishops and was able to force him to accede to the church's demands. Gregory VII's boldness was somewhat premature, though, and the emperor was later able to get his own back by invading Rome and driving out the pope (1084). But the long-term trend was now set. In 1095, Pope Urban II (r. 1088–1099) was strong enough to persuade the kings of Western Europe to go on crusade to recover the Holy Land from the Muslims, and papal power was revealed for all to see.

In the course of the twelfth century, the papacy grew ever stronger as a series of capable popes convened councils to establish new and tighter rules of church discipline.[76] In particular, they imposed celibacy on both priests and bishops, mainly as a way of preventing the alienation of church property in the form of dowries and inheritances given to members of clerical families. This was the era of Gratian, whose initial aim was to sort out the church's ancient legislation in order to make it consistent and applicable to the needs of his own time. It was also the age of Peter Lombard, who did much the same thing for theology. The result was the creation of universities where law and theology could be studied and where a cadre of ecclesiastical officials was produced to staff the burgeoning church administration. To this

---

75. In 1054, the pope and the patriarch excommunicated each other, but whether this applied to their churches (and not just to them personally) was a matter of debate. It is, however, indicative of the strongly personal nature of authority that the personal split between the leaders became a schism of the churches and has remained so ever since.

76. These were the first so-called "ecumenical" councils to be summoned by the pope and not by the emperor. They were also the first ones that the pope attended in person.

legislative inheritance the popes added further decretals of their own, which, along with the decisions of later church councils, formed the canon law of the medieval church. It was this canon law that became "tradition" in the minds of medieval theologians and that Martin Luther attacked in the early days of the Reformation.

Today we are used to hearing that this canonical tradition was a corrupting influence in the medieval church, but people at the time did not see it that way. When Othobon, the papal legate to the British Isles, addressed a council of British archbishops and bishops meeting in London on April 22, 1268, he described the relationship of the Bible to the decrees of popes and councils as follows:

> The commandments of God and the law of the Most Highest were given in ancient times, so that the creature who had broken the yoke and turned away from the peace of his God, by living in obedience to the law and commandment as his lamp and light, with the hope given [to him] like a shadow, in the promises made to the fathers, might wait for the coming of the King of Peace, the means of reconciliation and the pontiff who would restore all things. It is the dignity of the adopted children of the bride, and the glory of the sons of Holy Mother Church, that they should hear from it [i.e., the Bible] the commandments of life and in them keep their heart in the beauty of peace, the purity of decency and the practice of modesty, subjecting their evil desires to the control of reason. For the better performance of this task, decrees of the holy fathers, divinely promulgated by their own mouths and containing the rules of justice and the doctrines of equity, flowed out like broad rivers. The sacred constitutions of the supreme pontiffs, as well as those of the legates of that apostolic see and of the other prelates of Holy Church, have emerged like streamlets from the breadth of that river, according to the need of different times, so that new cures would arise for the new diseases spawned by human frailty.[77]

In other words, the God who had given his people hope of a coming Redeemer in the inspired Scriptures also inspired the leaders of the

---

77. The Latin text is printed in F. M. Powicke and C. R. Cheney, eds., *Councils and Synods, with Other Documents Relating to the English Church* (Oxford: Clarendon, 1964), 2:747. Note that Othobon used the same word "pontiff" (*pontifex*) for both Christ and the popes. In 1276, he briefly became pope himself, taking the papal name Hadrian V.

church to provide remedies for the ills of later times, a state of affairs that was intended to preserve God's people until Christ himself should return in judgment. The canonical tradition was regarded as a supplement to the Bible made necessary by the appearance of problems that the ancient texts had not envisaged. Thus it was to be received as a blessing that confirmed and extended the original deposit of faith and not rejected as a corruption that had distorted it. In Othobon's mind, the Bible, the church, and canon law enjoyed equal authority because they all came from God, even though they were mediated to the world by different people in different ways and for slightly different purposes.

CHALLENGES TO PAPAL AUTHORITY

Papal power reached its apogee in the time of Innocent III (r. 1198–1216), but in the course of the thirteenth century things began to go wrong. A series of untimely deaths led to a rapid turnover of popes and a consequent weakening of papal policy. The resurgence of Muslim power drove the crusaders out of Palestine, and the church could no longer persuade the kings of Europe to venture themselves in a lost cause. Financing the overextended papacy was another problem, and secular rulers found themselves having to resist the pope's claims to taxing their people (while at the same time exempting the clergy from secular taxation).[78]

By 1296, the conflict between the king of France and Pope Boniface VIII (r. 1294–1303) over this issue had grown so serious that the pope issued a bull (*Clericis laicos*) forbidding the secular taxation of church property. In 1302, he issued another bull (*Unam sanctam*), which stated that the spiritual power was superior to the temporal power and claimed that only those in communion with the Roman See would be saved. This produced a crisis. When the archbishop of Bordeaux was elected pope as Clement V (r. 1305–1314), the French king refused to let him go to Rome. Eventually, Clement V established himself at Avignon, where he was theoretically sovereign but practically a hostage of France. The papacy remained in Avignon until 1377,

---

78. For the details of this history, see Walter Ullmann, *A Short History of the Papacy in the Middle Ages* (London: Methuen, 1972), 251–78.

and it was during this period of its "Babylonian captivity" that critics made their first major challenges to its authority.

The most important attack on the church's claims came from Marsilius (Marsiglio) of Padua (ca. 1270–ca. 1342), who wrote a long treatise on government (*Defensor pacis*) in which he developed his theories of secular rule, making it clear that the popes and bishops of the church had far overstepped the bounds of their authority by seeking to dominate not merely spiritual but even temporal affairs. As Marsilius put it,

> Their insatiable appetite for temporal things caused them to be discontented with the things which the rulers have granted to them. . . . [A]nd what is the worst of all civil evils, the bishops have set themselves up as rulers and legislators, in order to reduce kings and peoples to intolerable and disgraceful slavery to themselves. For since most of these bishops are of humble birth, they do not know what secular leadership is when they reach the status of pontiff[,] . . . and consequently they become insufferable to all the faithful.[79]

Marsilius took the side of the temporal rulers in their struggle with the papacy over taxation, and in the process he investigated the history of the papal claims. He was able to point out that for many centuries, the popes and bishops of the church had lived under secular rule and had none of the pretensions that had come to be taken for granted in the fourteenth century.[80] His book caused a sensation, and the popes did what they could to suppress it. But there was too much truth in what Marsilius was saying, and too much sympathy for his position, for their opposition to succeed. Later on, when various Reformers began to challenge the papacy, their temerity was inevitably blamed on Marsilius, who inadvertently became the chief spokesman for an alternative concept of authority in and over the church.

Marsilius was more concerned with politics than with theology, but some of his contemporaries were already questioning the doctrinal

---

79. Marsilius of Padua, *Defensor pacis*, trans. Alan Gewirth (Toronto: University of Toronto Press, 1980), 340. See also Marsilius of Padua, *The Defender of the Peace*, ed. and trans. Annabel S. Brett, Cambridge Texts in the History of Political Thought (Cambridge: Cambridge University Press, 2005), 443.

80. This was the theme of his book *De translatione imperii*, which he wrote sometime after completing *Defensor pacis* in 1324.

principles on which the church based its concept of authority. William of Ockham asserted that the church recognized two distinct sources of authority: Scripture and an extrabiblical tradition that complemented it and could be traced back to the apostles.[81] Theology was the way Scripture was interpreted, and the bishops, particularly the pope, were appointed to apply it in any given circumstance. It was to this that theologians were referring when they spoke of the "authority of the church," so that by definition the church's authority was ultimately dependent on Scripture, even if it did not always look that way. In Ockham's mind, Scripture and the tradition of the church were mutually reinforcing, though they were distinct from each other to a degree that had not been recognized in the early church.[82]

In the next generation, the potential tension between these two principles was brought out by John Wyclif (ca. 1328–1384), who resolved it by claiming that the Bible *alone* was the authority for the laws of the church. If something could not be found in Scripture (like clerical celibacy or papal supremacy, for example), then it could not be demanded of the faithful as necessary for salvation. Wyclif also supported Marsilius, using the New Testament as his chief witness:

> Why is it necessary for Christ's priests to give such damnable attention to alien [i.e., secular] laws? That would be of no use to them unless they were intent on securing their ecclesiastical possessions which have been introduced over and above the Gospel. . . . [J]ust as the people in Christ's day were destroyed by the traditions of the Pharisees, it is only fitting now that the guidance of Christ's law and the mediation of spiritual leaders will be withdrawn if secular traditions are increasingly multiplied, and the lifestyles of the priests corrupted more and more by worldliness.[83]

The strictures of Marsilius and Wyclif against corruption in the church were matched on the other side by an increasing concern about

---

81. He developed this idea in his *Dialogus inter magistrum et discipulum*, ed. M. Goldast, *Monarchiae Sancti Romani Imperii sive Tractatum de iurisdictione imperiali, regia, et pontificia seu sacerdotali* (Frankfurt am Main: J. D. Zunner, 1668), 2:394–957.

82. See Oberman, *Harvest of Medieval Theology*, 361–422, for a full discussion of this issue.

83. John Wyclif, *De veritate Sacrae Scripturae* 2.20.150–51. Cf. John Wyclif, *On the Truth of Holy Scripture*, trans. Ian Christopher Levy (Kalamazoo, MI: Medieval Institute Publications, 2001), 280–81.

the spread of heresy. New ideas had been filtering into Western Europe ever since the Crusades, when Arabic learning, much of it originally in ancient Greek, was discovered and translated into Latin. This newly available material unsettled traditionally minded people, and the suspicion that the new learning was subversive was never fully laid to rest. The popes wanted heretics to be burnt at the stake, a form of punishment that was thought to be particularly appropriate.[84] This was a sensitive issue because it straddled the line between spiritual and temporal affairs. Heresy was a spiritual crime that could only be judged by the church, but burning at the stake was a temporal punishment that could only be administered by the state. The church's aim, therefore, was to make heresy a statutory crime, which would give the church power over the administration of secular justice. Many secular rulers objected to this as long as they could, but medieval governments were often weak and unable to resist pressure from the church for long. In England, for example, King Richard II (r. 1377–1399) refused to enact a heresy law—thus sparing Wyclif's life—but when his successor Henry IV (r. 1399–1413) usurped the throne, he needed allies. The church agreed to support him on condition that he enact a heresy law, which he did in 1401. As a result, the church was able to root out the followers of John Wyclif and put them to death, a privilege that it was not slow in exercising.

THE GREAT WESTERN SCHISM AND ITS AFTERMATH

Matters became further complicated after 1378, when the return of the popes to Rome led to a schism that lasted until 1415. For most of that time there were two popes—one in Rome and the other in Avignon—and for a while there were even three. How could papal authority over the church be implemented when nobody knew for sure who the true pope was? It was during this difficult time that Jan Hus (ca. 1369–1415) began to preach in Bohemia. Hus was influenced by Wyclif and also by a native Bohemian movement that objected to the recently introduced practice of withholding the cup from the laity at

---

84. Apparently, noblemen were beheaded and commoners were hanged, but since heresy was not a class-based crime, it was thought better to find one punishment that could be applied equally to all. Some also believed that the flames would purge a sinner's sins and make it possible for him or her to enter purgatory (and eventually heaven) rather than go to eternal damnation in hell.

Holy Communion. There was no scriptural basis for that practice, but Roman theologians argued that because a body must contain blood, the person who consumed the consecrated bread partook not only of Christ's body but also of his blood, making the cup unnecessary.[85] What authority did the church have to introduce (and make compulsory) a practice that was so clearly inconsistent with both the witness of the New Testament and the ancient tradition of the church?

The crisis came to a head at the Council of Constance (1414–1418), which the emperor summoned in order to end the schism and restore the unity of the church. The existing popes were deposed, a new one was elected as Martin V (r. 1417–1431), and the choice was ratified by the whole of Western Christendom. However, the council also condemned the teaching of John Wyclif and ordered Jan Hus to appear and give account of his own doctrine. Reassured of safe conduct from the emperor, Hus turned up, only to be condemned and burnt at the stake on the spot. The church simply ignored the emperor by invoking its own spiritual superiority—and got away with it.

The rest of the fifteenth century is a tale of how the popes did their best to recover the ground their predecessors had lost since 1302. One of the compromises at Constance had been a decision to hold councils every five years that would legislate for the church as a whole. This solution was supported by men like Pierre d'Ailly (1351–1420) and Jean Gerson (1363–1429), who rejected Wyclif's principle of *sola Scriptura* and held that the Holy Spirit was still revealing truth to the church through bishops who stood in the apostolic succession. The main difference between them and the supporters of papal authority was that they conceived this tradition as a collective inheritance, to be determined and defined by a council representing the entire episcopate, not by the pope alone. The popes understandably felt threatened by this and did what they could to neutralize these councils. One tactic, employed with great success by Eugenius IV (r. 1431–1447), was to force the Council of Basel, called in 1431, to transfer to Italy in order to make it easier for representatives of the Eastern church to come and submit to reunion with the West, which they did (at least on paper) in 1439. The council

---

85. It is possible that the original prohibition was motivated by hygienic considerations, but this is uncertain.

eventually made its way to Rome, but the conciliar movement had run out of steam. When it was dissolved in 1445, the whole experiment was abandoned, and papal supremacy was reasserted once more.

Ironically, it was at this moment that a fresh challenge to the papal claims emerged. Scholars from the Eastern church could point out that it had never accepted papal control and that the claims made by Rome were exaggerated, if not explicitly false. The Italian scholar Lorenzo Valla (ca. 1407–1457) also demonstrated that the papacy's claims to jurisdiction over the West were based on a number of forged documents. Composed sometime in the ninth century, probably in opposition to the heirs of Charlemagne, these documents claimed that when Constantine transferred the capital of the empire to Constantinople in 330, he left the pope in charge of the city of Rome and of the Western half of the empire![86]

Valla's discoveries made no practical difference at the time, but their long-term effect was considerable. A few years after he wrote, the printing press was invented, making it possible to disseminate information cheaply and reliably for the first time. Scholars took advantage of the new technology to search out manuscripts and publish them, making people aware of the importance of trying to recover the original documents. Before long, it was common knowledge that many manuscripts were corrupt, that ancient works were sometimes being circulated under the wrong names, and that forgery had at times been almost a way of life. The realization that for centuries the papacy had based its claims on a fraud inevitably discredited it in academic circles and made people long to know the truth. By the time of Erasmus (1466–1536), the importance of scholarly research into original sources was universally recognized, and their potential for destroying the myths accumulated over the centuries became a major weapon in the hands of the Protestant Reformers less than a century after Valla's death.

THE EVE OF THE REFORMATION

The dilemmas facing theologians are perhaps nowhere more clearly illustrated than in the writings of Gabriel Biel (ca. 1420–1495). On

---

86. Lorenzo Valla, *On the Donation of Constantine*, trans. G. W. Bowersock, I Tatti Renaissance Library 24 (Cambridge, MA: Harvard University Press, 2007).

the one hand, as we observed above, Biel followed William of Ock-ham's assertion that the church does not receive new truths but only elucidates what it has already inherited in Scripture, which contains everything necessary for salvation, whether it is clearly expressed as such or not. At the same time, Biel also claimed that the Bible does not contain the whole of revealed truth, because under the guidance of the unerring Holy Spirit, the church continually receives new inspiration, which it transmits to its faithful in the form of tradition.[87] Biel had a high opinion of canon law, and he insisted that all Christians ought to obey it because it was the way in which the church had promulgated the divine laws that it discerned by its reflection on Scripture.

The doctrine of purgatory gives us an example of how far this could be taken. Biel believed not only in the existence of purgatory but also in the power of the pope to deliver souls from it. At first he argued that the papacy's jurisdiction was limited to this life, denying that the pope had any authority to release the dead from their suffering. But after reflecting more deeply on the question, he concluded that because souls in purgatory were still part of the church militant (since they had not yet entered eternal glory), the pope could claim jurisdiction over them. Biel rested this extraordinary turnaround on a papal statement made in 1476, though it did not come to his attention until twelve years later![88] To a man like Biel, the popes' spiritual authority remained undimin-ished despite the revelations of Valla—indeed, with every new state-ment emanating from Rome, it grew clearer and more powerful. In the hierarchy of Christendom, the pope stood above councils because his office was higher than that of the bishops who constituted the councils. Needless to say, both popes and councils stood above the emperor, who was only a secular ruler, charged with implementing church doctrine but not with formulating it. The Bible retained its ancient prestige, but it was just one source of authority among many, and its true meaning could be known only by papally approved interpretation. One way or another, in Biel's theology the pope had reclaimed his authority over the church and, for all practical purposes, over the Scriptures too.

At this point something quite unexpected happened. Shortly before

---

87. For the details of this argument, see Oberman, *Harvest of Medieval Theology*, 397–408.
88. Ibid., 404–6.

Biel's death, Christopher Columbus discovered the Americas, and before long, Spain was laying claim to a continental empire. Thanks to a clever marriage policy, the Habsburg rulers of Austria managed to unite the Netherlands and Spain under their rule, and their combined financial resources made it possible for them to take over the Holy Roman Empire as well. That was not what the German princes (who had enjoyed considerable autonomy in that empire) wanted, and they began to look for ways of limiting the rise of Habsburg power. When Charles V (r. 1519–1556) was elected emperor, many of them were only too glad to support the spiritual revolt of Martin Luther, seeing in it a means of maintaining their independence. To complicate matters further, the new emperor had no desire to see the pope's authority rival his, and although he could not agree with Luther, he shared the Reformer's view that the papacy was in need of serious reform. Charles V was unable to silence Luther, but he did manage to capture Rome and imprison Pope Clement VII (r. 1523–1534), whom he did not release until he had extracted a promise from him to summon a council that would enact far-reaching changes in the structures of the church.[89]

When Luther posted his *Ninety-Five Theses* on the church door at Wittenberg, he was not attacking the church's official doctrine or even the institution of the papacy as such. What he claimed was that the popes had exceeded their jurisdiction by purporting to determine the fate of souls that had departed this life. Who were the popes to say who was in heaven, purgatory, or hell? What right did they have to transfer someone from one of these places to another, which is ultimately what indulgences claimed to be doing? How did they justify doctrines and practices that not only lacked any scriptural warrant but actually contradicted the biblical text? As the implications of these questions were debated, the reality sank in—the church was relying on a human authority that went beyond anything that God had commanded and even contradicted his Word from time to time. Luther came to understand that "tradition" could not be used to overturn the plain teaching of Scripture, and without fully realizing it, he moved toward the position

---

89. The council did not meet until 1545 (at Trent, in northern Italy), which was too late to heal the Protestant schism, though it did a great deal to correct the more blatant abuses in what remained of the Roman Catholic Church.

of Wyclif and Hus. The Protestant Reformation was a new thing—Luther never became a Wyclifite or a Hussite, and neither did the other sixteenth-century Reformers. But there was enough in what Wyclif and Hus had said that resembled what Luther was proclaiming that later generations saw the underlying links between them. The debates of late-medieval theology were not in themselves a reformation, but they created the intellectual climate in which real change was possible and that eventually produced a church that acknowledged only the Bible as its supreme authority in matters of faith and doctrine.

As for the emperor, Luther would probably have accepted his authority over the church had he become a Protestant, but that was never a realistic possibility. Instead, Luther sided with the German princes, granting them a voice in church affairs that was greater than anything known in pre-Reformation times. This pattern was repeated in Scandinavia and in England, whose monarchs were to become the heads of national churches that had to bow to their authority in all but purely spiritual matters.[90]

Conclusion

Luther and his fellow Protestants followed a line that can be traced back through Hus and Wyclif to Ockham and Marsilius of Padua, but circumstances obliged them to rework their inheritance in a more systematic way. They rejected conciliarism by asserting that councils could (and did) err, and of course they all renounced the pope's jurisdiction. While papal infallibility was not declared official dogma until 1870, nevertheless, the Reformers opposed Catholics whenever they appeared to be elevating the pope above the Scriptures.

But it soon became apparent that certain individuals were in danger of throwing the baby out with the bathwater. Some of the more radical groups wanted to deny the Trinity and the divinity of Christ on the ground that these were part of the corrupt tradition of the church and not doctrines that had been directly revealed by God in the Scriptures,

---

90. This is still the case, to varying degrees, in the state churches of England, Denmark, Norway, and Finland, where even matters of faith and doctrine are ultimately subject to the authority of the respective national parliaments, which could theoretically overrule anything the Bible or the church's tradition might require. It should, however, be added that if that were ever to happen, the most likely result would be the separation of church and state, as occurred in Sweden in 2000.

but the mainline Reformers recoiled from such an extreme. They came to realize that the church's extrabiblical tradition was a mixed bag—some of it was the result of ignorance and corruption, but much of it was a faithful interpretation of the meaning of revealed Scripture.

Unfortunately, the academic dichotomy between the Bible and tradition, which late-medieval theology had conceived, had grown to such a degree that it was almost impossible to exalt the one without discounting the other. Protestants erred on the side of the Bible and Catholics on the side of tradition, with little attempt being made to hold the middle ground. The result was that post-Reformation Catholicism grew even further away from the Scriptures than it had been before and that Protestants divided into hostile camps because they could not agree about what to do with pre-Reformation tradition(s). The medieval legacy thus created a series of divisions that continue to the present time, with little prospect that they will be overcome in the foreseeable future.

Resources for Further Study

PRIMARY SOURCES

Gratian. *The Treatise on Laws with the Ordinary Gloss.* Translated by Augustine Thompson and James Gordley. Studies in Medieval and Early Modern Canon Law 2. Washington, DC: Catholic University of America Press, 1993.

Lombard, Peter. *The Sentences.* Translated by Giulio Silano. 4 vols. Mediaeval Sources in Translation 42–43, 45, 48. Toronto: Pontifical Institute of Mediaeval Studies, 2007–2010.

Marsiglio of Padua. *Defensor minor and De translatione imperii.* Translated by Cary J. Nederman. Cambridge Texts in the History of Political Thought. Cambridge: Cambridge University Press, 1993.

Marsilius of Padua. *The Defender of the Peace.* Edited and translated by Annabel S. Brett. Cambridge Texts in the History of Political Thought. Cambridge: Cambridge University Press, 2005.

———. *Defensor Pacis.* Translated by Alan Gewirth. Toronto: University of Toronto Press, 1980.

Valla, Lorenzo. *On the Donation of Constantine.* Translated by G. W. Bowersock. I Tatti Renaissance Library 24. Cambridge, MA: Harvard University Press, 2007.

Wyclif, John. *On the Truth of Holy Scripture*. Translated by Ian Christopher Levy. Kalamazoo, MI: Medieval Institute Publications, 2001.

SECONDARY SOURCES

Brundage, James A. *Medieval Canon Law*. London: Longman, 1995.

Helmholz, R. H. *The Spirit of Classical Canon Law*. Athens: University of Georgia Press, 1996.

Lahey, Stephen E. *John Wyclif*. Great Medieval Thinkers. Oxford: Oxford University Press, 2009.

Leff, Gordon. *Heresy in the Later Middle Ages: The Relation of Heterodoxy to Dissent, c. 1250–c. 1450*. 2 vols. Manchester: Manchester University Press, 1967.

Le Goff, Jacques. *The Birth of Purgatory*. Chicago: University of Chicago Press, 1984.

Oberman, Heiko A. *The Harvest of Medieval Theology: Gabriel Biel and Late Medieval Nominalism*. 3rd ed. Durham, NC: Labyrinth, 1983.

Ozment, Steven. *The Age of Reform, 1250–1550: An Intellectual and Religious History of Late Medieval and Reformation Europe*. New Haven, CT: Yale University Press, 1980.

Prodi, Paolo. *The Papal Prince: One Body and Two Souls: The Papal Monarchy in Early Modern Europe*. Translated by Susan Haskins. Cambridge: Cambridge University Press, 1987.

Spade, Paul Vincent, ed. *The Cambridge Companion to Ockham*. Cambridge Companions to Philosophy. Cambridge: Cambridge University Press, 1999.

Ullmann, Walter. *A Short History of the Papacy in the Middle Ages*. London: Methuen, 1972.

Van Nieuwenhove, Rik. *An Introduction to Medieval Theology*. Cambridge: Cambridge University Press, 2012.

3

The Reformers and
Their Reformations

Carl R. Trueman and Eunjin Kim

ABSTRACT

The Reformation of the sixteenth century took various forms and exhibited numerous emphases in the places in which it took root. While the work of Luther in Germany was foundational to all that happened, the Reformations in Switzerland, Geneva, England, and Scotland were each given unique shape as Protestantism established itself in different social, economic, and political circumstances. Certain themes remained constant, such as the need for the church to be regulated by Scripture, but considerable diversity emerged on matters of the sacraments, church organization, and the relationship between the church and the civil magistrate.

Introduction

While the theology of the Reformation remains a vital source of thinking for evangelical Protestantism, knowledge of the history that gave this theology its shape is often weaker than it should be. Figures such as Luther and Calvin loom large in the popular evangelical imagination but often more as heroic symbols than firsthand theological guides. In addition, many scholars now recognize that *Reformation* in the singular is something of a misnomer. The political and ecclesiastical turbulence of the sixteenth century was highly variegated. It is true that the various traditions of magisterial Protestantism produced what can be described as a series of confessional consensuses—Lutheran, Reformed, and Anglican. Further, Reformation Catholicism produced a remarkably comprehensive and coherent doctrinal series of canons and decrees at the Council of Trent.[1] Yet educational backgrounds, political contexts, and even geographical conditions served to give the various instances of reformation a relatively diverse appearance. Thus, it is actually more appropriate to talk of European *Reformations*, as in the title of Carter Lindberg's well-known history of the period.[2]

In that light, this essay will survey the key movements in the magisterial Reformation: the Lutheran Reformation; the Swiss Reformation, including Geneva; the English and Scottish Reformations; and the Catholic Reformation as culminating in the Council of Trent.[3]

The Lutheran Reformation

The figure of Luther bestrides the popular image of the Reformation like no other. There is good reason for this. His life shaped the future of the Christian church in unique ways. Not only did his early protest against indulgences help to bring into the open the widespread disenchantment with the church, but also his personal approach to various concerns—authority, justification, the Lord's Supper—shaped the way the theological debates of the day were framed and prosecuted.

Born in 1483 in Eisleben, the son of a mine manager, Luther became an Augustinian monk in 1505 as the result of being caught in a terrifying thunderstorm. He was also ordained a priest, which meant that he would always have regular pastoral duties in addition to those

---

1. We use the term *Reformation Catholicism* in preference to the more traditional *Counter-Reformation Catholicism* because the Roman Catholic Church was not simply reacting to Protestantism but also attempting to produce a positive vision of church reform.
2. Carter Lindberg, *The European Reformations*, 2nd ed. (Malden, MA: Wiley-Blackwell, 2010).
3. The following sections of this chapter rely on the sources cited in the respective sections of the bibliography at the end of the chapter.

connected to his monastic vocation. In 1509, he transferred to the new University of Wittenberg, where he taught for much of his remaining life. A year later, a visit to Rome on business for his order confronted him not only with the heights of medieval piety, focused on relics, but also with the corruption of the Roman See.

Luther came to prominence when, in October 1517, he nailed his famous *Ninety-Five Theses* against indulgences to the door of the Castle Church in Wittenberg. In doing this, he was merely calling for a debate on the practice of allowing Christians to buy time off purgatory for themselves or their loved ones. This had become a pressing pastoral problem for Luther when Johann Tetzel (1465–1519) arrived nearby to sell indulgences. For Luther, this practice effectively turned the grace of God into a commodity to be bought or sold on the market, with no reference to repentance or faith.

The details of the subsequent events that this initially nondescript act precipitated have been well rehearsed many times. The *Ninety-Five Theses* became a popular tract and rallying point for opposition to Rome. In April 1518, Luther presided at a disputation in Heidelberg, where he most memorably articulated his famous distinction between the theologian of glory and the theologian of the cross. Put simply, the *theologian of glory* assumes that God is made in man's image and thus conforms to human expectations. So, for example, to please God, one does good works to earn his favor, as one would do with a fellow human being. The *theologian of the cross*, however, looks to God's revelation of himself on the cross to understand how God has chosen to be toward us. There God shows that he is strong through weakness and overcomes death not by avoiding it but by going through it. This counterintuitive God contradicts all human expectations.

After Heidelberg, Luther's move toward a definitive break with the medieval church both theologically and ecclesiastically continued apace. The church failed to take him into custody at the imperial Diet of Augsburg in late 1518. He debated with Johann Eck (1486–1543) at the University of Leipzig in 1519, at which point the issue of authority (i.e., *sola Scriptura*) emerged as a central Reformation concern. He wrote the three great manifestos of his reformation project in 1520, the year in which he was also excommunicated. And then in 1521, he was tried at, yet survived, the Diet of Worms.

What emerged in the four years after the posting of the *Ninety-Five Theses* were the central tenets of Luther's theology. Human beings are dead in sin, incapable of moving to God in their own strength. God himself in Christ has taken human flesh and died and risen again. The righteousness of Christ can be grasped by the believer as he trusts in God's Word, which unites him to Christ and leads to a joyful exchange of the believer's sins for Christ's righteousness.

Practically, this meant that the Word preached became central to Luther's understanding of the Christian life. The preacher had to proclaim first the law, to remind his hearers of how far short of God's holiness they fell, and then the gospel, to point them to the promise of salvation in Christ, who had done all things for them. This law-gospel, command-promise dialectic lay at the very heart of Luther's understanding of the Christian faith.

The 1520s started very positively for Luther. An heir of medieval eschatological expectation, Luther filled his writings with confidence that the Reformation heralded the imminent return of Christ. Yet as the decade wore on, the Lutheran Reformation suffered both external and internal setbacks. Iconclastic riots at Wittenberg in 1521–1522 hinted at more radical forces within the Reformation, and these became far more dangerous in the series of rebellions known as the Peasants' War of 1525. This conflict shattered the fragile anticlerical coalition of ministers, knights, and peasants on which the Lutheran movement had been built. Luther's own violent rejection of the peasants' cause also damaged his own reputation.

Two other events of significance also occurred in 1525. Luther married the former nun Katharina von Bora (1499–1552) and thus became the most high-profile former priest to contravene his vow of celibacy. More significantly from a theological perspective, he published his refutation of Erasmus's (1466–1536) work of 1524, *A Diatribe on Free Will*. Erasmus, under pressure from the church authorities to declare himself with regard to Luther, had published the work in order to show his opposition to the Lutheran Reformation. He targeted (and defended) two things that were central to Luther's theology: the bondage of the human will and the clarity or perspicuity of Scripture.

In Luther's response, *On the Bondage of the Will*, he explicated both the anti-Pelagian foundation of his soteriology and his understanding of the fundamental clarity of Scripture. Indeed, these two things lay at the heart of his dispute with Rome. The first undergirded justification by grace through the instrumentality of faith, which thus undercut the notion of sacramentally dispensed grace. This effectively shattered the authority of the medieval church, built as it was on the sacramental priesthood. The second was Luther's answer to the crisis of authority in the church: If the papacy and councils had erred, where could truth be found? Luther essentially replied by claiming that Scripture itself was sufficiently clear on vital points of doctrine that no teaching magisterium such as the papacy was necessary.

The other great theological development of the 1520s was the Eucharistic controversy with Huldrych Zwingli (1484–1531). Zwingli, the Reformer of Zurich, held to a strongly symbolic understanding of the Lord's Supper. For Luther, it was vital that Christ's flesh and blood be really present in the bread and the wine, for it was only God in the flesh who revealed God as gracious. If the Spirit but not the flesh was present, then the Lord's Supper was law, not gospel, and it brought nothing but condemnation and despair.

The controversy between Luther and Zwingli came to a head at Marburg Castle in 1529, when Philip, Landgrave of Hesse (1504–1567), brought leading Lutherans and Reformed theologians together in an effort to forge a pan-Protestant alliance against the forces of the Holy Roman Empire. The two sides agreed on fourteen and a half of fifteen theological points. The half point on which they disagreed related to the real presence of Christ in the sacrament. For Luther, this was nonnegotiable, and any compromise on the matter was a compromise of the gospel. Thus, the failure to reach agreement at Marburg was the origin of the formal break between Lutheran and Reformed churches.

Luther lived for a further seventeen years after Marburg. Perhaps the most important development of this time was the production of the Augsburg Confession, written by Philipp Melanchthon

(1497–1560) in 1530.[4] The Lutheran princes and cities of the Holy Roman Empire all subscribed to this standard, thus forming the basis of the Schmalkaldic League, a Lutheran defensive alliance designed to protect the territories and interests of the Lutheran states in the empire. In 1540, Melanchthon revised the Augsburg Confession in a way that softened the teaching on the real presence and thus made it more acceptable to the Reformed. Indeed, it was to this version—the *Variata*, or "Altered"—that Calvin subscribed. Nevertheless, the *Invariata*, or "Unaltered," remains the standard for Lutherans around the world today.

Luther's later years were notoriously marked by increasing anger and bitterness toward the Jews. In 1523, he had written a treatise that was remarkable for the times, *That Jesus Christ Was Born a Jew*, in which he had encouraged Christians to treat Jews with love and respect in order to win a hearing for the gospel. Twenty years later, in 1543, he wrote the violent *On the Jews and Their Lies*, which advocated extreme persecution of the Jews.

Luther's death in 1546 had two significant effects. First, the emperor was emboldened to attack and dramatically weaken the Schmalkaldic League. This struggle between empire and League continued until the Peace of Augsburg in 1555, which effectively divided the empire legally along confessional lines. The principle of the peace was that each region should have its religion determined by the confessional position of its prince. Thus was born the confessional state.

The second effect of Luther's death was a theological civil war within the Lutheran church itself for the ownership of Luther's legacy. The church split between the Philippists, or followers of Philipp Melanchthon, and the Gnesio ("Real") Lutherans under the leadership of men such as Matthias Flacius Illyricus (1520–1575). The former tended to be more concessive to Roman Catholicism in matters of aesthetics and also to be less insistent on the centrality of the real presence in ecumenical discussions. The latter were much more militant on the nonnegotiability of Luther's Eucharistic theology. The dispute was effectively brought to an end with the production of the Formula

---

4. Reformation scholars spell Melanchthon's first name variously as both Philip and Philipp; we have used Philipp in this volume for the sake of consistency.

of Concord in 1577, which, while not endorsing all of Illyricus's positions, was broadly speaking a victory for the Gnesios.

The Swiss Reformation

The Swiss Reformation followed a different path of reform than the one taken by Wittenberg. One distinction came from the political contexts of the two regions. Whereas the German imperial cities were dependent on the emperor's rule, the Swiss Confederation consisted of self-governing cities loosely bound by military alliances, which made them subject to the local people. Thus, for the success of the Reformation, Luther depended on the authorities to provide him with protection, while Zwingli directly involved himself in the political power of Zurich. Further, the two men had different intellectual backgrounds. Unlike Luther, who was trained as a medieval man in the monastery, Zwingli was a modern man trained as a humanist in the cities. The degree of influence of the two men also differed, as Zwingli, though influential, never achieved quite the dominating role that Luther did in the Lutheran Reformation.

Huldrych Zwingli was born on January 1, 1484—only about two months after Luther—in Wildhaus, Toggenburg, into a well-to-do peasant family. At age ten, he moved to Basel, and in 1498, he studied at the University of Vienna, only to return later to Basel, where he received his BA in 1504 and MA in 1506. Zwingli's thoughts were shaped by humanist endeavors to read classical texts and patristic authors and to study the original languages, all greatly influenced by the works of Erasmus. In 1506, upon completing his studies, he was ordained and called to be the parish priest of Glarus, where he served for the next ten years.

Experiences at Glarus were not all pleasant for Zwingli. The mercenary trade had been an economically successful exporting business for the Swiss Confederation. In 1510, however, Zwingli wrote his allegorical poem "The Ox," attacking the use of the Swiss army for foreign wars. Further, when he participated in the campaigns as the chaplain, he personally witnessed the devastating effects of mercenaries and was appalled by the deaths of thousands of Swiss soldiers. His opposition to such a practice placed him in tension with the magistrates of Glarus.

Yet he approved the use of mercenaries when it concerned defending the pope—from whom he was receiving a papal pension. In 1516, he was transferred to a parish in Einsiedeln, famous for the shrine of the Black Virgin. He spent much of his time mastering the biblical languages and reading Erasmus's Greek New Testament. A powerful preacher, Zwingli considered his preaching ministry to be a prophetic office. Having gained prominence for biblical preaching, he was called to Zurich in 1518 as the people's priest of the Great Minster. Before his appointment, the rumor had been that he was guilty of having a sexual affair with a daughter of a well-off citizen, to which he admitted, but even that was not enough to fail him for the job since his case was like many other priests in his day. In Zurich, he began preaching through the book of Matthew, gradually fertilizing the soil for the reform that would soon erupt there and in the Confederation.

If much of Luther's way of thinking was shaped by his existential crisis in search of certainty, Zwingli's thoughts were greatly shaped by the plague that swept Zurich in 1519–1520, which wiped out one-fourth of Zurich's population, including his brother. Having lost a quarter of his congregation and nearly dying from taking care of the sick, Zwingli became preoccupied with the providence of God. The traumatizing experience left him clinging to the doctrine of God's sovereignty, hoping that at the end of the day, God would somehow resolve all tragedy for the good.

The public Reformation in Zurich started in a peculiar way with the eating of sausages during Lent on March 9, 1522. Zwingli was at the house of the printer Christoph Froschauer (ca. 1490–1564) with some of his workers when they were served sausages. The group of gathered men self-consciously broke the Lenten fast by eating the meat, although Zwingli did not join them in the act. When the news of this scandalous rebellion had gone out, however, Zwingli, who was already an influential preacher of the Great Minster, pressed the issue by preaching on the topic of Christian freedom. He emphasized that Christians were free to make their own decisions on fasting because the Bible had not required it and that it was not the food but the faith of the believer that really mattered. A month later, his sermon was published as a pamphlet. In arguing for Christian freedom, he also pointed to the issue of clerical celibacy as having no foundation in Scripture, and he confronted the bishop of Constance with a petition. In April 1524, he married a widow, Anna Reinhart (1484–1538), publicly making his statement on the issue.

At the heart of these two matters—the "affair of the sausages" and clerical celibacy—was the question of what weight the authorities of church and Scripture held. Zwingli asserted that everything had to be judged by the Scripture, the notion of *sola Scriptura*, while the bishop argued that only the church should have the power to interpret the Scripture, prioritizing the authority of the church. The Confederate Diet at Baden accused Zwingli of heresy and found Zurich guilty of allowing Zwingli to preach nonsense. To resolve the conflict, the Zurich council decided to hold a public disputation. Zurich did not have a sophisticated university like Wittenberg. However, the purpose of this meeting was to be not an academic disputation but rather a public disputation, held in the vernacular and open to the local merchants, craftsmen, and common people. Representatives from other Swiss cities such as Bern and Basel joined. On January 29, 1523, six hundred people gathered, and Zwingli prepared his "Sixty-Seven Articles." With only the Hebrew, Greek, and Latin Bibles laid on his table, he magnificently defended his view on the primary authority of the Scripture, gripping the minds of the people and the magistrates and drawing them toward a favorable stance on the Reformation. As a result, the council ordered all Zurich preachers to preach from Scripture only. Yet it was not only the theological views that moved the magistrates to support Zwingli but also the broad political interests in curtailing the influence of clergy in the city and in the local autonomy.

The second disputation followed in October of that same year. Biblical preaching led people to seriously question the place of images, saints, and relics in the church, and even the legitimacy of the Mass. They responded by acts of iconoclasm, destroying church ornaments and tearing down crucifixes from the streets. In reaction to such violence, the magistrates called for a second disputation. In terms of the pace and method of reform, Zwingli argued that the change should occur top-down in an orderly way, implemented by the magistrates to the people, not vice versa. A few men who were present at the meeting, such as Konrad Grebel (ca. 1498–1526) and Balthasar Hubmaier (ca. 1480–1528), found Zwingli's method of reform too moderate, and they wished to pursue their own reform in a much more radical way. This eventually gave rise to the Anabaptist movement. On the use of the images, Zwingli and his friend Leo Jud (1482–1542) asserted that all images must be completely banned from churches. Even music was to be prohibited, setting forth a very simple form of worship and church aesthetics in Zurich. In 1525, the Mass was finally abolished and was replaced with Zwingli's liturgical text.

The rise of the Anabaptists generated serious problems for Zurich. What had begun as dissatisfaction with Zwingli's pace of reform gained momentum through some charismatic leaders who claimed to have the true church and began rebaptizing people into their community. They rejected infant baptism and separated God's salvation history in the Old Testament from the New in regard to the sacraments. The Anabaptists were considered extremely dangerous as they did not fit in socially, and many of them were drowned in Zurich. Such polemics prompted Zwingli to develop his thoughts on covenant, and his successor, Heinrich Bullinger (1504–1575), later formulated the concept into a more elaborate doctrine, arguing for continuity in God's salvation history.

Along with the ongoing debates, the doctrine of the Lord's Supper surfaced as the next great controversial point. Zwingli interpreted the "is" of Jesus's statement, "This is my body," in a symbolic way, insisting that the bread and wine *signified* Christ's body and blood. For him, Luther's argument on Christ's real presence seemed too close to transubstantiation. Further, Zwingli asserted that since the bodily Christ is seated at the right hand of the Father, Christ's flesh cannot be present in the bread and the wine. If Christ were bodily present in the elements, then the Lord's Supper would become an act of idolatry. For Zwingli, Christ was not really present in the Lord's Supper but was present in the hearts of believers through their faith. After a series of bitter exchanges between Luther and Zwingli, the clash culminated in the Colloquy of Marburg in 1529.

In the meantime, the efforts toward reformation spread rapidly throughout the Confederation. Printing and preaching were the two most important factors contributing to this movement. Other cities such as St. Gall and Appenzell adopted biblical preaching, which resulted in resistance against the Catholic states. Churches removed ornaments and sought a simple form of worship, following the example of Zurich. Politically, the conversions of Bern in 1528 and Basel in 1529 were particularly important for advancing the Reformation. The key leader in Basel was Johannes Oecolampadius (1482–1531), an expert in the church fathers and in biblical exegesis. Basel had a university where Erasmus taught until his death in 1536 and a printing press that disseminated Protestant writings and made ideas accessible to a wider audience in their own language. Bern possessed strong military power that would become crucial in leading the way to the reform of French-speaking lands, although the Bernese were willing to negotiate with the Catholics when their political wishes were met. Nonetheless, despite the different political intentions for adopting the Zwinglian cause, the religious ties that bound them caused the Protestant cities to unite. The alliance of the Catholic states, however, also strengthened in opposition to the new order. This deepened the Protestant-Catholic tensions to a point that made war inevitable. As a strong advocate of religious war, Zwingli took up the sword to fight against the Catholic enemies in the Second War of Kappel in 1531. He faced a brutal end, as his corpse was quartered and burnt. The war ended in a disaster and left a deep religious divide in the Swiss Confederacy, over which the Catholic power regained dominance.

The Swiss Reformation entered a time of confusion. Was there any hope of success for reform? The Confederation was divided, many of the Reformed cities switched back to Catholicism, those that remained Reformed blamed Zurich for the war, and Anabaptists were only aggravating the problems. It seemed that the Swiss Reformation had reached an impasse. Efforts to reconcile with the Lutherans emerged from Bern and Basel with the mediation of Strasbourg but concluded with only limited success. The key shift came from the leading Swiss Reformed cities as they began to engage in theological discussions with one another. The outcome of the first council of Reformed churches held in Basel was the First Helvetic Confession of 1536, which laid the groundwork for the future direction of the Swiss Reformed churches.

After Zwingli's death, Zurich appointed Heinrich Bullinger, in

1532, as his successor at the Great Minster. With Zwingli's controversial legacy in the background, Bullinger's difficult task was to move the Reformation forward by holding both the Zurich authorities and the Confederation together. His gift in writing, his emphasis on the interpretation of Scripture, his deeply pastoral concerns, and his political adeptness proved him to be the right man for the job. Soon he gained control of Zurich churches and became a man of great significance, whose influence extended to the whole of Western Europe, including England. His book *The Decades* (1549–1552) attained a wide popularity as the most important theological resource for pastors in the sixteenth century, even more so than Calvin's *Institutes*.

With Bullinger in the forefront, the Swiss Reformation entered a phase of theological development under new leadership, although it did not occur in uniformity. In Basel, after Oecolampadius died in 1531, Oswald Myconius (1488–1552) dominated the scene until a man with Lutheran sympathies named Simon Sulzer (1508–1585) arrived in 1548 to become the head of the church. He directed the Basel church toward Lutheran positions and opposed Calvin's theology, especially his doctrine on predestination. Once it reopened after the war, Basel University attracted Reformed and Lutheran students from all over Europe. In 1549, Wolfgang Musculus (1497–1563) arrived in Bern, where he wrote his most significant work, *Loci Communes*. In 1556, Peter Martyr Vermigli (1499–1562), an Italian refugee, was appointed as Old Testament professor in Zurich. His support for Calvin's view of double predestination led to the dismissal of Theodor Bibliander (1506–1564), who had taught in Zurich for thirty years. Predestination was one of the most hotly debated topics in the Swiss Reformation. Bullinger differed from Vermigli and Calvin as he refused to speak of God's election of the damned but rather emphasized election in relation to Christ as part of God's saving will toward his people. Although Geneva was not part of the Confederation, Calvin came to have a significant role in the Swiss Reformation as well. In 1549, Calvin and Bullinger coauthored the Consensus Tigurinus, or the Zurich Consensus, to reach an agreement on the Lord's Supper, in which they purposefully excluded their points of disagreement.

The theological development of the Swiss Reformation ripened into its full maturity with the Second Helvetic Confession of 1566. Originally written as a short confession of faith by Bullinger for Frederick III, Elector Palatine (1515–1576), it was revised as a confession for the whole Swiss church. The Reformed Confederates, as well as Geneva, accepted the document, but Basel's Lutheran sympathies prevented them from signing the confession until 1644. It gained wide international popularity as an orthodox Reformed confession over against the canons of Trent and the Lutheran Book of Concord.

By the time of Bullinger's death in 1575, the center stage of the Reformation had shifted to Geneva and the Low Countries. The legacy of the Swiss Reformation, however, lived on. According to Bruce Gordon, what distinguished the Swiss theologians was "an emphasis upon the historical dimension of God's salvation, the working out of God's eternal covenant."[5] The theological interests of the Swiss Reformation primarily centered on doctrines such as Christology and predestination in light of the sovereignty of God. The next generation of Swiss Reformers built on these doctrines of their predecessors with greater precision as academic institutions arose and the polemical context shifted from internal wrangling to focusing on their Lutheran and Catholic opponents.

The Genevan Reformation

If there was one place in Europe in the second half of the sixteenth century that was acknowledged as the best model of what a Reformed church should look like, it was Geneva. Young intellectuals from England, France, and the Low Countries, often fleeing persecution, traveled to Geneva to learn Reformed theology and to be trained as pastors. They returned to their native lands with their imaginations gripped by the new theological visions that they had seen and experienced in this holy city.

Central to the development of the Genevan Reformation was the Frenchman John Calvin (1509–1564). Born on July 10, 1509, at Noyon, Picardy, Calvin was twenty-six years younger than Luther. His ambitious father arranged benefices for young Calvin from the

---

5. Bruce Gordon, *The Swiss Reformation* (Manchester: Manchester University Press, 2002), 185.

local church to support his education. In August 1523, at the age of fourteen, Calvin went to Paris to study for the priesthood at the Collège de la Marche, where he studied Latin and rhetoric under one of the finest scholars of the day, Mathurin Cordier (ca. 1480–1564). The next year, he enrolled in the Collège de Montaigu as a student of Noel Beda (ca. 1470–1537). In 1528, however, Calvin's father suddenly instructed him to change his path to a legal career in pursuit of a more lucrative vocation. Calvin moved to Orléans, then to Bourges to study law, but when his father died in 1531, he immediately returned to his humanist studies. In fact, his first publication, a commentary on Seneca's *De Clementia* (1532), was a purely humanist work, representing Calvin as a man of letters.

Two incidents triggered Calvin's departure from France. First, in 1533, when his friend Nicholas Cop (ca. 1501–1540) preached a sermon attacking Paris theologians, Calvin was accused of being a coauthor and had to run to escape arrest. The second incident happened on October 1534, the Affair of the Placards. Posters attacking the Catholic Mass suddenly appeared in major cities of France, and one even made it into the king's bedchamber. In response, King Francis I (r. 1515–1547) arrested several hundred suspected Protestants and had nine of them executed, changing his policy of tolerance to one of persecution. Calvin fled for his life to Basel. It was here in 1536 that Calvin produced the first edition of his *Institutes of the Christian Religion*, a catechetical introduction that laid out six basic theological heads of faith. The fact that Calvin was a French exile greatly impacted his thoughts, as is clear, for example, in the prefatory letter addressed to Francis I in his *Institutes*, pleading for the toleration of French Protestants.

Calvin first arrived in Geneva when he made a detour on his route from Paris to Strasbourg. What had originally been planned as a one-night stay in Geneva changed into years of arduous pastoral work for him. On hearing the news that Calvin was in Geneva, William Farel (1489–1565) admonished him to stay, threatening that he would be under God's severe wrath if he did not comply. Reluctantly, Calvin accepted Farel's invitation and began his new pastoral career.

At the time of Calvin's arrival, Geneva was a city in its early phase of Reformed faith. Originally, Geneva had been under the rule of both the prince-bishop and the duke of Savoy. With the military support from Bern, however, Geneva gained its independence from the House of Savoy in 1526. The Genevan Council of 200 was established the next year. Bern converted to the Reformed cause in 1528, and it seemed natural for Geneva to follow the religion of its protector. Farel led public disputations and preached to drive Catholicism out of Geneva. On May 25, 1536, Genevans voted to accept the Reformed faith.

Calvin, having been appointed a pastor in Geneva, worked to establish a Reformed city. The fact that Genevans ratified the decision to accept the Reformed cause, however, did not mean that all citizens were ready to give up their old beliefs altogether. Under pressure from Bern, the Small Council in Geneva adopted the confession but refused to make subscription by oath mandatory for citizens. For Calvin, it was integral that the church leadership execute church discipline, but the Council also regarded this as a challenge to its authority. Furthermore, to add to the tensions, Pierre Caroli (1480–ca. 1545) attacked Calvin by labeling him an Arian. Calvin took an adamant stance against the oppositions. The quarrels finally blew up on Easter Sunday of 1538 when Calvin and Farel refused to administer the Lord's Supper, signaling a direct challenge against the magistrates. The Council kicked them out of Geneva, and the two men headed to Basel believing they had failed.

Not long after, another pastoring opportunity came to Calvin, this time through Martin Bucer (1491–1551) in Strasbourg. Bucer invited Calvin to pastor a church of French refugees, and Calvin accepted the offer. During his years in Strasbourg, Calvin saw through Bucer a model of the church with the freedom to appoint its own officers, execute its own discipline, and conduct its own liturgy—a model that he would later try to bring to Geneva. Further, Bucer's long-winded commentaries made Calvin aware of their drawbacks and led him to pursue a way of "lucid brevity" for his own commentaries. He resolved the issue by placing the theological discussions in a separate work, his *Institutes*, while dealing with only the exegesis of the text in his commentaries. In 1539, the second edition of the *Institutes* was published, followed by his commentary on Romans in 1540. He also married the widow of a refugee, Idelette de Bure (d. 1549), while in Strasbourg.

Meanwhile, Genevans came up against a problem that they lacked the skills to resolve. Cardinal Jacopo Sadoleto (1477–1547) wrote a letter to Geneva in March 1539, challenging them to return to the Catholic faith and accusing the Protestants of being innovative deviants from church tradition. The Genevan authorities knew no one more competent than Calvin to provide a convincing answer to Sadoleto. At their request, Calvin produced a brilliant piece of work, *Reply to Sadoleto*, asserting that it was the Protestants who had kept the historic tradition and that it was actually Catholicism that had abandoned the truth. Impressed by his performance, the Genevans decided to call him back. For Calvin, Geneva was a "place of torture" to which he dreaded returning.[6] On September 13, 1541, however, he returned to Geneva, where he would remain for the rest of his life.

Reform in Geneva accelerated. Within six weeks of his return, Calvin prepared the *Ecclesiastical Ordinances*, which the Council adopted as law with only a few modifications on November 20, 1541. One such adjustment concerned the frequency of the Lord's Supper. The Council, in accord with the Bernese liturgy, advocated quarterly administration, whereas Calvin desired weekly Communion. The document laid out a form of church order and society that Calvin had envisioned in Strasbourg. He argued for a fourfold ministry of pastors, teachers, elders, and deacons. The deacons took care of the poor and supervised charity. The teachers studied and taught Scripture, refuting false doctrines. Twelve lay elders were to be elected by the councils. And the pastors preached the Word, administered the sacraments, and played a role in church discipline. At the heart of Calvin's social reform was the Consistory, an institution made up of the elders and pastors for enforcing discipline and moral laws. Cursing, adultery, games of chance, and dancing were some of the cases that the Consistory dealt with. Another institution that was distinct to Geneva was the Company of Pastors. There the teachers and pastors gathered to discuss biblical texts and church issues. By setting up these different institutions, Calvin laid the foundation for a society based on the Word of God in every aspect of life.

Geneva, however, was not without its problems. As Catholicism

---

6. Calvin to Pierre Viret, May 19, 1540, in *Letters of John Calvin*, ed. Jules Bonnet (Philadelphia: Presbyterian Board of Publication, 1858) 1:187.

gained strength in France, French Protestants sought haven in Geneva. Since they were mostly intellectuals, these French immigrants provided skilled labor forces for Geneva, not to mention political support for Calvin. In fact, Calvin, a French exile himself, did not receive his citizenship until 1559. The high number of French immigrants and their strong presence created political and cultural tensions with the Genevan nobilities, who posed continuous threats to Calvin's authority.

Besides the internal political tensions, Geneva was continuously involved in theological controversies. In October 1551, a man named Jerome Bolsec (d. ca. 1584) attacked Calvin's doctrine of predestination. He was tried and banished from Geneva, but he fled to Bern, where he continued to complain about Calvin's teachings. This led Bern to ban preaching on predestination from the pulpit, which then became a pastoral issue for the Genevan pastors. Of all the controversies, however, the most famous was the Servetus affair. Michael Servetus (ca. 1511–1553) denied the orthodox teaching of the Trinity in such an innovative way that he made enemies of both Catholics and Protestants. He managed to escape from the custody of the Catholic Inquisition, but on his way to Naples, he stopped in Geneva, of all places, to stay overnight. He was captured and, unsurprisingly, accused of heresy. On October 27, 1553, he was burnt at the stake. After the incident, Sebastian Castellio (1515–1563), bitter toward Calvin for expelling him from Geneva, exacerbated the issue by writing a treatise against the capital punishment of heretics. The Bolsec and Castellio conflicts continued even after Calvin's death through the writings of his right-hand man and successor, Theodore Beza (1519–1605), who responded in Calvin's defense.

The opposition provided Calvin with stronger grounds for exerting further influence in Geneva. Theological education was vital for Calvin's idea of reform, and he recruited Beza, a professor of Greek at the Academy of Lausanne and also a French exile, to help establish the Geneva Academy in 1559. Calvin appointed Beza the first rector of the school, and under their leadership the Academy came to prominence as a training center for Protestant pastors and missionaries, most of whom were French refugees. That same year, Calvin's final Latin edition of the *Institutes* was published.

Although the Genevan Reformation had its distinctives, it must not be seen in isolation from the rest of the reform movement in various parts of Europe. Besides Geneva being the center of Reformed education from which many missionaries were sent, one connection to the wider European context was visible in Calvin's efforts to reconcile the Lutherans and Zwinglians, especially on the doctrine of the Lord's Supper. Calvin maintained a lifelong friendship with Melanchthon and in 1540 signed the Altered Augsburg Confession, the *Variata*, with the desire to bring the Lutheran and Swiss parties together. He made the same effort with the Zwinglians as he personally traveled to Zurich and coauthored the Consensus Tigurinus with Bullinger in 1549.

Of all of Calvin's achievements, his greatest influence was derived from his ability to interpret the Scripture. Preaching and exegesis were central to his theology. He preached twice on Sundays, on the New Testament in the mornings and occasionally on the Psalms in the afternoons. During the weekdays, he preached on the Old Testament. In addition to preaching, he also lectured at the Geneva Academy and wrote commentaries on almost every book of the Bible. He believed that his role as the preacher was to declare only what has been revealed in the Scripture and to expound it through careful study of each text. According to Calvin, the Scripture as the Word of God aroused a desire in people's hearts to devote their lives entirely to God and to conform to his will.

After suffering from chronic physical ailments, Calvin breathed his last on May 27, 1564. The heavy burden of maintaining the Reformed structure and teachings in Geneva fell on the shoulders of Theodore Beza. Trained as a skilled humanist and a lawyer, Beza shared with Calvin a profound interest in fighting for the Protestant cause not only in Geneva but also in France, and they became friends. Beza defended Calvin against opponents, while producing his own theological works. His most significant writing was *A Brief and Pithy Sum of the Christian Faith*, originally published in French in 1559 as a summary of major Reformed doctrines, which closely followed the structure and theology of Calvin's *Institutes*.

From 1564 to 1603, Geneva faced a time of political insecurity. To the south, the dukes of Savoy looked to recapture Geneva, and to the west, France had grown to be a massive Catholic nation. The threats of the Jesuits escalated the fear. In the summer of 1586, the duke of Savoy, Charles Emmanuel I (1562–1630), launched an attack against Geneva and enforced a blockade. Soon the city was financially broke, and the Council decided to close the Academy. Beza protested, making the case that closing the Academy would only benefit the Catholic enemies. This kept the Academy alive for another three months, but conditions degenerated to the point that all professors except Beza were forced to leave. As the only professor left, Beza lectured on the book of Job to the few remaining students until the outbreak of the plague in the summer of 1587 made the Savoyard armies retreat.

The threats of Savoy did not cease throughout the sixteenth century, and the Jesuits only made matters worse as they sought to bring Catholicism back to the rural areas of Geneva. Savoy attacked these regions, burning many Protestant churches and capturing pastors. In the midst of fear and insecurity, Catholic Mass was reestablished. Further, the Jesuits had spread a false rumor that Beza was dead and that he had converted to Catholicism on his deathbed along with the entire city of Geneva. The news alarmed many Protestants all over Europe who were holding on to Reformed faith despite persecutions. The Jesuit ploy, along with the Savoyards' intense pressure, largely succeeded, as several thousand people in the countryside of Geneva renounced the Protestant faith and embraced Catholicism.

The theological climate during Beza's years had also changed from Calvin's time. As the rector of the Geneva Academy, Beza had to be keenly sensitive to the polemical debates and languages of the wider European academic context. This meant new questions were being asked that had to be answered in defense of Reformed theology. Thus, Beza formed his arguments with greater precision than what appeared in Calvin's writings. The difference was not so much a result of Beza's deviation from Calvin's theology but rather his attempt to defend Reformed theology in his own polemical and pastoral context.

Beza faithfully labored to preserve Reformed theology until his death in 1605. As a result, Geneva stood firm as an internationally renowned center of Reformed faith, drawing students from all over Europe. Theologians and pastors consulted Geneva for theological clarifications. Beza ministered to the Genevan church until 1600, trained future pastors until 1599, and moderated the Company of Pastors until 1580, remaining the most influential figure in the Company as the mediator between the church and the city council until he died. Like Calvin, he emphasized the teaching and preaching of the Scripture, which was the fundamental basis for the success of the Genevan Reformation.

The English Reformation

The path to Reformation in England started earlier but developed more slowly than in Germany or Switzerland. In the fourteenth century, John Wyclif (ca. 1328–1384) had inspired both vernacular Bible translations and a movement of lay preaching and protest known as Lollardy. In addition, as an island, England had always enjoyed a certain political independence from both Rome and the Holy Roman Empire. In the fifteenth century, this had allowed English authorities to impose a series of legal restrictions on the activity of churchmen in England, essentially inhibiting the church from imposing the pope's will. During his reign, the first Tudor king, Henry VII (r. 1485–1509), curtailed the legal benefits of clergy, and thus, even before Lutheranism shook the Continent, the English crown had been increasingly assertive in how it related to the church.

It was under Henry VIII (r. 1509–1547) that England formally broke with Rome. This rupture was driven not primarily by theological reasons. Indeed, Henry VIII was to remain in doctrinal agreement with the medieval church on key issues such as justification and the sacraments even as he repudiated the claims of the papacy.

The origin of the break with Rome under Henry VIII was theological only in the most tangential way. Henry had obtained a special dispensation from the pope to marry his dead brother's widow, Catherine of Aragon (1485–1536). But when she produced no male heir, Henry saw this, and a series of miscarriages, as a sign of God's displeasure with the union. Thus, from the late 1520s onward, he pursued various strategies to obtain a divorce. Ultimately, the pope did not agree; Catherine was Spanish royalty, and the papacy could not afford to insult the Habsburgs. As a result, Henry used Parliament to pass a series of acts that removed England from papal jurisdiction and established an autonomous church.

During the 1530s, under the leadership of Archbishop of Canterbury Thomas Cranmer (1489–1556), the church moved in a very modestly Protestant direction. But from 1540 onward, any tendency to reform ceased, and Henry implemented something of a Catholic reaction (without the papacy). It was only with his death in 1547 that the English Reformation really started to advance. At that time, his young son, Edward VI (r. 1547–1553), became king, and those nobles in charge of protecting him pursued a self-consciously Protestant policy.

The key religious results of Edward's reign were the two Books of Common Prayer (1549 and 1552). Both were primarily the work of Thomas Cranmer. Indeed, while it is arguable that England produced no Protestant theologian of international stature in the late sixteenth century until William Perkins (1558–1602), it undoubtedly produced one of the greatest Protestant liturgists in Cranmer. Both books were, of course, subject to Parliamentary scrutiny, and as Parliament continued to have many Roman Catholic members, the first edition in particular retained a certain amount of traditionally Roman theology, such as the stipulation to swear an oath by the saints. The second edition was more Reformed, though it did retain certain elements that were obnoxious to those who looked to more strictly Reformed models of reformation, such as those in Zurich and Geneva, for their ecclesiastical inspiration.

With the death of Edward in 1553, his older sister Mary (r. 1553–1558) became queen to great popular acclaim—at least initially. Protestantism under Edward had earned the reputation of being something of a corrupt political movement. Mary moved to restore the papacy in England and also initiated the persecution of many associated with her brother's regime. Several hundred Protestants—including high-profile churchmen such as John Hooper (1495–1555), Hugh Latimer (ca. 1487–1555), Nicholas Ridley (ca. 1500–1555), and Thomas Cranmer himself—perished at the stake. Their deaths were immortalized by John Foxe (1516–1587) in his massive martyrology, *Acts and Monuments* (1563), a book that played a key part in rehabilitating the English Reformation in the popular mind from implications of corruption.

Mary's Catholic Reformation proved short-lived. Her attempt to reestablish monasticism failed and represented a misjudgment of the times. Not only had Roman Catholic nobility done rather well out of Henry's dissolution of the monasteries and thus had no incentive to see them reestablished, but also the rising religious order in the Roman church was the Jesuits. Jesuit piety and practice were built around the individual and were more in tune with the age than the older communal arrangements of the medieval orders. Mary also married Philip II (1527–1598) of Spain, which proved very unpopular politically. And above all were the burnings, which did more than anything else to win sympathy for the Protestant cause.

The final blow to the English Roman Catholic Reformation came when Mary and her close colleague, Cardinal Reginald Pole (1500–1558), died within hours of each other in 1558. Mary's death left her younger sister, the Protestant Elizabeth I (r. 1558–1603), as heir to the throne. The sheer length of Elizabeth's reign combined with her remarkable ability to govern secured the English Protestant settlement and also provided it with some of its distinctive character. A slightly revised Book of Common Prayer, two Books of Homilies, and the Thirty-Nine Articles of Religion articulated the heart of the Elizabethan Reformation vision.

This meant that English Protestantism exhibited certain unique features, compared with its Continental counterparts. While Reformed in doctrine, the church maintained several aesthetic and liturgical trappings that many Reformed individuals found unsatisfactory—particularly those who had spent time in exile under Mary at places like Zurich and Geneva. Thus, the major conflicts of the latter part of the sixteenth century in the English Reformation were less about theology proper and more about the nature of worship. Especially in the 1560s, there were serious disputes within the church over the issue of clerical vestments, which many saw as the vestiges of pre-Reformation Romanism. Though Elizabeth ultimately triumphed and imposed conformity to the Book of Common Prayer on the Church of England, a significant number of clergy were unhappy with this settlement. It was in this context that the movement later known as Puritanism emerged.

Puritanism, like most -isms, has proved hard for scholars to define.

The issues of vestments and aesthetics seem to have been major factors in its emergence. Another was Sabbatarianism, which emerged as a highly contentious theological issue in English circles in the late sixteenth century, fueled in part by the publication of *The Doctrine of the Sabbath, playnely layde forth*, by the English clergyman Nicholas Bownde (d. 1613) in 1595. Yet the definitional problem of Puritanism is complicated by the fact that there was no single distinctive point on which those known as Puritans all agreed. Rather, the term perhaps works best as a means of gathering together figures who exhibited certain family resemblances on the theological and ecclesiastical fronts.

Underlying the issue of vestments, of course, were perennial questions about church government and particularly the relationship of the church to the civil magistrate. Who had the power to set the standards for public worship? Were ministers to be selected by the church, by the state, or by some combination of the two? And was church discipline a matter purely for church courts, or did the magistrate have a significant role? In an era when religion was key to politics and indeed to social control, such questions were always going to be highly contentious and divisive. They also cut across doctrinal lines. Thus, men like Archbishop John Whitgift (ca. 1530–1604) and Thomas Cartwright (1535–1603), though both strong Calvinists on the matter of grace, were on opposite sides in the ecclesiological debates. Whitgift was a brutal opponent of anything that smacked of Puritanism or Presbyterianism, while Cartwright was a Presbyterian.

Theologically, the Thirty-Nine Articles provided a relatively uncontentious doctrinal standard for the church until the last decade of the sixteenth century. Then, a number of clergy began to press for a somewhat looser understanding of predestination and perseverance. While it would be anachronistic to call the work of such men as Peter Baro (1534–1599) "Arminianism," it was certainly an example of tendencies in post-Reformation Protestantism to move away from the more strictly Augustinian patterns of soteriology, which had marked the earlier development of Protestantism. Whitgift responded to Baro and company with the Lambeth Articles (1595), a doctrinal statement that reasserted a vigorous anti-Pelagianism. Composed without the queen's permission, however, they never achieved any official creedal status. Thus, the potential weaknesses in the Church of England's doctrinal position carried over into the seventeenth century.

The Scottish Reformation

If the English Reformation was driven and then controlled by the crown, the Scottish Reformation resulted more from the actions of the nobility. In the mid-sixteenth century, Scotland was closely allied to France and ruled by Mary of Guise (1515–1560), a French princess and the widow of James V (r. 1513–1542). The nobility saw Protestantism as a key element in their political aim to draw apart from France and draw closer to England.

Protestant theology started to arrive in Scotland in the 1520s with the advent of Lutheran books. Patrick Hamilton (ca. 1504–1528), a Lutheran, produced his work *Patrick's Places*, based on the *Loci Communes* of Melanchthon. Then, in the 1540s, George Wishart (ca. 1513–1546), a Zwinglian who translated the First Helvetic Confession into English, emerged as a fiery preacher of reform. But when Wishart was executed in 1546, a group of Protestants stormed St. Andrew's Castle and murdered Cardinal David Beaton (ca. 1494–1546), the churchman seen as responsible.

John Knox (ca. 1513–1572), a supporter of Wishart, arrived at the castle in April 1547 and became chaplain to the rebels. When the castle fell to the French, he and the others were taken captive and served as galley slaves before he was released into English custody in 1549. He went on to play a role as one of the more radical Protestant voices of the Edwardian Reformation.

After spending much of Mary's reign in exile on the Continent, where he pastored in both Frankfurt on the Main and Geneva, Knox developed a vision of reformation shaped both by the Reformed theology of Calvin and company and by the problem of the church's relationship to a hostile head of state. Thus, in the 1550s, he started to formulate his theory of just rebellion, which was predicated on the idea that an idolatrous monarch brought divine judgment on the nation and should thus be overthrown by the godly. One unfortunate literary expression of this theory was his *First Blast of the Trumpet against the Monstrous Regiment of Women* (1558), written while Mary was on the throne of England but not published until Elizabeth had succeeded her. The book's central argument, that women should not rule, was not well received by the new English monarch, and she banned Knox from England for life.

Knox returned to Scotland in 1559 and, in league with the Protestant nobility and with the support of the English, helped to drive the queen regent, Mary of Guise, and her French allies from Scotland. Then, in 1560, the Scottish Parliament instructed Knox and five other ministers (all with the first name John) to produce a confession of faith. The Scots Confession of 1560 was the result, and it remained the doctrinal standard of the Church of Scotland until it was supplanted by the Westminster Confession of Faith in the seventeenth century.

Central to Knox's vision of Reformation was the distinction between idolatry and true worship. Knox focused on the regulative principle of worship, whereby anything not specifically prescribed in the Bible (for example, kneeling at Communion) was considered to be idolatrous and thus forbidden. Therefore, Scottish Presbyterianism in its Knoxian form became known for its simplicity of worship and then later for its opposition to the Anglican Book of Common Prayer. What many of the English Puritans dreamed of was practically realized in the Scottish settlement.

This vision was embodied both in the teaching of the Scots Confession and in the First and Second Books of Discipline (1560, 1578), which sought both to establish the basic structure of church polity and to set forth the social ambition of the church, with a stated desire to establish parish schools. These documents all showed the influence of Geneva and reflected the increasing need for Protestants to consider issues not only of confession but also of organization and polity in order to guarantee the long-term establishment of the faith.

The Scottish settlement was by and large more Presbyterian than that in England not simply for theological reasons but also because it developed in the face of the opposition of the crown, first Mary of Guise, then her daughter, Mary, Queen of Scots (r. 1542–1567). The latter abdicated in 1567 and fled to England in 1568, leaving her infant son, James, to be crowned James VI of Scotland (r. 1567–1625). Knox preached the coronation sermon, signifying that the idea of the sovereign as Supreme Governor of the Church (as in the English settlement) was not only highly impractical but also theologically obnoxious. Presbyterianism, by acknowledging the close link of church and state but also emphasizing the spiritual authority of the church and its courts, thus comported well with the political dynamics of the Scottish Reformation.

Though James was tutored by the redoubtable Presbyterian intellectual George Buchanan (1506–1582) and was closely guarded by the nobility, he himself developed strong Erastian views and a firm belief in the divine right of kings. Thus, as he reached adulthood, he himself engaged in various attempts to bring Scotland into a more Episcopalian mold, triggering by way of reaction the rise in the early seventeenth century of Presbyterian radicalism, which was to bear fruit in the 1640s in the work of the Scottish delegates to the Westminster Assembly.

Other Reformations

As noted at the start of this chapter, the Reformations of Europe were as varied as the lands from which they emerged. France, with a strong monarchy, a vibrant intellectual culture at the University of Paris, and indeed, an interest in exerting independence from the Roman church, looked in the early sixteenth century like fruitful soil for Protestant reform. A sizeable Protestant minority, the Huguenots, did emerge to challenge the Catholic monarchy, but its power was decisively broken at the Saint Bartholomew's Day Massacre in 1572. France thereafter remained firmly in the grip of Catholicism.

Within the Holy Roman Empire itself, the Peace of Augsburg (1555) made transfer from one confessional constituency to another a relatively easy affair for individual provinces. The most dramatically fruitful example of this was the conversion of Frederick III, Elector Palatine, in the early 1560s from Lutheranism to the Reformed faith. The result was the production of the Heidelberg Catechism, which was intended as a document to which both Reformed and Philippists at the University of Heidelberg could subscribe. Thus, it has a generally irenic tone (except when combating Roman Catholic distinctives), and it avoids issues that would have divided Reformed and Phillipists, such as predestination.

Perhaps the most significant of the other "Reformations," however, was that of the Roman Catholic Church itself. It is easy for Protestants to forget that not all moves to address the church's theological and moral problems in the sixteenth century led to separate church bodies. Two aspects of Roman Catholic reform in particular deserve mention.

First, the founding of the Jesuits by Ignatius Loyola (1491–1556) and their rapid rise (they were officially recognized in 1540) were central to Catholic reform. Unlike medieval monasticism, built as it was on settled communities, both rural and urban, the Society of Jesus was modeled along military lines (Loyola had been a soldier) and promoted a piety designed for individuals, thus allowing its members to be highly mobile and to operate undercover in hostile territory. The order also required its members to take a vow to travel and thus had a strong missionary dynamic. This was later combined with an interest in education, making the Jesuits (in terms of sheer numbers and geographical extent) the greatest educational and missionary success story of the Reformation era. By 1600, they had 8,500 missionaries in twenty-six countries from South America to Japan.

Second was the Council of Trent. Called first by Pope Paul III (r. 1534–1549) in 1545, the council gathered for three sessions (1545–1547, 1551–1552, 1562–1563) in the city of Trento in modern-day northern Italy. Trent definitively established the Catholic Church's position on a number of doctrines, which had until then been left somewhat vague, most notably justification. Later sessions, dominated by the Jesuits, also established important educational reforms within the church. Thus, by the 1560s, the Roman Catholic Church had become a much more sharply defined body, and as a result, Protestants were also able to define themselves over against it. Hence, the 1560s saw the start of the great era of Protestant confessionalism.

Conclusion

The diversity of the European Reformations was much broader than can be reasonably covered in a brief survey chapter. Other significant movements for reform, Protestant and Catholic, emerged across the Continent in places such as the Netherlands, Scandinavia, Poland, Hungary, Spain, and Italy. While each of these exhibited its own distinctives, they all addressed common underlying theological, moral, political, and ecclesiastical concerns, allowing for a certain unity within the diversity.

This is clear even from the selection of Reformation narratives offered in this chapter. Germany, Switzerland, England, and Scotland differed in their social and political structures and in their specific pathways to reformation. Hence, we see different ways in which various Reformation movements related to the civil magistrate and to each other. England's Erastianism explicitly subordinated church policy to the needs of the state. In Wittenberg Luther tried to separate the spiritual realm of the church from the secular sphere of the magistrate as much as possible. Calvin struggled throughout his time in Geneva for the spiritual independence of the church, an independence he was never quite able to achieve. Each addressed a similar problem but answered it in a different way.

To this we should add a level of theological diversity. Most obvious was the division between Roman Catholics and Protestants on authority, but differences on the Lord's Supper, church polity, and liturgy also affected the way in which Protestants related to each other. Hence the bitter division between Luther and Zwingli on the matter of the Eucharist and the angry debates between Knox and the Anglican establishment over the provisions of the Book of Common Prayer. Reformation Protestantism itself was a theologically and liturgically diverse phenomenon.

Yet for all this, magisterial Protestants also exhibited a level of unanimity on key issues. Thus, justification by grace through faith by the imputed righteousness of Christ was a central doctrine not simply to Lutherans but also to the Reformed. Formal ecumenical consensus was achieved at points, albeit in an often contentious manner, as seen in the Augsburg Confession *Variata* and the Heidelberg Catechism. Further, when one looks at the large number of Reformed confessions produced by European churches in the sixteenth and seventeenth centuries, there is clearly an underlying and fairly elaborate consensus with regard to what constitutes the Reformed faith, from Edinburgh to Budapest and from the Netherlands to Poland.

The points of confessional consensus and division in the Reformation profoundly shaped the churches of the day. They continue to do so for both Roman Catholics and Protestants who live in a world that is, ecclesiastically speaking, the product of the religious and theological conflicts of the sixteenth century. Thus, knowledge of both the history and the theology of the European Reformations remains vital for the church's understanding of her identity and mission in the twenty-first century.

Resources for Further Study

GENERAL

Cameron, Euan. *The European Reformation*. 2nd ed. Oxford: Oxford University Press, 2012.

Greengrass, Mark. *Christendom Destroyed: Europe, 1517–1648*. Penguin History of Europe 5. New York: Viking, 2014.

Lindberg, Carter. *The European Reformations*. 2nd ed. Malden, MA: Wiley-Blackwell, 2010.

MacCulloch, Diarmaid. *The Reformation: A History*. New York: Penguin Books, 2005.

LUTHERAN REFORMATION

Brecht, Martin. *Martin Luther*. Translated by James L. Schaaf. 3 vols. Minneapolis: Fortress, 1985–1993.

Kolb, Robert. *Luther's Heirs Define His Legacy: Studies on Lutheran Confessionalization*. Brookfield, VT: Variorum, 1996.

———. *Martin Luther: Confessor of the Faith*. Christian Theology in Context. Oxford: Oxford University Press, 2009.

Kolb, Robert, Irene Dingel, and L'ubomír Batka, eds. *The Oxford Handbook of Martin Luther's Theology*. Oxford: Oxford University Press, 2014.

Lohse, Bernhard. *The Theology of Martin Luther: Its Historical and Systematic Development*. Translated by Roy A. Harrisville. Edinburgh: T&T Clark, 1999.

Oberman, Heiko A. *Luther: Man between God and the Devil*. Translated by Eileen Walliser-Schwarzbart. New Haven, CT: Yale University Press, 2006.

Preus, Robert D. *The Theology of Post-Reformation Lutheranism*. 2 vols. St. Louis, MO: Concordia, 1970–1972.

Steinmetz, David C. *Luther in Context*. 2nd ed. Grand Rapids, MI: Baker Academic, 2002.

Wengert, Timothy J., ed. *The Pastoral Luther: Essays on Martin Luther's Practical Theology*. Lutheran Quarterly Books. Grand Rapids, MI: Eerdmans, 2009.

SWISS REFORMATION

Gäbler, Ulrich. *Huldrych Zwingli: His Life and Work*. Philadelphia: Fortress, 1986.

Gordon, Bruce. *The Swiss Reformation*. Manchester: Manchester University Press, 2002.

Gordon, Bruce, and Emidio Campi, eds. *Architect of Reformation: An Introduction to Heinrich Bullinger, 1504–1575*. Texts and Studies in Reformation and Post-Reformation Thought. Grand Rapids, MI: Baker Academic, 2004.

Poythress, Diane. *Reformer of Basel: The Life, Thought, and Influence of Johannes Oecolampadius*. Grand Rapids, MI: Reformation Heritage Books, 2011.

Stephens, W. P. *The Theology of Huldrych Zwingli*. Oxford: Clarendon, 1986.

———. *Zwingli: An Introduction to His Thought*. Oxford: Clarendon, 1992.

GENEVAN REFORMATION

Gordon, Bruce. *Calvin*. New Haven, CT: Yale University Press, 2009.

Greef, Wulfert de. *The Writings of John Calvin: An Introductory Guide*. Translated by Lyle D. Bierma. Exp. ed. Louisville: Westminster John Knox, 2008.

Kingdon, Robert M. *Adultery and Divorce in Calvin's Geneva*. Harvard Historical Studies 118. Cambridge, MA: Harvard University Press, 1995.

Manetsch, Scott M. *Calvin's Company of Pastors: Pastoral Care and the Emerging Reformed Church, 1536–1609*. Oxford Studies in Historical Theology. New York: Oxford University Press, 2013.

———. *Theodore Beza and the Quest for Peace in France, 1572–1598*. Studies in Medieval and Reformation Thought 79. Leiden: Brill, 2000.

Muller, Richard A. *The Unaccommodated Calvin: Studies in the Foundation of a Theological Tradition*. Oxford Studies in Historical Theology. New York: Oxford University Press, 2000.

Naphy, William G. *Calvin and the Consolidation of the Genevan Reformation*. Manchester: Manchester University Press, 1994.

Selderhuis, Herman. *John Calvin: A Pilgrim's Life*. Translated by Albert Gootjes. Downers Grove, IL: IVP Academic, 2009.

Steinmetz, David C. *Calvin in Context*. New York: Oxford University Press, 1995.

ENGLISH AND SCOTTISH REFORMATIONS

Brigden, Susan. *New Worlds, Lost Worlds: The Rule of the Tudors, 1485–1603*. Penguin History of Britain 5. London: Penguin, 2002.

Collinson, Patrick. *The Elizabethan Puritan Movement*. Oxford: Clarendon, 1990.

———. *The Religion of Protestants: The Church in English Society, 1559–1625*. Oxford: Oxford University Press, 1994.

Dawson, Jane. *John Knox*. New Haven, CT: Yale University Press, 2015.

Duffy, Eamon. *The Stripping of the Altars: Traditional Religion in England, 1400–1580*. 2nd ed. New Haven, CT: Yale University Press, 2005.

MacCulloch, Diarmaid. *The Later Reformation in England, 1547–1603*. 2nd ed. London: Palgrave, 2001.

———. *Thomas Cranmer: A Life*. New Haven, CT: Yale University Press, 1998.

Marshall, Peter. *Reformation England, 1480–1642*. 2nd ed. Reading History. London: Bloomsbury Academic, 2012.

Part 2

REFORMATION
THEOLOGY

4

Sola Scriptura

Mark D. Thompson

ABSTRACT

Sola Scriptura is sometimes described as the formal principle of the Reformation. Certainly, an appeal to Scripture's final authority is a common thread throughout the writings of the major theological voices of the Reformation, despite their distinctive emphases and particular interests. This chapter examines the thought of Luther, Melanchthon, Zwingli, Bullinger, Calvin, and Cranmer on the authority of Scripture in an attempt to highlight both their common perspective and their unique contributions. It also argues that despite the genuinely revolutionary character of the Reformers' appeal to Scripture, it in fact relied on antecedently held convictions about the nature of Scripture and its right to determine Christian faith and practice.

Introduction

The theology of the Reformation has not always been studied on its own terms. That is hardly surprising since it is one of the pivotal points in the history of Christian theology. Later authors naturally have their own agendas with respect to it. Whether one is an enthusiast, convinced that the Reformation was an act of God that rescued the Christian churches from dangerous trajectories, or a revisionist, convinced that the real message of the Reformation is something else entirely, there is still a recognized value in being able to appeal to the Reformers. Contemporary accounts often seem driven by a desire to show that the commentator's own theology, or that of his or her particular Christian tradition, is a faithful contemporary rendering of the theology espoused by Luther, Calvin, or one of the other Reformers. But was Luther really an early biblical critic? Did Calvin really exclude other voices and leave us alone with the Bible? Did Cranmer or even Hooker really place the authority of Scripture alongside the authority of reason and tradition to form a "three-legged stool"? What did the sixteenth-century Reformers mean by the expression *sola Scriptura*? If none of us can escape our own presuppositions, at least we can ask the questions that might expose them.

There can be no doubt, however, that the issue of Scripture's authority and function in the churches and in the lives of individual Christians was the particular preoccupation of all the chief figures of the Reformation. From the Leipzig Disputation of 1519, at which Martin Luther (1483–1546) nailed his colors to the mast and insisted on the authority of Scripture over the authority of the church, tradition, or reason, to the Synod of Dort exactly one hundred years later, which, in the preface to its judgment, declared itself bound by a sacred oath to "take the Holy Scriptures alone as the rule of judgment," the Reformers and their immediate heirs kept returning to this subject.[1] Consequently, any attempt to present a holistic account of the Reformation teaching on revelation and the authority of Scripture is bound to be inadequate. There is simply too much ground to cover. Instead, this chapter will, after a brief glance at the context of the Reformation discussion, concentrate on the contributions made by Luther, Melanchthon, Zwingli, Bullinger, Calvin, and Cranmer. These are the major voices of the mainstream Reformation. In examining their thoughts on

---

1. At Leipzig, Luther cited Augustine and Nicolò de' Tudeschi (Panormitanus) in arguing for the authority of "the divine Scripture, which is the infallible word of God," over against "the authority of the word of councils, which are creaturely and liable to err." Martin Luther, *Disputatio I. Eccii et M. Lutheri Lipsiae habita* (1519), WA 2:30–35; *The Articles of the Synod of Dort*, trans. Thomas Scott (Harrisonburg, VA: Sprinkle, 1993), 246.

the issue *in seriatim*, we will clearly see both their essential agreement and their distinctive emphases.

Biblical Authority in the Late-Medieval Period

Luther's appeal to the authority of Scripture, along with that of the other Reformers, would not have gained any traction if it had not echoed an existing sentiment. Confessing the authority of Scripture was common among not only the Reformers but also the Roman theologians. *Sacra pagina*, the study of the sacred page, was a very prominent aspect of theological endeavor in the medieval period. If Thomas Aquinas (1225–1274) is taken as the representative character of medieval scholastic theology, it must also be remembered that he wrote commentaries on almost every book of the Bible. Studies by Beryl Smalley and her student Gillian Evans have demonstrated the extent and profundity of the medieval engagement with Scripture and raised questions about the trite caricatures of pre-Reformation exegesis.[2] Aquinas was not alone. Many of the great scholastic theologians thought deeply about the nature and function of Scripture as well as the most appropriate way to expound it.

Medieval theologians often took as their starting point Augustine's classic statements about the authority of the Scriptures. Three in particular would be regularly quoted in both the medieval and Reformation periods. In 397, Augustine wrote *Against the Basic Letter of the Manichees*, in which he explained, "Indeed I would not have believed the Gospel except the authority of the Catholic Church roused me to action."[3] From the context of this quote, it is clear that Augustine was not insisting on a contingent authority of Scripture, one that depended on the prior authority of the church. Instead, he was insisting that the church that promotes the gospel rejects the doctrine of the Manichaeans. In this light the claim that Mani was a genuine apostle of Jesus Christ had to be seen as spurious. The enduring principle to which he was appealing was that the catholic church is the proper context for reading, understanding, and appealing to Scripture. Indeed, it was in this context that Augustine himself came to faith in Christ as the

2. Beryl Smalley, *The Study of the Bible in the Middle Ages*, 3rd ed. (Oxford: Blackwell, 1983); G. R. Evans, *The Language and Logic of the Bible: The Earlier Middle Ages* (Cambridge: Cambridge University Press, 1984).
3. Augustine, *Contra Epistolam Manichaei Quam Vocant Fundamenti* 1.5 (6), in *PL* 42:176.

church pointed him to the Scriptures. Yet this church sat under the authority of apostolic teaching in the Scriptures, not over it. It pointed to the authoritative text as it fulfilled its own role as guardian and witness; it did not invest that text with authority. The other frequently cited comments of Augustine make this point clear.

Three years after this work, Augustine wrote a treatise on baptism in the wake of continuing questions about the Donatists. In it he clarified the relationship of Scripture to other, later writings, even the writings of those given authority within the church:

> However, who does not know that the sacred canon of Scripture, both of the Old and New Testament, is contained within its own established limits, and that it is to be preferred to all later letters of bishops to such a degree, that it ought not to be possible to doubt or dispute at all, whether anything established as written in it is true or right? But on the other hand, the letters of bishops which have been written or are being written, since the closing of the canon, may be refuted if there be anything in them which by chance deviates from the truth.[4]

Augustine clearly understood the canon of Scripture to be unique, bearing an authority that stood over all other writing. In a letter to Jerome in 405, he drew a firm and explicit connection between this understanding and a commitment to the complete and utter truthfulness of Scripture:

> I have learnt to ascribe to those books which are of canonical rank, and only to them, such reverence and honour, that I firmly believe that no single error due to the author is found in any of them. And when I am confronted in these books with anything that seems to be at variance with truth, I do not hesitate to put it down either to the use of an incorrect text, or to the failure of a commentator rightly to explain the words, or to my own mistaken understanding of the passage.[5]

These three comments by Augustine—and other similar statements, such as his opening comments in *De Genesi ad litteram* (393/4)—

---

4. Augustine, *De Baptismo contra Donatistas Libri Septem*, in *CSEL* 51:178.11–21.
5. Augustine, *Epistulae* 82.3, in *CSEL* 33:354.

reappear regularly in the writings of influential medieval theologians, as well as in the work of the magisterial Reformers. However, more needed to be said, particularly about the unique authority of the Scriptures and the way this related to the authority of the church. The Abbey of St. Victor in Paris was a significant center for this continuing discussion. Hugh of St. Victor (ca. 1096–1141) wrote extensively on the purpose and function of this authoritative Scripture, in one instance stating,

> The only Scripture that is rightly called divine is that which is inspired by the Spirit of God and issued by those who speak by the Spirit of God; it makes humanity divine, reforming it to the likeness of God by instructing in knowledge and exhorting to love. Whatever is taught in it is truth; whatever is commanded is goodness; whatever is promised is happiness.[6]

Unsurprisingly, Hugh accented the ultimate divine origin of Scripture, which he understood gave Scripture its authority. Richard of St. Victor (d. 1173), at one time Hugh's student, also underlined the authority of the Scriptures in an intriguing interpretation of the transfiguration narrative in Matthew 17:

> If now you believe you see Christ transfigured, do not easily believe what you see in him or hear from him, unless Moses and Elijah concur. We know that any testimony stands by the mouth of two or three. Any truth that the authority of the Scriptures does not confirm is suspect in my eyes; I do not receive Christ in His brightness, unless Moses and Elijah are standing by. . . . I do not receive Christ without a witness. No apparent revelation is ratified without the testimony of Moses and Elijah, without the authority of the Scriptures.[7]

This intriguing paragraph is certainly worthy of careful analysis. It does raise questions about the nature and significance of the incarnation.

---

6. Hugh of St. Victor, *De scripturis et scriptoribus sacris* 1, in *PL* 175:10–11A; English translation by Hugh Feiss.

7. Richard of St. Victor, *Book of the Twelve Patriarchs* 81, in *PL* 196:57BD. English translation from Hugh Feiss, *On Love: A Selection of Works of Hugh, Adam, Achard, Richard, and Godfrey of St Victor*, Victorine Texts in Translation 2 (New York: New City, 2012), 48–49.

However, Richard clearly defends the practice, even in the New Testament, of citing Scripture in order to establish the truth and significance of the gospel.

The Victorines did have considerable influence in later centuries, and Peter Lombard's (ca. 1090–1160) *Sententiae in IV libris* was undoubtedly the single most influential medieval textbook in theology, as evidenced by the widely used university degree of *baccalaureus sententarius*, or "Bachelor of the Sentences" (taken even by Luther!). But Aquinas remains the giant of the era. Aquinas famously applied Aristotelian concepts of causality to explain both the divine origin of and the genuine human involvement in the production of Scripture. In his *Quodlibetal Questions*, he acknowledged that God was the principal author of Holy Scripture but went on to insist that "there is nothing repugnant about the notion that [a] man, who is the instrumental cause of Scripture, should in one expression mean several things."[8] This would prove a rather unsatisfactory way of construing the relationship between God's involvement and that of human beings in the production of Scripture. It left open the possibility that Moses, David, the prophets, and the apostles were all entirely passive, making no conscious contribution of their own to the texts attributed to them.

Aquinas was, however, entirely unambiguous about the authority that pertains to canonical Scripture. He anchored this authority in the reality of revelation to the prophets and apostles:

> Argument from authority is the method most appropriate to this teaching in that its premises are held through revelation; consequently it has to accept the authority of those to whom revelation was made. . . .
>
> All the same, holy teaching also uses human reasoning, not indeed to prove the faith, for that would take away from the merit of believing, but to make manifest some implications of its message. . . .
>
> Yet holy teaching employs such authorities only in order to provide as it were extraneous arguments from probability. Its own proper authorities are those of canonical Scripture, and these it

---

8. Thomas Aquinas, *Quodlibet VII*, 6.1, ad 5, Corpus Thomisticum, Textum Taurini, 1956 ed., accessed January 1, 2015, http://www.corpusthomisticum.org/q07.html.

applied with convincing force. It has other proper authorities, the doctors of the Church, and these it looks to as its own, but for arguments that carry no more than probability.

For our faith rests on the revelation made to the Prophets and Apostles who wrote the canonical books, not on revelation, if such there be, made to any other teacher.[9]

Later in the *Summa*, dealing with the sin of lying, Aquinas was more succinct in relating the authority of Scripture to its truthfulness.

That either in the Gospels or anywhere else in the canonical Scriptures falsehood is asserted or that their authors lied is inadmissible; it would put an end to the certainty of faith, which rests on the authoritativeness of Sacred Scripture.[10]

A generation after Aquinas, Henry of Ghent (ca. 1217–1293) resolved at least one of the issues surrounding Aquinas's treatment of the subject. Henry has been credited with being the first to speak of the double authorship of Scripture.[11] The human authors were not mere "technicians and note-takers" but "secondary authors." Nevertheless, the sentences of Scripture, as well as the quality and form of the words they used, were derived from God. Henry, like Aquinas and almost all his contemporaries, drew the necessary inference:

[For this reason,] we must believe the Holy Scriptures simply and absolutely more than the church because the truth itself in Scripture is always kept steadfast and unchangeable and no one is allowed to add to, subtract from, or change it.[12]

Of course, the theological judgments of its leading thinkers were only one factor in the complex mass that was medieval Catholicism. The picture was somewhat complicated by the development of the exegetical tradition in two distinct directions, even though they arose from common assumptions about the authority and relevance of the

9. Thomas Aquinas, *Summa Theologiae* 1a.1.8
10. Aquinas, *Summa Theologiae* 2a2ae.110.3.
11. Rein Fernhout, *Canonical Texts: Bearers of Absolute Authority: Bible, Koran, Veda, Tipitaka: A Phenomenological Study* (Leiden: Brill, 1994), 104.
12. Cited in Hermann Schüssler, *Der Primat der Heiligen Schrift als theologisches und kanonistisches Problem im Spätmittelalter* (Wiesbaden: Franz Steiner, 1977), 57n53.

Scriptures: (1) toward a fourfold exegesis (the *Quadriga*, identifying literal, allegorical, tropological, and anagogical senses in the text) and (2) toward a heightened emphasis on the "literal" interpretation of the text (e.g., greater attention to the historical events to which the Old Testament referred). There was, in the end, no single exegetical tradition in the medieval period but rather a variety of emphases.[13]

More pressing, though, was the way the official pronouncements of the church could stand in stark contrast to statements by its doctors. In the struggle between the church and the empire, the papacy made increasingly expansive claims for power over all other authorities. The extent to which these could reach became obvious in the first officially endorsed response to Luther's *Ninety-Five Theses*, Sylvestro Prierias's (ca. 1456–1523) *On the Power of the Papacy*, in which the third thesis or *fundamentum* brazenly declared, "Whoever does not hold fast to the teachings of the Roman Church and of the Pope as the infallible rule of faith, from which even Holy Scripture draws its strength and authority, is a heretic."[14]

Prierias may have been extreme, but he was not exceptional. After all, the notion that tradition was a distinct second source of authoritative teaching alongside Scripture did not emerge *de novo* at the Council of Trent. Indeed, Gabriel Biel (ca. 1420–1495), professor of theology at the University of Tübingen, justified this view by citing the writings of Basil of Caesarea (ca. 330–379).[15] In a context where people increasingly appealed not only to Scripture but also to an unwritten apostolic tradition embodied in the pronouncements of the church, Luther's appeal to Scripture alone was genuinely revolutionary. It significantly challenged the theological consensus at the turn of the sixteenth century, as well as the theory and practice of the Roman church. So the lines of continuity must not be overdrawn.

---

13. Richard A. Muller, "Biblical Interpretation in the Era of the Reformation: The View from the Middle Ages," in *Biblical Interpretation in the Era of the Reformation: Essays Presented to David C. Steinmetz in Honor of His Sixtieth Birthday*, ed. Richard A. Muller and John L. Thompson (Grand Rapids, MI: Eerdmans, 1996), 11–12.

14. Sylvestro Prierias, *De potestate papae dialogus*, quoted in Latin and English in Heiko A. Oberman, *The Reformation: Roots and Ramifications*, trans. Andrew C. Gow (Edinburgh: T&T Clark, 1994), 124.

15. Gabriel Biel, *Expositio* (1488; repr., Basel, 1515), cited in Heiko A. Oberman, "Quo Vadis, Petre? Tradition from Irenaeus to *Humani Generis*," in *The Dawn of the Reformation: Essays in Late Medieval and Early Reformation Thought* (Edinburgh: T&T Clark, 1986), 281n50.

Yet those lines were certainly present, particularly when it came to a common understanding of the ultimate origin of Scripture in God's revelatory activity and divine inspiration and of the truthfulness and authority that attaches to the biblical text as a result. The theology of the Reformers did not arise in a vacuum, nor did it lack substantial connection with what had come before. This is what made argument on the basis of Scripture possible. This is why Luther could hope, as he most certainly did in the early years of the Reformation (though ultimately in vain), that the pope and the church of Rome would accept his arguments and reform themselves. But the stark realities of vested interests and a commitment to institutional authority, which in practice rivaled and ultimately undermined this common commitment to the authority of Scripture, would press themselves hard on Luther and all the Reformers before too long.

Coining the Term: Luther on Biblical Authority

Martin Luther's commitment to the final authority of Scripture, an authority by which all other authorities are to be judged, is clear from the earliest years of his teaching and writing ministry. Within a year of publishing both his *Disputation against Scholastic Theology* (September 1517) and his *Ninety-Five Theses against the Power of Indulgences* (October 1517), Luther was summoned to an interview with Tommaso de Vio, or Cardinal Cajetan (1469–1534), following the Diet of Augsburg in October 1518. When Cajetan challenged him on the basis of the church's teaching, Luther insisted, "The truth of Scripture comes first. After that is accepted one may determine whether the words of men can be accepted as true."[16] It is clear that Luther was not dismissing the authority of "the words of men" but rather submitting them to what he regarded as a higher authority, "the truth of Scripture." Throughout his ministry Luther would cite the fathers and the creeds and even some decisions of the early church councils in support of his teaching, but he did not consider them decisive. Yet they were also more than merely illustrative. Insofar as they faithfully expressed the teaching of Scripture, they were to be

---

16. Martin Luther, *Acta Augustana* (1518), WA 2:21.5–6; LW 31:282.

regarded as authoritative. Scripture was not the *only* authority but rather the *final* authority.

That this is what Luther meant by the slogan *sola Scriptura* was made even clearer a few years later when, in the wake of Leo X's (r. 1513–1521) threat of excommunication, he wrote *An Assertion of All the Articles* (1520):

> I do not want to throw out all those more learned [than I], but *Scripture alone* to reign, and not to interpret it by my own spirit or the spirit of any man, but I want to understand it by itself and its spirit.[17]

This is one of the very first occurrences of the phrase *sola Scriptura* from the pen of a Reformer. Luther wrote again in these terms in his preface to Melanchthon's notes on Romans in 1522, though this time he put the phrase in the mouth of Melanchthon:

> You say, "*scripture alone* must be read without commentaries." You say this correctly about the commentaries of Origen, Jerome, and Thomas. They wrote commentaries in which they handed down their own ideas rather than Pauline or Christian ones. Let no one call your annotations a commentary [in that sense] but only an index for reading Scripture and knowing Christ, on account that up to this point no one has offered a commentary which surpasses it.[18]

It is clear that Luther was familiar with the expression and the conviction underlying it from the earliest years of the Reformation. But once again, it is important not to import a modern notion of biblical proof texts into Luther's approach to the place of Scripture in theology and church practice. He did not simply support his assertions with a string of biblical references. True, like theologians in all centuries, Luther was not averse to citing *dicta probanta* (i.e., proof texts). The express words of Scripture were decisive. He was more than willing to argue the precise meaning of a particular text—his debate with Zwingli at Marburg in 1529 over Jesus's statement "This is my body" (Matt.

---

17. Martin Luther, *Assertio omnium articulorum M. Lutheri per bullam Leonis X. novissimam damnatorum* (1520), WA 7:98.40–99.2.

18. Martin Luther, *Vorwort zu den Annotationes Philippi Melanchthonis in epistolas Pauli ad Romanos et Corinthios* (1522), WA, vol. 10, bk. 2, 310.12–17.

26:26) is sufficient evidence of that.[19] Earlier, in 1525, he had written on the same subject and insisted that the plain words of Scripture must stand:

> This then is our basis. Where Holy Scripture is the ground of faith we are not to deviate from the words as they stand nor from the order in which they stand, unless an express article of faith compels a different interpretation or order. For else, what would happen to the Bible?[20]

But Luther would also tease out the meaning of a text, using the arguments of those who had gone before him and his own reasoning to lay bare the significance and consequences of what the Bible teaches. He recognized other subsidiary and contingent authorities, not alongside but under the rule of Scripture, which remained his final authority. These other authorities included not only the church fathers but also a number of significant medieval theologians. He also recognized that reasoning from and about the text of Scripture was a critical element in the entire process. Proper inferences from what is said in Scripture, always subject to testing against the biblical text itself, appear throughout Luther's writings. His willingness to reason from the Scriptures (following the example of Paul in Acts 17:2) is evident as early as the famous statement made at the Diet of Worms in May 1521:[21]

> Unless I am convinced by the testimony of the Scriptures or by evident reason—for I can believe neither pope nor councils alone, as it is clear that they have erred repeatedly and contradicted themselves—I consider myself conquered by the *Scriptures* adduced by me and my conscience is captive to the Word of God.[22]

So for Luther, Scripture itself remained the final authority, but this did not eliminate all appeal to the fathers, the creeds, and the decisions

19. For a helpful account see Martin Brecht, *Martin Luther*, trans. J. L. Schaaf, vol. 2, *Shaping and Defining the Reformation, 1521–1532* (Minneapolis: Fortress, 1990), 325–34.
20. Martin Luther, *Wider die himmlischen Propheten von den Bildern und Sakrament* (1525), WA 18:147.23–26; LW 40:157.
21. For Luther, this often meant very specifically "to prove the New Testament from the Old." Martin Luther, *Epistel S. Petri gepredigt und außgelegt* (1523), WA 12:274.24–32; LW 30:18–19.
22. Martin Luther, *Verhandlungen mit D. Martin Luther auf dem Reichstage zu Worms* (1521), WA 7:838.4–7; LW 32:112.

of the church. Reading Scripture is a fellowship activity in which the voices of those who have read before us need to be heard attentively. The individualism of later centuries is only anachronistically read into Luther's appeal to *sola Scriptura*. Neither did the final authority of Scripture do away with all need for applying human reason to the meaning of the text. Luther could certainly make use of logic in constructing a theological argument from time to time (especially when arguing with the Swiss), and his stand at Worms did after all include the phrase "or by evident reason."[23] But, critically, both an appeal to the fathers and the application of reason could be questioned on the basis of the plain reading of the text of Scripture. Scripture alone must reign. Our consciences are not captive to any other authority than the Word of God.

Human reason had its own challenges, of course. Yes, it could and should serve a ministerial function in helping the believer to understand the Word of God. Nevertheless, Luther was convinced that it was the undisciplined exercise of reason that led to many of the errors he perceived in his time, and he refused to let reason be an isolated or final test of truth. In 1532, long after the initial heat of the clash with Rome had died down a little, Luther lectured on Psalm 45, insisting that

> this should be the first concern of a theologian: that he be a good textualist, as it is called, and that he hold fast to the first principle, not to dispute or philosophise in sacred matters. For if one were to operate with rational and plausible arguments in this area, it would be easy for me to distort every article of faith as well as Arius, the Sacramentarians, and the Anabaptists. But in theology we must only hear and believe and be convinced in our heart that "God is truthful, no matter how much what God says in his word might appear absurd to reason."[24]

As is clear in the quotations above, all this was built, as far as Luther was concerned, on the prior conviction that Scripture was

23. See, for instance, Martin Luther, *Vom Abendmahl Christi, Bekenntnis* (1528), WA 26:275.33–34, 323.13–327.4, 437.30–445.17; *LW* 37:134, 211–14, 294–303.
24. Martin Luther, *Praelectio in Psalmum 45* (1532), WA, vol. 40, bk. 2, 593.30–36; *LW* 12:288.

indeed the written Word of God. Even given Luther's insistence that the Word must be *preached* and not just *read*,[25] he had no doubt that the text of Scripture was itself the Word of God. Twentieth-century notions of Scripture containing God's Word ought not to be read back into Luther, as Karl Barth did in his misreading of a comment by Luther in his *Adventspostille*—"it holds God's word"; in fact, this comment has been shown to refer to "the soul in all its distress," not to "Holy Scripture."[26] Luther's own repeated testimony is clear. In 1522, he wrote, "I think that the pope himself, with all his devils, even though he suppresses every word of God, cannot deny that St Paul's word is God's word and that his order is the order of the Holy Spirit."[27] Twenty years later, in 1542, while commenting on Genesis, Luther spoke of how he firmly believed, even if weakly, that "the Holy Spirit Himself and God, the Creator of all things, is the Author of this book."[28]

He could speak interchangeably of "Scripture" and "the Word of God," as he did frequently in his debate with Erasmus in 1525: "I say with respect to the *whole of Scripture*, I will not have *any part of it* called obscure. . . . Christ has not so enlightened us as deliberately to leave *some part of his word* obscure."[29] He could also put the two expressions alongside each other, not to signify two different entities but in order to impress on his readers the identity of Scripture as the Word of God. So in 1521, in the fourth of his responses to the papal bull threatening his excommunication, he wrote,

> Do not make your own ideas into articles of faith as that abomination at Rome does. For then your faith may become a nightmare. Hold to Scripture and the word of God. There you will find truth

25. Luther's most strident expression of this emphasis on the orality of the Word is found in his 1526 lecture on Mal. 2:7. Martin Luther, *Praelectiones in Malachiam* (1526), WA 13:686.6–12; *LW* 18:401.

26. Martin Luther, *Adventspostille* (1522), WA, vol. 10, bk. 1, pt. 2, 75.1–10; Karl Barth, *Kirchliche Dogmatik*, vol. 1, pt. 2, 544 (for an English translation, see Karl Barth, *Church Dogmatics*, trans. G. W. Bromiley, ed. G. W. Bromiley and T. F. Torrance, vol. 1, pt. 2 [London: T&T Clark, 2004], 492). See the discussion in Mark D. Thompson, *A Sure Ground on Which to Stand: The Relation of Authority and Interpretive Method in Luther's Approach to Scripture*, Studies in Christian History and Thought (Carlisle: Paternoster, 2004), 88–89.

27. Martin Luther, *Wider den falsch genannten geistlichen Stand des Papsts und der Bischöfe* (1522), WA, vol. 10, bk. 2, 139.15–18; *LW* 39:277.

28. Martin Luther, *Genesisvorlesung* (1535–1545), WA 43:618.31–33; *LW* 5:275.

29. Martin Luther, *De servo arbitrio* (1525), WA 18:656.15–16, 18–20; *LW* 33:94, 95.

and security—assurance and a faith that is complete, pure, sufficient and abiding.[30]

Eighteen years later, in the midst of a lecture on Genesis 19, he warned of the danger of "evading Holy Scripture" and concluded by urging, "Let us not change the word of God."[31]

Luther did famously speak of three forms of the Word of God but not in the same way that Karl Barth would four centuries later. As Luther put it,

> Thus we must know that the word of God is spoken and revealed in a threefold manner. First, by God the Father in the saints in glory and in Himself. Second, in the saints in this life in the Spirit. Third, through the external word and tongue addressed to human ears.[32]

This is not a strict progression of incarnate Word, inscripturated Word, proclaimed Word. Luther moved from the direct, unmediated voice of the Father in glory, to the Word mediated by the Spirit to the believer in human history, to the Word mediated by the public text and proclamation in the world. However, at other points Luther did come close to Barth's threefold formula. He insisted that Christ the incarnate Word of God is to be distinguished from Scripture and from preaching by the fact that only he is "in substance God."[33] Even so, Luther remained devoted to the Bible, and his lifelong, serious attention to Scripture as the Word of God, to be believed and obeyed as from the lips of God himself, never descended into bibliolatry.

Luther's focus remained what he believed to be the focus of Scripture—the testimony to and word of Christ in both law and gospel. Famously for Luther, the central interpretive principle when discussing either the Old Testament or the New was "what promotes Christ" (*was Christum treibet*).[34] It was a principle, Luther insisted, that arose from

---

30. Martin Luther, *Grund und Ursach aller Artikel D. Martin Luthers* (1521), WA 7:455.21–24; LW 32:98.

31. Luther, *Genesisvorlesung* (1535–1545), WA 43:87.37–40; LW 3:297.

32. Martin Luther, *Dictata super Psalterium* (1513–1515), WA 3:262.6–9; LW 10:220.

33. Martin Luther, "Substantialiter Deus," *Tischreden* #5177 (August 1540), WATr 4:695.16–696.2; LW 54:395.

34. "All the genuine sacred books agree in this, that all of them preach and promote Christ. And that is the true test by which to judge all books, when we see whether or not they promote Christ." Luther *Vorrede auf die Episteln S. Jacobi und Judas* (1522), WADB 7:384.25–27; LW 35:396.

Scripture itself and particularly from the words and example of Christ in places like John 5:39 and Luke 24:27:

> Now the gospels and epistles of the apostles were written for this very purpose. They want themselves to be our guides, to direct us to the writings of the prophets and of Moses in the Old Testament so that we might there read and see for ourselves how Christ is wrapped in swaddling cloths and laid in the manger, that is, how he is comprehended in the writings of the prophets. It is there that people like us should read and study, drill ourselves, and see what Christ is, for what purpose he has been given, how he was promised, and how all Scripture tends toward him. For he himself says in John 5, "If you believed Moses, you would also believe me, for he wrote of me." Again, "search and look up the Scriptures, for it is they that bear witness to me."[35]

This principle was also a particular application of Luther's even more fundamental approach to biblical interpretation: "Scripture is its own interpreter" (*Scriptura sui ipsius interpres*).[36] The Scripture itself must direct our attention to its central point and provide us with the key to understanding each of its parts and how it fits together as a coherent whole, and in Luther's view, Christ was that key. In 1525, he asked, "Take Christ out of the Scriptures and what will you find left in them?"[37] Ten years later he insisted, "Holy Scripture, especially the New Testament, always promotes faith in Christ and magnificently proclaims him."[38]

With this focus on Christ and a settled commitment to the "analogy of Scripture" (a comparison of Scripture with Scripture), Luther was able to insist that Scripture is clear. This tenet formed an important part of his argument against Erasmus in *The Bondage of the Will* (1525). It was why he could confidently make theological assertions, something Erasmus considered inappropriate given the divine mystery and its

---

35. Martin Luther, *Eyne kleyn unterricht, was man ynn den Euangelijs suchen und gewartten soll, Kirchenpostille* (1522), WA, vol. 10, bk. 1, pt. 1, 15.1–10; LW 35:122.
36. The expression is found, among other places, in Luther, *Assertio omnium articulorum M. Lutheri per Bullam Leonis X. novissimam damnatorum* (1520), WA 7:97.20–24.
37. Luther, *De servo arbitrio* (1525), WA 18:606.29; LW 33:26.
38. Martin Luther, *In epistolam S. Pauli ad Galatas Commentarius* (1535), WA, vol. 40, bk. 1, 254.17–18; LW 26:146.

expression in the profundity of Scripture. A Christian man delights in assertions, Luther responded, but he immediately insisted that he was speaking about "the assertion of those things which have been divinely transmitted to us in the sacred writings."[39] Theological assertions are possible because God has effectively communicated his truth in the Scriptures. Of course, Luther did not deny that some passages in Scripture are difficult, and he embraced the ancient practice of explaining difficult passages in light of plain passages. He would unpack what he meant by the clarity of Scripture and go some way toward explaining why a clear passage did not inexorably lead to universal assent by distinguishing between two types of clarity:

> To put it briefly, there are two kinds of clarity in Scripture, just as there are also two types of obscurity: one external and pertaining to the ministry of the Word, the other located in the understanding of the heart. If you speak of the internal clarity, no man perceives one iota of what is in the Scriptures unless he has the Spirit of God. . . . If, on the other hand, you speak of the external clarity, nothing at all is left obscure or ambiguous, but everything there is in the Scriptures has been brought out by the Word into the most definite light, and published to all the world.[40]

Luther's approach to the authority, nature, and function of Scripture set many of the directions for those who followed. It was not a radical break with the official teaching of the church in the centuries prior to the Reformation. The divine origin of Scripture, its authority and truthfulness, and its central focus on Christ, were all themes he held in common with the theological consensus he inherited. An appeal to Scripture was also commonplace in the theological writing and official documents of the church. Luther's radicalism came rather from following through the consequences of these convictions in his revision of the theological curriculum at Wittenberg and in his critique of contemporary church practice. He was prepared to question what

39. "For it is not the mark of a Christian mind to take no delight in assertions; on the contrary a man must delight in assertions or he will be no Christian. [. . .] I am speaking, moreover, about the assertion of those things which have been divinely transmitted to us in the sacred writings." Luther, *De servo arbitrio* (1525), WA 18:603.10–12, 14–15; LW 33:19–20.
40. Luther, *De servo arbitrio* (1525), WA 18:609.4–7, 12–14; LW 33:28.

was being taught and practiced in the Roman church on the basis of his sustained engagement with the text of Scripture. *Sola Scriptura* meant for him that all other authorities, as venerable as they may be, stand under the authority of Scripture and are to be tested by what is taught in Scripture. At the point of the final word, Scripture stands alone. Other Reformers would build on Luther's insights in the light of the challenges that inevitably came.

Following the Trajectory: Melanchthon on Biblical Authority

Phillip Melanchthon (1497–1560), Luther's colleague at the University of Wittenberg, pursued each of these lines of argument but characteristically sought greater systematic clarity. On September 19, 1519, not long after the Leipzig Disputation between Luther, Johann Eck (1486–1543), and Andreas Karlstadt (c. 1480–1541), Melanchthon replied to twenty-four propositions submitted by the dean of the theology faculty as part of his examination for the *baccalaureus biblicus*. Three of the propositions are particularly noteworthy:

16. It is not necessary for a Catholic to believe any other articles of faith than those to which Scripture is a witness.
17. The authority of councils is below the authority of Scripture.
18. Therefore not to believe in the "*character indelibilis,*" transubstantiation, and the like is not open to the charge of heresy.[41]

Undoubtedly, Melanchthon was deeply affected by the exchange at Leipzig, particularly between Luther and Eck. It gave him an entirely new perspective on the authorities of antiquity who had dominated his humanist training. His response to Eck's personal attack against him, published a month before the baccalaureal disputation, spelled out more fully his understanding of the relationship between the authority of Scripture and the authority of the church fathers in particular:

First, it is not in my heart to detract from the authority of anyone in any way. I revere and honour all the lights of the church, those illustrious defenders of Christian doctrine. Next, I consider it to be

41. Philipp Melanchthon, *Melanchthon: Selected Writings*, ed. Elmer E. Flack and Lowell J. Satre, trans. Charles L. Hill (Minneapolis: Augsburg, 1962), 18.

important that the opinions of the holy fathers when they differ, as they do, be judged by Scripture, not vice versa, [which would result in] Scripture suffering violence from [their] diverse judgments. There is a single and simple sense of Scripture, as also the heavenly truth is most simple, which brings together a thread of Scripture and prayer. To this end we are commanded to philosophize in the divine Scriptures, that we might assess the opinions of men and decrees against the touchstone. . . . [T]he Scripture of the heavenly Spirit, which is called canonical, is one, pure and true in all things.[42]

Melanchthon's humanist training made his concern for the patristic authorities unexceptional. They remained authoritative, and their efforts in defending Christian doctrine were to be honored. However, there was an authority higher than any of them, a touchstone against which they were all to be tested. Here, very clearly, Melanchthon enthusiastically adopted the theological directions set by Luther.

The reason underlying this difference between Scripture, on the one hand, and the texts of the fathers and decrees of the church, on the other, is found in the origin of Scripture. Melanchthon put it succinctly when writing to John Hess of Nuremberg a year later:

We know what has been set forth in the Canonical Books is the doctrine of the Holy Spirit. We do not know that what is decided by the councils is the doctrine of the Holy Spirit unless it agrees with Scripture.[43]

Earlier in this important letter Melanchthon expressed his commitment to the clarity of Scripture (another important theme of Luther's, as we have seen), anchoring it in the character and will of God:

On the contrary, the merciful Spirit of God has designed that Scripture be understood by all of the faithful with as little difficulty as possible. I beg you, let us not permit divine Scripture to become Egyptian hieroglyphs. The Son of God took upon himself flesh in order that he might not be unknown. And how much more has he

---

42. Philipp Melanchthon, *Defensio contra Johannem Eckium* (1519), CR 1:113–14, 115.
43. Philipp Melanchthon, *Epistolas ad Hessum* (February 1522), CR 1:143; *Melanchthon: Selected Writings*, 53.

willed to be known through the Scriptures which, as a sort of image of himself, he has left to us for a perpetual possession![44]

Melanchthon's major work, his *Loci Communes*, first published in 1521, did not treat the doctrine of Scripture as a distinct locus. However, his introduction to the locus treating the difference between the old and new covenants in the third edition (1543) included a statement about the divine purpose behind Scripture and incorporated the law-gospel dialectic that Luther had made famous:

> Thus we should understand that it is a great blessing of God that He has given to His church a certain Book, and He preserves it for us and gathers His church around it. Finally, the church is the people who embrace this Book, hear, learn, and retain as their own its teachings in their worship life and in the governing of their morals. Therefore where this Book is rejected, the church of God is not present, as is the case among the Mohammedans; or where its teachings have been suppressed or false interpretations set forth, as has happened among heretics. Therefore we must read and meditate upon this Book so that its teachings may be retained, as we are often commanded regarding the study of it, e.g., 1 Tim. 4:13, "Devote yourself to reading"; Col. 3:16, "Let the Word of Christ dwell in you richly." The Holy Spirit testifies that it is His will that the doctrine and the divine testimonies be put in writing, e.g., Ps. 102:18, "This shall be written for the generations to come, and the people who shall be created shall praise the Lord."
>
> Therefore we should love and cultivate the study of this divinely given Book. First, we should know its substance and that there are two kinds of teaching contained in the entire Book, the Law and the promise of grace, which is properly called the Gospel. This distinction is a light to the entire Scripture and was taught even before Moses.[45]

Though he unpacked none of these at any length, Melanchthon touched on the source of Scripture in God, the confidence in approaching it that is anchored in the benevolence of the God who has given

---

44. Melanchthon, *Epistolas ad Hessum*, CR 1:141; *Melanchthon: Selected Writings*, 51.
45. Philipp Melanchthon, *Loci Communes* (1543), CR 21:801; Melanchthon, *Loci Communes 1543*, trans. J. A. O. Preus (St. Louis, MO: Concordia, 1992), 117.

it, the preservation of it by God, and the role of the Scriptures in the local congregation. He was more direct, and more succinct, in the first edition:

> Articles of faith must be judged simply in accordance with the canon of Holy Scripture. What has been put forth outside Scripture must not be held as an article of faith.[46]

Melanchthon went on to explain why:

> Now, how shall we know the source of what men decree if it cannot be accurately weighed according to Scripture? For it is surely agreed that what the Scriptures confirm originated in the Holy Spirit. . . . Paul enjoins the Thessalonians: "Test everything; hold fast what is good." And elsewhere he orders that the spirits be tested to see whether they are from God. I ask you how we shall test the spirits unless they are measured against a definite standard, surely that of Scripture; for Scripture alone is definitely agreed to have been established by the Spirit of God.[47]

Similar arguments are found in Melanchthon's 1539 treatise *The Church and the Authority of the Word*. However, he was able to develop them in more detail as he sought to defend the pious "against the sophistry of those who falsely quote the testimonies of the dogmas of antiquity and of the church in defense of wicked dogmas."[48] He anticipated the objection that "if the authority of the church is repudiated, then too great license is conceded to the haughtiness of ingenious persons," and in response, Melanchthon wrote,

> To this I respond that just as the Gospel enjoins us to hear the church, so I always say that that assembly within which the Word of God has been honoured, and which is called the church, must be heard, as we also order our pastors to be heard. Let us, therefore hear the church when she teaches and admonishes, but not believe merely because of the authority of the church. For the church does

---

46. Melanchthon, *Loci Communes* (1522), CR 21:131; *Melanchthon and Bucer*, ed. Wilhelm Pauck, LCC 19 (London: SCM, 1969), 63.
47. Melanchthon, *Loci Communes* (1522), CR 21:131; *Melanchthon and Bucer*, 63.
48. Philipp Melanchthon, *De Ecclesia et de Autoritate Verbi Dei* (1539), CR 23:642; *Melanchthon: Selected Writings*, 186.

not originate articles of faith; she only teaches and admonishes. But we must believe because of the Word of God when, to be sure, admonished by the church, we understand that a particular opinion has been handed down in the Word of God truly and without sophistry.[49]

Melanchthon's treatment of the authority of Scripture, most often in the context of repudiating the final authority of church dogma, certainly follows closely the trajectory set by Luther. It is not an entire repudiation of other theologies, except insofar as they are treated as final authorities. All other claims must be tested against Scripture, and wherever there is a difference, Scripture must reign supreme.

Powerful and Effective: Huldrych Zwingli on Biblical Authority

Huldrych Zwingli (1484–1531) always argued that he came to his theology before and independently of Martin Luther. Indisputably the original Swiss Reformer, he produced the first treatise on the nature and function of Scripture in the Protestant era. On September 6, 1522, only sixteen months after the Diet of Worms, Zwingli published his sermon *Die Klarheit und Gewissheit des Wortes Gottes* (*The Clarity and Certainty of the Word of God*). The sermon begins with an introductory meditation on humanity created in the image of God, leading to the following conclusion:

> So then we have come to the point where, from the fact that we are the image of God, we may see that there is nothing which can give greater joy or assurance or comfort to the soul than the Word of its creator and maker. We can now apply ourselves to understand the clarity and infallibility of the Word of God.[50]

The body of the sermon is structured around two characteristics of Scripture: the certainty or power of the Word of God and the clarity of the Word of God. Though the expression "Word of God" is favored by Zwingli throughout the sermon, his use of the text of Scripture and his

---

49. Melanchthon, *De Ecclesia et de Autoritate Verbi Dei*, CR 23:603; *Melanchthon: Selected Writings*, 142.
50. Huldrych Zwingli, *Von der gewüsse oder kraft des worts gottes* (1522), in ZSW 1:352–53; English translation in *Zwingli and Bullinger: Selected Translations with Introductions and Notes*, ed. G. W. Bromiley, LCC 24 (Philadelphia: Westminster, 1953), 68.

own explicit comments—"We speak of Scripture, and this came from God and not from men"[51]—demonstrate that he did not distinguish the two in quite the same way as some twentieth-century theologians. This is evident in one extended comment about Christ and the Word:

> For the one who says [this] is a light of the world. He is the way, the truth and the light. In his Word we can never go astray. We can never be deluded or confounded or destroyed in his Word. If you think there can be no assurance or certainty for the soul, listen to the certainty of the Word of God. The soul can be instructed and enlightened—note the clarity—so that it perceives that its whole salvation and righteousness, or justification is enclosed in Jesus Christ.[52]

In the first section, Zwingli repeatedly insisted that the Word of God, spoken or written, would unfailingly effect the purpose of God:

> The word of God is so sure and strong that if God wills all things are done the moment that he speaks his Word.[53]

> Nothing is too hard or distant for the Word of God to accomplish.[54]

> The Word of God is so alive and strong and powerful that all things have necessarily to obey it, and that as often and at the time that God himself appoints.[55]

He provided a series of examples from both the Old and New Testaments as evidence of the efficacy of the Word of God.

Zwingli then turned to the clarity of Scripture. Three years later Luther would speak of a twofold clarity: the external clarity effected by the Spirit in the text and the internal clarity brought about by the Spirit in the human heart. Zwingli's focus was more singular. His interest was

---

51. Zwingli, *Von der gewüsse oder kraft des worts gottes*, in ZSW 1:382; *Zwingli and Bullinger*, 92.
52. Zwingli, *Von der gewüsse oder kraft des worts gottes*, in ZSW 1:372; *Zwingli and Bullinger*, 84.
53. Zwingli, *Von der gewüsse oder kraft des worts gottes*, in ZSW 1:352; *Zwingli and Bullinger*, 68.
54. Zwingli, *Von der gewüsse oder kraft des worts gottes*, in ZSW 1:355; *Zwingli and Bullinger*, 70.
55. Zwingli, *Von der gewüsse oder kraft des worts gottes*, in ZSW 1:356; *Zwingli and Bullinger*, 71.

in the power of the Word of God to enlighten and bring understanding: "When the Word of God shines on the human understanding, it enlightens it in such a way that it understands and confesses the Word and knows the certainty of it."[56] This was in effect a particular application of the power or efficacy of the Word of God. Precisely because it is the Word *of God*, the sovereign God (Zwingli spoke of "as often and at the time that God himself appoints" in the first section), it is able to bring the understanding from darkness to light. The believer "must be *theodidacti*, that is, taught of God, not of men."[57] The directness of God's address through his Word is the key to the light that comes from God's Word. Here Zwingli moved close to the concept of Scripture's self-authentication, an idea most often associated with Calvin. God so enlightened Abraham with his word "that he knew it to be the Word of God."[58] Zwingli ended the work with twelve instructions on "the way to come to a true understanding of the Word of God and to a personal experience of the fact that you are taught of God."[59]

Of particular note is the way Zwingli gave prominence to the work of the Spirit. First Corinthians 2:12–13 and 1 John 2:27 were significant biblical texts for him in this regard, enabling him to explain precisely how the believer is "taught by God" in and through the Scriptures:

> Note that the gifts which God gives are known by the Spirit of God, not by the clever display of the words and wisdom of man, which is the spirit of this world. . . . God reveals himself by his own Spirit, and we cannot learn of him without his Spirit. . . . [T]his anointing is the same as the enlightenment and gift of the Holy Ghost.[60]

Zwingli's pastoral practice needs to be put alongside his writing to get a fuller picture of his commitment to the authority of Scripture and in particular to its efficacy in transforming the lives of men and women

---

56. Zwingli, *Von der gewüsse oder kraft des worts gottes*, in *ZSW* 1:361; *Zwingli and Bullinger*, 75.

57. Zwingli, *Von der gewüsse oder kraft des worts gottes*, in *ZSW* 1:377; *Zwingli and Bullinger*, 89.

58. Zwingli, *Von der gewüsse oder kraft des worts gottes*, in *ZSW* 1:363; *Zwingli and Bullinger*, 76.

59. Zwingli, *Von der gewüsse oder kraft des worts gottes*, in *ZSW* 1:383; *Zwingli and Bullinger*, 93.

60. Zwingli, *Von der gewüsse oder kraft des worts gottes*, in *ZSW* 1:369, 370; *Zwingli and Bullinger*, 82.

and the community of which they are a part. Zwingli began his preaching ministry in the Great Minster at Zurich with a continuous exposition of the Gospel of Matthew. In the twelve years he exercised this ministry, he preached through most of the Bible. He also established the *Prophezei*, a school of the prophets, in which the text of the Old Testament was read in Latin, Hebrew, and Greek (the Septuagint) before being expounded in Latin for the educated and then in German for the citizens of the city. Zwingli hoped that Scripture would permeate every aspect of life, and he built ministry structures to make that possible.

Near the end of his life, Zwingli drafted a confession to be presented before Emperor Charles V at the Diet of Augsburg. Though the emperor refused to receive it, it nevertheless provides an insight into Zwingli's theology near the end of his life. He did not treat the doctrine of Scripture in a discrete section. However, as he summed up his confession, he made a statement that gives ground for concluding that he stood with Luther in a commitment to *sola Scriptura*, understood as the sole final authority of Scripture over a real but contingent authority of the church and its teachers:

> The above I firmly believe, teach and maintain, not from my own oracles, but from those of the Divine Word; and, God willing, I promise to do this as long as life controls these members, unless someone from the declarations of Holy Scripture, properly understood, explain and establish the reverse as clearly and plainly as we have established above. For it is no less grateful and delightful than fair and just for us to submit our judgments to the Holy Scriptures, and the Church deciding according to them by the Spirit.[61]

Pastoral Guidance: Heinrich Bullinger on Biblical Authority

Heinrich Bullinger (1504–1575), Zwingli's successor in Zurich, was influential not only in the Swiss Confederation but also in England. In 1586, the Convocation of the province of Canterbury directed that Bullinger's *Decades* (a collection of fifty sermons delivered to the pastors

---

61. Huldrych Zwingli, *Fidei ratio* (1530), in *ZSW*, vol. 6, pt. 2, 815; Samuel M. Jackson, *Huldreich Zwingli: The Reformer of German Switzerland, 1484–1531*, 2nd ed. (New York: Putnam, 1903), 481.

of Zurich at their *Prophezei*) be read by "every minister having cure, and being under the degrees of master of arts, and batchelors of law, and not licensed to be a public preacher."[62] The first three sermons of the first "decade" concerned the Word of God and incorporated material previously published as *De scripturae sanctae auctoritate*.[63]

Bullinger's first sermon contained this definition of "the word of God":

> But in this treatise of ours, the word of God doth properly signify the speech of God, and the revealing of God's will; first of all uttered in a lively-expressed voice by the mouth of Christ, the prophets and apostles; and after that again registered in writings, which are rightly called "holy and divine scriptures." The word doth shew the mind of him out of whom it cometh: therefore the word of God doth make declaration of God. But God of himself naturally speaketh truth; he is just, good, pure, immortal, eternal: therefore it followeth that the word of God also, which cometh out of the mouth of God, is true, just, without deceit and guile, without error or evil affection, holy, pure, good, immortal, and everlasting.[64]

This definition, though unexceptional in its historical context, brings the speech of God and the Scriptures into the closest possible relation. There can be no doubt that when Bullinger spoke of the Word of God, he had in mind the text of the Bible as well as the voice of God heard by Moses and the prophets. He insisted that "the doctrine and writings of the prophets have always been of great authority among all wise men throughout the world," and this because "they took not their beginning of the prophets themselves, as chief authors; but were inspired from God out of heaven by the Holy Spirit of God."[65] Likewise, he stated, "Although therefore that the apostles were men, yet

62. Thomas Harding, "Advertisement," in *The Decades of Henry Bullinger, Minister of the Church of Zurich*, trans. H. I., ed. Thomas Harding, Parker Society for the Publication of the Works of the Fathers and Early Writers of the Reformed English Church 7–10 (1587; repr., Cambridge: Cambridge University Press, 1849), viii.

63. Heinrich Bullinger, *De scripturae sanctae auctoritate, certitudine, firmitate, et absoluta perfectione* (Zurich: Froschouer, 1538).

64. Heinrich Bullinger, *Sermonum Decades quinque, de potissimis Christianae religionis capitibus* (Zurich: Froschoveri, 1557), 1; *Decades of Henry Bullinger*, 37.

65. Bullinger, *Sermonum Decades quinque*, 4; *Decades of Henry Bullinger*, 50.

their doctrine, first of all taught by a lively expressed voice, and after that set down in writing with pen and ink, is the doctrine of God and the very true word of God."[66]

The same concerns for truthfulness and reliability discernible in the writings of Luther, Melanchthon, and Zwingli were repeated by Bullinger in this sermon. Likewise, we see the same concern that the Scripture be allowed to do its work, enabling and providing guidance in how to live:

> Let us therefore in all things believe the word of God delivered to us by the scriptures. Let us think that the Lord himself, which is the very living and eternal God, doth speak to us by the scriptures. Let us for evermore praise the name and goodness of him, who hath vouchedsafe so faithfully, fully, and plainly to open to us, miserable mortal men, all the means how to live well and holily.[67]

In the second sermon again it is clear that Bullinger did not exclude Scripture when speaking of the Word of God—the Word of God was to be read and heard:

> Where, by the way, we see our duty; which is, in reading and hearing the word of God, to pray earnestly and zealously that we may come to that end, for the which the word of God was given and revealed unto us.[68]

Bullinger had no doubt about that end or purpose:

> In the word of God, delivered to us by the prophets and apostles, is abundantly contained the whole effect of godliness, and what things soever are available to the leading of our lives rightly, well and holily. . . . What is he, therefore, that doth not confess that all points of true piety are taught us in the sacred scriptures?[69]

Bullinger went on to ground this observation in Paul's classic statement about the inspiration and the utility of the Scriptures in 2 Timothy 3:16–17. He had no difficulty in understanding that the phrase

---

66. Bullinger, *Sermonum Decades quinque*, 5; *Decades of Henry Bullinger*, 54.
67. Bullinger, *Sermonum Decades quinque*, 5; *Decades of Henry Bullinger*, 56–57.
68. Bullinger, *Sermonum Decades quinque*, 6; *Decades of Henry Bullinger*, 61.
69. Bullinger, *Sermonum Decades quinque*, 6; *Decades of Henry Bullinger*, 61.

"all Scripture" in those verses included the emerging New Testament as well as the Old:

> I do not think that any one is such a sot, as to interpret these words of Paul to be spoken only touching the old Testament; seeing it is more manifest than the day-light, that Paul applied them to his scholar Timothy, who preached the gospel, and was a minister of the new Testament.[70]

Bullinger's sermon treated the sufficiency of Scripture in this connection. He was aware that Jesus spoke many things to his disciples that were not recorded by the apostles in the pages of the New Testament. Nevertheless, citing John 20:30–31 in support of this claim, Bullinger insisted that "by this doctrine which [John] contained in writing, that faith is fully taught, and that through faith there is granted by God everlasting life."[71] His target was undoubtedly the oral tradition and the suggestion that the church is also led, and necessarily so, by apostolic teaching not contained in the Scriptures:

> John therefore did let pass nothing which belongeth to our full instructing in the faith. Luke did omit nothing. Neither did the rest of the apostles and disciples of our Lord Jesus Christ suffer any thing to overslip them. Paul also wrote fourteen sundry epistles: but yet the most of them contained one and the selfsame matter. Whereby we may very well conjecture, that in them is wholly comprehended the absolute doctrine of godliness.[72]

This led Bullinger to a statement that fits in entirely with the position on the final authority of Scripture that we have seen in Luther, Melanchthon, and Zwingli. In slightly more colorful language, Bullinger challenged the contemporary appeal to oral tradition, particularly with reference to the touchstone of Scripture:

> As for those which do earnestly affirm, that all points of godliness were taught by the apostles to the posterity by word of mouth, and not by writing, their purpose is to set to sale their own, that

---

70. Bullinger, *Sermonum Decades quinque*, 6; *Decades of Henry Bullinger*, 62.
71. Bullinger, *Sermonum Decades quinque*, 7; *Decades of Henry Bullinger*, 62.
72. Bullinger, *Sermonum Decades quinque*, 7; *Decades of Henry Bullinger*, 63.

is, men's ordinances instead of the word of God. But against this poison, my brethren, take this unto you for a medicine to expel it. Confer the things, which these fellows set to sale under the colour of the apostles' traditions, taught by word of mouth and not by writing, with the manifest writing of the apostles; and if in any place you shall perceive those traditions to disagree with the scriptures, then gather by and by, that it is the forged invention of men, and not the apostles' tradition.[73]

It is a theme Bullinger would pick up in later work, most notably his *Summa christenlicher Religion* from 1556. There he insisted that "the holy biblical writing has enough authority and standing of itself and does not need to be made trustworthy by the church or by human beings."[74] In between these two works, in 1544, he wrote an open letter to Johann Cochlaeus (1479–1552) in which he even argued that "the books of the Old and New Testaments are indisputably called by the ancients canonical and authentic, as someone says *autopistoi*, making faith for themselves, even without arguments, having the supposition of truth and authority."[75] He was arguably the first Protestant writer to use the language of *self-authentication*.

There is, of course, a difference of emphasis between Bullinger's writing on Scripture and that of Luther in particular. Whereas Luther was concerned that we read and hear the gospel of our salvation and understand that it is only by faith in Christ crucified and risen that God deals with our sin, Bullinger's emphasis was on discovering how we should live. Profitable reading is reading that bears the fruit of true godliness:

> If therefore that the word of God do sound in our ears, and therewithal the Spirit of God do shew forth his power in our hearts, and that we in faith do truly receive the word of God, then hath the word of God a mighty force and a wonderful effect in us. For it driveth away the misty darkness of errors, it openeth our eyes, it converteth and enlighteneth our minds, and instructeth us most full and absolutely in truth and godliness.[76]

---

73. Bullinger, *Sermonum Decades quinque*, 7; *Decades of Henry Bullinger*, 64.
74. Heinrich Bullinger, *Summa christenlicher Religion* (Zurich: Froschouer, 1556), 7b.
75. Heinrich Bullinger, *Ad Ioannis Cochlei De Canonicae Scripturae* (Zurich: Froschouer, 1544), 10b.
76. Bullinger, *Sermonum Decades quinque*, 7; *Decades of Henry Bullinger*, 67.

Bullinger dealt at greater length with the use of Scripture in the third sermon in the *Decades*. There he set forth important principles of right interpretation such as attending to genre, interpreting within the framework of the articles of faith and the proper goal of love toward God and our neighbor, paying attention to context (e.g., "we mark upon what occasion every thing is spoken, what goeth before, what followeth after, at what season, in what order, and of what person any thing is spoken"),[77] comparing passages with one another in light of the divine author's self-consistency, and keeping prayer in the paramount place.

Of particular importance in this sermon is a justification of the place of godly exposition, affirmed alongside Bullinger's ongoing commitment to the clarity of Scripture. Having concluded that "the scripture is difficult or obscure to the unlearned, unskilful, unexercised, and malicious or corrupted wills, and not to the zealous and godly readers or hearers thereof," he insisted,

> But, though the scripture be manifest and the word of God be evident, yet, notwithstanding, it refuseth not a godly or holy exposition; but rather an holy exposition doth give a setting out to the word of God, and bringeth forth much fruit in the godly hearer.[78]

Bullinger's chief concerns followed very closely those of Zwingli and the German Reformers. Where he developed their comments on Scripture—in his bold treatment of its sufficiency, in his pastoral emphasis on the effect of Scripture in producing godliness, and in his introduction of the term *autopistos*—he was evidently traveling in a similar trajectory.

The Self-Attesting Word of God: John Calvin on Biblical Authority

John Calvin (1509–1564) was unquestionably the single most influential theologian of the Reformation era. Indeed, his *Institutio Religionis Christianae* (*Institutes of the Christian Religion*) stands out as one of the most enduring accounts of biblical doctrine in the past two

77. Bullinger, *Sermonum Decades quinque*, 7; *Decades of Henry Bullinger*, 77–78.
78. Bullinger, *Sermonum Decades quinque*, 9; *Decades of Henry Bullinger*, 72.

thousand years. However, it must be remembered that the work was expanded and reordered in significant ways over the years, from 516 small format pages divided into six chapters in the first edition of 1536 to eighty chapters divided into four books in both the definitive Latin edition of 1559 and Calvin's own French translation of it a year later. Originally, the work lacked a discrete treatment of the origin, nature, and use of Scripture. He first addressed these questions substantially in the expanded introduction on the knowledge of God in the 1539 edition, three times larger than the first and published while Calvin was in exile in Strasbourg. Yet many of the familiar lines of Calvin's approach to the subject were evident even at this early stage.

Calvin spoke of the authority of Scripture deriving from the simple reality that God speaks in it:

> But while no daily revelations are given from heaven anymore, the Scriptures alone remain, wherein it pleased the Lord to consecrate his truth to everlasting remembrance; it must also be noticed how they will justly receive authority among believers and be heard as the living voices of God himself.[79]

This authority and the notion of truth associated with it, Calvin insisted, is not something conferred by the church or by human reason. On the one hand, this authority is intrinsic to the Scriptures themselves; on the other, it is the result of the Spirit's testimony to the believer's heart. While in some measure echoing Luther's appeal to the "internal clarity of Scripture," this appeal to the Spirit's work in convicting Christians of the authority of Scripture would be a major feature of all of Calvin's future discussions about biblical authority. As he explained in 1539,

> If we desire to take care for our consciences in the best way, so that they may not waver by continual doubt, we must derive the authority of Scripture from something higher than human reasons, indications, or conjectures. That is from the inner testifying of the Holy Spirit, for although it gains reverence for itself by its own majesty,

---

79. John Calvin, *Institutes of the Christian Religion* (1539), 1.21, CR 29:293; the translation is a slightly modified form of that in Henk van den Belt, *The Authority of Scripture in Reformed Theology: Truth and Trust*, Studies in Reformed Theology 17 (Leiden: Brill, 2008), 18.

still it only then really impresses us seriously when it is sealed by the Spirit to our hearts.[80]

It is evident from another piece from Calvin's pen that year, his response to Cardinal Sadoleto on behalf of the citizens of Geneva, that Calvin was aware of the danger of an appeal to the Spirit severed from the Word. He had seen the consequence of this approach in the radical edge of the Reformation. Calvin recognized a similarity between the Anabaptists and the pope at this critical point ("the principal weapon with which they both assail us is the same"): both boast of the Spirit, either in directing the teaching office of the Roman church or directly enlightening the mind, will, and words of the individual Christian without paying appropriate attention to the Word of God.[81] But the touchstone against which the teaching of those in either group is to be tested remains the Word.

The inseparable bond of Spirit and Scripture/Word would be a distinctive feature of all of Calvin's writings on this subject from this point on. As Calvin stated, "It is no less unreasonable to boast of the Spirit without the Word than it would be absurd to bring forward the Word itself without the Spirit."[82] The authority of the Word is sealed to our hearts by the Spirit:

> Scripture then only will suffice to give a saving knowledge of God when its certainty is founded on the inward persuasion of the Holy Spirit.[83]

> The Word is the instrument by which the Lord dispenses the illumination of his Spirit to believers.[84]

Another enduring feature of Calvin's theology introduced at this point was his use of arguments (*argumenta*) for the authority of Scripture, though he insisted that these were secondary, confirmatory aids (*posterior adminicula*). Calvin was obviously, even at this early stage,

---

80. Calvin, *Institutes* (1539), 1.24, *CR* 29:295; translation from van den Belt, 18–19.
81. John Calvin, *Responsio ad Sadoletum* (1539), *CR* 33:393; translation from *A Reformation Debate: Sadoleto's Letter to the Genevans and Calvin's Reply*, ed. John C. Olin (Grand Rapids, MI: Baker, 1976), 61.
82. Calvin, *Responsio ad Sadoletum* (1539), *CR* 33:393–94; translation from Olin, 61.
83. Calvin, *Institutes* (1539), 1.33, *CR* 29:300; translation from van den Belt, 28.
84. Calvin, *Institutes* (1539), 1.36, *CR* 29:303; translation from van den Belt, 34.

attempting to tread a fine line. On the one hand, Scripture stands above and beyond need for "proofs." "We seek no arguments, or probabilities on which to rest our judgment," he wrote, "but we subject our judgment and intellect to it as to something that is above all doubt."[85] On the other hand, God has provided these confirmations (e.g., the majestic simplicity of Scripture, the consensus of the church), which, while not the ground of Scripture's authority, are aids to faith:

> There are other reasons, neither few nor weak, by which the dignity and majesty of the Scriptures themselves are not only asserted by pious minds, but brilliantly vindicated against the schemes of the oppressors: but they are not sufficient in themselves to provide a firm faith, until the heavenly Father places reverence for them above all doubt by manifesting himself there.[86]

Calvin held the testimony of the Spirit and the confirmations together in a careful and constructive tension: "This, then, is a persuasion which needs no reasons; a knowledge with which the highest reason agrees."[87] In this way the authority of Scripture was not undermined by his argument for it.

In what would become (and was in Calvin's mind) the definitive edition of the *Institutes*, that of 1559, Calvin developed his thinking on Scripture even further. His extended treatment of the knowledge of God at the beginning of book 1 became a continuous, careful argument for the necessity of Scripture. Calvin insisted that each person has an innate knowledge of God since each is created in the image of God: "There is within the human mind, and indeed by natural instinct, an awareness of divinity."[88] Why? Calvin's answer was simple: "God has sown a seed of religion in all men."[89] Nevertheless, he insisted, "While some may evaporate in their own superstitions and others deliberately and wickedly desert God, yet all degenerate from the true

---

85. Calvin, *Institutes* (1539), 1.24, CR 29:295; translation from van den Belt, 20.

86. Calvin, *Institutes* (1539), 1.33, CR 29:300; translation slightly modified from van den Belt, 28.

87. Calvin, *Institutes* (1539), 1.24, CR 29:296; translation slightly modified from van den Belt, 21.

88. John Calvin, *Institutes of the Christian Religion* (1559) 1.3.1, CR 30:36; John Calvin, *Institutes of the Christian Religion*, ed. John T. McNeill, trans. Ford Lewis Battles, Library of Christian Classics 20 (Philadelphia: Westminster, 1960), 1:43.

89. Calvin, *Institutes* (1559), 1.4.1, CR 30:38; translation from Battles, 1:47.

knowledge of him."[90] Similarly, Calvin acknowledged that God "not only sowed in men's minds that seed of religion of which we have spoken but revealed himself and daily discloses himself in the whole workmanship of the universe."[91] But once again, human sinfulness keeps us from knowing God through this "dazzling theatre" of God's glory:

> But although the Lord represents both himself and his everlasting Kingdom in the mirror of his works with very great clarity, such is our stupidity that we grow increasingly dull toward so manifest testimonies, and they flow away without profiting us.[92]

In the light of such epic failure to respond appropriately to the work of God within us and around us, "it is needful that another and better help be added to direct us aright to the very Creator of the universe."[93] Calvin's conclusion is well known:

> Just as old or bleary-eyed men and those with weak vision, if you thrust before them a most beautiful volume, even if they recognize it to be some sort of writing, yet can scarcely construe two words, but with the aid of spectacles will begin to read distinctly; so Scripture, gathering up the otherwise confused knowledge of God in our minds, having dispersed our dullness, clearly shows us the true God. This, therefore, is a special gift, where God, to instruct the church, not merely uses mute teachers but also opens his own most hallowed lips.[94]

Tied to the necessity of Scripture is God's willingness to speak to us in terms that are appropriate to our weakness. Rather than leaving us in our self-imposed ignorance, God has descended to us and effectively communicated with us. Calvin's doctrine of accommodation took account of both our creatureliness and our fallenness. So, a little later in the *Institutes*, dismissing the misunderstanding of the Anthropomorphites, Calvin explained,

---

90. Calvin, *Institutes* (1559), 1.4.1, CR 30:38; translation from Battles, 1:47.
91. Calvin, *Institutes* (1559), 1.5.1, CR 30:41; translation from Battles, 1:51–52.
92. Calvin, *Institutes* (1559), 1.5.11, CR 30:49; translation from Battles, 1:63.
93. Calvin, *Institutes* (1559), 1.6.1, CR 30:53; translation from Battles, 1:69.
94. Calvin, *Institutes* (1559), 1.6.1, CR 30:53; translation from Battles, 1:70.

For who even of slight intelligence does not understand that, as nurses commonly do with infants, God is wont in a measure to "lisp" in speaking to us? Thus such forms of speaking do not so much express clearly what God is like as accommodate the knowledge of him to our slight capacity. To do this he must descend far beneath his loftiness.[95]

The language of Scripture's self-authentication, though introduced into the discussion by Bullinger, is most often associated with Calvin—and especially with a very significant passage in these early chapters of the 1559 edition of the *Institutes*. In it Calvin does not so much hold the testimony of the Spirit alongside the proofs of Scripture's authority, the way he did in the 1539 edition, as he holds together the testimony of the Spirit and self-attestation of the Scripture. After all, "the highest proof of Scripture derives in general from the fact that God in person speaks in it."[96] It is surely significant that at the point at which Calvin introduces this language, he makes clear that Scripture, not God, is self-attested:

Let this therefore stand: those whom the Holy Spirit has inwardly taught, truly find rest in Scripture; it is indeed *autopistos*—it should not be submitted to demonstration by proofs—while it still owes the certainty that it deserves among us to the testimony of the Spirit. For even if it wins reverence for itself by its own majesty, it seriously affects us only when it is sealed upon our hearts through the Spirit.[97]

In 1559, Calvin first established that the ground of the believer's confidence (*acquiescere*, "to rest") in Scripture is the self-attestation of Scripture but that this testimony must be sealed to our hearts through the Spirit. Only then did Calvin go on to talk about the sufficiently firm but limited proofs to strengthen confidence (*fides*, "faith") in Scripture.[98]

Alongside these developments and clarifications of the doctrine

---

95. Calvin, *Institutes* (1559), 1.13.1, *CR* 30:90; translation from Battles, 1:121.

96. Calvin, *Institutes* (1559), 1.7.4, *CR* 30:58; translation from Battles, 1:78.

97. Calvin, *Institutes* (1559), 1.7.5, *CR* 30:60; translation based on Battles, 1:80, but takes into account insights in van den Belt, 51–58.

98. The heading of book 1, chap. 8 reads, "So far as human reason goes, sufficiently firm proofs are at hand to establish the credibility of Scripture." Calvin, *Institutes* (1559), 1.8, *CR* 30:61; translation from Battles, 1:81.

of Scripture, Calvin spoke in terms very much identical to the earlier Reformers, especially when, later in the *Institutes*, he addressed the question of how Scripture's authority is properly related to the church's authority. Indisputably, the Council of Trent's decree on Holy Scripture, published thirteen years earlier (April 8, 1546), was in Calvin's mind as he redrafted these chapters. He had, after all, written an *Antidote to the Council of Trent* in 1547. He summarized the two positions, that of the Roman church and that of the Reformation churches, succinctly: "This, then, is the difference. Our opponents locate the authority of the church outside God's Word; but we insist that it be attached to the Word, and do not allow it to be separated from it."[99] A few pages earlier, Calvin had spelled out what this meant for distinguishing the ministry of the apostles and that of their successors:

> Yet this, as I have said, is the difference between the apostles and their successors: the former were sure and genuine scribes of the Holy Spirit, and their writings are therefore to be considered oracles of God; but the sole office of others is to teach what is provided and sealed in the Holy Scriptures. We therefore teach that faithful ministers are now not permitted to coin any new doctrine, but that they are simply to cleave to that doctrine to which God has subjected all men without exception. When I say this, I mean to show what is permitted not only to individual men but to the whole church as well.[100]

Calvin's extraordinary theological gifts enabled him to develop the insights of those who had written before him, maintaining rather than deviating from the directions set by Luther, Melanchthon, Zwingli, and Bullinger. He certainly added new dimensions as he faced new challenges and explored the consequences of the primary authorship of Scripture by God. However, the evidence suggests that, in most cases, even those new dimensions were not without precedent. Most important of all, while hermeneutical emphases would develop in distinctive ways in Lutheran and Reformed circles, a common commitment to the final authority of Scripture would remain.

---

99. Calvin, *Institutes* (1559), 4.8.13, *CR* 30:855; translation from Battles, 2:1162.
100. Calvin, *Institutes* (1559), 4.8.9, *CR* 30:851–2; translation from Battles, 2:1157.

The Word That Transforms:
Thomas Cranmer on Biblical Authority

While Calvin was exercising an international ministry in Geneva, Thomas Cranmer (1489–1556) was trying to negotiate the delicate political situation of Tudor England. Cranmer, the first Protestant archbishop of Canterbury, was the principal drafter of the Forty-Two Articles of Religion (to become the Thirty-Nine Articles under Elizabeth I) and the Book of Common Prayer, and he also authored a number of the sermons in the Books of Homilies, including "A Fruitfull Exhortation to the Readyng and Knowledge of Holy Scripture." Since the statements in the Forty-Two Articles on Scripture remained unchanged between the Edwardian and Elizabethan editions, we can simply explore the text of the Thirty-Nine Articles as a reflection of Cranmer's views. This has the added benefit that it was the Thirty-Nine Articles to which subscription *ex animo* ("from the heart") was required for centuries in the Church of England and many of its dominions (and in some places still is today).

Two of the Thirty-Nine Articles touch on the authority of Scripture:

> VI. Holy Scripture conteyneth all thinges necessarie to saluation: so that whatsoeuer is not read therein, nor may be proued therby, is not to be required of anye man, that it shoulde be beleued as an article of the fayth, or be thought requisite [as] necessarie to saluation. . . .

> XX. The Church hath power to decree Rites or Ceremonies, and aucthoritie in controuersies of fayth: And yet it is not lawfull for the Church to ordayne any thyng that is contrarie to Gods worde written, neyther may it so expounde one place of scripture, that it be repugnaunt to another. Wherefore, although the Churche be a witnesse and a keper of holy writ: yet, as it ought not to decreee any thing agaynst the same, so besides the same, ought it not to enforce any thing to be beleued for necessitie of saluation.[101]

Article 6 finishes with an extensive canonical list, which includes the Apocrypha as books that "the Churche doth reade for example

---

101. Philip Schaff, *The Creeds of Christendom: With a History and Critical Notes*, vol. 3, *The Evangelical Protestant Creeds*, rev. David S. Schaff (1877; repr., Grand Rapids, MI: Baker, 2007), 489, 500.

of lyfe and instruction of manners: but yet doth it not applie them to establishe any doctrene." What is more interesting is the statement that if anything is not read in or proved by Scripture, it is not to be set up as a binding article of faith. Here in confessional form is the principle of *sola Scriptura*. Proposed articles of faith are to be tested by the plain reading of Scripture—"read therein" and "proued therby." If what is proposed is found to be against the teaching of Scripture, it may not stand, and it may not be insisted on. Neither the church nor the king may bind the conscience of believers beyond what can be read or proved on the basis of Holy Scripture. Yet the article was not narrowly biblicist: it spoke very specifically about "all thinges necessarie to saluation" and "article[s] of the fayth." These are what must be read in or proved on the basis of Holy Scripture.

This principle becomes clearer in article 20 with its acknowledgment that "the Church hath power to decree Rites or Ceremonies, and aucthoritie in controuersies of fayth." Cranmer could hardly have written otherwise, given the relationship of church and state in England. Yet a statement like this was not unusual in other Reformation confessions. The ordering of common life was the prerogative of the church so long as what was instituted did not contravene the Word of God. The settling of religious controversy was a collective activity of believers rather than a single solitary believer, no matter what his title. Therefore, this too rightly fell within the responsibility of the church. Christians could be confident with such an arrangement precisely because of the next line: "It is not lawfull for the Church to ordayne any thyng that is contrarie to Gods worde written."

The identification of Scripture as "Gods worde written" is significant even if it is rather unexceptional. The authority carried by Scripture is directly related to this identification. Since this is God's Word, not simply a human response of one kind or other to God's Word, it carries God's own authority. Just as important, since it is all of God's Word written, then an assumption of consistency and coherence—a fundamental unity of the Scriptures in their unfolding witness to Christ—directs the way it is to be read and applied. The Continental Reformers spoke of Scripture as its own interpreter, and the Thirty-Nine Articles fleshed out what this means for the church: the church may not so expound one part of Scripture that it conflicts or contradicts another. This was Cranmer's fundamental hermeneutical principle. As we will see, his related homily explained the appropriate response when one part of Scripture was hard to understand.

Of further interest in this article is the way it describes the church: "a witnesse and keper of holy writ." Here Cranmer revealed his understanding of Augustine's famous quote mentioned earlier. The church does not convey authority to the Scripture. It most certainly should not interpose itself between the believer and Scripture. Instead, its responsibilities lie in preserving the Scripture in order to ensure it is handed on to another generation and is drawing the attention of men and women to what is written there. A "witnesse" and "keper" does not control the written Word; instead, it guards it and facilitates serious sustained engagement with it.

Much of this tightly expressed thinking is unpacked in the homily "A Fruitfull Exhortation to the Readyng and Knowledge of Holy Scripture." The Thirty-Nine Articles themselves point to the Homilies to expound what can only be presented by them in summary form (see article 35, with its emphasis on the Second Book of Homilies, which is to be added to the first and read for the edification of the congregation). This particular homily is suffused with a lively confidence in Scripture as the Word of God, which is not simply a source of knowledge but a life-transforming power:

> The wordes of holy scripture be called wordes of everlastyng life: for they be Gods instrument, ordeyned for the same purpose. They have power to converte through Gods promise, and thei be effectual through Gods assistence; and, beyng received in a faithfull harte, thei have ever an heavenly spirituall woorkyng in them.[102]

These words expose a particular concern of Cranmer regarding the doctrine of Scripture. The matter of where Scripture fits in a hierarchy of authorities was certainly important, and Cranmer addressed it in

---

102. Ronald B. Bond, ed., *Certain Sermons or Homilies (1547); and, A Homily against Disobedience and Wilful Rebellion (1570): A Critical Edition* (Toronto: University of Toronto Press, 1987), 62.

the Articles of Religion, but more important from Cranmer's point of view was the way Scripture brings about a transformation of life both in the individual believer and in the community at large. "The power to converte" was not just a poetic flourish but rather a heartfelt conviction, one that echoes what we have already read in Hugh of St. Victor and Heinrich Bullinger. God has made promises about the effficacy of his Word that need to be taken seriously:

> This Woorde whosoever is diligent to reade, and in his harte to printe that he readeth, the great affeccion to the transitory thynges of this worlde shalbe minished in hym, and the greate desire of heavenly thynges, that bee therein promised of God, shall increase in hym. And there is nothyng that so muche establisheth our faithe and trust in God, that so much conserveth innocencie and purenesse of the harte, and also of outwarde godly life and conversacion, as continual readyng and meditacion of Gods Woorde.[103]

This confidence that regular exposure to the Scriptures would bring about radical transformation was reflected in Cranmer's emphasis on the lectionary that he created to supplement the services of the Book of Common Prayer. According to one of the prefaces of that book, if the lessons were read each day as appointed, then the whole Old Testament would be read through once per year, the New Testament twice per year, and the Psalms once per month. The entire structure of the liturgical life of the Church of England was designed to provide the context for Scripture to make a radical impact on the minds and hearts and wills of sinful people.

The second part of this homily treats two objections that Cranmer anticipated might keep people from this "continual readyng and meditacion of Gods Woorde." He insisted that they were "vaine and fained excuses," and yet he set out to answer them. They were, first, that through ignorance one might fall into error, and second, that Scripture is just too hard to understand. His responses are two of the most ornate passages of the homily, and they bring theological commitment and pastoral concern together in a unique way.

First, on the danger of falling into error, Cranmer explained,

---

103. Bond, *Certain Sermons*, 63.

And if you be afraied to fal into error by readyng of Holy Scripture, I shall shewe you how you maie reade it without daunger of error. Reade it humbly with a meke and a lowly harte, to thintent you maie glorifie God, and not your self, with the knowledge of it; and reade it not without daily praiyng to God, that he would directe your readyng to good effecte; and take upon you to expounde it no further then you can plainly understande it. . . . Presumpcion and arrogancie is the mother of all error: and humilitie nedeth to feare no error. For humilitie will onely searche to knowe the truthe; it will searche and will conferre one place with another: and where it cannot fynd the sense, it will praie, it will inquire of other that knowe, and will not presumpteously and rasshely define any thyng whiche it knoweth not. Therfore, the humble man maie searche any truthe boldely in the Scripture without any daunger of error.[104]

Second, on the fear of a scripture that is too hard to understand, Cranmer responded,

If we reade once, twise or thrise, and understande not, let us not cease so, but still continue readyng, praiyng, askyng of other and so by still knockyng, at the laste the doore shalbe opened, as Sainct Augustyne saieth. Although many thyngs in the Scripture bee spoken in obscure misteries, yet there is no thyng spoken under darke misteries in one place, but the selfe same thyng in other places is spoken more familiarly and plainly to the capacitie bothe of learned and unlearned. And those thynges in the Scripture that be plain to understande and necessarie for salvacion, every mannes duetie is to learne theim, to print theim in memorye, and effectually to exercise theim; and as for the obscure misteries, to be contented to bee ignoraunt in theim untill suche tyme as it shall please God to open those thynges unto hym.[105]

Cranmer's largest private notebook, his "Great Commonplaces," gives further evidence of his convictions regarding the origin and authority of Scripture. "Scripture comes not from the church," he wrote, "but from God and has authority by the Holy Spirit."[106] A little further

---

104. Bond, *Certain Sermons*, 65.
105. Bond, *Certain Sermons*, 66.
106. "Cranmer's Great Commonplaces," British Library Royal MS 7.B.XI, fol. 8v. I am very thankful to my friend Ashley Null for drawing my attention to Cranmer's comments about Scripture in the "Great Commonplaces."

along he added, "The authority of the Scriptures is from God, the author, and not from man nor from men. . . . [T]he authority of Scripture ought not to be made subordinate to the judgments of the church, but the church itself ought to be judged and governed by the Scriptures."[107] The wider evidence of the "Great Commonplaces" amply demonstrates Cranmer's humanist regard for the writings of the church fathers and the councils. However, these statements and others make clear that at least by the time he wrote the "Great Commonplaces," Cranmer had moved to a position in line with that of the other mainstream voices of the Reformation. He understood, with them, the disastrous pastoral consequences of other words introduced alongside, rather than subordinate to, Scripture:

> If anything were the Word of God other than Holy Scripture, we could not be certain of God's Word. If we be uncertain of the Word of God, the Devil might be able to make for us a new word, a new faith, a new church, a new God, indeed make himself God, as he has done up to now. For this is the foundation of the Antichrist's kingdom. If the church and the Christian faith did not rely upon the certain word of God as a firm foundation, no one could know whether he had faith, whether he were in the church of Christ or the synagogue of Satan.[108]

Conclusion

Sola Scriptura, the conviction that Scripture stands alone as the final authority by which every other claim to Christian truth is tested, has long been described as the formal principle of the Reformation, with *sola fide*, justification by faith alone, as its material principle.[109] Whether the Reformers themselves would have been comfortable with such a distinction is a moot point. What is more important is the abundance of evidence that, whatever their distinctives, each of the major voices we have examined from this period shared an understanding of Scripture as the Word of God, which bears the authority of the God

---

107. "Cranmer's Great Commonplaces," fol. 32v.
108. "Cranmer's Great Commonplaces," fol. 22v.
109. The distinction goes back at least to Philip Schaff, *The Principle of Protestantism as Related to the Present State of the Church* (Chambersburg, PA: German Reformed Church, 1845), 54, 70–71.

whose written Word it is and which does not do away with all other authorities but is the final test of them. It is the good Word of a good God, and it is a precious treasure in which those saved by Christ and indwelt by his Spirit delight.

Resources for Further Study

PRIMARY SOURCES

Bullinger, Heinrich. *The Decades of Henry Bullinger, Minister of the Church of Zurich*. Translated by H. I. Edited by Thomas Harding. Parker Society for the Publication of the Works of the Fathers and Early Writers of the Reformed English Church 7–10. 1587. Reprint, Cambridge: Cambridge University Press, 1849–1852.

Calvin, John. *Institutes of the Christian Religion*. Edited by John T. McNeill. Translated by Ford Lewis Battles. 2 vols. Library of Christian Classics 20–21. 1559 edition. Philadelphia: Westminster, 1960.

Cranmer, Thomas. *Certayne Sermons or Homilies*. S. I.: Edwarde Whitchurche, 1547.

Luther, Martin. *The Bondage of the Will, 1525: The Annotated Luther Study Edition*. Edited by Volker Leppin and Kirsi I. Stjerna. Minneapolis: Fortress, 2016.

Melanchthon, Philipp. *Defense against Johann Eck*. In *Melanchthons Werke in Auswahl*, edited by Robert Stupperich, 1:13–22. 1519. Reprint, Gütersloh: Bertelsmann, 1951.

Zwingli, Huldrych. *Of the Clarity and Certainty of the Word of God*. In *Zwingli and Bullinger: Selected Translations with Introductions and Notes*, edited by G. W. Bromiley, 49–95. Library of Christian Classics 24. 1522. Reprint, Philadelphia: Westminster, 1953.

SECONDARY SOURCES

Belt, Henk van den. *The Authority of Scripture in Reformed Theology: Truth and Trust*. Studies in Reformed Theology 17. Leiden: Brill, 2008.

Horton, Michael. "Knowing God: Calvin's Understanding of Revelation." In *John Calvin and Evangelical Theology: Legacy and Prospect*, edited by Sung Wook Chung, 1–31. Milton Keynes: Paternoster, 2009.

Lillback, Peter A., and Richard B. Gaffin Jr. *Thy Word Is Still Truth: Essential Writings on the Doctrine of Scripture from the Reformation to Today*. Phillipsburg, NJ: P&R, 2013.

Null, Ashley. "Thomas Cranmer and the Anglican Way of Reading Scripture." *Anglican and Episcopal History* 75, no. 4 (2006): 488–526.

Stephens, W. P. "Authority in Zwingli—in the First and Second Disputations." *Reformation and Renaissance Review* 1, no. 1 (1999): 54–71.

Thompson, Mark D. *A Sure Ground on Which to Stand: The Relation of Authority and Interpretive Method in Luther's Approach to Scripture.* Studies in Christian History and Thought. Carlisle: Paternoster, 2004.

5

The Holy Trinity

Michael Reeves

ABSTRACT

This chapter argues that the mainstream Protestant Reformers did not accept the doctrine of the Trinity only to ignore it; rather, Reformation theology was built on (and shaped by) explicitly Trinitarian foundations. After a brief look at the late-medieval context, it describes the challenges that the Trinitarianism of Luther and the early Reformers presented to the Roman Catholic theology of their day. It then shows how, in the theology of Calvin and the Reformed tradition, the triune being of God came to constitute the shape of all Christian belief. It concludes with an examination of anti-Trinitarianism and the response of the Counter-Reformation.

Introduction

One could be forgiven for thinking that the Trinity was not a doctrine especially relevant to the Reformers or the Reformation. After all, the Trinity was historically well-trodden ground, an area of agreement accepted by Protestant and Roman Catholic alike. The major issues of Trinitarianism had already been discussed; the major heresies, from Sabellianism to Arianism, had already been refuted. Other doctrines

(Scripture and justification, for example) had not yet been subjected to such scrutiny or debate, and by the sixteenth century, it was they that needed to undergo that same enlightening disputation. And so, if the theologians and councils of the early postapostolic church had already enshrined and defined Trinitarian language about God, what need was there for the Reformers to say any more than amen? They could simply accept the orthodox formulations of the doctrine of God and give their attention to areas of more pressing concern.

Certainly, that story seems to bear out in the secondary literature. The views of the Reformers on the Trinity receive very short shrift in almost every standard introduction to Reformation thought. For example, *The T&T Clark Companion to Reformation Theology*, an impressive topical guide, devotes chapters to subjects as abstruse as "Superstition, Magic, and Witchcraft," yet leaves no room for an examination of the Trinity—or even anything on the doctrine of God at all.[1] *The Oxford Encyclopedia of the Reformation* includes an article on anti-Trinitarianism but not on Trinitarianism.[2] Alister McGrath's textbook *Reformation Thought* makes no mention of the Trinity as a subject of any substantial, renewed thought.[3] Paul Althaus's classic and otherwise rather compendious *The Theology of Martin Luther* gives less than two pages to the Reformer's thoughts on the Trinity, thoughts summed up by this statement: "Luther accepts the orthodox doctrine of the Trinity because he knows that it is supported by the Scripture."[4] The strong impression given is that while Luther finally affirmed belief in the Trinity, it was not particularly valuable to him, and it certainly did not affect his theology in any substantial way. Richard Muller, whose *Post-Reformation Reformed Dogmatics* actually proves an exception to the rule, writes,

> There is no history of the doctrine of the Trinity that covers the era adequately. The trinitarian thought of the Reformers and their

1. David M. Whitford, ed., *The T&T Clark Companion to Reformation Theology* (London: T&T Clark, 2012).
2. Hans J. Hillerbrand, ed., *The Oxford Encyclopedia of the Reformation*, 4 vols. (New York: Oxford University Press, 1996).
3. Alister E. McGrath, *Reformation Thought: An Introduction*, 1st ed. (Oxford: Basil Blackwell, 1988).
4. Paul Althaus, *The Theology of Martin Luther*, trans. Robert C. Schultz (Philadelphia: Fortress, 1966), 199.

orthodox successors has, in fact, received comparatively little treatment, except for a few scattered essays on the views of the more famous Reformers and virtually no analysis of the thoughts on the Trinity among their immediate successors in the late sixteenth century.[5]

Yet if, as the secondary literature tends to imply, the Reformers were rather vacantly nodding along to the doctrine of the Trinity without seeing its worth and import, we should be concerned. That other issues—such as justification—were more urgent is one thing, but if the Reformers failed wholesale to see the connection between especially the doctrine of God and the doctrine of salvation, that would call into question the overall coherence and depth of Reformation theology. Christian doctrines, after all, do not float freely or independently from one another: alter your understanding of the person of Christ, and you must alter your view of the work of Christ; change your soteriology, and you must change your view of the Christian life; and so on. How much more so with the doctrine of God, the One who constitutes the very ground and logic of the Christian faith. The "urgent" soteriological issues of the Reformation simply cannot be understood in abstraction from the doctrine of the Trinity. As John Webster has put it,

> Soteriology is a derivative doctrine, and no derivative doctrine may occupy the material place which is properly reserved for the Christian doctrine of God, from which alone all other doctrines derive. The question from which soteriology takes its rise, and which accompanies each particular soteriological statement, is: *Quis sit deus?*[6]

Indeed, writes Gerald Bray,

> The great issues of Reformation theology—justification by faith, election, assurance of salvation—can be properly understood *only*

5. Richard A. Muller, *Post-Reformation Reformed Dogmatics*, vol. 4, *The Triunity of God* (Grand Rapids, MI: Baker Academic, 2003), 24.
6. John Webster, "'It Was the Will of the Lord to Bruise Him': Soteriology and the Doctrine of God," in *God of Salvation: Soteriology in Theological Perspective*, ed. Ivor J. Davidson and Murray A. Rae (Burlington, VT: Ashgate, 2011), 16.

against the background of Trinitarian theology which gave these matters their peculiar importance.[7]

It will be my contention in this chapter that Reformation theology at its best was not so atomistic or truncated as is commonly implied. The ever more explicit Trinitarianism of the Reformers was not simply a reaction to the threat of anti-Trinitarianism; rather, it constituted the very mold and temper of Reformation theology. For this to be more readily apparent, we need to start out with a brief look at the medieval context the Reformers found themselves facing.

Peter Lombard, Thomas Aquinas, and the Medieval Context

Catholic Trinitarian theology in the so-called Middle Ages stood squarely on the shoulders of Augustine, with the Father seen as the prime Lover, the Son as the Beloved, and the Spirit as the personal Love they share. The writings of Anselm (1033–1109), Bernard of Clairvaux (1090–1153), and the Victorines all have an unmistakably Augustinian—and thus richly Trinitarian—flavor to them.

Or take Peter Lombard (ca. 1090–1160), whose systematic work *Four Books of Sentences* would stand as a (often *the*) core textbook for the schools of the High and Late Middle Ages. In what appears a striking move to us today, Lombard *starts* his doctrine of God (which stands at the head of his magnum opus) with a discussion of the Trinity. Only when he has given considerable time to the three persons of the Trinity and their relations does he proceed to discuss the knowledge, power, and will of God. This thoroughgoing Augustinian Trinitarianism took an important practical turn in Lombard's thought. Developing Augustine's idea that the Spirit *is* the Love of God, he proposed that the love *we* have for God and neighbor is actually the Holy Spirit himself, working in us (Rom. 5:5).[8] In other words, for Lombard, the Christian life was one of being caught up in the Spirit to share in God's own triune life and love.

These emphases would be reversed significantly by Thomas Aquinas

---

7. Gerald Bray, *The Doctrine of God*, Contours of Christian Theology (Leicester: Inter-Varsity Press, 1993), 197–98, italics added.
8. Peter Lombard, *The Sentences, Book 1: The Mystery of the Trinity*, trans. Giulio Silano, Mediaeval Sources in Translation 42 (Toronto: Pontifical Institute of Mediaeval Studies, 2007), 17.1.

(1225–1274). With Aristotle's writings made more readily available in the twelfth century, Aquinas proposed a system in which he sought to bring Aristotelianism and Christianity into a harmony. Aquinas held that in the natural realm Aristotle was so generally trustworthy that he could provide reliable philosophical foundations on which theology could build. Christian theology could then extend Aristotle's logic into analysis of the supernatural realm (of which, lacking divine revelation, Aristotle was ignorant).

This theological model meant that Aquinas differed substantially from Lombard when he came to discuss the doctrine of God in his *Summa Theologiae.* Instead of starting with the Trinity, Aquinas sought first to determine what unaided reason could know of God. Only after spending the bulk of his time proving from reason the existence, unity, perfection, goodness, infinity, immutability, simplicity, and omniscience of God did he consider the Trinity. And then he was quite brief.

Just as Lombard's Trinitarianism had practical consequences, so Aquinas could not so relegate the Trinity without fallout. The difference can be felt in how Aquinas viewed God's grace. Whereas Lombard had identified the grace of God as the very presence of the Spirit in us, moving us with his own love, Aquinas believed in "created grace." The idea that the Spirit might be loving *through* us struck Aquinas as a violation of our human integrity. If that were the case, he thought, it would not be *us* loving, and so it would not be *us* who could be counted righteous. Instead, God gives to us some *thing* that enables us to love: "When people are said to have the grace of God, there is signified *something* bestowed on them by God."[9]

Here were two claims that would, by the sixteenth century, be deeply embedded in Roman Catholic theology and that the Reformers would repeatedly pit themselves against:

1. The grace of God is not something whereby God sovereignly rescues otherwise helpless sinners; it is something whereby he enables us in ourselves to be meritorious.
2. The gift of God is something other than God himself.

9. Thomas Aquinas, *Summa Theologica* (Westminster, MD: Christian Classics, 1981), 1a2ae.110.1, italics added.

Because Aquinas gave preeminence to an Aristotelian, unrelational doctrine of God, his soteriology inevitably defaulted away from the idea of God giving us *himself* by his Spirit. What God seemed to offer, and what people thus began to desire, was this other thing, this "created grace."

Aquinas was soon canonized by the Roman Catholic Church and his theology enshrined. The *Summa Theologiae* was said to have been laid alongside the Scriptures on the altar at the Council of Trent, where Aquinas was awarded the title Universal Doctor of the Church. Not that all agreed with his overall theological model: William of Ockham (ca. 1287–ca. 1347), for example, ardently rejected Aquinas's Aristotelian foundations. Yet Ockham's nominalist belief that there were no shared natures made it impossible for him to see how three divine persons might share one nature. He was left taking on faith a doctrine that otherwise seemed nonsensical and therefore irrelevant! The leading lights of late-medieval Roman Catholicism were effectively sidelining the doctrine of the Trinity, and the effects could be felt in the church's everyday life of administering enabling grace.

Martin Luther and the Early Reformation

It would be easy to gain the impression that during the 1520s and 1530s, the first Reformers treated the Trinity as a doctrine to be hissed at.[10] And certainly they tended to be hesitant about the use of traditional, extrascriptural terminology (words such as Trinity, *homoousios*, *ousia*, and *hypostasis*). In 1521, Martin Luther wrote,

> Although the Arians were in error in regard to the faith, yet— whether their motives were good or bad—they rightly demanded that no new, nonscriptural word be allowed in dogmatic formulations. The integrity of Scripture must be guarded, and a man ought not to presume that he speaks more safely and clearly with his mouth than God spoke with his mouth.[11]

There was more to their nervousness than the matter of manmade theological terms, however. Philipp Melanchthon's comments in the

---

10. See Reinhold Seeburg, *The History of Doctrines*, trans. Charles E. Hay (Grand Rapids, MI: Baker, 1977), 2:303.
11. Martin Luther, *Against Latomus*, LW 32:244.

opening pages of his *Loci Communes* (also 1521) make Luther's look mild:

> We do better to adore the mysteries of Deity than to investigate them. . . . Paul writes in 1 Cor. 1:21 that God wishes to be known in a new way, i.e., through the foolishness of preaching, since in his wisdom he could not be known through wisdom. Therefore, there is no reason why we should labor so much on those exalted topics such as "God," "The Unity and Trinity of God," "The Mystery of Creation," and "The Manner of the Incarnation." What, I ask you, did the Scholastics accomplish during the many ages they were examining only these points? Have they not, as Paul says, become vain in the disputations (Rom. 1:21), always trifling about universals, formalities, connotations, and various other foolish words?[12]

Yet this reaction (shared by other early Reformers such as Martin Bucer) was not against Trinitarianism as such but against the amount of philosophical speculation that had grown up around the doctrine of God and that had too little grounding in scriptural exegesis.[13] Back in 1517, shortly before posting his more famous *Ninety-Five Theses*, Luther had posted his "Disputation against Scholastic Theology," taking square aim at Aquinas's nonbiblical, Aristotelian foundations:

> 43. It is an error to say that no man can become a theologian without Aristotle. This in opposition to common opinion.
> 44. Indeed, no one can become a theologian unless he becomes one without Aristotle. . . .
> 50. Briefly, the whole Aristotle is to theology as darkness is too light. This in opposition to the scholastics.[14]

What Luther, Melanchthon, and Bucer were really seeking in the early years of the Reformation was an application of the principle of *sola Scriptura* to the doctrine of God. Far from questioning the triunity of God, they were defending the idea that God is known truly not through the unaided efforts of fallen human minds but through the preaching

12. Philipp Melanchthon, *Loci Communes Theologici*, in *Melanchthon and Bucer*, ed. Wilhelm Pauck, LCC (Philadelphia: Westminster, 1969), 21.
13. See Simo Knuuttila and Risto Saarinen, "Luther's Trinitarian Theology and Its Medieval Background," *Studia theologica*, 53 (1999): 3–12.
14. Martin Luther, "Disputation against Scholastic Theology" (1517), *LW* 31.12.

of Christ in the gospel. Indeed, twenty years later, when Melanchthon was prepared to write explicitly on the unity and triunity of God in the final edition of his *Loci Communes* (1543), that same concern could still be found. Christ, he said,

> did not wish God to be sought by idle and vagrant speculations, but He wills that our eyes be fixed on the Son who has been manifested to us, that our prayers be directed to the eternal Father who has revealed himself in the Son whom he has sent.[15]

In other words, if the church was to be reformed by Scripture (i.e., *sola Scriptura*), the God made known to her must be the God made known in Scripture. Thus was born a defining mark of Reformational Trinitarianism: it would be grounded and proved not philosophically but exegetically.[16] Ongoing debate about the Trinity would make the Reformers ever happier to use traditional terms such as *hypostasis* and *ousia* but only insofar as those words actually illuminated the meaning of Scripture. A clear example of this can be seen in *The Old Faith, an Evident Probacion out of the Holy Scripture, that the Christian Fayth . . . hath Endured sens the Beginning of the Worlde*, by the Zurich Reformer Heinrich Bullinger.[17] In many ways, Bullinger set a Reformation course with this work, laying out a strong and thorough exegetical case that both Old and New Testaments testify to a God who is three persons in one being.

To say that Reformational Trinitarianism was ardently exegetical does not imply that it was therefore doctrinally naïve. As early as 1520, Luther recognized the controlling primacy of the doctrine of God, calling the Trinity "the highest article on which all others hang."[18] Eight years later, in his Large Catechism, he explained how and why this was the case, thus unfolding the radically Trinitarian shape of his overall theology:

---

15. Philipp Melanchthon, *Loci Communes, 1543*, trans. J. A. O. Preus (St. Louis, MO: Concordia, 1992), 18.

16. See Christine Helmer, "Luther's Trinitarian Hermeneutic and the Old Testament," *Modern Theology*, 18, no. 1 (2002): 49–73.

17. Heinrich Bullinger, *The Old Faith* (1537), in *Writings and Translations of Myles Coverdale, Bishop of Exeter*, trans. Miles Coverdale, ed. George Pearson, Parker Society for the Publication of the Works of the Fathers and Early Writers of the Reformed English Church 13 (Cambridge: Cambridge University Press, 1844), 1–83.

18. Martin Luther, *Treatise on Good Works* (1520), WA 7:214.27.

The Creed was once divided into 12 articles. . . . [W]e shall sum-
marise the entire Christian faith in three chief articles, according
to the three persons in the Godhead, on whom everything that we
believe is focused. . . . The Creed might be summed up very briefly
in these few words: "I believe in God the Father, who created me;
I believe in God the Son, who redeemed me; I believe in God the
Holy Spirit, who sanctifies me."[19]

In Luther's explanation, the first article ("I believe in God the Father")
answers the basic question, what kind of God do you have? with the
answer that he is a Father and that "we may look into His fatherly
heart and sense how boundlessly He loves us."[20] The second article
("I believe in Jesus Christ, his only Son") speaks of the Redeemer who
has "brought us back into our Father's favor and grace."[21] The third,
and lengthiest, article ("I believe in the Holy Spirit") comprehends the
entire Christian life, the Spirit being the One who sets us apart and
makes us holy.

Luther was being quite clear that revelation, justification, and salvation—those flashpoints of the Reformation—all found their proper
context and shape within a Trinitarian schema. Our knowledge of God
is not a philosophical prize but the gift of a God who reveals himself
through his Son to be Fatherly. Our salvation is not a self-appropriated
blessing but the compassionate rescue of that Son, who comes from
the Father to shelter us with his righteousness. Our Christian life is not
about obtaining God's reward by our works but about the Spirit laying hold of our hearts and bringing us to Christ. That is to say, all the
gratuity and comfort of the gospel that Luther would fight for in the
Reformation found its source in the triune nature of God.

Summing up, Luther wrote,

In these three articles God Himself has revealed and disclosed the
deepest profundity of His fatherly heart, His sheer inexpressible
love. He created us for the very purpose that He might redeem
us and make us holy. And besides giving and entrusting to us

19. Martin Luther, *Getting into Luther's Large Catechism: A Guide for Popular Study*, ed.
F. Samuel Janzow (St. Louis, MO: Concordia, 1978), 68.
20. Ibid., 70.
21. Ibid., 71.

everything in heaven and on earth, He has given us His Son and His Holy Spirit in order to bring us to Himself through them. For, as we explained earlier, we were totally unable to come to a recognition of the Father's favor and grace except through the Lord Christ, who is the mirroring image of the Father's heart. Without Christ we see nothing in God but an angry and terrible Judge. But we could know nothing of Christ either, if it were not revealed to us by the Holy Spirit.[22]

There are two momentous challenges here to the theology that Aquinas had helped bring into the mainstream of late-medieval Roman Catholicism. First, in regard to revelation, knowledge of God here starts not with reason but with the preaching of Christ, who is revealed to us by the Spirit. Second, in regard to salvation, the gift of God is not "created grace" but God himself: "Besides giving and entrusting to us everything in heaven and on earth, He has given us His Son and His Holy Spirit in order to bring us to Himself through them."

The first point, about revelation, is just what provided Luther with his ability to critique so much of the theology of his day. Since our knowledge of God and his gospel is a gracious gift, our reason cannot be determinative in theology: God's Word must decide and determine the truth.

The second point, about salvation, was no less significant for Luther himself. As a young man, Luther had prayed to saints, but he had never dared pray to God. The very thought of having direct communion with God, speaking to "the most-gracious Father, through Jesus Christ his Son" as any priest would have to do when celebrating Mass, terrified him when he was ordained in 1507. That had to change if God "has given us His Son and His Holy Spirit in order to bring us to Himself." The nature of God entailed a particular shape to salvation and the Christian life: united to Christ by the Spirit, we are brought before the Father to know and enjoy him as the Son always has.

Moreover, the fact that God gives us his very Spirit and not merely some enabling grace was of seminal importance in Luther's soteriology for yet another reason. That we need the Spirit—the very Giver of life

---

22. Ibid., 77.

himself—proves that we do not have life in ourselves. That is, fallen sinners need more than a bit of enabling; they need a life they do not naturally possess. Thus, the first thing Luther wrote regarding the Spirit in his Small Catechism was this: "'I believe in the Holy Spirit.' What does this mean? 'Answer: I believe that by my own reason or strength I cannot believe in Jesus Christ, my Lord, or come to him. But the Holy Spirit has called me through the Gospel.'"[23] The giving of the Spirit means that salvation is not a cooperative effort, God assisting merely weak sinners; it is a divine rescue, God raising the dead. More than any assistance, sinners need a radical regeneration—something that cannot come from the flesh but can only come from the Spirit through the gospel. As Luther put it in his 1520 *Treatise on Good Works*, "We never read that the Holy Spirit was given to anybody because he had performed some works, but always when men have heard the gospel of Christ and the mercy of God."[24]

William Tyndale

The same theme looms large in the writings of William Tyndale, the English Reformer and Bible translator. Recognizing that our problem as sinners is a radical one rooted in "the heart, with all the powers, affections, and appetites, wherewith we can but sin," Tyndale saw that our only solution is "the Spirit, which looseth the heart."[25] Only the very Spirit of God through the gospel, he maintained, could so "loose" the heart as to free it from love of self and win it to an unfeigned love of God. Thus, unless the believer "had felt the infinite mercy, goodness, love, and kindness of God, and the fellowship of the blood of Christ, and the comfort of the Spirit of Christ in his heart, he could never have forsaken any thing for God's sake."[26]

All told, Tyndale's own break with the superficial ritualism of his upbringing was inextricably intertwined with his robust Trinitarianism. Full-blooded Trinitarian thinking was, from the first, a stamp of

---

23. Martin Luther, "The Small Catechism," WA 30:1.317.
24. Luther, *Treatise on Good Works*, LW 44:30.38–39.
25. William Tyndale, "A Prologue upon the Epistle of St. Paul to the Romans," in *The Works of William Tyndale* (Edinburgh: Banner of Truth, 2010), 1:489; see also *The Parable of the Wicked Mammon*, in *The Works of William Tyndale*, 1:52.
26. Tyndale, "Prologue," 1:109.

Tyndale's reforming message. Witness this appeal from *The Parable of the Wicked Mammon*, the tract that was smuggled into England alongside so many copies of his English translation of the New Testament:

> If thou wilt therefore be at peace with God, and love him, thou must turn to the promises of God, and to the gospel, which is called of Paul, in the place before rehearsed to the Corinthians, the ministration of righteousness, and of the Spirit. For faith bringeth pardon, and forgiveness freely purchased by Christ's blood, and bringeth also the Spirit; the Spirit looseth the bonds of the devil, and setteth us at liberty.[27]

Likewise, Tyndale says in *A Pathway into the Holy Scripture*, "When Christ is thuswise preached . . . [hearts] begin to wax soft and melt at the bounteous mercy of God, and kindness shewed of Christ. For when the evangelion is preached, the Spirit of God entereth into them."[28]

John Calvin

While other Reformers have merely endured their Trinitarianism being overlooked, John Calvin was actually accused of anti-Trinitarianism in his own day. His early reluctance to employ traditional theological terminology and his ensuing refusal to subscribe to the Athanasian Creed led to his being charged with Arianism and Sabellianism. The charges never stuck, being rather obviously politically motivated, and Calvin in any case had quickly come round to appreciate the classical terms. In the first edition of his *Institutes of the Christian Religion* (1536), he wrote,

> The heretics bark that *ousia*, *hypostaseis*, essence, persons, are names invented by human decision, nowhere read or seen in the Scriptures. But since they cannot shake our conviction that three are spoken of, who are one God, what sort of squeamishness is it to disapprove of words that explain nothing else than what is tested and sealed by Scripture![29]

---

27. Tyndale, *Parable*, 1:48.
28. William Tyndale, *A Pathway into the Holy Scripture*, in *The Works of William Tyndale*, 1:19.
29. John Calvin, *Institutes of the Christian Religion* (1536 ed.), trans. Ford Lewis Battles, H. H. Meeter Center for Calvin Studies (Grand Rapids, MI: Eerdmans, 1975), 2.8.45–46.

Most scholars today broadly agree with Michael O'Carroll's verdict that of all the Reformers, Calvin developed "the fullest, most evidently traditional and orthodox Trinitarian theology."[30]

One of the earliest indications of the depths of Calvin's Trinitarianism—how informative it was and how integrated it was into the body of his theology—can be found in his 1539 response to the open letter from Cardinal Sadoleto to the people of Geneva. Working with the Thomistic assumption that the gift of God is something other than God himself, Sadoleto was understandably troubled by the Reformers' doctrine of salvation by grace alone. What possible motivation for holiness would that leave people? Calvin replied,

> If he who has obtained justification possesses Christ, and at the same time Christ never is where his Spirit is not, it is obvious that gratuitous righteousness is necessarily connected with regeneration. Therefore, if you would duly understand how inseparable faith and works are, look to Christ, who, as the apostle teaches (1 Cor. 1:30), has been given to us for justification and for sanctification. Wherever, therefore, that righteousness of faith which we maintain to be gratuitous is, there too Christ is; and where Christ is, there too is the Spirit of holiness who regenerates the soul to newness of life. On the contrary, where zeal for integrity and holiness is not in force, there neither the Spirit of Christ nor Christ himself are present. Wherever Christ is not, there is no righteousness, and indeed no faith; for faith cannot lay hold of Christ for righteousness without the Spirit of sanctification.[31]

Since the gift of God is Christ, who cannot be separated from the Spirit, Sadoleto's objections had no traction within Calvin's Trinitarianism.

30. Michael O'Carroll, *Trinitas: A Theological Encyclopedia of the Holy Trinity* (Collegeville, MN: Liturgical Press, 1987), 194. See also Edward A. Dowey Jr., *The Knowledge of God in Calvin's Theology* (Grand Rapids, MI: Eerdmans, 1994), 125–26, 146; Wilhelm Niesel, *The Theology of Calvin*, trans. Harold Knight (Grand Rapids, MI: Baker, 1980), 54–57; T. H. L. Parker, *The Doctrine of the Knowledge of God: A Study in the Theology of John Calvin* (Edinburgh: Oliver and Boyd, 1952), 61–62; B. B. Warfield, "Calvin's Doctrine of the Trinity," in *Calvin and Augustine*, ed. Samuel G. Craig (Philadelphia: Presbyterian and Reformed, 1974), 187–284; Philip W. Butin, *Revelation, Redemption, and Response: Calvin's Trinitarian Understanding of the Divine-Human Relationship* (New York: Oxford University Press, 1995); T. F. Torrance, "Calvin's Doctrine of the Trinity," chap. 3 in *Trinitarian Perspectives: Toward Doctrinal Agreement* (Edinburgh: T&T Clark, 1994); Christoph Schwöbel, "The Triune God of Grace: The Doctrine of the Trinity in the Theology of the Reformers," in *The Christian Understanding of God Today: Theological Colloquium on the Occasion of the 400th Anniversary of the Foundation of Trinity College, Dublin*, ed. J. M. Byrne (Dublin: Columba, 1993), 49–64.

31. John Calvin and Jacopo Sadoleto, *A Reformation Debate: Sadoleto's Letter to the Genevans and Calvin's Reply*, ed. John C. Olin (Grand Rapids, MI: Baker, 1966), 68.

God's triune nature had so impressed itself on Calvin's soteriology that he could preach salvation by grace alone unhesitatingly, unhampered by the fear that it might lessen zeal for holiness. Antinomianism simply could not grow in such soil.

To see the place of the Trinity in Calvin's mature theology, we must of course look to his *Institutes*. The first edition (1536) very much followed the traditional structure of a catechism; however, by the final and definitive edition (1559), he had entirely reorganised his material into an elegantly creedal and expressly Trinitarian shape:

- Book 1: "The Knowledge of God the Creator" (corresponding to the first section of the Apostles' Creed, "I believe in God the Father almighty")
- Book 2: "The Knowledge of God the Redeemer in Christ" (corresponding to the second section of the Apostles' Creed, "I believe in Jesus Christ his only Son our Lord")
- Book 3: "The Way in Which We Receive the Grace of Christ" (corresponding to the third section of the Apostles' Creed, "I believe in the Holy Spirit")[32]
- Book 4: "The External Means or Aids by Which God Invites Us into the Society of Christ and Holds Us Therein" (corresponding to the section of the Apostles' Creed on "the holy catholic Church")

What this structure suggests (and what its contents then prove) is that, far from Calvin simply reacting to either accusations of heresy or the anti-Trinitarian teachings of men like Michael Servetus, he was Trinitarian, root and branch. By the time he came to write the 1559 edition of the *Institutes*, the Trinity was no longer treated simply as one doctrine among others: in Calvin's mind, the triune being of God had come to constitute the shape of *all* Christian belief. In that sense, there is a stark difference between Aquinas's *Summa Theologiae*, with its sidelining of the doctrine of the Trinity, and Calvin's *Institutes*, which receives its very form from it.

Book 1 contains Calvin's explanation of the Trinity as a discrete

---

32. Though Calvin does not treat the person of the Spirit specifically, he explains in the title of the first chapter of book 3 that the things already spoken of concerning Christ (in book 2) "Profit Us by the Secret Working of the Spirit."

topic: "In Scripture, from the creation onward, we are taught one essence of God, which contains three persons."[33] There he examines God's nature and persons, the suitability of such terms as "persons," the deity of the Son and deity of the Spirit, and God's oneness and threeness, and he also spends time refuting anti-Trinitarianism.

Two matters here have caused some debate: (1) Calvin's claim that each person of the Trinity is *autotheos* ("God of himself"), and (2) the extent to which Calvin was influenced by Eastern theology, especially Gregory of Nazianzus (ca. 329–ca. 389). We will consider both.

First, against any quasi-Arian notion that the Son has only a derived, secondary deity, Calvin argued that, like the Father, the Son has divinity "from himself." Even in Calvin's day this confused some, who felt that Calvin was denying that the Son is *begotten* of the Father, "true God *of* true God," as stated in the Niceno-Constantinopolitan Creed. But Calvin was making a distinction between the person of the Son and his divine being. The *person* of the Son *is* begotten of the Father, but his divine being exists of itself. Calvin explained,

> Therefore we say that deity in an absolute sense exists of itself; whence likewise we confess that the Son since he is God, exists of himself, but not in respect of his Person; indeed, since he is the Son, we say that he exists from the Father. Thus his *essence* is without beginning; while the beginning of his *person* is God himself.[34]

Second, T. F. Torrance, Gerald Bray, and Robert Letham have all suggested that Calvin was in many ways indebted to the Cappadocian Fathers in his Trinitarianism.[35] A. N. S. Lane, however, has expressed the need for caution with this theory.[36] The main point here is to recognize that Calvin, unlike medieval Western theologians such as Aquinas, was concerned primarily with the *persons* of God (Father,

---

33. Calvin, *Institutes*, 1.13.
34. Ibid., 1.13.25, italics added. For a clear analysis of Calvin's position and the subsequent debate, see Brannon Ellis, *Calvin, Classical Trinitarianism, and the Aseity of the Son* (Oxford: Oxford University Press, 2012).
35. T. F. Torrance, "The Doctrine of the Holy Trinity in Gregory Nazianzen and John Calvin," in *Trinitarian Perspectives: Toward Doctrinal Agreement* (Edinburgh: T&T Clark, 1994), 21–40; Bray, *The Doctrine of God*, 197–224; Robert Letham, *The Holy Trinity: In Scripture, History, Theology, and Worship* (Phillipsburg, NJ: P&R, 2004), 252–68.
36. A. N. S. Lane, *John Calvin: Student of the Church Fathers* (Grand Rapids, MI: Baker, 1999), 1–13, 83–86.

Son, and Spirit), not the *essence* of God. He did not give time—as had been traditional—to considering the existence, nature, or attributes of God but almost immediately turned to look at the persons, writing with verve that

> God also designates himself by another special mark to distinguish himself more precisely from idols. For he so proclaims himself the sole God as to offer himself to be contemplated clearly in three persons. Unless we grasp these, only the bare and empty name of God flits about in our brains, to the exclusion of the true God.[37]

More striking, though, than his specific treatment of the Trinity in chapter 13 is the fact that the *entirety* of book 1 of the *Institutes* forms part of a larger Trinitarian argument. The book is about "The Knowledge of God the Creator," meaning knowledge of God *the Father* in particular. So conspicuous, in fact, is Calvin's emphasis on the fatherhood of God that it drove J. S. Lidgett to observe that Calvin was sounding out a note "which has not been heard since Irenaeus."[38]

Our problem as sinners in a fallen world, Calvin wrote, is that in "this ruin of mankind *no one now experiences God either as Father* or as Author of salvation, or favorable in any way, until Christ the Mediator comes forward to reconcile him to us."[39] Only the converted (or "pious") mind now "acknowledges him as Lord and Father."[40] In other words, true, saving knowledge of God means knowing the Creator as our Father. Indeed, we do not truly understand God's work as Creator or his providence (and so we have no comfort) unless we understand that it is a *fatherly* work. Thus "we ought in the very order of things [in creation] diligently to contemplate God's fatherly love."[41] "To conclude once for all," Calvin continued, "whenever we call God the Creator of heaven and earth, let us at the same time bear in mind that . . . we are indeed his children, whom he has received into his faithful protection to nourish and educate."[42]

37. Calvin, *Institutes*, 1.13.2.
38. J. S. Lidgett, *The Fatherhood of God in Christian Truth and Life* (Edinburgh: T&T Clark, 1902), 253.
39. Calvin, *Institutes*, 1.2.1, italics added.
40. Ibid., 1.2.2; cf. 2.6.1; 3.6.3.
41. Ibid., 1.14.2.
42. Ibid., 1.14.22.

Book 2 concerns the Son and his redemption, a story that is ultimately about the Son returning us "to God our Author and Maker, from whom we have been estranged, in order that he may again begin to be our Father."[43] In keeping with the logic of book 1, where the work of the Creator was intimately bound up with his identity as the Father, so here the identity of the Son is critical to rightly understanding his work. The redemption of the Son has the final aim of sharing that sonship:

> His task was so to restore us to God's grace as to make of the children of men, children of God; of the heirs of Gehennna, heirs of the Heavenly Kingdom. Who could have done this had not the self-same Son of God become the Son of man, and had not so taken what was ours as to impart what was his to us, and to make what was his by nature ours by grace?[44]

It was precisely this Trinitarian account of redemption that provided Calvin with the theological weight he needed, as a pastor, to give people real assurance before God. Standing on our own before the Almighty, even enabled by grace, we could never have confidence, unless filled with the most vain presumption: "To be sure, the inheritance of heaven belongs only to the children of God [cf. Matt. 5:9–10]. Moreover, it is quite unfitting that those not engrafted into the body of the only-begotten Son are considered to have the place and rank of children."[45] But "the Son of God, to whom it wholly belongs, has adopted us as his brothers."[46]

Book 3 examines the Spirit's application of the Son's redemption to believers. The book opens with the question, "How do we receive those benefits which the Father bestowed on his only-begotten Son—not for Christ's own private use, but that he might enrich poor and needy men?" The answer: through "the secret energy of the Spirit, by which we come to enjoy Christ and all his benefits. . . . To sum up, the Holy Spirit is the bond by which Christ effectually unites us to himself."[47] To

---

43. Ibid., 2.6.1.
44. Ibid., 2.12.2.
45. Ibid., 2.6.1.
46. Ibid., 2.12.2.
47. Ibid., 3.1.1.

explain this, Calvin noted what titles are given to the Spirit in Scripture, suggesting that the first title of the Spirit is the

> "Spirit of adoption" because he is the witness to us of the free benevolence of God with which God the Father has embraced us in his beloved only-begotten Son to become a Father to us; and he encourages us to have trust in prayer. In fact, he supplies the very words so that we may fearlessly cry, "Abba, Father!" [Rom. 8:15; Gal. 4:6].[48]

According to Calvin, the Spirit unites us to Christ in order that the Father might embrace us as children in his beloved Son. Calvin could hardly demonstrate more how he worked the Trinity right through his theology into his soteriology. And such statements are no blip in Calvin's writings overall; the Father's adoption of believers in Christ runs like a unifying thread throughout Calvin's *ordo salutis*.[49] According to Sinclair Ferguson, Calvin "does not treat sonship as a separate locus of theology precisely because it undergirds everything he writes."[50] The theme of adoption becomes yet more noticeable in his commentaries. So Calvin wrote in his commentary on Romans, "Our salvation *consists* in having God as our Father."[51]

God's election, for example, is a topic Calvin saw as closely linked to adoption:

> It is not from a perception of anything that we deserve, but because our heavenly Father has introduced us, through the privilege of adoption, into the body of Christ. In short, the name of Christ excludes all merit, and everything which men have of their own; for when he says that we are chosen in Christ, it follows that in ourselves we are unworthy.[52]

---

48. Ibid., 3.1.3.
49. See Richard A. Muller, *Calvin and the Reformed Tradition: On the Work of Christ and the Order of Salvation* (Grand Rapids, MI: Baker Academic, 2012).
50. Sinclair B. Ferguson, "The Reformed Doctrine of Sonship," in *Pulpit and People: Essays in Honor of William Still*, ed. Nigel M. De S. Cameron and Sinclair B. Ferguson (Edinburgh: Rutherford House, 1986), 81. See also Nigel Westhead, "Adoption in the Thought of John Calvin," *SBET* 13, no. 2 (1995): 102–15; Howard Griffith, "The First Title of the Spirit: Adoption in Calvin's Soteriology," *EvQ* 73, no. 2 (2001): 135–53.
51. John Calvin, *Calvin's Commentaries* (1844–1856; repr., Grand Rapids, MI: Baker, 1993), 19:301 (Rom. 8:17).
52. Ibid., 21:198 (Eph. 1:4).

And again,

> When our Lord engraveth his fear in our hearts by his Holy Spirit, and such an obedience towards him, as his Children ought to perform unto him, this is as if he should set upon us the seal of his election, and as if he should truly testify that he hath adopted us and that he is a Father unto us.[53]

Election, in other words, is precisely the ratification of God's gracious adoption.[54]

Also, when he wrote of justification, he cast it as inexplicable if not grounded in our adoption:

> Paul surely refers to justification by the word "acceptance" when in Eph. 1:5–6 he says: "We are destined for adoption through Christ according to God's good pleasure, to the praise of his glorious grace by which he has accounted us acceptable and beloved" [Eph. 1:5–6 p.] That means the very thing that he commonly says elsewhere, that "God justifies us freely" [Rom. 3:24].[55]

And when he concluded his chapter on justification by faith, he selected a filial illustration to summarize the doctrine, an image of approaching our Father "clothed" by the Spirit in the righteousness of Christ:

> As [Jacob] did not of himself deserve the right of the first-born, concealed in his brother's clothing and wearing his brother's coat, which gave out an agreeable odor [Gen. 27:27], he ingratiated himself with his father, so that to his own benefit he received the blessing while impersonating another. And we in like manner hide under the precious purity of our first-born brother, Christ, so that we may be attested righteous in God's sight. . . . And this is indeed the truth, for in order that we may appear before God's face unto salvation we must smell sweetly with his odor, and our vices must be covered and buried by his perfection.[56]

As to our future, why is it that those who are elect and righteous in Christ are still subject to death, pain, and evil? Again, Calvin's answer

---

53. John Calvin, *Sermons on Election and Reprobation*, trans. John Field (Audubon, NJ: Old Paths Publications, 1996), 98–99.
54. Calvin, *Institutes*, 3.22.4.
55. Ibid., 3.11.4.
56. Ibid., 3.11.23.

was bound up with our adoption: we continue to suffer here "because the fruit of our adoption is as yet hid."[57] We must be confidently patient and endure a while longer until that day when "we shall partake of it in common with the only-begotten Son of God."[58]

Book 4, which treats the church, could reasonably be expected to have a less obviously Trinitarian feel. But in fact, Calvin's examination of the sacraments as signs of the gospel gave him an opportunity to recapitulate the overall Trinitarian shape of our salvation:

> All the gifts of God proffered in baptism are found in Christ alone. Yet this cannot take place unless he who baptizes in Christ invokes also the names of the Father and the Spirit. For we are cleansed by his blood because our merciful Father, wishing to receive us into grace in accordance with his incomparable kindness, has set this Mediator among us to gain favor for us in his sight. But we obtain regeneration by Christ's death and resurrection only if we are sanctified by the Spirit and imbued with a new and spiritual nature. For this reason we obtain and, so to speak, clearly discern in the Father the cause, in the Son the matter, and in the Spirit the effect, of our purgation and our regeneration.[59]

Indeed, believed Calvin, baptism stands at the beginning of our faith precisely as the pledge of its Trinitarian nature: the Father adopting us through his Son and renewing us through his Spirit. Calvin explained,

> There are good reasons why *the Father, the Son, and the Holy Spirit*, are expressly mentioned; for there is no other way in which the efficacy of *baptism* can be experienced than when we begin with the unmerited mercy of *the Father*, who reconciles us to himself by the only begotten *Son*; next, Christ comes forward with the sacrifice of his death; and at length, *the Holy Spirit* is likewise added, by whom he washes and regenerates us, (Titus 3:5,) and, in short, makes us partakers of his benefits. Thus we perceive that God cannot be truly known, unless our faith distinctly conceive of Three Persons in one essence; and that the fruit and efficacy of *baptism* proceed from God *the Father* adopting us through his

57. *Calvin's Commentaries*, 22:205 (1 John 3:2).
58. Ibid., 19:301 (Rom. 8:17).
59. Calvin, *Institutes*, 4.15.6.

Son, and, after having cleansed us from the pollutions of the flesh through *the Spirit*: creating us anew to righteousness.[60]

For Calvin, in other words, the very shape and goodness of the gospel—of the entire Christian faith—was molded by and grounded in the triune nature of God.

Trinitarianism in the Reformed Tradition

Evidences of the Trinitarianism of the subsequent Reformed movement in the history of the sixteenth century are far too numerous to catalog here. Yet two cases stand out as specially worthy of mention: the Heidelberg Catechism and the early development of Reformed covenantal theology.

The Heidelberg Catechism, perhaps the best known of all the Reformed catechisms, provides a good example of how deeply embedded and how pastorally vital Trinitarian thinking became for Reformed theology, even as early as 1563, when it was written. After some questions dealing with man's misery and redemption, the central section of the catechism is devoted to God the Father, God the Son, and God the Holy Spirit. More revealing, though, is the rich Trinitarianism of its memorable first answer:

> What is your only comfort in life and death?
>   That I, with body and soul, both in life and in death, am not my own, but belong to my faithful Saviour Jesus Christ, who with his precious blood has fully satisfied for all my sins, and redeemed me from all the power of the devil; and so preserves me that without the will of my Father in heaven not a hair can fall from my head; yea, that all things must work together for my salvation. Wherefore, by his Holy Spirit, he also assures me of eternal life, and makes me heartily willing and ready henceforth to live unto him.[61]

The logic of the answer shows that the names Christ, Father, and Spirit have not been inserted mechanically, merely to do theological due diligence; rather, the comfort of the believer is revealed as irreducibly

---

60. *Calvin's Commentaries*, 17:385 (Matt. 28:19).
61. "The Heidelberg Catechism," in *The School of Faith: The Catechisms of the Reformed Church*, ed. and trans. Thomas F. Torrance (London: James Clarke, 1959), 68.

Trinitarian. Assurance of salvation, the knowledge of God's providential care, and the Spirit's renewal of the believer—all hallmarks of Reformed theology—receive their rationale from the fact that God is (and so acts as) Father, Son, and Spirit. As in the theology of Calvin himself, the Trinity was not being kept merely as one topic of theology among others; the triune being of God was being treated as the matrix for *all* theology.

The other particularly noteworthy instance of Trinitarian thinking in sixteenth-century Reformed theology can be found in the early development of the idea of a *covenant of redemption*. This was the doctrine that in eternity the Father had entered into a covenantal agreement with the Son to save the elect, the Father appointing and the Son agreeing to be the Redeemer. The details need not concern us here, but the idea grew out of a deeper belief that was foundational in Reformed theology: that all of God's ways in both creation and salvation flow out of the very nature and identity of God. Since God is triune, the root and branches of salvation can be properly explained only in Trinitarian ways. The covenant of redemption would be an increasingly strong feature of later, seventeenth-century Reformed theology, but the origins of the concept can be found earlier, in the writings of theologians such as Caspar Olevian and Jerome Zanchi.[62] Zanchi would also produce the largest Reformational work of Trinitarian analysis and polemic with his *De tribus Elohim*.[63] This was a compendious and (in keeping with previous Reformational Trinitarianism) strongly exegetical work, laying out a sizable number of texts that refer to a plurality of persons in both New Testament and Old. (The title refers to the fact that the one God Jehovah is the triune Elohim.) Following Calvin's scripturally driven lead, Zanchi placed his discussion of the Trinity *before* that of God's essence and attributes.

---

62. See Caspar Olevian, *De substantia foederis gratuiti inter Deum et electos* (Geneva: Eustathium Vignon, 1585); Hieronymus Zanchius, "De natura Dei," in *Omnium operum theologicorum* (Geneva: Crispinus, 1619), 6:1.11–13; Richard A. Muller, "Toward the Pactum Salutis: Locating the Origins of a Concept," *MAJT* 18 (2007): 11–65; Lyle D. Bierma, *German Calvinism in the Confessional Age: The Covenant Theology of Caspar Olevianus* (Grand Rapids, MI: Baker, 1996), 107–12; R. Scott Clark, *Caspar Olevian and the Substance of the Covenant: The Double Benefit of Christ*, Rutherford Studies in Historical Theology (Edinburgh: Rutherford House, 2005), 177–80.

63. Hieronymus Zanchius, *De tribus Elohim*, vol. 1 of *Operum theologicorum D. Hieronymi Zanchii* (Heidelberg: Stephanus Gamonetus and Matthaeus Berjon, 1605).

Anti-Trinitarianism: Servetus, Socinus, and the Radical Reformers

As early as the 1520s, men such as Ludwig Hätzer (1500–1529) and Christian Entfelder (fl. 1530–1535) were teaching anti-Trinitarian doctrine in opposition to both Rome and the magisterial Reformers. Perhaps the best known of these early Reformation-age anti-Trinitarians was Michael Servetus (ca. 1511–1553). A descendant of Jewish *conversos*, Servetus hailed from Spain, a country that, with its large Jewish and Muslim populations, had long been especially receptive to anti-Trinitarianism. The title of his first and last works—*On the Errors of the Trinity* (1531) and *The Restoration of Christianity* (1553)—make clear his agenda: he wanted to restate the doctrine of God along non-Trinitarian lines so as to restore Christianity to his vision of its original purity. According to Servetus, the apostles had taught that the Father alone is God: Jesus is "Son" only insofar as he has a supernatural origin, and the Spirit is but the impersonal power of God. And, he was clear, if the church threw its Trinitarianism overboard, it would need to recalibrate every other doctrine, from its Christology to its doctrines of justification and the sacraments.

However, the name that would become synonymous with anti-Trinitarianism—and that would come to be spoken with horror across Europe—was that of Faustus Socinus (1539–1604). If anything, Socinus was stronger than Servetus in his anti-Trinitarianism. Like Servetus, he saw the Spirit as the impersonal power of God, but he held Christ to be a mere man conceived by the Spirit and only in that sense eligible to be called the "Son of God." Jesus Christ was not God in any real sense. As with Servetus, the result was a radical—and inevitable—reworking of the very structure of Christianity: Jesus was construed as a teacher, not a Savior; the cross was a martyrdom, not an atonement. Socinus proved once again that without grounding in the triune being of God, the gospel becomes a graceless thing.

How true to the Reformation were these anti-Trinitarians? In 1962, George Williams popularized an expression with the title of his book *The Radical Reformation*.[64] The term could be taken to imply

---

64. George Huntston Williams, *The Radical Reformation* (London: Weidenfeld & Nicolson, 1962).

a movement that was radically true to the Reformation project. In other words, where the magisterial Reformers would stop short or hesitate, the radical Reformers (of whom the Anabaptists were the most numerous and renowned) would push on for a more thorough-going reformation of the church. That was certainly how most radicals saw themselves. Among these radicals, Williams included the anti-Trinitarians, a designation that again fit the self-identification of men like Servetus and Socinus. Others, like the Unitarian historian E. M. Wilbur, have argued explicitly that they were simply pushing the project of reformation to its logical conclusions.[65] Yet as the decades of the sixteenth century wore on, the sheer volume of polemic produced by the Trinitarian Reformers against these "radicals" proves that the mainstream Reformers, at least, vehemently denied the faithfulness of such radicals to the Reformation.

What are we to make of this? The way forward is to ask the following question: Where the magisterial Reformers desired a reformation of the church *by the Word of God* (i.e., *sola Scriptura*), by what standard did the anti-Trinitarians wish to reform the church? Richard Muller has argued that "the antitrinitarian position is characterized by a radical biblicism coupled with a renunciation of traditional Christian and philosophical understandings of substance, person, subsistence, and so forth, as unbiblical accretions."[66] Certainly the literature of the anti-Trinitarians, like that of the original Arians, is replete with biblicist language and argument; however, underneath that biblicist surface seems to lie a deeper rationalism. These anti-Trinitarians repeatedly made key doctrinal moves on the basis of logical inference and *only then* supported them exegetically.

Take, for example, Socinianism's Racovian Catechism. Before even getting to the doctrine of God, it recommends as a principle of exegesis that we reject "every interpretation which is repugnant to right reason, or involves a contradiction."[67] Then, when the doctrine of God is ad-

---

65. E. M. Wilbur, *A History of Unitarianism* (Cambridge, MA: Harvard University Press, 1945–1952), 1:12–18.
66. Muller, *Post-Reformation Reformed Dogmatics*, 4:75.
67. Thomas Rees, ed. and trans., *The Racovian Catechism: With Notes and Illustrations, Translated from the Latin; to Which Is Prefixed a Sketch of the History of Unitarianism in Poland and the Adjacent Countries* (London: Longman, Hurst, Orme, and Brown, 1818), 18.

dressed, we find ourselves immediately confronted, not with biblical texts but with reason:

> What is it to know that God is one only?
>
> This you may of yourself easily understand—that there cannot be more beings than one who possesses supreme dominion over all things.[68]

As to the question of the Trinity, it frames it in this way:

> Prove to me that in the one essence of God, there is but one Person?
>
> This indeed may be seen from hence, that the essence of God is one, not in kind but in number. Wherefore it cannot, in any way, contain a plurality of persons, since a person is nothing else than an individual intelligent essence. Wherever, then, there exist three numerical persons, there must necessarily, in like manner, be reckoned three individual essences; for in the same sense in which it is affirmed that there is one numerical essence, it must be held that there is also one numerical person.[69]

Given, then, that Socinianism was deferring to a different final authority (reason, not Scripture), it would be entirely inaccurate to see it as a straight continuation of the Protestant reforming trajectory. Certainly, from the perspective of the Reformers, it was instead a *false* reformation, calling the church not back to apostolic purity but away to a different supreme authority, a different god, and so a different gospel.

Rome's Counter-Reformation

In 1550, the English Reformer Roger Hutchinson wrote his *The Image of God*, arguing with extensive biblical referencing that all false teaching was a by-product of distorting the doctrine of the Trinity.[70] From Arianism to transubstantiation to Rome's doctrine of priesthood, all, he sought to prove, were inextricably linked to a defective doctrine of

---

68. Ibid., 26.

69. Ibid., 33.

70. Roger Hutchinson, *The Image of God, or Laie Mans Book, in Whych the Right Knowledge of God Is Disclosed* (London: John Day, 1550), in *The Works of Roger Hutchinson, Fellow of St. John's College, Cambridge, and afterwards of Eton College, A.D. 1550*, Parker Society for the Publication of the Works of the Fathers and Early Writers of the Reformed English Church 22 (Cambridge: Cambridge University Press, 1842), 1–208.

God. Hutchinson was by no means a theologian of the same caliber as Luther or Calvin, but his argument fits well with their shared insistence that the triune being of God underpinned and shaped all Reformation theology. Yet it was an especially barbed argument. Rome, after all, had never thought of herself as anything less than Trinitarian, and Roman Catholic authors, like the Reformers, opposed the anti-Trinitarians. How, then, did Rome respond to this revitalized and vibrant Trinitarianism among the Reformers?

In the early days, there were a few individuals—the Catholic Evangelicals and *Spirituali*—who made doctrinal overtures in the direction of the Reformers. But as Rome's position hardened, *doctrinal* reform came to be viewed with increasing suspicion. The Council of Trent (1545–1563), Rome's official theological response to the Reformation, simply did not concern itself with the doctrine of God. The Counter-Reformation (or "Catholic Reformation") would consist predominantly of monastic observantism, preachers emphasizing Christian morality and the imitation of Christ, church discipline, and the effective care of souls. In other words, it was essentially about attaining a purer practical performance of the same, unreformed theology. Or take those works most especially vital to and representative of Counter-Reformation spirituality, Ignatius of Loyola's (1491–1556) *Spiritual Exercises* or the writings of Teresa of Avila (1515–1582) or John of the Cross (1542–1591): when placed alongside Reformational works like Calvin's *Institutes*, they seem comparatively unscathed by Trinitarian thought. Roman Catholicism in the Counter-Reformation, it appears, tended not to recognize the Trinitarian foundations of the Reformers' theological critiques and thus never answered them.

Yet Trinitarian those foundations surely were: from the day Luther referred to the doctrine of the Trinity as "the highest article on which all others hang," the best Reformational theology was profoundly and ineradicably Trinitarian.[71] Foundations are commonly hidden by the structures they support, and so it is not entirely surprising that the secondary literature on Reformation theology has tended to miss them, concentrating instead on more obvious areas of disagreement. From

---

71. Luther, *Treatise on Good Works*, WA 7:214.27.

revelation to salvation, however, the theology and pastoral practice of the mainstream Reformation drew its life and logic from the soil of Trinitarian thought.

Resources for Further Study

PRIMARY SOURCES

Calvin, John. *Institutes of the Christian Religion.* Edited by John T. Mc-Neill. Translated by Ford Lewis Battles. 2 vols. Library of Christian Classics 20–21. 1559 edition. Philadelphia: Westminster, 1960.

Calvin, John, and Jacopo Sadoleto. *A Reformation Debate: Sadoleto's Letter to the Genevans and Calvin's Reply.* Edited by John C. Olin. Grand Rapids, MI: Baker, 1966.

Lombard, Peter. *The Sentences.* Translated by Giulio Silano. 4 vols. Mediaeval Sources in Translation 42–43, 45, 48. Toronto: Pontifical Institute of Mediaeval Studies, 2007–2010.

Luther, Martin. *Getting into Luther's Large Catechism: A Guide for Popular Study.* Edited by F. Samuel Janzow. St. Louis, MO: Concordia, 1978.

Melanchthon, Philip. *Loci Communes Theologici.* In *Melanchthon and Bucer,* edited by Wilhelm Pauck, translated by Lowell J. Satre, 3–152. Library of Christian Classics 19. Philadelphia: Westminster, 1969.

Rees, Thomas, ed. and trans. *The Racovian Catechism: With Notes and Illustrations, Translated from the Latin; to Which Is Prefixed a Sketch of the History of Unitarianism in Poland and the Adjacent Countries.* London: Longman, Hurst, Orme, and Brown, 1818.

Zanchi, Hieronymus. *De tribus Elohim.* Translated by Ben Merkle. Wenden House of New Saint Andrews College. Accessed June 10, 2016. http://www.nsa.edu/academics/wenden-house-project/zanchis-de-tribus-elohim/.

SECONDARY SOURCES

Bray, Gerald. *The Doctrine of God.* Contours of Christian Theology. Leicester: Inter-Varsity Press, 1993.

Butin, Philip W. *Revelation, Redemption, and Response: Calvin's Trinitarian Understanding of the Divine-Human Relationship.* New York: Oxford University Press, 1995.

Dowey, Edward A., Jr. *The Knowledge of God in Calvin's Theology.* Grand Rapids, MI: Eerdmans, 1994.

Ferguson, Sinclair B. "The Reformed Doctrine of Sonship." In *Pulpit and People: Essays in Honor of William Still,* edited by Nigel M. De S. Cameron and Sinclair B. Ferguson, 81–88. Edinburgh: Rutherford House, 1986.

Griffith, Howard. "'The First Title of the Spirit': Adoption in Calvin's Soteriology." *Evangelical Quarterly* 73, no. 2 (2001): 135–53.

Letham, Robert. *The Holy Trinity: In Scripture, History, Theology, and Worship.* Phillipsburg, NJ: P&R, 2004.

Muller, Richard A. *Post-Reformation Reformed Dogmatics: The Rise and Development of Reformed Orthodoxy, ca. 1520 to ca. 1725.* Vol. 4, *The Triunity of God.* Grand Rapids, MI: Baker Academic, 2003.

———. "Toward the Pactum Salutis: Locating the Origins of a Concept." *Mid-America Journal of Theology* 18 (2007): 11–65.

Parker, T. H. L. *The Doctrine of the Knowledge of God: A Study in the Theology of John Calvin.* Edinburgh: Oliver and Boyd, 1952.

Schwöbel, Christoph. "The Triune God of Grace: The Doctrine of the Trinity in the Theology of the Reformers." In *The Christian Understanding of God Today: Theological Colloquium on the Occasion of the 400th Anniversary of the Foundation of Trinity College, Dublin,* edited by J. M. Byrne, 49–64. Dublin: Columba, 1993.

Torrance, T. F. "Calvin's Doctrine of the Trinity." Chap. 3 in *Trinitarian Perspectives: Toward Doctrinal Agreement.* Edinburgh: T&T Clark, 1994.

———. "The Doctrine of the Holy Trinity in Gregory Nazianzen and John Calvin." Chap. 2 in *Trinitarian Perspectives: Toward Doctrinal Agreement.* Edinburgh: T&T Clark, 1994.

Warfield, B. B. "Calvin's Doctrine of the Trinity." In *Calvin and Augustine,* edited by Samuel G. Craig, 187–284. Philadelphia: Presbyterian and Reformed, 1974.

Westhead, Nigel. "Adoption in the Thought of John Calvin." *Scottish Bulletin of Evangelical Theology* 13, no. 2 (1995): 102–15.

6

The Being and Attributes of God

Scott R. Swain

ABSTRACT

The doctrine of God's being and attributes was not a disputed article at the time of the Reformation. It was not for that reason a neglected topic. Early Protestant theologians devoted significant attention to the doctrine of God's being and attributes in their polemical engagement with Rome regarding salvation and grace and the church and its worship. The doctrine also received significant attention in the various genres of constructive Protestant theology, such as biblical commentaries, *loci communes*, sermons, and catechisms, which were designed to meet the pedagogical and pastoral needs of the burgeoning reform movement in the academy and the church. In terms of doctrinal development, the Reformation provided a new context for elaborating the Christian doctrine of God that, relative to its late-medieval context, brought traditional teaching about God into more direct contact with its scriptural source and drew from that teaching more immediate application to pastoral ends, even as it offered numerous occasions for appropriating the sources and distinctions of patristic and medieval theology.

Introduction

Early Protestant rhetoric might suggest that the Reformation was a time of revolutionary significance for the doctrine of God. Martin Luther contrasted the "Aristotelian or philosophical god" of "the Jews, the Turks, and the papists" with "our God . . . whom the Holy Scriptures show."[1] Luther also spoke of "God's dying, God's martyrdom, God's blood, and God's death,"[2] and such language has led many interpreters to conclude that his theology undermines, in effect if not by intention, the traditional doctrine of divine impassibility.[3] In similar fashion, Philipp Melanchthon criticized traditional authorities on the doctrine of God, concluding that "John of Damascus philosophizes too much" and that Peter Lombard "prefers to pile up the opinions of men rather than to set forth the meaning of Scripture."[4] And John Calvin regarded the scholastic distinction between God's "absolute power" (*potentia absoluta*) and "ordained power" (*potentia ordinata*) as a "shocking blasphemy" because it implied "that God is a tyrant who resolves to do what he pleases, not by justice, but through caprice."[5] Examples of such rhetoric could be multiplied.

Rhetoric, however, can be misleading. The doctrine of God was not a point of direct conflict between Protestants and Rome during the "tempestuous epoch"[6] of the Reformation. When it came to "the lofty articles of divine majesty" (i.e., the doctrine of the triune God and the doctrine of the person of Jesus Christ), Luther insisted, "These articles are not matters of dispute or conflict, for both sides confess

---

1. Martin Luther, *Lectures on Genesis Chapters 21–25*, LW 4:145.
2. Martin Luther, *On the Councils and the Church* (1539), LW 41:104.
3. For one particularly sophisticated argument in this regard, see Eberhard Jüngel, *God as the Mystery of the World: On the Foundation of the Theology of the Crucified One in the Dispute between Theism and Atheism*, trans. Darrell L. Guder (Edinburgh: T&T Clark, 1983), 55–104.
4. Philipp Melanchthon, *Loci Communes* (1521), in *Melanchthon and Bucer*, ed. Wilhelm Pauck, LCC 19 (Philadelphia: Westminster, 1969), 20.
5. John Calvin, *Commentary on the Book of the Prophet Isaiah*, trans. William Pringle (repr., Grand Rapids, MI: Baker, 1998), 2:152. God's "absolute power" (*potentia absoluta*) refers to "the omnipotence of God limited only by the law of noncontradiction," whereas God's "ordained power" (*potentia ordinata*) refers to "the power by which God creates and sustains the world according to his *pactum* . . . with himself and creation. In other words, a limited and bounded power that guarantees the stability and consistency of the orders of nature and grace." Richard A. Muller, *Dictionary of Latin and Greek Theological Terms: Drawn Principally from Protestant Scholastic Theology* (Grand Rapids, MI: Baker, 1985), 231–32.
6. Huldrych Zwingli, *An Exposition of the Faith*, in *Zwingli and Bullinger: Selected Translations with Introductions and Notes*, ed. G. W. Bromiley, LCC 24 (Philadelphia: Westminster, 1953), 245.

them."[7] A survey of early Protestant confessions reveals a similar perspective. Early Protestant churches affirmed the main contours of Nicene Christianity when it came to the doctrine of God, confessing the eternal subsistence of three distinct persons in one simple, eternal, immutable, all-powerful, all-wise, and all-merciful God, the Creator and preserver of all things, the Redeemer of his church, and the highest good of the creature. The Augsburg Confession (1530) thus declares,

> The churches among us teach with complete unanimity that the decree of the Council of Nicea concerning the unity of the divine essence and concerning the three persons is true and is to be believed without any doubt. That is to say, there is one divine essence which is called God and is God: eternal, incorporeal, indivisible, of immeasurable power, wisdom, and goodness, the creator and preserver of all things, visible and invisible. Yet, there are three persons, coeternal and of the same essence and power: the Father, the Son, and the Holy Spirit.[8]

Similar statements appear in Reformed confessions of the sixteenth century. The First Helvetic Confession (1536) holds that "there is one only, true, living and almighty God, one in essence, threefold according to the persons, who has created all things out of nothing by his Word, that is, by his Son, and by his providence justly, truly and wisely rules, governs and preserves all things."[9] The French Confession of Faith (1559) asserts that "there is but one God, who is one sole and simple essence, spiritual, eternal, invisible, immutable, infinite, incomprehensible, ineffable, omnipotent; who is all-wise, all-good, all-just, and all-merciful," and "that in this one sole and simple divine essence . . . there are three persons: the Father, the Son, and the Holy Spirit."[10] Likewise, the Scots Confession (1560) acknowledges

> one God alone, to whom alone we must cleave, whom alone we must serve, whom only we must worship, and in whom alone

---

7. Martin Luther, "Smalcald Articles," pt. 1, in Robert Kolb and Timothy J. Wengert, eds., *The Book of Concord: The Confessions of the Evangelical Lutheran Church* (Minneapolis: Fortress, 2000), 300.
8. "The Augsburg Confession" (Latin text), art. 1, in Kolb and Wengert, *Book of Concord*, 37.
9. "The First Helvetic Confession of Faith of 1536," art. 6, in Arthur C. Cochrane, ed., *Reformed Confessions of the Sixteenth Century* (Louisville: Westminster John Knox, 2003), 101.
10. "The French Confession of Faith," art. 1, 6, in Cochrane, *Reformed Confessions*, 144, 146.

we put our trust. Who is eternal, infinite, immeasurable, incomprehensible, omnipotent, invisible; one in substance and yet distinct in persons, the Father, the Son, and the Holy Ghost. By whom we confess and believe all things in heaven and earth, visible and invisible, to have been created, to be retained in their being, and to be ruled and guided by his inscrutable providence for such end as his eternal wisdom, goodness, and justice have appointed, and to the manifestation of his own glory.[11]

Though Faustus Socinus initiated a theological trajectory that would result in a thoroughgoing revision of the doctrine of God in the seventeenth century,[12] a revisionist tendency in the doctrine was not universal even among the radical Reformers. Balthasar Hubmaier, for example, expressed a fairly traditional sensibility when it came to the divine attributes. In answer to the question, what is God? Hubmaier's catechism responded, "He is the highest good, almighty, all-wise, and all-merciful," who manifests his omnipotence in creation, his all-encompassing wisdom in providence, and his all-encompassing mercifulness "by his sending his only-begotten Son."[13] Furthermore, the revisionist rhetoric of the magisterial Reformers cited above is, on closer analysis, easy to harmonize with the more traditional language of the Protestant confessions. Recent Luther scholarship demonstrates that the Wittenberg Reformer's language regarding the suffering of God is unexceptional when viewed within the broader context of traditional Christological discourse and that Luther self-consciously employed classical Trinitarian and Christological metaphysical concepts designed to preserve rather than to undermine divine impassibility in his talk about the suffering of God.[14] Moreover, Calvin's scorn for the distinction between God's absolute and ordained power is probably best understood not as an absolute rejection of the distinction per se, the substance of which he employed throughout his writings, but as a

11. "The Scots Confession," chap. 1, in Cochrane, *Reformed Confessions*, 166.
12. George Huntston Williams, *The Radical Reformation*, 3rd ed., Sixteenth Century Essays and Studies 15 (Kirksville, MO: Truman State University Press, 2000), 979–90; Richard A. Muller, *Post-Reformation Reformed Dogmatics: The Rise and Development of Reformed Orthodoxy, ca. 1520 to ca. 1725*, vol. 3, *The Divine Essence and Attributes* (Grand Rapids, MI: Baker Academic, 2003), 91–92.
13. Balthasar Hubmaier, *A Christian Catechism*, in CCFCT 2:676.
14. David J. Luy, *Dominus Mortis: Martin Luther and the Incorruptibility of God in Christ* (Minneapolis: Fortress, 2014).

rejection of certain perceived abuses of the distinction in late-medieval theology.[15]

While the doctrine of God was considered an undisputed article in the Reformation era, that did not relegate it to the sideline of Protestant theological reflection. Early Protestant theologians devoted significant attention to God's being and attributes, convinced that a proper understanding of "what God is, how he is known, where and how he has revealed himself, and both if and why he hears our pleas and cries" was absolutely essential to Christian life and worship.[16] The doctrine played a crucial role in Protestant polemics on topics such as salvation and grace, as well as the church and its worship. The doctrine also received significant attention in the various genres of constructive Protestant theology, such as biblical commentaries, *loci communes*, sermons, and catechisms, which were designed to meet the pedagogical and pastoral needs of the burgeoning reform movement in the academy and the church. Indeed, Herman Selderhuis suggests that John Calvin's commentaries on the Psalms display an "utterly *theocentric*" perspective.[17]

In terms of doctrinal development, therefore, the Reformation did not witness substantive revision to the doctrine of God confessed by the church catholic in previous centuries. The Reformation did provide a new context for elaborating the Christian doctrine of God that, relative to its late-medieval context, brought traditional teaching about God into more direct contact with its scriptural source and drew from that teaching more immediate application to pastoral ends, even as it offered numerous occasions for appropriating the sources and distinctions of patristic and medieval theology. In what follows we will trace several of the major features of early Protestant teaching about God's being and attributes, leaving the other major topic in Protestant

---

15. Richard A. Muller, *The Unaccommodated Calvin: Studies in the Foundation of a Theological Tradition*, Oxford Studies in Historical Theology (New York: Oxford University Press, 2000), 41–42, 47, 51–52; Paul Helm, *John Calvin's Ideas* (Oxford: Oxford University Press, 2004), chap. 11.

16. Philipp Melanchthon, *Loci Communes* (1555), in *Melanchthon on Christian Doctrine: Loci Communes 1555*, trans. and ed. Clyde L. Manschreck (Grand Rapids, MI: Baker, 1982), 3.

17. Herman J. Selderhuis, *Calvin's Theology of the Psalms*, Texts and Studies in Reformation and Post-Reformation Thought (Grand Rapids, MI: Baker Academic, 2007), 285, italics original. As we will see more fully below, Calvin's biblical commentaries provide more ample discussion of the divine attributes than what may be found in his *Institutes of the Christian Religion*.

teaching about God—the distinction between the three persons—to be discussed in chapter 5 of this volume.[18]

The Knowledge of God's Being and Attributes

GOD INCOMPREHENSIBLE, ACCOMMODATED, AND BEHELD

The doctrine of God's utter incomprehensibility frames the entryway to early Protestant theological treatments of God's being and attributes. In his commentary on Genesis 6:5–6, wherein he discusses the nature of divine revelation at length, Luther states, "God in his essence is altogether unknowable; nor is it possible to define or put into words what he is, though we burst at the effort."[19] Melanchthon likewise affirmed that the knowledge of God is "so high that one cannot express it in words."[20] Divine incomprehensibility is not a reason to ignore the study of God, Wolfgang Musculus nevertheless insisted, because "there is nothing which with greater danger we may be ignorant of." Instead, God's utter incomprehensibility requires that students of theology approach the doctrine of God with fear and circumspection.[21] Heinrich Bullinger asserted, "Therefore the saints, if in any other matters belonging to God, then in this especially, are humble, modest, and religious; understanding that his eternal and incomprehensible power and unspeakable majesty are altogether incircumscriptible, and cannot be comprehended by any name whatsoever."[22]

God is incomprehensible according to universal Protestant confession. The knowledge of God is possible, however, because God stoops down to reveal himself to creatures in terms that they are capable of understanding, though not in terms that are capable of exhausting the truth of God's unfathomable being. God is "altogether unknowable," but, Luther reminds us, "God lowers himself to the level of our weak

---

18. Elsewhere I have discussed the doctrine of the Trinity in the era of the Reformation. See Scott R. Swain, "The Trinity in the Reformers," in *The Oxford Handbook of the Trinity*, ed. Gilles Emery and Matthew Levering (Oxford: Oxford University Press, 2011), 227–39.

19. Martin Luther, *Lectures on Genesis Chapters 6–14*, LW 2:45.

20. Melanchthon, *Loci Communes* (1555), 86. For a similar approach, see Peter Martyr Vermigli, *Commentary on Aristotle's Nicomachean Ethics*, ed. Emidio Campi and Joseph C. McLelland, Sixteenth Century Essays and Studies (Kirksville, MO: Truman State University Press, 2006), 136.

21. Wolfgang Musculus, *Common Places of Christian Religion* (London: R. Wolfe, 1563), 1 (p. 1, col. 2–p. 2, col. 1).

22. Heinrich Bullinger, *The Decades of Heinrich Bullinger*, ed. Thomas Harding (1849–1852; repr., Grand Rapids, MI: Reformation Heritage Books, 2004), 2:126.

comprehension and presents himself to us in images, in coverings, as it were, in simplicity adapted to a child, that in some measure it may be possible for him to be known by us."[23] According to Bullinger,

> No tongue either of angels or of men can fully express what, who, and what manner God is, seeing that his majesty is incomprehensible and unspeakable; yet the scripture, which is the word of God, attempering itself to our imbecility, doth minister unto us some means, forms, and phrases of speech, by them to bring to us some such knowledge of God as may at leastwise suffice us while we live in this world.[24]

The accommodated nature of revelation played an important role in Luther's doctrine of God. Luther distinguished God in the accommodated form of his self-revelation (God "clothed in his Word") from God outside this accommodated form (God "naked in his majesty"):

> God in his own nature and majesty is to be left alone; in this regard, we have nothing to do with him, nor does he wish us to deal with him. We have to do with him as clothed and displayed in his Word, by which he presents himself to us. That is his glory and beauty, in which the Psalmist proclaims him to be clothed (cf. Ps. 21.5).[25]

Although his rhetoric is susceptible to misinterpretation, the point of Luther's distinction was not to suggest the existence of two different gods: "the God of the philosophers," characterized by transcendent majesty, and "the God of Jesus Christ," characterized by lowliness and humility. According to Luther, the majesty of God's eternal, immortal, and omnipotent nature is a source of great comfort to sinners insofar as God pledges to be their God in the gospel.[26] The point of Luther's

---

23. Luther, *Lectures on Genesis Chapters 6–14*, LW 2:45.

24. Bullinger, *Decades*, 2:129–30. Cf. Peter Martyr Vermigli, *The Common Places of Peter Martyr Vermilius*, trans. Anthonie Marten (London: Henry Denham and Henry Middleton, 1583), 1.12.1.

25. Martin Luther, *The Bondage of the Will*, trans. J. I. Packer and O. R. Johnston (Old Tappan, NJ: Fleming H. Revell, 1957), 4.10; cf. Luther, *Lectures on Genesis Chapters 6–14*, LW 2:45. For further discussion, see Roland F. Ziegler, "Luther and Calvin on God: Origins of Lutheran and Reformed Differences," *CTQ* 75, no. 1 (2011): 64–76; and Steven Paulson, "Luther's Doctrine of God," in *The Oxford Handbook of Martin Luther's Theology*, ed. Robert Kolb, Irene Dingel, and Ľubomír Batka (Oxford: Oxford University Press, 2014), 194–98.

26. Martin Luther, *Selected Psalms II*, LW 13:91–93. Forde helpfully summarizes the matter: "In Luther's theology the attributes of divinity such as divine necessity, immutability, timelessness, impassibility, and so forth, function as masks of God's hiddenness. That means that they func-

distinction was to identify two different *modes* in which God may be known and to direct us away from one mode of knowledge to the other.[27] To elaborate on this point, Luther appropriated the scholastic distinction between God's "will of good pleasure" (*voluntas bene-placiti*) and his "will of the sign" (*voluntas signi*):[28]

> An investigation of this essential and divine will, or of the Divine Majesty, must not be pursued but altogether avoided. This will is unsearchable, and God did not want to give us an insight into it in this life. He merely wanted to indicate it by means of some coverings: Baptism, the Word, the Sacrament of the Altar. These are the divine images and "the will of the sign." Through them God deals with us within the range of our comprehension. Therefore these alone must engage our attention. "The will of his good pleasure" must be completely discarded from consideration unless you are a Moses, a David, or some similar perfect man, although these men, too, viewed "the will of his good pleasure" without ever diverting their eyes from "the will of the sign."[29]

In Luther's theology, the distinction between God "clothed" and "naked" ultimately served the pastoral end of promoting evangelical consolation: "In these images we see and meet a God whom we can bear, one who comforts us, lifts us up into hope, and saves us. The other ideas about 'the will of his good pleasure,' or the essential and eternal will, slay and condemn."[30] Luther's antispeculative, pastoral motive echoed across the spectrum of early Protestant thought.[31]

---

tion on the one hand as wrath, as attack on human pretense, and on the other hand ultimately as comfort, as backup for the proclamation." Gerhard O. Forde, "Robert Jenson's Soteriology," in *Trinity, Time, and Church: A Response to the Theology of Robert W. Jenson*, ed. Colin E. Gunton (Grand Rapids, MI: Eerdmans, 2000), 137.

27. Compare this notion with Luther's distinction between being a "theologian of glory" and being a "theologian of the cross" in his "Heidelberg Disputation."

28. God's "will of good pleasure" (*voluntas beneplaciti*) refers to God's hidden and eternal decree regarding all things that will occur in his external works. God's "will of the sign" (*voluntas signi*) refers to that aspect of God's eternal will that he is pleased to reveal to creatures. The distinction between the will of good pleasure and the will of the sign is developed differently in Lutheran and Reformed theological traditions. See Muller, *Dictionary of Latin and Greek Theological Terms*, 331–33.

29. Luther, *Lectures on Genesis Chapters 6–14*, LW 2:47. See also Luther, *Lectures on Genesis Chapters 21–25*, LW 4:143–45.

30. Luther, *Lectures on Genesis Chapters 6–14*, LW 2:48.

31. Melanchthon, *Loci Communes* (1521), 21–22; Bullinger, *Decades*, 2:130; Peter Martyr Vermigli, *Philosophical Works: On the Relation of Philosophy to Theology*, trans. and ed. Joseph C. McLelland, Sixteenth Century Essays and Studies 39 (Kirksville, MO: Thomas Jefferson University Press, 1996), 151.

Given that God accommodates the knowledge of his unfathomable being to us in the humble form of revelation, early Protestant theologians regularly warned against the folly of the Anthropomorphites, who "sin against the nature of God by clothing it with a body."[32] Calvin acknowledged that "Scripture often ascribes to him a mouth, ears, eyes, hands, and feet."[33] "Such forms of speaking," he nevertheless insisted, "do not so much express clearly what God is like as accommodate the knowledge of him to our slight capacity."[34] Reformation theologians not only blocked the deduction from biblical anthropomorphism that God has human *body parts*, they also blocked the deduction from biblical anthropopathism that God has human *emotions*. Again commenting on Genesis 6:6, Luther stated, "One should not imagine that God has a heart or that he can grieve." God's grief in Genesis 6 refers to the effect of God's wrath on the spirits of the patriarchs, "who perceived in their hearts that God hated the world because of its sins and intended to destroy it"—it does not refer to "the divine essence."[35] The accommodated nature of revelation thus holds both promise and peril for creaturely wayfarers when it comes to the doctrine of God: promise, insofar as it enables God to be known; peril, insofar as we may be tempted to confuse the Creator with the creature.

The accommodated nature of revelation was not the Reformers' last word regarding the knowledge of God's incomprehensible being and attributes. Early Protestant theologians affirmed traditional catholic teaching that the accommodated, mediated form of our knowledge of God will one day give way to an unmediated knowledge of God in the beatific vision. Thus Luther affirmed, "On the Last Day those who have died in this faith will be so enlightened by heavenly power that they will see even the Divine Majesty itself."[36] According to Peter Martyr Vermigli, we will grasp God's incomprehensible es-

---

32. Vermigli, *Philosophical Works*, 140.
33. John Calvin, *Institutes*, 1.13.1.
34. Ibid. For further discussion of Calvin's views of divine accommodation, see Helm, *John Calvin's Ideas*, chap. 7; and Jon Balserak, *Divinity Compromised: A Study of Divine Accommodation in the Thought of John Calvin*, Studies in Early Modern Religious Reforms 5 (Dordrecht: Springer, 2006). Cf. Vermigli, *Philosophical Works*, 148.
35. Luther, *Lectures on Genesis Chapters 6–14*, LW 2:49.
36. Ibid., LW 2:49. See also Bullinger, *Decades*, 2:130, 142–43.

sence not through our senses but rather through spiritual perception, and even then, our finite minds will not fully fathom God's infinite perfection.[37] Until the day we behold God's face in unmediated bliss, Luther encourages us to lay hold of God's self-revelation in Jesus Christ: "We must come to the Father by that way which is Christ himself; he will lead us safely, and we shall not be deceived."[38] Bullinger similarly counsels, "Let the knowledge of Christ suffice and content us."[39]

SOURCES OF THE KNOWLEDGE OF GOD

Reformation theologians traced the knowledge of God's incomprehensible majesty to various sources. In a sermon titled, "Of God; Of the True Knowledge of God, and Of the Diverse Ways How to Know Him; That God is One in Substance, and Three in Persons," Heinrich Bullinger devoted extensive space to discussing the various means by which God reveals himself to creatures.[40] According to Bullinger, "The first and chiefest way to know God is derived out of the very names of God attributed to him in the holy scripture"—a methodological principle observed across the board in early Protestant theology and to which we will return below.[41] God also makes himself known "by visions and divine mirrors, as it were in a certain parable, while by *Prosopography, Prosopoeia*, or mortal shapes he is set before our eyes."[42] But "the most evident and excellent way and mean to know God," Bullinger insisted, "is laid forth before us in Jesus Christ, the Son of God incarnate and made man." The Swiss Reformer drew support for this claim from John 14:9 ("Whoever has seen me has seen the Father"), a common proof text for this early Protestant methodological principle.[43] In discussing the varied means by which God reveals himself to us, Bullinger also affirmed that God makes himself known "out of the contemplation of his works" and "by the sayings or sentences uttered

---

37. Vermigli, *Philosophical Works*, 140, 148.
38. Luther, *Lectures on Genesis Chapters 6–14*, LW 2:49.
39. Bullinger, *Decades*, 2:147.
40. For similar discussions, see Melanchthon, *Loci Communes* (1555), 5–7; Musculus, *Common Places*, 1.1 (p. 2, col. 2–p. 3, col. 2); Vermigli, *Philosophical Works*, 18–29, 138–54.
41. Bullinger, *Decades*, 2:130.
42. Ibid., 2:138.
43. Ibid., 2:147. See also Luther, *Lectures on Genesis Chapters 6–14*, LW 2:49; Melanchthon, *Loci Communes* (1555), 3–4; Vermigli, *Philosophical Works*, 151.

by the mouths of the prophets and apostles," the latter providing the source of "the true knowledge of God" as "one in essence, and three in persons."[44]

The knowledge of God revealed through the divine names and supremely through Jesus Christ in Holy Scripture far outstrips that which is revealed through God's works, both in content and efficacy.[45] Early Protestant theologians nevertheless accorded a significant role to general revelation in producing a true but limited knowledge of God, even among non-Christian philosophers.[46] Commenting on Romans 1:19, Vermigli argued that God had implanted common notions (*prolepseis*) in the human mind "through which we are led to conceive noble and exalted opinions about the divine nature."[47] The presence of these common notions explains how philosophers arrived at a knowledge of God's being and attributes by observing "the wonderful properties and qualities of nature" and by considering "the series of causes in their relation to effects."[48] Indeed, Vermigli argued that when people reflect on "the noblest qualities" of the human soul, such as justice, wisdom, truth, and righteousness, and duly consider how human beings depend on God, they would conclude that these perfections reside in God, who is their "chief and principal author."[49] Though Vermigli was aware of Cicero's attempt to refute this kind of argument, he believed that Psalm 94:9 ("He who planted the ear, does he not hear? He who formed the eye, does he not see?") established it beyond any doubt: "We learn from this not to withhold from the divine nature whatever is perfect and absolute in us."[50]

---

44. Bullinger, *Decades*, 2:150, 153–54.
45. Vermigli, *Philosophical Works*, 27, 150–51.
46. Luther, *Lectures on Genesis Chapters 21–25*, LW 4:145; Luther, *Lectures on Romans: Glosses and Scholia*, LW 25:154, 156–57; Luther, *Bondage*, 2.4; Melanchthon, *Loci Communes* (1555), 5–6, 39–41, 86; Musculus, *Common Places*, 1.1 (p. 2, cols. 1–2).
47. Vermigli, *Philosophical Works*, 20. For similar treatments, see Melanchthon, *Loci Communes* (1555), 5–6; Calvin, *Institutes*, 1.3.1.
48. Vermigli, *Philosophical Works*, 21.
49. Ibid., 22. Compare with Thomas Aquinas, *Summa Theologiae* 1a.13.2.
50. Vermigli, *Philosophical Works*, 22. Karl Barth criticized early Protestant theology for appealing to general revelation and philosophical proofs in the doctrine of God, suggesting that this appeal ultimately "paved the way for the Enlightenment with all that that involved." Barth, *Church Dogmatics*, trans. G. W. Bromiley, ed. G. W. Bromiley and T. F. Torrance, vol. 2, pt. 1 (Edinburgh: T&T Clark, 1957), 266 (see his entire discussion from 259–72). What Barth's criticism failed to grasp, however, was that the Reformers both derived and confirmed their arguments regarding general revelation through biblical exegesis, as Vermigli's appeal to Rom. 1:19 and Ps. 94:9 illustrates.

Let God Be God: The Creator-Creature
Distinction and Divine Simplicity

The distinction between true and false gods, and thus between Creator and creature, was of fundamental importance in early Protestant teaching about God.[51] "This is the first doctrine in the first command concerning right knowledge of God," Melanchthon insisted.[52] Protestant theologians judged Rome's failure to observe this distinction to be a root cause of many of its errors. According to Luther, because the medieval scheme of salvation taught that human works were capable of meriting divine grace, it robbed God "of the glory of his deity" by refusing to acknowledge his sole sufficiency as the One "who dispenses his gifts freely to all."[53] In similar fashion, Zwingli argued that Rome's teaching regarding the veneration of the saints and the efficacy of the sacraments wrongly ascribed "to the creature that which belongs solely to the Creator."[54]

The Creator-creature distinction also informed constructive exposition of the divine attributes, preeminently in the form of the doctrine of divine simplicity. Following the basic shape of Nicene orthodoxy, Martin Bucer's "Tetrapolitan Confession" affirmed that the Godhead "admits no distinction other than of persons."[55] Calvin similarly stated, "When we profess to believe in one God, under the name God is understood a single, simple essence."[56] Melanchthon more fully spelled out the significance of divine simplicity for our understanding of the divine attributes: "In God, power, wisdom, righteousness, and other virtues are not contingent things, but are one with the Being; divine Being is divine power, wisdom, and righteousness, and these virtues are not separated from the Being."[57]

51. The title of this section comes from Philip S. Watson, *Let God Be God! An Interpretation of the Theology of Martin Luther* (Eugene, OR: Wipf & Stock, 2000).

52. Melanchthon, *Loci Communes* (1555), 86; see also 7.

53. Martin Luther, *Lectures on Galatians* (1535), LW 26:127. Charles Arand discusses the significance of the Creator-creature distinction in Luther's commentaries on the Apostles' Creed in his Small and Large Catechisms. See Charles P. Arand, "Luther on the Creed," *LQ* 20 (2006): 1–25.

54. Zwingli, *Exposition of the Faith*, 249. For the role of the Creator-creature distinction in Zwingli's theology, see W. P. Stephens, *Zwingli: An Introduction to His Thought* (Oxford: Clarendon, 1992). Note the similar concern in Melanchthon, *Loci Communes* (1555), e.g., 7, 86.

55. "Tetrapolitan Confession," chap. 2, in Cochrane, *Reformed Confessions*, 56.

56. Calvin, *Institutes*, 1.13.20.

57. Melanchthon, *Loci Communes* (1555), 8.

Vermigli put the doctrine of divine simplicity to serious philosophical and theological use throughout his *Commentary on Aristotle's Nicomachean Ethics* and, in doing so, drew on a wide range of classical, patristic, and medieval philosophical and theological sources. In discussing the divine ideas, the eternal patterns according to which the divine craftsman creates and sustains all that exists, the Italian Reformer engaged Plato, Aristotle, Augustine, Boethius, and Averroës, among others.[58] While Vermigli argued that the divine ideas accounted for the diversity of creatures that inhabit God's world, he also insisted, following Augustine and others, that they must be "one and uniform" in God due to his absolute simplicity. He concluded,

> Thus Idea may be understood by us in three ways: First, as something that is contained in the divine essence and so is one and uniform. Second as a practical object of the divine mind, in which case it would also be one and uniform, since God's contemplation of himself is a unique and single action that reveals to him everything at once. Third, it may be understood as a Form and pattern, but in this case we must assume the existence of many various ideas since they would present many distinct patterns of numerous creatures of different species.[59]

Later in the same work, in discussing the question of whether Aristotle's ten metaphysical categories applied to God's being, Vermigli's commitment to the doctrine of divine simplicity led him to adopt the position of Dionysius and "certain wise (and quite numerous) scholastic theologians [who] were reluctant to enclose God in Aristotelian categories."[60] According to Vermigli, "God is above all these categories as being their efficient cause."[61] He is therefore "both everything and nothing" in relation to the categories: "He is every-

---

58. See Vermigli, *Commentary*, 137–44, 172.

59. Ibid., 143. Compare with Francis Turretin, *Institutes of Elenctic Theology*, ed. James T. Dennison Jr., trans. George Musgrave Giger (Phillipsburg, NJ: P&R, 1992–1997), 4.1.8–12.

60. Vermigli, *Commentary*, 156. Aristotle's ten categories of being (i.e., substance, quality, quantity, relation, position, habit, place, time, action, and passion) received widespread attention in classical Trinitarian thought, with theologians taking various positions on the degree and manner in which they might be appropriated in theological discourse. See, for example, Augustine, *The Trinity* 5.2; Boethius, *De Trinitate* 4.1–9; Peter Lombard, *Sentences* 1.8.6–8. For an overview of the medieval discussion, see Marilyn McCord Adams, "The Metaphysics of the Trinity in Some Fourteenth Century Franciscans," *Franciscan Studies* 66, no. 1 (2008): 101–68.

61. Vermigli, *Commentary*, 158.

thing, since whatever exists participates in him; at the same time he is nothing, though not in the sense of defect, as if he lacks substance or, if I may put it, essence, but rather because he is beyond anything that exists."[62]

Zwingli's *Exposition of the Faith* provides another clear example of how the Creator-creature distinction and its accompanying doctrine of divine simplicity functioned in early Protestant thinking about God.[63] The article "Of God and the Worship of God" addresses the importance of distinguishing the Creator from his creatures in order that we might trust the former and use the latter for God's glory.[64] "To sum up," he said, "the source of our religion is to confess that God is the uncreated Creator of all things, and that he alone has power over all things and freely bestows all things."[65] According to Zwingli, the Creator's unique and transcendent nature determines the way we must think about divine goodness. God's goodness, he explained, is simple: "We know that this God is good by nature, for whatever he is he is by nature."[66] Furthermore, because it is simple, God's goodness is "both loving, kind and gracious, and also holy, just and impassible."[67] Zwingli introduced divine impassibility at this point to set up the final section in his discussion of divine goodness, where he treated the supreme expression of God's goodness in giving his Son "not merely to reveal to, but actually to bestow upon,

62. Ibid., 157. Vermigli's discussion offers further evidence against the charge, recently stated with great force by Brad Gregory, that the Reformation inaugurates a fall from classical "metaphysics of participation." Brad S. Gregory, *The Unintended Reformation: How a Religious Revolution Secularized Society* (Cambridge, MA: Harvard University Press, 2012). For further evidence against Gregory's thesis, see Richard A. Muller, "Not Scotist: Understandings of Being, Univocity, and Analogy in Early-Modern Reformed Thought," *RRR* 14, no. 2 (2012): 127–50; Scott R. Swain, "Lutheran and Reformed Sacramental Theology, Seventeenth–Nineteenth Centuries," in *The Oxford Handbook of Sacramental Theology*, ed. Hans Boersma and Matthew Levering (Oxford: Oxford University Press, 2015), 362–79.
63. This paragraph is adapted from Scott Swain, "Zwingli, Divine Impassibility, and the Gospel," *reformation21* (blog), The Alliance of Confessing Evangelicals, January 23, 2015, http://www.reformation21.org/blog/2015/01/zwingli-divine-impassibility-a.php. Used by permission of the Alliance of Confessing Evangelicals and the author.
64. In distinguishing God, who is to be "trusted" and "enjoyed," from creatures, who are to be "used" in the enjoyment of God, Zwingli drew on an Augustinian distinction, set forth in *On Christian Teaching*, that came to dominate the shape of medieval theology through its structural influence on Peter Lombard's *Sentences*. Zwingli put the distinction to polemical use in arguing that Roman Catholic theologians "unwittingly disregard" the distinction by commending the trust and enjoyment of sacraments, which are creatures, rather than of God. *Exposition of the Faith*, 247–49.
65. Zwingli, *Exposition of the Faith*, 249.
66. Ibid. For similar statements regarding the nonadventitious nature of divine goodness, see Vermigli, *Commentary*, 137; Musculus, *Common Places*, 1 (p. 8, col. 2–p. 9, col. 1).
67. Zwingli, *Exposition of the Faith*, 249.

the whole earth both salvation and renewal."[68] Zwingli argued that we cannot fully appreciate God's motivation for the incarnation and atoning work of his Son apart from a proper understanding of God's simple and impassible goodness. He stated,

> For inasmuch as his goodness, that is, his justice and mercy, is impassible, that is, steadfast and immutable, his justice required atonement, but his mercy forgiveness, and forgiveness newness of life. Clothed therefore with flesh, for according to his divine nature he cannot die, the Son of the Most High King offered up himself as a sacrifice to placate irrevocable justice and to reconcile it with those who because of their consciousness of sin dared not enter the presence of God on the ground of their own righteousness. He did this because he is kind and merciful, and these virtues can as little permit the rejection of his work as his justice can allow escape from punishment. Justice and mercy were conjoined, the one furnishing the sacrifice, the other accepting it as a sacrifice for sin.[69]

For Zwingli, God's simple and impassible goodness enables us to appreciate the deep divine foundation and motive for the Son of God's death on the cross and for our redemption thereby. It also provides an occasion for marveling in gratitude:

> Who can sufficiently estimate the magnanimity of the divine goodness and mercy? We had merited rejection, and he adopts us as heirs. We had destroyed the way of life, and he has restored it. The divine goodness has so redeemed and restored us that we are full of thanks for his mercy and just and blameless by reason of his atoning sacrifice.[70]

The Divine Names

The divine names revealed in Holy Scripture served as one of the most important sources for the early Protestant doctrine of God.[71] Because God's simple and incomprehensible being is not susceptible to summation in one name or definition, God accommodates himself to us

---

68. Ibid., 250.
69. Ibid.
70. Ibid., 250–51.
71. Bullinger, *Decades*, 2:130. Muller, *Post-Reformation Reformed Dogmatics*, 3:246–54.

through manifold names.[72] Consistent with their understanding of the accommodated nature of revelation, the Reformers acknowledged the radical disproportion between the way Scripture uses terms such as *goodness, power, wisdom,* and *glory* with reference to God and the way we ordinarily use these terms with reference to creatures. Musculus thus encourages us to "forbeare all comparisons, and acknowledge that his goodness, wisedome, greatnes, majestie, power and glorie, is incomparable, passing great, and his continuance infinite."[73] The radical disproportion between God and creatures, however, did not limit the divine names from being a significant resource for constructive theology. Quite to the contrary, the divine names were often treated as sources from which the full range of divine attributes, along with deep Christian consolation, could be drawn. Bullinger said of the name El Shaddai revealed in Genesis 17:1, "Whatever things have been said in the Holy Scripture about the unity, power, majesty, goodness, and glory of God are included in this one expression of the covenant: 'I am the all-sufficient Lord.'"[74] As we will see more fully below, Calvin derived from the revealed name of God in Exodus 3:14 the attributes of divine glory, self-existence, eternity, incomprehensibility, being, and omnipotence.[75] And Luther saw in the "single little word 'shepherd'" from Psalm 23 "almost all the good and comforting things that we praise in God."[76]

The Reformers' exposition of the divine names exhibits linguistic sophistication and broad familiarity with the history of biblical interpretation, both Christian and Jewish. Commenting on Genesis 17:1 and the name El Shaddai, Luther said that El "indicates the might and power of God," demonstrating that God "alone is powerful, is all-sufficient of himself, has power over everything, needs no one's help, and is able to give all things to all." As for Shaddai, Luther displayed awareness of the medieval Jewish interpretation that viewed the name

72. Vermigli, *Common Places*, 1.13.1. See also Vermigli, *Commentary*, 156–57; Bullinger, *Decades*, 2:126–28, citing Tertullian; Musculus, *Common Places*, 1.3.2 (p. 4, col. 2).
73. Musculus, *Common Places*, 1 (p. 9, col. 1). See also Muller, "Not Scotist," 131.
74. Heinrich Bullinger, *A Brief Exposition of the One and Eternal Testament or Covenant of God*, in Charles S. McCoy and J. Wayne Baker, *Fountainhead of Federalism: Heinrich Bullinger and the Covenantal Tradition* (Louisville: Westminster John Knox, 1991), 112.
75. John Calvin, *Commentaries on the Last Four Books of Moses: Arranged in the Form of a Harmony*, trans. Charles William Bingham (repr., Grand Rapids, MI: Baker, 1998), 1:73–74.
76. Martin Luther, *Selected Psalms I*, LW 12:152.

as a compound of the pronoun "who" and the noun "sufficiency," but he found this interpretation unconvincing on a lexical level.[77] Bullinger and others, however, followed this interpretation of the name:

> Therefore God is that he, to whom nothing is lacking, which in all things and unto all things is sufficient to himself; who needeth no man's aid, yea, who alone had all things which do appertain to the perfect felicity both of this life and of the world to come; and which only and alone can fill and suffice all his people and other creatures.[78]

The name of God revealed in Exodus 3:14 has been regarded by many Protestant theologians as God's "most excellent" name.[79] In Calvin's exegesis of this divine name, we witness once again an example of linguistic competence, historical awareness, and theological sophistication. Calvin commented on the grammar of this verse, noting that "the verb in the Hebrew is in the future tense, 'I will be what I will be'; but it is of the same force as the present, except that it designates the perpetual duration of time."[80] He also observed that "immediately afterwards, contrary to grammatical usage, he used the same verb in the first person as a substantive, annexing it to a verb in the third person; that our minds may be filled with admiration as often as his incomprehensible essence is mentioned."[81] Calvin was unimpressed by Platonic readings of this verse, which suggested "that this one and only Being of God absorbs all imaginable essences," for such interpretations too easily lended themselves to the idolatrous conclusion that "the multitude of false gods" are derived, downstream as it were, from God's supereminent being.[82] How should this divine name be interpreted? Calvin concluded,

> Wherefore, in order rightly to apprehend the one God, we must first know, that all things in heaven and earth derive at his will their essence, or subsistence from One, who truly is. From this Being all

---

77. Martin Luther, *Lectures on Genesis Chapters 15–20*, LW 3:80–81.
78. Bullinger, *Decades*, 2:135. See also Bullinger, *Brief Exposition*, 109; Vermigli, *Common Places*, 1.12.2.
79. Muller, *Post-Reformation Reformed Dogmatics*, 3:248–49.
80. Calvin, *Commentaries on the Last Four Books of Moses*, 73.
81. Ibid.
82. Ibid.

power is derived; because, if God sustains all things by his excellency, he governs them also at his will. And how would it have profited Moses to gaze upon the secret essence of God, as if it were shut up in heaven, unless, being assured of his omnipotence, he had obtained from thence the buckler of his confidence? Therefore God teaches him that he alone is worthy of the most holy name, which is profaned when improperly transferred to others; and then sets for his inestimable excellency, that Moses may have no doubt of overcoming all things under his guidance.[83]

Calvin's treatment of Exodus 3:14 is noteworthy insofar as it reveals how his rather sparse discussion of the divine names in the *Institutes of the Christian Religion*[84] is balanced out by the more elaborate exposition of his biblical commentaries.[85]

Bullinger offers what might anachronistically be called a "canonical reading" of the divine names El Shaddai and Yahweh by means of commentary on Exodus 6:3: "I appeared to Abraham, to Isaac, and to Jacob, as God Almighty, but by my name the LORD I did not make myself known to them." According to Bullinger, this verse should not be read to claim "that the patriarchs had not heard or known the name Jehovah: for that name began to be called upon in the time of Seth, immediately after the beginning of the world."[86] Bullinger instead glossed the meaning of the verse in light of his exegetical conclusions regarding the two divine names El Shaddai and Yahweh:

> Therefore it seemeth that the Lord meant thus in effect: "I opened myself unto the patriarchs as God Schaddai, who am able in all things sufficiently to fill them with all goodness; and therefore I promised them a land that floweth with milk and honey: but in my name Jehovah I was not yet known unto them, that is, I did not perform unto them that which I promised." For we have heard already, that he is called Jehovah of that which he maketh to be; and therefore he bringeth his promise to performance. "Now therefore"

---

83. Ibid., 73–74.
84. See Calvin, *Institutes*, 1.10.1–3, 1.12.1–2. Though Calvin's discussion of the divine attributes in the *Institutes* is meager, B. B. Warfield observes that a wide range of divine attributes are discussed in scattered places across the *Institutes*. See Warfield, "Calvin's Doctrine of God," in *Calvin and Calvinism* (repr., Grand Rapids, MI: Baker, 1981), chap. 3.
85. Muller, *The Unaccommodated Calvin*, 152–54.
86. Bullinger, *Decades*, 2:136.

(saith he) "I will indeed fulfil my promise, and shew myself to be, not only *Deum Schaddai*, an all-sufficient or almighty God, but also to be Jehovah, an essence or being eternal, immutable, true, and in all things like myself, or standing to my promise."[87]

The two distinct meanings of the divine names El Shaddai and Yahweh thus underwrote the two distinct phases of God's historical relation to his people, namely, promise and fulfillment. In Bullinger's exegesis, the divine names took on not only a theological but also a redemptive-historical significance.

Bullinger's exposition of the divine names also exhibits a pastoral or practical motive. Within the same context of his discussion of the names El Shaddai and Yahweh, Bullinger reminded his readers that God also calls himself "the God of Abraham, the God of Isaac, and the God of Jacob" (Ex. 3:15). When we hear that this divine name is to be memorialized "throughout all generations" (Ex. 3:15), it reminds us that "all the excellent and innumerable benefits which God bestowed on our forefathers" are promised to us as well: "For he will be our God, even as he was theirs, if so be we do believe in him as they did believe. For to us that believe he will be both Schaddai and Jehovah, eternal and immutable truth, being, life, and heaped-up store of all manner good things."[88] As Bullinger said elsewhere, "It is not sufficient to have believed that God exists or even that he is all-sufficient unless you further believe that the same omnipotent God, the creator of all things, is your God, indeed the rewarder of all who seek him."[89] In early Protestant thought, the divine names were integral to the fabric of a practical, covenant theology.

Luther's commentaries on the Psalms reveal a similar practical motive. In his exposition of Psalm 111:4, he encouraged Christians to draw consolation rather than dread from the Lord's Supper by considering the various divine names that Scripture presents to us. "The names 'God' and 'Lord' contain something terrifying," Luther tells us, "for they are the names of majesty"—a label with which we are already familiar.

---

87. Ibid.
88. Ibid., 2:136–37.
89. Bullinger, *Brief Exposition*, 109.

But the surnames "gracious and merciful" contain pure comfort and joy. I do not know if God anywhere in the Scriptures lets himself be called by lovelier names. So anxiously does he want to impress on our heart the sweet words that we really ought to accept and honor his remembrance with joy and love, praise and thanks.[90]

Driving the point home, Luther then exhorted his readers,

Do not give him a different name in your heart or make him anything else in your conscience. You would do him an injustice and a great wrong, and yourself the great harm. For if you call him something else or think of him otherwise in your heart, you make him a liar and reject this verse; for then you believe your deceitful heart more than you do God and his sweet and tender words.[91]

Luther drew a similar contrast between God's "majestic" names and his "friendly" names in his commentary on Psalm 23. "Some of the other names which Scripture gives God"—such as Lord, King, and Creator—

sound almost too splendid and majestic and at once arouse awe and fear when we hear them mentioned. . . . The little word "shepherd," however, is not of that kind but has a very friendly sound. When the devout read or hear it, it immediately grants them a confidence, a comfort, and a sense of security that the word "father" and others grant when they are attributed to God.[92]

As we noted above, it is important to remember that Luther's contrast between God's "majestic" and "friendly" names was relative, not absolute, for he also commended God's majesty as a source of consolation to the believer.[93]

Conclusion

The doctrine of God played a significant role in the constructive, polemical, and pastoral theology of the Protestant Reformation. Drawing on resources from across classical philosophical and theological

90. Luther, *Selected Psalms II, LW* 13:374.
91. Ibid., *LW* 13:374–75.
92. Luther, *Selected Psalms I, LW* 12:152.
93. Luther, *Selected Psalms II, LW* 13:91–93.

traditions, Protestant theologians expounded with great learning and conviction the doctrine of God as historically confessed by catholic Christians. Their exposition exhibited patient and detailed attention to the biblical and exegetical bases from which the doctrine of God derives, even as it engaged freely with philosophical arguments that they deemed part of God's bounteous self-revelation to creatures. Without exception, early Protestant theology also displayed a profound commitment to pastoral care, encouraging Christians to take heart that this great God is their God and to live for the honor of God's name. These characteristics of the Reformation doctrine of God were further developed during the era of Protestant orthodoxy.[94]

It is a lamentable situation, therefore, that many who consider themselves heirs of Reformation theology have found themselves of late taking an increasingly ambivalent stance toward the doctrine of God that early Protestants confessed and proclaimed. The attributes of divine simplicity, aseity, eternity, immutability, impassibility, goodness, love, grace, mercy, justice, and wrath, along with the ways these attributes inform God's engagement with us as Creator, Redeemer, and Consummator, do not enjoy widespread embrace among contemporary Protestants, at least in their traditional forms. Nor are they regularly discussed or defended within the context of biblical exegesis and pastoral care.

Theology is not permitted to despair in situations of lament, however, and that for reasons ultimately related to the doctrine of God. Theology concerns itself with the God "who gives life to the dead and calls into existence the things that do not exist" (Rom. 4:17). Commenting on Romans 4, Calvin stated, "We do not sufficiently exalt the power of God, unless we think it to be greater than our weakness. Faith then ought not to regard our weakness, misery, and defects, but to fix wholly its attention on the power of God alone."[95] Following Calvin's counsel, therefore, and also the example of the Protestant pastors, exegetes, and

---

94. See Muller, *Post-Reformation Reformed Dogmatics*, vol. 3, *The Divine Essence and Attributes*; Sebastian Rehnman, "The Doctrine of God in Reformed Orthodoxy," in *A Companion to Reformed Orthodoxy*, ed. Herman J. Selderhuis, Brill's Companions to the Christian Tradition 40 (Leiden: Brill, 2013), 353–401; Dolf te Velde, *The Doctrine of God in Reformed Orthodoxy, Karl Barth, and the Utrecht School: A Study in Method and Content*, Studies in Reformed Theology 25 (Leiden: Brill, 2013).

95. John Calvin, *Commentaries on the Epistle of Paul the Apostle to the Romans*, trans. John Owen (repr., Grand Rapids, MI: Baker, 1998), 181.

theologians who confessed this God before us, theology does well to entrust itself to the Lord God Almighty. And in times of need, theology may also take the prayers of these trusted teachers on its lips:

> God grant that we may truly know, and religiously worship, the high, excellent, and mighty God, even so, and such, as himself is. For hitherto I have, as simply, sincerely, and briefly as I could, discoursed of the ways and means how to know God, which is in substance one, and three in persons: and yet we acknowledge and do freely confess, that in all this treatise hitherto there is nothing spoken worthy of or comparable to his unspeakable majesty. For the eternal, excellent, and mighty God is greater than all majesty, and than all the eloquence of all men; so far am I from thinking that I by my words do in one jot come near unto his excellency. But I do humbly beseech the most merciful Lord, that he will vouchsafe of his inestimable goodness and liberality to enlighten in us all the understanding of our minds with sufficient knowledge of his name, through Jesus Christ our Lord and Saviour. Amen.[96]

Resources for Further Study

PRIMARY SOURCES

Bullinger, Heinrich. *The Decades of Heinrich Bullinger*. Edited by Thomas Harding. 2 vols. 1849–1852. Reprint, Grand Rapids, MI: Reformation Heritage Books, 2004.

Calvin, John. *Institutes of the Christian Religion*. Edited by John T. McNeill. Translated by Ford Lewis Battles. 2 vols. Library of Christian Classics 20–21. 1559 edition. Philadelphia: Westminster, 1960.

Cochrane, Arthur C., ed. *Reformed Confessions of the Sixteenth Century*. Louisville: Westminster John Knox, 2003.

Luther, Martin. *Lectures on Genesis*. Vols. 1–8 in *Luther's Works*. Edited by Jaroslav Pelikan and Helmut T. Lehmann. Philadelphia: Fortress; St. Louis, MO: Concordia, 1955–1986.

Melanchthon, Philipp. *Loci Communes* (1555). In *Melanchthon on Christian Doctrine: Loci Communes 1555*. Translated and edited by Clyde L. Manschreck. Grand Rapids, MI: Baker, 1982.

---

96. Bullinger, *Decades*, 2:173.

Musculus, Wolfgang. *Common Places of Christian Religion*. London: R. Wolfe, 1563.

Vermigli, Peter Martyr. *The Common Places of Peter Martyr Vermilius*. Translated by Anthonie Marten. London: Henry Denham and Henry Middleton, 1583.

Zwingli, Huldrych. *An Exposition of the Faith*. In *Zwingli and Bullinger: Selected Translations with Introductions and Notes*, edited by G. W. Bromiley, 239–79. Library of Christian Classics 24. Philadelphia: Westminster, 1953.

SECONDARY SOURCES

Kolb, Robert. *Luther and the Stories of God: Biblical Narratives as a Foundation for Christian Living*. Grand Rapids, MI: Baker Academic, 2012.

Luy, David J. *Dominus Mortis: Martin Luther and the Incorruptibility of God in Christ*. Minneapolis: Fortress, 2014.

Muller, Richard A. *Post-Reformation Reformed Dogmatics: The Rise and Development of Reformed Orthodoxy, ca. 1520 to ca. 1725*. Vol. 3, *The Divine Essence and Attributes*. Grand Rapids, MI: Baker Academic, 2003.

———. *The Unaccommodated Calvin: Studies in the Foundation of a Theological Tradition*. Oxford Studies in Historical Theology. New York: Oxford University Press, 2000.

Stephens, W. P. *Zwingli: An Introduction to His Thought*. Oxford: Clarendon, 1992.

7

Predestination and Election

Cornelis P. Venema

ABSTRACT

The Reformation doctrine of predestination and election was based on scriptural teaching, and represents a continuation of a long-standing Augustinian legacy. Contrary to the teaching of Pelagianism and semi-Pelagianism, which grant a measure of human autonomy and free will in the believer's response to the gospel call to faith and repentance, the doctrine of predestination undergirds the teaching of salvation by grace alone through the work of Christ alone. The leading theologians of the Reformed tradition taught that salvation was rooted in God's gracious choice in and for Christ to save some fallen sinners and to grant them the gift of faith.

Introduction

A commonly held prejudice regarding Reformation theology is that the doctrine of predestination and election was the peculiar focus of Reformed theologians, especially its leading theological figure, John Calvin. Whereas the Protestant Reformation, both in its Lutheran and Reformed expressions, especially emphasized the doctrine of free justification by grace alone through faith alone, the Reformed branch of the Reformation was distinguished by its special interest in the topic of predestination. This prejudice has led some historians of Reformation theology to pit the Lutheran and Reformed traditions over against each other: the Lutheran retaining a special focus on the doctrine of justification, which is the "article of the standing and falling of the church" (*articulus stantis et cadentis ecclesiae*), and the Reformed substituting a kind of predestinarian metaphysic that deduces the entire corpus of theology from the governing principle of God's sovereign will. In this interpretation of the two traditions, the religious impulse of the Reformation—the rediscovery of the gospel of God's free acceptance of sinners on the basis of the righteousness of Christ alone—was imperiled by an austere and foreboding view of the absolute sovereignty of God. The fresh wind of Luther's rediscovery of justification by faith alone was threatened by a doctrine of predestination that removed the focus from God's revealed will in the gospel of Jesus Christ and replaced it with a focus on the hidden and inscrutable decree of the triune God.

I do not intend here to resolve this prejudice, which has played a significant role in the interpretation of Reformation theology. However, it deserves mention at the outset of this chapter on the doctrine of predestination and election in Reformation theology for at least three reasons.

First, since the Reformation was born out of a renewed attention to the teaching of Scripture, it was bound to include a renewed consideration of the scriptural teaching on predestination and election. Though the language does not belong to the sixteenth century's theological vocabulary, historians of the Reformation period often speak of the doctrine of Scripture as its "formal principle." Over against the medieval Roman Catholic Church, which privileged the church's official interpretation of apostolic tradition (whether in written or unwritten form), the Reformers insisted that Christian theology must be normed by the teaching of Scripture, properly interpreted. The church's dogmatic pronouncements must always stand the test of Scripture and must be revised where they are at variance with scriptural teaching. For this reason, the leading theologians of the Protestant Reformation were obliged to address the doctrine of predestination and election. For example, since the apostle Paul's epistle to the Romans was a particularly important source for the Reformation's articulation of the doctrine of justification, it was scarcely possible that the Reformers could ignore the doctrine of predestination, which forms an important part of the teaching of Romans.

Second, the central theme of the Reformation, the doctrine of free justification, was born out of a rediscovery of the gospel of salvation by grace alone (*sola gratia*). Contrary to the medieval Roman Catholic Church's teaching that fallen human beings retain a free will that is able to "cooperate" with God's grace and "merit" further grace, even eternal life, the Reformers insisted that fallen human beings are incapable of performing any saving good.[1] According to the teaching of the leading Reformers, salvation begins and ends with God's gracious initiatives in Christ. Only those who are brought to faith through the work of the Holy Spirit and the word of the gospel, are able to embrace the promise of the gospel, the forgiveness of sins, and free acceptance with God. Human merits, achievements, and performances contribute nothing to the salvation of fallen sinners. The Reformation doctrine of justification emphasized that the righteousness of Christ, freely granted and imputed to believers who embrace the gospel promise, is the sole basis for the believer's right standing with God. The Pelagian and semi-Pelagian teaching that fallen sinners have the wherewithal to cooperate freely with God's gracious initiative in Christ or the capacity to perform good works that constitute a partial basis for salvation was roundly condemned by Reformation theology.

These features of the Reformation doctrine of salvation were bound to raise the question that the doctrine of predestination and election addresses. After all, if fallen sinners are unable to save themselves or perform any works that contribute to their salvation, then their salvation is ultimately authored by God alone, who takes the initiative to provide for and effect the salvation of believers through the work of Christ. As we shall observe in the course of expositing the Reformation views, the doctrine of predestination and election naturally finds

---

1. The following statement of the Council of Trent, which treats the way in which fallen sinners can freely cooperate with God's grace and dispose themselves for justification, is representative of the Roman Catholic view: "They, who by sins are alienated from God, may be disposed through his quickening and assisting grace, to convert themselves to their own justification, by freely assenting to and co-operating with that said grace." Philip Schaff, *The Creeds of Christendom: With a History and Critical Notes*, vol. 2, *The Greek and Latin Creeds*, rev. David S. Schaff (1877; repr., Grand Rapids, MI: Baker, 1985), 92.

its home within the context of acknowledging human inability and affirming the gospel of God's undeserved grace in Jesus Christ. The same theological emphases that gave impetus to the doctrine of justification undergirded the Reformation doctrine of election.

And third, though the Reformation was born from a renewed study of Scripture, it was also deeply rooted in a long-standing Augustinian legacy, especially in Western Christian theology. The doctrine of predestination and election found its most thorough patristic expression in the great church father Augustine's polemical writings against Pelagianism and semi-Pelagianism.[2] While Augustine's doctrine of justification did not coincide entirely with that of the sixteenth-century Reformers, his doctrine of predestination and election, as it was formulated over against Pelagianism, was an important source for the Reformation view.[3] Indeed, among most of the primary authors of Reformation theology, Augustine's doctrine of predestination and election was a key component in their polemic against medieval semi-Pelagianism and every form of a doctrine of salvation based (wholly or partly) on human works. The Reformers were biblical in their approach to theology, but they were also catholic and traditional in their claim to represent the historic teaching of the Christian church.[4] Invoking Augustine's teaching on the doctrine of predestination was, accordingly, an important component in their defense of the catholicity of the teachings both that salvation comes by grace alone and that salvation finds its source in the eternal counsel of the triune God.

2. For Augustine's doctrine, see Augustine, *Four Anti-Pelagian Writings*, trans. John A. Mourant and William J. Collinge, Fathers of the Church 86 (Washington, DC: Catholic University of America Press, 1992); Donato Ogliari, *Gratia et Certamen: The Relationship between Grace and Free Will in the Discussion of Augustine with the So-Called Semipelagians* (Leuven: University Press, 2003); J. B. Mozley, *A Treatise on the Augustinian Doctrine of Predestination*, 2nd ed. (New York: E. P. Dutton, 1878).

3. In the fourteenth century, Augustine's views were embraced and defended by Thomas Bradwardine and Gregory of Rimini, who anticipated the views of the Reformers of the sixteenth century. For treatments of medieval Augustinianism, see Heiko A. Oberman, *Archbishop Thomas Bradwardine, a Fourteenth-Century Augustinian: A Study of His Theology in Its Historical Context* (Utrecht: Kemink & Zoon, 1958); Gordon Leff, *Bradwardine and the Pelagians: A Study of His "De Causa Dei" and Its Opponents* (Cambridge: Cambridge University Press, 1957); and P. Vigneaux, *Justification et predestination au XIVe siècle: Duns Scot, Pierre d'Auriole, Guillaume d'Occam, Gregoire de Rimini* (Paris: Librairie Philosophique J. Vrin, 1981).

4. Cf. Heinrich Bullinger, *Der Alt Gloub* [The old faith] (Zurich: Froschouer, 1537). Bullinger's treatise is a striking example of the Reformer's claim not to novelty but to a rediscovery of the "old faith" of the Christian church. For a treatment of this essay and its significance, see Cornelis P. Venema, "Heinrich Bullinger's *Der Alt Gloub* ('The Old Faith'): An Apology for the Reformation," *MAJT* 15 (2004): 11–32.

For these reasons, it is not surprising that the Reformers, in the course of rediscovering the gospel of salvation by grace apart from any human works, also rediscovered the scriptural and Augustinian doctrine of predestination and election. The Reformation wanted to underscore the truth that God alone authors and accomplishes the redemption of his people through the work of Christ. In defending the truth of grace alone and Christ alone, they insisted that the work of Christ had deep roots in God's own loving determination from before the foundation of the world to save his elect people in Christ.

Predestination and Election: Some Preliminary Definitions

Before I turn to a survey of the doctrine of predestination and election in the writings of several key sixteenth-century Reformers, I need to offer a few brief definitions of terms that are pertinent to the doctrine.

The term *predestination* derives from a Latin root, *praedestinatio*, which is a composite of *prae-*, "before," and *destinare*, "to destine" or "to ordain." Within the framework of historic Christian theology, the doctrine of predestination concerns God's eternal purpose or will for the salvation or the nonsalvation of fallen sinners. Traditionally, the doctrine of predestination was treated in the system of theology as a part of the broader doctrine of providence (as a "special providence," *providentia specialis*). Whereas the doctrine of providence treats God's sustenance and governance of all created things, the doctrine of predestination especially focuses on God's eternal purpose regarding the salvation of fallen human beings. The doctrine fundamentally assumes that all things occur within history according to God's eternal purpose. In the Christian distinction between the triune God, who is the Creator of all things and the sole Redeemer of his people, and the created world, the entire creation in its existence and history is governed by God's counsel and not by chance or fate.[5]

In the history of theology, predestination is ordinarily viewed as

---

5. Cf. Benjamin B. Warfield, *The Plan of Salvation*, rev. ed. (Grand Rapids, MI: Eerdmans, n.d.), 14: "That God acts upon a plan in all his activities, is already given in Theism. On the establishment of a personal God, this question is closed. For person means purpose: precisely what distinguishes a person from a thing is that its modes of action are purposive, that all it does is directed to an end and proceeds through the choice of means to that end." Warfield's study remains a masterful presentation of the doctrine of predestination and election.

consisting of two elements, *election* and *reprobation* (double predestination or *gemina praedestinationis*). Election, from the Latin word
electio, "to choose out of," refers to God's choice to save some fallen
sinners and to grant them faith in Jesus Christ as Savior. Reprobation,
from the Latin word *reprobatio*, "to reject," refers to God's choice not
to save others but to leave them in their sins. The decree or purpose of
God to elect or to reprobate expresses God's sovereign freedom either
to save and grant faith in Jesus Christ to some or to not save and thus
to leave others in their sins. A distinction is also often drawn between
election, a positive expression of God's gracious will to grant salvation
to otherwise undeserving sinners, and reprobation, a negative expression of God's just determination to "pass by" some of the fallen human
race, all of whose members are justly worthy of condemnation and
death for their sins. In this understanding, reprobation is not exactly
parallel to election but is a manifestation of God's justice.[6] Although
God's will is the ultimate reason for the salvation of some and the
nonsalvation of others, the proximate reason for the nonsalvation of
the reprobate is their own sinfulness. Election especially reveals God's
mercy, whereas reprobation reveals his justice.

In the history of Christian theology, two related terms are employed
to distinguish the doctrine of predestination from alternative views
regarding God's work in the salvation of sinners. Since a robust doctrine of predestination and election accents the truth that salvation is
grounded in God's gracious and sovereign choice, this doctrine is a
form of *monergism*. The only effective cause in the beginning and effecting of conversion is God's sovereign grace. This stands in contrast
to *synergism*, which teaches that the divine and human wills cooperate
in the believer's response to the gospel. Synergism implies that the salvation of believers is not solely authored by God in consequence of his
electing purpose. Instead, salvation ultimately depends on the free and
independent cooperation of the human will in embracing the gospel
promise of salvation in Christ.

---

6. For this reason, a distinction is sometimes drawn between what is termed *preterition* (from the
Lat. *praeterire*, "to pass by"), which is an expression of God's negative will not to save the reprobate,
and *condemnation*, which is an expression of God's justice in punishing the reprobate for their sin.
In the closing portion of this chapter, I will have occasion to address the difference that emerged
in later Reformed theology between *infralapsarianism* and *supralapsarianism*. The infralapsarian
position especially emphasizes that God's will in respect to the reprobate is an instance of preterition.

Luther and Lutheranism

Since Luther (1483–1546) and Lutheranism represent the first branch of the Protestant Reformation, it is appropriate to begin with a sketch of the doctrine of predestination as it was articulated by Luther and his followers. While Lutheranism is not ordinarily associated with the doctrine of predestination,[7] the topic does emerge expressly in two significant contexts: first, Luther's well-known treatise against Erasmus, *The Bondage of the Will*,[8] and second, in subsequent debates within the developing Lutheran tradition regarding the freedom of the human will in receiving the grace of Jesus Christ.

MARTIN LUTHER: *DE SERVO ARBITRIO*

The most important, and controversial, source for Martin Luther's treatment of the doctrine of predestination is undoubtedly his response to Erasmus of Rotterdam (1466–1536), who had written a criticism of Luther's teaching in 1524 titled *The Freedom of the Will*.[9] Although Erasmus was committed to a moral and humanistic program of church reform, he was strongly opposed to Luther's early insistence that fallen human beings have no freedom of the will in respect to their response to the gospel.[10] In Erasmus's judgment, it was essential that human beings retain the freedom to respond favorably or unfavorably to the gospel. Without a clear emphasis on such freedom, the gospel could only be an occasion for human irresponsibility and antinomianism. If fallen sinners were unable to do (or to not do) what the gospel requires,

---

7. For example, Werner Elert claims that predestination was at best "a merely auxiliary thought" in Luther's theology. Elert, *The Structure of Lutheranism*, trans. Walter A. Hensen (St. Louis, MO: Concordia, 1962), 1:123.

8. For an English translation of this work, see *LW* 33. For an extensive treatment of Luther's work, including a history of its reception in the developing Lutheran tradition, see Robert Kolb, *Bound Choice, Election, and Wittenberg Theological Method: From Martin Luther to the Formula of Concord*, Lutheran Quarterly Books (Grand Rapids, MI: Eerdmans, 2005).

9. For an English translation of Erasmus's *De libero arbitrio*, see Ernst F. Winter, ed. and trans., *Erasmus-Luther: Discourse on Free Will* (New York: Continuum, 1961), 3–94. For recent studies of the exchange between Erasmus and Luther, written by respected Lutheran theologians, see Gerharde O. Forde, *The Captivation of the Will: Luther vs. Erasmus on Freedom and Bondage*, ed. Steven D. Paulson, Lutheran Quarterly Books (Grand Rapids, MI: Eerdmans, 2005); and Kolb, *Bound Choice*, 11–28.

10. Even by 1521, Luther made the following claim in his *Assertion of All Articles*: "It is a profound and blind error to teach that the will is by nature free and can, without grace, turn to the spirit, seek grace, and desire it. Actually, the will tries to escape from grace and rages against it when it is present. . . . These teachings [concerning free will] have been invented in order to insult and detract from the grace of God." *LW* 32:93.

God's favor toward believers or disfavor toward unbelievers would be baseless. Furthermore, if God were to condemn sinners who are incapable of performing what the gospel requires of them, he would be manifestly unjust.

Luther's response to Erasmus is strikingly summarized in two significant passages from *The Bondage of the Will*:

> Christian faith is entirely extinguished, the promises of God and the whole gospel are completely destroyed, if we teach and believe that it is not for us to know the necessary foreknowledge of God and the necessity of the things that are come to pass. For this is the one supreme consolation of Christians in all adversities, to know that God does not lie, but does all things immutably, and that his will can neither be resisted nor changed nor hindered.[11]

> But now, since God has taken my salvation out of my hands into his, making it depend on his choice and not mine, and has promised to save me, not by my own work or exertion but by his grace and mercy, I am assured and certain both that he is faithful and will not lie to me, and also that he is too great and powerful for any demons or any adversities to be able to break him or to snatch me from him. "No one," he says, "shall snatch them out of my hand because my Father who has given them to me is greater than all" [John 10:28–29]. So it comes about that, if not all, some and indeed many are saved, whereas by the power of free choice none at all would be saved, but all would perish together.[12]

Several aspects of Luther's view of predestination and election are present in these representative passages. In the first place, Luther started from the conviction that God is a personal God and the almighty Creator of all that exists. As the Creator and Lord of all creation, God is ultimately responsible for all that takes place in the world that he created and oversees by his providence. As Luther expressed it,

> He is God, and for his will there is no cause or reason that can be laid down as a rule or measure for it since there is nothing equal or

11. Martin Luther, *The Bondage of the Will*, LW 33:43.
12. Ibid., *LW* 33:289.

superior to it, but it is itself the measure of all things. For if there were any rule or measure or cause or reason for it, it could no longer be the will of God.[13]

The God who reveals his mercy and grace in Jesus Christ in the fullness of time is at the same time the One who works his will and purpose in all things, including the salvation of fallen sinners:

> For the will of God is effectual and cannot be hindered, since it is the power of the divine nature itself; moreover it is wise, so that it cannot be deceived. Now, if his will is not hindered, there is nothing to prevent the work itself from being done, in the place, time, manner and measure that he himself both foresees and wills. If the will of God were such that, when the work was completed, the work remained but the will ceased—like the will of men, which ceases to will when the house they wanted is built, just as it also comes to an end in death—then it could be truly said that things happen contingently and mutably. But here the opposite happens; the work comes to an end and the will remains.[14]

In his representation of God's sovereign, predestinating will, Luther frequently distinguished between God's "hidden" and "revealed" will, between *Deus absconditus* and *Deus revelatus*. By means of this distinction, Luther aimed to emphasize that the all-governing will of God is perfect and righteous, even though it remains somewhat inscrutable and beyond our comprehension:

> For if his righteousness were such that it could be judged to be righteous by human standards, it would clearly not be divine and would in no way differ from human righteousness. But since he is the one true God, and is wholly incomprehensible and inaccessible to human reason, it is proper and indeed necessary that his righteousness should be incomprehensible.[15]

---

13. Ibid., *LW* 33:181.
14. Ibid., *LW* 33:38.
15. Ibid., *LW* 33:290. For assessments of this distinction in Luther's theology, see Paul Althaus, *The Theology of Martin Luther*, trans. Robert C. Schultz (Philadelphia: Fortress, 1966), 274–86; and David C. Steinmetz, *Luther in Context*, 2nd ed. (Grand Rapids, MI: Baker Academic, 2002), 23–31.

While there is no discrepancy between what we know of God's will in the gospel concerning Christ and what remains inaccessible to us, we can never fully comprehend or fathom the depths of God's will.

In the argument of *The Bondage of the Will*, Luther rarely spoke explicitly of God's predestination or election. Interestingly, he did not even offer an exposition of passages like Romans 9 or Ephesians 1, which are among the most significant scriptural testimonies to the doctrine.[16] However, he did clearly teach that fallen sinners are incapable of turning themselves toward God in faith and repentance, unless God himself graciously grants them these gifts according to his purpose of election. Predestination belongs to the word of the gospel and not to the law because it refers to God's gracious choice of some fallen sinners to be his children through the work of Christ. In the spiritual realm of redemption, God alone is able to convert the will and choice of fallen sinners so that they embrace the gospel promise in faith. In this realm,

> man is not left in the hand of his own counsel but is directed and led by the choice and counsel of God, so that just as in his own realm he is directed by his own counsel, without regard to the precepts of another, so in the Kingdom of God he is directed by the precepts of another without regard to his own choice.[17]

While Luther emphasized the means of grace that the Spirit of God uses to draw sinners into fellowship with Christ and also insisted that the gospel word is always one that expresses God's desire that all sinners be saved, his understanding of the sinful will's bondage led him to ascribe the salvation of believers entirely to the sovereign choice of God.

Philipp Melanchthon and Later Lutheranism

Next to Luther, Philipp Melanchthon (1497–1560) was arguably the most formative figure in the development of Lutheran theology during the sixteenth century. Melanchthon's growing reluctance to treat the doctrine of predestination and election and his apparent modification

---

16. See Steinmetz, *Luther in Context*, 12–22, for an insightful analysis of the difference between Luther and Augustine's comments on Romans 9 in their respective writings. Steinmetz identifies areas where Luther differs from Augustine, especially in his concern that the doctrine of predestination might serve to undermine the believer's assurance of salvation.

17. Luther, *Bondage*, *LW* 33:118–19.

of Luther's views in *The Bondage of the Will* contributed significantly to the muting of the doctrine in subsequent Lutheran theology.[18]

In the first edition (1521) of his principal theological work, *Loci Communes*, Melanchthon set forth a fairly robust form of the doctrine of predestination, which coincided with the view Luther espoused in *The Bondage of the Will*.[19] In this edition of the *Loci*, Melanchthon linked the doctrine directly with the gospel of justification by grace alone through the work of Christ alone. Salvation is by grace alone, and the work of Christ benefits only those whom God chooses to save by granting them faith in Christ. However, in subsequent editions of the *Loci* and in his other writings, Melanchthon shifted the location of the doctrine to the doctrine of the church, and placed increasing emphasis on the universal promises of the gospel that are presented in the Word and sacraments. Fearful that the doctrine of predestination would undermine the presentation of the gospel promise in Word and sacrament, Melanchthon began to view the doctrine with greater reserve. Furthermore, in his formulation of the doctrine of the bondage of the will, Melanchthon expressed views that modified the strong statements of Luther.

In his reflections on the role of the will in the believer's response to the gospel, Melanchthon's position engendered a protracted controversy about "synergism" among Lutheran theologians that would be formally settled only by the Formula of Concord in 1576.[20] Melanchthon's emphasis on the cooperation of the human will in the believer's response to the gospel prompted considerable debate since it arguably compromised the sovereignty of God in granting faith to fallen sinners. Rather than emphasizing God's sovereign work as the sole basis for

---

18. For a treatment of Melanchthon's relationship with Luther, see Timothy J. Wengert, "Melanchthon and Luther / Luther and Melanchthon," *Lutherjahrbuch* 66 (1999): 55–88, and Wengert, "Philip Melanchthon's Contribution to Luther's Debate with Erasmus over the Bondage of the Will," in *By Faith Alone: Essays on Justification in Honor of Gerhard O. Forde*, ed. Joseph A. Burgess and Marc Kolden (Grand Rapids, MI: Eerdmans, 2004), 110–24. For a treatment of Melanchthon's early comments on predestination in Romans 9, see Robert Kolb, "Melanchthon's Influence on the Exegesis of his Students," in *Philip Melanchthon (1497–1560) and the Commentary*, ed. Timothy J. Wengert and M. Patrick Graham (Sheffield, England: Sheffield Academic Press, 1997), 194–215.

19. Philipp Melanchthon, *Loci Communes* (1521), in *Melanchthon and Bucer*, ed. Wilhelm Pauck, LCC 19 (Philadelphia: Westminster, 1969), 25–26: "I think it makes considerable difference that young minds are immediately imbued with this idea that all things come to pass, not according to the plans and efforts of men but according to the will of God."

20. For an extensive treatment of the controversy, see Kolb, *Bound Choice*, 106–34.

the believer's response to the gospel, synergism emphasized the active cooperation of the human will in conversion. In the course of the synergism controversy, the Lutheran tradition stopped short of embracing Melanchthon's view and insisted that believers respond in faith to the gospel only by virtue of the sovereign work of the Holy Spirit.[21]

Rather than attempt to sort out the complicated history of Lutheran debates regarding the doctrine of predestination, the bondage of the will, and Melanchthon's modifications of Luther's insights, the Lutheran tradition's consensus on the doctrine can best be determined by considering the Augsburg Confession and the Formula of Concord.

Since Melanchthon was the principal author of the Augsburg Confession, the first and most formative of the confessional documents of the Lutheran tradition, a consideration of its teaching is instructive to ascertaining the view of Melanchthon particularly and of Lutheranism generally. The Augsburg Confession makes no explicit mention of the doctrine of predestination or election. However, after an early article on the doctrine of justification, which emphasizes that sinners are justified before God by grace alone and not "by their own powers, merits, or works,"[22] the confession strongly repudiates the error of Pelagianism. In the article that treats the freedom of the will, the confession insists that fallen sinners have no freedom "to work the righteousness of God, or a spiritual righteousness, without the Spirit of God; because the natural man receiveth not the things of the Spirit of God (1 Cor. 2:14). But this is wrought in the heart when men do receive the Spirit of God through the Word."[23] The teaching of the Pelagians, namely, "that by the powers of nature alone, without the Spirit of God, we are able to love God above all things," is explicitly condemned. Though these statements do not expressly affirm the doctrine of God's election of some to salvation, they correspond closely to the burden of

21. In the second and third editions of his *Loci Communes*, Melanchthon began to speak of "three causes of good action": the Word of God, the Holy Spirit, and "the human will which assents to and does not reject the Word of God." *Melanchthons Werke in Auswahl*, ed. Robert Stupperich, vol. 2, bk. 1 (Gütersloh: Bertelsmann, 1955), 243. See also Kolb, *Bound Choice*, 91–95. Employing Aristotle's scheme of causes, Melanchthon identified the Word of God as the "instrumental," the Spirit as the "creative," and the human will as the "material" cause of conversion. Whether Melanchthon's formulations are truly synergistic remains a matter of debate among his interpreters.
22. "The Augsburg Confession," art. 4, in Schaff, *Creeds of Christendom*, vol. 3, *The Evangelical Protestant Creeds*, 10.
23. "The Augsburg Confession," art. 18, in Schaff, *Creeds of Christendom*, 3:18.

Luther's teaching that believers are saved by God's free decision and grace, not on the basis of their own works or initiative.

The Formula of Concord, which was written to settle a series of doctrinal disputes within Lutheranism toward the end of the sixteenth century, is more directly relevant to understanding the Lutheran view of predestination and election. The Formula of Concord does not address the doctrine of predestination directly, and it clearly views the nonsalvation of some fallen sinners who do not come to faith in a way that is "asymmetrical" with the salvation of those whom God wills to save. Whereas the salvation of believers is entirely the fruit of God's gracious initiative and the work of the Spirit, the nonsalvation of others is the result of their irresponsible refusal to embrace the free promises of the gospel.

Nevertheless, in its handling of the synergistic controversy, the Formula of Concord offers a mild corrective to the followers of Melanchthon. In its descriptions of the work of God's grace in the salvation of believers and the bondage of the human will apart from the work of the Spirit, the Formula of Concord corresponds significantly to the earlier themes of Luther's *Bondage of the Will*.[24] In article 2, which treats the controversy regarding the freedom of the will, the Formula rejects the teaching that fallen sinners can "apply and prepare [themselves] unto the grace of God" in response to the Word and sacraments. Unless the Holy Spirit regenerates through the means of grace, the "unregenerate will of man is not only averse from God, but has become even hostile to God, so that it only wishes and desires those things, and is delighted with them, which are evil and opposite to the divine will."[25] The bondage of the will of fallen sinners prevents them from cooperating with God's grace ministered through the Word, unless the Spirit first draws them and makes them willing. In its defense of this view of the bondage of the will, the Formula of Concord cites Augustine's claim that God in the conversion "of unwilling men makes willing men," and it identifies only two "efficient causes" in conversion, the Holy Spirit and the Word of God.[26] In doing so, the Formula

---

24. Kolb, *Bound Choice*, 248–58.
25. "The Formula of Concord," art. 2, in Schaff, *Creeds of Christendom*, 3:107.
26. Ibid., art. 2, in Schaff, *Creeds of Christendom*, 3:113.

254 Cornelis P. Venema

of Concord took exception to Melanchthon's apparent synergism between the three causes of conversion, the Holy Spirit (the creative
cause), the Word of God (the instrumental cause), and the consenting
will of man (the material cause).

Therefore, although the Lutheran confessions do not directly affirm a doctrine of sovereign and gracious election, they do affirm that
the salvation of fallen sinners, who are unable to convert themselves
without a prior working of the Holy Spirit through the Word, happens
entirely according to God's gracious purpose. Admittedly, the Lutheran
tradition generally follows Melanchthon's reticence to speak of predestination and election, fearful that this might mitigate the clarity of the
gospel in distinction from the law. And yet, in clearly affirming salvation by grace alone through the gracious initiative of God in Christ,
and in opposing any synergistic view of the relation between the work
of God's grace and the will of fallen sinners, Lutheranism presents a
moderate Augustinian monergism. However, in order to preserve the
universal grace that is communicated in the gospel, the Lutheran tradition generally refrains from affirming any doctrine of reprobation or
divine purpose to pass by nonelect persons, leaving them in their sins.

The Reformed Doctrine of Predestination and Election[27]

The reticence to articulate a fulsome doctrine of predestination and
election in the Lutheran tradition was not shared by the leading theologians of the Reformed tradition in the sixteenth century. Although
there was a considerable diversity of formulation among Reformed
theologians, a general consensus obtained among them that the salvation of fallen sinners is the fruit of God's gracious electing purpose.
Testimony to this consensus is given in the principal confessional documents of the Reformed churches. For the purpose of my survey of the

---

27. For general surveys of the doctrine of predestination in Reformed theology, see Harry Buis,
Historic Protestantism and Predestination (Philadelphia: Presbyterian & Reformed, 1958); Richard A. Muller, *Christ and the Decree: Christology and Predestination in Reformed Theology from
Calvin to Perkins*, Studies in Historical Theology 2 (1986; repr., Grand Rapids, MI: Baker, 1988);
Cornelis Graafland, *Van Calvijn tot Barth: Oorsprong en ontwikkeling van de leer der verkiezing
in het Gereformeerd Protestantisme* [From Calvin to Barth: The origin and development of the
doctrine of election in Reformed Protestantism] ('s-Gravenhage, The Netherlands: Uitgeverij Boekencentrum, 1987); Pieter Rouwendal, "The Doctrine of Predestination in Reformed Orthodoxy,"
in *A Companion to Reformed Orthodoxy*, ed. Herman J. Selderhuis, Brill's Companions to the
Christian Tradition 40 (Leiden: Brill, 2013), 553–89.

Reformed doctrine of predestination, I will offer a summary of two leading figures, John Calvin of Geneva (1509–1564) and Heinrich Bullinger of Zurich (1504–1575). While these two theologians confirm a broad consensus of teaching among the Reformed theologians of the period, their differences also illustrate the diversity of opinion that remained on some points.

PREDESTINATION IN THE THEOLOGY OF JOHN CALVIN[28]

In the history of the interpretation of Calvin's theology, it has often been argued that predestination was the center and organizing principle of Calvin's theology. For a number of nineteenth- and twentieth-century theologians, the doctrine of predestination was regarded as the "central dogma" of Calvin's theology, the root from which all other doctrines were allegedly drawn.[29] Even in the popular imagination, the one feature of Calvin's theology that is most often emphasized is his doctrine of double predestination.

Despite the general assumption that predestination is at the center of Calvin's theology, it is noteworthy that Calvin treats the doctrine in his most important theological work, *Institutes of the Christian Religion*, toward the end of an extended discussion on the Holy Spirit's work in uniting believers to Christ and communicating to them the

---

28. Among the many sources on Calvin's doctrine of predestination, the following are especially valuable: Muller, *Christ and the Decree*, 17–38; Paul Jacobs, *Prädestination und Verantwortlichkeit bei Calvin* (Kasel: Oncken, 1937); Fred H. Klooster, *Calvin's Doctrine of Predestination* (Grand Rapids, MI: Baker, 1977); François Wendel, *Calvin: The Origins and Development of His Religious Thought* (New York: Harper & Row, 1963), 263–83; Carl R. Trueman, "Election: Calvin's Theology of Election and Its Early Reception," in *Calvin's Theology and Its Reception: Disputes, Developments, and New Possibilities*, ed. J. Todd Billings and I. John Hesselink (Louisville: Westminster John Knox, 2012), 97–120; R. Scott Clark, "Election and Predestination: The Sovereign Expressions of God (3.21–24)," in *A Theological Guide to Calvin's Institutes: Essays and Analysis*, ed. David W. Hall and Peter A. Lillback, Calvin 500 Series (Phillipsburg, NJ: P&R, 2008), 90–122.

29. For representative presentations of the thesis that predestination is a "central dogma" in Calvin's theology and in later Calvinism, see Alexander Schweizer, *Die Protestantischen Centraldogmen in ihrer Entwicklung innerhalb der reformierten Kirche*, 2 vols. (Zurich: Orell, Füssli, 1854–56); Hans Emil Weber, *Reformation, Orthodoxie Und Rationalismus*, vol. 1, pt. 1, *Von Der Reformation Zur Orthodoxie* (Gütersloh: Gerd Mohn, 1937); Graafland, *Von Calvijn tot Barth*; Ernst Bizer, *Frühorthodoxie und Rationalismus* (Zurich: EVZ Verlag, 1963). For critical, persuasive refutations of this thesis, see Muller, *Christ and the Decree*, esp. 1–13, 177–82; Muller, "The Use and Abuse of a Document: Beza's *Tabula Praedestinationis*, the Bolsec Controversy, and the Origins of Reformed Orthodoxy," in *Protestant Scholasticism: Essays in Reassessment*, ed. Carl R. Trueman and R. Scott Clark (Carlisle: Paternoster, 1999), 33–61; Willem J. van Asselt and Eef Dekker, "Introduction," in *Reformation and Scholasticism: An Ecumenical Enterprise*, ed. Willem J. van Asselt and Eef Dekker, Texts and Studies in Reformation and Post-Reformation Thought (Grand Rapids, MI: Baker Academic, 2001), 11–43.

benefits of Christ's saving work.[30] Although Calvin originally treated
the doctrine of predestination in the context of the doctrine of providence, in the final edition of the *Institutes* he discussed it within the
context of soteriology (the doctrine of salvation) and ecclesiology (the
doctrine of the church). In this way, Calvin emphasized how predestination confirms that the believer's salvation is born entirely of God's
gracious purposes in Christ and how it undergirds the believer's assurance of God's favor.

Calvin opened his treatment of predestination by noting that "the
covenant of life is not preached equally among all men, and among
those to whom it is preached, it does not gain the same acceptance
either constantly or in equal degree."[31] The topic of predestination
and election is, therefore, unavoidable. How are we to explain that
some respond to the call of the gospel in the way of faith, while others
refuse to believe? The ultimate explanation must be found in God's
"free mercy" and "eternal election," which are the fountainhead of
all of God's saving graces in Christ. If we fail to ascribe the difference between those who believe and are saved and those who remain
unwilling to believe to "God's mere generosity," we will dishonor
God's sheer grace in saving us and will fail to rest our comfort in God
alone.[32] Consequently, Calvin argued that we must give attention to
the scriptural doctrine of predestination and election. In doing so, we
face two dangers. On the one hand, there is the danger of excessive
curiosity regarding the doctrine, which can easily lead us to go beyond
the limits of what Scripture reveals concerning God's eternal election.
On the other hand, there is the danger of undue reticence, which fails
to acknowledge that what the Spirit of God has revealed in the Word
is for our comfort and blessing.

The title of Calvin's first chapter on the doctrine of predestination

30. For helpful analyses of the significance of where Calvin placed the doctrine of predestination in the *Institutes*, see Richard A. Muller, "The Placement of Predestination in Reformed Theology: Issue or Non-Issue?," *CTJ* 40, no. 2 (2005): 184–210; Paul Helm, "Calvin, the 'Two Issues,' and the Structure of the *Institutes*," *CTJ* 42, no. 2 (2007): 341–48.

31. Calvin, *Institutes*, 3.21.1. In addition to Calvin's treatment of predestination in the *Institutes*, the following sources offer an extensive presentation of his view: John Calvin, *The Bondage and Liberation of the Will: A Defence of the Orthodox Doctrine of Human Choice against Pighius*, ed. A. N. S. Lane, trans. G. I. Davies, Texts and Studies in Reformation and Post-Reformation Thought 2 (Grand Rapids, MI: Baker, 1996); Calvin, *Concerning the Eternal Predestination of God*, trans. J. K. S. Reid (Louisville: Westminster John Knox, 1997).

32. Calvin, *Institutes*, 3.21.1.

in the *Institutes* clearly identifies what is at issue: "Eternal election, by which God has predestined some to salvation, others to destruction."[33] The ultimate reason that some believe and are saved through Christ must be ascribed to God's purpose of election. While it is true that God is omniscient and knows all events prior to their occurrence, it is not true that election amounts to no more than God's foreknowledge of who will believe in response to the preaching of the gospel. As Calvin defined it,

> We call predestination God's eternal decree, by which he compacted within himself what he willed to become of each man. For all are not created in equal condition; rather, eternal life is foreordained for some, eternal damnation for others. Therefore, as any man has been created to one or the other of these ends, we speak of him as predestined to life or to death.[34]

In the scriptural descriptions of God's purpose of election, a distinction may be drawn between "degrees of election." In the case of the people of Israel, God chose them corporately and granted to them many common blessings and privileges. However, to this general election of Israel as a people, we must "add a second, more limited degree of election, or one in which God's more special grace was evident, that is, when from the same race of Abraham God rejected some but showed that he kept others among his sons by cherishing them in the church."[35] When the apostle Paul speaks of God's "purpose of election" in Romans 9–11, he speaks of this second, proper purpose of God to save a certain number of individuals from among the larger number of the people of Israel.

According to Calvin, God's decision to save some is based entirely on his "freely given mercy," whereas his decision not to save others is based on his "just and irreprehensible but incomprehensible judgment":

> As Scripture, then, clearly shows, we say that God once established by his eternal and unchangeable plan those whom he long before determined once for all to receive into salvation, and those whom, on the other hand, he would devote to destruction. We assert that,

---

33. Ibid., 3.21.
34. Ibid., 3.21.5.
35. Ibid., 2.21.6.

with respect to the elect, this plan was founded upon his freely given mercy, without regard to human worth; but by his just and irreprehensible but incomprehensible judgment he has barred the door of life to those whom he has given over to damnation.[36]

When the apostle Paul treats the doctrine of election in Romans 9–11, he ascribes the salvation of some to God's undeserved mercy, which is revealed in his purpose of election, and he ascribes the nonsalvation of others to God's just decision to leave them in their sins. Contrary to those who affirmed election but not reprobation, Calvin argued that

> it will be highly absurd to say that others acquire by chance or obtain by their own effort what election alone confers on a few. Therefore, those whom God passes over, he condemns; and this he does for no other reason than that he wills to exclude them from the inheritance which he predestines for his own children.[37]

Although there is not an exact symmetry between election and reprobation—election reveals God's undeserved mercy, reprobation reveals God's justice in leaving some in their sin—the ultimate explanation for the salvation of some and not others rests in God's electing purpose.

In the concluding chapter of his relatively brief exposition of the doctrine of predestination in the *Institutes*, Calvin identified and responded to several common objections against the doctrine. Among these objections, two are of special importance.

The first objection Calvin considered was the claim that this doctrine makes God out to be a "tyrant." Against this objection, Calvin insisted that the will of God is perfectly just, even as God is just and is himself the standard of all righteousness. Though we may not be able to fathom the depths of God's will, we may not regard it as arbitrary or unjust. When God chooses not to save some, it must always be remembered that the "cause" of their condemnation lies in themselves.[38]

---

36. Ibid., 3.21.7.
37. Ibid., 3.23.1. In this passage, Calvin clearly has in view the Lutheran position, which affirms election but not reprobation.
38. Ibid., 3.23.3: "Let them not accuse God of injustice if they are destined by his eternal judgment to death, to which they feel—whether they will or not—that they are led by their own nature of itself. How perverse is their disposition to protest is apparent from the fact that they deliberately suppress the cause of condemnation, which they are compelled to recognize in themselves, in order to free themselves by blaming God."

The second objection was that the doctrine of election takes the "guilt and responsibility" away from sinners in respect to their salvation. According to this objection, if God's will is the ultimate reason for the nonsalvation of the reprobate, then "why should God impute those things to men as sin, the necessity of which he has imposed by his predestination?"[39] In his reply to this objection, Calvin did not hesitate to insist that the nonsalvation of some sinners is due to God's foreordination, and that even the fall of the human race into sin was a result of God's decree.[40] For Calvin, it was not enough to say that God simply "permitted" Adam's fall or that the nonsalvation of the reprobate had no other explanation than their own willful sinfulness. While it is true that the "cause and occasion" for the nonsalvation of the reprobate must be "found in themselves," Calvin declared, "I shall not hesitate, then, simply to confess with Augustine that 'the will of God is the necessity of things,' and that what he has willed will of necessity come to pass, as those things which he has foreseen will truly come to pass."[41] We must acknowledge that "man falls according as God's providence ordains, but he falls by his own fault."[42] God does indeed justly and freely determine not to save some. But this must not become the occasion for removing from the sinner the blame for his or her condemnation:

> By his own evil intention, then, man corrupted the pure nature he had received from the Lord; and by his fall he drew all his posterity with him into destruction. Accordingly, we should contemplate the evident cause of condemnation in the corrupt nature of humanity—which is closer to us—rather than seek a hidden and utterly incomprehensible cause in God's predestination.[43]

In Calvin's exposition of the doctrine of election, he placed special emphasis on the comfort that believers may derive from this doctrine.

---

39. Ibid., 3.23.6.
40. Muller notes, "Unlike many of his contemporaries and successors, Calvin did not shrink from the conclusion that permission and volition are one in the mind of an eternal and utterly sovereign God: reprobation could not be viewed simply as a passive act of God. . . . Nevertheless, in view of Calvin's emphasis on knowledge of God, reprobation does not appear the exact coordinate of election." *Christ and the Decree*, 24–25.
41. Calvin, *Institutes*, 3.23.8.
42. Ibid., 3.23.9.
43. Ibid., 3.23.3.

The doctrine of predestination and election must be handled judiciously and in a way that not only ascribes glory to God for his free grace in Christ but also comforts believers and assures them of the certainty of their salvation. Since God's purpose of election is made known through the gracious call of the gospel, Christ is the "mirror" of our election. Only as believers place their trust in Christ will they find the comfort and assurance that election properly affords them:

> If we seek God's fatherly mercy and kindly heart, we should turn our eyes to Christ, on whom alone God's Spirit rests. . . . Accordingly, those whom God has adopted as his sons are said to have been chosen not in themselves but in his Christ; for unless he could love them in him, he could not honor them with the inheritance of his Kingdom if they had not previously become partakers of him. But if we have been chosen in him, we shall not find assurance of our election in ourselves; and not even in God the Father, if we conceive him as severed from his Son. Christ, then, is the mirror wherein we must, and without self-deception may, contemplate our own election.[44]

As Calvin understood it, the scriptural teaching regarding predestination especially emphasizes that believers are saved by God's grace alone, and it affords believers a solid basis for the assurance of God's favor.

PREDESTINATION IN THE THEOLOGY OF HEINRICH BULLINGER

Unlike John Calvin, who is commonly regarded as the leading theologian of the Reformed churches in the sixteenth century, Heinrich Bullinger is viewed as a "Reformer in the wings."[45] Bullinger, who

---

44. Ibid., 3.24.5. Calvin's emphasis on the comfort of the doctrine of predestination is a common theme among the Reformed theologians of the period. Predestination, in a manner similar to the doctrine of justification by faith alone, is a teaching that simultaneously honors God's initiative of grace in salvation and undergirds the believer's confidence in that grace. By contrast, the Roman Catholic Church at the Council of Trent rejected the possibility of such assurance for believers unless by way of exception one is given a "special revelation" of God's electing grace: "No one, moreover, so long as he is in this mortal life, ought so far to presume as regards the secret mystery of divine predestination, as to determine for certain that he is assuredly in the number of the predestinate; as if it were true, that he that is justified, either can not sin any more, or, if he do sin, that he ought to promise himself an assured repentance; for except by special revelation, it can not be known whom God hath chosen unto himself." In Schaff, *Creeds of Christendom*, 2:103.

45. This language derives from David C. Steinmetz's *Reformers in the Wings* (Philadelphia: Fortress, 1971). For a useful introduction to Bullinger's reformatory work and thought, see Bruce

succeeded Zwingli as the leading pastor of the Reformed churches in Zurich, is nonetheless a fitting figure to include in this survey of the doctrine of predestination in Reformation theology. Next to Calvin, no Reformed theologian was more influential during the sixteenth century. And on the doctrine of predestination, Bullinger offers a more moderately stated version of classic Augustinianism than that of Calvin.

In studies of Reformation theology, Bullinger's doctrine of predestination has elicited considerable controversy.[46] Since Bullinger expressed reservations about Calvin's formulations and declined to come strongly to Calvin's defense in the Bolsec controversy,[47] interpreters of Bullinger have debated whether he differed substantially from Calvin on the doctrine of predestination. Some have even argued that Bullinger privileged the doctrine of the covenant over that of election and was the "fountainhead" of an alternative theological tradition to that stemming from Calvin.[48] While I do not believe there are substantial, or insuperable, differences between Bullinger and Calvin, there is no doubt that Bullinger expressed himself more reservedly on this doctrine.

The best source for ascertaining Bullinger's mature teaching on the doctrine of predestination and election is the Second Helvetic Confession (*Confessio helvetica posterior*). Although Bullinger wrote on the topic of predestination on several occasions throughout his life, the

---

Gordon and Emidio Campi, eds., *Architect of Reformation: An Introduction to Heinrich Bullinger, 1504–1575*, Texts and Studies in Reformation and Post-Reformation Thought (Grand Rapids, MI: Baker Academic, 2004).

46. For general studies of Bullinger's doctrine of predestination, which provide an account of the debate regarding the compatibility of his view with that of Calvin, see Cornelis P. Venema, *Heinrich Bullinger and the Doctrine of Predestination: Author of 'the Other Reformed Tradition'?*, Texts and Studies in Reformation and Post-Reformation Thought (Grand Rapids, MI: Baker Academic, 2002); Muller, *Christ and the Decree*, 39–47; and Peter Walser, *Die Prädestination bei Heinrich Bullinger im Zussamenhang mit seiner Gotteslehre* (Zurich: Zwingli Verlag, 1957).

47. The controversy over the doctrine of predestination in Geneva commenced when Jerome Bolsec, an ex-Carmelite monk and physician, publicly attacked Calvin's doctrine of predestination on October 16, 1551. For original source materials and treatments of the controversy, see Philip E. Hughes, *The Register of the Company of the Pastors of Geneva in the Time of Calvin* (Grand Rapids, MI: Eerdmans, 1966), 133–86; Philip C. Holtrop, *The Bolsec Controversy on Predestination, From 1551–1555: The Statements of Jerome Bolsec, and the Response of John Calvin, Theodore Beza, and Other Reformed Theologians*, vol. 1, bks. 1 and 2, *Theological Currents, the Setting and Mood, and the Trial Itself* (Lewiston, NY: Edwin Mellen, 1993); and Venema, *Heinrich Bullinger*, 58–63.

48. J. Wayne Baker, *Heinrich Bullinger and the Covenant: The Other Reformed Tradition* (Athens: Ohio University Press, 1980). My study *Heinrich Bullinger and the Doctrine of Predestination* offers an extensive and critical assessment of the claim that Bullinger authored another Reformed tradition that privileged the doctrine of covenant over that of election.

Second Helvetic Confession sets forth themes that Bullinger consistently emphasized when treating this doctrine. This confession, which
Bullinger probably began to write in 1561,[49] contains a comprehensive
summary of his understanding of the Reformed faith. Bullinger wrote
the Second Helvetic Confession not only as a statement of his personal
confession but also as a summary and defense of the "catholic" faith
of the Reformed churches. When he first penned this confession, Bullinger intended that it be affixed to his will as a kind of bequest to the
Reformed churches that he had served as pastor. Little could he have
anticipated the extent to which the Confession would be received and
embraced among the Reformed churches on the Continent.[50]

In the sequence of topics treated in his confession, Bullinger took
up the doctrine of predestination in a separate chapter, which follows
chapters on the doctrines of providence, the fall into sin, and the freedom of the will, and which precedes a chapter on the person and work
of Christ. Thus, the doctrine of predestination is framed between the
topics of human sinfulness and God's gracious purpose to save his
people in Christ. Predestination and election belong not to the doctrine
of theology proper but to the doctrines of soteriology and Christology.
By virtue of this arrangement of topics, Bullinger's presentation of the
doctrine of predestination is infralapsarian in form. God's gracious
election answers the need of fallen sinners, who are incapable of restoring themselves to favor with God or taking the initiative in response to
the gospel's call to faith.[51]

God's work of redemption finds its ultimate source in God's election
to save his people in Christ. Only the monergism of sovereign electing
grace can redress the situation of fallen human beings, whose wills,

---

49. Ernst Koch, "Die Textüberlieferung Der Confessio Helvetica Posterior Und Ihre Vorge-
schichte," in *Glauben und Bekennen: Vierhundert Jahre Confessio Helvetica Posterior*, ed. Joachim
Staedtke (Zurich: Zwingli Verlag, 1966), 17.

50. The Second Helvetic Confession was translated into fifteen languages and published in more
than 115 editions. It is arguably the most widely disseminated of the Reformed symbols of the sixteenth century. The English translations in what follows are taken from *The Book of Confessions*,
2nd ed. (Office of the General Assembly of the United Presbyterian Church in the United States of
America, 1970). In the following, I will cite the confession by chapter. The Latin text of the Second
Helvetic Confession can be found in Wilhelm Niesel, *Bekenntnisschriften und Kirchenordnungen
der nach Gottes Wort reformierten Kirche* (Zurich: A. G. Zollikon, 1938), 219–75.

51. "The Second Helvetic Confession," chap. 9: "For the evangelical and apostolic Scripture
requires regeneration of whoever among us wishes to be saved. Hence our first birth from Adam
contributes nothing to our salvation. . . . Wherefore, man not yet regenerate has no free will for
good, no strength to perform what is good."

though free from any external compulsion to evil, have no capacity to perform what is good. Predestination is defined as God's election to save his people *in Christ* and is not treated within the context of the divine decree as an aspect of the doctrine of God. Breaking from the traditional order of theological topics followed by Thomas Aquinas and earlier scholasticism, Bullinger viewed predestination not simply as a special providence (*providentia specialis*) but as the fountainhead of God's saving work in Christ. For Bullinger, predestination answered the question, How can fallen sinners, who have no free will or capability of responding in faith to the gospel on their own, be saved through faith in Christ?[52] The only explanation for the salvation of those who embrace the gospel promise in Christ is that God has freely chosen to grant them salvation and to grant faith through the work of the Holy Spirit with the gospel.

Although the doctrine of predestination includes, at least formally, the two elements of election and reprobation, Bullinger particularly emphasized the positive expression of God's decree, the election of some to salvation in Christ: "From eternity God has freely, and of his mere grace, without any respect to men, predestined or elected the saints whom he wills to save in Christ."[53] Elaborating on this definition of predestination, which focuses on God's gracious purpose to save the elect in Christ, Bullinger closely associated election with the person and work of Christ. Christ is not only the Mediator who provides for the salvation of the elect but also the ground and source of God's electing grace. According to Bullinger, those whom God predestines are elect, "not directly, but in Christ, and on account of Christ, in order that those who are now ingrafted into Christ by faith might also be

---

52. As Muller states, "Juxtaposition of predestination with sin and the problem of the will represents a powerful affirmation of soteriological monergism: human inability answered directly by the electing will of God." *Christ and the Decree*, 44. Of special importance in the Confession's treatment of anthropology is Bullinger's comment on "curious questions" (*curiosae quaestiones*) that arise in considering Adam's fall into sin: "Other questions, such as whether God willed Adam to fall, and similar questions we reckon among curious questions (unless perchance the wickedness of heretics, or of other churlish men compels us also to explain them out of the Word of God, as the godly teachers of the Church have frequently done), knowing that the Lord forbade man to eat of the forbidden fruit and punished his transgression." "The Second Helvetic Confession," chap. 8. In this statement, Bullinger obliquely criticized Calvin's inclusion of the fall within God's decree and echoed an argument that he had previously advanced in his correspondence with Calvin during the controversy with Bolsec.

53. "The Second Helvetic Confession," chap. 10.

elected."[54] With this language, Bullinger did not intend to suggest that God's gracious election is on the ground of faith. Even though there is a close correlation between election and the believer's union with Christ by faith, faith itself is God's gift to the elect that enables them to have fellowship with Christ.[55] Consistent with his emphasis on the positive expression of God's predestination of the elect unto salvation, Bullinger offered only one observation about reprobation, namely, describing the reprobate as those who are "outside of Christ."[56] Though it might be possible to infer from God's election of some to salvation that this logically entails the nonelection or reprobation of others, Bullinger was content to note simply that they are reprobate on account of their not having fellowship with Christ.

After defining the doctrine of predestination as God's free election of his people in and on account of Christ, Bullinger turned to pastoral questions that often surface in respect to God's purpose of election. With respect to the question concerning the scope of election, Bullinger emphasized that "we must hope well of all and not rashly judge any man to be a reprobate."[57] Rather than speculating about the relative number of the elect, whether they be few or many, we should encourage everyone to "strive to enter by the narrow door" (Luke 13:24). Although Bullinger did not use the expression in the Second Helvetic Confession, his insistence both that no one be rashly considered reprobate and that believers hold out hope for all reflects his frequent claim that God is a "lover of man" (*philanthrōpos*) who bears malice toward no one. And although he did not explicitly speak of the universal promises of God, he did speak of God's promises "which apply to all the faithful" and ought to be the occasion for the believer's confidence before God.[58]

Bullinger concluded his consideration of election by addressing the important question of the believer's assurance or knowledge of election. Consistent with the close and intimate conjunction of election with Christ, Bullinger noted that the believer's relationship with Christ

54. Ibid.
55. Ibid.
56. Ibid. The Latin reads, "Reprobi vero, qui sunt extra Christum."
57. Ibid.
58. Ibid.

is the basis for any assurance of election. We may not ask whether or not we are elect from eternity "outside of Christ" (*extra Christum*).[59] Rather, we are called to believe through the preaching of the gospel promise in Christ. For "it is to be held as beyond doubt that if you believe and are in Christ, you are elected."[60] For Bullinger, "being elect" and "being in Christ" were correlated, just as "being rejected" and "being outside of Christ" through unbelief were correlated. Employing imagery used by Calvin to answer the question of having assurance of election, Bullinger asserted, "Let Christ, therefore, be the looking glass [*speculum*], in whom we may contemplate our predestination. We shall have a sufficient and clear testimony that we are inscribed in the Book of life if we have fellowship with Christ, and he is ours and we are his in true faith."[61] It is in this sense of our election being joined to our fellowship with Christ that admonitions are not in vain. As Augustine has shown, "both the grace of free election and predestination, and also salutary admonitions and doctrines, are to be preached."[62] Consequently, Bullinger concluded his discussion of predestination and election with Saint Paul's admonition to work out our salvation with fear and trembling.

Though Bullinger demonstrated greater reserve in the Second Helvetic Confession than in some prior instances in his consideration of the subject of reprobation—his definition of predestination there speaks only of election, not reprobation—his reluctance to draw a direct connection between God's will and the condemnation of those who are outside Christ certainly follows a pattern evident in his other writings. The pastoral quality of Bullinger's handling of the doctrine is also evident in the way the Second Helvetic Confession stresses such themes as the good hope believers should have for the salvation of all sinners, not rashly judging anyone a reprobate; the erroneous assumption that the number of the elect is only few; the importance of

---

59. Ibid.

60. Ibid.

61. Ibid. The Latin reads, "Christus itaque sit speculum, in quo praedestinationem nostram contemplemur. Satis perspicuum et firmum habebimus testimonium, nos in libro vitae inscriptos esse, si communicaverimus cum Christo, et is in vera fide noster sit, nos eius simus." Cf. Calvin, *Institutes*, 3.24.5.

62. "The Second Helvetic Confession," chap. 10. As in his other writings on the subject of predestination, Bullinger's references to Augustine's writings show that he stands in the Augustinian exegetical and theological tradition.

the means God uses in the accomplishment of his saving purposes; and the assurance of election through fellowship with Christ. Though these themes were by no means unique to Bullinger's formulation of the doctrine of predestination among the Reformed theologians of the mid-sixteenth century, including Calvin, the pastoral and homiletical manner in which Bullinger treated the doctrine of predestination in the Second Helvetic Confession bears many telltale traces of his distinctive view.[63]

PREDESTINATION IN THE THEOLOGY OF HULDRYCH ZWINGLI AND PETER MARTYR VERMIGLI

While our survey of the doctrine of predestination among Reformed theologians in the sixteenth century has focused on Calvin and Bullinger, a number of other influential figures addressed the doctrine in their writings. Two of these theologians, Huldrych Zwingli and Peter Martyr Vermigli, deserve brief attention.

Zwingli's treatment of predestination is located within the framework of the doctrine of God's providence. In his most important treatment of the doctrine, Zwingli began with a general definition of providence: "Providence is the enduring and unchangeable rule over and direction of all things in the universe."[64] God is the good, wise, and just Ruler and Sustainer of all things, so that nothing takes place in the course of history that lies outside his providential care and rule. According to Zwingli, "God is all-knowing, all-powerful, and good.

---

63. For a discussion of how two of Calvin's contemporaries, Wolfgang Musculus (1497–1563) and Peter Martyr Vermigli (1499–1562), treated the doctrine of predestination, see Muller, *Christ and the Decree*, 39–75. While Muller finds these theologians employing a more "scholastic form" in their handling of the doctrine, he rejects the claim that this form materially affects their understanding of predestination or represents a movement away from Calvin's close association of the doctrine with Christology and soteriology. As in Calvin and Bullinger's theology, "predestination and Christology both serve to focus and to ground the soteriological structure and themselves both develop out of the context of an overarching concern to delineate the pattern of divine working in the economy of salvation." *Christ and the Decree*, 68. For Musculus's doctrine of predestination, see Wolfgang Musculus, *Common Places of Christian Religion* (London: R. Wolfe, 1563, 1578); Musculus, *Loci communes sacrae theologiae* (Basel: Johannes Hervagius, 1560, 1568, 1573). For Vermigli's doctrine, see *The Common Places of D. Peter Martyr Vermigli* (London: Denham, 1583); Vermigli, *Loci Communes D. Petri Martyris Vermigli* (London, 1576; rev. ed. 1583); Frank A. James III, *Peter Martyr Vermigli and Predestination: The Augustinian Inheritance of an Italian Reformer*, Oxford Theological Monographs (Oxford: Clarendon, 1998).

64. Huldrych Zwingli, *On Providence and Other Essays*, ed. William John Hinke (1922; repr., Durham, NC: Labyrinth, 1983), 136. For a survey of Zwingli's doctrine of predestination, see Gottfried W. Locher, *Zwingli's Thought: New Perspectives*, Studies in the History of Christian Thought 25 (Leiden: Brill, 1981), 121–41.

Hence nothing escapes His notice, nothing evades His orders and His sway, nothing which He does is anything but good."[65] Predestination is the aspect of God's providence that pertains to God's good and gracious will to grant salvation to the elect. In the strictest sense, predestination focuses especially on God's gracious election, which displays his undeserved mercy toward those whom he is pleased to save from the fallen human race, and not on his determination to leave others in their lost condition. Whereas gracious election especially displays God's mercy, God's determination not to save the nonelect displays his justice. Consequently, Zwingli defined election as "the free disposition of the divine will in regard to those that are to be blessed."[66] Though God's gracious election has as a corollary the nonelection of those whom God righteously condemns by leaving them in their sins, Zwingli clearly distinguished this feature of God's providence from his merciful and good election of some unto salvation. In spite of Zwingli's reluctance to treat God's determination not to save some as parallel to God's determination to save the elect, his decision to formulate the doctrine of election within the context of God's providential determination of all things troubled his successor, Bullinger.[67] Because Zwingli located his treatment of predestination in the context of his emphasis on God's all-inclusive providence, Bullinger feared that his doctrine did not sufficiently emphasize God's goodness and grace in the election of his people in Christ.

Peter Martyr Vermigli's doctrine of predestination is also worthy of notice.[68] Vermigli was one of a number of influential Italian theologians (including his good friend Girolamo Zanchius) who exercised an important influence on the early development of the Reformed theological

---

65. Zwingli, *On Providence*, 180.

66. Ibid., 184.

67. Bullinger expressed his concern regarding Zwingli's doctrine of providence in his correspondence with Calvin regarding the controversy over Jerome Bolsec's doctrine of predestination in Geneva. When Bolsec criticized Calvin's teaching, he argued that his view of predestination was similar to that of Bullinger. In his correspondence with Calvin, Bullinger expressed dissatisfaction with Calvin and Zwingli's incautious statements on the subject of predestination and providence. For a review of this correspondence, see Venema, *Heinrich Bullinger*, 58–63.

68. The most comprehensive treatment of Vermigli's life and writings remains C. Schmidt, *Peter Martyr Vermigli, Leben und ausgewählte Schriften* (Elberfeld: R. L. Friderichs, 1858). For a brief sketch of his life, see David C. Steinmetz, "Peter Martyr Vermigli," in *Reformers in the Wings*, 151–61. For a summary of his correspondence with Bullinger, see Marvin W. Anderson, "Peter Martyr, Reformed Theologian (1542–1562): His Letters to Heinrich Bullinger and John Calvin," *SCJ* 4, no. 1 (1973): 41–64.

tradition.[69] The most important statement of Vermigli's doctrine of predestination is provided in his *Loci Communes*, a collection of Vermigli's lectures, treatises, and disputations that was posthumously published by Robert Masson in 1576.[70] Masson organized these writings according to the order of Calvin's *Institutes*, though without distorting the basic structure of Vermigli's thought.[71] In his treatment of the doctrine of predestination, Vermigli followed a far more "scholastic" and rationalistic pattern than the one we have witnessed thus far in Calvin and Bullinger's writings.[72] He began with an introductory discussion of two matters: the suitability of the doctrine of predestination for preaching and teaching, and the "logician's question" of whether or not there is a divine predestination.[73] Only after addressing these matters and offering a defense against the objection that predestination leads to a doctrine of "fatal necessity" (*necessitatem quidem fatalem*)[74] did Vermigli take up directly the subject of predestination. In doing so, he began with a broad and general statement of predestination and then spoke of a positive will of God in election and a negative or permissive will of God in reprobation.

In his initial definition of predestination, Vermigli maintained that God in his divine counsel (*consilium*) destined or appointed all things to their particular end.[75] Though the divine counsel includes the election of some and the reprobation of others, Vermigli proceeded to link divine predestination most especially with election and formulated the doctrine of reprobation with the use of the scholastic doctrine of God's "permissive" or "passive" will. In his formal definition of predestina-

69. For more recent treatments of Vermigli's doctrine of predestination, particularly within the framework of his Aristotelian scholasticism, see John Patrick Donnelly, *Calvinism and Scholasticism in Vermigli's Doctrine of Man and Grace*, Studies in Medieval and Reformation Thought 18 (Leiden: Brill, 1976), esp. 3–41, 116–49; Muller, *Christ and the Decree*, 57–75; J. C. McClelland, "The Reformed Doctrine of Predestination: According to Peter Martyr," *SJT* 8, no. 3 (1955): 255–71; James, *Vermigli and Predestination*; Frank A. James III, "Peter Martyr Vermigli: At the Crossroads of Late Medieval Scholasticism, Christian Humanism and Resurgent Augustinianism," in Trueman and Clark, *Protestant Scholasticism*, 62–78.
70. Vermigli, *Loci communes*. References to Vermigli's treatise on predestination in the following notes are from the revised edition of 1583.
71. Thus Muller, *Christ and the Decree*, 58.
72. Donnelly and James document the influence on Vermigli's thought of Aquinas and Scotus among the scholastics and of the more explicitly developed doctrine in Gregory of Rimini and Martin Bucer among the Reformers. Donnelly, *Calvinism and Scholasticism*, 125–29; James, "Peter Martyr Vermigli," 52–78.
73. Vermigli, *Loci communes*, 3.1.1.
74. Ibid., 3.1.5.
75. Ibid., 3.1.5.

tion, Vermigli emphasized God's counsel to exhibit his love toward his own in Christ:

> I say, therefore, that predestination is the most wise counsel [*pro-positum*] of God by which he has decreed firmly from before all eternity to call those whom he has loved in Christ to the adoption of sons, to be justified by faith; and subsequently to glorify through good works, those who shall be conformed to the image of the Son of God, that in them the glory and mercy of the Creator might be declared.[76]

By contrast, in his definition of reprobation, Vermigli maintained that, though it had its source in the divine will from eternity, it was a passive act of God in which he withheld his love from the nonelect. He accordingly denied a direct or efficient will of God in reprobation. Those whom God chose not to save are fallen sinners whom he passed by in the divine decree. Thus, Vermigli defined reprobation as God's decree in eternity "not to have mercy on those whom he has not loved."[77]

Though this represents only a sketch of Vermigli's doctrine of predestination, it illustrates some of the differences between Vermigli's doctrine and the one Bullinger espoused. Unlike Bullinger, Vermigli cast the doctrine of predestination in a far more scholastic form, exhibiting considerable dependence on a Thomist construction of the divine counsel with its distinction between God's "efficient" and "permissive" will. Vermigli, in his careful and extended exposition of the divine will, insisted that all things fall within the scope of the divine counsel, whether by way of direct and positive willing or by way of indirect or permissive willing. He was also prepared to develop more explicitly the decree of reprobation, linking it with God's passive will and acknowledging that it parallels in some, though not all, respects God's decree of election. In these emphases, he exhibited a willingness to explore rather explicitly and fully, in the manner of the scholastic tradition, the diverse aspects of the divine counsel. In so doing, he distinguished himself from the more cautious and restrained handling

---

76. Ibid., 3.1.11. Translation by James, "Peter Martyr Vermigli," 75.
77. Vermigli, *Loci communes*, 3.1.5.

of the doctrine by Bullinger, at least as represented by the sources we have considered here.

However, it should also be noted that Vermigli's doctrine approximated Bullinger's in some respects more than that of Calvin. For example, he shared Bullinger's basically infralapsarian presentation of predestination: God's election to save some assumes the fall of all men into sin (*homo creatus et lapsus*). Also, by linking predestination positively with election and only passively with reprobation, he shared Bullinger's resistance to positing any direct connection between God's will and the nonsalvation of the reprobate. The fact that some are not saved cannot be ascribed to God's efficient will; they are merely left in their fallen condition, a condition for which God bears no ultimate responsibility. God's will in relation to the reprobate is merely passive, not active.[78] Similarly, with Bullinger, Vermigli resisted any attempt to draw a positive connection between God's predestination and the fall of Adam into sin.

PREDESTINATION IN THE REFORMED CONFESSIONS

Undoubtedly, the most important sources for ascertaining the Reformed doctrine of predestination in the sixteenth century are the official confessions that were adopted by the Reformed churches. In addition to the Second Helvetic Confession, discussed above with reference to Bullinger, the following confessions offer insight into the Reformed understanding of the doctrine toward the close of the first, and most formative, period of the Reformation: the Gallican (French) Confession of 1559, the Scots Confession of 1560, the Heidelberg Catechism of 1563, and the Belgic Confession of 1567. In each of these confessions, the doctrine of predestination is set forth in order to underscore the doctrinal themes of human inability, salvation by grace alone through the work of Christ, the eternal purpose that underlies God's gracious provision for salvation in Christ, and the comfort that this teaching affords the believer. In the interest of brevity, I will cite the most im-

---

78. As Muller states, "Reprobation remains a negative will, a decision to withhold mediation and to leave some men to a fate of their own making. Clearly, the scholastic foundation of Vermigli's argument is not the cause of a more rigid formulation of predestination but of a less overtly deterministic conception of the decrees." *Christ and the Decree*, 66. Muller correctly makes this point against the claim of John Patrick Donnelly that Vermigli's doctrine of predestination was more strict than that of Calvin. "Calvinist Thomism," *Viator* 7 (1976): 445, 448.

portant statements of the doctrine in these confessions and will then offer a synthesis of their common teaching.[79]

> The Gallican Confession: "We believe that from this corruption and general condemnation in which all men are plunged, God, according to his eternal and immutable counsel, calleth those whom he hath chosen by his goodness and mercy alone in our Lord Jesus Christ, without consideration of their works, to display in them the riches of his mercy; leaving the rest in this same corruption and condemnation to show in them his justice."[80]

> The Scots Confession: "The same eternal God and Father, who by grace alone chose us in his Son Christ Jesus before the foundation of the world was laid, appointed him to be our head, our brother, our pastor, and the great bishop of our souls."[81]

> The Heidelberg Catechism: "What do you believe concerning the *holy catholic church*? That the Son of God, out of the whole human race, from the beginning to the end of the world, gathers, defends, and preserves for Himself, by His Spirit and Word, in the unity of the true faith, a Church chosen to everlasting life; and that I am, and forever shall remain, a living member thereof."[82]

> The Belgic Confession: "We believe that, all the posterity of Adam being thus fallen into perdition and ruin by the sin of our first parents, God then did manifest Himself such as He is; that is to say, merciful and just: merciful, since He delivers and preserves from this perdition all whom He in His eternal and unchangeable counsel of mere goodness has elected in Christ Jesus our Lord, without any respect to their works; just, in leaving others in the fall and perdition wherein they have involved themselves."[83]

---

79. For a more complete exposition of the Reformed confessions on the doctrine of predestination, see Jan Rohls, *Reformed Confessions: Theology from Zurich to Barmen*, trans. John Hoffmeyer, Columbia Series in Reformed Theology (Louisville: Westminster John Knox, 1998), 148–66.

80. "The Gallican Confession," art. 12, in Schaff, *The Creeds of Christendom*, 3:366–67.

81. "The Scots Confession," 3.08, in *Book of Confessions*. Though the doctrine of predestination in the Scots Confession is stated moderately and focuses only on God's gracious election of believers in Christ, it is noteworthy that John Knox, one of its principal authors, wrote a lengthy, strong defense of predestination: *An answer to a great number of blasphemous cauillations written by an Anabaptist, and aduersarie to Gods eternal predestination* (Geneva: Crespin, 1560).

82. "The Heidelberg Catechism," in *The Good Confession: Ecumenical Creeds and Reformed Confessions* (Dyer, IN: Mid-America Reformed Seminary, 2013), 103.

83. "The Belgic Confession," art. 16, in *Good Confession*, 41.

These confessional statements share several common themes. All of them view the person and work of Christ, not only in the provision of salvation but also in its communication to believers by the work of his Spirit, to be rooted in God's eternal purpose of election. They also start from the conviction that all human beings are fallen in Adam and are unwilling and incapable of turning toward God in faith and repentance, unless God draws them according to his mercy and grace. The doctrine of predestination focuses primarily on God's merciful election to save his people. Although the doctrine includes both a decree of election and reprobation (*gemina praedestinationis*), there is an asymmetry between these two aspects of God's counsel. Election involves God's positive and merciful decision in and for the sake of Christ to save his people. Reprobation involves God's just decision to "leave" others in their sins, and to condemn them for their own sinfulness. Without broaching the more speculative question of the relative order of the elements within God's decree, these confessions represent the doctrine of predestination in a decidedly "infralapsarian" manner: the decree contemplates the human race in its fallen condition so that the proper occasion and cause for the condemnation of the reprobate is their own sin and unworthiness. Furthermore, the two primary themes that the doctrine of predestination accentuates are the glory of God, who alone authors the salvation of believers, and the comfort of believers, who may confidently rest in the assurance of God's grace and mercy as they are revealed in the gospel.

Predestination in Early Reformed Orthodoxy

After the initial codification of the doctrine of predestination in the Reformed confessions of the mid-sixteenth century, several important theologians articulated the doctrine in the period of early Reformed orthodoxy. Though these theologians continued the earlier period's diversity of formulation, they generally reflected a more developed and "scholastic" formulation of the doctrine of predestination and the decrees of God.[84] In doing so, they set the stage for the early seventeenth-

---

84. In addition to Musculus and Vermigli, two contemporaries of Calvin who treated the doctrine of predestination in a more "scholastic" fashion, another important transitional figure in the development of early Reformed orthodoxy was Girolamo Zanchius. For treatments of Zanchius's doctrine of predestination, see Muller, *Christ and the Decree*, 110–25; Venema, *Heinrich Bullinger*, 79–86.

century controversies among the Reformed churches, which were addressed at the Synod of Dort in 1618–1619 and the Westminster Assembly in 1643–1645.[85] Since the confessions produced by these seventeenth-century assemblies of the Reformed churches take us beyond the sixteenth century, I will merely identify three important topics that emerged during this period.

First, in this period the precise order of the elements of God's decree became a topic for theological discussion, especially in the writings of Theodore Beza and William Perkins, two theologians who vigorously defended the Reformed doctrine of predestination.[86] While Reformed theologians exhibited no significant difference of opinion on the order in which God's purpose was executed in history, the distinction between infralapsarianism and supralapsarianism reflected two different views of the order of the distinct elements that are included within God's eternal decree. Whereas infralapsarianism views God's decree to elect or not elect to salvation as "below" (*infra*) or logically subsequent to his decree to permit the fall into sin (*lapsus*), supralapsarianism views God's decree of predestination as "above" (*supra*) or logically prior to his decree regarding the fall. In the infralapsarian position, the objects of God's decree are created and are fallen sinners (*homo creatus et lapsus*); in the supralapsarian position, the objects of God's decree are uncreated and are unfallen sinners (*homo creabilis et labilis*). The order of the elements in God's decree in the infralapsarian scheme is as follows:

1. The decree to glorify himself in the creation of the human race
2. The decree to permit the fall

85. For a survey of this period and the debates regarding the doctrine of predestination, see Rouwendal, "Predestination in Reformed Orthodoxy," 568–89.

86. For Beza's doctrine of predestination, see Theodore Beza, *Tabula Praedestinationis* (Geneva, 1555); John S. Bray, *Theodore Beza's Doctrine of Predestination*, Bibliotheca Humanistica & Reformatorica 12 (Nieuwkoop: De Graaf, 1975); Muller, *Christ and the Decree*, 79–96; Muller, "Use and Abuse of a Document," 33–61. For Perkins's doctrine of predestination, see William Perkins, *The Workes of . . . Mr. William Perkins*, vol. 2, *A Golden Chaine, or the Description of Theologie*, and *A Treatise of the Manner and Order of Predestination* (Cambridge, 1612–1619); Muller, *Christ and the Decree*, 149–71; Muller, "Perkins' *A Golden Chaine*: Predestinarian System or Schematized Ordo Salutis?," *SCJ* 9, no. 1 (1978): 69–81. Perkins's *A Golden Chaine* was written as an elaboration of Beza's *Tabula Praedestinationis*. In his assessment of Perkins's scholastic elaboration of the doctrine of predestination, Muller concludes that "though the statement of the doctrine of predestination has become more elaborate in a scholastic sense and, indeed, more speculative in terms of its statement of logical priorities, it has not become more deterministic than that of Calvin, nor has it become any less christologically oriented." *Christ and the Decree*, 170.

3. The decree to elect some of the fallen human race to salvation and to pass by others and condemn them for their sins
4. The decree to provide salvation for the elect through Jesus Christ

The order of the elements in God's decree in the supralapsarian scheme is as follows:

1. The decree to glorify himself through the election of some and the nonelection of others
2. The decree to create the elect and the reprobate
3. The decree to permit the fall
4. The decree to provide salvation for the elect through Jesus Christ

While the difference between the infralapsarian and supralapsarian views became an occasion for theological discussion in the period of early Reformed orthodoxy, it is significant that the seventeenth-century confessions that offer the final and most comprehensive codification of the Reformed view, the Canons of Dort and the Westminster Standards, do not grant confessional status to either view. These confessions tend to express the doctrine of predestination in an infralapsarian manner, viewing election as a positive expression of God's will to save some out of the fallen human race and reprobation as a negative expression of God's will to "pass by" others and to condemn them for their sins. The debate regarding the order of the elements within God's decree evidences a more scholastic, even speculative, approach to the doctrine of predestination in the period of early Reformed orthodoxy. However, it did not produce any substantial change in the Reformed tradition's confessional consensus regarding the doctrine.

Second, another topic that emerged in this period was associated with the theology of Theodore Beza (1519–1605), who sought to defend Calvin's doctrine against his critics. In addition to several important works on the doctrine of predestination, Beza was an important transitional figure in later Reformed discussions of the relation between God's purpose of election and the extent or design of Christ's work of atonement. During the course of his conflict with the Lutheran theologian, Jacob Andreae, Beza criticized the traditional formula that

Christ's death was "sufficient for all, but efficient only for the elect."[87] In Beza's estimation, this formula was ambiguously stated, since the preposition "for" in the statement could be variously interpreted. To remove any ambiguity, Beza insisted that Christ's death was intended to provide only for the salvation of the elect. While Beza acknowledged the sufficiency and perfection of the work of Christ, he was among the first to explicitly teach the doctrine of definite or particular atonement. Since Calvin did not explicitly address the question of the extent or design of Christ's work of atonement,[88] at least not in the fashion in which Beza did during this controversy, some students of the history of Reformed theology have raised the question whether the later Reformed doctrine of definite atonement, which was codified in the second head of doctrine of the Canons of Dort, is consistent with the teaching of Calvin and the earlier Reformed tradition. In studies of the development of Reformed theology in this period, the question of the continuity or discontinuity of doctrine between Calvin and later Reformed orthodoxy has been cast as a question of "Calvin and the Calvinists."[89] Some interpreters argue that Beza and theologians of

---

87. For an account of the conflict, see Theodore Beza, *Ad Acta Colloqui Montisbelgardensis Tubingae edita, Theodori Bezae responsionis* (Geneva: Joannes le Preux, 1588); Jill Raitt, *The Colloquy of Montbéliard: Religion and Politics in the Sixteenth Century* (New York: Oxford University Press, 1993). In his defense of Beza's doctrine of predestination, William Perkins also emphasized the divine intention in providing and applying Christ's work of redemption to the elect. See Muller, *Christ and the Decree*, 168.

88. Though Calvin was familiar with the expression "sufficient for all, efficient for the elect" (*pro omnibus . . . sufficientiam; sed pro electis . . . ad efficaciam*), which was found in Peter Lombard's *Sentences*, he did not find it an adequate formulation. See Calvin's comments on 1 John 2:2 in *Calvin's Commentaries* (1844–1856; repr., Grand Rapids, MI: Baker, 1981), 22:173. For treatments of the extent or design of the atonement in Calvin and later Calvinism, see W. Robert Godfrey, "Reformed Thought on the Extent of the Atonement to 1618," *WTJ* 37, no. 2 (1975): 133–71; Pieter L. Rouwendal, "Calvin's Forgotten Classical Position on the Extent of the Atonement: About Efficiency, Sufficiency, and Anachronism," *WTJ* 70, no. 2 (2008): 317–35; G. Michael Thomas, *The Extent of the Atonement: A Dilemma for Reformed Theology from Calvin to the Consensus (1536–1675)*, Paternoster Biblical and Theological Monographs (Carlisle: Paternoster, 1997); Brian G. Armstrong, *Calvinism and the Amyraut Heresy: Protestant Scholasticism and Humanism in Seventeenth-Century France* (Madison: University of Wisconsin Press, 1969); Muller, *Christ and the Decree*, 33–35; Roger Nicole, *Moyse Amyraut (1596–1664) and the Controversy on Universal Grace: First Phase (1634–1637)* (PhD diss., Harvard University, 1966). In my judgment, Muller's comments on the implications of Calvin's view of particular election and the priestly intercession of Christ are especially appropriate: "It is superfluous to speak of a hypothetical extent of the efficacy of Christ's work [in Calvin's theology] beyond its actual application. As shown in the doctrine of election, salvation is not bestowed generally but on individuals. The Gospel appeal is universal but Christ's intercession, like the divine election, is personal, individual, particular." *Christ and the Decree*, 35. Though Calvin did not explicitly address the extent of the atonement in the manner of later writers, it seems evident that his doctrine of predestination and of Christ's work of atonement pointed in this direction.

89. For interpretations of the Reformed tradition that seek to contrast Calvin with later Calvinism, see R. T. Kendall, *Calvin and English Calvinism to 1649* (Oxford: Oxford University Press,

the orthodox period diverged from Calvin's more Christocentric view of predestination. However, the claims of these interpreters who pit Calvin against the later Calvinists have been ably refuted. While the theologians of the orthodox period cast Calvin's doctrine in a more scholastic form, they did not abandon Calvin's emphasis on election in Christ. There are also intimations of the later doctrine of definite atonement in Calvin's writings.[90]

And third, the debate regarding the degree of continuity or discontinuity between Calvin's view of predestination and that of Reformed orthodoxy has highlighted a long-standing question regarding the Reformed tradition's doctrine of predestination: Does the doctrine of predestination, especially in the period of orthodoxy, increasingly take on the character of a "central dogma"? As noted in the introduction to this chapter, several nineteenth- and early twentieth-century interpreters of Reformation theology advanced the thesis that Calvin and the Reformed tradition set forth a predestinarian theology that differed significantly from the Lutheran tradition with its focus on the doctrine of justification.[91] According to these interpreters, the Reformed tradition articulated a theology that began from the starting point of God's sovereign predestinating will. All the elements or topics of the Reformed system of theology were then logically deduced or derived from this point of departure. The doctrine of the decree of God was transmuted into a "decretalism" that subordinated Christology, the study of the person and work of Christ, and pneumatology, the study of the Holy Spirit's communication of the benefits of Christ's work to believers, to the doctrine of God.[92]

Among recent interpreters of the Reformed doctrine of predestina-

1979); Basil Hall, "Calvin against the Calvinists," in *John Calvin: A Collection of Distinguished Essays*, ed. G. E. Duffield, trans. G. S. R. Cox and P. G. Rix, Courtenay Studies in Reformation Theology 1 (Grand Rapids, MI: Eerdmans, 1966), 19–37; Armstrong, *Calvinism and the Amyraut Heresy*. For a compelling refutation of this approach, see Richard A. Muller, "Calvin and the 'Calvinists': Assessing Continuities and Discontinuities between the Reformation and Orthodoxy," Part 1, *CTJ* 30, no. 2 (1995): 345–75, and Part 2, *CTJ* 31, no. 1 (1996): 125–60; Muller, *The Unaccommodated Calvin: Studies in the Foundation of a Theological Tradition*, Oxford Studies in Historical Theology (New York: Oxford University Press, 2000), 3–8; Muller, *Christ and the Decree*, esp. 175–82; Paul Helm, *Calvin and the Calvinists* (Edinburgh: Banner of Truth, 1982); Carl R. Trueman, "Calvin and Calvinism," in *The Cambridge Companion to John Calvin*, ed. Donald K. McKim (Cambridge: Cambridge University Press, 2004), 225–44.
    90. See Muller, *Christ and the Decree*, 35, 175–82.
    91. See note 29 above.
    92. See Richard A. Muller, "The Myth of 'Decretal Theology,'" *CTJ* 30, no. 1 (1995): 159–67.

tion, Richard Muller has offered an extensive and compelling case against the "central dogma" thesis. According to Muller's interpretation of the Reformed tradition, there were significant antecedents to the Reformed view in the patristic and medieval periods, and there were considerable differences of accent and teaching among Reformed theologians throughout the sixteenth and seventeenth centuries. While continuities and discontinuities of formulation were present throughout this period, the difference between the early formulation of the doctrine in Calvin and his contemporaries and the later formulation of the orthodox period was largely a matter of casting similar doctrinal positions in a more "scholastic" form. However, the scholastic method and form of the orthodox period did not produce a fundamentally different theological position on the doctrine of predestination. Compared to Calvin's formulation of the doctrine, the later orthodox formulation was no more reflective of a decretalism or predestinarian metaphysic than Calvin was. Like Calvin and earlier Reformed theologians, the doctrine of predestination was intimately linked and correlated with typical Reformation emphases on salvation by grace alone through the work of Christ alone. Since fallen human sinners are incapable of saving themselves, and since the faith required to benefit from Christ's saving work is a gracious gift of God, they formulated the doctrine of predestination in order to provide a theological account of the divine provision of Christ as Mediator and the efficacy of his saving work for his people.

Summary and Concluding Observations

While my survey of the doctrine of predestination in the sixteenth-century Reformation offers only a broad overview of the doctrinal formulations of this period, it does provide a basis for a few concluding observations.

In the first place, the Reformation doctrine of predestination and election was based on an engagement with the teaching of Scripture and represents a continuation of a long-standing Augustinian legacy. Contrary to the teachings of Pelagianism and semi-Pelagianism, which grant a measure of human autonomy and free will in the believer's response to the gospel call to faith and repentance, the doctrine of predestination emphasizes the themes of salvation by grace alone and the divine initiative in providing salvation through the work of Christ alone. Rather than representing a deflection from the doctrine of justification through faith alone, the doctrine of predestination articulates the Reformation's primary concern to root the doctrines of Christology and ecclesiology in God's determination to grant salvation to fallen sinners in Christ, none of whom are capable of taking the initiative in turning toward God or responding favorably to the call of the gospel. Though the Reformed theologians of the sixteenth century were more apt to articulate the doctrine in a fulsome manner than other streams of Reformation theology, the doctrine of predestination was not unique to the Reformed tradition but was expressed as well by Luther and Lutheranism especially in the early part of the sixteenth century.

Furthermore, despite the diverse ways that sixteenth-century Reformed theologians formulated the doctrine of predestination, several common themes are evident, which were codified in the principal Reformed confessions of the period. While the doctrine of predestination was never a "central dogma" or organizing principle of Reformed theology, it did find common acceptance among the leading theologians of the period. Even though more scholastic features of the doctrine surfaced only late in the sixteenth century—such as the question of the relative order of the elements within God's eternal counsel or decree or the question of the design underlying Christ's work of atonement—several features of the doctrine were commonly embraced. Though some theologians formulated the doctrine of double predestination more rigorously than others, the leading theologians of the Reformed tradition affirmed both God's merciful election of some and his just nonelection or reprobation of others. On the one hand, they insisted that salvation and the work of Christ in providing salvation were rooted in God's gracious choice in and for Christ to save some fallen sinners and to grant them the gift of faith whereby to embrace the gospel promise. And on the other hand, they affirmed God's just determination to leave others in their lost estate and to condemn them on account of their sins and willful disobedience. In this respect, the Reformed theologians of the period commonly recognized the asymmetry that obtains between

God's gracious choice to save some and his just choice not to save others.

Finally, the doctrine of predestination and election was closely linked with two emphases that also belong to the doctrine of justification. The first of these emphases was the honor of God as the sole Savior of his people. The doctrine of predestination militates against any view of salvation that grants to fallen sinners any part in contributing to their own salvation. In Calvin's treatment of the doctrine, for example, predestination expresses most clearly that the salvation of God's people is born from God's undeserved generosity in Christ alone.[93] The second of these emphases was the comfort that derives from the doctrine of election. Far from undermining the believer's assurance of salvation, the doctrine of predestination and election affords believers a solid basis of comfort. When the knowledge of God's grace toward us in Christ is viewed as the only proper "mirror" of election, then what follows is an assurance of God's grace and mercy that hangs not on the thin thread of our choice and perseverance but on the unbreakable chain of God's sovereign grace and mercy. If God loves his people in Christ from all eternity, then nothing will be able to sever them from his love or frustrate the realization of his good purpose to save them.

Resources for Further Study

PRIMARY SOURCES

Augustine. *Four Anti-Pelagian Writings*. Trans. John A. Mourant and William J. Collinge. Fathers of the Church 86. Washington, DC: Catholic University of America Press, 1992.

Calvin, John. *The Bondage and Liberation of the Will: A Defence of the Orthodox Doctrine of Human Choice against Pighius*. Edited by A. N. S. Lane. Translated by G. I. Davies. Texts and Studies in Reformation and Post-Reformation Thought 2. Grand Rapids, MI: Baker, 1996.

———. *Calvin's Commentaries*. Vol. 22, *Commentaries on the Epistle of Paul the Apostle to the Hebrews; Commentaries on the Catholic Epistles*. Translated by John Owen. 1844–1856. Reprint, Grand Rapids, MI: Baker, 1981.

---

93. See Calvin, *Institutes*, 3.21.1.

————. *Concerning the Eternal Predestination of God*. Translated by J. K. S. Reid. Louisville: Westminster John Knox, 1997.

————. *Institutes of the Christian Religion*. Edited by John T. McNeill. Translated by Ford Lewis Battles. 2 vols. Library of Christian Classics 20–21. 1559 edition. Philadelphia: Westminster, 1960.

Luther, Martin. *Luther's Works*. Edited by Jaroslav Pelikan and Helmut T. Lehmann. American ed. 82 vols. (projected). Philadelphia: Fortress; St. Louis, MO: Concordia, 1957–.

SECONDARY SOURCES

Bray, John S. *Theodore Beza's Doctrine of Predestination*. Bibliotheca Humanistica & Reformatorica 12. Nieuwkoop: De Graaf, 1975.

Clark, R. Scott. "Election and Predestination: The Sovereign Expressions of God (3.21–24)." In *A Theological Guide to Calvin's Institutes: Essays and Analysis*, edited by David W. Hall and Peter A. Lillback, 90–122. Calvin 500. Phillipsburg, NJ: P&R, 2008.

Graafland, Cornelis. *Van Calvijn tot Barth: Oorsprong en ontwikkeling van de leer der verkiezing in het Gereformeerd Protestantisme* [From Calvin to Barth: The origin and development of the doctrine of election in Reformed Protestantism]. 's-Gravenhage, The Netherlands: Uitgeverij Boekencentrum, 1987.

Jacobs, Paul. *Prädestination und Verantwortlichkeit bei Calvin*. Kasel: Oncken, 1937.

James, Frank A., III. *Peter Martyr Vermigli and Predestination: The Augustinian Inheritance of an Italian Reformer*. Oxford Theological Monographs. New York: Oxford University Press, 1998.

Klooster, Fred H. *Calvin's Doctrine of Predestination*. Grand Rapids, MI: Baker, 1977.

Kolb, Robert. *Bound Choice, Election, and Wittenberg Theological Method: From Martin Luther to the Formula of Concord*. Lutheran Quarterly Books. Grand Rapids, MI: Eerdmans, 2005.

Muller, Richard A. *Christ and the Decree: Christology and Predestination in Reformed Theology from Calvin to Perkins*. Studies in Historical Theology 2. 1986. Repr., Grand Rapids, MI: Baker, 1988.

Nicole, Roger. *Moyse Amyraut (1596–1664) and the Controversy on Universal Grace: First Phase (1634–1637)*. PhD diss., Harvard University, 1966.

Rouwendal, Pieter. "The Doctrine of Predestination in Reformed Orthodoxy." In *A Companion to Reformed Orthodoxy*, edited by Herman J. Selderhuis, 553–89. Brill's Companions to the Christian Tradition 40. Leiden: Brill, 2013.

Trueman, Carl R. "Election: Calvin's Theology and Its Early Reception." In *Calvin's Theology and Its Reception: Disputes, Developments, and New Possibilities*, edited by J. Todd Billings and I. John Hesselink, 97–120. Louisville: Westminster John Knox, 2012.

Venema, Cornelis P. *Heinrich Bullinger and the Doctrine of Predestination: Author of 'the Other Reformed Tradition'?* Texts and Studies in Reformation and Post-Reformation Thought. Grand Rapids, MI: Baker Academic, 2002.

Warfield, Benjamin B. *The Plan of Salvation*. Rev. ed. Grand Rapids, MI: Eerdmans, n.d.

8

Creation, Mankind, and the Image of God

Douglas F. Kelly

ABSTRACT

As we survey the teaching of the major sixteenth-century Reformers on creation, mankind, and the image of God, we find a general unanimity (with only minor differences) among them on God's creation of humankind, followed by man's fall and the divine restoration. All interpreted the early chapters of Genesis and related New Testament passages (as in Romans 5 and 1 Corinthians 15) in historico-literal fashion that avoided allegorism. For the most part, the Reformers were in line with the great Western theological tradition on man's creation, fall, and redemption—especially with Augustine (though they criticized him in places). Usually, they were not very far from Peter Lombard and Thomas Aquinas, although—unlike Thomas—they saw no difference between "image" and "likeness" and took more seriously the effects of the fall on the human mind. Most of the Protestant Reformers based their doctrine on serious exegetical work and took advantage of many of the linguistic advances provided by the Renaissance. These sixteenth-century theologians laid a firm intellectual foundation for all later interpretation of Holy Scripture on the question of Psalm 8: "What is man?"

Introduction

The foundational doctrine of Scripture is the creation of all things out of nothing by the living God. The Bible begins not with an argument for God's existence but with his creation of the universe. Genesis 1:1 says, "In the beginning, God created the heavens and the earth." Creation of all things by God is assumed as the basis of all reality, and frequently celebrated by the Law, the Prophets, and the Wisdom Literature.

Creation is as foundational to the New Testament as it is to the Old. In the New Testament, the prologue to John's Gospel states, "In the beginning was the Word, and the Word was with God, and the Word was God. He was in the beginning with God. All things were made through him, and without him was not any thing made that was made" (John 1:1–3). According to Hebrews 11:3, "By faith we understand that the universe was created by the word of God, so that what is seen was not made out of things that are visible."

The books of the New Testament rely heavily on the Genesis account of both creation and the early history of the human race. It has been pointed out that some 165 passages in Genesis are either directly quoted or definitely alluded to in the New Testament.[1] Nearly every writer of the New Testament refers somewhere to the first eleven chapters of Genesis, and nowhere is there the slightest suggestion that any of them regarded the teaching of these chapters as mythical or allegorical. Christ himself referred on at least six occasions to matters related in these early chapters of Genesis, and he understood them to be truthful and relevant accounts that provided the background of the creation and fall of the humanity he came to redeem.[2]

Scripture and the Reformers' Theology
Hold Together Creation and Redemption

The Bible is rightly called "the book of redemption," and the context of redemption is God's creation of the cosmos as pure and perfect.

---

1. See Henry M. Morris, *The Genesis Record: A Scientific and Devotional Commentary on the Book of Beginnings* (Grand Rapids, MI: Baker, 1976), 21, 22.
2. Ibid.

By the third chapter of Genesis, the fall of mankind and the rest of the universe (which Adam represented) had occurred. Creation and fall demonstrated the origin of evil and the need for God to redeem mankind and the cosmos out of that destructive evil. The Creator God becomes the Redeemer of his own well-loved handiwork that had fallen into sin, which had then brought guilt, judgment, decay, and death. The first promise of the gospel is found in Genesis 3:15, when the Lord promises our first mother, Eve, that a descendant of hers will reverse the effects of the fall, at immense cost to himself and loss to the Evil One, thereby winning the victory over sin, death, and final judgment.

The gospel can never be understood apart from this creational context, followed by the fall and then the long development of the various phases of the overarching redemptive covenant of grace, which vouchsafes full and final redemption by the same God who created it all to begin with! As Athanasius once said, only someone so infinitely great as the Creator would be powerful enough and wise enough to redeem such a created order, at the center of which are his image bearers, humankind, all of whom are descendants of Adam and Eve.[3]

The General Approach of the Reformers

Calvin tied together creation, fall, and redemption in the opening "argument" of his *Commentary on Genesis*:

> And, in fact, though Moses begins, in this Book, with the Creation of the World, he nevertheless does not confine us to this subject. For these things ought to be connected together; that the world was founded by God, and that man, after he had been endued with the light of intelligence, and adorned with so many privileges, fell by his own fault, and was thus deprived of all the benefits he had obtained; afterwards, by the compassion of God, he was restored to the life he had forfeited, and this through the loving-kindness of Christ; so that there should always be some assembly on earth, which being adopted into the hope of the

---

3. Athanasius, *De Incarnatione* 7.

celestial life, might in this confidence worship God. The end to which the whole scope of the history tends is to this point, that the human race has been preserved by God in such a manner as to manifest his special care for his Church. For this is the argument of the Book.[4]

Bullinger covered much the same ground in tying creational and redemptive themes together, for example, in the first sermon of his *First Decade*.[5] And in doing so, he and his friend Calvin were not far from parts of Saint Augustine's *City of God* (although they critiqued some aspects of his teaching).

It was similar with Philipp Melanchthon, another follower of Augustine and Luther's assistant and successor, as well as a friend of Calvin and Bullinger (who met through some of the Lutheran-Calvinist colloquies and who read each other's writings). Melanchthon placed creation, and especially man's creation in the image of God, in the context of God's election of his church.[6] His teacher, Martin Luther, had at an earlier time also clearly set the gospel in the context of creation, fall, and promise.[7]

CREATION AND THE ATTRIBUTES OF GOD

The sixteenth-century Protestant Reformers generally followed in the train of many church fathers and several of the medieval scholastics (with some critique of both) in emphasizing the original goodness of creation and its fallenness as the context for its redemption by Christ, the agent of creation. They understood that for all its vastness and complexity, the created order is temporal and finite and is directly dependent on a power outside it and above it. This transcendent power, whose creative work is the beginning of the first chapter of Genesis, was held to be the triune God (though some felt that one could not

---

4. John Calvin, *Calvin's Commentaries*, vol. 1, *Commentary on Genesis*, trans. John King (1844–1856; repr., Grand Rapids, MI: Baker, 1979), 64.

5. Heinrich Bullinger, *The First Decade*, in *The Decades of Heinrich Bullinger*, ed. Thomas Harding (1849–1852; repr., Grand Rapids, MI: Reformation Heritage Books, 2004), 42, 43.

6. Philipp Melanchthon, *Initia doctrinae physicae*, CR 13, 199. This work is helpfully discussed by Dino Bellucci, *Science de La Nature et Réformation: La physique au service de la Réforme dans l'enseignement de Philippe Mélanchthon* (Roma: Edizioni Vivere In, 1998), 129–94.

7. Martin Luther, "Preface to the Old Testament" (1523, rev. 1545), in *Martin Luther's Basic Theological Writings*, ed. Timothy F. Lull, 2nd ed. (Minneapolis: Fortress, 2005), 114–15.

derive the Trinity from Genesis 1:26 alone).[8] Elohim alone is eternal and infinite, dependent on nothing outside himself.

In other words, they saw that God's eternal self-existence (traditionally called *aseity*—i.e., who exists in and by himself, without dependence on anything outside his own being) is demonstrated (1) in the work of creation, and (2) in the names he is given in the books of Moses, especially those that relate the work of creation.

(1) Creation out of Nothing Demonstrates God's Self-Existence

John Calvin, for instance, pointed out that the precise Hebrew verb used for God's creation (*bara*) refers to making all things out of nothing—sometimes in the later theological tradition, termed *absolute creation*—and is a miracle reserved to God, whereas a different verb, *yatsar*, means "to frame or form" (with preexistent materials)—later called *secondary creation. Bara* (in the Qal stem) is used in Scripture only for describing God's activity, while *yatsar* can be used to describe the activity of either humans or God.[9]

In his *Sermons on Genesis Chapters 1–11*, Calvin summarized this point in simpler terms to his congregation in Geneva:

> That is why Moses says God created the heaven and the earth. Now, when he uses the word "create," he indicates there is no being unless it exists in God alone. . . . This word "create" tells us that

---

8. John Calvin, however, thought it was ill founded to make this direct identification between Elohim and the Trinity—see his *Commentary on Genesis*, 1:70. And yet elsewhere, in his *Institutes*, Calvin did mention that the phrase "Let us make man in our image" suggests that more than one person subsists in God (1.13.24). Calvin probably meant that while we may not read the full New Testament doctrine of the Trinity back into the Old, yet aspects of it are intimated. Zwingli, who was exegetically less careful than Calvin (whose ministry began some years after Zwingli's death), taught that the phrase "Let us make man in our image" (Gen. 1:26) refers to the Trinity in his 1522 sermon *Of the Clarity and Certainty or Power of the Word of God*, translated into English in *Zwingli and Bullinger: Selected Translations with Introductions and Notes*, ed. G. W. Bromiley, LCC 24 (Philadelphia: Westminster, 1953), 59. Bullinger similarly found evidence for the Trinity in Gen. 1:26 in the third sermon of his *Fourth Decade*, in *The Decades of Henry Bullinger*, 2:135. Bullinger's usage of Old Testament texts to establish the doctrine of the Trinity is carefully discussed by Mark Taplin, "Bullinger on the Trinity: 'Religionis Nostrae Caput et Fundamentum,'" in *Architect of Reformation: An Introduction to Heinrich Bullinger, 1504–1575*, ed. Bruce Gordon and Emidio Campi, Texts and Studies in Reformation and Post-Reformation Thought (Grand Rapids, MI: Baker Academic, 2004), 67–99. Luther taught in his *Lectures on Genesis*, commenting on Gen. 1:26, that "Let us make" refers to the counsels within the Trinity, but his remarks on Gen. 3:22 are judicious, where he states that Gen. 1:26 indicates "a plurality of persons, or . . . the Trinity," yet adds, "But these mysteries are more definitely unfolded in the New Testament." *Lectures on Genesis Chapters 1–5*, LW 1:58–59, 223.

9. Calvin, *Commentary on Genesis*, 1:70.

existence resides only in him. For everything which had a beginning is not of itself, that is, it has nothing proper to itself but derives its being from something else.[10]

(2) God's Self-Existence Suggested by His Names

The various names ascribed to God in Genesis and Exodus—Elohim and particularly the "covenant (or redemptive) name" that he gives to his chosen people, Yahweh (or Jehovah)—were understood to indicate God's eternal self-existence. This was nothing new with the Reformers. The church fathers had long before seen the significance of these divine names. One of the earliest of the Protestant Reformers, William Tyndale, translator of all the New Testament and the earlier portions of the Old (whose work was largely taken on by the translators of the 1611 Authorized Version), discussed the significance of the name Jehovah: "Jehovah is God's name, neither is any creature so called. And is as much to say as one that is of himself, and dependeth of nothing. Moreover, as oft as thou seest LORD in great letters (except there be an error in the printing) it is in Hebrew *Jehovah*, thou that art, or he that is."[11]

Bullinger discussed this name similarly:

Among all the names of God that is the most excellent which they call *Tetragrammaton*, that is (if we may so say), the four-lettered name: for it is compounded of the four spiritual letters, and is called *JEHOVAH*. It is derived of the verb-substantive, *Hovah*, before which they put *Jod*, and make it Jehovah, that is to say, Being, or I am, as he that is *autousia*, a being of himself; lacking nobody's aid to make him to be, but giving to be unto all manner of things; to wit, eternal God, without beginning and ending, in whom we live, we move, and have our being. To this do those words especially belong. . . . And God said to Moses, I am that I am; or, I will be that I will be. . . . That is, I am God that will be, and he hath sent me who is himself Being, or Essence, and God everlasting.[12]

---

10. John Calvin, *Sermons on Genesis 1:1–11:4: Forty-Nine Sermons Delivered in Geneva between 4 September 1559 and 23 January 1560*, trans. Rob Roy McGregor (Edinburgh: Banner of Truth, 2009), 10, 11.

11. From Tyndale's ca. 1530 *Pentateuch*, quoted in David Daniell, *William Tyndale: A Biography* (New Haven, CT: Yale University Press, 1994), 284.

12. Sermon 3 of *The Fourth Decade*, in *The Decades of Henry Bullinger*, 2:130, 131.

Or as Calvin says, "Deity in an absolute sense exists of itself."[13] The meaning of the divine names indicates this essential quality of the living God: aseity. God alone is God; he alone possesses the attributes of eternity and self-existence, of omnipotent and omniscient power. These attributes are never to be ascribed to what he created by that transcendent power.

Teaching of the Reformers Contrasted to Later Evolutionary Theories

Before we survey the Reformers' teaching on the divine image in humankind, we must briefly consider the massive intellectual gap between their confidence in the plain meaning of Holy Scripture and the post-Enlightenment rejection of its authority as regards its historical and scientific truth claims. The eighteenth-century Enlightenment (especially in its later phases), placed the powers of human reason above the divine revelation in such a way that it rejected much of the biblical worldview and replaced it with current theories of those who were at that time in the intellectual vanguard.

For that reason, particularly with the development of deism (which excluded God's intervention in the natural world), many outright rejected the miraculous and especially the biblical accounts of divine creation within the space of six days only a few thousand years ago. Those who felt that they needed to come to terms with these early forms of what would later be called "secularism" were faced with the hard problem of proposed reinterpretations of miracles and divine creation. The two worldviews were incompatible: belief in divine intervention and belief in secularism (also known as naturalism) rendered contrary accounts of the meaning of nature in general and the significance of mankind in particular.

Any serious reading of the Reformers will show that they developed their doctrine on the basis of the traditional biblical worldview with its commitment to God's intervention into the natural realm and his accurate account of it in Holy Scripture. Of course, Luther, Calvin, and the other Reformers were well aware of ancient forms of secularist

---

13. Calvin, *Institutes*, 1.13.25.

explanations of the cosmos, such as the atomic theories of Democritus and Lucretius, which had no recourse to God, nor to any miracles he might perform in the world. But they wrote off these atheistic theories and believed that with the truth of the Scriptures, they were standing in the divinely revealed light by which alone they could make sense of nature and mankind.

What they would have made of deism and evolutionism some two or three hundred years after their time is impossible to say for certain. But it may be a fair observation to suggest that their commitment to the plain teaching of the Holy Scriptures on the world and on God's image bearers would have rendered them no more friendly to the post-Enlightenment philosophers than to the ancient atomistic writers, although this suggestion does not constitute proof.

Yet there is this important difference as concerns Reformation-era believers and ancient philosophy: it was not difficult for Christian thinkers to reject it in the sixteenth century; nearly their whole medieval culture had done so long before. But it is much harder for Christians today to reject the *modern* forms of ancient Greek atomic and evolutionary theory. That is because most of Western culture since approximately 1800 has felt that it has had to submit to what it understood to be the scientific interpretation of natural reality.[14] By the mid- and late nineteenth century, to question the reigning scientific claims about the world and how it works was generally thought to put one into the category of ignorance and obscurantism (in a way that traditional rejection of the pre-Socratics did not), and thereby possibly to render their presentation of the gospel incredible to their own generation.

---

14. T. F. Torrance has done groundbreaking work on the real meaning of science, as in his *Theological Science* (London: Oxford University Press, 1969). He demonstrates that true science is *not* the same as the still popular theories of post-Newtonian dualism (which rejected out of hand divine creation and other miracles). He notes that this later form of deism has since the 1920s been surpassed by the new physics brought in by Einstein. A particularly helpful survey of this difference is his essay "Newton, Einstein, and Scientific Theology," chap. 8 in Torrance, *Transformation and Convergence in the Frame of Knowledge: Explorations in the Interrelations of Scientific and Theological Enterprise* (Grand Rapids, MI: Eerdmans, 1984), 263–83. It may well be that many Christian theologians, in their sincere eagerness to be in accordance with "science," have all too rapidly, and without careful consideration, uncritically accepted a sort of popular science that does not reflect the current reading of much science since the 1920s. They may have been on safer ground to have followed the Reformers in their acceptance of the plain historico-literal reading of Scripture.

That is why so many Christian interpreters of Genesis 1–11 felt it no longer necessary to accept the plain meaning of the biblical texts on the creation of the cosmos and of Adam and Eve. In reinterpreting the foundational doctrines of Scripture, they therefore no longer needed to rely directly on how Luther, Calvin, Bullinger, and the other Reformers expounded these passages.

So as we study the details of Reformational teaching on man in the image of God, it is helpful to keep in mind the bigger picture, namely, a worldview that rejects a large part of what these church teachers believed and taught on creation. But this is not the place to expound in any depths these crucial presuppositional differences that always lie near the surface of how we read the Reformers' doctrine of creation and the image of God and directly influence what we make of their teaching.[15]

So without tracing the development of the post-Enlightenment interaction between changing views of science and Christian theology, one salient reference might be sufficient to show what happened when so much of the church capitulated to evolutionary teaching in the nineteenth century. Nigel Cameron, for instance, in his *Evolution and the Authority of the Bible*, shows how nearly every Protestant commentator in Great Britain within twenty years of the publication of Darwin's *The Origin of Species* drastically reintepreted Genesis 1–11 to allow for evolutionary theory.[16] But one breathes a totally different atmosphere in the commentaries on Genesis of Luther, Calvin, and Capito, the Strasbourg Reformer and friend of John Calvin.[17]

Let me suggest a few points that, I would argue, demonstrate that what the Reformers wrote on creation and the image of God is finally incompatible with evolutionary theory. First, they sought to base their teaching on a straightforward historico-literal interpretation of the

15. Following many others, I have sought to deal with it in some detail elsewhere, in *Creation and Change: Genesis 1.1–2.4 in the Light of Changing Scientific Paradigms* (Fearn, Ross-shire, Scotland: Mentor, 1997).

16. Nigel M. De S. Cameron, *Evolution and the Authority of the Bible* (Exeter: Paternoster, 1983).

17. Wolfgang Capito, *Hexameron, Sive Opus Sex Dierum* (Argentiae [Strasbourg], 1539 (unfortunately, only in Latin). It is a superb exposition of the early chapters of Genesis, and it ties them in to Job, the Psalms, Romans, and other biblical books. Capito also draws much material from rabbinical sources, especially their theories of the connection of "wisdom" to the work of God's creation.

relevant text of Scripture. They did so in opposition to much of the medieval allegorical renderings of the biblical texts. They believed that what the various texts of Scripture set forth was to be understood by means of a plain reading of the Hebrew and Greek originals.

Thus, in their commentaries on Genesis, for example, Luther and Calvin plainly accepted the teaching of direct creation of all things by God in the space of six days only a few thousand years ago.[18] That is the definite meaning of the sacred text. To stretch out the age of the cosmos to billions of years (in order to accommodate the vast ages required by evolutionary theory) requires a new sort of "creative" allegorical procedure that was never practiced by Luther or Calvin.

Second, in their commentaries on Genesis and Romans, and elsewhere, the magisterial Reformers taught the central significance of the headship of Adam over the human race, and thus the significance of his fall (in which all his posterity fell with him) as the background to the glorious work of redemption through Christ, the second Adam. The first Adam's sin brought decay, disease, and death, according to the Scriptures, and that is the account of sin and salvation that the Reformers followed. Sin was the origin of evil; it was not the context of the prefallen world.

They understood the place of Adam, God's first image bearer, and his rebellion and its consequences to be crucial to understanding what Christ, as the last Adam, has done to restore us. A viewpoint of mankind gradually evolving into something like "the image of God" from a lower species in a world already marked by struggle and death is contrary to all that the Reformers taught.

Third, from all that they wrote, the Reformers could not have accepted the tacit transfer of the attributes of God to the self-sufficient evolutionary process.[19] But that is precisely what happens in openly atheistic evolutionary teaching, although the theistic evolutionists seek to avoid it as best they can. Yet the theistic evolutionists, for all their good intentions, are unable to take such a straightforward reading of the biblical text as did the Reformers.

---

18. Calvin expounds this position in his *Institutes*, 1.14.
19. Note the references quoted immediately above bearing on this issue from Bullinger and Calvin.

Without forgetting the big picture of incompatible worldviews, let us now, in the train of the Reformers, go on to see what the plain historical meaning of the relevant biblical texts teaches us about man's creation in the image of God. Let us humbly say with Samuel of old, "Speak, LORD, for thy servant heareth" (1 Sam. 3:9). That attitude lies at the foundation of the Reformational doctrine of the image of God.[20]

The Content of the Image of God in Mankind

The sixteenth-century Reformers generally agreed that man was created in innocence and beauty by God on the sixth day of creation.

MARTIN LUTHER (1483–1546) AND HULDRYCH ZWINGLI (1484–1531)

The earliest Reformer, Martin Luther, was clear about this. In one of his sermons, he spoke of the purity of this original image in mankind:

> Such an image of God Adam was when first created. He was, as to the soul, truthful, free from error, and possessed of true faith and knowledge of God; and as to the body holy and pure, that is, without the impure, unclean desires of avarice, lasciviousness, envy, hatred, etc. And all his children—all men—would have so remained from their birth if he had not suffered himself to be led astray by the devil and to be ruined.[21]

In his *Lectures on Genesis 1–5*, Luther spoke of the dignity of mankind above all other creatures, indicated by the speaking of God within himself as a "divine counsel" befitting a very important work.[22] Luther then drew from Augustine's *On the Trinity* (books 9–11), in saying that

---

20. There is growing evidence that although evolutionary theory is still the majority reading of our "scientific culture," evolution is no longer beyond serious scientific and philosophical challenge. Up to the 1950s, a majority of evangelicals thought that it was intellectually irresponsible to argue against evolution in favor of a literal view of six-days creation. But since the 1960s much significant work has been done against evolutionary theory and for special creation. It started among fundamentalist "creation scientists" and then by the 1980s went more mainstream with the "intelligent design" scientists, lawyers, and philosophers. Only time will tell whether this is the beginning of a paradigm shift, but if so, the commitment of the Reformers to the historico-literal teaching of Genesis on man's creation in the divine image may once again become widespread.

21. *Sermons of Martin Luther*, ed. John Nicholas Lenker, vol. 8, *Sermons on Epistle Texts for Trinity Sunday to Advent with an Index of Sermon Texts in Volumes 1–8* (Grand Rapids, MI: Baker, 1989), 309.

22. Luther, *Lectures on Genesis Chapters 1–5*, LW 1:55–61.

the image of God is the powers of the soul—memory, the mind, or intellect, and will. . . . Therefore the image of God, according to which Adam was created, was something far more distinguished and excellent, since obviously no leprosy of sin adhered either to his reason or to his will. Both his inner and his outer sensations were all of the purest kind.[23]

Zwingli's account of the image was much the same as Luther's, though with less detail. He placed the image primarily in the mind, discussing it in his *Of the Clarity and Certainty or Power of the Word of God*.[24]

WILLIAM TYNDALE (1494–1536)

The early English Reformer William Tyndale is most noted for his superb translation of the whole New Testament and of the first half of the Old into clear and beautiful English, working from the best Greek and Hebrew texts of his time (rather than from the Latin Vulgate). His translations, as David Daniell has stated, are "the foundation of all succeeding English Bibles, including the celebrated 1611 Authorized Version, or King James Version, of which the New Testament is 83 per cent Tyndale."[25]

Tyndale was, in many respects, a follower of much, though not all, that Luther wrote, particularly in matters relating to justification by faith. Donald Dean Smeeton has sought to minimize the influence of Luther over Tyndale, in the interests of rooting him in the work of Wyclif and the Lollards.[26] But David Daniell has critiqued this emphasis of Smeeton, who, he argues, "detaches Tyndale far too eagerly from Luther."[27]

Either way, what Luther taught concerning man's creation in the image of God was probably carried forward by Tyndale in the relatively few places where he mentioned it. Usually, he referred to the image of God in the context of our relationship to Christ. Typically, in his second letter to Frith, Tyndale exhorted, "Bear the image of

---

23. Ibid., *LW* 1:62.
24. Zwingli, *Of the Clarity and Certainty or Power of the Word of God*, 59–68.
25. David Daniell, "Introduction," in William Tyndale, *The Obedience of a Christian Man*, ed. David Daniell (London: Penguin, 2000), xix.
26. Donald Dean Smeeton, *Lollard Themes in the Reformation Theology of William Tyndale*, Sixteenth Century Essays and Studies 6 (Kirkville, MO: Sixteenth Century Journal Publishers, 1986).
27. Daniell, *William Tyndale: A Biography*, 393n24.

Christ in your mortal body, that it may at his coming be made like to His."[28] And in his prologue to the Sermon on the Mount, he wrote, "To believe in Christ's blood for the remission of sin . . . [is] the new generation [i.e., new birth] and image of Christ."[29] In his *Obedience of a Christian Man*, he said, referring to Colossians 3, "Ye have put on the new man which is renewed in the image of him that made him (that is to say Christ)."[30]

But Tyndale also ascribed the image directly to God the Father. Earlier in his prologue to the Sermon on the Mount, he spoke of us loving "our brethren for our Father's sake, because they be created after his image."[31] In his prologue to the Gospel of Matthew, he combined "image of God" both in terms of our creation in the image of the Father and in terms of our Christian duty to show mercy.[32]

JOHN CALVIN (1509–1564)

The teaching of John Calvin on the image of God is, of course, much fuller and more systematic than that of Tyndale, who, though an able theologian, flourished earlier in the Reformation and served primarily as a translator and so wrote occasional books and essays. Calvin, the magisterial biblical expositor and theologian, held that as far as man is concerned, "the proper seat of his [i.e., God's] image is in the soul."[33] Calvin understood "soul" and "spirit" to be essentially the same and viewed it as "separable from the body."[34] He believed that the human conscience, which fears judgment, is a witness to the sense of a human's immortality.[35]

In Calvin's exposition of Genesis 1:26, he denied any real difference in meaning between "image" and "likeness." Unlike the second-century Saint Irenaeus, Saint Augustine, and some of the medieval scholastics who followed Irenaeus and Augustine, Calvin rightly saw,

---

28. Robert Demaus, *William Tyndale: A Biography* (1871; repr., Nashville: Cokesbury, 1927), 429, 430.

29. Ibid., 398.

30. Tyndale, *Obedience of a Christian Man*, 149.

31. *William Tyndale: Selected Works* (1831; repr., Lewes, East Sussex: Focus Christian Ministries, 1986), 136.

32. Ibid., 304.

33. Calvin, *Institutes*, 2.15.3.

34. Ibid., 1.15.2.

35. Ibid.

working from a Renaissance understanding of Hebrew, that "image" and "likeness" were parallel words, explanatory of one another (or *epexegetical*, to use a more modern word): "First, we know that repetitions were common among the Hebrews, in which they express one thing twice; then in the thing itself, there is no ambiguity, simply man is called God's image because he is like God."[36] Calvin went on to discuss the original parallel terms in Hebrew (*tselem* and *demuth*):

> For, when God determined to create man in his image, which was a rather obscure expression, he for explanation repeats it in this phrase, "According to his likeness," as if he were saying that he was going to make man, in whom he would represent himself as in an image, by means of engraved marks of likeness.[37]

Thomas F. Torrance argues that Calvin employed the word "engraved" in the sense of "mirroring" God, rather than possessing the image in and of himself.[38] This seems to be consistent with Calvin's concept in the *Institutes*: "Man was created therefore in the image of God, and in him the Creator was pleased to behold as in a mirror His own glory."[39] But at the same time, Calvin insisted that the image is *internal* to man: "The likeness must be within, in himself. It must be something which is not external to him, but is properly the internal good of the soul."[40] Thus, it is far more than the merely superficial shining of a face on a glass. That is, who we are and how we are to live are shaped by the character of our Creator God.

Being made in the image of God's character is seen in our obligation to reflect the Lord's kindness to all people: "We are not to consider that men merit of themselves but to look upon the image of God in all men, to which we owe all honor and love. . . . Therefore, whatever man you meet, who needs your aid, you have no reason to refuse to help him."[41]

---

36. Ibid., 1.15.3.
37. Ibid.
38. "There is no doubt that Calvin always thinks of the *imago* in terms of a *mirror*. Only while the mirror actually reflects an object does it have the image of that object. There is no such thing in Calvin's thought as an *imago* dissociated from the act of reflecting. He does use such expressions as *engrave* and *sculptured*, but only in a metaphorical sense and never dissociated from the idea of the mirror." T. F. Torrance, *Calvin's Doctrine of Man* (London: Lutterworth, 1949), 36–37.
39. Calvin, *Institutes*, 2.12.6.
40. Ibid., 1.15.4.
41. Ibid., 3.7.6.

Calvin interpreted Genesis 1:26 in light of the New Testament discussion of the renewal of the vitiated image in Christ. Thus, it is necessary to look at the incarnate Christ, in order to "see more plainly those faculties in which man excels, and in which he ought to be thought the reflection of God's glory" (Calvin referred to Eph. 4:24 and Col. 3:10). He added,

> Now we are to see what Paul chiefly comprehends under this renewal. In the first place he posits knowledge, then pure righteousness and holiness. From this we infer that, to begin with, God's image was visible in the light of the mind, in the uprightness of the heart, and in the soundness of all the parts.

After quoting 2 Corinthians 3:18, he stated, "Now we see how Christ is the most perfect image of God; if we are conformed to it, we are so restored that with true piety, righteousness, purity, and intelligence we bear God's image."[42]

Calvin did not totally deny that some sparkling of God's image shone in man's body[43] or that dominion over the rest of the created order was connected to it,[44] but he did not lay emphasis on either of these two aspects, instead focusing on the spiritual: "The glory of God peculiarly shines forth in human nature where the mind, will, and all the senses, represent the divine order."[45]

HEINRICH BULLINGER (1504–1575)

Bullinger and Calvin were colleagues and friends. Calvin led the church in Geneva, and Bullinger (successor of Zwingli) led the church in Zurich. Both were exemplars of Reformational preaching; their

---

42. Ibid., 1.15.4.

43. Calvin stated briefly in the *Institutes*, 1.15.4, that "there was no part of man, not even the body itself, in which some sparks did not glow." Earlier he said, as he quoted Ovid: "And if anyone wishes to include under 'image of God' the fact that, 'while all other living things being bent over look earthward, man has been given a face uplifted, bidden to gaze heavenward and to raise his countenance to the stars,' I shall not contend too strongly." *Institutes*, 1.15.3, quoting Ovid, *Metamorphoses* 1.84ff.

44. Calvin referred to mankind (male and female) being given dominion over the animals, but with very little discussion, in his *Sermons on Genesis 1–11*: "Now for the second kind of benediction: God gives the man and the woman dominion and mastery over the animals. . . . God says, 'Behold, I have made you lords and masters even over all of the animals. Not only will you live off the fruits of the land, but you will also rule over the birds of the air." *Sermons on Genesis 1:1–11:4*, 104.

45. Calvin, *Commentary on Genesis*, 1:96.

commitment to Holy Scripture was the same; and both were Augustinian in theology. Bullinger's preaching was very influential on the
Church of England in the latter part of the sixteenth century.[46]

Bullinger was like Calvin in that he primarily located the image
of God that is in man in the soul. Drawing on Genesis 2:7, Bullinger
stated, "For the breath of life doth signify the living and reasonable
soul, that is to say, the soul of man, which thou seest breathed or
poured into the body when it is fashioned."[47]

Bullinger saw two aspects of the soul: physical vivification and intellectual guidance. The soul, in the first sense, animates the body, so
that "it comprehendeth the powers vegetative and sensitive, whereby
it giveth life to the body."[48] But it also has intellectual powers for
human life in God's image: "Moreover, the soul hath two parts, distinguished in offices, and not in substance; namely, Understanding
and Will; and thereby it directeth man."[49] Elsewhere he said, "There
was in our father Adam before his fall the very image and likeness of
God; which image, as the apostle expoundeth it, was a conformity
and participation of God's wisdom, justice, holiness, truth, integrity,
innocency, immortality, and eternal felicity."[50] Like Calvin here, and
unlike Augustine, Bullinger understood "image" and "likeness" to be
parallel, not different.

PIERRE VIRET (1511–1571)

Pierre Viret of Lausanne was a close colleague of Calvin and frequent
correspondent, and at one time he even served as Calvin's assistant
in Geneva. Viret wrote the fullest and perhaps the most interesting

---

46. Bullinger's famous fifty sermons, *The Decades*, were translated in their entirety into English
by 1577. As Thomas Harding explains, "In 1588 the Archbishop of Canterbury, John Whitgift,
drew up instructions for those called to the ministry, which he entitled *Orders for the better increase
of learning in the inferior Ministers*. Junior clergymen and those wishing to be licensed as public
preachers who did not have a theological education were told to procure a Bible, a copy of Bullinger's *Decades*, and a blank-paged exercise book. The Archbishop told the candidates that they
must read a chapter of the Bible every day, making notes of what they had learned in their exercise
book. Each week, they should read through one of Bullinger's books and make appropriate notes
on what they had learned; then, once a quarter, they should meet with their tutor to discuss their
reading and notes and receive his further instructions." Harding, "Introduction," in *The Decades
of Henry Bullinger*, 1:lxvi.
47. Bullinger, sermon 10 of *The Fourth Decade*, in *The Decades of Henry Bullinger*, 2:375.
48. Ibid., 2:376.
49. Ibid.
50. Bullinger, sermon 10 of *The Third Decade*, in *The Decades of Henry Bullinger*, 1:394.

account of man's creation in the image of God of any leader of the sixteenth-century Reformation. In the third volume of his works (published in French in 2013), Viret devoted almost 350 pages to various aspects of man's creation in the image of God.[51]

He believed that the "executive divine counsel" mentioned in Genesis 1:26 implies a discussion within the Trinity, although, Viret added, the reference this early in Scripture to the Trinity is "somewhat vague."[52] He stated that since, unlike other creatures, man is both physical and spiritual, he is a sort of "microcosm" of the whole world.[53]

Viret devoted the major part of this treatise to an outline, in considerable detail, of "the exterior edifice of the human body."[54] Much of his interest in the body was because the Lord planned it to be a worthy temple for the incarnation of his Son. As though this were a manual of gross anatomy, Viret covered such parts of the body as ligaments, cartilages, and nerves.[55] He listed man's two feet and legs as enabling him to stand upright and his hands as "the cause of science and wisdom."[56] He briefly mentioned the sexual organs, the stomach, and the womb for the passing on and nourishment of physical life.[57] He dealt with the flesh, with muscles, and with glands. He discussed the providence of God in forming women's breasts (and the glands that sustain them). He talked about the usefulness of one's hair. He stated how physical beauty is joined to the utility and commodity of the human body.[58]

Viret then expounded at large our five bodily senses: sight, hearing, smell, taste, and touch.[59] It is unnecessary to survey his teaching here, except to note that he went on to discuss the instruments of our five senses as particularly reflecting the life of the triune God. For example,

---

51. Pierre Viret, *Instruction Chrétienne, Tome Troisième*, ed. Arthur-Louis Hofer (Lausanne: L'Age D'Homme, 2013), 405–742.

52. Ibid., 428.

53. Viret's words for this are that man is "l'image de tout le monde et de tout l'univers qui et en lui" ("the image of the whole world, and of the whole universe which is in him," author's trans.). Ibid., 430.

54. Ibid., 475–743.

55. Ibid., 479, 489–93, 507–13.

56. Ibid., 494–95.

57. Ibid., 511–12. Luther also spoke of some of the details of the blessings of childbearing in his *Lectures on Genesis Chapters 1–5, LW* 1:200–203.

58. Viret, *Instruction Chrétienne*, 513, 515–26, 529–32.

59. Ibid., 534–82.

he showed how the tongue and the usefulness of the human languages reflect the triune God, in whom is "the Word."[60] Often, in these pages, Viret engaged in creative analogies, such as, for instance, his comparison of the necessity of physical nourishment for our bodies and the usefulness of the sacraments.[61]

Without entering into the details, we find Viret describing and spiritually applying the nose, the face, and the members of the human body that are attributed to God. He talked about the brain and our interior sensations and within that section offered interesting insights on common sense, memory, imagination, and how the Evil One disturbs us inwardly.[62]

As an assessment, I would deem that his long and far-ranging survey of man's bodily and mental life is, so far as I can tell, correct, and though not allegorical (i.e., it accepts the full reality of both the physical aspects of the body and the events of the text of Scripture without evacuating the significance of either one of them), it is certainly more "creative" than most of the Calvinist wing of the Reformation. Perhaps we could think of Viret's long disquisition on the image of God in man as a sort of massive meditation on David's marvel over human nature in Psalm 139. Viret certainly sought to think through the relationship of soul/spirit/mind and body and to give fuller attention to the body itself, issues that Reformed theology from the sixteenth century to the twenty-first may have tended to neglect.

JOHN KNOX (CA. 1513–1572)

The great Scottish Reformer John Knox spent several formative years as a colleague of Calvin when he was in exile in Geneva during the persecuting regime of Queen Mary Tudor. The thought of Calvin deeply marked Knox's theology ever afterward. While Knox gave little detailed attention to the image of God in his works, we can find his teaching on this matter accurately represented in the 1560 Scots Confession, of which he was the primary author (though five other men, all named John, assisted in its formulation). It presents this doctrine in article 2:

60. Ibid., 583–611.
61. Ibid., 631–38.
62. Ibid., 649–743.

We confess and acknowledge this our God to have created man, to wit, our first father Adam, to his own image and similitude, to whom he gave wisdom, lordship, justice, free-will, and clear knowledge of himself, as that in the whole nature of man there could be noted no imperfection. From which honour and perfection, man and woman did both fall: the woman being deceived by the Serpent, and man obeying the voice of the woman, both conspiring against the Sovereign Majesty of God, who in expressed words had before threatencd death, if they presumed to eat of the forbidden tree.[63]

CONTINENTAL CONFESSIONS

The teaching of three Continental confessions, one of them Lutheran and two of them Calvinist, essentially agree with what is said in the Scots Confession concerning man's creation in the divine image.

The Formula of Concord

The leading successors of Luther drew together (in German) in 1576 the Formula of Concord. In article 1 of the "Epitome" section, "Concerning Original Sin," the Formula affirms, "We believe, teach, and confess that there is a distinction between the nature of man itself, not only as man was created of God in the beginning pure and holy and free from sin, but also as we now possess it after our nature has fallen."[64] It adds in the same article, "And today no less God acknowledges our minds and bodies to be his creatures and work; as it is written (Job x. 8): 'Thy hands have made me and fashioned me together round about.'"[65]

The Gallican Confession (or The Confession of La Rochelle)

This confession of the French Reformed Church was prepared by Calvin and his pupil Antoine de Chandieu (ca. 1534–1591) and was revised by a synod at Paris in 1559. It was approved by a synod at La Rochelle in 1571. It states in article 9, "We believe that man was created pure and

63. Philip Schaff, *The Creeds of Christendom: With a History and Critical Notes*, vol. 3, *The Evangelical Protestant Creeds*, rev. David S. Schaff (1877; repr., Grand Rapids, MI: Baker, 1996), 440.
64. Ibid., 3:98.
65. Ibid., 3:99.

perfect in the image of God, and that by his own guilt he fell from the grace which he received, and is thus alienated from God."[66]

The Belgic Confession

This confession was composed (in French) by Guy de Brès (1522–1567) in 1561 for the Reformed churches of Flanders and the Netherlands. Its teaching on the image of God in man is no different from the other three confessions cited above. In article 14 it affirms, "We believe that God created man out of the dust of the earth, and made and formed him after his own image and likeness, good, righteous, and holy, capable in all things agreeably to the will of God."[67]

The Deforming of the Image of God in Man by the Fall

The fall of Adam and Eve in the garden of Eden brought devastating results for the image of God, which they bore. Some of the Reformed confessions actually begin with the fall of Adam (although they obviously accept his perfect creation by God). That is the case with the Church of England's major confession, the Thirty-Nine Articles, and with the influential Heidelberg Catechism.

THE THIRTY-NINE ARTICLES (1562) AND THE HEIDELBERG CATECHISM (1563)

Article 9 reads,

> Original sin standeth not in the following of Adam (as the Pelagians do vainly talk); but it is the fault and corruption of every man, that naturally is engendered of the offspring of Adam, whereby man is very far gone from original righteousness, and is of his own nature enclined to evil, so that the flesh lusteth always contrary to the spirit, and therefore in every person born into this world, it deserveth God's wrath and damnation.[68]

In like fashion, the Heidelberg Catechism begins the story of man with the fall. It was written in 1563 by two German followers of Calvin,

---

66. Ibid., 3:365.
67. Ibid., 3:398.
68. Ibid., 3:492, 493.

Zacharius Ursinus (1534–1583) and Caspar Olevianus (1536–1587). An early question asks:

> Question 6:
>   Did God create man thus wicked and perverse?
>
> Answer:
>   No; but God created man good, and after his own image—that is, in righteousness and true holiness; that he might rightly know God his Creator, heartily love him, and live with him in eternal blessedness, to praise and glorify him.[69]

Both of these church documents are in the mainstream of the teaching of the Protestant Reformers on man's fall.

MARTIN LUTHER ON THE DESTRUCTION OF THE IMAGE

At times, Luther seemed to say that the image of God in man was totally lost in the fall, as in his *Lectures on Genesis*: "But through sin both the similitude and the image were lost."[70] Yet he did not always go that far. In the same *Lectures on Genesis*, he admitted that at least some aspects of it have remained:

> Thus even if this image has been almost completely lost, there is still a great difference between the human being and the rest of the animals. . . . Therefore even now, by the kindness of God, this leprous body has some appearance of the dominion over the other creatures. But it is extremely small and far inferior to that first dominion, when there was no need of skill or cunning.[71]

In the Smalcald Articles, he gave even grimmer details on the effects of the fall on mankind:

> We must confess, as Paul says in Rom. 5:11, that sin originated from one man, Adam, by whose disobedience all men were made sinners, and subject to death and the devil. This is called original sin or capital sin. The fruits of this sin are afterwards the evil

---

69. Ibid., 3:309.
70. Luther, *Lectures on Genesis Chapters 1–5*, LW 1:338.
71. Ibid., 67.

deeds which are forbidden in the Ten Commandments. . . . This hereditary sin is so deep a corruption of nature, that no reason can understand it, but it must be believed from the revelation of the Scriptures, Ps. 51:5; Rom. 5:12 sqq.; Ex. 33:3; Gen. 3:7 sqq.[72]

BULLINGER ON THE DEFACING OF THE IMAGE

Bullinger used the language of "defacing" the image of God. He wrote,

> Original sin is the inheritably descending naughtiness or corruption of our nature, which doth first make us endangered to the wrath of God, and then bringeth forth in us those works which the scripture calleth the works of the flesh. Therefore this original sin is neither a deed, nor a word, nor a thought; but a disease, a vice, a depravation, I say, of judgment and concupiscence; or a corruption of the whole man, that is, of the understanding, will, and all the power of man. . . . This sin taketh beginning at and of Adam; and for that cause it is called the inheritably descending naughtiness and corruption of our nature.[73]

JOHN CALVIN ON THE CORRUPTION OF THE IMAGE OF GOD

Calvin taught that we can best understand what the image of God in us was originally like by considering its restoration in Christ:

> There is no doubt that Adam, when he fell from his state, was by this defection alienated from God. Therefore, even though we grant that God's image was not totally annihilated and destroyed in him, yet it was so corrupted that whatever remains is frightful deformity. Consequently, the beginning of our recovery of salvation is in that restoration which we obtain through Christ, who also is called the Second Adam for the reason that he restores us to true and complete integrity. . . . Now God's image is the perfect excellence of human nature which shone in Adam before his defection, but was subsequently so vitiated and almost blotted out that nothing remains after the ruin except what is confused, mutilated, and disease-ridden.[74]

---

72. "The Smalcald Articles," pt. 3, art. 1, in *The Book of Concord*, quoted in *A Compend of Luther's Theology*, ed. Hugh T. Kerr (Philadelphia: Westminster, 1943), 84.
73. Bullinger, *The Third Decade*, in *The Decades of Henry Bullinger*, 1:385.
74. Calvin, *Institutes*, 1.15.4.

Calvin held that mind, will, and affections, though deformed, remained in fallen Adam but that pure righteousness and holiness were lost (especially in light of Eph. 4:24 and Col. 3:10).[75]

Calvin and Luther's accounts of the effects of the fall were very different from that of Thomas Aquinas (1225–1274). Thomas, following Alexander of Hales (ca. 1185–1245), taught that even within the unfallen human, a gift of grace was needed to enable man to control his "lower powers" (or passions) by his higher reason.[76] Since we can no longer do so, Thomas concluded that this "superadded gift" was lost in the fall and that we became prey to all the destructive passions of sin.[77]

But there is no indication in the text of Genesis of any such prefall struggle between passions of the body and the mind (or soul). Such would not really be in harmony with the original, total goodness of the creation. Calvin's, Luther's, and Bullinger's teaching on the radical effects of the fall on the whole human person (rather than the loss of a superadded gift of grace) was much more in line with a plain exegesis of the Hebrew Old Testament and Greek New Testament Scriptures.

Thomas's account of the fall was actually not as superficial as some have suggested. He did speak of "the wounding of nature," which damaged the ability of the intellect to receive the truth, and asserted that this called for "the light of grace."[78] He did not teach that man's mind is unfallen. Nevertheless, Thomas did place his major emphasis on the loss of the superadded gift and did not take so seriously as later Reformational exegetes the devastating effects of the fall on God's image bearers. Thus he developed a rather different account of the sovereign work of regenerating grace in the fallen human personality.[79]

Certainly Thomas did not go as far as the later Nominalists, such

---

75. Ibid.

76. Alexander of Hales calls this prefall grace *donum superadditum naturae*. *Summa Theologica* 2.91.1.3.

77. Thomas, *Summa Theologiae* 2a2ae.164.2.

78. Ibid., 2a2ae2.4. This has been carefully discussed by Arvin Vos in *Aquinas, Calvin, and Contemporary Protestant Thought: A Critique of Protestant Views on the Thought of Thomas Aquinas* (Grand Rapids, MI: Eerdmans, 1985).

79. A survey of the Roman Catholic theory of "the superadded gift" is discussed and critiqued in a lucid way by John Murray, "Man in the Image of God," in *Collected Writings of John Murray*, vol. 2, *Systematic Theology* (Edinburgh: Banner of Truth, 1977), 41–45.

as Gabriel Biel, who in Pelagian fashion claimed that if—after the fall—people's consciences are intellectually confused so that their wills are misguided, then their confusion excuses their sin,[80] and if they seek to do right on their own lights, they can do so.[81] In opposition to this sort of late-medieval Pelagianism, the 1530 Augsburg Confession was representative of Reformation theology when it said: "They [i.e., the Protestants] condemn the Pelagians and others, who teach that by the powers of nature alone, without the Spirit of God, we are able to love God above all things; also to perform the commandments of God, as touching the substance of our actions."[82]

The Reformers were not the first to do battle with Pelagian views of human nature. They knew that they were in line with the numerous writings of Augustine against the Pelagians. Calvin, for example, quoted Augustine's *Against Pelagius and Caelestius* in demonstrating that "grace is prior to works."[83]

Although Thomas was never so far from the Genesis teaching of the radical effects of the fall as Biel and the Nominalists, nonetheless, the Reformers rejected much of his position as not faithfully reflecting Genesis on this matter. Melanchthon, for instance, denied the teaching of the fifth session of the Council of Trent, which followed Thomas in positing this tendency of the lower nature to assert its power over the higher nature of man, generally called "concupiscence."[84] Unlike the scholastics, Melanchthon taught that the major element of the deformed image was not a "privation" (of the superadded gift of original righteousness) but a quantity of internal disorders, such as doubt, omissions, and the spirit of revolt against God.[85]

---

80. Gabriel Biel, *II Sent.* 22.2.2.1: "Invincible ignorance going before an act of the will, whether positive or negative, whether of law or of fact, simply excuses from sin, not only in that matter, but totally" (author's trans.).

81. Biel, *II Sent.* 22.2.2.4: "The infidel does what is in himself, while he conforms to reason and seeks with his whole heart and seeks to be illumined to knowledge of the truth, righteousness, and goodness" (author's trans.). I owe these references to Biel to Heiko A. Oberman, *The Harvest of Medieval Theology: Gabriel Biel and Late Medieval Nominalism*, 3rd ed. (Durham, NC: Labyrinth, 1983), 131. See Oberman's discussion of this deviation from Scripture, as well as from the patristic and Thomistic heritage, in ibid., 131–45.

82. "The Augsburg Confession," art. 18, quoted in Schaff, *Creeds of Christendom*, 3:19.

83. Calvin, *Institutes*, 2.3.7.

84. Council of Trent, session 5, can. 5 (DH §792).

85. Philipp Melanchthon, *Loci praecipui theologici nunc denuo cura et diligentia summa recogniti multisque in locis copiose illustrati* (*Loci Communes, tertia aetas*), in *Melanchthons Werke in Auswahl* [*Studien-Ausgabe*], ed. Robert Stupperich (1559; repr., Gütersloh: Bertelsmann, 1955), 2.1.264, 37–265. This is expounded in Bellucci, *Science de La Nature et Réformation*, 543–54.

The Image of God and Immortality

Calvin was typical of both traditional Catholic[86] and Reformed theology in connecting human immortality with our creation in the image of God:

> Now, unless the soul were something essential, separate from the body, Scripture would not teach that we dwell in houses of clay [Job 4:19] and at death leave the tabernacle of the flesh, putting off what is corruptible. . . . For surely these passages and similar ones that occur repeatedly not only clearly distinguish the soul from the body, but by transferring to it the name "man" indicate it to be the principal part.[87]

Bullinger devoted much of a long sermon to the reality and blessings of life after death. But his emphasis was not as much on the "natural immortality" of the soul (in terms, let us say, of Platonic argument) as it was on the believer in the context of the providence of God, which in unseen mercy, safely brings him through every kind of earthly evil, with his eye on the goal of immortal glory through and with Christ.[88]

The Scots Confession affirms the immortality of the soul (both of the elect and of the reprobate) in article 17. Similarly, the Heidelberg Catechism in question 16 speaks of the believer passing through death to life.

Without surveying the many biblical passages in both Testaments pertaining to the immortality of the soul, let us note only this crucial text: "the blessed and only Potentate, the King of kings, and Lord of

---

86. Peter Lombard (ca. 1090–1160), "Master of Sentences," provided the major theological textbook used in European universities for the next five hundred years, and the Reformers would have read his work as students. Lombard, in line with Augustine (whom he so often quoted) and the entire patristic tradition, taught the immortality of the soul, as when he quoted Augustine's *Enarrationes in Psalmos*, on Ps. 48:15, sermon 2, referring to the death of Christ: "The death which men fear is the separation of the soul from the flesh, and the death which they do not fear is the separation of the soul from God." Lombard, *The Sentences, Book 3: On the Incarnation of the Word of God*, trans. Giulio Silano, Mediaeval Sources in Translation 45 (Toronto: Pontifical Institute of Mediaeval Studies, 2008), 21.68. Lombard's main focus was not so much on the immortality of the soul (which, of course, he accepted) but on the state of man's body, which was animated by the soul. He wrote that "the body of man before sin was mortal and immortal . . . because it was able to die and not to die." Lombard, *The Sentences, Book 2: On Creation*, trans. Giulio Silano, Mediaeval Sources in Translation 43 (Toronto: Pontifical Institute of Mediaeval Studies, 2008), 19.3.

87. Calvin, *Institutes*, 1.15.2.

88. Bullinger, sermon 1 of *The Third Decade*, in *The Decades of Henry Bullinger*, vol. 1, pt. 2, 2–111.

lords; Who only hath immortality" (1 Tim. 6:15–16 KJV). In other words, the triune God alone is *essentially immortal*, but he grants immortality to his image bearers in a derivative way to mirror, as dependent creatures, his immortality. Human immortality is not the essence of created image bearers but is an aspect of their mirroring of God. That is, their relationship to God is what gives them immortality.

Patristics scholar George Dragas shows that this was the teaching of Saint Athanasius in the fourth century: "It seems clear that the human person is not for Athanasius a possession of a human creature, *per se*, but a dynamic gift which is maintained by the Creator Logos. Athanasius speaks of it as a gift, when he tells us that the *kat' eikona* ['according to the image'] involves the transmission of the power of the Logos."[89]

The Restoration of the Image of God in Mankind

Calvin was representative of the magisterial Reformation when he wrote in his *Commentary on 2 Corinthians*, specifically discussing 3:18, "Observe that the purpose of the Gospel is the restoration in us of the image of God which had been cancelled by our sin, and that this restoration is progressive and goes on during our whole life. . . . Thus the apostle speaks of progress which will be perfected only when Christ appears."[90] Calvin, in company with other Reformers, emphasized the ministry of the Holy Spirit in the renewal of the image of God in the believer. T. F. Torrance accurately summarizes Calvin: "Man's answer is the work of the Holy Spirit, who through the Word forms the image anew in man, and forms his lips to acknowledge that he is a child of the Father."[91]

---

89. George Dion Dragas, *Saint Athanasius of Alexandria: Original Research and New Perspectives*, Patristic Theological Library 1 (Rollinsford, NH: Orthodox Research Institute, 2005), 9. Again, without my entering into the details, many Protestant theologians in the twentieth century denied the immortality of the soul. Whether this denial was related to the materialistic philosophy of the nineteenth and twentieth centuries, in the spirit of the New Testament Sadducees, would require a substantial volume in itself to resolve fairly. However, I will mention here two works of excellent scholarship that discuss and defend a careful biblical reading of the immortality of the soul: G. C. Berkouwer, "Immortality," chap. 7 in *Man: The Image of God* (Grand Rapids, MI: Eerdmans, 1962), and John W. Cooper's more recent *Body, Soul, and Life Everlasting: Biblical Anthropology and the Monism-Dualism Debate* (Vancouver, BC: Regent College Publishing, 1995).
90. John Calvin, *The Second Epistle of Paul the Apostle to the Corinthians and the Epistles to Timothy, Titus and Philemon*, trans. T. A. Smail, ed. David W. Torrance and Thomas F. Torrance (Grand Rapids, MI: Eerdmans, 1964), 50.
91. Torrance, *Calvin's Doctrine of Man*, 80.

Luther wrote in the same vein:

> But now the Gospel has brought about the restoration of that image. Intellect and will indeed have remained, but both very much impaired. And so the Gospel brings it about that we are formed once more according to that familiar and indeed better image, because we are born again into eternal life or rather into the hope of eternal life by faith, that we may live in God and with God and be one with Him, as Christ says (John 17:21).[92]

In a sermon on Ephesians 4:22–28, Luther spoke of the Christian life as a joyful recovery from the brokenness of iniquity:

> Nor can anyone hope for remedy except the Christians, who through faith in Christ begin again to have a joyful and confident heart toward God. They thus enter again into their former relation and into the true paradise of perfect harmony with God and of justification; they are comforted by his grace. Accordingly they are disposed to lead a godly life in harmony with God's commandments and to resist ungodly lusts and ways. . . . He, therefore, that would be a Christian should strive to be found in this new man created after God . . . in the very essence of righteousness and holiness.[93]

We find in both Luther and Calvin the concept that the aspect of the image of God that was lost in the fall ("righteousness and holiness") will be restored in believers. While Calvin more strongly (but also Luther to a certain degree) held that the ontological aspects of the image remained, though seriously defaced, the ethical aspects of it were lost. These are now being restored in the believer through the work of sanctification (based on gratuitous justification by faith).

Zwingli had been less forceful than Luther (and later Calvin) on the damage done by the fall to the image, but in a 1524 sermon, he also affirmed that regeneration is a new creation after the likeness of Christ.[94] But his successor, Bullinger, was crystal clear, both on the effects of the fall and on the restoration of the image in Christian

---

92. Luther, *Lectures on Genesis Chapters 1–5*, LW 1:64.
93. Luther, *Sermons of Martin Luther*, 8:310.
94. The sermon was titled, "Answer," which is discussed in *Zwingli and Bullinger*, 51–53.

experience. Concerning its restoration, he wrote, in the context of Christ's incarnation, "For as by his taking of flesh, he joined man to God; so, by dying in the flesh with sacrifice, he cleansed, sanctified, and delivered mankind; and, by giving him his Holy Spirit, he made him like again in nature to God, that is, immortal, and absolutely blessed."[95]

Melanchthon mirrored Luther, Bullinger, and Calvin in setting forth the importance of the redeemed taking action as the Spirit restores the image in them. He applied Romans 6:12 ("Let not sin therefore reign in your mortal body, to make you obey its passions") to our human responsibility: "Sin is present in the regenerated, but their resistance to it keeps it from reigning. Believers thus remain in the grace of God."[96]

This grace of the triune God is restoring mankind to the divine image through the work of Father, Son, and Holy Spirit, which involves first the sovereign divine initiative and then the self-denying experience of life in the church with a loving openness to a lost world. It takes place in a renewed life: "In sum, from looking at Jesus Christ, the perfect image of God, we learn that the proper functioning of the image includes being directed toward God, being directed toward the neighbor, and ruling over nature."[97]

Resources for Further Study

PRIMARY RESOURCES

Bullinger, Heinrich. *The First Decade.* In *The Decades of Heinrich Bullinger*, edited by Thomas Harding, 1:36–192. 1849–1852. Reprint, Grand Rapids, MI: Reformation Heritage Books, 2004.

Calvin, John. *Calvin's Commentaries.* Vol. 1, *Commentary on Genesis.* Translated by John King. 1844–1856. Reprint, Grand Rapids, MI: Baker, 1979.

———. *Institutes of the Christian Religion.* Edited by John T. McNeill. Translated by Ford Lewis Battles. 2 vols. Library of Christian Classics 20–21. 1559 edition. Philadelphia: Westminster, 1960.

95. Bullinger, sermon 1 of *The First Decade*, in *The Decades of Henry Bullinger*, 1:42–43.
96. Melanchthon, *Loci praecipui theologici* (*Loci Communes, tertia aetas*), 2.1.275, 10 (author's trans.).
97. Anthony A. Hoekema, *Created in God's Image* (Grand Rapids, MI: Eerdmans, 1994), 75.

————. *Sermons on Genesis 1:1–11:4: Forty-Nine Sermons Delivered in Geneva between 4 September 1559 and 23 January 1560*. Translated by Rob Roy McGregor. Edinburgh: Banner of Truth, 2009.

Lenker, John Nicholas, ed. *Sermons of Martin Luther*. Vol. 8, *Sermons on Epistle Texts for Trinity Sunday to Advent with an Index of Sermon Texts in Volumes 1–8*. Grand Rapids, MI: Baker, 1989.

Luther, Martin. *Luther's Works*. Vol. 1, *Lectures on Genesis Chapters 1–5*. Edited by Jaroslav Pelikan. St. Louis, MO: Concordia, 1958.

Melanchthon, Philip. *Initia doctrinae physicae*. In vol. 13 of *Corpus Reformatorum*, edited by C. G. Brettschneider and H. E. Bindseil, 179–412. Halle: Schwetschke, 1846.

————. *Loci praecipui theologici nunc denuo cura et diligentia summa recogniti multisque in locis copiose illustrati* (*Loci Communes, tertia aetas*). In *Melanchthons Werke in Auswahl* [*Studien-Ausgabe*], edited by Robert Stupperich, 2.1.164–2.2.780. 1559. Reprint, Gütersloh: Bertelsmann, 1955.

Tyndale, William. *The Obedience of a Christian Man*. Edited by David Daniell. London: Penguin, 2000.

Viret, Pierre. *Instruction Chrétienne, Tome Troisième*. Edited by Arthur-Louis Hofer. Lausanne: L'Age D'Homme, 2013.

Zwingli, *Of the Clarity and Certainty or Power of the Word of God*. In *Zwingli and Bullinger: Selected Translations with Introductions and Notes*, edited by G. W. Bromiley, 49–95. Library of Christian Classics 24. Philadelphia: Westminster, 1953.

SECONDARY RESOURCES

Berkouwer, G. C. *Man: The Image of God*. Grand Rapids, MI: Eerdmans, 1962.

Cameron, Nigel M. De S. *Evolution and the Authority of the Bible*. Exeter: Paternoster, 1983.

Cooper, John W. *Body, Soul, and Life Everlasting: Biblical Anthropology and the Monism-Dualism Debate*. Vancouver, BC: Regent College Publishing, 1995.

Daniell, David. *William Tyndale: A Biography*. New Haven, CT: Yale University Press, 1994.

Demaus, Robert. *William Tyndale: A Biography*. 1871. Reprint, Nashville: Cokesbury, 1927.

Hoekema, Anthony A. *Created in God's Image*. Grand Rapids, MI: Eerd-
    mans, 1994.

Kelly, Douglas F. *Creation and Change: Genesis 1.1–2.4 in the Light of
    Changing Scientific Paradigms*. Fearn, Ross-shire, Scotland: Mentor,
    1997.

Morris, Henry M. *The Genesis Record: A Scientific and Devotional Com-
    mentary on the Book of Beginnings*. Grand Rapids, MI: Baker, 1976.

Murray, John. "Man in the Image of God." In *Collected Writings of John
    Murray*, vol. 2, *Systematic Theology*, 41–45. Edinburgh: Banner of
    Truth, 1977.

Oberman, Heiko A. *The Harvest of Medieval Theology: Gabriel Biel and
    Late Medieval Nominalism*. 3rd ed. Durham, NC: Labyrinth, 1983.

Schaff, Philip. *The Creeds of Christendom: With a History and Critical
    Notes*. Vol. 3, *The Evangelical Protestant Creeds*. Revised by David S.
    Schaff. 1877. Reprint, Grand Rapids, MI: Baker, 1996.

Smeeton, Donald Dean. *Lollard Themes in the Reformation Theology of
    William Tyndale*. Sixteenth Century Essays and Studies 6. Kirkville,
    MO: Sixteenth Century Journal Publishers, 1986.

Torrance, T. F. *Calvin's Doctrine of Man*. London: Lutterworth, 1949.

———. *Theological Science*. London: Oxford University Press, 1969.

9

The Person of Christ

Robert Letham

ABSTRACT

Christology was not a source of friction between Rome and the Reformers. The main issues in the sixteenth century affected the innovative position of Luther and Lutheranism on the nature of the hypostatic union and its impact on the Lord's Supper. They asserted that divine attributes were communicated to Christ's humanity. The Reformed countered by insisting that, because of the bodily ascension, Christ transcended the limits of the humanity he had assumed. This difference affected the controversy over the presence of Christ in the Lord's Supper.

Introduction

Christology was not a major issue between the Reformers and the Roman church. Both accepted the classic Christological dogma as it had been worked out in the fifth, sixth, and seventh centuries. In this the church in both East and West affirmed that the eternal Son of God had, in the incarnation, taken a complete human nature into personal union such that the assumed humanity was, and is, the humanity of the eternal Son. In answer to the question as to *who* Jesus of Nazareth was, the answer was that he was the Son of God. When asked of *what* he consisted, the reply was that he was simultaneously fully God and fully human. Thus, the church confessed personal identity and continuity between one member of the Trinity and the incarnate one, the human nature having no existence apart from its assumption in the virginal conception. On this both sides agreed. The only slight question surrounded Calvin's attribution of *autotheos* (aseity) to the Son, in his opposition to the Italian anti-Trinitarian Valentine Gentile.[1] However, the leading Roman Catholic theologian Robert Bellarmine acknowledged Calvin's orthodoxy on this point.[2] Besides, this is more a matter of Trinitarianism than Christology. The main area of concern related to the differences between Lutheran and Reformed Christologies, which affected their respective views on the Eucharist. These were expressed in the writings of representatives of the two confessions and reached a head in three colloquies: Marburg in 1529, Malbronn in 1564, and Montbéliard in 1586. Accordingly, we will focus here on the theological issues surrounding the Eucharist. Additionally, we will note how some Anabaptists held to heterodox ideas on the heavenly flesh of Christ.

Martin Luther and the Communication of Attributes

For Luther, Christ was the key to interpreting Scripture. In his "Preface to the Epistles of St. James and St. Jude," he stated that he could not accept that James was written by an apostle or was canonical since "it does not once mention the Passion, the resurrection, or the Spirit of Christ," messages that a true apostle would proclaim, "and that is the true test by which to judge all books, when we see whether or not they inculcate Christ"—"for all Scriptures show us Christ."[3] Whoever the author is, if the book does not teach Christ, it is not apostolic.[4] Luther regarded the Old Testament as a book about Christ, bearing witness to him as both law and promise.[5] Thus, in his "Preface to the Old

1. On Calvin's doctrine of *autotheos*, see "John Calvin," in chap. 5, "The Trinity," by Michael Reeves (p. 200).
2. Robert Letham, *The Holy Trinity: In Scripture, History, Theology, and Worship* (Phillipsburg, NJ: P&R, 2004), 256–57.
3. Martin Luther, "Preface to the Epistles of St. James and St. Jude," LW 35:396.
4. See Martin Luther, *Commentary on Psalm 45*, LW 12:260; Luther, *Against Latomus*, LW 32:229–30.
5. Paul Althaus, *The Theology of Martin Luther*, trans. Robert C. Schultz (Philadelphia: Fortress, 1966), 92.

Testament," he said, "The prophets are nothing else than administrators and witnesses of Moses and his office, bringing everyone to Christ through the law," so that "if you would interpret well and confidently, set Christ before you, for he is the man to whom it all applies, every bit of it."[6]

Althaus is correct in stating that distinctive to Luther is his pervasive focus on salvation[7] and that for Luther, "the true knowledge of Christ consists in recognizing and grasping God's will for me in Christ's will for me and God's work to save me in Christ's work for me."[8] Atkinson claims that this is "the dynamic of his theology."[9]

As Althaus remarks, Luther "expressly accepts the great ecumenical creeds of Greek and Latin theology. Apart from individual concepts he expresses no criticism of the traditional christological dogmas."[10] Commenting on Philippians 2:6, Luther stated, "The term 'form of God' here does not mean the essence of God because Christ never emptied himself of this."[11] Luther's grasp of the twin dogmas of *anhypostasia*[12] and *enhypostasia*[13] is clear and important for his Christology for it forms the basis for his peculiar ideas of the *communicatio idiomatum*,[14] which is integral to his whole Christology. He wrote,

> Since the divinity and humanity are one person in Christ, the Scriptures ascribe to the divinity, because of this personal union, all that happens to humanity, and vice versa. And in reality it is so. Indeed,

6. Martin Luther, "Preface to the Old Testament," *LW* 35:247; James Atkinson, *Martin Luther and the Birth of Protestantism* (1968; repr., Atlanta: John Knox, 1982), 95–102.
7. Althaus, *Theology of Martin Luther*, 181–86.
8. Ibid., 189.
9. Atkinson, *Martin Luther*, 127. See also Gerhard Ebeling, *Luther: An Introduction to His Thought*, trans. R. A. Wilson (London: Collins, 1972), 235.
10. Althaus, *Theology of Martin Luther*, 179.
11. Martin Luther, "Two Kinds of Righteousness," *LW* 31:301.
12. This is the dogma that the human nature of Christ has no personal existence of its own, apart from the union into which it was assumed in the incarnation. This means that the Son of God united himself not with a human being (which would entail two separate personal entities) but with a human nature.
13. This is the dogma promulgated at the Second Council of Constantinople (553) that the eternal Son is the person of the incarnate Christ, who took into union a human nature conceived by the Holy Spirit in the womb of the Virgin Mary. Behind this dogma lies the biblical teaching that man is made in the image of God and thus is ontologically compatible with God on a creaturely level. Thus, the Son of God provides the personhood for the assumed human nature.
14. The communication of idioms stems from the fact that Christ is the Son of God, who has added human nature in the incarnation. Consequently, attributes of both deity and humanity are predicable of the person of Christ. Classic Christology asserted that these two natures are indivisibly united in the person of Christ but yet retain their distinct identity. The issue raised by Luther and his followers was whether divine attributes are communicated to Christ's *human* nature.

you must say that the person (pointing to Christ) suffers and dies. But this person is truly God, and therefore it is correct to say: the Son of God suffers. Although, so to speak, the one part (namely, the divinity) does not suffer, nevertheless the person, who is God, suffers in the other part (namely, in the humanity).[15]

He used a number of analogies. The king's son is wounded when only his leg is wounded; Solomon is wise, whereas it is only his soul that is wise; Peter is grey, although only his head is grey. So the person of Christ is crucified according to his humanity.[16]

All this is soundly in line with the classic dogma. However, Luther added a distinctively new twist. For him, Christ possessed the full range of divine attributes according to his human nature, and these were communicated to his humanity by virtue of the hypostatic union. Thus Christ, according to his human nature, possessed the attributes of divine majesty. Luther did not understand Philippians 2:6–7 to refer to the preexistent Christ emptying himself, as the exegetes of the early church did, but thought it referred to the attitude of the earthly Christ. He constantly emptied himself throughout his earthly life.[17] He was "unwilling to use his rank against us, unwilling to be different from us," and "although he was free . . . he made himself servant of all [Mark 9:35]."[18] This is an ongoing self-emptying leading to the cross.[19]

While Luther stressed the *genus majestaticum*—that the divine attributes are communicated to the humanity of Christ—as the presupposition of his self-emptying in history, Althaus considers that this is in conflict not only with the biblical picture of Christ and with Luther's acceptance of the ecumenical creeds but especially with the *enhypostasia*. But, Althaus argues, the *genus majestaticum* is balanced by Luther's acceptance of the *genus tapeinoticon*—God in Christ shared the weakness, suffering, and humiliation of Jesus. For Luther, God suffers in Christ, and he saw it as an incomprehensible mystery.[20]

This came to a head in Luther's doctrine of the real presence of

---

15. Martin Luther, *Confession concerning Christ's Supper*, LW 37:210.
16. Ibid., LW 37:211.
17. Luther, "Two Kinds of Righteousness," *LW* 31:301–2; Martin Luther, *The Freedom of a Christian*, LW 31:366.
18. Luther, "Two Kinds of Righteousness," *LW* 31:301.
19. Ibid., *LW* 31:300–303.
20. Althaus, *Theology of Martin Luther*, 196–98.

Christ in the Lord's Supper, where Luther held emphatically that the body and blood of Christ are present corporeally in, with, and under the bread and wine, due to their partaking of the divine attribute of omnipresence. Christ's flesh is not fleshly—that is, under the curse of God and requiring rebirth—but spiritual, since Christ was born of the Holy Spirit, and so it is God's flesh that gives life to all who eat it in faith.[21]

Luther's basic Christological thought was that there is no God apart from Christ, and therefore, the humanity of Christ is omnipresent. The right hand of God is not to be located in one place but is everywhere: "Where is the Scripture which limits the right hand of God in this fashion to one place?"[22] Citing Psalm 139, Luther stated,

> The Scriptures teach us . . . that the right hand of God is not a specific place in which a body must or may be . . . but is the almighty power of God, which at one and the same time can be nowhere and yet must be everywhere. . . . For if it were at some specific place, it would have to be there in a circumscribed and determinate manner . . . so that it cannot meanwhile be at any other place. But the power of God cannot be so determined and measured, for it is uncircumscribed and immeasurable, beyond and above all that is and may be. . . . On the other hand it must be essentially present at all places, even in the tiniest tree leaf.[23]

Luther concluded that Christ—at the right hand of God—is present at the same time in heaven and in the Supper, for "it is contrary neither to Scripture nor to the articles of faith for Christ's body to be at the same time in heaven and in the Supper."[24]

Luther attacked Zwingli's idea of *alloiosis*, in which one nature is taken for the other.[25] What we want, Luther fumed, "is Scripture, and sound reasons, not [Zwingli's] snot and slobber."[26] He strongly defended himself against the claim that he mingled the natures. Rather,

---

21. Martin Luther, *That These Words of Christ, "This Is My Body," Still Stand Firm against the Fanatics*, LW 37:98–100, 124. See also Luther, *Confession concerning Christ's Supper*, LW 37:236–38.
22. Luther, *That These Words of Christ*, LW 37:56.
23. Ibid., LW 37:57.
24. Ibid., LW 37:55.
25. Luther, *Confession concerning Christ's Supper*, LW 37:209–10.
26. Ibid., LW 37:212.

his opponents threatened to divide the person. However, there is evidence that Luther had not understood Zwingli, thinking that he had confined the right hand of God to a single space in heaven.[27]

It will help us to grasp how Luther came to these conclusions by knowing that he considered there to be three possible forms of presence. First, an object is locally or circumscriptively in a place, where the object and the space fit precisely. This applies to people, who occupy particular locations. Second, an object is present definitively or in an uncircumscribed way, where it can occupy more room or less. Such was the risen Christ, who passed through the stone sealing his grave and through locked doors. Angels too are not confined to particular spaces. Third, God alone occupies places repletively, being present in all places at all times, filling them while not being measured by any one of them. So we cannot confine our thoughts on the presence of Christ to one mode of presence only. Since the risen Christ was present definitively, it makes sense to take "this is my body" as it stands. Wherever Christ is, he is present as God and as man; if this were not so, he would be divided. Rather, he is one person with God, besides which there is nothing higher.[28] Since he is one indivisible person with God, wherever God is, he must be also. This is a mystery known only to God; Luther only wrote about it to show "what crass fools our fanatics are."[29] So he raved, "Get out of here, you stupid fanatic, with your worthless ideas!"[30]

Luther expressed these ideas vehemently at the Colloquy of Marburg (1529), where he came into sharp conflict with Zwingli. Before we examine what happened there, we need to inquire into Zwingli's Christology.

Huldrych Zwingli and *Alloiosis*

In his broader theology, Zwingli's stress was on God rather than man, so in his Christology, it was on Christ as God. As a result, whereas Luther emphatically asserted the unity of Christ's person, Zwingli distinguished sharply between the two natures. This led Luther to accuse

27. Ibid., *LW* 37:212–13.
28. Ibid., *LW* 37:215–18, 221–22.
29. Ibid., *LW* 37:223.
30. Ibid., *LW* 37:220.

him of holding that a mere man had died for us.[31] This sharp distinction—almost separation—between the natures is clear in Zwingli's *Commentary on True and False Religion* (1525). There he wrote that Christ is our salvation according to his divine nature, not according to his humanity.[32] So in John 6 he referred the flesh and blood simply to the gospel, the eating and drinking to faith: "This, then, is the third sure mark that Christ is not speaking here of sacramental eating; for He is only in so far salvation unto us as He was slain for us; but He could be slain only according to the flesh and could be salvation bringing only according to his divinity."[33] Much of this section is devoted to establishing that John 6 does not refer to sacramental eating, but in doing so, Zwingli came close to the Nestorian separation of the natures.[34] It follows that he regarded the phrase "this is my body" to mean "this signifies the body."[35] In the Eucharistic debate with Luther, Zwingli so stressed the distinction of the two natures—while holding to unity of the person—that Luther accused him of Nestorianism.[36]

On the *communicatio idiomatum*, Zwingli argued that there is attributed to one of the natures what is accomplished by the other. This is a figure of speech on the basis of the unity of the person of Christ and does not represent an actual transfer of attributes.[37] Zwingli's most usual word in this connection was *alloiosis*, indicating that where we refer to one nature, we also understand the other, or when we name both, yet we understand only one. Consequently, Zwingli resisted Luther's belief in the ubiquity of Christ's humanity. This points to the root of the clash with Luther. While Luther held together the two natures to such an extent that it could be doubted whether he had done justice to the humanity, Zwingli distinguished them to a point where one could ask whether he had an adequate grasp of the unity of the person.

This clash underlay the sacramental controversy. While in an early

---

31. W. P. Stephens, *The Theology of Huldrych Zwingli* (Oxford: Clarendon, 1986), 111.

32. Huldrych Zwingli, *Commentary on True and False Religion*, ed. Samuel Macaulay Jackson and Clarence Nevin Heller (1929; repr., Durham, NC: Labyrinth, 1981), 204.

33. Ibid., 205.

34. Ibid., 199–211.

35. Ibid., 226–30.

36. Ibid., 113–14.

37. Ibid., 205.

work, his *Exposition of the Articles* (1523), Zwingli had held that the Eucharist strengthens faith, he abandoned this position by the time he wrote his *Commentary on True and False Religion* (1525).[38] It was from that time that the controversy with Luther developed. Zwingli's main argument, evidenced by the record of debate at Marburg, was focused on the ascension. For him, the body of Christ could only be in one place. Since the ascension, he has been at the right hand of God, *in loco*. Therefore, he cannot be corporeally present in the Eucharist. Neither can the omnipotence of God or the will of Christ make his body ubiquitous.[39] Repeatedly at Marburg, Zwingli had recourse to what he thought was the clear meaning of John 6:63, "It is the Spirit who gives life; the flesh is no help at all. The words that I have spoken to you are spirit and life." However, he read this text, as he did wider theological issues, through the lens of his Neoplatonism, which made it difficult for him to see how material entities could be the channel of spiritual realities.[40] He agreed that Christ was present in the Supper but could not accept that this was in a bodily form.[41] Christ's body is human and has human characteristics, and so it is bound by the limitations of space and time.

In his short treatise *On the Lord's Supper* (1526), it is clear that Zwingli accentuated the human nature, treating the two natures as virtually autonomous. He considered that Christ experiences this or that according to his natures rather than his person. Accordingly, Christ experienced the ascension in his human nature only, so he is now absent and his body and blood cannot be present in the sacrament. Only Christ's divine nature is ubiquitous, or else he would have had no need to ascend. Consequently, the body of the ascended Christ is in one place and cannot be present simultaneously in the Supper. Therefore the clause "this is my body" is a trope.[42]

Bromiley agrees in his introduction to this work that "it must be admitted that Zwingli did tend towards that isolation of the distinc-

38. Stephens, *Theology of Zwingli*, 222.
39. Ibid., 238.
40. Robert Letham, "Baptism in the Writings of the Reformers," *SBET* 7, no. 2 (1989): 21–44.
41. Stephens, *Theology of Zwingli*, 252.
42. Huldrych Zwingli, *On the Lord's Supper*, in *Zwingli and Bullinger: Selected Translations with Introductions and Notes*, ed. G. W. Bromiley, LCC 24 (London: SCM, 1953), 212, 214–15, 219–27.

tive natures or aspects both of Christ himself and also of the Word and sacraments."[43] Later, however, in *An Exposition of the Faith* (1529), Zwingli did display an orthodox statement of Christology.[44]

The Colloquy of Marburg (1529)

The Colloquy was called by Philip, Landgrave of Hesse, so as to present a united Protestant front against Emperor Charles V. The emperor had reached accord with the pope and the king of France, rendering the Protestants vulnerable. Philip wanted theological agreement as a basis for a defensive alliance. The talks stalled over the nature of the presence of Christ in the Lord's Supper. Underlying these differences were deeper Christological issues. In particular, their differences over the *communicatio idiomatum* highlight the significantly different Christologies of the two Reformers, which, in turn and among other things, affected their views of the Eucharist. As Atkinson points out, Luther was almost Eutychian, mingling divine and human, whereas Zwingli bordered on Nestorianism.[45] Luther had a strong doctrine of the hypostatic union; Zwingli's focus was on the distinctiveness of Christ's humanity, although his overall concentration was on his deity.

In part, this impasse reflected earlier developments in patristic Christology. Chalcedon (451) had highlighted the two natures "coming together" to form one person, one and the same Christ. This had created problems for the followers of Cyril of Alexandria (ca. 378–444), the leading figure behind the rejection of Nestorius, and led many to defect, thinking that Chalcedon had made too many concessions to the Nestorians. The Second Council of Constantinople (553) resolved many such questions by the twin dogmas of *anhypostasia* and *enhypostasia*, asserting the unity and continuity of the person of Christ, the assumed humanity being the Son's humanity. In this sense, Zwingli could be seen in Chalcedonian terms as highlighting the two-natures dogma, whereas Luther had a stronger grasp of the enhypostatic resolution.[46]

43. G. W. Bromiley, "Introduction to *On the Lord's Supper*," in *Zwingli and Bullinger*, 183.
44. Huldrych Zwingli, *An Exposition of the Faith*, in *Zwingli and Bullinger*, 251–53.
45. Atkinson, *Martin Luther*, 269.
46. For more on the Colloquy of Marburg, see especially the translation of the record of debate recorded by Rudolph Collini in B. J. Kidd, ed., *Documents Illustrative of the Continental Reformation* (Oxford: Clarendon, 1918), 247–54.

Lutheranism after Luther

JOHANNES BRENZ (1499–1570)

Brenz's main work on Christology was his *De personali unione duarum naturam in Christo* (1561).[47] He built his idea of the *communicatio idiomatum* on the patristic doctrine that deity and humanity are inseparably and indivisibly conjoined. As the Son of God from eternity had immense power, so now does the Son of Man. It is mere human wisdom that opposes the idea that the humanity is everywhere that the deity is. When the Word was made flesh, all the majesty of his deity was poured in. Brenz saw that this was effective from the moment of conception. Those who said that this is contrary to the nature of the human body needed to submit to the Word of God, for the glory of the body of Christ is not from his humanity but from the deity.[48]

Hence, for Brenz the divine attributes were communicated to Christ's humanity from conception, and the power he was given after the resurrection, he had beforehand. Human reason cannot comprehend it. It is based on the hypostatic union, whereby the properties of the one nature are communicated to the other, the humanity's power being from the deity, not from itself. Brenz was aware of the problems this would cause, so he insisted that the humanity is not changed into divinity, for the properties of both natures remain. So in terms of geometrical space, Christ is not everywhere. At root, the ascension was not to another corporeal or worldly place but was to the omnipotence and majesty of God.[49] It is hard to see how Brenz's argument is compatible with the account of Christ in the Gospels.

MARTIN CHEMNITZ (1522–1586)

Martin Chemnitz presented a more sophisticated construction than Brenz, avoiding some of his obvious flaws. In *De duabus naturis in Christo* (1578)[50] and its English translation, *The Two Natures of Christ*

---

47. Johannes Brenz, *De Personali Unione Duarum Naturarum in Christo, et Ascensu Christi in Coelum, ac Sessione Eius ad Dexteram Dei Patris. Qua Vera Corporis et Sanguinis Christi Praesentia in Coena Explicata Est, & Confirmata* (Tübingen: Viduam Ulrichi Morhadi, 1561), 4–15.
48. Ibid., 4, 4b–5, 5b, 6a–7b.
49. Ibid., 7b, 8a, 11a–b, 12a, 15a–b.
50. Martin Chemnitz, *De Duabus Naturis in Christo: De Hypostatica Earum Unione: De Communicatione Idiomatum, et de Aliis Quaestionibus Inde Dependentibus* (Lipsiae: Ramba, 1578).

(1971),[51] he presents the clearest and most careful exposition of the Lutheran position.

Chemnitz considered there to be a threefold aspect to the communication of attributes. The first type, resulting from the hypostatic union, entails the attribution of properties of Christ's natures to his person *in concreto*. Second are things attributed to the person according to both natures, when both natures perform in communion with the other what is proper to them.[52] Chemnitz's third category is the most significant for our purposes. Countless "supernatural qualities and qualities even contrary to the common condition of human nature are given and communicated to Christ's human nature."[53] Scripture testifies that the humanity assumed in the incarnation retains its essential attributes, but because the hypostatic union is exalted above every name and given all power in heaven and earth, his flesh is life giving. Since Christ's divine nature dwells personally in the assumed nature, it would be blasphemous to think that in this hypostatic union the humanity of Christ is left only in its merely natural state and that it had received nothing beyond its essential attributes, powers, and faculties. Scripture asserts that Christ was anointed above his fellows. These infused gifts are not the essential attributes of the divine nature but are his workings outside the divine nature infused into the human nature so that they inhere in it formally, habitually, and subjectively, an instrument suitable for the deity. There are echoes here of the distinction between the essence of God and his workings expounded by the Cappadocians in the Trinitarian crisis of the fourth century and expressed later in Orthodox theology by Gregory Palamas as a distinction between essence and energies. Chemnitz reinforced his comments by extensive citations from the fathers. These gifts are not only created, finite, or habitual gifts but are also the very attributes of the divine nature of Christ, attributes belonging to the deity itself but given according to the assumed human nature. So Christ, according to his human nature, has been given omnipotence, which properly belongs to the divine nature. The divinity has the kind of communion with the humanity that fire has when it communicates

---

51. Martin Chemnitz, *The Two Natures in Christ*, trans. J. A. O. Preus (1578; repr., St. Louis, MO: Concordia, 1971).
52. Ibid., 215–40.
53. Ibid., 241–42.

its essence and heat to burn iron, without any commingling. The glory of the Only Begotten did not always reveal itself in its fullness through the assumed flesh at the time of his humiliation, but when the humiliation was laid aside, Christ was exalted according to the human nature and so entered glory.[54]

Chemnitz was clear that there is no mixture or change in either nature. The divine attributes communicated to the humanity are not possessed essentially by the human nature; otherwise, the divine nature would be commuted. Properties of one nature cannot become the properties of the other. Any idea of this essential communication of divine attributes must be rejected. There is no equalization of natures, no communication of essences or natures. On the other hand, Chemnitz also rejected any denial that the majesty is communicated to the assumed nature, with the corollary that the humanity in the hypostatic union has no share in divine attributes. He also opposed the claim that the divine attributes relate only to the person and are given only verbally to Christ as man, the humanity having no communion in them at all. Antiquity was united on this, he claimed, while the Reformed had been evasive, saying that these gifts were given to the person of Christ but not to the human nature, as if the person exists outside the united natures, so that the person has something either or both natures do not have.[55]

Chemnitz agreed that this is a mystery, received by us in faith. It takes place through interpenetration, like fire in heated iron, the whole majesty of Christ's deity shining forth in the humanity, working with it and through it, with no commingling, so that the assumed nature can give life and rule over all things. He cited the fathers profusely—Athanasius, Cyril, Justin, Ambrose, Eusebius, Theodoret, and Leo I, as well as the Third Council of Constantinople (680–681). In sum, the communication flows out of the hypostatic union, not the other way round. This safeguards against the idea that the whole Trinity became incarnate.[56]

A. B. Bruce thinks that Chemnitz had probably no theoretical dif-

---

54. Ibid., 243–44, 247–56, 259, 263–64.
55. Ibid., 267, 270, 278–83.
56. Ibid., 288–89, 292–312.

ference from the Reformed.[57] In fact, I suggest, Chemnitz had a better grasp of the classic doctrine of the incarnation than Zwingli and many of the Reformed. His basic premise was the hypostatic union, rather than the two natures, a perspective more in keeping with the ultimate patristic Christological resolution. His view of ubiquity was nuanced too. Christ *is able to be present* when, where, and how he pleases. This is a hypothetical or optional omnipresence, as Bruce calls it.[58] Chemnitz saw it as a logical deduction from the hypostatic union, after which the Logos is not outside the flesh. It follows that Christ's human nature is always intimately and inseparably present to the Logos, with the possibility of being present at will to any part of the creation. Chemnitz maintained that in his state of humiliation, Christ only occasionally used these gifts, but after his ascension, he entered into their full use. Brenz, on the other hand, thought that in possessing these gifts from conception, he used them furtively.[59]

THE FORMULA OF CONCORD (1576) AND PHILIPP MELANCHTHON

Differences between Brenz and Chemnitz aroused controversy. The Formula of Concord attempted a resolution, with Chemnitz prominent. The result, in article 8, was something of a fudge. Opposing positions were placed side by side and troublesome questions passed over in silence. No distinction was made between essential and accidental properties of the human nature. This uneasy juxtaposition of incompatible elements left the underlying problems unresolved.[60]

Article 8 states the controversy as "whether the divine and human nature in the attributes of each are in mutual communication REALLY, that is, truly and in every fact and deed, in the person of Christ, and how far that communication extends."[61] The sacramentarians, or the Reformed, the Formula claimed, consider that neither nature communicates to the other anything proper to it but that the communication

57. A. B. Bruce, *The Humiliation of Christ in Its Physical, Ethical, and Official Aspects*, 5th ed. (Edinburgh: T&T Clark, 1905), 98.
58. Ibid., 99.
59. Ibid., 100–102.
60. Ibid., 104–6.
61. Philip Schaff, *The Creeds of Christendom: With a History and Critical Notes*, vol. 3, *The Evangelical Protestant Creeds*, rev. David S. Schaff (1877; repr., Grand Rapids, MI: Baker, 1966), 147–59.

is purely nominal. They consider that God has nothing in common with humanity, nor humanity with divinity, a charge of effective Nestorianism.

In opposition, the Formula affirmed that the natures are personally united so completely that the Son of God and Son of Man are one and the same. The natures are not mingled or changed but retain their own essential attributes. Therefore, the divine attributes of omniscience, omnipresence, and omnipotence never become attributes of the humanity. On the other hand, the union is not a conjunction where neither nature has anything personally in common with the other, for it is the highest communion God has with man—like glowing iron, body and soul. Due to the personal union with the Son, God is man and man is God. Mary bore not a mere man but the true Son of God and is rightly called the Mother of God. It was not a mere man that suffered and died but the person of the Son of God. He suffered according to his human nature, assumed into the unity of his divine person. According to his human nature, the Son of Man is exalted to the right hand of God.

In his humiliation Christ divested himself of his divine majesty and did not always use it until after the resurrection, when he laid aside the form of a servant but not the human nature. Therefore, now he is omniscient, omnipotent, and omnipresent not only as God but also as man. Hence he can be present in his body and blood in the Supper according to the mode of the right hand of God. This presence is not physical or Capernaitic (i.e., transubstantiation) but is true and substantial.

In turn, the Formula repudiated, among other things, the position that the personal union is only a figure of speech and that the *communicatio idiomatum* is only verbal, without any corresponding fact. It rejected the notion that the humanity has become infinite and so is everywhere present with the divine nature, or that it has been made equal to the divine. It denied the claims that it is impossible for Christ to be in more places than one with his body, that humanity alone suffered for us and thus the Son of God had no communication with the human nature, or that he is present to us only by his divinity. It also rejected those who assert that the Son does not accomplish omnipotent works in and with his humanity, that according to his humanity he is incapable of the properties of the divine nature, and that the power given to Christ according to his humanity has no communication with the omnipotence of God. It further denied that there are limits on what he can know, such that Christ even now does not have a perfect knowledge of God and his works and that he cannot know what has been from eternity, what is everywhere, and what will be to eternity.

While concentrating on the period after 1600, Schmid sums up Lutheran Christology: "A real communion of both natures is thereby asserted, in consequence of which the two natures sustain no merely outward relations to each other" but "a true and real impartation and communion."[62]

Bruce makes some telling criticisms. Why, he asks, is the communication not reciprocal? He correctly points to its being one-way, from divine to human, for there is no corresponding claim that attributes of Christ's humanity are communicated to his deity. In so doing, it threatens the humanity of Christ, for the humiliation, while soteriologically necessary, is Christologically impossible.[63] This is evident, I suggest, since Christ, if omnipresent, omnipotent, and omniscient according to his humanity, can hardly be said to have been in a state of humiliation! As Bruce concludes, in its zeal for the deification of Christ's humanity, the Lutheran Christology robs us of the incarnation.[64]

Strikingly, Philipp Melanchthon (1497–1560) moved to a Reformed position on this issue over the years. In his 1521 *Loci Communes*, he wrote nothing on the person of Christ, as he was concerned with the works of Christ and the immediate issues in the Reformation. He later discussed the bodily ascension in his commentary on Colossians, while expounding the third chapter.[65] The 1555 *Loci* are clearly Reformed, especially in the section "De coena Domini" ("On the Lord's Supper").[66] He rejected the communication of attributes from one nature to another.[67]

---

62. Heinrich Schmid, *The Doctrinal Theology of the Evangelical Lutheran Church*, trans. Charles A. Hay and Henry E. Jacobs, 3rd ed. (1899; repr., Minneapolis: Augsburg, 1961), 309, 310.

63. Bruce, *Humiliation of Christ*, 106–12.

64. Ibid., 113–14.

65. Philipp Melanchthon, "Enarratio Epistolae Pauli ad Colossenses Praelecta, 1556," in *Operum omnium* (Wittenberg: Zacharia Schürerio et eius sociis, 1601), 4:358.

66. Philipp Melanchthon, *Loci Communes Theologici* (1555; repr., Basel: Ioannem Operinum, 1562), 41–44, 402–17.

67. Philipp Melanchthon, *Loci Communes* (1555), in *Melanchthon on Christian Doctrine: Loci Communes 1555*, trans. and ed. Clyde L. Manschreck (Grand Rapids, MI: Baker, 1965), 34.

Reformed Christology

A. B. Bruce sums up the characteristics of Reformed Christology in contrast to the Lutheran in its stress on the reality of Christ's humanity and the state of humiliation. As in orthodox Christology, Christ has two natures, a twofold mind and a twofold will. In virtue of the hypostatic union, whatever is said of Christ is said of his person, sometimes in respect to both natures, sometimes in respect to one or the other. In terms of the divine nature, the difference is between concealment in the state of humiliation and open manifestation after the ascension. In his exaltation, the humanity lost some accidental properties—hunger, thirst, and the like—while others were perfectly developed—glory, majesty, strength, wisdom, and virtue—and the essential properties retained.[68]

Bruce thinks that Reformed Christology differed from Lutheran Christology in relation to the nature of the union. The Lutherans accused the Reformed of viewing the natures as if they were two boards without any real communion, whereas the Reformed, for their part, stressed the communication of charisms—wisdom and virtue as qualities produced by the Logos through his Spirit. Bruce's question is, how does this do justice to the union? Why shouldn't these graces result from the union of the Logos with the humanity? Why should they be communicated in a roundabout way by the Holy Spirit? Does this not make the union itself purely external?[69] This is a pressing matter, as we shall see.

Prominent in Reformed Christology is the Son's emptying (*exinanition*), applied to his divine nature not by divestiture but by concealment (*occultatio*). From this arose the idea of a double life of the Logos—the *logos totus extra Jesum* and the *logos totus in Jesu*—one unaffected by the incarnation, another self-controlled in the man Jesus Christ.[70]

JOHN CALVIN (1509–1564) AND THE *EXTRA CALVINISTICUM*

In his *Institutes*, Calvin asked why it was necessary for the Mediator to be God and become man. He connected the incarnation to the whole of redemption:

68. Bruce, *Humiliation of Christ*, 114–16, 118–20.
69. Ibid., 120–24.
70. Ibid., 125–26.

The situation would surely have been hopeless had the very majesty of God not descended to us, since it was not in our power to ascend to him. Hence, it was necessary for the Son of God to become for us "Immanuel, that is, God with us" [Isa. 7:14, Matt. 1:23], and in such a way that his divinity and our human nature might by mutual connection grow together [*ut mutua coniunctione eius divinitas et hominum natura inter se coalescerent*].[71]

Here *coalesco* implies the ontological priority of the natures rather than the person, which runs counter to the eventual conclusion of the Second Council of Constantinople and has a Nestorian ring to it. So Christ took "what was ours as to impart what was his to us, and to make what was his by nature ours by grace."[72]

Calvin continued, drawing the indissoluble connection between incarnation and atonement:

The second requirement of our reconciliation with God was this: that man, who by his disobedience had become lost, should by way of remedy counter it with obedience, satisfy God's judgment, and pay the penalties for sin. Accordingly our Lord came forth as true man and took the person and name of Adam in order to take Adam's place in obeying the Father, to present our flesh as the price of satisfaction to God's righteous judgment, and, in the same flesh, to pay the penalty we had deserved. . . . In short, since neither as God alone could he feel death, nor as man alone could he overcome it, he coupled human nature with divine that to atone for sin he might submit the weakness of the one to death; and that, wrestling with death by the power of the other nature, he might win victory for us.[73]

Thus "our common nature with Christ is the pledge of our fellowship with the Son of God; and clothed with our flesh he vanquished sin and death together that the victory and triumph might be ours."[74]

Later Calvin expounded the *communicatio idiomatum*. Christ was free from all corruption not just because he was born of the Virgin but

---

71. Calvin, *Institutes*, 2.12.1. For the Latin, see Peter Barth, ed., *Joannis Calvini Opera Selecta* (Munich: C. Kaiser, 1926–1959), 3:437.
72. Calvin, *Institutes*, 2.12.2.
73. Ibid., 2.12.3.
74. Ibid.

because he was sanctified by the Spirit that the generation might be pure and undefiled as would have been true before Adam's fall. . . . Here is something marvelous: the Son of God descended from heaven in such a way that, without leaving heaven, he willed to be borne in the virgin's womb, to go about the earth, and to hang upon the cross; yet he continually filled the world even as he had done from the beginning![75]

Calvin stressed that the Son was not restricted to the human nature he assumed into union but that he transcended it. This is what Lutherans were to call the *extra Calvinisticum*. However, some have argued that Calvin so stressed the two natures that he appeared to flirt with Nestorianism. Christ's divinity is so joined and united with his humanity (*ita coniunctam unitamque humanitati divinitatem*) that each retains its distinctive nature unimpaired, and yet these two natures constitute one Christ (*ex duabus illis unus Christus constituatur*).[76] Calvin appears to equalize the natures, with the possible implication that the humanity existed prior to the union insofar as the union is formed out of the two. This impression is reinforced by his consideration that the *communicatio* was a figure of speech. In the same section he wrote that Scripture sometimes attributes to Christ what applies solely to his humanity, sometimes what belongs to his divinity, sometimes what embraces both natures but fits neither alone: "And they so earnestly express this union of the two natures that is in Christ as sometimes to interchange them. This figure of speech is called by the ancient writers 'the communicating of properties.'"[77] The Lutherans considered this a reality rather than a trope.

While Calvin said that passages comprehending both natures at once set forth Christ's true substance most of all—such as John 1:29; 5:21–23; 8:12; 9:5; 10:11; 15:1—he remarked that "the name 'Lord' exclusively belongs to the person of Christ only in so far as it represents a degree midway between God and us."[78] It seems that Calvin thought the person is a union of two natures rather than an action of the eternal Son in adding human nature.

---

75. Ibid., 2.13.4.
76. Ibid., 2.14.1.
77. Ibid.
78. Ibid., 2.14.3.

This tendency is particularly evident in Calvin's comments on 1 Corinthians 15:27. There he stated that at the end Christ "will transfer it [the kingdom] in some way or other [*quodammodo*] from his humanity to his glorious divinity,"[79] as if the natures have some degree of autonomy. It is this that lies at the root of the Reformed tradition of attributing the union of natures and the works performed by Christ to the Holy Spirit rather than to the union established in the Son himself, for if the incarnation were simply a coalescence of two natures, the union would be subsequent to the natures, almost a conjunction, and so would require an outside agent to effect and maintain it.[80]

Calvin agreed with Zwingli that the human body of Christ is in one place, in heaven. In his *Second Defence of the Pious and Orthodox Faith concerning the Sacraments in Answer to the Calumnies of Joachim Westphal* (1556), he wrote that to say, as Westphal did, that "the body which the Son of God once assumed, and which . . . he raised to heavenly glory, is ἄτοπος (without place) is indeed very ἄτοπος (absurd)."[81] Rather, Calvin said, "In order to gain possession of Christ he must be sought in heaven," since "the body . . . which he once offered in sacrifice, must now be contained in heaven, as Peter declares."[82] This is so since the body, while it is "carried above the heavens is exempt from the common order of nature, it does not however cease to be a true body."[83] Where he differed from Zwingli was that he considered that Christ "not only fills heaven and earth, but also miraculously unites us to himself in one body, so that the flesh, though it remains in heaven, is our food."[84] Westphal had argued that Calvin shut Christ up in heaven like Zwingli did.

---

79. Calvin on 1 Cor. 15:27, in *CNTC* 9:327.

80. Calvin was accused of Nestorian leanings. Thomas Weinandy recognizes that Calvin was forced to statements like these in order to defend the integrity of the two natures. Thomas G. Weinandy, *Does God Suffer?* (Notre Dame, IN: University of Notre Dame Press, 2000), 188. He agrees with Willis when the latter says that Calvin lacked a clear concept of the ontological foundation of the incarnation. Edward David Willis, *Calvin's Catholic Christology: The Function of the So-Called Extra Calvinisticum in Calvin's Theology*, Studies in Medieval and Reformation Thought 2 (Leiden: E. J. Brill, 1966), 61–100.

81. John Calvin, *Second Defence of the Pious and Orthodox Faith concerning the Sacraments in Answer to the Calumnies of Joachim Westphal*, in *Selected Works of John Calvin*, vol. 2, *Tracts and Letters, Part 2*, ed. Henry Beveridge and Jules Bonnet, trans. Henry Beveridge (1849; repr., Grand Rapids, MI: Baker, 1983), 2:282.

82. Ibid., 2:285.

83. Ibid., 2:290.

84. Ibid., 2:295.

In reply Calvin argued, "If believers would find Christ in heaven, they must begin with the word and sacraments."[85] Thus, "Christ, by the incomprehensible agency of his Spirit, perfectly unites things disjoined by space, and thus feeds our souls with his flesh, though his flesh does not leave heaven, and we keep creeping on the earth."[86] So Calvin went beyond Zwingli in asserting that the distance between Christ's body in heaven and we on earth is overcome by the Holy Spirit. However, in distinction from Luther and the Lutherans, this feeding occurs not in direct relation to the incarnation, to the hypostatic union and the communion of natures resulting from it, but by the distinct agency of the Spirit. Union with Christ is not a consequence flowing directly from the incarnation.

In his *Clear Exposition of Sound Doctrine concerning the True Partaking of the Flesh and Blood of Christ in the Holy Supper in order to dissipate the mists of Tileman Heshusius* (1561), Calvin was even clearer. Here he attributed the life we receive to the flesh of Christ, with the Spirit as the agent who effects this. Hence, he said that the flesh Christ assumed is life giving since it is the source of spiritual life for us.[87] While the body of Christ is absent in terms of place, we have a real spiritual participation in it, "every obstacle from distance being surmounted by his divine energy."[88] In passing, Calvin acknowledged that it is incomprehensible to us how the body of Christ is in one place but yet the person of Christ is omnipresent.[89] He mentioned his adoption of the scholastic dictum—*totus ubique sed non totum*—"the whole Christ everywhere but not wholly."[90] Hesshus, he maintained, perverted what he had said by stating that the human nature is everywhere and Christ's human nature can exist in different places wherever he chooses.[91] On the contrary,

> to our having substantial communion with the flesh of Christ there is no necessity for any change of place, since, by the secret virtue of the Spirit, he infuses his life into us from heaven. Distance does

85. Ibid., 2:296.
86. Ibid., 2:299.
87. Ibid., 2:507.
88. Ibid., 2:510.
89. Ibid., 2:514.
90. Ibid., 2:514–15.
91. Ibid., 2:515.

not at all prevent Christ from dwelling in us, or us from being one with him, since the efficacy of the Spirit surmounts all natural obstacles.[92]

From Scripture it is clear that the body of Christ is finite:

> We deny not that the whole and entire Christ in the person of the mediator fills heaven and earth. I say *whole*, not *wholly* (*totus, non totum*) because it were absurd to apply this to his flesh. The hypostatic union of the two natures is not equivalent to a communication of the immensity of the Godhead to the flesh, since the peculiar properties of both natures are perfectly accordant with unity of person.[93]

Citing previous work, Calvin stated that while the humanity of Christ is in heaven, the right hand of God does not signify a place but rather the power the Father has given Christ to rule the cosmos. "For Christ by his ascension to heaven entered on the possession of the dominion given him by the Father"; he is far removed in terms of bodily presence "yet fills all things . . . by the agency of his Spirit."[94] "For wherever the right hand of God, which embraces heaven and earth, is diffused," Calvin explained, "there the spiritual presence of Christ himself is present by his boundless energy, though his body must be contained in heaven, according to the declaration of Peter."[95] As a parting shot, Calvin retorted, "When he [Hesshus] says that certain properties are common to the flesh of Christ and to the Godhead, I call for a demonstration which he has not yet attempted."[96]

Calvin's insistence, shared by the Reformed, that the Son is not confined to the humanity he assumed was to be dubbed by the Lutherans in the next century "that Calvinistic beyond [*extra-Calvinisticum*]."[97] However, it was hardly an innovation. David Willis, investigating Calvin's sources, unearthed extensive evidence from patristic and medieval

---

92. Ibid., 2:518–19.
93. Ibid., 2:557–58.
94. Ibid., 2:558–59.
95. Ibid., 2:561.
96. Ibid., 2:561.
97. See Willis, *Calvin's Catholic Christology*, passim; Willis, "Extra-Calvinisticum," in *Encyclopedia of the Reformed Faith*, ed. Donald K. McKim (Louisville: Westminster John Knox, 1992), 132–33.

writers[98] to conclude that it represented "a consensus of the ancient fathers."[99] Indeed, he adds, "the term 'extra-Calvinisticum' is not an exclusive mark distinguishing the Christology of Calvin from other Christologies of the one Catholic Church. . . . Rather, the doctrine sustains the correct Catholic interpretations of the Biblical witness to Christ."[100] The "fact is that the 'extra-Calvinisticum' is a medium for expressing the unity of the person of Jesus Christ without displacing mystery with speculation."[101] Consequently, "the 'extra-Calvinisticum,' because of its widespread and ancient usage could just as well be called the 'extra-Catholicum.'"[102]

Notwithstanding this assessment, the pressure of debate may have driven Calvin on occasions to the type of unguarded comment to which we have drawn attention above. It appears that the Lutherans had a stronger grasp of the patristic doctrine of the hypostatic union as this had come to expression in the sixth century at the Second Council of Constantinople, but the Reformed had understood better the distinctness of the natures. However, the forces of controversy have a habit of polarizing opinions.

Peter Martyr Vermigli (1499–1562)

Vermigli's Christology is unfolded in his *Dialogus de utraque in Christo natura* (1561).[103] Vermigli was keenly aware of the reality of Christ's humanity in its postascension state. His dialogue accurately portrays the differences between the Lutheran and Reformed confessions. He insisted that we cannot remove mass, size, bodily disposition, parts, features, and limbs, which are part of the human makeup, from the body of Christ. The human body is abolished when one takes away such things.[104]

---

98. For instance, he cites Lombard, Aquinas, Duns Scotus, Occam, Biel, Lefevre, Augustine, Origen, Theodore of Mopsuestia, and Athanasius. Willis, *Calvin's Catholic Christology*, 26–58.

99. Ibid., 49.

100. Ibid., 99.

101. Ibid., 100.

102. Ibid., 153.

103. Pietro Martire Vermigli, *Dialogus de Utraque in Christo Natura . . . : Illustratur & Coenae Dominicæ Negotium, Perspicuisque . . . Testimoniis Demonstratur Corpus Christi Non Esse Ubique* (Tiguri: C. Froschoverus, 1561).

104. Peter Martyr Vermigli, *The Peter Martyr Library*, vol. 2, *Dialogue on the Two Natures in Christ*, trans. and ed. John Patrick Donnelly, Sixteenth Century Essays and Studies 31 (Kirksville, MO: Thomas Jefferson University Press and Sixteenth Century Journal Publishers, 1995), 12.

Vermigli affirmed the adherence of the Reformed churches to the first six ecumenical councils. His imaginary Lutheran interlocutor replied that Vermigli did not want to affirm their consequences. Since the deity and humanity are inseparable in the one person of Christ, wherever the Godhead is, there is the humanity. Vermigli rejected these conclusions; they exhibited the flaw of equivocation. The Lutheran, he said, understands the human nature as if the whole of the divine nature is included in it or as if the human nature were filled out and spread out equally with the divine. This is not far from Eutyches, who held to only one nature. Rather, he argued, the Reformed believe that the humanity is inseparable from the divinity, so that "it in no wise restricts the divinity within its own narrow limits nor so expands itself so that it fills every place where the divinity exists."[105] The Lutheran opponent could not avoid a commingling between the natures. He thought the person is torn apart if the deity is held to be where the humanity is not present. But, Vermigli maintained, while the body of Christ is in heaven and no longer dwells on earth, still the Son of God is in the church and everywhere: "He is never so freed from his human nature that he does not have it engrafted in him and joined in the unity of his person in the place where the human nature is."[106]

Vermigli used a variety of arguments—such as the relationship of head to body, and the orbits of planets—to argue that the unity of things is not destroyed when there is an intervening spatial distance. He denied that this means setting the deity off from the humanity. The divine nature is everywhere by virtue of its immensity, and it always has the humanity conjoined to it. But the humanity is not present in every place that the divinity fills. The divine Word fills all things, but the humanity hypostatically united to it is confined to its own place. The Lutheran countered by claiming that this means that Vermigli posits two persons, one hypostasis where the humanity is united to the deity and another where the deity is spread throughout the human nature.[107] Vermigli would have none of this. The unity of the person is retained in such a way that the properties of the natures remain distinct

---

105. Ibid., 23.
106. Ibid., 24.
107. Ibid., 24–25.

but not mixed.[108] We preach neither a separation of the deity from the humanity or vice-versa, he insisted. Wherever the human nature is, it is sustained in the divine person. The deity is not limited by the human body since it fills all things.[109]

On the properties of the natures in Christ, Vermigli made copious references to the fathers.[110] In support he cited Cyril of Alexandria, John of Antioch, Leo I, Theodoret, Ambrose, and Augustine.[111] He referred to Cyril speaking of Christ dying according to his humanity, by which he meant that the nature that the Word made its own through the incarnation suffered and died.[112] He cited Augustine's letter to Dardanus, in which he said that scriptural statements are so proper to one of Christ's natures that they cannot be attributed to the other without allowances for their terminology and manner of speaking.[113] Further, he had recourse to Cyril's *Fifth Dialogue on the Trinity*, where he warned against attributing to Christ's humanity qualities uniquely belonging to the Godhead or human attributes to the divine nature; instead, Cyril urged his readers to "cultivate a terminology that distinguishes and befits each one."[114]

From this, Vermigli discussed the Lutheran commitment to ubiquity. The Lutheran asked whether, if we grant to the humanity, because of the hypostatic union, life-giving sanctifying power, why not also grant to it ubiquity? Vermigli replied that while such faculties perfect rather than destroy human nature, it is impossible to make humanity coextensive with the Godhead without making it infinite and so destroying it. The opponent insisted that Lutherans do not believe the human nature is everywhere intrinsically—it does not have that power from itself. Instead, the Word communicates that power to it because of the hypostatic union. Citing Brenz, he said that the body of Christ does not fill all things as a human body but as an assumed body. Vermigli responded by declaring that the divine hypostasis does not rob the assumed body of being a real human body. The Lutheran

---

108. Ibid., 26.
109. Ibid., 28.
110. Ibid., 39–89.
111. Ibid., 51–59.
112. Ibid., 61–65.
113. Vermigli, *Dialogue on the Two Natures*, 66; PL 33:835.
114. Vermigli, *Dialogue on the Two Natures*, 67; PG 75:973.

then mentioned the three types of ubiquity traceable back to Luther: local, replete, and personal. After the Son of God became incarnate, it necessarily follows that the humanity assumed into the unity of his person is everywhere by a personal ubiquity (*ubiquitate personali*). Vermigli thought this very strange.[115]

On the ascension of Christ into heaven, Vermigli wrote that Christ is not human in heaven before the ascension. The burden of proof was on the Lutherans to show that Christ could have ascended according to his humanity if he was already present there. Someone who is everywhere has nowhere to go! The divine hypostasis of Christ could not ascend because he was infinite and had already occupied everything. But Christ's humanity had fixed dimensions and truly ascended into heaven. The angel announced that his body was not in the tomb. Christ was not with Lazarus when he died. Vermigli concluded that for the Lutherans, given their notion of ubiquity, the ascension was only in appearance and for display.[116]

THE COLLOQUY OF MALBRONN (1564)

The Colloquy of Malbronn was called after controversies arose in the Palatinate following Heidelberg's defection from Lutheranism to the Reformed faith. However, instead of reaching any resolution on Christology or the Lord's Supper, positions only hardened as a result. Among the Lutherans, it led to a detachment of Philippists (followers of Melanchthon) from the Wurttemburgers (Gnesio-Lutherans).[117]

At this time, the Lutherans called their opponents *Calviniani* rather than *Zwingliani*.[118] Recently there had occurred the Consensus Tigurinus (1549), where Calvin made concessions to Bullinger on the Eucharist,[119] and the Peace of Augsburg (1555), in which only Lutherans and Roman Catholics were to be tolerated in Europe.[120] Calvin

---

115. Vermigli, *Dialogue on the Two Natures*, 89–107, esp. 89–91.

116. Ibid., 107–11.

117. The chief figures for the Lutherans were Johannes Brenz, Jacob Andraeus, and Theodore Schnapff, and for the Reformed were Zacharias Ursinus, Caspar Olevian, Immanuel Tremellius, and Boquinas.

118. Willis, *Calvin's Catholic Christology*, 11.

119. Paul E. Rorem, "The Consensus Tigurinus (1549): Did Calvin Compromise?," in *Calvinus Sacrae Scripturae Professor: Calvin as Confessor of Holy Scripture; Die Referate Des Congrès International Des Recherches Calviniennes Vom 20. Bis 23. August 1990 in Grand Rapids*, ed. Wilhelm H. Neuser (Grand Rapids, MI: Eerdmans, 1994), 72–90.

120. Willis, *Calvin's Catholic Christology*, 13.

claimed his views were consistent with the Augsburg Confession in his *Final Admonition to Westphal.*[121] At Malbronn, Caspar Olevian introduced the figure of "Antwerp and the ocean" to defend the Reformed position, the ocean representing the Son of God who exists also beyond the bounds of the flesh he assumed.[122] Yet through all these disparate developments, the divide between Lutherans and Reformed remained.

THE COLLOQUY OF MONTBÉLIARD (1586)

The Christological issues increasingly assumed prominence in this controversy at the Colloquy of Montbéliard, since it was in the nature of Christ that the underlying sacramental differences lay. As Raitt observes, "From the Maulbronn Colloquy 1564 through the bitter battles about the meaning of *kenōsis* in the first quarter of the seventeenth century, discussions of the Lord's Supper, which meant discussions of the manner of Christ's presence, became christological arguments."[123] At Montbéliard the chief antagonists were Jacob Andraeus for the Lutherans and Theodore Beza for the Reformed. For Andraeus, there was no great difference in Christ before and after the resurrection, due to the communication of divine attributes to the human nature.[124] In contrast, as Willis observes, the Reformed analogies, such as the comparison between Antwerp and the ocean, seemed incongruous. Behind these lay the intention to state that the humanity is finite or it is not humanity, even when hypostatically united to the infinite Creator. From 1586, this *extra* was seen by the Lutherans as definitively Calvinist, although it had been opposed since 1564.[125] All this brings us back to Luther's insistence that "neither in heaven or on earth do I . . . know Christ outside this flesh."[126] This meant that for the Lutherans the Son does not exist beyond the bounds of the assumed humanity, which in turn entails the humanity's ubiquity.

---

121. CO 9:148.
122. Willis, *Calvin's Catholic Christology*, 15.
123. Jill Raitt, *The Colloquy of Montbéliard: Religion and Politics in the Sixteenth Century* (New York: Oxford University Press, 1993), 110.
124. Ibid., 84.
125. Willis, *Calvin's Catholic Christology*, 16–18, 23.
126. Martin Luther, *Scholia in Esaiam prophetam,* cap. 1–41, in vol. 22 of *Die Martini Lutheri Exegetica Opera Latina,* ed. Christoph von Elsperger und Heinrich Schmidt (Erlangen: Heyder, 1860), 60. This is also cited by Willis from the WA series.

THEODORE BEZA (1519–1605)

In his comments on the debates at Montbéliard, Beza reacted strongly to the calumny that he acknowledged only a verbal *communicatio idiomatum* in Christ, not a real one.[127] It is verbal only insofar as it is a form of predication (*genus praedicationis*) on account of the unity of the person, by which concrete attributes of either nature are attributed to the indivisible person. He called Chemnitz's claim that the gifts communicated to the humanity of Christ are immense to be "untrue, ungodly, and blasphemous."[128] He denied that the hypostatic union negates the human nature or that the divine properties are communicated to it. Christ's elevation to the right hand of God was not the result of the incarnation as such but rather occurred at the end of the time of humiliation. Andraeus, like Chemnitz, regarded the *communicatio* to be the result of the hypostatic union.[129] In turn, Beza contended that the presence of the flesh of Christ in the Eucharist is due not to the hypostatic union but to the words of institution of the sacrament. The substance of Christ's body was absent from heaven when he was on earth, and now that he is in heaven, it is absent from earth. His flesh is powerful and efficacious in a wonderful and impenetrable mystery. Whereas in his own marginal notes on the Colloquy, Andraeus repeatedly claimed that Beza agreed with Nestorius, Beza for his part accused Andraeus of confusing and mixing the deity and humanity.[130] In short, he held that Andraeus's claim about the communication of real and essential properties between the natures was "untrue and absurd."[131]

For Beza, in Christ's person the humanity receives nothing from the divinity, nor vice versa. He argued that there is no real communication between the deity and humanity.[132] However, as unsatisfactory as the Lutheran position may be, for some critics Beza sounded far too close to Nestorianism, as his Christology was more a conjunction of two natures than an incarnation.

---

127. Theodore Beza, *Ad Acta Colloquii Montisbelgardensis Responsionis*, 3rd ed. (Geneva: Ioannes le Preux, 1589), 17–18, 79–80, 163–67.
128. Ibid., 80 (author's trans.).
129. Ibid., 163.
130. Ibid., 164.
131. Ibid., 165 (author's trans.).
132. Ibid., 167.

Anabaptist Christology

Anabaptist Christology followed a different course. Some groups accepted the classic Christological settlement, but others, particularly the Dutch, adopted a variety of heterodox ideas. The Schleitheim Articles (1527) have nothing on Christology.[133] A Confession of Faith by Jörg Muller (1534) is orthodox.[134] On the other hand, article 6 of the Swiss Brethren Confession of Hesse (1578) says Jesus Christ is "a son of God," "like God in might, power and glory," "the first-born of all creatures"—which is clearly heterodox.[135] Moreover, articles 2–5 are not explicitly Trinitarian. These statements are a studied departure from the Christian tradition.[136] Among north German and Dutch confessions, the Kampen Confession (1545) is ambiguous, capable of an Arian interpretation.[137] The 1591 Concept of Cologne's paragraph on Christ is also ambiguous—Christ was incarnate "through the power of the Almighty," implying that he was less than almighty.[138] In view of the fact that the church had pronounced clearly on these issues, ambiguity tells its own story.

A key figure in the Dutch Anabaptist tradition was Melchior Hofmann (ca. 1495–ca. 1544). Karl Koop, in his comments on the Concept of Cologne, states that

> many Dutch anabaptists were influenced by Melchior Hofmann's doctrine of the incarnation that recognized that Christ became human, but assumed that his flesh was "heavenly" and did not come from Mary. Most Dutch anabaptist leaders, such as Menno Simons and Dirk Philips held some version of this Melchiorite doctrine, while south German anabaptists . . . generally followed the understanding of the wider church.[139]

On the other hand, in the Waterlander Confession (1577), the Melchiorite doctrine does not appear, suggesting that the Waterlanders

133. Karl Koop, ed., *Confessions of Faith in the Anabaptist Tradition, 1527–1660*, Classics of the Radical Reformation 11 (Kitchener, Ontario: Pandora, 2006), 23–33.
134. Ibid., 35–44.
135. Ibid., 56.
136. Ibid., 60.
137. Ibid., 97–98.
138. Ibid., 119.
139. Ibid., 115.

were at odds with it; this is supported by its orthodox statement on Christology.[140]

In its orthodox forms, Anabaptism tended toward a sharp distinction between the two natures, similar to Zwingli and Karlstadt. It was useful in defending a doctrine of the Lord's Supper in which Christ is absent and the Holy Spirit is the medium of the divine presence, thus securing a purely spiritualized view of reality.[141] Thus Balthasar Hubmaier (ca. 1480–1528) held that after the ascension, the Son was and is absent from history and the Supper.[142] This represents a radically dualist view of the world. However, this reading of Hubmaier has been challenged by MacGregor, who argues that Hubmaier was indebted to Luther and used Luther's "distinction between the definitive presence of God and the repletive presence of God," by which Christ fills all space-time locations without being restricted.[143] He concluded that both "definitive and repletive presence" apply also to the human nature of Christ, whose "physical body is definitively present at the right hand of God" while it is "repletively present at all points in the space-time universe without being limited by it."[144] But he did not go on to relate this to the Lord's Supper.[145]

Caspar Schwenkfeld (1489–1561) held that the primordial humanity of Christ was not creaturely and so was potentially available for all believers who were spiritually perceptive.[146] Indeed, Schwenkfeld held that those who thought that Christ as man in glory was a creature were more accursed than Eutychians. He recognized nothing of creation or creatureliness in Christ—"I cannot consider the Man Christ with his body and blood to be a creation or a creature."[147] Schwenkfeld's stress was on the unity of Christ's person to such an extent as effectively to erase the humanity.

---

140. Ibid., 123–27.
141. John D. Rempel, *The Lord's Supper in Anabaptism: A Study in the Christology of Balthasar Hubmaier, Pilgram Marpeck, and Dirk Philips*, Studies in Anabaptist and Mennonite History (Scottdale, PA: Herald, 1993), 34–35.
142. Ibid., 66–67.
143. Kirk R. MacGregor, "The Eucharistic Theology and Ethics of Balthasar Hubmaier," *HTR* 105, no. 2 (2012): 228.
144. Ibid., 228–29.
145. Ibid., 229.
146. George Huntston Williams and Angel M. Mergal, eds., *Spiritual and Anabaptist Writers*, LCC 25 (London: SCM, 1957), 162.
147. Ibid., 180.

Pilgram Marpeck (ca. 1495–1556), who had a basically orthodox Christology, opposed Schwenkfeld in debates in 1538 and 1539.[148] While Schwenkfeld held that the Son always had two natures, he believed the Son needed to be born not of a woman but only *in* a woman. Marpeck had only a limited *communicatio idiomatum*, due to the distinction of the natures, which he correctly held to continue after the ascension, but for Schwenkfeld the *communicatio* removed any distinction.[149] In Schwenkfeld's thought, from conception the uncreated humanity of Christ was progressively deified so that we, receiving it in the Supper, progress to deification ourselves.[150]

Others went further than Schwenkfeld, who had a concern to operate within confessional boundaries. Dietrich (or Dirk) Philips (1504–1568), in *The Church of God* (ca. 1560), considered it impossible for the flesh of Christ to be formed of the seed of Mary, for if that were so, he could not be the Living Bread that came down from heaven.[151] Melchior Hofmann, who probably influenced Schwenkfeld, argued that the Virgin Mary played no role in providing Jesus with human flesh; rather, Jesus "passed through Mary like water through a pipe."[152] If Mary had contributed anything, Jesus would have been tainted with creatureliness.[153] This was a denial of the human flesh of Christ and an assertion that he had one nature, not two.[154] Menno Simons followed Hofmann throughout his career. He taught that Christ was a single person, not two, indicating his failure to understand the Christological teaching of the church, since he understood anything creaturely to entail a separate identity and thus dual persons. Since the Son of Man came down from heaven, he concluded that the entire Christ—deity and humanity—has his origin in heaven, not on earth.[155] Williams traces the origins of these ideas to a Strasbourg gardener, Clement Zeigler, who taught that Christ

---

148. Rempel, *Lord's Supper in Anabaptism*, 108–19; C. Arnold Snyder, *Anabaptist History and Theology: An Introduction* (Kitchener, Ontario: Pandora, 1995), 357–58.
149. Rempel, *Lord's Supper in Anabaptism*, 114.
150. George Huntston Williams, *The Radical Reformation* (Philadelphia: Westminster, 1975), 332–35.
151. Ibid., 238–39.
152. Snyder, *Anabaptist History and Theology*, 357.
153. Ibid., 357.
154. Williams, *Radical Reformation*, 329–31.
155. Snyder, *Anabaptist History and Theology*, 359–60.

brought his body from heaven and gained visibility from the flesh provided by Mary.[156]

Conclusion

The differences among various Anabaptist groupings reflect the degree to which the respective spokesmen accepted or disregarded the historic confessional commitments of the church on Christology. However, many of the radical leaders had little commitment to the tradition of the church. Consequently, many old heresies resurfaced, and new ones emerged.

Overall, the Lutherans and the Reformed, while as committed to the ecumenical dogma as Rome was, tended to accentuate opposite sides of the classic confessional statements. The former, with a strong grasp of the hypostatic union, were held by the Reformed to jeopardize the reality of Christ's humanity. On the other hand, in their concern for the integrity of both natures, at times the Reformed appeared to have a loose view of the union.

Resources for Further Study

Primary Sources

Beza, Theodore. *Ad Acta Colloquii Montisbelgardensis Responsionis*. 3rd ed. Geneva: Ioannes le Preux, 1589.

Brenz, Johannes. *De Personali Unione Duarum Naturarum in Christo, et Ascensu Christi in Coelum, ac Sessione Eius ad Dexteram Dei Patris. Qua Vera Corporis et Sanguinis Christi Praesentia in Coena Explicata Est, & Confirmata*. Tübingen: Viduam Ulrichi Morhadi, 1561.

Bromiley, G. W., ed. *Zwingli and Bullinger: Selected Translations with Introductions and Notes*. Library of Christian Classics 24. London: SCM, 1953.

Calvin, John. *Calvin's Commentaries*. Vol. 9, *The First Epistle of Paul the Apostle to the Corinthians*. Translated by David W. Torrance and John W. Fraser. Grand Rapids, MI: Eerdmans, 1960.

———. *Institutes of the Christian Religion*. Edited by John T. McNeill. Translated by Ford Lewis Battles. 2 vols. Library of Christian Classics 20–21. 1559 edition. Philadelphia: Westminster, 1960.

---

156. Williams, *Radical Reformation*, 326–29.

———. *Tracts and Letters, Part 2*. Vol. 2 of *Selected Works of John Calvin*. Edited by Henry Beveridge and Jules Bonnet. Translated by Henry Beveridge. 1849. Reprint, Grand Rapids, MI: Baker, 1983.

Chemnitz, Martin. *The Two Natures in Christ*. Translated by J. A. O. Preus. 1578. Reprint, St. Louis, MO: Concordia, 1971.

Koop, Karl, ed. *Confessions of Faith in the Anabaptist Tradition, 1527–1660*. Classics of the Radical Reformation 11. Kitchener, Ontario: Pandora, 2006.

Luther, Martin. *Confession concerning Christ's Supper*. In *Luther's Works*. Vol. 37, *Word and Sacrament III*, edited by Robert H. Fischer, 151–372. 1528. Reprint, Philadelphia: Fortress, 1961.

———. *The Freedom of a Christian*. In *Luther's Works*. Vol. 31, *Career of the Reformer I*, edited by Harold J. Grimm, 327–77. 1520. Reprint, Philadelphia: Fortress, 1957.

———. "Preface to the Epistles of St. James and St. Jude." In *Luther's Works*. Vol. 35, *Word and Sacrament I*, edited by E. Theodore Bachman, 395–98. 1546. Reprint, Philadelphia: Fortress, 1960.

———. "Preface to the Old Testament." In *Luther's Works*. Vol. 35, *Word and Sacrament I*, edited by E. Theodore Bachman, 233–333. 1523. Reprint, Philadelphia: Fortress, 1960.

———. *That These Words of Christ, "This Is My Body," Etc., Still Stand Firm against the Fanatics*. In *Luther's Works*. Vol. 37, *Word and Sacrament III*, edited by Robert H. Fischer, 3–150. 1527. Reprint, Philadelphia: Fortress, 1961.

———. "Two Kinds of Righteousness." In *Luther's Works*. Vol. 31, *Career of the Reformer I*, edited by Harold J. Grimm, 293–306. 1519. Reprint, Philadelphia: Fortress, 1957.

Melanchthon, Philipp. *Loci Communes* (1555). In *Melanchthon on Christian Doctrine: Loci Communes 1555*. Translated and edited by Clyde L. Manschreck. Grand Rapids, MI: Baker, 1965.

———. *Loci Communes Theologici*. 1555. Reprint, Basel: Ioannem Operinum, 1562.

Vermigli, Peter Martyr. *The Peter Martyr Library*. Vol. 2, *Dialogue on the Two Natures in Christ*. Translated and edited by John Patrick Donnelly. Sixteenth Century Essays and Studies 31. Kirksville, MO: Thomas Jefferson University Press and Sixteenth Century Journal Publishers, 1995.

Williams, George Huntston, and Angel M. Mergal, eds. *Spiritual and Anabaptist Writers*. Library of Christian Classics 25. London: SCM, 1957.

Zwingli, Huldrych. *Commentary on True and False Religion*. Edited by Samuel Macaulay Jackson and Clarence Nevin Heller. 1929. Reprint, Durham, NC: Labyrinth, 1981.

SECONDARY SOURCES

Raitt, Jill. *The Colloquy of Montbéliard: Religion and Politics in the Sixteenth Century*. New York: Oxford University Press, 1993.

Rempel, John D. *The Lord's Supper in Anabaptism: A Study in the Christology of Balthasar Hubmaier, Pilgram Marpeck, and Dirk Philips*. Studies in Anabaptist and Mennonite History 33. Scottdale, PA: Herald, 1993.

Rorem, Paul E. "The Consensus Tigurinus (1549): Did Calvin Compromise?" In *Calvinus Sacrae Scripturae Professor: Calvin as Confessor of Holy Scripture; Die Referate Des Congrès International Des Recherches Calviniennes Vom 20. Bis 23. August 1990 in Grand Rapids*, edited by Wilhelm H. Neuser, 72–90. Grand Rapids, MI: Eerdmans, 1994.

Willis, Edward David. *Calvin's Catholic Christology: The Function of the So-Called Extra Calvinisticum in Calvin's Theology*. Studies in Medieval and Reformation Thought 2. Leiden: E. J. Brill, 1966.

10

The Work of Christ

Donald Macleod

ABSTRACT

Beginning with the observation that the doctrine of justification by
faith is incomplete without a clear doctrine of the work of Christ,
this chapter uses Calvin's concept of the threefold office (*munus
triplex*) as the framework for a summary of the Reformers' doctrine
of the mediatorial activity of Jesus, with special emphasis on their
understanding of the atonement. It notes the key points at which
Protestantism challenged Roman Catholic dogma with regard to
the priesthood of Christ, assesses Aulén's argument that Luther, as
distinct from the other Reformers, preached a "classical" doctrine
of the atonement, and concludes with reflections on Luther's insistence on a "theology of the cross."

Introduction

Few would deny that the key rediscovery of the Reformation was the
doctrine of justification by faith. As Calvin pointed out in his *Reply
to Cardinal Sadolet*, this was the "first and keenest subject of controversy between us," and he added, "Wherever the knowledge of it is
taken away, the glory of Christ is extinguished, religion abolished, the

Church destroyed, and the hope of salvation utterly overthrown."[1] Yet the phrase *justification by faith* is always incomplete, because it leaves unanswered the question, faith in what? It was on this question that Romanism and Protestantism divided. The Council of Trent never denied that justification was by faith. What it denied was that it was by faith *alone* and in Christ *alone*. It was on these that Rome's anathemas fell.[2] But in the Protestant doctrine was always something more fundamental than justification, namely, the work of the Redeemer. It was on this that justification rested and in this that faith trusted. Sinners, wrote Luther, "must be justified without merit [of their own] through faith in Christ, who has merited this for us by his blood, and has become for us a mercy-seat by God."[3]

It was only natural, then, that the Reformers would give prominence to the work of Christ, and particularly to the doctrine of the atonement, but neither Luther, Melanchthon, Bucer, Zwingli, nor Bullinger ever gave it the systematic treatment it received at the hands of John Calvin. Calvin devoted six chapters of his *Institutes*[4] to this subject, and in the course of his discussion, he introduced into Reformation theology the widely influential concept of the *munus triplex*. It seems appropriate, then, to use Calvin's doctrine as the point of entry into the wider Reformation doctrine.

Christ the Only Mediator

The Latin term *munus triplex* points not to "the three offices" of Christ but to a threefold office. There is one office, that of Mediator, but this one office (Lat. *officium*, "duty") includes the three functions of Prophet, Priest, and King. The biblical idea of a mediator occurs as early as Deuteronomy 5:5, where Moses speaks of himself as standing between Yahweh and Israel in order to receive the divine word and

---

1. John Calvin, *John Calvin: Tracts and Letters*, ed. Henry Beveridge and Jules Bonnet, trans. Henry Beveridge (1844; repr., Edinburgh: Banner of Truth, 2009), 1:41.
2. See canons 9 and 11 of the sixth session of the Council of Trent in, e.g., Philip Schaff, *The Creeds of the Greek and Latin Churches* (London: Hodder and Stoughton, 1877), 112–13.
3. From Luther's "Prefaces to the New Testament," *LW* 35:373. Cf. Melanchthon, who stated, "When we say that we are justified by faith, we are saying nothing else than that for the sake of the Son of God we receive remission of sins and are accounted as righteous." Philipp Melanchthon, *The Chief Theological Topics: Loci Praecipui Theologici*, 2nd English ed., trans. J. A. O. Preus (St. Louis, MO: Concordia, 2011), 157.
4. Calvin, *Institutes*, 2.12–17.

pass it on to the people; the reason why it had to be done through a mediator was that the people, confronted with the awesomeness of Sinai, were "afraid because of the fire." Calvin saw this as one signal instance of the principle of accommodation: "Whereas God sendeth his worde by the hand of men, he doeth it in respect of men's default and infirmitie."[5] But the need for a Mediator arose not only from our limited human capacities but also from our dire spiritual plight. Through the fall of Adam humanity has become degenerate, accursed, and miserably enslaved. "The whole human race," wrote Calvin, "perished in the person of Adam." Consequently, our "original excellence and nobility" "would be of no profit to us, but would rather redound to our greater shame, until God, who does not recognize as his handiwork men defiled and corrupted by sin, appeared as Redeemer in the person of his only-begotten Son."[6] Accordingly, "apart from the Mediator, God never showed favor toward the ancient people, nor ever gave hope of grace to them."[7]

The specific term "mediator" (Gk. *mesitēs*) is applied to Christ in such New Testament passages as 1 Timothy 2:5; Hebrews 8:6; 9:15; and 12:24. And it is applied to him not as one mediator among many but as sole Mediator. He is the "*one* mediator between God and men" (1 Tim. 2:5). This was a key point in the controversy with Rome. Over against the practice of praying to the Blessed Virgin and to the saints, the Reformers argued strenuously that "since Christ is proposed to us as the only Mediator, through whom we ought to approach God, those who, passing him by, or postponing him, betake themselves to the saints, have no excuse for their depravity."[8] In his commentary on 1 Timothy 2:5, Calvin referred to the fact that "from the beginning men have departed further and further from God by inventing for themselves one mediator after another," but what is particularly interesting is the reason he alleged for this development: "the erroneous notion that God was at a great distance from them, and so they did not know where to turn for help." The antidote to this is that in Christ

---

5. *The Sermons of M. John Calvin upon the Fifth Booke of Moses called Deuteronomie*, trans. Arthur Golding (London, 1583; facsimile repr., Edinburgh: Banner of Truth, 1987), 183.
6. Calvin, *Institutes*, 2.6.1.
7. Ibid., 2.6.2.
8. Calvin, *Tracts and Letters*, 1:96.

God has come down to us and is present with us: "If it were deeply impressed on the hearts of all men that the Son of God holds out to us the hands of a brother and is joined to us by sharing our nature, who would not choose to walk in this straighter highway rather than wander in uncertain and rough byways?" Calvin added, "Thus, whenever we pray to God, if the thought of his sublime and inaccessible majesty fills our minds with dread, let us also remember the man Christ who gently invites us and takes us by the hand, so that the Father whom we had dreaded and feared becomes favourable and friendly to us." The "Roman sophists," however, were busy contriving all manner of ways to obscure this truth: "The name is so hateful to them that if anyone so much as mentions Christ's mediatorship without bringing in the saints, he at once falls under suspicion of heresy."[9]

Exactly the same sentiments had already been expressed in the Augsburg Confession (1530), which declared (art. 21),

> It cannot be proved from the Scriptures that we are to invoke saints or seek help from them. "For there is one mediator between God and men, Christ Jesus" (1 Tim. 2:5), who is the only saviour, the only highpriest, advocate, and intercessor before God (Rom. 8:34). He alone has promised to hear our prayers.

The highest form of divine service (Lat. *cultus*), therefore, is "sincerely to seek and call upon this same Jesus in every time of need."[10] In the Apology of the Augsburg Confession, drafted by Melanchthon in 1531, the invocation of the saints is declared to be "simply intolerable, for it transfers to the saints honour belonging to Christ alone. It makes them mediators and propitiators."[11] The Apology may even have been the source from which Calvin drew when he attributed the invocation of saints to a misplaced dread of God, and even of Christ himself: "Men suppose," it declares, "that Christ is more severe and the saints more

---

9. Calvin on 1 Tim. 2:5, in *CNTC* 9:210–11. Cf. article 12 of the Genevan Confession, which states, "We reject the intercession of the saints as a superstition invented by men contrary to Scripture, for the reason that it proceeds from mistrust of the sufficiency of the intercession of Jesus Christ." John Calvin, "The Genevan Confession (1536)," in *Calvin: Theological Treatises*, trans. J. K. S. Reid, LCC 22 (London: SCM, 1954), 29.
10. See Theodore G. Tappert, ed. and trans., *The Book of Concord: The Confessions of the Evangelical Lutheran Church* (Philadelphia: Fortress, 1959), 47.
11. Ibid., 230.

approachable; so they trust more in the mercy of the saints than in the mercy of Christ, and they flee from Christ and turn to the saints."[12]

It is within the overarching concept of Christ as Mediator that Calvin developed both his understanding of the two natures of Christ and his doctrine of the threefold office: "The office enjoined upon Christ by the Father consists of three parts. For he was given to be prophet, king and priest."[13] It is noteworthy that Calvin offered no exposition of the phrase "the office enjoined on Christ." Even when we might have expected the texts he was commenting on (e.g., Heb. 3:2; 5:4) to serve as a prompt, he contented himself with saying that the Father has called him, appointed him, and set him over us;[14] or, commenting on Psalm 2:7, he merely stated that "Christ was made King by God the Father."[15] Perhaps most surprising of all is that when he commented on the words of Psalm 89:3 ("I have made a covenant with my chosen"), he limited himself to the covenant made with David.[16] What is striking here is not only the absence of any reference to what later Reformed theologians referred to as the covenant of redemption (the eternal agreement between the Father and the Son that lay behind the mission and work of Christ) but also the absence of any sense of a need for such a covenant. There is not even the germ of what John Owen would later call "Federal Transactions between the Father and the Son."[17] Even when he came closest to discussing the commissioning of Jesus, Calvin appeared to confine it to his earthly life: "We are speaking of Christ in so far as he has put on our flesh, and is thus the Servant of the Father for the carrying out of his commands."[18] Yet, while Calvin made no explicit mention of a pretemporal appointment or undertaking, the very word *officium* implies that Christ came not on some undefined mission but as one charged with a specific duty.

To some extent this absence of any reference to a pretemporal

---

12. Ibid., 231.
13. Calvin, *Institutes*, 2.15.1.
14. Calvin on Heb. 3:2 and 5:4, in CNTC 12:35, 60.
15. John Calvin, *Commentary on the Book of Psalms*, trans. James Anderson (Edinburgh: Calvin Translation Society, 1845–1849), 1:17 (*ad* Ps. 2:7).
16. Ibid., 3:421.
17. John Owen, *An Exposition of Hebrews*, ed. William H. Goold (Edinburgh: Johnstone & Hunter, 1855), 2:77–97.
18. John Calvin, *The Epistle of Paul the Apostle to the Hebrews and the First and Second Epistles of St. Peter*, 35 (*ad* Heb. 3:2).

covenant reflects Calvin's position on the timeline of Reformed theology: fully developed covenant theology would not come until a century later.[19] Still, more is at stake here than mere methodology. Christ himself clearly set his ministry in a covenantal context (Matt. 26:28), and key aspects of his work are hard to understand except against the background of an agreement between himself and the Father. How, for example, did the Son come to be sent, and how did there come to be a work given him to do (John 17:4)? Above all, there is the mystery of Christ's relationship with his people. How was he appointed their representative, surety, and substitute? And how did they come to be coheirs with God's only Son? In view of such questions, what the covenant of redemption offered was not a speculation too far but a coherent answer to questions arising out of the biblical material itself.

Precedents for the *Munus Triplex*

Calvin first introduced the idea of the *munus triplex* into the *Institutes* in the 1539 edition, but there were some precedents for it in earlier Christian thought. Calvin himself acknowledged that "the papists use these names, too,"[20] and in the course of explaining the title Christ, article 2 of the Catechism of the Council of Trent (1566) explicitly declared, "When Jesus Christ our Saviour came into the world, He assumed these three characters of Prophet, Priest and King," having been anointed for these functions by his heavenly Father.[21] The general tendency, however, had been to speak of a twofold office of Priest and King, even though as early as the beginning of the fourth century the *munus triplex* had already appeared in Eusebius, who described Christ as "the sole High Priest of the universe, the sole King of all creation, and of prophets the sole Archprophet of the Father."[22] Chrysostom also referred to Christ's "three dignities" as King, Prophet, and Priest,[23]

---

19. On the early roots of federal theology, see, for example, William Klempa, "The Concept of Covenant in Sixteenth- and Seventeenth-Century Continental and British Reformed Theology," in *Major Themes in the Reformed Tradition*, ed. Donald K. McKim (Grand Rapids, MI: Eerdmans, 1992), 94–107.

20. Calvin, *Institutes*, 2.15.1.

21. *The Catechism of the Council of Trent*, published by command of Pope Pius V, trans. Jeremiah Donovan (Baltimore: Fielding Lucas, 1829), 34.

22. Eusebius, *The History of the Church from Christ to Constantine*, trans. G. A. Williamson (Harmondsworth, UK: Penguin, 1965), 43.

23. Quoted in John Frederick Jansen, *Calvin's Doctrine of the Work of Christ* (London: James Clarke, 1956), 30.

but these were passing allusions rather than systematic formulae. Medieval theologians continued to speak in terms of a *munus duplex*, although there is an enigmatic instance of the threefold office in Aquinas, who mentioned the offices of Lawgiver (Lat., *legislator*), Priest, and King all concurring in Christ.[24] But, again, this appears to have been but part of a one-off response to an objection. Luther, Melanchthon, and Bullinger all continued the medieval usage. In *The Freedom of a Christian*, Luther, for example, referred to Christ as "the true and only first-born of God the Father and the Virgin Mary and true king and priest."[25] The only exception among Reformation theologians was Osiander, who wrote, "We must understand this of His office that He is Christ, that is, Master, King, and High Priest. For as Christ means anointed, and only prophets, kings and priests were anointed, so one sees that all three offices apply to Him."[26]

When Calvin himself wrote the first edition of the *Institutes* in 1536, he still spoke only of the twofold office of King and Priest, and, like Osiander, linked the offices to the anointing: as the Spirit has poured himself out fully on him,

> so do we believe in short that by this anointing he was appointed king by the Father to subject all power in heaven and on earth, that in him we might be kings, having sway over the devil, sin, death and hell. Then we believe that he was appointed priest, by his self-sacrifice to placate the Father and reconcile him to us, that in him we might be priests.[27]

In the 1539 edition of the *Institutes*, Calvin alluded to the fact that prophets, as well as kings and priests, were anointed, and in the 1545 edition, he clearly linked the "office of the chief prophet" to the kingship and priesthood of Christ.[28] But the arrangement had already become explicit in Calvin's Catechism of the Church of Geneva (Fr. ed.

---

24. Aquinas, *Summa Theologiae* 3a.22.1 *ad* 3, translation from Saint Thomas Aquinas, *Summa Theologica*, trans. Fathers of the English Dominican Province (Notre Dame, IN: Christian Classics, 1981), 4:2136.

25. *LW* 31:353.

26. Quoted in Jansen, *Calvin's Doctrine of the Work of Christ*, 37. The quotation comes from a work by Osiander published in 1530.

27. John Calvin, *Institutes of the Christian Religion* (1536 ed.), trans. Ford Lewis Battles, rev. ed., H. H. Meeter Center for Calvin Studies (Grand Rapids, MI: Eerdmans, 1986), 54.

28. See Jansen, *Calvin's Doctrine of the Work of Christ*, 41–42.

1541; Lat. 1545), where, to the question, "What force, then, has the name of Christ?" he gave the answer, "It signifies that he is anointed by his Father to be King, Priest and Prophet."[29] In the definitive 1559 edition of the *Institutes*, Calvin devoted a whole chapter to introducing the three offices of King, Priest, and Prophet.[30]

After Calvin, the threefold office became a key formula in Reformed catechesis and theology. It was adopted in answers 31 and 32 of the Heidelberg Catechism (published in 1563, while Calvin was still alive) and from there passed into Ursinus's widely influential *Commentary*, first published in 1591 but embodying the substance of university lectures delivered between 1561 and 1577.[31] And even before the publication of Ursinus's *Commentary*, William Perkins's *Golden Chain* (1590) took it for granted that "Christ's office is threefold—priestly, prophetical, regal."[32] It was adopted by the Westminster Confession of Faith (8.1), the Westminster Larger Catechism (42–45), and the Westminster Shorter Catechism (23–26), and also by Reformed systematicians from Ussher to Hodge and from Berkhof to Grudem.[33] Indeed, its influence ranged far beyond the bounds of Reformed orthodoxy, as Jansen points out: "Men as different as Schleiermacher and Brunner, Gerhard and Turretin, Bavinck and Newman, have all made use of it."[34]

Calvin clearly did not adopt the *munus triplex* out of deference to any prior authority, nor did he take it up because it corresponded neatly to man's threefold spiritual need (knowledge, forgiveness, and deliverance). Instead, as we have seen, he deduced it from the title Messiah, drawing on its basic meaning of "anointing." Christ was first and foremost "the anointed one," and Calvin noted that in the

---

29. In *Calvin: Theological Treatises*, 95. However, in his *Commentary on Hebrews* (published in 1549), Calvin reverted to the twofold office when commenting on Heb. 4:14: "When the Son of God was sent to us, He was given a twofold character, that of Teacher and that of Priest." Calvin, *The Epistle of Paul the Apostle to the Hebrews and the First and Second Epistles of St. Peter*, 54.
30. Calvin, *Institutes*, 2.15.
31. *The Commentary of Dr. Zacharias Ursinus on the Heidelberg Catechism*, trans. G. W. Williard (1852; repr., Phillipsburg, NJ: Presbyterian and Reformed, n.d.).
32. William Perkins, *A Golden Chain*, in *The Works of William Perkins*, ed. Ian Breward, Courtenay Library of Reformation Classics 3 (Appleford: Sutton Courtenay, 1970), 204.
33. James Ussher, *A Body of Divinitie* (London, 1653), 166–86; Charles Hodge, *Systematic Theology* (New York: Scribner, 1871–1873), 2:459–609; Louis Berkhof, *Systematic Theology* (London: Banner of Truth, 1959), 356–414; Wayne Grudem, *Systematic Theology: An Introduction to Biblical Doctrine* (Leicester: Inter-Varsity Press, 1994), 624–31.
34. Jansen, *Calvin's Doctrine of the Work of Christ*, 16.

Old Testament, three specific functionaries were anointed: kings, such as Saul (1 Sam. 10:1) and David (1 Sam. 16:13); priests, especially the high priest (Ex. 29:7); and prophets. Calvin's claim that under the law prophets as well as kings and priests were anointed with oil may seem somewhat dubious: there were, after all, no formal Old Testament prescriptions for the anointing of prophets. But there could be no doubt that they spoke by the Spirit, and this became explicit in Isaiah 61:1, where the prophet cries, "The Spirit of the Lord GOD is upon me, because the LORD has anointed me to bring good news to the poor."[35] It was with these very words that Jesus himself began his prophetic ministry in the synagogue at Nazareth (Luke 4:18–19).

The Mediator: Both True God and True Man

The Reformers' doctrine of the work of Christ rested on a strong Chalcedonian foundation. They were unanimous that the Mediator was both true God and true man. Luther expressed it memorably in his *Lectures on Romans* (*ad* Rom. 1:3–4): "For from the very beginning of Christ's conception, on account of the union of the two natures, it has been correct to say: 'This God is the Son of David, and this Man is the Son of God.'"[36] Melanchthon, bolder still, wrote, "God suffered, was crucified, and died; you must not think that the human nature alone is Redeemer, and not the whole Son of God. For even though the divine nature is not tortured, does not die, yet you must understand that this Son Himself, coeternal with the Father, is the Redeemer."[37]

But not only did they assert the reality of both natures, they were also at pains to show why both were essential to his work. Calvin devoted a whole chapter of his *Institutes* (2.12) to this question. The Mediator had to be true man because he had to be able to sympathize with his people and because the penalty due to sin had to be suffered in the same flesh as had sinned; and he had to be true God because his mission was to swallow up death, "and who but the Life could do this? It was his task to rout the powers of world and air. Who but a power higher than world and air could do this?"[38] "In short," he concluded,

35. Calvin, *Institutes*, 2.15.2.
36. *LW* 25:147.
37. Melanchthon, *Chief Theological Topics*, 2.8.
38. Calvin, *Institutes*, 2.12.2.

4—356 Donald Macleod

"since neither as God alone could he feel death, nor as man alone could he overcome it, he coupled human nature with divine that to atone for sin he might submit the weakness of the one to death; and that, wrestling with death by the power of the other nature, he might win victory for us."[39]

Luther did not address the necessity of the two natures with the same directness as Calvin.[40] He did lay down, however, that "Christ had to come as a second Adam, bequeathing his righteousness to us through a new spiritual birth in faith, just as the first Adam bequeathed sin to us through the old fleshly birth."[41] In *The Babylonian Captivity of the Church*, he linked the necessity of the incarnation to Jesus's words in Luke 22:20, "This cup that is poured out for you is the new covenant in my blood." Taking the Vulgate's *testamentum* at face value as meaning a "last will and testament," he concluded that if God made a testament, it was necessary that he should die, "but God could not die unless he became man."[42] But it was on the necessity of the Mediator's deity that Luther laid the most stress. Commenting on Galatians 3:13 in his 1535 *Lectures on Galatians*, he wrote,

> Here you see how necessary it is to believe and confess the doctrine of the divinity of Christ. When Arius denied this, it was necessary also for him to deny the doctrine of redemption. For to conquer the sin of the world, death, the curse, and the wrath of God in Himself—this is the work, not of any creature but of the divine power. Therefore it was necessary that He who was to conquer these in Himself should be true God by nature.[43]

In his *Plain Exposition of the Twelve Articles of the Christian Faith* (published in Italian in 1542), Peter Martyr Vermigli likewise underlined the importance of the Messiah's divinity: "If Christ were only human, we should be forbidden to hope in him."[44] Ursinus, too,

39. Ibid., 2.12.3.
40. However, see chap. 9, "The Person of Christ," by Robert Letham, which gives a detailed treatment of Luther's Christology.
41. Luther, "Prefaces to the New Testament," LW 35:375.
42. LW 36:37–8.
43. LW 26:282.
44. Peter Martyr Vermigli, *The Peter Martyr Library*, vol. 1, *Early Writings: Creed, Scripture, Church*, trans. Mariano Di Gangi and Joseph C. McLelland, ed. Joseph C. McLelland, Sixteenth Century Essays and Studies 30 (Kirksville, MO: Sixteenth Century Journal Publishers, 1994), 33.

took up the question, "What kind of a Mediator is he?" and answered, "Our Mediator must be man—very man, deriving his nature from our race, and retaining it for ever—a perfectly righteous man, and very God."[45] His argument, however, was that to be an appropriate "middle person," Christ had to relate to both parties, "having both natures, the divine and the human, in the unity of his person, that he may truly be a middle person, and mediator between God and men."[46] Perkins, in contrast, adhered to Calvin's argument: the union of the two natures in Christ was essential to his mediation, "for by this union it cometh to pass that his humanity did suffer such death upon the cross in such sort as he could neither be overcome, nor perpetually overwhelmed by it."[47]

As Calvin's successors developed the *munus triplex*, they insisted that after his incarnation the Mediator not only possessed both natures but also acted according to both natures—and did so at every point in his work. They were careful, however, to do justice to the unity of his person. All the actions and experiences of the Mediator were actions of the one Son of God. It was he, as a divine person, who spoke, acted, and suffered; indissolubly linked to this was the doctrine that it was himself, the divine Son, who was offered in sacrifice for the sins of the world. Luther had already stressed this (though for polemical purposes, arising out of his debate with Zwingli): "It is the person who does and suffers everything, the one thing according to this nature and the other thing according to the other nature."[48]

It was precisely this principle that Calvin invoked to explain Paul's use of the phrase "his own blood" in Acts 20:28: "Paul attributes blood to God, because the man Jesus Christ, who shed his blood for us, was also God."[49] One characteristic application of this was that the extraordinary magnitude of the sacrifice highlighted the gravity of sin. Melanchthon, for example, wrote, "For what could be a more terrible sign of the wrath of God than that he could not be satisfied with any

---

45. Ursinus, *Commentary on the Heidelberg Catechism*, 95.
46. Ibid.
47. Perkins, *A Golden Chain*, 200.
48. Martin Luther, *That These Words of Christ, "This Is My Body," Still Stand Firm against the Fanatics*, LW 37:3–150. Quotation on 37:123.
49. John Calvin, *The Acts of the Apostles 14–28*, trans. John W. Fraser (Grand Rapids, MI: Eerdmans, 1966), 184.

sacrifice except the death of his own Son?"[50] Conversely, to imagine that remission of sins could be secured by our own works was to minimize sin: "For human blindness and self-security do not understand the enormity of the wrath of God against sin, and therefore this blindness imagines that this wrath can be assuaged by human discipline."[51]

Defining the Relationship between the Two Natures

But by the end of the sixteenth century, theologians had taken the discourse a stage further. Perkins, for example, laid down that "Christ maketh intercession according to both natures."[52] Ursinus probed somewhat further as well, arguing that Christ was anointed according to each nature, and was therefore Prophet, Priest, and King in respect to each nature. And since, in terms of the communication of properties, the attributes of each nature were to be attributed *to the person*, it followed that it was appropriate to speak of God suffering according to his humanity, and of the man, Christ, being omnipotent, eternal, and omnipresent according to his divinity.[53]

By the time of Turretin's *Institutes of Elenctic Theology* (Geneva, 1688), this question was receiving extended treatment in Protestant Reformed dogmatics.[54] But it required clarification. While each act or experience of the Mediator is an act or experience of the one Son of God, each act is not to be attributed to each nature. For example, the Son did not uphold the universe according to his human nature; nor, as Zwingli pointed out in his *Exposition of the Faith* (1536), did he hunger and thirst according to his divine;[55] nor, yet again, could he be ignorant according to his divine nature. And while the divine Son tasted death, the divine nature neither died nor suffered (Reformation theologians accepted unquestioningly the doctrine of divine impassibility).

At this point, however, we should recall the precise terminology

50. Melanchthon, *Chief Theological Topics*, 153.
51. Ibid., 161.
52. Perkins, *A Golden Chain*, 207.
53. Ursinus, *Commentary on the Heidelberg Catechism*, 172. Notice the contrast with Lutheranism, which saw a communication of the attributes at the level of the two natures. See chap. 9, "The Person of Christ," by Robert Letham.
54. Francis Turretin, *Institutes of Elenctic Theology*, ed. James T. Dennison Jr., trans. George Musgrave Giger (Phillipsburg, NJ: P&R, 1992–1997), 1:379–84.
55. See *Zwingli and Bullinger: Selected Translations with Introduction and Notes*, ed. G. W. Bromiley, LCC 24 (Philadelphia: Westminster, 1953), 251.

used by Chalcedon to define the relation between the two natures in the person of Christ. They are not distinct agencies, but they run together, "both concurring [Gk. *suntrecho*] into [or in?] One Person and One Hypostasis."[56] This means that even when a particular act or function is peculiar to one nature, there is a "concurrence" of the other. For example, while the government of the universe is first and foremost a function of Christ's divine nature, he governs as the Incarnate One and gathers into his government all the compassion he has learned from sharing our life on earth. Were he not God, he could not stand in the center of the throne (Rev. 5:6), but were he not man, he could not sympathize with our weaknesses (Heb. 4:15). This concurrence applies to every action we ascribe to the incarnate Mediator. The two natures run together, distinct but not separated, united in one person but not confused. At every point, even approaching the cross (and, indeed, on the cross), there was a divine loving and a human loving, a divine choosing and a human choosing, a divine knowing and a human knowing.

Yet this idea of the concurrence of both natures in the work of Christ carries its own dangers. One is the temptation to ascribe his actions now to one nature and then to another. We see this already in Zwingli, who pronounced that the cry "My God, my God, why have you forsaken me?" (Matt. 27:46) was the voice of his human nature, but the prayer "Father, forgive them" (Luke 23:34) was "the voice of inviolable deity."[57] This requires a discrimination few of us possess: suffice that it was *he* who cried and *he* who prayed. But the even greater danger is that we lose sight of the ministry of the Holy Spirit in the life of the Mediator. We are too quick to invoke his divine nature as the explanation for the supernatural acts and aspects of his life and to speak, as Ursinus did, of the divine nature supporting the human, sustaining it in the sorrows and pains that it endured and raising it from death to life.[58] This is obviously plausible, but the New Testament ascribes his resurrection, for example, not to "his own" divine nature but to the action of the Father and the Spirit (Rom. 8:11) and to the

---

56. T. H. Bindley, ed., *The Oecumenical Documents of the Faith*, 3rd ed. (London: Methuen, 1925), 233.
57. *Zwingli and Bullinger*, 252.
58. Ursinus, *Commentary on the Heidelberg Catechism*, 216.

fact that once he had atoned for sin, death no longer had a claim on him (Rom. 6:9; cf. 4:25).

We must remember, too, the conditions under which Jesus exercised his earthly ministry. He was here in a state of *kenosis*, his glory veiled, operating not in the form of God but in the form of a servant, his divine splendor not "clung to" but so veiled that human observers saw only the human.[59] This cannot mean simply that though his powers were deployed, they were concealed. It must mean that they were concealed by *not* being deployed: kept *in retentis* (or restraint) but in abeyance, not absolutely but in relation to the work he had to accomplish in the flesh. He was not to draw on his divine powers to relieve his own hunger, to protect himself from exhaustion, or to ascertain the time of his second coming. He had taken flesh and blood and would be like his brothers and sisters in all things. He had come as the last Adam, to render a human obedience, and he would render it with the resources available to humanity. He would be tempted just like us (apart from yielding), and he would repel the Devil using the very same weapons as are available to his people.

It is Melanchthon who negotiated this aspect of the Lord's life most skillfully, taking his cue from a phrase in Irenaeus: "the Word remaining *quiescent*, that he might be capable of being tempted, dishonoured, crucified, and of suffering death."[60] Melanchthon explained, "The divine nature indeed was not mutilated or dead but was obedient to the Father, *remained quiet*, yielded to the wrath of the eternal Father against the sin of the human race, *did not use its power or exercise its strength*." Then, commenting on Paul's reference (Phil. 2:6) to Christ's having "equality with God," he observed that though Christ was equal to the Father in power and wisdom, he did not insist on using this equality; "that is, when He was sent to be obedient to God in suffering, He did not act contrary to the bidding, did not use his power to thwart his calling, but 'emptied Himself.'"[61]

---

59. Cf. Calvin's comment on Phil. 2:7: "Christ, indeed, could not renounce His divinity, but He kept it concealed for a time, that under the weakness of the flesh it might not be seen." Calvin, in *CNTC* 11:248.
60. Irenaeus, *Against Heresies*, 3.19, in *Ante-Nicene Fathers*, ed. Alexander Roberts and James Donaldson, rev. A. Cleveland Coxe (repr., Grand Rapids, MI: Eerdmans, 1993), 1:449. Italics added.
61. Melanchthon, *Chief Theological Topics*, 27–28.

The underlying concern here is to insist that Christ did not, and (under his "rules of engagement") could not, draw on his divine wisdom and power to mitigate the harshness of his conditions of service. He was here in the form of a servant, and in that form, and subject to its limitations, he had to be obedient, even to death.

Understanding the Son's Divine Power

How, then, are we to account for the extraordinary features of the life of Jesus: his supernatural knowledge, for example, his miracles, and the resoluteness with which he endured the cross? Do we have to invoke the support of his divine nature? This is what Zwingli did when he referred Christ's healing miracles to his "divine power and not the human."[62]

But this is hardly necessary. Surely the key point in the life of Jesus is that he came into this world as the Anointed One, possessed of a messianic endowment fully sufficient to equip him for every aspect of his work? And can his "mighty acts" not be explained by this endowment, the person-to-person ministry of the Holy Spirit, through whom the Father had promised to uphold him (Isa. 42:1)? It was this same Spirit who had enabled Moses, David, and Elijah to transcend the ordinary powers of human nature, and we may surely believe that he came upon the Messiah in unique measure because of his unique identity, his unique office, and his unique responsibilities. It was never to his divine nature that he prayed, even *in extremis*, but to "Abba" (Mark 14:36), and it was not to his divine nature that he ascribed his mighty acts but to the Holy Spirit (Matt. 12:28; cf. Acts 2:22; 10:38).

On the other hand, even while he lived in a state of *kenosis*, the work of Christ could not be confined within the limits of the life he lived as a human being. This is the doctrine that came to be known as the *extra Calvinisticum* (the *extra* pointing not to something additional but to something "outside"). Christ, Calvin insisted, was active beyond the confines of his human nature:

> For even if the Word in his immeasurable essence united with the nature of man into one person, we do not imagine that he was confined therein. Here is something marvellous: the Son of God

---

62. *Zwingli and Bullinger*, 251.

> descended from heaven in such a way that, without leaving heaven, he willed to be borne in the virgin's womb, to go about the earth, and to hang upon the cross; yet he continuously filled the world even as he had done from the beginning.[63]

In other words, during his earthly life the activity of the Logos transcended his human existence, so that even while his divine form was veiled from human eyes, he was still upholding the universe by his almighty power. But this activity, although transcending his humanity, was still mediatorial. His omnipotence, omniscience, and omnipresence served his people; and these divine perfections are needed still, because not even the glorified human nature of Christ is sufficient by itself for the burdens of mediatorship.

The *extra Calvinisticum* was not, however, shared by all the Reformers. Where Calvin argued that the deity of Christ transcended his humanity, Luther argued that the humanity itself possessed divine attributes, particularly the attribute of ubiquity. This clearly could not apply to Christ's body while he was on earth, but now that Christ has risen and ascended, his body sits at God's right hand, and "the right hand of God is not a specific place in which a body may or must be, such as on a golden throne, but is the almighty power of God, which at one and the same time can be nowhere and yet must be everywhere."[64] Luther clung to this "right hand" as an irrefutable warrant for his view that the body of Christ is ubiquitous: if the right hand of God is everywhere, the body of Christ is everywhere. But it is not only the doctrines of Calvin and Luther that are different; the concerns behind these doctrines are also radically divergent. Calvin was rebutting the "impudence" that objects to the incarnation on the ground that "if the Word of God became flesh, then he was confined within the narrow prison of an earthly body" (and, by implication, in no position to uphold the universe).[65] Luther was seeking a foundation for his perfervid belief that the body of Christ is present at the Lord's Supper: "Christ's body and blood are at the same time in heaven and in the Supper."[66]

---

63. Calvin, *Institutes*, 2.13.4.
64. Luther, *That These Words of Christ*, LW 37:59.
65. Calvin, *Institutes*, 2.13.4.
66. For Luther's extended defense of this position, see his anti-Zwinglian treatise *That These Words of Christ*, LW 37:3–150. Quotation on 59.

Christ as Prophet

The Old Testament had promised a prophet like Moses (Deut. 18:18), and in the mind of Jesus's contemporaries the idea of the Messiah was closely associated with a special prophetic ministry. The Samaritan woman, for example, remarks, "When the Messiah comes, he will teach us all things" (John 4:25, author's trans.). In accordance with this expectation, Christ comes, as Calvin remarked, "anointed by the Spirit to be herald and witness of the Father's grace."[67] It has to be stressed that this ministry is itself an essential part of the Mediator's work of redemption. Jansen, in accordance with his thesis that although Calvin announced a threefold office, he never made any real use of it, downplays the ministry of Christ as Prophet, arguing that nowhere in his commentaries and sermons does Calvin make Christ's work as Preacher and Teacher a separate messianic dignity alongside the offices of King and Priest.[68] The emphasis falls, he maintains, on the kingly and priestly offices, and his prevailing usage is to summarize Christ's work under the formula of *munus duplex* rather than *munus triplex*.

It is probably true that Calvin never saw the threefold office as a dogmatic formula that he was bound to adhere to whenever he discussed the work of Christ, and it is also true that he frequently wrote only in terms of a twofold office. However, even when he did so, he did not invariably limit it to Christ's priestly and kingly ministries. For example, commenting on Hebrews 3:1–2 and its comparison between Christ and Moses, he spoke of Christ sustaining a double honor, but the double honor is not that of Priest and King but that of Doctor and Priest. Moses, he wrote, "performed the office of prophet and doctor, Aaron that of priest: but both duties are laid on Christ."[69] As for the contention that Calvin made little systematic use of the threefold office, it is notable that he did use it in his Genevan Catechism, and it may well be that it was in the realm of catechesis that the formula was most useful—which is no doubt why it was adopted by the Heidelberg

---

67. *Institutes*, 2.15.2.
68. Jansen, *Calvin's Doctrine of the Work of Christ*, 61.
69. Calvin, *The Epistle of Paul the Apostle to the Hebrews and the First and Second Epistles of St. Peter*, 34.

Catechism, by the Larger and Shorter Catechisms of the Westminster Assembly, and by such early Scottish catechisms as that of John Craig.[70]

Nevertheless, however interesting the question of Calvin's use of the *munus triplex* formula may be, the real issue is the importance of Jesus's ministry as Prophet, Teacher, and Preacher. Jansen sets up an antithesis between Christ being the *herald* of the kingdom and *being* the kingdom, argues that teaching was not a separate messianic work, and suggests that it is unsafe to speak of Christ as Prophet, since unlike other prophets he does not "convey" another's word, but *is* the Word: "He is not given a revelation—He is the revelation." He concludes, "Christ's revelatory character belongs not under the *de officiis*, but under the *de persona*, permeating as it does both his kingly and priestly work."[71]

The import of this argument is that revelation was merely incidental to redemption, but this overlooks the fact that one of the great needs of fallen man's humanity was the need for light and wisdom. A Redeemer had to bring revelation as well as forgiveness and deliverance. And that revelation could not be incidental to his redeeming work; it had to be an integral part of it, or, as B. B. Warfield put it, a component part of the series of redemptive acts by which the merciful God saves men.[72] This does not prejudice in any way the truth that Christ is simultaneously Revealer, Revelation, and Revealed One.

It is in accordance with his revealing work that the Messiah was anointed specifically to be a preacher (Luke 4:18), was regularly called a teacher (John 3:2; 11:28; 13:13), was addressed as "Teacher" (Matt. 8:19, Mark 4:38), called himself a teacher (Matt. 23:8), was called a prophet (Matt. 21:11; John 6:14; Acts 3:22), delivered a memorable sermon setting forth the ethics of the kingdom (Matthew 5–7), and spent the last hours of his life instructing his disciples in the deepest mysteries of his kingdom (John 13–17).

Whatever, then, the use made by Calvin of the *munus triplex* formula, he was fully justified in speaking of Christ as a prophet and

---

70. See Thomas F. Torrance, ed. and trans., *The School of Faith: The Catechisms of the Reformed Church* (London: James Clarke, 1959), 97–165.

71. Jansen, *Calvin's Doctrine of the Work of Christ*, 85, 101–2. Quotations on 101–2.

72. B. B. Warfield, "The Biblical Idea of Revelation," in Warfield, *The Inspiration and Authority of the Bible*, ed. Samuel G. Craig (Philadelphia, NJ: P&R, 1948), 80.

in portraying this prophetic ministry as an essential element in his mediatorial work. Later sixteenth-century Reformed theologians followed his example. Perkins defined the office as "that whereby he, immediately from his Father, revealeth his word and all the means of salvation comprised in the same," and added, "For this cause Christ is called the doctor, lawgiver and counsellor of his Church."[73] Ursinus spoke to the same effect: "Christ is the greatest and chief prophet, and was immediately ordained of God, and sent by him from the very commencement of the church in Paradise, for the purpose of revealing the will of God to the human race."[74]

The key truth here is that in Christ God speaks. This follows not only from his mediatorial anointing but also from his identity as the Son of God: a point emphasized by the writer to the Hebrews when he declares that God has in these last days spoken by a Son (Heb. 1:2). And Jesus himself emphasized it when he announced that no one knows the Father except the Son (Matt. 11:27). His divine sonship put him in a unique position in terms of the classic Old Testament conception of the prophet (Heb. *nabi*) as one who had an audience with God and came forth as his appointed spokesman.

CHRIST'S PROPHETIC MINISTRY AS TEACHER

However, we have to remind ourselves once again that while Jesus was the Son of God for the entirety of his earthly ministry, he was the Son of God in servant from. This is one of the key points at which Calvin invoked his concept of accommodation. Drawing on Irenaeus, he wrote, "The Father, himself infinite, becomes finite in the Son, for he has accommodated himself to our little measure lest our minds be overwhelmed by the immensity of his glory."[75] This calls in question the phraseology used by Perkins when he spoke of Christ revealing his word "immediately from his Father."[76] In Christ, the voice of God is heard through the voice of a man, who declares what he, as man, has

---

73. Perkins, *A Golden Chain*, 208.
74. Ursinus, *Commentary on the Heidelberg Catechism*, 173.
75. Calvin, *Institutes*, 2.6.4. See also Ford Lewis Battles, "God Was Accommodating Himself to Human Capacity," in *Readings in Calvin's Theology*, ed. Donald K. McKim (Eugene, OR: Wipf and Stock, 1998), 21–42.
76. Perkins, *A Golden Chain*, 208.

received and assimilated, and who passes it on in a way that bears on it the unmistakable impress of his own incarnate personality. What we hear is not the voice of august, omniscient deity; nor is it the voice of Moses or Isaiah, or of Paul or John. It is the voice of Jesus, uniquely anointed and uniquely intimate with the Spirit, yet meek and lowly in heart, speaking with self-authenticating authority and clothing his message in unforgettable forms. Yet it is not a voice that is able, or authorized, to answer all our questions. There are still "secret things" that belong to the Lord our God (Deut. 29:29)—such as the day and the hour of Christ's parousia (Mark 13:32). But nothing has been kept secret that his church needs to know.

A second key point is that Christ comes as the Prophet of *good news*. This is a theme on which Melanchthon labored in his chapter on "The Gospel" in the original (1521) edition of *Loci Communes*,[77] though his whole approach is governed, inevitably, not by the *munus triplex* but by Luther's antithesis between law and gospel. Additionally, he is responding to the "godless sophists" who proclaimed that "Christ has become the successor of Moses and has given a new law, and that this new law is called the gospel."[78] Indeed, one wonders whether Lutheranism's comparative neglect of Christ's work as Prophet is linked to fears about linking Christ to Moses, and thus to the law.[79] On the other hand, Melanchthon was careful not to compromise the authority of Moses and distinguished him clearly from the advocates of Pharisaic righteousness.[80] He conceded, too, that Christ "expounds law, for grace cannot be preached without law."[81] He insisted, however, that the primary or proper office of Christ is not to establish the law

---

77. It appears to be this edition that is published in *Melanchthon and Bucer*, ed. Wilhelm Pauck, LCC 19 (Philadelphia: Westminster, 1969). The text of the *Loci* went through no fewer than seventy-five editions, and as the editor of Melanchthon's *Chief Theological Topics* points out in his introduction, "The differences between the editions were sometimes very great." Preus, ed., *Chief Theological Topics*. For example, the early editions did not contain the chapter on "God," from which some earlier quotations in this article were taken, while the chapter on "The Gospel" (locus 7) in later editions lacked the polemical sharpness of the early years of the Reformation.

78. *Melanchthon and Bucer*, 74.

79. See, for example, Luther's warning: "See to it, therefore, that you do not make a Moses out of Christ, or a book of laws and doctrines out of the gospel, as has been done before and as certain prefaces put it, even those of St. Jerome." "Preface to the New Testament," *LW* 35:360.

80. Cf. Luther: "Christ is without doubt a divine lawgiver and his doctrine is divine law, which no authority can change or dispense with." *Explanations of the Ninety-Five Theses* (1517), *LW* 31:88.

81. *Melanchthon and Bucer*, 75.

but to bestow grace: Moses is legislator and judge; Christ is the Savior, bestowing grace and forgiveness. And this grace, said Melanchthon, is not some quality in us "but rather the very will of God, or the goodwill of God toward us."[82]

Calvin repeated this emphasis, declaring that Christ was anointed to be the herald and witness of the Father's grace.[83] A generation later, the English Puritan John Preston would encapsulate this message in his paraphrase of the Marcan form of the Great Commission: "Go and tell every man without exception, that there is good news for him."[84] It is this message that brings relief to those frustrated, as Luther was, in their efforts to keep the law; and it is in this revelation of grace that faith puts its trust. "Where the pledge of the divine love towards us is wanting," wrote Calvin, commenting on Galatians 4:6, "there is assuredly no faith."[85] This is reflected in the answer given to question 21 of the Heidelberg Catechism, "What is true faith?" It is "a hearty trust, which the Holy Ghost works in me by the Gospel, that not only to others but to me also forgiveness of sins, everlasting righteousness and salvation, are freely given by God, only for the sake of Christ's merit."

Third, the revelation given through Christ is final and definitive. This applies not only to his teaching during his life on earth but also to the whole prophetic ministry he exercises in his capacity as Mediator, including the word he spoke (as *incarnandus* ["to be incarnate"] but not yet *incarnatus* ["incarnate"]) through the Old Testament and the tradition he handed down to the apostles after his resurrection (1 Cor. 11:23; 15:3–8; Gal. 1:11–12) with the express intention that they should deliver it to the church. Calvin was adamant on the finality of this revelation: the perfect doctrine Christ has brought has made an end to all prophecies. "Outside of Christ," he wrote, "there is nothing worth knowing, and all who by faith perceive what he is like have grasped the whole immensity of heavenly benefits."[86] The *finality* of the revelation was thus made to rest on its *perfection*.

82. Ibid., 87.
83. Calvin, *Institutes*, 2.15.2.
84. John Preston, *The Breast-Plate of Faith and Love* (1634; facsimile repr., Edinburgh: Banner of Truth, 1979), 8.
85. John Calvin, *Galatians, Ephesians, Philippians and Colossians*, in CNTC, 11:75.
86. Calvin, *Institutes*, 2.15.2.

"Neither the universal Church nor priests nor councils," wrote Melanchthon, "have the right to change or decree anything about faith. Articles of faith must be judged simply in accordance with the canon of Holy Scripture."[87] The point was repeated in such later Reformed creeds as the Westminster Confession, which declared that nothing was to be added to Scripture by "traditions of men."[88] This would exclude, for example, the approach to theology proposed in John Henry Newman's *Essay on the Development of Christian Doctrine*, which argued that the Christian creed may be expanded by "longer time and deeper reflection" and that this legitimizes the introduction into Catholic dogma of articles not even hinted at in the apostolic writings.[89]

But an external revelation is not enough. There must also be an internal work of the Holy Spirit illuminating the Word and sealing it on the human heart. "Nature does not assent to the Word of God, and moreover is not moved by it," wrote Melanchthon.[90] All it can attain to is historical faith or mere opinion: "What, therefore, is faith? It is constantly to assent to every word of God; this cannot be unless the Spirit of God renews and illuminates our hearts."[91] Luther made the same point, though in a context where he saw teaching as part of the priestly rather than the prophetic ministry of Christ: "Nor does he only pray and intercede for us but he teaches us inwardly through the living instruction of his Spirit, thus performing the two real functions of a priest."[92] It was this same doctrine that Calvin encapsulated in his doctrine of the inner testimony of the Holy Spirit: "The same Spirit, therefore, who has spoken through the mouths of the prophets must penetrate into our hearts to persuade us that they faithfully proclaimed what had been divinely commanded."[93]

---

87. Melanchthon, *Loci Communes*, 63.
88. WCF 1.6.
89. John Henry Newman, *An Essay on the Development of Christian Doctrine* (1845; repr., Harmondsworth, UK: Penguin Books, 1974).
90. *Melanchthon and Bucer*, 91.
91. Ibid., 92.
92. Martin Luther, *The Freedom of a Christian*, LW 31:354. This reflects the fact that in the Old Testament the priests were the day-to-day instructors of the people.
93. Calvin, *Institutes*, 2.7.4. See also Calvin's sermon on Isa. 53:13, where he states, "The prophet expressly affirms that the outward voice which invites is of no avail unless the special gift of the Spirit accompanies it." John Calvin, *Sermons on Isaiah's Prophecy of the Death and Passion of Christ*, trans. and ed. T. H. L. Parker (London: James Clarke, 1956), 46.

CHRIST'S PROPHETIC MINISTRY THROUGH PREACHERS

Linked to this teaching is the doctrine that Christ's prophetic anointing "was diffused from the Head to the members."[94] This doctrine followed from the fact that he received his anointing "not only for himself that he might carry out the office of teaching, but for his whole body, that the power of the Spirit might be present in the continuing preaching of the gospel."[95] Did the Reformers, then, regard not only the *written* but also the *preached* word as the Word of Christ? Luther certainly did, insisting that where the preacher faithfully expounds Scripture, his word is the Word of God: "Now I and any man who speaketh Christ's Word may freely boast that his mouth is Christ's mouth. I am certain that my word is not mine but Christ's."[96] The same sentiment is recorded in his *Table Talk*: "Somebody asked, 'Doctor, is the Word that Christ spoke when he was on earth the same in fact and in effect as the Word preached by a minister?' The doctor [Luther] replied, 'Yes, because he said, He who hears you hears me' [Luke 10:16]."[97] In his "Preface to the Epistles of James and Jude," he even went so far as to claim that this was true regardless of the personal qualities of the preacher: "Whatever preaches Christ would be apostolic, even if Judas, Annas, Pilate and Herod were doing it."[98] It is the content that matters.

The same note was sounded by Calvin, even though he was at pains to insist that human interpreters of the Word are an accommodation to our weakness "in that he [God] prefers to address us in human fashion through interpreters in order to draw us to himself, rather than to thunder at us and drive us away."[99] Nevertheless, when we hear his ministers speaking, it is just as if he himself spoke: "It is a singular privilege that he deigns to consecrate to himself the mouths and tongues of men in order that his mouth may resound in them." This depends, of course, on "the fact that the preacher shall declare only what has been revealed and recorded in Holy Scripture."[100]

94. Calvin, *Institutes*, 2.15.2.
95. Ibid.
96. Quoted in Karl Barth, *Church Dogmatics*, trans. G. T. Thomson, vol. 1, pt. 1 (Edinburgh: T&T Clark, 1936), 107.
97. *LW* 54:394.
98. *LW* 35:396.
99. Calvin, *Institutes*, 4.1.5.
100. T. H. L. Parker, *Calvin's Preaching* (Edinburgh: T&T Clark, 1992), 22.

Preaching "borrows" its status as the Word of God from Scripture, and the pulpit then becomes the throne from which God governs our souls: "Let us bear in mind," declared Calvin in one of his sermons on Deuteronomy, "that the doctrine which we receive from God is as the speech of a king."[101]

This notion does not mean that the preacher, simply as such, is an extension of the prophetic ministry of Christ. But it does mean that Christ continues to exercise *his* prophetic ministry through the preacher.

Christ as Priest

Calvin's initial discussion of the priestly office of Christ was more or less in proportion to his comments on the prophetic and kingly offices in the same chapter.[102] However, he extended his treatment into the two subsequent chapters, following the lines of the Apostles' Creed and pausing reverently over the clauses "suffered under Pontius Pilate, was crucified, dead and buried; he descended into hell." There is a much briefer, but no less rich, treatment of these same clauses in Peter Martyr Vermigli, whose exposition of the creed reflects Calvin's theological outlook.[103] We shall glance at this later.

Christ's Priestly Work in the Atonement

Calvin's focus on the crucifixion of Christ should not obscure the fact that he ascribed our redemption to "the whole course of his obedience": "from the time he took on the form of a servant he began to pay the price of liberation in order to redeem us."[104] Yet Calvin insisted that when it comes to defining the way of salvation "more exactly," Scripture "ascribes this as peculiar and proper to Christ's death."

But would Christ have come had it not been necessary to lay down his life as an atonement for sin? Calvin addressed, with considerable thoroughness and rigor (and obvious irritation), what he called Osiander's "speculation" that Christ would still have become man even

---

101. John Calvin, *Sermons on Deuteronomy*, trans. Arthur Golding (1583; facsimile repr., Edinburgh: Banner of Truth, 1987), 1192.
102. Calvin, *Institutes*, 2.15.6.
103. Vermigli, *Early Writings*, 15–79.
104. Calvin, *Institutes*, 2.16.5.

if sin had never entered the world.[105] To Calvin, this was a frivolous novelty: all Scripture proclaimed that it was in order to be a Redeemer that Christ was clothed with flesh. The Messiah was promised from the beginning only to restore the fallen world, and when he did actually come, he himself declared (e.g., Matt. 18:11) that the reason for his advent was that by his death he might appease God and deliver us from death to life. He concluded that since the Spirit declares that these two, the sin of man and the advent of Christ, are joined together by God's eternal decree, "it is not lawful to enquire further how Christ became our redeemer and the partaker of our nature."[106]

But what was it that prompted God to show favor to our fallen world? Calvin was at pains to root his doctrine of reconciliation firmly in eternal divine love and to insist that this love preceded the expiatory sacrifice of Christ. "By his love," he wrote, "God the Father goes before and anticipates our reconciliation in Christ." He continued,

> For it was not after we were reconciled to him through the blood of his Son that he began to love us. Rather, he has loved us before the world was created. . . . The fact that we were reconciled through Christ's death must not be understood as if his Son reconciled us to him that he might now begin to love those whom he hated.[107]

On the contrary, we have been reconciled to him who loves us.

Yet Calvin was equally conscious that Christ as Priest must reckon seriously with the anger of God: no one can seriously consider what he is without feeling "God's wrath and hostility toward him." Associated with this comes the need for an assurance that there is some means by which God may be appeased, but no common assurance will do, "for God's wrath and curse always lie upon sinners until they are absolved of guilt. Since he is a righteous Judge, he does not allow his law to be broken without punishment, but is equipped [Lat. *armatus*] to avenge it."[108]

But here, Calvin suggested, there is "some sort of contradiction."[109] How could we be objects of God's love and mercy and simultaneously

---

105. Ibid., 2.12.4–7.
106. Ibid., 2.12.5.
107. Ibid., 2.16.4.
108. Ibid., 2.16.1.
109. Ibid., 2.16.1.

objects of his wrath and vengeance? Or, as the "contradiction" is expressed by Paul Helm, "How could God at any time be an enemy if he eternally loved us?"[110] An appropriate response to this would have been that love and anger are not opposites: love can be angry, sometimes very angry. It is love and hatred that are opposites, and while God's children were by nature objects of his wrath (Eph. 2:3), they were never objects of his hatred. Besides, even after we are freely forgiven and adopted into God's family we can, as the Westminster Confession of Faith says, still "fall under God's fatherly displeasure."[111]

But Calvin chose a different route, arguing that such expressions as God being man's enemy, man being under a curse, and man being estranged from God "have been accommodated to our capacity [so] that we may better understand how miserable and ruinous our condition is apart from Christ."[112] In other words, biblical talk of God's being angry belongs to the same category as God repenting.

This, surely, is a dangerous road. "No repentance can belong to God," declared Calvin in his commentary on Jonah. It is simply a mode of speaking, used only with regard to our human comprehension. Similarly, when Scripture speaks of God's wrath it is accommodating itself to "the grossness of our understanding," because we cannot otherwise be terrified and thus be humbled before God and repent: "For as we *conceive* God to be angry, whenever he summons us to his tribunal, and shows to us our sins; so also we *conceive* him to be placable, when he offers the hope of pardon."[113]

As these words make clear, the concepts of wrath and propitiation stand or fall together. If the one is but a manner of speaking, so is the other; and so, eventually, are all the key concepts of the doctrine of the atonement. Even the divine love will have to be demythologized as a mere anthropomorphism designed to accommodate our human finitude. Instead, surely, we must cling to the fact that our love is but a faint reflection of the divine and our anger against evil but a faint reflection of his.

---

110. Paul Helm, *John Calvin's Ideas* (Oxford: Oxford University Press, 2004), 393.
111. WCF 11.5.
112. Calvin, *Institutes*, 2.16.2.
113. John Calvin, *Commentaries on the Twelve Minor Prophets* (1846–1849; repr., Edinburgh: Banner of Truth, 1986), 3:115. Italics added.

THE DESCENT INTO HELL

Calvin also devoted considerable attention to the statement of the Apostles' Creed that Christ "descended into hell."[114] This was not an issue on which the Reformers were unanimous. For example, Luther oscillated between Jesus descending into hell after his death in order to swallow up death and hell, and Christ merely suffering in Gethsemane and on Calvary.[115] Zwingli, in his *Exposition of the Faith*, understood the descent as referring primarily to the reality of Jesus's death, "for to be numbered among those who have descended into hell means to have died," but then he extended this to include the idea that the power of Christ's atonement penetrated even to the underworld—in support of this suggestion he cited 1 Peter 3:19, taking it to mean that the gospel was preached to the dead, "that is, to those in Hades who from the beginning of the world had believed in divine warnings, like Noah."[116] According to Peter Martyr Vermigli, the descent into hell indicates that when the soul of Christ departed from his body, it "descended into the lower regions," where it experienced the same conditions as other souls separated from their bodies, namely, "association with the saints or with the company of the condemned." Both of these groups, he declared, were confronted with the presence of Christ's soul. To those believers who had awaited salvation through Christ, he brought consolation. To those condemned to eternal perdition (and here Vermigli also cited 1 Pet. 3:19), he brought rebuke for their obstinacy and unbelief.[117]

Calvin was remarkably insistent on the importance of this article, declaring that if it were left out of the creed, much of the benefit of Christ's death would be lost.[118] He dismissed both the idea that "hell" here simply means the grave and the idea that Christ descended to the *limbus patrum* ("the limbo of the fathers") to deliver the souls of the patriarchs, excluded from the life of glory until delivered by the passion of Christ.[119] Instead, he defined the descent into hell as an

---

114. Calvin, *Institutes*, 2.16.8–12.
115. Luther, *Freedom of a Christian*, LW 31:352. See Paul Althaus, *The Theology of Martin Luther*, trans. Robert C. Schultz (Philadelphia: Fortress, 1966), 207.
116. *Zwingli and Bullinger*, 251–52.
117. Vermigli, *Early Writings*, 43–44.
118. Calvin, *Institutes*, 2.16.8.
119. Aquinas, *Summa Theologiae* 3a.52.2.

expression of the spiritual torment that Christ underwent for us: "He had to grapple hand to hand with the armies of hell and the dread of everlasting death." What is noteworthy, however, is that Calvin placed this descent *before* the death of Christ, not after. He descended into hell *on the cross*. Not only, says Calvin, was Christ's body given as the price of our redemption, but also "he paid a greater and more excellent price in suffering in his soul the terrible torments of a condemned and forsaken man."[120] The lowest point of this "hell" was his being forsaken by the Father: "Surely no more terrible abyss can be conceived than to feel yourself forsaken and estranged from God; and when you call upon him not be heard. It is as if God himself had plotted your ruin."[121]

This understanding of the descent into hell was shared by key figures among Calvin's successors. Ursinus, for example, offered a concise but comprehensive discussion in his *Commentary* on question 44 of the Heidelberg Catechism, concluding that "it signifies those extreme torments, pains and anguish, which Christ suffered in his soul." At the same time he was careful to link this descent into hell to our salvation:

> To believe in Christ, who descended into hell, is to believe that he sustained for us, in his own soul, hellish agonies and pains, and that extreme ignominy which awaits the ungodly in hell, that we might never descend thither, nor be compelled to suffer the pains and torments which all the devils and reprobates will for ever suffer in hell.[122]

It is in Christ's experience of this anguish that Calvin saw the clearest refutation of Apollinarianism. Echoing Gregory of Nazianzus's (ca. 329–ca. 389) dictum "the unassumed is the unhealed," Calvin wrote, "Unless his soul shared in the punishment, he would have been the Redeemer of bodies alone." And while careful to deny that Christ ever experienced "a despair contrary to faith," yet there was in Christ "a weakness pure and free." This becomes particularly clear in Gethsemane, where we must confess Christ's sorrow, "unless we are

---

120. Calvin, *Institutes*, 2.16.10. The phraseology may be indebted to Luther, who spoke of Christ experiencing "the anxiety and the terror of a frightened conscience which feels eternal wrath." Quoted in Althaus, *Theology of Martin Luther*, 205.

121. Calvin, *Institutes*, 2.16.11.

122. Ursinus, *Commentary on the Heidelberg Catechism*, 231–32.

ashamed of the cross." This, he concluded, is our wisdom, "duly to feel how much our salvation cost the Son of God."[123]

THE EXTENT OF THE ATONEMENT

In contrast to his immediate successors in the Reformed tradition, Calvin offered no discussion of the extent of the atonement. During the twentieth century it became fashionable to argue that Calvin taught universal redemption and that the doctrine of "limited atonement" was a pernicious innovation introduced by Theodore Beza—an argument advanced by John Cameron and Moïse Amyraut even in the seventeenth century.[124] It is tempting for admirers of Calvin to respond with the counterargument that Calvin was already a proponent of the doctrine of definite atonement, but the precise question of whether Christ died to obtain redemption "for all men and for every man" was never before Calvin's mind, and it is unsafe to cite him on an issue he never addressed directly. It is certainly not difficult to glean from the vast Calvin corpus statements to the effect that Christ died for all, but then, as Cunningham pointed out, "No Calvinist, not even Dr. Twisse, the great champion of high Supralapsarianism, has ever denied that there is a sense in which it may be affirmed that Christ died for all men."[125]

The most pertinent fact here is that when Calvin commented on those passages commonly cited in support of universal redemption he did not take the opportunity to press home a universal-redemption exegesis. This is all the more remarkable in view of the fact that such

---

123. Calvin, *Institutes*, 2.16.12. In his 1535 *Lectures on Galatians*, Luther expressed the same sentiment when discussing Gal. 2:20: "Therefore it is an intolerable blasphemy to think up some work by which you presume to placate God, when you see that he cannot be placated except by this immense, infinite price, the death and blood of the Son of God, one drop of which is more precious than all creation." *LW* 26:176.

124. See, for example, Basil Hall, "Calvin against the Calvinists," in *John Calvin: A Collection of Distinguished Essays*, ed. G. E. Duffield, trans. G. S. R. Cox and P. G. Rix, Courtenay Studies in Reformation Theology 1 (Appleford: Sutton Courtenay, 1966), 19–37; R. T. Kendall, *Calvin and English Calvinism to 1649* (Oxford: Oxford University Press, 1979), esp. 3–28; Brian G. Armstrong, *Calvinism and the Amyraut Heresy: Protestant Scholasticism and Humanism in Seventeenth-Century France* (Eugene, OR: Wipf and Stock, 2004), esp. 127–39. See *contra*, Paul Helm, "Calvin, Indefinite Language, and Definite Atonement," in *From Heaven He Came and Sought Her: Definite Atonement in Historical, Biblical, and Pastoral Perspective*, ed. David Gibson and Jonathan Gibson (Wheaton, IL: Crossway, 2013), 97–120; Raymond A. Blacketer, "Blaming Beza: The Development of Definite Atonement in the Reformed Tradition," in Gibson and Gibson, *From Heaven He Came and Sought Her*, 97–141.

125. William Cunningham, "Calvin and Beza," in *The Reformers and the Theology of the Reformation* (Edinburgh: T&T Clark, 1862), 396.

scholars as R. T. Kendall argue not only that Christ died indiscriminately for all but that this doctrine was fundamental to his theology, undergirding his whole understanding of faith.[126] Yet Calvin's exegesis of such passages as 1 Timothy 2 and 1 John 2 is exactly the same as is found later in the work of advocates of definite atonement. For example, commenting on the words "God willeth that all men should be saved" (1 Tim. 2:4), he dismissed "the childish illusion of those who think that this passage contradicts predestination," and concluded that "the apostle's meaning here is simply that no nation of the earth and no rank of society is excluded from salvation, since God wills to offer the Gospel to all without exception."[127] He approached 1 John 2:2 in the same way, arguing that when the apostle spoke of Christ as the propitiation for the sins of the whole world,

> his purpose was only to make this blessing common to the whole Church. Therefore, under the word "all" he does not include the reprobate, but refers to all who would believe and those who were scattered throughout various regions of the earth. For, as is meet, the grace of Christ is really made clear when it is declared to be the only salvation of the world.[128]

Given that many suppose Beza to be the real author (or villain) of the doctrine of "limited atonement," it is fascinating that his younger contemporary Ursinus was already teaching a carefully worded doctrine of definite atonement at the University of Heidelberg between 1561 and 1577 (as witnessed by his *Commentary on the Heidelberg Catechism*, which, though published only in 1616, set forth the substance of his Heidelberg lectures). There is no reason to think that Ursinus was part of Beza's circle; his affinities appear to have been with Melanchthon and Peter Martyr Vermigli. Nor did the question of the extent of the atonement arise out of the Heidelberg Catechism itself. Yet he faced it directly, addressing the issue of "seemingly opposite" passages of Scripture by invoking the classic distinction between the

---

126. As Kendall notes, "Fundamental to the doctrine of faith in John Calvin is his belief that Christ died indiscriminately for all men." *Calvin and English Calvinism*, 13.

127. Calvin, *The Second Epistle of Paul the Apostle to the Corinthians and the Epistles to Timothy, Titus and Philemon*, 209.

128. John Calvin on 1 John 2:2, in *CNTC* 5:244.

sufficiency of the atonement and its efficacy and by laying down that while the atonement is *sufficient* to expiate the sins of all men, its *efficacy* is limited to the elect and was intended to be so:

> He willed to die for the elect alone as touching the efficacy of his death, that is, he would not only sufficiently merit grace and life for them alone, but also effectually confers these upon them, grants faith, and the Holy Spirit, and brings it to pass that they apply to themselves, by faith, the benefits of his death, and so obtain for themselves the efficacy of his merits.[129]

THE NECESSITY OF THE ATONEMENT

But while he offered no pronouncement on the extent of the atonement, Calvin did address the question of its *necessity*. The precise form of this question as addressed by Calvin was, why was it necessary for the Mediator to be both God and man? However, this was part of the wider question posed by Anselm: "By what logic or necessity did God become man, and by his death, as we believe and profess, restore life to the world, when he could have done this through the agency of some other, angelic or human, or simply by willing it?"[130] Why did redemption have to be secured at such a price?

Calvin answered in terms of what has been labeled "consequent hypothetical necessity."[131] There was no absolute necessity, only a necessity stemming from the heavenly decree on which man's salvation depended: "Our most merciful Father decreed what was best for us."[132] Calvin was drawing a careful distinction here. God was under no necessity to save the human race; it was a matter of sovereign clemency prompted by unconditional eternal love. But it followed from this commitment that there had to be atonement, because God, to use Anselm's terms, could not simply have "willed" the salvation of the world,

---

129. Ursinus, *Commentary on the Heidelberg Catechism*, 223. Calvin had reservations about the sufficiently/efficiently distinction: "The common solution does not avail, that Christ suffered sufficiently for all, but efficaciously only for the elect." Calvin, *Concerning the Eternal Predestination of God*, trans. J. K. S. Reid (London: James Clarke, 1961), 148; cf. 103.

130. Anselm, *Cur Deus Homo*, 1.1. English trans., *Why God Became Man*, in *Anselm of Canterbury: The Major Works*, ed. Brian Davies and G. R. Evans (Oxford: Oxford University Press, 1998), 265.

131. John Murray, *Redemption: Accomplished and Applied* (Grand Rapids, MI: Eerdmans, 1955), 11.

132. Calvin, *Institutes*, 2.12.1.

and Calvin is absolutely clear as to the reason why: "God's righteous curse bars our access to him, and God in his capacity as judge is angry toward us. Hence, an expiation must intervene in order that Christ as priest may obtain God's favour for us and appease his wrath. Thus Christ to perform this office had to come forward with a sacrifice."[133]

This same question was addressed by Peter Martyr Vermigli, who asked, "Does it not seem strange to you that if God could reconcile the world to himself in some easier way, he chose to do it by exposing his Son to these sufferings?" His basic response was that no other way could have satisfied the justice of God. But he amplified this point, highlighting three further truths, which, he said, are to be "noted carefully": first, that by this bitter means God highlighted how great a debt our sins incurred, when so severe a retribution was required; second, were it not for the punishment undergone by Christ, the human conscience could not be assured of its freedom from condemnation; and third, in Christ's suffering we see a demonstration of perfect patience, obedience, and love. This last point led him to expatiate on the way that this demonstration strengthens us in every affliction: "Who shall refuse to drink of that chalice that he sees his Lord Jesus Christ so willingly drain for the salvation of others?"[134] Vermigli was clearly aware that while the cross is first and foremost expiatory, this does not preclude its also having exemplarist force.

The Sufficiency of the Atonement

There remains the issue of the finality of Christ's self-sacrifice on the cross: a question raised in an acute form by the Roman Catholic doctrine of the Mass. The Council of Trent defined the Mass as a sacrifice, laid down that in this "divine sacrifice" Christ was reimmolated "in an unbloody manner," and went on to declare that this sacrifice is truly

---

133. Ibid., 2.15.6. But Calvin appeared to take a different view in his commentary on John 15:13: "God could have redeemed us by a word or a wish, save that another way seemed to Him best for our sakes: that by not sparing His own and only-begotten Son He might testify in His person how much He cares for our salvation." Later Reformed divines such as Jerome Zanchius and Samuel Rutherford, arguing from the premise of God's absolute freedom, believed that God, had he chosen, could have left sin unpunished. Lutheran divines appear not to have addressed the question of the *necessity* of the atonement. As we have seen, however, Luther himself did declare that God could not be placated "except by this immense, infinite price, the death and blood of the Son of God." *Lectures on Galatians* (1535), LW 26:176.

134. Vermigli, *Early Writings*, 41.

propitiatory. By it God is appeased, and by it we obtain mercy and find grace. The victim, the council continued, is one and the same, the bread having been converted by the mystery of transubstantiation into the body, blood, soul, and divinity of the Son of God and Christ now offering by the ministry of the priests the same sacrifice as he himself offered on the cross.[135]

Every detail in this construction was anathema to the Reformers. They denied that the Mass was a sacrifice, that those "ministering at the altar" were acting in the capacity of priests, and that the Mass was in any sense propitiatory. Above all they denied that there was any need for any further sacrifice. The one sacrifice on the cross was perfect and therefore absolutely final. In the *Babylonian Captivity of the Church*, Luther described "the common belief that the Mass is a sacrifice" as the greatest and most "dangerous stumbling block of all."[136] In his later treatise *This Is My Body*, he also wrote, "It is quite certain that Christ cannot be sacrificed over and above the one single time he sacrificed himself."[137] Melanchthon struck the same note: "In the whole world there was only one propitiatory sacrifice, namely, the suffering or death of Christ." And in support of this he cited Hebrews 10:10, which he rendered, "We have been sacrificed through the sacrifice of the body of Christ once for all."[138]

But again, it is in Calvin that we find the most systematic treatment. Already in the first edition of the *Institutes* (1536), he described as "a most pestilential error" the belief that the Mass is a sacrifice offered in order to obtain the forgiveness of sins. The key principle here is the exclusive priesthood of Christ: only the Son of God could offer up the Son of God, because he alone was divinely appointed Priest, and he had no successor: "Christ, being immortal, needs no vicar to replace him. . . . [T]he Father designated him 'priest forever, according to the order of Melchizedek,' that he should discharge an everlasting priesthood."[139]

These points are amplified in the definitive 1559 edition of the *Institutes*. The honor of the priesthood, wrote Calvin, "was competent

---

135. See "The Canons and Decrees of the Council of Trent," session 22, chaps. 1–2, and canons 1–4, in Schaff, *Creeds of the Greek and Latin Churches*, 176–79, 184–85.
136. LW 36:51.
137. LW 37:143.
138. Melanchthon, *Chief Theological Topics*, 280.
139. Calvin, *Institutes of the Christian Religion* (1536 ed.), 115.

to none but Christ, because by the sacrifice of his death he wiped away our guilt and made satisfaction for sin."[140] And when he proceeded in book 4 to discuss the Mass, he prefaced his remarks with the observation that he was contending against the opinion that has "infected the whole world," namely, that the Mass is a work by which the priest offers up Christ as an expiatory victim, thereby meriting God's favor and reconciling us to God. Calvin's judgment was uncompromising: this notion "inflicts signal dishonour upon Christ, buries and oppresses his cross, consigns his death to oblivion [and] takes away the benefit which came to us from it."[141] Then, citing the words "It is finished" from John 19:30, he declared, "By his one sacrifice all that pertains to our salvation has been accomplished and fulfilled." "Are we," he challenged, "to be allowed daily to sew innumerable patches upon such a sacrifice, as if it were imperfect, when he has so clearly commended its perfection?" Then, drawing on Hebrews 9–10, he concluded, "In the whole discussion the apostle contends not only that there are no other sacrifices, but that this one was offered only once and is never to be repeated."[142] There is only one sacrifice, so that our faith may be made fast to his cross.[143]

Christ as King: Was Luther Classic Rather Than Anselmic?

Calvin, Melanchthon,   Vermigli, Ursinus, and Perkins all appear to be firmly in the tradition of Anselm, proclaiming the cross as a vicarious sacrifice offered to make satisfaction for our sins. But did Luther hold a different view?[144] This is the argument of Gustaf Aulén,[145] who maintains that this "Latin" or "Western" doctrine of the atonement, deriving from Anselm, was a radical departure from the "classic" doctrine of the early fathers, who saw the atonement primarily as a victory over

---

140. Calvin, *Institutes*, 2.15.6.
141. Ibid., 4.18.1.
142. Ibid., 4.18.3.
143. Ibid., 4.18.6. One of the pillars of the Roman Catholic argument in favor of the doctrine of the Mass as sacrifice was the statement of Gen. 14:18 that Melchizedek as priest of God Most High brought out "bread and wine." On this, see Calvin's *Commentaries on the First Book of Moses Called Genesis*, trans. John King (Edinburgh: Calvin Translation Society, 1847–1850), 1:388–91.
144. For an overview of Luther's understanding of Christ's work as reconciler, see Althaus, *Theology of Martin Luther*, 201–23.
145. Gustaf Aulén, *Christus Victor: An Historical Study of the Three Main Types of the Idea of the Atonement*, trans. A. G. Herbert (London: SPCK, 1965), 101–22. For a critique of Aulén, see Althaus, *Theology of Martin Luther*, 218–23.

sin, death, and the Devil, a view expressed most famously in Gregory of Nyssa's *Great Catechism*.[146] Through sin, man had become the property of the Devil, and the only condition on which the Devil would release him was the payment of a ransom. But where could a ransom for such a prize be found? In none other than God himself, who, in the person of his Son, became the ransom paid to the Devil. In the course of the transaction, however, a certain deception had to be practiced: "In order to secure that the ransom would be easily accepted the Deity was hidden under the veil of our nature so that, as with ravenous fish, the hook of the Deity might be gulped down along with the bait of flesh," and thus "he who first deceived man by the bait of sensual pleasure is himself deceived by the presentment of the human form."[147]

Is it this doctrine, emphasizing the kingly idea of victory to the neglect of the priestly idea of sacrifice, that we hear in Luther? We certainly hear clear echoes of it, even to the extent that he adopted Nyssa's imagery of the deception of the Devil, including the idea of Christ's humanity as the bait on the hook. The Devil swallows Christ but cannot digest him, "for Christ sticks in his gills, and he must spew Him out again, as the whale the prophet Jonah, and even as he chews Him the devil chokes himself and is slain, and is taken captive by Christ."[148] It is doubtful whether the use of such language is to the great Reformer's credit, though it is easy to imagine a rustic audience enjoying a preacher making fun at the Devil's expense. But then, the theme of victory and deliverance is also clear in Luther's more nuanced statements. For example, in his Small Catechism (1529) he declared, "I believe that Jesus Christ . . . delivered me and freed me from all sins, from death, and from the power of the devil."[149] He spoke to similar effect in his Large Catechism (2.2): the tyrants and jailers have now been routed, because Christ "has snatched us, poor lost creatures, from the jaws of hell, won us, made us free and restored us to the Father's favour and grace."[150] The same note is sounded again in *The Freedom of a Christian*, where Luther spoke of "a blessed struggle and victory

146. Gregory of Nyssa, *Select Writings and Letters of Gregory, Bishop of Nyssa*, NPNF, 2nd ser., vol. 5, ed. Philip Schaff and Henry Wace (Grand Rapids, MI: Eerdmans, 1983), 471–509.
147. Gregory of Nyssa, *The Great Catechism*, NPNF, 2nd ser., 5:24, 26.
148. Quoted in Aulén, *Christus Victor*, 104.
149. Tappert, *Book of Concord*, 345.
150. Ibid., 414.

and salvation and redemption."[151] It was precisely to overcome sin, death, and the pains of hell that Christ descended into hell, and since death and hell could not swallow him up, they were swallowed up by him in a mighty "duel": "For his righteousness is greater than the sins of all men, his life stronger than death, his salvation more invincible than hell."[152] The duel theme occurs again in his 1535 *Commentary on Galatians* (*ad* Gal. 3:13), and by that time it had become the "wondrous duel" (*mirabile duellum*), with the deception theme still there in the background. The Devil attacked Christ and wanted to devour him, along with the whole human race,

> but because life was immortal, it emerged victorious when it had been conquered, conquering and killing death in turn. About this wondrous duel the church beautifully sings: "It was a great and dreadful strife when death with life contended." The Prince of life, who died, is alive and reigns. Through Christ, therefore, death is conquered and abolished in the whole world, so that now it is nothing but a picture of death.[153]

These are memorable statements of the divine power deployed in our salvation and of Christ's victory over the powers of evil, and it would be easy to quote many more. But statements to the same effect also abound in Calvin, though without Luther's vivid language. In the first edition of the *Institutes*, Calvin related Christ's anointing specifically to his kingship: "We believe in short that by this anointing he was appointed king by the Father to subject all power in heaven and on earth [Ps. 2:1–6], that in him we might be kings, having sway over the devil, sin, death and hell."[154] In the 1559 edition, the discussion of Christ's kingship focused mainly on the spiritual nature of the benefits it confers on the church, but Calvin was still at pains to emphasize that Christ was called Messiah especially by virtue of his kingship and that as such he would be the eternal protector and defender of his people. Since he rules, Calvin said, more for our own sake than his, "let us not doubt that we shall always be victorious over the devil, the world

---

151. *LW* 31:351.
152. *LW* 31:252.
153. *LW* 26:281.
154. Calvin, *Institutes of the Christian Religion* (1536 ed.), 54.

and every kind of harmful thing."[155] It follows from this that "the devil, with all the resources of the world, can never destroy the church, founded as it is on the eternal throne of Christ."[156]

The treatment of the kingship in the *Institutes* is comparatively brief, but the topic itself recurs frequently in Calvin. Indeed, Jansen goes so far as to claim that "the regal conquest over the devil, death and sin" is Calvin's most recurrent theme and even that Calvin is "one with Luther in stressing the 'classic' view of the atonement."[157] What is undeniable is that in his *Commentaries* Calvin took every opportunity to expatiate on the Messiah's triumphant kingship. There is a fine example of this in his *Commentary on Colossians* (*ad* Col. 2:15), where he referred to the cross as a triumphal march in which Christ paraded his enemies and as a triumphal car "in which he appeared illustriously":

> For although in the cross there is nothing but curse, this was nevertheless so swallowed up by the power of the Son of God, that it has put on, as it were, a new nature. For there is no tribunal so magnificent, no kingly throne so stately, no show of triumph so distinguished, no chariot so lofty, as the gibbet on which Christ subdued death and the devil, the prince of death; more, has utterly trodden him under His feet.[158]

This lofty register is sustained in Calvin's *Sermons on Isaiah's Prophecy of the Death and Passion of Christ*. In his seventh sermon (on Isa. 53:12), Calvin used language redolent of Luther's "duel": Christ has plundered his enemies and has held them bound and pinioned, powerless to resist him.[159] And in his first sermon (on Isa. 52:13–15), he declared that on the cross ("an infamous gallows"), Jesus Christ has not only vanquished the Devil "but has shown that we can now glory in that we are acquitted from all condemnation, that sin has no more dominion over us and that all the devils in hell have to withdraw their case against us completely."[160]

Among non-Lutherans, this emphasis was not confined to Calvin.

---

155. Calvin, *Institutes*, 2.15.4.
156. Ibid., 2.15.3.
157. Jansen, *Calvin's Doctrine of the Work of Christ*, 88.
158. Calvin, *Galatians, Ephesians, Philippians and Colossians*, in *CNTC*, 11:336.
159. Calvin, *Isaiah's Prophecy*, 137.
160. Ibid., 38.

Geneva and Zurich were agreed on it, as witnessed by article 4 of the Consensus Tigurinus (the Zurich Agreement), drafted jointly by Calvin and Bullinger, which declared that Christ "is to be considered as a king, who enriches us with all kinds of blessings, governs and defends us by his power, provides us with spiritual weapons, delivers us from all harm, and rules and guides us by the sceptre of his mouth."[161] And in his sermon "Concerning the Temptations of Christ in the Wilderness," the Scottish Reformer John Knox used language fully as dramatic as Luther's. He pictured Christ challenging the Devil:

> Lo, I am a man like to my brethren, having flesh and blood, and all properties of man's nature, sin, which is thy venom, excepted. Tempt, try, and assault me. I offer thee here a place most convenient,—the wilderness:—there shall be no mortal creature to comfort me against thy assaults; thou shalt have time sufficient to do what thou canst; I shall not fly the place of battle. If thou become victor, thou may still continue in possession of thy kingdom in this wretched world: but if thou canst not prevail against me, then must thy prey and unjust spoil be taken from thee; thou must grant thyself vanquished and confounded, and must be compelled to leave off from all accusations of the members of my body; for to them doth appertain the fruit of my battle; my victory is theirs, as I am appointed to take the punishment of their sins in my body.[162]

But if victory and conquest are key themes in Calvin, Bullinger, and Knox, expiation, propitiation, and substitution are no less so in Luther. Indeed, Luther's 1535 *Commentary on Galatians* (*ad* Gal. 3:13) offers the most brilliant exposition of the doctrine of penal substitution in the history of Christian theology. The core idea is imputation: "God has laid our sins, not upon us but upon Christ his Son."[163] Luther developed this idea with extraordinary energy and daring. "And all the prophets," he wrote, "saw this, that Christ was to become the greatest

---

161. Quoted in John Calvin, *Tracts and Treatises*, vol. 2, *On the Doctrine and Worship of the Church*, trans. Henry Beveridge, ed. Thomas F. Torrance (1849; repr., Grand Rapids, MI: Eerdmans, 1958), 213.

162. *The Select Practical Writings of John Knox* (Edinburgh: Banner of Truth, 2011), 182–83. For the original (unmodernized) text, see *The Works of John Knox*, ed. David Laing (1855; repr., Edinburgh: Banner of Truth, 2014), 4:103.

163. *LW* 26:279.

thief, murderer, adulterer, robber, desecrator, blasphemer, etc., there has ever been anywhere in the world." He continued,

> Now He is not the Son of God, born of the Virgin. But He is a sinner, who has and bears the sin of Paul, the former blasphemer, persecutor and assaulter; of Peter, who denied Christ; of David, who was an adulterer and a murder. . . . In short, He has and bears all the sins of all men in His body—not in the sense that He has committed them but in the sense that He took these sins, committed by us, upon His own body, in order to make satisfaction for them with His own blood.

"Whatever sins," he concluded, "I, you and all of us have committed or may commit in the future, they are as much Christ's own as if He Himself had committed them."[164]

Of course, Luther's overriding concern was with justification by faith: "This is how we must magnify the doctrine of Christian righteousness in opposition to the righteousness of the Law and of works."[165] Faith puts its trust in this vicarious sin bearing, knowing that "our sin must be Christ's own sin or we shall perish eternally."[166] But the underlying truth is that the concept of victory and the concept of sacrifice, far from being antitheses, are interrelated and interdependent elements in the one great biblical doctrine of the atonement. It was precisely by bearing the curse that Christ redeemed us from it and delivered us from the Devil, as is made unmistakably clear in Hebrews 2:14–18, which declares that it was in order to expiate the sins of the people that Christ took flesh and blood and that it was by means of that expiation that he destroyed the Devil. Once sin was expiated—once Christ took it off them and bore it himself—Satan lost the power to carry "the children" down to hell with himself. It is to this "fortunate exchange"[167] that we owe our deliverance: "He took those sins, committed by us, upon his own body, in order to make satisfaction for them with his own blood."[168] The result, as Calvin put

---

164. *LW* 26:277–78.
165. *LW* 26:280.
166. *LW* 26:278.
167. *LW* 26:284.
168. *LW* 26:277.

it, is that Christ "has freed us from a diabolical tyranny," and now we have to deal only with an adversary who has no power against us: "The devil himself has been laid so low as to be of no more account, as if he did not exist."[169]

This is why we may speak of Christ's priestly work as foundational. Both the prophetic ministry and the kingly rule of Christ bear directly only on the human race. His priestly work of expiation, on the other hand, is directed Godward, and on this act of expiation, restoring our communion with God, everything hinges. "The powers with which Christ struggled had their power and authority only through God's wrath," writes Paul Althaus. "This is why Luther in discussing Christ's work, places primary emphasis on its relationship to God's wrath and thus to our guilt rather than on its relationship to demonic powers."[170] Hence Luther's explicit order: "The freedom by which we are free of the wrath of God forever is greater than heaven and earth and all creation. *From this there follows the other freedom*, by which we are made free through Christ from the Law, from sin, death, the power of the devil, hell, etc."[171] First, freedom from the wrath, then (and only then), freedom from the powers.

The Theology of the Cross

Despite, then, his stress on conquest and victory, Luther's primary mission was to promote not a theology of glory but a "theology of the cross."[172] This is the phrase he used in the Heidelberg Disputation (May 1518),[173] and as Moltmann points out, he chose it "in order to find words for the Reformation insight of the liberating gospel of the crucified Christ, in contrast to the *theologia gloriae* of the mediaeval institutional church."[174] The phrase poses a sharp antithesis: "A theologian of glory calls evil good and good evil. A theologian of the cross calls the thing what it actually is."[175] But what are the

---

169. Calvin, *The Epistle of Paul to the Hebrews and the First and Second Epistles of St. Peter*, 31.
170. Althaus, *Theology of Martin Luther*, 220.
171. Luther, *Lectures on Galatians* (1535), *LW* 27:4. Italics added.
172. For a fuller exposition of Luther's theology of the cross, see Althaus, *Theology of Martin Luther*, 25–34; Jürgen Moltmann, *The Crucified God: The Cross of Christ as the Foundation and Criticism of Christian Theology*, trans. R. A. Wilson and John Bowden (London: SCM, 2001), 62–79.
173. For the "Heidelberg Disputation," see *LW* 31:35–70.
174. Moltmann, *The Crucified God*, 67.
175. Luther, "Heidelberg Disputation," *LW* 31:53.

points of the antithesis? Luther offered answers in his "Proofs of the Thesis."[176]

First, the theology of the cross differs radically from the theology of glory in what it understands by "the knowledge of God." Luther's starting point here was Romans 1:20, where Paul declares that God's invisible qualities can be known from what he has made. It is such knowledge that "the wisdom of the world" (1 Cor. 1:20) seeks, and Luther did not deny its validity: "That wisdom is not of itself evil."[177] God's invisible nature can indeed be seen and recognized in his works.[178] What he did deny was, first, that God's works are the primary source of theological knowledge, and second, that recognition of God's invisible qualities (such as his divinity, power, and justice) can make one "worthy or wise."[179] On the contrary, argued Luther, no one deserves to be called a theologian unless he "comprehends the visible and manifest things of God seen through suffering and the cross."[180] What Luther was doing here was to introduce a new definition of "work." It is not in the majestic and glorious work of creation that real wisdom is to be found but in the work of Christ, humiliated and shamed. Here Luther recalled the moment (John 14:8) when Philip asked Jesus, "Show us the Father." That was spoken, said Luther, according to the theology of glory, which assumes that any divine epiphany will be resplendent might and majesty. But Christ set aside "this flighty thought" and directed Philip to himself: "Whoever has seen me has seen the Father" (John 14:9).[181] The glory makes himself visible not in "lofty mountain grandeur" but in servant form, washing feet and laying down his life.[182]

Second, the theology of the cross differs from the theology of glory in its understanding of justification. The theology of glory boasts in its works, the works of the law, and takes credit for them, forgetting that the "law brings the wrath of God, kills, reviles, accuses, judges,

---

176. Ibid., *LW* 31:39–70.
177. Ibid., *LW* 31:55. Cf. his comment on Rom. 1:19: "This was their error, that they did not worship this divinity untouched, but changed and adjusted it to their desires and needs." Luther, *Lectures on Romans: Glosses and Scholia*, *LW* 25:157.
178. Luther, *Lectures on Romans*, *LW* 25:154 (*ad* Rom. 1:20).
179. Luther, "Heidelberg Disputation," *LW* 31:52.
180. Ibid., *LW* 31:53.
181. Ibid., *LW* 31:53.
182. "O Lord My God, When I in Awesome Wonder," original Swedish poem by Carl G. Boberg, translated and adapted from a Russian version into English by Stuart K. Hine, 1949.

and condemns everything that is not in Christ."[183] The theology of the cross, on the other hand, leaves no room for boasting, because it knows that "man must utterly despair of his own ability before he is prepared to receive the grace of Christ."[184] The righteous man, consequently, is not the man who does much but the man who, without work, believes much in Christ. "The law says, 'do this,' and it is never done. Grace says, 'believe in this,' and everything is already done," because Christ has fulfilled all the laws of God and because we also fulfill everything through him.[185]

Third, the theologian of the cross expects that he himself will be crucified, because he is identified with the weakness and folly of God, who "can be found only in suffering and the cross."[186] Yet he will choose the "good of the cross," while those who hate the cross pursue wisdom, glory, and power. It is remarkable how central this is to Luther's psyche. For example, in his comment on Galatians 6:14 ("But far be it from me to boast except in the cross of our Lord Jesus Christ"), where we would expect an exultant exposition of Calvary, instead Luther explained, "'The cross of Christ' does not mean, of course, the wood that Christ carried on his shoulders and to which he was then nailed. No, it refers to all the sufferings of the faithful, whose sufferings are the sufferings of Christ." He continued,

> It is helpful to know this so that we are not overly sad or even completely desperate when we see our enemies persecuting, excommunicating, and murdering us, or when we see the heretics hating us so bitterly. Then we should think that, following the example of Paul, we ought to glory in the cross *which we have received because of Christ*, not because of our own sins.[187]

Such suffering, however, is not merely the inevitable consequence of faithfulness to one's calling. It is an essential element in the formation of a theologian of the cross: the suffering man "is the only man who is able to enter into community with God."[188] No one can be a theo-

183. Luther, "Heidelberg Disputation," *LW* 31:41.
184. Ibid., *LW* 31:40.
185. Ibid., *LW* 31:41, 56.
186. Ibid., *LW* 31:53.
187. Luther, *Lectures on Galatians* (1535), *LW* 27:134.
188. Althaus, *Theology of Martin Luther*, 28.

logian of the cross unless he has first been crucified with Christ. Then, "emptied through suffering," he neither boasts if he does good works, nor is he disturbed if God does not do good works through him. Dying and rising again with the Son of Man, he knows that "it is impossible for a person not to be puffed up by his good works unless he has first been deflated and destroyed by suffering and evil until he knows that he is worthless and that his works are not his but God's."[189]

It is precisely because Luther was a theologian of the cross that he could write, "*Crux probat omnia*":[190] "The cross is the test of everything." It is the test of our sense of the gravity of sin; it is the test of such doctrines as divine impassibility; it is the test of our Christian lifestyles; and above all, it is the test of our preaching—it claims the central place and is to be reiterated with urgent and unwearying emphasis. To mute or obscure or marginalize it is a betrayal of Paul's programmatic motto, "We preach Christ crucified" (1 Cor. 1:23). But no less is it a betrayal of the Reformation, which set aside every human work and proclaimed the work of Christ as the only foundation for Christian assurance and hope.

Resources for Further Study

PRIMARY SOURCES

Bromiley, G. W., ed. *Zwingli and Bullinger: Selected Translations with Introduction and Notes*. Library of Christian Classics 24. Philadelphia: Westminster, 1953.

Calvin, John. *Calvin: Theological Treatises*. Translated by J. K. S. Reid. Library of Christian Classics 22. London: SCM, 1954.

———. *Institutes of the Christian Religion*. Edited by John T. McNeill. Translated by Ford Lewis Battles. 2 vols. Library of Christian Classics 20–21. 1559 edition. Philadelphia: Westminster, 1960 (esp. 2.15–17, 4.18).

———. *Institutes of the Christian Religion* (1536 ed.). Translated by Ford Lewis Battles. Rev. ed. H. H. Meeter Center for Calvin Studies. Grand Rapids, MI: Eerdmans, 1986.

---

189. Luther, "Heidelberg Disputation," *LW* 31:53.

190. Martin Luther, WA 5:179. The remark occurs in Luther's comment on Ps. 5:11 in the course of his second series of lectures on the Psalms (1519–1521). This series was not included in the 55-volume Concordia edition of *Luther's Works*.

———. *Reply to Cardinal Sadolet.* In *John Calvin: Tracts and Letters*, edited by Henry Beveridge and Jules Bonnet, translated by Henry Beveridge, 1:25–68. 1844. Reprint, Edinburgh: Banner of Truth, 2009.

———. *Sermons on Isaiah's Prophecy of the Death and Passion of Christ.* Translated and edited by T. H. L. Parker. London: James Clarke, 1956.

Luther, Martin. *The Babylonian Captivity of the Church.* In *Luther's Works.* Vol. 36, *Word and Sacrament II*, edited by Abdel Ross Wentz, 3–126. Philadelphia: Fortress, 1959.

———. "Heidelberg Disputation." In *Luther's Works.* Vol. 31, *Career of the Reformer I*, edited by Harold J. Grimm, 38–70. Philadelphia: Fortress, 1957.

———. *Lectures on Galatians* (1535). Vol. 26 in *Luther's Works.* Edited by Jaroslav Pelikan. St. Louis, MO: Concordia, 1963.

Melanchthon, Philipp. *The Chief Theological Topics: Loci Praecipui Theologici 1559.* 2nd English ed. Translated by J. A. O. Preus. St. Louis, MO: Concordia, 2011.

Pauck, Wilhelm, ed. *Melanchthon and Bucer.* Library of Christian Classics 19. Philadelphia: Westminster, 1969.

Perkins, William. *A Golden Chain.* In *The Works of William Perkins*, edited by Ian Breward, 175–259. Courtenay Library of Reformation Classics 3. Appleford: Sutton Courtenay, 1970.

Schaff, Philip. *The Creeds of the Greek and Latin Churches.* London: Hodder and Stoughton, 1877.

Tappert, Theodore G., ed. and trans. *The Book of Concord: The Confessions of the Evangelical Lutheran Church.* Philadelphia: Fortress, 1959.

Ursinus, Zacharias. *The Commentary of Dr. Zacharias Ursinus on the Heidelberg Catechism.* Translated by G. W. Williard. 1852. Reprint, Phillipsburg, NJ: Presbyterian and Reformed, n.d.

Vermigli, Peter Martyr. *The Peter Martyr Library.* Vol. 1, *Early Writings: Creed, Scripture, Church.* Translated by Mariano Di Gangi and Joseph C. McLelland. Edited by Joseph C. McLelland. Sixteenth Century Essays and Studies 30. Kirksville, MO: Sixteenth Century Journal Publishers, 1994.

Secondary Sources

Althaus, Paul. *The Theology of Martin Luther.* Translated by Robert C. Schultz. Philadelphia: Fortress, 1996.

Armstrong, Brian G. *Calvinism and the Amyraut Heresy: Protestant Scholasticism and Humanism in Seventeenth-Century France.* Eugene, OR: Wipf and Stock, 2004.

Aulén, Gustaf. *Christus Victor: An Historical Study of the Three Main Types of the Idea of the Atonement.* Translated by A. G. Herbert. London: SPCK, 1965.

Battles, Ford Lewis. "God Was Accommodating Himself to Human Capacity." In *Readings in Calvin's Theology*, Donald K. McKim, 21–42. Eugene, OR: Wipf and Stock, 1998.

Franks, R. S. *The Work of Christ: A Historical Study of Christian Doctrine.* London: Nelson, 1962.

Helm, Paul. *Calvin at the Centre.* Oxford: Oxford University Press, 2010.

Jansen, John Frederick. *Calvin's Doctrine of the Work of Christ.* London: James Clarke, 1956.

Kendall, R. T. *Calvin and English Calvinism to 1649.* Oxford Theological Monographs. Oxford: Oxford University Press, 1979.

Lindberg, Carter, ed. *The Reformation Theologians: An Introduction to Theology in the Early Modern Period.* Oxford: Blackwell, 2002.

McKim, Donald K. *Introducing the Reformed Faith: Biblical Revelation, Christian Tradition, Contemporary Significance.* Louisville: Westminster John Knox, 2001.

———, ed. *Major Themes in the Reformed Tradition.* Grand Rapids, MI: Eerdmans, 1992.

Parker, T. H. L. *Calvin's Preaching.* Edinburgh: T&T Clark, 1992.

Van Buren, Paul. *Christ in Our Place: The Substitutionary Character of Calvin's Doctrine of Reconciliation.* Eugene, OR: Wipf and Stock, 2002.

Whitford, David M., ed. *T&T Clark Companion to Reformation Theology.* London: Bloomsbury, 2014.

11

The Holy Spirit

Graham A. Cole

ABSTRACT

The pneumatologies of four magisterial Reformers (Luther, Zwingli, Calvin, and Cranmer) and a radical one (Simons) are explored in this chapter with respect to their views on the nature of God as Trinity, specifically focusing on the personhood and deity of the Holy Spirit. The chapter highlights commonalities and differences. All five believed that the Holy Spirit of God was active in salvation, in sanctification, in our response to the Word, and in the sacraments. The magisterial Reformers, however, saw a positive relationship between church and state that the persecuted radical Reformers did not. For Simons the only true church was a believers' church. Luther, Zwingli, Calvin, Cranmer, and Simons believed that the Holy Spirit is the great applier of the salvation whose architect is the Father and whose accomplisher is the Son.

Introduction

Approaching the past is never done without an angle of vision. Nor is the past approached without selectivity. In this case the doctrine of the Holy Spirit (pneumatology) is the subject and not a particular person's theology in general. Moreover, this study focuses on four magisterial Reformers and one radical Reformer. The magisterial Reformers "tried to work within existing ecclesial structures or develop new ones that were specially connected to kings or princes or the state."[1] In contradistinction, radical Reformers "resisted forms of the church that were too closely connected to the state and its power."[2] The magisterial Reformers chosen include Martin Luther (1483–1546), Huldrych Zwingli (1484–1531), John Calvin (1509–1564), and Thomas Cranmer (1489–1556). The radical Reformer chosen is Menno Simons (1496–1561).[3] While this approach sets Reformation movements in the background rather than in the foreground, they will not be out of sight.[4]

Five questions in particular animate this chapter:

1. How do Luther, Zwingli, Calvin, Cranmer, and Simons view the Spirit in relation to the triune Godhead?
2. How does each view the Spirit's relation to the Word of God?
3. How does each view the Spirit's relation to the sacraments?
4. How does each view the Spirit's role in salvation, especially sanctification?
5. How does each understand the Holy Spirit's relation to the church?

The approach is thus systematic.[5]

---

1. F. LeRon Shults and Andrea Hollingsworth, *The Holy Spirit* (Grand Rapids, MI: Eerdmans, 2008), 44.

2. Ibid., 44–45. Interestingly, Anthony C. Thiselton describes these Reformers as "the major reformers" rather than the magisterial ones in his very fine *The Holy Spirit—In Biblical Teaching, through the Centuries, and Today* (Grand Rapids, MI: Eerdmans, 2013), 255–69. Significantly too, in his history of the doctrine, Thiselton does not treat the radical Reformers in their own right but as the objects of the major Reformers' ire, which is a surprising lacuna. Menno Simons, for example, goes unmentioned.

3. According to Olson, the radical Reformers fell into three distinct groups: the Anabaptists, the Spiritualists, and the anti-Trinitarian rationalists. Roger E. Olson, *The Story of Christian Theology: Twenty Centuries of Tradition and Reform* (Downers Grove, IL: IVP Academic, 1999), 415. The present chapter will not treat all the subgroups.

4. For an overview of Reformation theology, see David Bagchi and David C. Steinmetz, eds., *The Cambridge Companion to Reformation Theology* (Cambridge: Cambridge University Press, 2004). It is beyond my brief chapter to consider the Catholic Reformation, but for a brief treatment of pneumatology and the Catholic Reformation, or Counter-Reformation, see Veli-Matti Kärkkäinen, ed., *Holy Spirit and Salvation: The Sources of Christian Theology* (Louisville: Westminster John Knox, 2010), 177–84.

5. There are limitations in employing such a method. Another limitation in this chapter arises from the sources drawn upon for each of the Reformers on view. Each deserves a monograph in his own right, and the source material is voluminous: treatises, sermons, commentaries, catechisms, liturgies, and correspondence. Selectivity has been inescapable. The strength lies in delimiting the focus in a manageable way. This is a chapter in a book, not a book. The weakness is that I am

A Common Trinitarian Faith

The Reformers considered in this chapter, whether magisterial or radical, were committed to belief in the triune God. They affirmed the oneness of the Godhead and the threeness of the persons. Thus they also affirmed the deity and personhood of the Holy Spirit.

The magisterial Reformers saw their views of God and Christ as no mere novelty. They prized the faithful Christian past. Carl L. Beckwith accurately claims,

> The mainline Reformers never hesitated in accepting the decrees of the ecumenical councils on the doctrine of the Trinity and Christ or the great creeds from the early church. There was no dispute on these matters. The need for creed was simply assumed. Indeed, the Lutherans placed the Apostles' Creed, Nicene, and Athanasian creeds before their own confessional documents in the *Book of Concord*. A similar move is made in the Thirty-Nine Articles. Even though Calvin never promoted the Nicene Creed in the same official manner, he most certainly embraced its content and significance.[6]

So too Roger Olson and Christopher Hall rightly argue, "For the most part the Protestant reformers considered the doctrine of the Trinity a settled matter and refused to reconsider its essential content as expressed in the Nicene Creed and worked out in the writings of Augustine."[7]

Luther, Zwingli, Calvin, and Cranmer were not impressed with scholastic Trinitarian speculation. Even so, they were prepared to use nonbiblical language such as *person* in the articulation of the doctrine, as well as draw on the fathers of the early church. In their view the

---

approaching these figures with my questions, not necessarily theirs. For example, Martin Luther's formulation of justification by faith alone was characterized later by others as "the article of the standing or falling of the church" (*articulus stantis et cadentis ecclesiae*). See Richard A. Muller, *Dictionary of Latin and Greek Theological Terms: Drawn Principally from Protestant Scholastic Theology* (Grand Rapids, MI: Baker, 1986), 46. The same could not be said of Luther's doctrine of the Holy Spirit. An alternative approach would have been to adopt the method of problematic elucidation. For an example of this approach, see E. Osborn, "Elucidation of Problems as a Method of Interpretation – 1," *Colloquium* 8, no. 2 (1976): 24–32, and "Elucidation of Problems as a Method of Interpretation – 2," *Colloquium* 9, no. 2 (1976): 10–18. In short, this method seeks to discover the problematic that Luther, Zwingli, Calvin, Cranmer, and Simons wrestled with and how successfully they addressed it. The strength of this approach is that it squarely situates a magisterial or a radical Reformer's theology in his *Sitz im Leben* ("situation in life").

6. Carl L. Beckwith, "The Reformers and the Nicene Faith: An Assumed Catholicity," in *Evangelicals and the Nicene Faith: Reclaiming the Apostolic Witness*, ed. Timothy George (Grand Rapids, MI: Baker Academic, 2011), 65.

7. Roger E. Olson and Christopher A. Hall, *The Trinity* (Grand Rapids, MI: Eerdmans, 2002), 67.

Holy Spirit was a distinct person of the triune Godhead, and they embraced the Western position on the *filioque* clause, which posits that the Spirit proceeds from the Father *and the Son*. In this they stood in marked contrast to anti-Trinitarian teachers such as Michael Servetus (ca. 1511–1553) and Faustus Socinus (1539–1604), the latter of whom viewed the Holy Spirit as neither a person nor a deity but "an activity of God."[8]

Radical Reformer Menno Simons likewise affirmed the triune God but sought to articulate that faith in strictly biblical categories and language.[9] Olson and Hall are right to argue that "clearly, Menno Simons and the other major Anabaptist leaders were at least minimally orthodox in terms of their belief in the Trinity."[10] Simons was comfortable in stating that the Holy Spirit "proceeds from the Father through the Son, although he remains with God and in God."[11] This form of words resonates with the Eastern position on the *filioque* question, but there is little evidence of any direct borrowing from them.

Our discussion now turns to pneumatology per se.

Luther and the Spirit

At an earlier time in Luther scholarship, it was argued that Luther had little interest in or contribution to make to pneumatology.[12] After all, for Luther justification by faith alone was "the article of the standing or falling of the church," as Alsted was to state it in the seventeenth century. However, the work of Regin Prenter in the 1950s challenged this consensus. He contended that "the concept of the Holy Spirit completely dominates Luther's theology."[13] More recent scholarship takes Prenter's point but balances it with the rediscovery of Luther's accent on union with Christ (more below).[14]

---

8. Ibid., 76, 79.
9. Timothy George points out that Simons was not always consistent in this respect. Simons employed, for instance, the patristic category of *person* when speaking of Christ. *Theology of the Reformers*, rev. ed. (Nashville: Broadman, 2013), 289–90.
10. Olson and Hall, *The Trinity*, 74.
11. Quoted in George, *Theology of the Reformers*, 290.
12. For a superb, up-to-date bibliography on Luther of both primary and secondary works, see ibid., 107–11.
13. Regin Prenter, *Spiritus Creator*, trans. John M. Jensen (Philadelphia: Muhlenberg, 1953), ix.
14. See the useful discussion in Veli-Matti Kärkkäinen, *Pneumatology: The Holy Spirit in Ecumenical, International, and Contextual Perspective* (Grand Rapids, MI: Baker Academic, 2002), 79–80. Strangely, Kärkkäinen refers to "Reginald" [*sic*] Prenter. Ibid., 79.

The Spirit and the Word

Luther believed that his Bible was the Word of God. He also believed that there was a vital nexus between that Word and the Holy Spirit. He argued in the Smalcald (also referred to as Schmalcald) Articles,

> In these matters, which concern the external spoken Word, we must hold firmly to the conviction that God gives no one his Spirit or grace except through or with the external Word which comes before. Thus we shall be protected from the enthusiasts—that is, from the spiritualists who possess the Spirit without and before the Word and who therefore judge, interpret, and twist the Scriptures or spoken Word according to their pleasure. Thomas Münzer did this. . . . Accordingly, we should and must constantly maintain that God will not deal with us except through his external Word and sacrament. Whatever is attributed to the Spirit apart from such Word and sacrament is of the devil.[15]

However, to appreciate this Word, the Spirit's ministry is essential. Luther made this contrast in his commentary on Galatians, where he described "the common people, which have no love to the word, but contemn it, as though it pertained nothing at all unto them. But whosoever do feel any love or desire to the word, let them acknowledge with thankfulness, that this affection is poured unto them by the Holy Ghost."[16]

Not all his contemporaries were impressed by Luther's insistence on the objectivity of the Word. The radical Anabaptist Thomas Müntzer (1489–1525), mentioned in the Luther quote above, is a case in point.[17] He claimed that Luther "knows nothing of God, even though he may swallow one hundred Bibles." Luther famously replied in kind: "I wouldn't listen to Thomas Münzer if he swallowed the Holy Ghost, feathers and all." Müntzer appealed to the Spirit. Luther appealed to Word and Spirit in inseparable nexus. In Luther's eyes Müntzer was

---

15. "Schmalcald Articles," 3.8.3–12, in Kärkkäinen, *Holy Spirit and Salvation*, 156–57.

16. Luther, *Commentary on Galatians*, quoted in Hugh T. Kerr, ed., *A Compend of Luther's Theology* (Philadelphia: Westminster, 1974), 70.

17. Müntzer's stature as a theologian has been undergoing a reassessment. In fact, according to Matheson, "Müntzer may be the outstanding theologian of the Radical Reformation." Peter Matheson, "Müntzer, Thomas (ca. 1489–1525)," in *The Dictionary of Historical Theology*, ed. Trevor A. Hart (Grand Rapids, MI: Eerdmans, 2000), 382.

"an unstable 'Schwärmer,' or 'visionary,' whilst for Münzer, Luther was 'Dr Liar.'"[18]

THE SPIRIT AND THE SACRAMENTS

Luther's doctrine of the sacraments is more heavily freighted with Christology than with explicit pneumatology. Regarding baptism Luther argued, "For it is not man's baptism, but Christ's and God's baptism, which we receive by the hand of a man; just as every other created thing that we make use of by the hand of another, is God's alone."[19] In relation to the Lord's Supper, this Christological accent—especially his doctrine of the ubiquity of Christ's humanity—came to the fore in his celebrated debates with Zwingli. However, Luther did not neglect pneumatology in his sacramental theology, as can be seen in this claim that is worth quoting again: "Accordingly, we should and must maintain that God will not deal with us except through his external Word and sacrament. Whatever is attributed to the Spirit apart from such Word and sacrament is of the devil."[20] This claim was originally made about baptism in debate with the Anabaptists, but it applies *mutatis mutandis* to the Lord's Supper as well.

THE SPIRIT AND SALVATION

For Luther, the accomplishment of Christ on the cross for our salvation is of no effect unless the Holy Spirit takes what Christ has done and applies it to us. Luther maintained,

> Neither you nor I could ever know anything of Christ, or believe in him and take him as our Lord, unless these were offered to us and bestowed on our hearts through the preaching of the Gospel by the Holy Spirit. The work is finished and completed, Christ has acquired and won the treasure for us by his sufferings, death, and resurrection, etc. But if the work remained hidden and no one knew of it, it would have been in vain, all lost. In order that this treasure might not be buried but put to use and enjoyed, God has caused the Word to be published and proclaimed, in which

18. Ibid., 381–82. Note that spellings of "Müntzer" in the secondary literature vary.
19. Luther, *The Babylonian Captivity of the Church*, in Kerr, *Compend of Luther's Theology*, 65.
20. "Schmalcald Articles," 3.8.3–12, in Kärkkäinen, *Holy Spirit and Salvation*, 156–57.

he has given the Holy Spirit to offer and apply to us this treasure of salvation.[21]

In his usually colorful way, Luther used picture language. He spoke of Christ's work as a treasure. Treasure is useless if out of sight and buried. It is the Spirit who brings the treasure to light and makes it our own.

The work of the Spirit is for the one and the many, and that work does not cease with the initial expression of faith. In expounding the third article of the Apostles' Creed in his Small Catechism, Luther stated,

> I believe that I cannot by my own reason or strength believe in Jesus Christ, my Lord, or come to Him; but the Holy Ghost has called me by the Gospel, enlightened me with His gifts, sanctified and kept me in the true faith; even as He calls, gathers, enlightens, and sanctifies the whole Christian Church on earth, and keeps it with Jesus Christ in the one true faith; in which Christian Church He forgives daily and richly all sins to me and all believers, and at the last day will raise up me and all the dead, and will give to me and to all believers in Christ everlasting life. This is most certainly true.[22]

The scope of the Holy Spirit's role in salvation extends from the initial call through the heard gospel to the last day itself. The benefits of that role are for Luther and for all believers in Christ. Luther was no individualist.

The Spirit and the Church

Luther was a churchman. For him Christianity was no solo affair. Through the Spirit he belonged to a body, the body of Christ. He wrote of the church in his Large Catechism as follows:

> It is called together by the Holy Spirit in one faith, mind, and understanding. It possesses a variety of gifts, yet united in love without sect or schism. Of this community I also am a part and member, a participant and co-partner in all the blessings it possesses. I was

---

21. Martin Luther, "The Large Catechism," The Apostles' Creed, art. 3, pars. 38–39, in Kärkkäinen, *Holy Spirit and Salvation*, 158.
22. Luther, "Small Catechism," in Kerr, *Compend of Luther's Theology*, 65.

brought to it by the Holy Spirit and incorporated into it through the fact that I heard and still hear God's Word, which is the first step in entering it. . . . Until the last day the Holy Spirit remains with the holy community or Christian people. Through it he gathers us, using it to teach and preach the Word.[23]

Clearly, for Luther the Holy Spirit's work was vital for the very existence and life of the church understood as the community (*Gemeinde*) of faith, not as a building and not as an institution. This quotation also displays what for Luther was one of the two marks of the true church, namely, the faithful preaching of God's Word. Indeed, the Spirit is the preacher.[24]

Zwingli and the Spirit

Our focus now turns to Huldrych Zwingli, from Wittenberg to Zurich.[25] Of the five figures considered in this chapter, he was the only one to die on the battlefield (wielding a double-headed axe during the Battle of Kappel in 1531).[26] Importantly, Zwingli was not only a soldier; he was also an acute theologian whose teaching about the Holy Spirit is still worth weighing.

The Spirit and the Word

Zwingli prized the Word of God written but not to the neglect of the Holy Spirit, as the following shows:

Whether the Spirit of God is with you is demonstrated above all, by whether his word is your guide, and by whether you do nothing except what is clearly stated in the word of God so that scripture is your master and not you, masters of scripture. . . . Whenever we

---

23. Luther, "Large Catechism," Creed, art. 3, pars. 47–53, in Kärkkäinen, *Holy Spirit and Salvation*, 161–62.

24. One of Luther's congregational hymns addressed to the Holy Spirit—"Come, God Creator, Holy Spirit"—has this verse:

6. Teach us the Father well to know,
Likewise his only Son our Lord,
Thyself to us believing show,
Spirit of both, aye adored.

See *Martin Luther: Hymns, Ballads, Chants, Truth* (St. Louis, MO: Concordia, 2009), compact disc. The hymn is a ninth-century Latin work that Luther both translated and restructured.

25. For a superb, up-to-date bibliography on Zwingli of both primary and secondary works, see George, *Theology of the Reformers*, 167–68.

26. Ibid., 115.

give heed to the word, we acquire pure and clear knowledge of the will of God and are drawn to him by his Spirit and transformed into his likeness.[27]

For Zwingli, Scripture was the Word of God in general and the Spirit's Word in particular. A sure sign of the Spirit's presence with the believer is whether she or he is living under the authority of that Word. Obedience to the Word of God leads to transformation by the Spirit into the divine likeness. Zwingli evidenced a strong sense of the connectivity between Word and Spirit.

THE SPIRIT AND SALVATION

For Zwingli, turning ourselves to God is beyond human capability. The heavenly Father must draw us to himself. Zwingli wrote in relation to educating youth, "Yet it is still the case, in the words of St. Paul, that 'faith cometh by hearing, and hearing by the Word of God,' though this does not mean that very much can be accomplished by the preaching of the external word apart from the internal address and compulsion of the Spirit."[28] What part then does the Christian educator have to play in this? Zwingli counseled prayer: "Therefore it is necessary not merely to instill faith into the young by the pure words which proceed from the mouth of God, but to pray that he who alone can give faith will illuminate by his Spirit those whom we instruct in his word."[29] There are a number of classic theological ideas in Zwingli's work: the external call of the preacher and the internal call of the Spirit, faith as a divine gift, and the need for the hearers of the Word to experience the illumination of the Spirit.

Zwingli's articulation of his soteriology is also startling in places. At times he wrote in a way that an Eastern Orthodox theologian would applaud. For example, he stated, "That a person is drawn to God by God's Spirit and deified, becomes quite clear from scripture."[30] Zwingli

---

27. Huldrych Zwingli, *The Defense of the Reformed Faith*, in Kärkkäinen, *Holy Spirit and Salvation*, 163.
28. Huldrych Zwingli, "Of the Education of Youth," in *Zwingli and Bullinger: Selected Translations with Introductions and Notes*, ed. G. W. Bromiley, LCC 24 (Philadelphia: Westminster, 1953), 104.
29. Ibid.
30. Zwingli, *Defense of the Reformed Faith*, in Kärkkäinen, *Holy Spirit and Salvation*, 165.

in this proposition was not abolishing the Creator-creature distinction; rather, this claim echoed Athanasius: Jesus became what we are that we might become what he is. By grace the believer is restored to the image of God. Such belief is the work of the Holy Spirit. Zwingli wrote, "For no one knows or believes that Christ suffered for us, save those whom the Spirit within has taught to recognize the mystery of divine goodness. For such alone receive Christ. Hence nothing gives confidence in God except the Spirit."[31] Assurance of salvation is Spirit dependent.

The Spirit, the Church, and the Sacraments

Like Luther, Zwingli believed that where the Word is faithfully preached and the sacraments duly administered, there is the church. However, their very different understandings of the Lord's Supper meant that Zurich and Wittenberg took very different directions regarding the nature of this sacrament. Timothy George captures the difference in this striking way: "Luther emphasized the 'This is' in the words of institution, while Zwingli stressed the 'Do this.'"[32]

For Zwingli, without the Spirit, who grants faith, sacraments can only evoke "historical faith" (*fides historica*) and not saving faith. He wrote in relation to the Lord's Supper (though his words apply *mutatis mutandis* to baptism as well): "First, because no external things but only the Holy Spirit can give that faith which is trust in God. The sacraments do give faith, but only historical faith."[33] For Zwingli, "faith must be present already before we come."[34] Regarding baptism, the crucial baptism is the baptism of the Spirit, for without that baptism there is no salvation.[35] Such a baptism does not require water; the baptism of the Spirit is "the baptism of inward teaching, calling, and cleaving to God."[36]

---

31. Huldrych Zwingli, "On Providence," in Kärkkäinen, *Holy Spirit and Salvation*, 167.

32. George, *Theology of the Reformers*, 153. To explore the so-called Supper strife, fascinating though it is, would take us well beyond our brief.

33. Zwingli, *An Exposition of the Faith*, in *Zwingli and Bullinger*, 260. For Zwingli and other Reformers on baptism, see Robert Letham, "Baptism in the Writings of the Reformers," *SBET* 7, no. 2 (1989): 21–44.

34. Zwingli, *Exposition of the Faith*, 261. See Bruce A. Ware, "The Meaning of the Lord's Supper in the Theology of Ulrich Zwingli (1484–1531)," in *The Lord's Supper: Remembering and Proclaiming Christ until He Comes*, ed. Thomas R. Schreiner and Matthew R. Crawford (Nashville: B&H Academic, 2010).

35. Huldrych Zwingli, "Of Baptism," in *Zwingli and Bullinger*, 136.

36. Ibid., 133. Zwingli's attempts to fit infant baptism into this theological framework is well discussed in George, *Theology of the Reformers*, 146–47. Luther faced a similar challenge.

Calvin and the Spirit

With Calvin we move from Wittenberg and Zurich to Geneva—and arguably to the most significant contributor to pneumatology on view in this chapter.[37] In fact, Calvin has been described by B. B. Warfield as "pre-eminently the theologian of the Holy Spirit." Warfield placed Calvin in a line of luminaries:

> In the same sense in which we may say that the doctrine of sin and grace dates from Augustine, the doctrine of satisfaction from Anselm, the doctrine of justification by faith from Luther—we must say that the doctrine of the work of the Holy Spirit is a gift from Calvin to the church.[38]

To that gift we now turn our attention.

THE SPIRIT AND THE WORD

Calvin saw the closest of relations between Scripture and the Holy Spirit, so much so that Willem Balke argues that "the inseparability of the Word and Spirit was one of Calvin's cardinal teachings."[39] The heading to chapter 7 of book 1 of his *Institutes* supports Balke's claim: "Scripture Must Be Confirmed by the Witness of the Spirit. Thus May Its Authority Be Established as Certain."[40] Calvin went on to argue,

> But I reply: the testimony of the Spirit is more excellent than all reason. For as God alone is a fit witness of himself in his Word, so also the Word will not find acceptance in men's hearts before it is sealed by the inward testimony of the Spirit. The same Spirit, therefore, who has spoken through the mouths of the prophets must penetrate

---

37. For a superb, up-to-date bibliography on Calvin of both primary and secondary works, see George, *Theology of the Reformers*, 259–64. It is extraordinary that in his *Pneumatology: The Holy Spirit in Ecumenical, International, and Contextual Perspective*, Veli-Matti Kärkkäinen has no section per se on Reformed pneumatology and only one reference to Calvin in the book, according to the index.

38. Benjamin Breckinridge Warfield, "John Calvin the Theologian," in *Calvin and Augustine*, ed. Samuel G. Craig (Philadelphia: Presbyterian and Reformed, 1956), 485.

39. Willem Balke, as quoted in a fine article by Eifon Evans, "John Calvin: Theologian of the Holy Spirit," *R&R* 10, no. 4 (2001): 94.

40. Calvin, *Institutes*, 1.7. Balke's claim is also supported by Calvin's commentaries. For example, in commenting on Ezekiel, Calvin writes, "That we may know that the external word is of no avail by itself, unless animated by the power of the Spirit." John Calvin, *Commentary on the First Twenty Chapters of the Book of the Prophet Ezekiel*, trans. Thomas Myers (Edinburgh: Calvin Translation Society, 1849), 108.

into our hearts to *persuade* us that they faithfully proclaimed what had been divinely commanded.[41]

This important statement exhibits Calvin's seminal contribution to the nexus between bibliology and pneumatology: the idea of the internal witness of the Spirit (*testimonium Spiritus sancti internum*).

The Spirit's internal witness in Calvin's view is stronger than reason. He contended that "we ought to seek our conviction in a higher place than human reasons, judgments, or conjectures, that is, in the secret testimony of the Spirit." Again, he argued,

> Let this point therefore stand: that those whom the Holy Spirit has inwardly taught truly rest upon Scripture, and that Scripture indeed is self-authenticated; hence, it is not right to subject it to proof and reasoning. And the certainty it deserves with us, it attains by the testimony of the Spirit. For even if it wins reverence for itself by its own majesty, it seriously affects us only when it is sealed upon our hearts through the Spirit.[42]

Here are some familiar themes in Calvin: the witness of the Spirit, its inward nature, its secret character, the Spirit's illuminative work vis-á-vis Scripture, and the self-authenticating nature of Scripture.

The idea of a self-authenticating Scripture raises questions about the coherence of Calvin's discussion. The argument appears to involve an appeal to both Word and Spirit, with the Spirit authenticating the Word, on the one hand, and Scripture authenticating itself, on the other—the latter case seeming to suggest that Scripture has a life of its own. Yet Calvin's argument is that the Spirit with the Word is the key. Indeed, the Spirit is the great persuader that this Scripture is in fact the Word of God.[43]

THE SPIRIT AND THE SACRAMENTS

For Calvin, the sacraments—baptism and the Lord's Supper—are used by the Holy Spirit to confirm and increase faith. The activity of the

---

41. Calvin, *Institutes*, 1.7.4.
42. Ibid.
43. On the Spirit as persuader, and with acknowledged indebtedness to Calvin, see the discussion in Bernard L. Ramm, *The God Who Makes a Difference: A Christian Appeal to Reason* (Waco, TX: Word Books, 1972), 38–44.

Spirit is a necessary condition for their efficacy: "They only perform their office aright when they are accompanied by the Spirit, that internal Teacher, by whose energy alone our hearts are penetrated, our affections moved, and an entrance is opened for the sacraments into our souls."[44]

"Baptism," Calvin explained, "is the sign of the initiation, by which we are received into the society of the Church, in order that, engrafted in Christ, we may be reckoned among God's children."[45] In baptism God's promises are on display: "Thus, the free pardon of sins and the imputation of righteousness are first promised us, and then the grace of the Holy Spirit to reform us to newness of life."[46] The role of faith, however, is not neglected by Calvin: "But from this sacrament, as from all others, we obtain only as much as we receive in faith."[47]

Pneumatology also figures in Calvin's understanding of the Lord's Supper. According to Calvin, the risen Christ's presence at the Lord's Supper is to be understood in pneumatological terms. In his *Institutes* he maintained, "Yet a serious wrong is done to the Holy Spirit, unless we believe that it is through his incomprehensible power that we come to partake of Christ's flesh and blood." He further argued,

> Even though it seems unbelievable that Christ's flesh, separated from us by such great distance, penetrates to us, so that it becomes our food, let us remember how far the secret power of the Holy Spirit towers above all our senses, and how foolish it is to measure his immeasurableness by our measure. What, then, our mind does not comprehend, let faith conceive: that the Spirit truly unites things separated in space.[48]

For Calvin, the Lord Jesus is at the right hand of the Father. However, his Spirit is with us and in us. Thus Christ is present by his Spirit. There is a real presence but not one to be reduced to the bread and wine. In this Calvin parted company with both the Catholics and the Lutherans.

Calvin summarized his position with his usual lucidity in what he described as "a brief summary":

---

44. Calvin, *Institutes*, 4.19.9.
45. Ibid., 4.15.1.
46. Ibid., 4.15.5.
47. Ibid., 4.15.15.
48. Ibid., 4.17.10.

My readers now possess, collected into summary form, almost everything that I have thought should be known concerning these two sacraments, whose use has been handed down to the Christian church from the beginning of the New Testament even to the end of the world; that is, that baptism should be, as it were, an entry into the church, and an initiation into faith; but the Supper, should be a sort of continual food on which Christ spiritually feeds the household of faith.[49]

Importantly for Calvin, though, "the sacraments profit not a whit without the power of the Holy Spirit."[50]

The Spirit and Salvation

In Calvin's soteriology, unless the believer is united to Christ in some real way, then the benefits of Christ's obedience (*obedientia Christi*) are lost to us.[51] However, if the Holy Spirit joins us to Christ like a branch is joined to the vine, then all the benefits Christ has gained are ours. In this vein, Calvin began book 3 of his *Institutes* by raising a question:

We must examine this question. How do we receive these benefits which the Father bestowed on his only-begotten Son—not for Christ's own private use but that he might enrich poor and needy men? First, we must understand that as long as Christ remains outside of us, and we are separated from him, all that he has suffered and done for the salvation of the human race remains useless and of no value for us. Therefore, to share with us what he has received from the Father, he had to become ours and to dwell within us. For this reason, he is called "our head" [Eph. 4:15], and "the first-born among many brethren" [Rom. 8:29]. We also, in turn, are said to be "engrafted into him" [Rom. 11:17], and to "put on Christ" [Gal. 3:27]; for, as I have said, all that he possesses is nothing to us until we grow into one body with him. . . . To sum up, the Holy Spirit is the bond by which Christ effectually unites us to himself.[52]

---

49. Ibid., 4.18.19.
50. Ibid., 4.14.9.
51. This point is well made by Lewis B. Smedes, *Union with Christ: A Biblical View of the New Life in Jesus Christ*, 2nd ed. (Grand Rapids, MI: Eerdmans, 1983), 11.
52. Calvin, *Institutes*, 3.1.1. Calvin's heading for chap. 1 of book 3 is, "The Things Spoken concerning Christ Profit Us by the Secret Working of the Spirit," and that of the first section is, "The Holy Spirit as the Bond That Unites Us to Christ."

This is rich pneumatology![53] According to Lewis Smedes, Calvin's claim that as long as Christ remains outside us, the salvation he brings is of no use to us "controls Calvin's entire discussion of the grace of sanctification and justification."[54] Significantly, though, Calvin did not neglect the human agent in his treatment of union with Christ. In the same place he argued, "It is true that we obtain this by faith."[55] However, this faith, Calvin contended, "is the principal work of the Holy Spirit."[56]

THE SPIRIT, COMMON GRACE, AND CULTURE

Calvin had a full-orbed theology, as the *Institutes* show. He believed not only in God the Redeemer (book 2) but also in God the Creator (book 1). In his theology the order of creation and the order of redemption were not divorced. He was no Manichaean, as though life as a creature was without value.

In his *Institutes* Calvin distinguished between fallen humanity's grasp of earthly or inferior things and humanity's failure to grasp heavenly or superior things.[57] In the broken creation postfall, human reason was still competent to differing degrees, as evidenced by the mechanical arts, manual arts, liberal arts, medical arts, mathematical science, rhetoric, and so forth. These arts and sciences are the products of our natural endowments, which are the gift of God.[58] They also show "some remains of the divine image."[59] Even so, when it comes to the knowledge of God and salvation, the philosophers "are blinder than moles."[60]

Calvin was writing about what a later theology would term *common grace*. Common grace is God's general kindness toward his fallen image bearers.[61] Special grace or saving grace, on the other hand, in Reformed thought, is God's unmerited saving kindness toward his elect in reconciling them to himself. The Holy Spirit is intimately involved in both. Take common grace, for example. Calvin traced whatever

---

53. A surprising lacuna in George, *Theology of the Reformers*, is that he makes no reference to union with Christ by the Spirit in his treatment of Calvin's doctrine of life in the Spirit, 231–43.
54. Smedes, *Union With Christ*, 10.
55. Calvin, *Institutes*, 3.1.1.
56. Ibid., 3.1.4.
57. Ibid., 2.2.13.
58. Ibid., 2.2.14–16.
59. Ibid., 2.17.
60. Ibid., 2.18.
61. Donald K. McKim, *Westminster Dictionary of Theological Terms* (Louisville: Westminster John Knox, 1996), 120.

art, science, or skill fallen humanity shows to the work of the Holy Spirit. In fact, he asserted that in despising such gifts, we "dishonor the Spirit."[62] This is strong language. Furthermore, he argued, "If the Lord has willed that we be helped in physics, dialectic, mathematics, and the like disciplines, by the work and ministry of the ungodly, let us use this assistance. For if we neglect God's gift freely offered in these arts, we ought to suffer just punishment for our sloths."[63]

Calvin appealed to the Scriptures to justify his position, but his choice of evidence is surprising. He discussed the tabernacle of the wilderness period and the skill and knowledge of Bezalel and Oholiab used in its construction (Ex. 31:2; 35:30). Their knowledge and skill came from the Spirit. The argument is somewhat obscure: if their excellence comes from the Spirit, then so too does the highest excellence in human life.[64] There is a difference between the godly and the ungodly, though. The Spirit is said to indwell believers, making them holy temples by his presence. The ungodly are not so. Yet the Spirit has not left them bereft of his influence: "Nonetheless he fills, moves, and quickens all things by the power of the same Spirit, and does so according to the character he bestowed on each kind by the law of creation."[65]

The Spirit, the Church, and the Sacraments

For Calvin, the church included both the visible and the invisible. He wrote in relation to the creed, "The article in the Creed in which we profess to 'believe the church' refers not only to the visible church (our present topic) but also to all God's elect, in whose number are also included the dead."[66] Baptism is the unrepeatable rite of initiation into the church, and the Lord's Supper is the ongoing feasting on the risen Christ at the right hand of the Father by faith through the Holy Spirit. Writing of the sacraments (baptism and Lord's Supper), Calvin noted,

> We believe this communication to be (a) mystical, and incomprehensible to human reason, and (b) spiritual, since it is effected by the Holy Spirit; to whom, since he is the virtue of the living God, proceeding

---

62. Calvin, *Institutes*, 2.2.15.
63. Ibid., 2.2.16.
64. Ibid.
65. Ibid.
66. Ibid., 4.1.2.

from the Father and the Son, we ascribe omnipotence, by which he joins us to Christ our Head, not in an imaginary way, but most powerfully and truly, so that we become flesh of his flesh and bone of his bone, and from his vivifying flesh he transfuses eternal life into us.[67]

This statement is rich in theological freight. Calvin's affirmation of *filioque* is on view, as is his realist understanding of union with Christ as pneumatologically effected. Moreover, the deity of the Spirit is affirmed, as omnipotence can only be predicated of deity.

Cranmer and the Spirit

For all his liturgical genius, few scholars would maintain that Archbishop Thomas Cranmer stood at the forefront of Reformation theology. Jonathan Dean writes,

> Thomas Cranmer was not one of the Reformation's great original thinkers or theologians. He did not, as Martin Luther, unleash the energies of a whole generation in a monumental movement of religious change. He was no Calvin, defining the contours of reformed theology and practice through a massive and meticulous systematic exposition intended for the guidance of future generations. Nor was he even an Ulrich Zwingli, reimagining the Eucharist in controversial and dynamic fashion.[68]

So why consider Cranmer? Again, Jonathan Dean supplies a helpful observation: "If not the most brilliant or critical leader of the varied Reformation movements of the sixteenth century, his work is by far the most influential in the lives of the ordinary Christians he so cared about, and it has enjoyed a much greater longevity."[69]

Granted, Cranmer was no Luther or Zwingli or Calvin. However,

---

67. John Calvin, "Summary of Doctrine concerning the Ministry of the Word and the Sacraments," in *Calvin: Theological Treatises*, trans. J. K. S. Reid, LCC 22 (Louisville: Westminster John Knox, 2006), 171.

68. Jonathan Dean, ed., *God Truly Worshipped: Thomas Cranmer and His Writings* (Norwich: Canterbury Press, 2012), 1. J. I. Packer adds a needed nuance here: "It is true that he [Cranmer] was neither prolific nor original nor argumentative, but this does not of itself mark him down as a second rater. . . . If Cranmer's services [1549 and 1552 especially] pass muster as masterpieces of Christian worship, there is at least a presumption that the theology behind them is also in the master class." "Introduction," in *The Works of Thomas Cranmer*, ed. G. E. Duffield (Philadelphia: Fortress, 1965), xvii–xviii.

69. Dean, *God Truly Worshipped*, 1.

he knew what the needs of the English church were and strove to meet them in a biblically informed and theologically adroit way. Gerald Bray captures this well:

> The historic formularies were designed by Archbishop Cranmer
> . . . to give the English Church a solid grounding in the three fun-
> damental areas of life—*doctrine, devotion and discipline.* The Ar-
> ticles provided its doctrinal framework, the Prayer Book settled
> the pattern of its devotional life and the Ordinal outlined what
> was expected of the clergy, whose role was the key to the Church's
> discipline.[70]

Regarding the Prayer Book (also known as the Book of Common Prayer), Stephen Neill offers an astute observation. First, he makes this general point: "Nothing is more striking in the Reformation than the recovery of the almost forgotten doctrine of the Holy Spirit." Next, he turns his attention to Cranmer in particular: "Of Cranmer's special interest in this doctrine the Prayer Book itself, with its constant references to the Holy Spirit, is evidence."[71]

What, then, was Cranmer's pneumatology? We begin our discussion with his doctrine of the Word of God.

The Spirit and the Word

Like the other magisterial Reformers, Cranmer had a high view of biblical authority. His high view of Scripture is patent in article 5 of the Forty-Two Articles, which reads,

> Holy Scripture containeth all things necessary to Salvation: so that
> whatsoever is neither read therein, nor may be proved thereby,
> although it be sometime received of the faithful, as Godly, and
> profitable for an order, and comeliness: Yet no man ought to be
> constrained to believe it as an article of faith, or repute it requisite
> to the necessity of Salvation.[72]

---

70. Gerald Bray, *The Faith We Confess: An Exposition of the Thirty-Nine Articles* (London: Latimer, 2009), 1. Emphasis originally bold but here italicized. Cranmer was martyred in 1556, so the articles to be considered are the Forty-Two Articles of 1553, and the Prayer Book is that of 1552.

71. Stephen Neill, *Anglicanism*, 4th ed. (New York: Oxford University Press, 1982), 79.

72. In Dean, *God Truly Worshipped*, 165. The Forty-Two Articles were first written in Latin by Cranmer. As Gerald Bray points out, "The forty-two articles were not just position statements

The Bible for Cranmer was in the first instance a gospel book. For him it was *norma normans* ("the norming norm"). He was aware that other authorities have their place in Christianity but only as *norma normata* ("ruled norms," i.e., ruled by Scripture). General councils of the church, for example, bear some weight, but they can and have erred in the past. This is so, according to article 22 of the Forty-Two Articles, because such councils have not always been "governed with the Spirit and the Word of God."[73]

In Cranmer's view, the Scriptures were not only to be read by the learned. In his preface to the Bible, he contended, "For the holy ghost hath so ordered and tempered the scriptures, that in them as well publicans, fishers, and shepherds may find their edification, as great doctors their erudition."[74] Above all, whether we are learned or unlearned, Scripture is the Holy Spirit's instrument by which the knowledge of salvation comes to us: "For as mallets, hammers, saws, chisels, axes, and hatchets, be the tools of their occupation; so be the books of the prophets, and Apostles, and all holy writers inspired by the holy ghost, the instruments of our salvation."[75] Moreover, it is the Spirit who provides epistemic certitude as to scriptural truthfulness: "There is the illumination of the holy ghost, the end of all our desires, and the very light whereby the verity of scriptures is seen and perceived."[76]

The Spirit and Salvation

Like Luther, Zwingli, and Calvin, Cranmer held a robust view of divine sovereignty and was a predestinarian in his soteriology.[77] He was, in fact, a Protestant Augustinian.[78] Article 17 of the Forty-Two Articles expresses the Cranmerian position and is the longest of the articles. I quote *in extenso*:

on disputed points of doctrine but a general exposition of what he [Cranmer] thought the church ought to believe." See Bray, *Faith We Confess*, 8.

73. In Dean, *God Truly Worshipped*, 169–70.
74. Thomas Cranmer, "Preface to the Bible," in Duffield, *Works of Thomas Cranmer*, 35.
75. Ibid.
76. Ibid.
77. On Cranmer as a predestinarian, see the definitive biography by Diarmaid MacCulloch, *Thomas Cranmer: A Life* (New Haven, CT: Yale University Press, 1996), 211.
78. A point well made by Ashley Null, *Thomas Cranmer's Doctrine of Repentance: Renewing the Power to Love* (Oxford: Oxford University Press, 2006), 215, 251.

Predestination to Life is the everlasting purpose of God, whereby (before the foundations of the world were laid) he hath constantly decreed by his counsel secret to us, to deliver from curse and damnation those whom he hath chosen in Christ out of mankind, and to bring them by Christ to everlasting salvation, as vessels made to honour. Wherefore, they which be endued with so excellent a benefit of God be called according to God's purpose *by his Spirit* working in due season: they through Grace obey the calling: they be justified freely: they be made sons of God by adoption: they be made like the image of his only-begotten Son Jesus Christ: they walk religiously in good works, and at length, by God's mercy, they attain to everlasting felicity.

As the godly consideration of Predestination, and our Election in Christ, is full of sweet, pleasant, and unspeakable comfort to godly persons, and such as feel in themselves *the working of the Spirit of Christ*, mortifying the works of the flesh, and their earthly members, and drawing up their mind to high and heavenly things, as well because it doth greatly establish and confirm their faith of eternal Salvation to be enjoyed through Christ, as because it doth fervently kindle their love towards God: So, for curious and carnal persons, *lacking the Spirit of Christ*, to have continually before their eyes the sentence of God's Predestination, is a most dangerous downfall, whereby the Devil doth thrust them either into desperation, or into recklessness of most unclean living, no less perilous than desperation.

Furthermore, we must receive God's promises in such wise, as they be generally set forth to us in holy Scripture: and, in our doings, that Will of God is to be followed, which we have expressly declared unto us in the Word of God.[79]

The import of the three pneumatological references here is manifold. The Spirit is the applier of God's salvific purposes whether one has on view justification, adoption, transformation into Christ's likeness, the production of good works in the Christian life, or the safe arrival of the elect in the world to come. Furthermore, as for sanctification, the Holy Spirit at work puts to death the works of the flesh, sets our minds on

---

79. In Dean, *God Truly Worshipped*, 168. Italics added.

things above, establishes and confirms our faith in eternal salvation, and kindles our love for God. Finally, if one lacks the Holy Spirit, then this doctrine when contemplated may foster despair or a reckless lifestyle.

On the matter of justification, Cranmer was a *solifidian* ("faith alone"). As article 11 of the Forty-Two Articles states, "Justification by only faith in Jesus Christ, in that sense as it is declared in the homily of Justification, is a most certain, and wholesome doctrine for Christian men."[80] Ashley Null well sums up Cranmer's position on justification and the Holy Spirit's relation to it: "The believer's faith laid hold of the extrinsic righteousness of Christ on which basis his sins were pardoned. At the same time the Holy Spirit indwelt the believer, stirring in him a love for God out of gratitude for the assurance of salvation."[81] A wholesome doctrine indeed!

One of the theological issues facing Cranmer was how to understand the role of good works in the life of faith. He was very clear that works done before justification count for naught before God, as article 12 shows:

> Works done before the grace of Christ, and the inspiration of his Spirit, are not pleasant to God, forasmuch as they spring not of faith in Jesus Christ, neither do they make men meet to receive grace, or (as the School-authors say) deserve grace of congruity: yea, rather, for that they are not done as God hath willed and commanded them to be done, we doubt not but they have the nature of sin.

Divine grace and the working of the Holy Spirit are necessary conditions for God-pleasing works done by the believer. Cranmer was no Pelagian.

Cranmer was pastorally aware that Christians do sin after being justified by grace. Sinless perfectionism was not a part of his theology, as article 15 of the Forty-Two Articles makes plain:

> Not every deadly sin willingly committed after Baptism is Sin against the Holy Ghost, and unpardonable; wherefore the place

---

80. Ibid., 167.
81. Ashley Null, *Cranmer's Doctrine*, 252. Null argues that Cranmer's strong doctrine of "unconditional election" protected "the utter gratuity of this saving faith." Ibid.

for penance, is not to be denied to such as fall into sin after Baptism. After we have received the Holy Ghost, we may depart from grace given, and fall into sin, and by the grace of God we may arise again, and amend our lives. And therefore they are to be condemned, which say, they can no more sin as long as they live here, or deny the place of penitence to such as truly repent, and amend their lives.[82]

Even so, for Cranmer there is the unpardonable sin against the Holy Spirit, and according to article 16, it occurs "when a man of malice, and stubbornness of mind doth rail upon the truth of God's word manifestly perceived, and being enemy thereunto persecuteth the same."[83] Such men and women are under a divine curse.

The Spirit, the Church, and the Sacraments

The Anglicanism that emerged during the sixteenth-century Reformation in England was a Reformed Western Catholicism. It remained a liturgical church informed by the ecclesiastical year. The language of sacraments was retained but reformed. How did Cranmer, then, understand the role of the Spirit in the two dominical sacraments of baptism and the Lord's Supper?

In Cranmer's view, the Holy Spirit plays a vital role in the sacramental life of the church. Geoffrey Bromiley captures this when he writes of Cranmer's Eucharistic theology: "Therefore no account can be satisfactory which does not do justice to the fact and mission of the Holy Spirit in relation to Jesus Christ."[84] Again, Bromiley is accurate: "The office of the Holy Spirit is not merely to give us a symbolic reminder of Christ's person and work, but to make Him our contemporary, so that in the signs we are genuinely confronted with Christ and His redemption."[85] These words could have equally been written of Cranmer's baptismal theology. Article 27, "Of Baptism," affirms,

Baptism is not only a sign of profession and mark of difference, whereby Christian men are discerned from other that be not chris-

82. In Dean, *God Truly Worshipped*, 167–68.
83. Ibid., 168.
84. G. W. Bromiley, *Thomas Cranmer: Theologian* (New York: Oxford University Press, 1956), 83.
85. Ibid., 82.

tened; but is also a sign of our new birth, whereby as by an instrument, they that receive baptism rightly are grafted into the Church; the promises of forgiveness of sin, and our adoption to be the sons of God by the Holy Ghost [*sic*], are visibly signed and sealed; faith is confirmed; and grace increased by virtue of prayer unto God. The custom of the Church to christen young children is to be commended and in any wise to be retained in the Church.[86]

Cranmer rejected transubstantiation root and branch.[87] Moreover, as with Zwingli and Calvin, Cranmer believed that the ascended Christ was in heaven at the right hand of the Father. He did not embrace the ubiquitism theory of Luther concerning Christ's humanity sharing in the divine attribute of omnipresence through the *communicatio idiomatum* ("communication of properties"). However, he did believe that Christ was in a sense present at the Lord's Supper. Bromiley underlines Cranmer's understanding well: "He [Christ] is not now present as incarnate, but crucified, resurrected and ascended He is present by the Spirit."[88] Diarmaid MacCulloch helpfully describes Cranmer's mature view of Christ's presence from 1548 on as a "spiritual presence" through "the gift of the Holy Spirit" in contradistinction to a "real presence."[89]

Menno Simons and the Spirit

Menno Simons was not the most theologically astute of the Anabaptist writers, but he was "the most outstanding leader."[90] In discussing Simons's pneumatology, some new themes emerge beyond what we have seen thus far with the magisterial Reformers. In particular, unlike Luther, Zwingli, Calvin, and Cranmer, Simons rejected infant baptism.

86. "The Forty-Two Articles," in *Documents of the English Reformation, 1526–1701*, ed. Gerald Bray (Cambridge: James Clarke, 2004), 301, https://books.google.com/books?id=UGi6WWtz kJYC&pg. I have altered the text in Bray's translation from the Latin at one point. He placed "by the Holy Ghost" in brackets, indicating that it was a later addition. However, the Latin of 1553 reads "*per Spiritum Sanctum*." Consequently, I have removed his brackets.
87. In Cranmer's reading of church history, Satan was unleashed, as in Revelation 20, about a thousand years after Christ, and the Fourth Lateran Council of 1215 that officially endorsed the doctrine of transubstantiation was evidence of that loosing of Satan. See Graham A. Cole, "Cranmer's Views on the Bible and the Christian Prince: An Examination of His Writings and the Edwardian Formularies" (ThM thesis, University of Sydney, 1983), 49–54.
88. Bromiley, *Thomas Cranmer: Theologian*, 79.
89. MacCulloch, *Cranmer*, 392.
90. This is the judgment of George, *Theology of the Reformers*, 269. For a superb, up-to-date bibliography on Simons of both primary and secondary works, see ibid., 323–25.

And as an Anabaptist, Simons made the ban (more below) a third mark
of the true church alongside the faithful preaching of the Word and the
sacraments duly administered.[91]

THE SPIRIT AND THE WORD

In Simons's thought, the inspired Word of Scripture is the *norma normans* ("norming norm"). He expressed himself this way:

> We certainly hope no one of a rational mind will be so foolish a
> man as to deny the whole Scriptures, both the Old and New Testa-
> ments, were written for our instruction, admonitions, and correc-
> tion, and that they are the true scepter and rule by which the Lord's
> kingdom, house, church, and congregation must be ruled and gov-
> erned. Everything contrary to Scripture, therefore, whether it be in
> doctrines, beliefs, sacraments, worship, or life, should be measured
> by this infallible rule and demolished by this just and divine scepter,
> and destroyed without any respect of persons.[92]

Like the magisterial Reformers, Simons held a high view of biblical
authority. Interestingly, though, for him the canonical Word extended
to the apocryphal writings. In this he was out of step with most of the
magisterial Reformers.[93] At the same time, he did not privilege reason
like the evangelical rationalists did, nor did he accent the Spirit within
like the Spiritualists did.[94]

Simons made no claims to any kind of privileged experiential access

---

91. George makes this point well in *Theology of the Reformers*, 310.

92. Menno Simons, "Foundations," quoted in *Anabaptism in Outline: Selected Primary Sources*,
ed. Walter Klaassen, Classics of the Radical Reformation 3 (Waterloo, ON: Herald, 1981), 151.

93. This aspect of Simons's theology is well discussed in George, *Theology of the Reformers*,
291. Magisterial Reformer Thomas Cranmer thought the Apocrypha worth reading with profit but
that no doctrine should be built on it. Article 6 of the Book of Common Prayer reads,

> And the other Books (as Hierome [Jerome] saith) the Church doth read for example of life
> and instruction of manners; but yet doth it not apply them to establish any doctrine; such
> are these following:
>   The Third Book of Esdras, The rest of the Book of Esther,
>   The Fourth Book of Esdras, The Book of Wisdom,
>   The Book of Tobias, Jesus the Son of Sirach,
>   The Book of Judith, Baruch the Prophet,
>   The Song of the Three Children, The Prayer of Manasses,
>   The Story of Susanna, The First Book of Maccabees,
>   Of Bel and the Dragon, The Second Book of Maccabees.

94. George, *Theology of the Reformers*, 269. See also the discussion by Werner O. Packull,
"An Introduction to Anabaptist Theology," in Bagchi and Steinmetz, *Cambridge Companion to
Reformation Theology*, 194–219, esp. 218.

to the mysteries of God. He wrote, "Brethren, I tell you the truth and lie not. I am no Enoch. I am no Elijah. I am not one who sees visions. I am no prophet who can teach and prophesy otherwise than what is written in the Word of God and understood in the Spirit."[95] This is an impressive epistemic modesty.

THE SPIRIT AND THE SACRAMENTS

As one would expect of an Anabaptist, Simons held that only those who could confess the faith could be proper candidates for baptism. He wrote, "The church of Christ [is] made up of true believers, broken in their hearts by the mill of the divine Word, baptized with the water of the Holy Ghost, and with the fire of pure, unfeigned love made into one body."[96] Such confession had to come from the heart. He argued, "Oh, no, outward baptism avails nothing so long as we are not inwardly renewed, regenerated, and baptized with the heavenly fire and the Holy Ghost of God."[97]

With regard to the Lord's Supper, Simons became lyrical: "Oh, the delightful assembly and Christian marriage feast . . . where hungry consciences are fed with the heavenly bread of the divine Word, with the wine of the Holy Ghost, and where the peaceful, joyous souls sing and play before the Lord."[98]

THE SPIRIT AND SALVATION

For Simons, the new birth was of paramount salvific importance, and the Holy Spirit has a pivotal role in the event and the discipleship that arises from it.[99] Regarding the conversion process, he wrote that "the heart is pierced and moved through the Holy Ghost with unusual regenerating, renewing, vivifying power, which produces first of all fear of God."[100] He described the Christian life that flows from regeneration in these terms:

95. Quoted in George, *Theology of the Reformers*, 295.
96. Quoted in ibid., 308.
97. Simons, "Foundations," in Klaassen, *Anabaptism*, 188.
98. Quoted in George, *Theology of the Reformers*, 309.
99. Max Göbel wrote in 1848, "The essential and distinguishing characteristic of this [Anabaptist] church is its great emphasis upon the actual personal conversion and regeneration of every Christian through the Holy Spirit." Quoted in George, *Theology of the Reformers*, 280.
100. Quoted in George, *Theology of the Reformers*, 281.

These regenerated people have a spiritual king over them who rules them by the unbroken scepter of His mouth, namely, with His Holy Spirit and Word. He clothes them with the garment of righteousness of pure white silk. He refreshes them with the living water of His Holy Spirit and feeds them with the Bread of Life.[101]

According to Roger Olson, "Menno's [own] heartfelt conversion involving conscious repentance and trust in Jesus Christ followed by a filling of the Holy Spirit became the paradigm for the early Anabaptist theology of salvation."[102]

The Spirit, the Church, and the Ban

In Simons's ecclesiology, the church is a believer's church rather than a mixed body (*corpus per mixtum*). He wrote,

They verily are not the true congregation of Christ who merely boast of his name. But they are the true congregation of Christ who are truly converted, who are born from above of God, who are of a regenerate mind by the operation of the Holy Spirit through the hearing of the divine Word, and become the children of God, have entered into obedience to him, and live unblamably in his holy commandments, and according to his holy will with all their days, or from the moment of their call.[103]

The Word must be heard to be responded to. Infants are incapable of this. So for Simons, "those who maintain that the baptism of irrational children is a washing of regeneration do violence to the Word of God, resist the Holy Ghost, make Christ a liar and his holy apostles."[104] Why so? He argued, "For Christ and his apostles teach that regeneration, as well as faith, comes from God and his Word, which Word is not to be taught to those who are unable to hear or understand, but to those who have the ability both to hear and understand."[105]

The accent on the congregation being pure and true fits with the

101. Menno Simons, "The New Birth," in Kärkkäinen, *Holy Spirit and Salvation*, 189.
102. Olson, *The Story of Christian Theology*, 423.
103. Quoted in George, *Theology of the Reformers*, 300.
104. Menno Simons, "Foundations," in Klaassen, *Anabaptism*, 187.
105. Ibid.

Anabaptist notion of the ban. George Williams and Angel Mergal note, "Baptism and the ban were the two keys controlling the entry to and the exit from the regenerate church of Anabaptism." How so? "By [re]baptism one entered the church. By the ban the wayward member was extruded. Only the pure could participate in the communion of the celestial flesh of Christ."[106]

For Simons, the strictures of Matthew 18:15–18 constituted a defining characteristic of a pure church. Those who strayed in doctrine and conduct had no place in a holy assembly. They were to be excluded and shunned. The rhetoric is strong yet not without feeling:

> But now the Holy Spirit does not teach us to destroy the wicked, as did Israel, but that we should sorrowfully expel them from the church, and that in the name of the Lord, by the power of Christ and the Holy Spirit, since a little leaven leavens the whole lump. . . . Therefore the Holy Spirit has abundantly taught us to separate such from among us.[107]

This ban was to be widely applied to family, husbands, wives, parents, and children. In practice, though, Simons did on occasion counsel leniency.[108]

References to the Holy Spirit abound in Simons's articulation of the ban. To receive those who have lapsed, by, for example, eating with them, is to reject the Holy Spirit. To shun the lapsed is to follow the counsel of the Holy Spirit. To do so with a view to their hopeful reformation is also to follow the counsel of the Holy Spirit. To obey the Holy Spirit in practicing the ban is to never be made ashamed. Indeed, the Holy Spirit ordained the ban.[109]

Conclusion

We have considered four magisterial Reformers (Luther, Zwingli, Calvin, and Cranmer) and one radical Reformer (Simons). In so doing,

---

106. George Huntston Williams and Angel M. Mergal, eds., *Spiritual and Anabaptist Writers*, LCC 25 (Louisville: Westminster John Knox, 2006), 261.

107. Menno Simons, "Account of Excommunication," in Klaassen, *Anabaptism*, 229.

108. The ban is well discussed in George, *Theology of the Reformers*, 312.

109. For the substance of this paragraph, I am indebted to Menno Simons, "On the Ban: Questions and Answers by Menno Simons," in Williams and Mergal, *Spiritual and Anabaptist Writers*, 263–71, passim.

both Continental and English Reformations have been in view. All agreed on the nature of God as Trinity and therefore on both the personhood and the deity of the Holy Spirit. All agreed that the Holy Spirit of God was active in salvation, in sanctification, in our responding to the Word, and in the sacraments. The magisterial Reformers, however, saw a nexus between church and state that the radical Reformers rejected. The magisterial Reformers were also comfortable with the practice of infant baptism, while the radical Reformers were not. For the radical Reformers, the only true church was a believers' church. Of particular interest is how the relationship between God's Word written and the ministry of the Spirit were to be construed. Some of the radical Reformers privileged the inner Word (the Spiritualists) or reason (the evangelical rationalists) over the external Word in ways that the magisterial Reformers did not. In contrast, the magisterial Reformers accented the external Word. In that respect, Menno Simons was more like the magisterial Reformers than a Servetus or Schwenkfeld. All our selected personages placed immense theological value on the person and work of the Holy Spirit as the great applier of the salvation planned by the Father and accomplished through the Son.

Resources for Further Study

PRIMARY

Bromiley, G. W., ed. *Zwingli and Bullinger: Selected Translations with Introductions and Notes.* Library of Christian Classics 24. Philadelphia: Westminster, 1953.

Calvin, John. *Institutes of the Christian Religion.* Edited by John T. McNeill. Translated by Ford Lewis Battles. 2 vols. Library of Christian Classics 20–21. 1559 edition. Philadelphia: Westminster, 1960.

Cranmer, Thomas. *Works.* Cambridge: Parker Society, 1844–1846.

Dillenberger, John, ed. *Martin Luther: Selections from his Writings.* Garden City, NY: Doubleday, 1961.

Duffield, G. E., ed. *The Work of Thomas Cranmer.* Philadelphia: Fortress, 1965.

Kärkkäinen, Veli-Matti, ed. *Holy Spirit and Salvation: The Sources of Christian Theology.* Louisville: Westminster John Knox, 2010.

Klaassen, Walter, ed. *Anabaptism in Outline: Selected Primary Sources.* Classics of the Radical Reformation 3. Waterloo, ON: Herald, 1981.

Simons, Menno. *The Complete Works of Menno Simons.* London: Forgotten Books, 2012.

Williams, George Huntston, and Angel M. Mergal, eds. *Spiritual and Anabaptist Writers.* Library of Christian Classics 25. Louisville: Westminster John Knox, 2006.

SECONDARY

Bagchi, David, and David C. Steinmetz, eds. *The Cambridge Companion to Reformation Theology.* Cambridge: Cambridge University Press, 2004.

George, Timothy. *Theology of the Reformers.* Rev. ed. Nashville: B&H, 2013.

Hart, Trevor A., ed. *The Dictionary of Historical Theology.* Grand Rapids, MI: Eerdmans, 2000.

Hughes, Philip E. *Theology of the English Reformers.* 2nd ed. Grand Rapids, MI: Baker, 1980.

Kärkkäinen, Veli-Matti. *Pneumatology: The Holy Spirit in Ecumenical, International, and Contextual Perspective.* Grand Rapids, MI: Baker Academic, 2002.

12

Union with Christ

J. V. Fesko

ABSTRACT

Sixteenth-century theologians of every stripe (Lutheran, Reformed, Roman Catholic, Arminian, and Socinian) advocated the doctrine of union with Christ. Protestant theologians (Lutheran and Reformed) echoed earlier medieval formulations of the doctrine, especially that of Bernard of Clairvaux, but distinguished between justification and sanctification in order to argue that the believer's justification rests solely on the imputed righteousness of Christ. This stands in contrast to Roman Catholic formulations and to later post-Reformation developments, such as those from Jacobus Arminius and Faustus Socinus. Roman Catholic and Arminian views maintained the importance and necessity of union with Christ but conflated justification and sanctification. Socinians maintained that believers are united to God through an impersonal power that flows to Christ, not the personal indwelling of Christ by the Spirit. These divergent views provide a backdrop to appreciate the unique features of Protestant formulations of union with Christ.[1]

1. I would like to thank Korey Maas and Robert Kolb for reading an initial draft of this chapter and offering helpful feedback, comments, and suggested sources.

Introduction

A cursory reading of the New Testament quickly impresses on the reader the frequency of the phrase "in Christ" (or "in him"), which denotes the doctrine of union with Christ.[2] This phrase appears repeatedly throughout the Pauline corpus, which has naturally produced significant reflection on this doctrine throughout the history of the church but especially within the Protestant Reformation, which has been characterized as a renaissance of Paulinism. But what, precisely, did the Protestant Reformers teach with respect to the doctrine of union with Christ? How did they define it? And more broadly, how did Reformation formulations compare with Roman Catholic, Arminian, and Socinian views? Before we proceed, it is important to present a garden-variety definition of the doctrine to establish its parameters. As tempting as it might be to quote a contemporary source or definition, it is methodologically preferable to employ an early-modern definition so that historic Reformation views take center stage rather than later versions of the doctrine.

One such example comes from Girolamo Zanchi (1516–1590), a second-generation Reformer. Zanchi explained union with Christ in a personal confession, one that was intended to supersede the Second Helvetic Confession (1566), written by Heinrich Bullinger (1504–1575). Zanchi's confession, therefore, was written for wide acceptance and presents what he believed were common convictions about the doctrine. Zanchi wrote that participation in righteousness and salvation depends wholly on a necessary communion with Christ. He described this union as threefold: "One, which was once made in our nature; another, which is daily made in the persons of the elect, which yet go astray from the Lord; and the last, which shall be likewise with the Lord in our persons when they shall be present with him, namely, when God shall be all in us all." The first union entails the Son's incarnation as a human being. The second union is when Christ mystically indwells believers, which Peter calls participation in the divine nature (2 Pet. 1:4). The third union is the sinner's glorification.[3] Immediately

---

2. E.g., Constantine R. Campbell, *Paul and Union with Christ: An Exegetical and Theological Study* (Grand Rapids, MI: Zondervan, 2012).

3. Girolamo Zanchi, *De Religione Christiana Fides – Confession of Christian Religion*, ed. Luca Baschera and Christian Moser, Studies in the History of Christian Traditions 135 (Leiden:

evident from this description and functional definition is that union with Christ has a broader scope than contemporary versions of the doctrine. Zanchi's statements encompass Christology, soteriology, and eschatology, whereas contemporary definitions sometimes focus largely on soteriology.[4]

With this basic description in hand, this chapter will proceed to examine Reformation views on union with Christ, primarily through chief Reformation figures, such as the Lutheran theologians Martin Luther (1483–1546), Philipp Melanchthon (1497–1560), Andreas Osiander (1498–1552), and Martin Chemnitz (1522–1586), and the Reformed theologians Peter Martyr Vermigli (1499–1562), John Calvin (1509–1564), Wolfgang Musculus (1497–1563), and Zanchi. By sampling formulations from these Lutheran and Reformed theologians, we will be able to identify the chief elements and contours of union with Christ according to the Reformers. The second part of the essay will compare and contrast Protestant formulations with those offered by Roman Catholic theologians, primarily through the lens of the Council of Trent (1545–1563), and will also briefly examine the Socinian views on union with Christ, primarily through the writings of Faustus Socinus (1539–1604) and the Racovian Catechism (1605), as well as through the works of Jacobus Arminius (1560–1609). Though Socinian views and Arminius's formulation of union lie beyond the Reformation, they nevertheless provide greater historical context by which we can appreciate and better understand Protestant opinions in the Reformation. If we were merely to examine Protestant understandings, it would be like painting a lone figure on a blank canvas. As interesting as the lone figure might be, only the surrounding context of the painting tells the rest of the story. Comparing and contrasting Roman Catholic, Socinian, and Arminian views of union with Christ with Protestant constructions in the Reformation will demonstrate their unique features.

Brill, 2007), 12.5. Archaic English has been updated in this and all subsequent quotations from Zanchi's *De Religione*.

4. Cf., e.g., Wayne Grudem, *Systematic Theology: An Introduction to Biblical Doctrine* (Grand Rapids, MI: Zondervan, 1994), 840; John M. Frame, *Systematic Theology: An Introduction to Christian Belief* (Phillipsburg, NJ: P&R, 2013), 913–14; Gerald Bray, *God Is Love: A Biblical and Systematic Theology* (Wheaton, IL: Crossway, 2012), 620–25. See the more expansive treatment offered in Michael Horton, *The Christian Faith: A Systematic Theology for Pilgrims on the Way* (Grand Rapids, MI: Zondervan, 2011), 587–619.

Medieval Forerunners

In any survey of early modern Protestant teaching, it is important to note that the Reformation was not a complete break with the theological past. The Reformation was a *reform* movement, which means that it sought to correct errors, not create an entirely new understanding of the Bible. Such an observation is necessary when we consider the doctrine of union with Christ. Some, as of late, have presented the doctrine as if it were unique to the Reformation, and specifically to the groundbreaking insight of John Calvin.[5] But such a narrative has more to do with Reformation lore and myth than the actual facts of history. Long before the Reformation, theologians such as Thomas Aquinas (1225–1274) and Thomas à Kempis (1380–1471) wrote of union with Christ.[6] Aquinas contended that the incarnation establishes a union between God and man (generally considered) through the hypostatic union of Christ's two natures.[7] One of the most famous theologians to expound on the doctrine, however, was Bernard of Clairvaux (1090–1153), which he did famously in his sermons on the Song of Songs.[8] Bernard's sermons are replete with references to the doctrine of union with Christ. In fact, Bernard discussed union in terms of a twofold grace: repentance and perseverance.[9]

One of the more important works for understanding the vast array of views during the Middle Ages is that of Jean Gerson (1363–1429) and his treatise *De Mystica Theologia Speculativa* (*On Mystical Speculative Theology*).[10] In his work Gerson identified a number of different extant views, such as that of Peter Lombard (ca. 1090–1160), who proposed that union is the indwelling of the Holy Spirit by which

---

5. E.g., William B. Evans, *Imputation and Impartation: Union with Christ in American Reformed Theology*, Studies in Christian History and Thought (Eugene, OR: Wipf & Stock, 2009), 7n1; Richard B. Gaffin Jr., "Justification and Union with Christ," in *A Theological Guide to Calvin's Institutes: Essays and Analysis*, ed. David W. Hall and Peter A. Lillback, Calvin 500 Series (Phillipsburg, NJ: P&R, 2008), 248; Charles Partee, *The Theology of John Calvin* (Louisville: Westminster John Knox, 2008), 19n65, 24–27, esp. 27.

6. Thomas à Kempis, *The Imitation of Christ* (London: Oxford University Press, 1906), 4.2.6, 4.4.2; Richard A. Muller, *Calvin and the Reformed Tradition: On the Work of Christ and the Order of Salvation* (Grand Rapids, MI: Baker Academic, 2012), 205.

7. Thomas Aquinas, *Summa Theologica* (repr., Allen, TX: Christian Classics, 1948), 3a.1.2.

8. Bernard of Clairvaux, *On the Song of Songs*, trans. Kilian Walsh and Irene M. Edmonds, 4 vols., Cistercian Fathers 4, 7, 31, 40 (Kalamazoo: Cistercian Publications, 1971–1980).

9. Ibid., sermon 3.3; cf. Dennis E. Tamburello, *Union with Christ: John Calvin and the Mysticism of St. Bernard* (Louisville: Westminster John Knox, 1994), 48.

10. Jean Gerson, *Selections from "A Deo Exivit," "Contra Curiositatem Studentium," and "De Mystica Theologia Speculativa,"* ed. and trans. Steven E. Ozment (Leiden: Brill, 1969).

sinners are able to love God. In this manner, God is in us, and we are in God.[11] Gerson identified another view, one that employed a number of different analogies to express the doctrine, such as when a drop of water is released into a bottle of strong wine—the drop of water loses its properties and is absorbed completely into the wine. Such is the nature of union with Christ according to Augustine (354–430), claimed Gerson.[12] Gerson attributed another variation to Bernard, who argued that through love the human soul forsakes itself and its body and passes completely over into God.[13] This particular imagery and expression eventually made its way into the early writings of a young Martin Luther, in his 1517 lectures on Romans.[14]

Another voice that would eventually feed into the development of Reformation views on union with Christ was the head of Luther's monastic order, Johann von Staupitz (ca. 1460–1524). In his 1517 sermon "Eternal Predestination and Its Execution in Time," Staupitz expounded the doctrines of election and justification and joined them together under the rubric of union with Christ. Staupitz employed the analogy of marriage to describe the union between Christ and the believer. As two people become one in marriage, so it is with Christ and the believer. Christ says to the church or the believer, "'I accept you as Mine, I accept you as My concern, I accept you into Myself.' And conversely the Church, or the soul, says to Christ, 'I accept You as mine, You are my concern, I accept you into myself.'"[15] Staupitz, like Aquinas before him, also connected union with Christ to the incarnation.[16]

All these medieval theologians (Bernard, Aquinas, Gerson, and Staupitz) employed the doctrine of union with Christ. Gerson also noted that there are various ways of explaining the nature of the union between Christ and the believer. Another feature of these medieval views was to

---

11. Gerson, *Selections from "Mystica Theologia,"* 87n15; cf. Peter Lombard, *The Sentences, Book 1: The Mystery of the Trinity,* trans. Giulio Silano, Mediaeval Sources in Translation 42 (Toronto: Pontifical Institute of Medieval Studies, 2007), 17.4.

12. Gerson, *Selections from "Mystica Theologia,"* 87n19; cf. Augustine, *Confessions,* trans. Henry Chadwick (Oxford: Oxford University Press, 1991), 7.10.

13. Gerson, *Selections from "Mystica Theologia,"* 53.

14. Ibid., 87n20; Martin Luther, *Lectures on Romans: Glosses and Scholia,* LW 25:364.

15. Johann von Staupitz, "Eternal Predestination and Its Execution in Time," in *Forerunners of the Reformation: The Shape of Late Medieval Thought,* ed. Heiko A. Oberman, trans. Paul L. Nyhus, Library of Ecclesiastical History (Cambridge: James Clark, 1967), 187; Staupitz, *Libellus de Executione Eterne Predestinationis: Fratris Ioannis de Staupitz* (Nuremburg: Peypus, 1517), 9.56.

16. Staupitz, "Eternal Predestination," 188; Staupitz, *Eterne Predestinationis,* 9.61.

connect union not merely to soteriology but also to Christology, namely, through the hypostatic union. The Son becomes united to all humanity in a general, not redemptive, sense, by virtue of his incarnation.

Reformation Perspectives on Union with Christ

LUTHERAN VIEWS

When we cross the threshold of the Reformation, popularly associated with October 31, 1517, the day Luther nailed his *Ninety-Five Theses* to the castle door at Wittenberg, we find many of the same *union with Christ* themes in the theology of the Protestant Reformers. But where medieval theologians failed to distinguish between the doctrines of justification and sanctification, Protestant theologians took a different path. Luther famously wrote of an *iustitia aliena*, an "alien righteousness." That is, when a believer is declared righteous before the divine bar, the verdict does not rest on his own good works but on the alien righteousness of Jesus.[17] Justification was not, therefore, accomplished by faith formed by love (*fides charitatae formata*) or faith working by love—a common view among medieval theologians such as Lombard and Aquinas.[18] Rather, Luther argued that Christ, not love, was the form of faith.[19] In this respect, Luther contended, "Christ who is grasped by faith and who lives in the heart is the true Christian righteousness."[20] On account of this alien righteousness, the perfect righteousness of Christ, God accounts believers righteous.[21]

With this emphasis on Christ's alien righteousness, Luther enveloped his understanding of justification in the doctrine of union with Christ:

> So far as justification is concerned, Christ and I must be so closely attached that He lives in me and I in Him. What a marvelous way

---

17. See Mark Mattes, "Luther on Justification as Forensic and Effective," in *The Oxford Handbook of Martin Luther's Theology*, ed. Robert Kolb, Irene Dingel, and L'ubomír Batka (Oxford: Oxford University Press, 2014), 264–73; Klaus Schwarzwäller, "Verantwortung des Glaubens: Freiheit und Liebe nach der Dekalogauslegung Martin Luthers," in *Freiheit als Liebe bei Martin Luther / Freedom as Love in Martin Luther*, ed. Dennis O. Bielfeldt and Klaus Schwarzwäller (Frankfurt am Main: Lang, 1995), 133–58. I am grateful to Robert Kolb for alerting me to these sources.

18. Lombard, *Sentences, Book 1: The Mystery of the Trinity*, 3.23.3; Aquinas, *Summa Theologiae* 2a2ae.4.3.

19. Martin Luther, *Lectures on Galatians* (1535), LW 26:129.

20. Ibid., *LW* 26:130.

21. Ibid., *LW* 26:132–33.

of speaking! Because He lives in me, whatever grace, righteousness, life, peace, and salvation there is in me is all Christ's: nevertheless, it is mine as well, by the cementing and attachment that are through faith, by which we become as one body in the Spirit.[22]

Unlike his medieval predecessors, Staupitz excepted, Luther grounded justification in alien righteousness. But like his medieval forebears, he articulated his understanding of redemption under the rubric of union with Christ. However, just because Luther distinguished justification and sanctification did not mean that he slighted the latter. For Luther, union with Christ was the context from which the believer could proceed to manifest good works. Employing imagery that hearkens back to Bernard, Luther described union and sanctification in the following manner:

> By faith we are in Him and He is in us (John 6:56). This Bridegroom, Christ, must be alone with His bride in his private chamber, and all the family and household must be shunted away. But later on, when the Bridegroom opens the door and comes out, then let the servants return to take care of them and serve them food and drink. Then let works and love begin.[23]

For Luther, union with Christ was the ring that envelops the gem, the ultimate source and fountain of a believer's sanctification and good works.[24]

Given Luther's status as a first-generation Reformer, he had the benefit and freedom to plow fallow ground—to be a trailblazer. It fell upon other theologians, such as Philipp Melanchthon, Luther's colleague and co-Reformer, to defend the theological fortress that Luther built. For example, Melanchthon was responsible for writing the Augsburg Confession (1530), the first confessional expression of Lutheran theology. Moreover, throughout his writings Melanchthon vigorously defended the doctrine of imputed righteousness. Given the great lengths to which he went to defend the forensic nature of justification, some erroneously conclude that Melanchthon did not hold to a doctrine of union with

---

22. Ibid., *LW* 26:167–68.
23. Ibid., *LW* 26:137–38.
24. Ibid., *LW* 26:131–32.

Christic.[25] They suggest, rather, that justification was simply a stand-alone doctrine.[26] And rather than have union with Christ serve as the all-encompassing rubric through which the believer receives justification and sanctification, Melanchthon supposedly believed that justification was the source and cause of sanctification.[27] History, however, reveals a different picture.

Melanchthon believed that in salvation, there were two chief benefits or "things" (*zwei Ding*)—the forgiveness of sins and the gift of God's indwelling presence—and that Christ obtains both things through his merit.[28] Melanchthon described union with Christ in the following manner:

> We do not say that God is present in them like the power of the sun at work upon the veins of the earth, but that the Father and the Son are actually present, breathing the Holy Spirit into the heart of the believer. This presence or indwelling is what is called spiritual renewal. This personal union, however, is not the same as the union of the divine and human natures in Christ but is an indwelling like someone living in a separable domicile in this life.[29]

Melanchthon held that believers were indwelled by Christ and therefore in union with him. But like Luther before him, he wanted to ensure that the ground for the believer's acceptance before the divine bar was found solely in Christ and his obedience.[30]

One of the important points to note about Melanchthon's statements concerning union with Christ is that he made them in the context of debates with Andreas Osiander.[31] Osiander was a professor at the University of Königsberg who created controversy with his doctrines of justification and union with Christ. Unlike Luther and Melanch-

---

25. E.g., Alister E. McGrath, *Iustitia Dei: A History of the Christian Doctrine of Justification*, 3rd ed. (Cambridge: Cambridge University Press, 2005), 238.

26. Richard B. Gaffin Jr., *By Faith, Not by Sight: Paul and the Order of Salvation*, 2nd ed. (Phillipsburg, NJ: P&R, 2013), 56–57.

27. Mark A. Garcia, *Life in Christ: Union with Christ and Twofold Grace in Calvin's Theology* (Milton Keynes: Paternoster, 2008), 145–46, 248.

28. Philipp Melanchthon, "Iudicum de Osiandro 1552, no. 5017," in *CR* 7:893–94.

29. Philipp Melanchthon, "Confutation of Osiander (September 1555)," in *Documents from the History of Lutheranism, 1517–1750*, ed. Eric Lund (Minneapolis: Fortress, 2002), 208.

30. Ibid.

31. For a historical survey of the Osiander debate within Lutheran circles, see Timothy J. Wengert, *Defending the Faith: Lutheran Responses to Andreas Osiander's Doctrine of Justification, 1551–1559*, Spätmittelalter, Humanismus, Reformation 65 (Tübingen: Mohr Siebeck, 2012).

thon, Osiander denied that justification was a forensic declaration and instead claimed that it required divine indwelling so that believers would share in Christ's personal and essential righteousness. Osiander's view was justification not by imputed righteousness but by indwelled righteousness, or justification by union with Christ.[32] As much as Melanchthon vigorously rejected Osiander's view, this did not mean that he therefore entirely scuttled the doctrine of union with Christ in favor of a stand-alone doctrine of justification.[33] Melanchthon wrote, "We clearly affirm the presence or indwelling of God in the reborn."[34] Yet he carefully stipulated the relationship between indwelling and justification in the following manner:

> Although God dwelt in Moses, Elijah, David, Isaiah, Daniel, Peter, and Paul, nevertheless none of them claimed to be righteous before God on account of this indwelling or the effecting of their renewal but on account of the obedience of the Mediator and his gracious intercession, since, in this life, the remnants of sin were still in them.[35]

Melanchthon believed Osiander erred by shifting the ground of justification away from the alien righteousness of Christ and moving it to the believer, which was the problem with the Roman Catholic doctrine of justification. Melanchthon explained,

> Osiander especially makes an issue of this article and contends that man is righteous on account of the indwelling of God, or on account of the indwelling of God, not on account of the obedience of the Mediator, and not by the imputed righteousness of the Mediator through grace. He corrupts the proposition "By faith we are justified" into "By faith we are prepared that we may become just by something else," that is, the indwelling of God. Thus in reality he

32. Timothy J. Wengert, "Philip Melanchthon and John Calvin against Andreas Osiander: Coming to Terms with Forensic Justification," in *Calvin and Luther: The Continuing Relationship*, ed. R. Ward Holder, Refo500 Academic Studies 12 (Göttingen: Vandenhoeck & Ruprecht, 2013), 64; cf. Andreas Osiander, *Disputatio de Iustificatione (1550)*, in *Gesamtausgabe* (Gütersloh: Gütersloher Verlagshaus, 1994), 9:422–47.
33. In his 1556 commentary on Romans, Melanchthon spent twelve columns of text in the *Corpus Reformatorum* edition to refute Osiander's view before he exposited the doctrine of justification. Wengert, "Melanchthon and Calvin," 65–66; cf. CR 15:855–67.
34. Melanchthon, "Confutation of Osiander," 208.
35. Ibid., 208–9.

is saying what the papists say: "We are righteous by our renewal," except that he mentions the cause where the papists mention the effect. We are just when God renews us.[36]

Melanchthon was concerned that justification by union with Christ—that is, indwelling—was scarcely different from Roman Catholic views. Osiander, he believed, made justification rely on the cause (the indwelling presence of Christ) while the Roman Catholics made justification rely on the effect (the good works produced by the presence of Christ through the disposition of a *habitus*, or infused righteousness).[37] Both views compromised the alien nature of Christ's imputed righteousness. So Melanchthon maintained the doctrine of union with Christ but distinguished between imputed righteousness and divine indwelling so as not to move the legal ground of justification away from Christ to the believer. Melanchthon's rejection of Osiander's views were received positively by the Lutheran confessional tradition and were substantively incorporated into the Formula of Concord (1577).[38] Moreover, the Formula of Concord also commended Luther's 1535 commentary on Galatians as a "wonderful, magnificent exposition" of the "lofty and sublime article on justification before God," which means that the framers of the Formula maintained the compatibility of Melanchthon's and Luther's views on justification and union with Christ.

Before we proceed to discuss Reformed views on union, we should note that some Lutheran theologians, such as Martin Chemnitz, discussed the doctrine in connection with the incarnation. Chemnitz believed that salvation required not only the imputation of Christ's righteousness but also the incarnation. Through the incarnation, the divine Son of God assumed human nature and thus united divinity and humanity, "so that we might be less in doubt that His flesh is of the same substance with our own and that we might be rendered certain that the incarnation of the Son of God contributes toward the restora-

---

36. Ibid., 209.
37. Wengert, "Melanchthon and Calvin," 66.
38. See "The Solid Declaration of the Formula of Concord," art. 3, in Robert Kolb and Timothy J. Wengert, eds., *The Book of Concord: The Confessions of the Evangelical Lutheran Church*, trans. Charles P. Arand et al. (Minneapolis: Fortress, 2000), 573; cf. Charles P. Arand, James Nestingen, and Robert Kolb, eds., *The Lutheran Confessions: History and Theology of the Book of Concord* (Minneapolis: Fortress, 2012), 217–26.

tion of our own conception, birth, and entire nature."[39] In this respect, Chemnitz believed that the incarnation telegraphed the future union between the sinner and God.[40] For Chemnitz, union with Christ and the incarnation went hand in hand:

> For Christ imparts and lavishes His blessings on us by the communi-cation of Himself and by union with Himself. He does not do this by the communication and sharing of only His divine nature but also by that of His flesh and blood (which are expressly mentioned sev-eral times in John 6). Faith which grasps, holds, and applies Christ to itself lays hold not only on His divine nature but particularly on that nature which is related to us and of the same substance with us, in and through which He accomplished the work of redemption.[41]

Chemnitz maintained the doctrine of an imputed righteousness and, like Luther and Melanchthon, emphasized that this alien righteous-ness came through union with Christ—a fellowship, communion, or *koinonia* between Christ and the believer by which the latter shares in the divine nature (2 Pet. 1:4).[42]

Reformed Views

In the Reformed wing of the Protestant Reformation, theologians were equally eager to affirm the doctrine of union with Christ.[43] One Re-formed theologian who wrote about the doctrine was John Calvin. As a second-generation Reformer, Calvin burst onto the scene with the publication of his 1536 *Institutes of the Christian Religion*.[44] This

39. Martin Chemnitz, *The Two Natures in Christ*, trans. J. A. O. Preus, vol. 6 of *Chemnitz's Works* (St. Louis, MO: Concordia, 2007), 56.

40. Olli-Pekka Vainio, *Justification and Participation in Christ: The Development of the Lu-theran Doctrine of Justification from Luther to the Formula of Concord (1580)*, Studies in Medieval and Reformation Traditions 130 (Leiden: Brill, 2008), 139. For trenchant criticisms of Vainio's overall thesis and the weakness of its prosecution at key points, see Timothy J. Wengert, "Review of *Justification and Participation in Christ*," *Renaissance Quarterly* 61, no. 4 (2008): 1305–7.

41. Chemnitz, *Two Natures*, 332.

42. Ibid., 309; cf. Chemnitz, *Examination of the Council of Trent, Part 1*, trans. Fred Kramer, vol. 1 of *Chemnitz's Works* (St. Louis, MO: Concordia, 2007), 462; Chemnitz, *Loci Theologici, Parts 2–3*, trans. J. A. O. Preus, vol. 8 of *Chemnitz's Works* (St. Louis, MO: Concordia, 2008), 813–1042; cf. Vainio, *Justification and Participation*, 150–61.

43. For a survey of various Reformed theologians on union with Christ, see J. V. Fesko, *Beyond Calvin: Union with Christ and Justification in Early Modern Reformed Theology (1517–1700)*, Reformed Historical Theology 20 (Göttingen: Vandenhoeck & Ruprecht, 2012).

44. John Calvin, *Institutes of the Christian Religion* (1536 ed.), trans. Ford Lewis Battles, H. H. Meeter Center for Calvin Studies (Grand Rapids, MI: Eerdmans, 1975).

initial edition of the *Institutes* is a rather slim volume in contrast to the definitive 1559 edition; it has chapters on the law, the Apostles' Creed, the Lord's Prayer, the sacraments, the five false sacraments, and Christian liberty. Calvin did not treat the doctrine of justification, for example, in this initial edition. By 1539, however, when Calvin issued a second, expanded edition, he incorporated union with Christ into his newly added chapter on justification. Calvin famously wrote,

> Christ, being given to us by the goodness of God, is apprehended and possessed by us by faith, by a participation of whom we receive especially two benefits. In the first place, being by his innocence reconciled to God, we have in heaven a propitious Father instead of a judge; in the next place, being sanctified by his Spirit, we devote ourselves to innocence and purity of life.[45]

From one vantage point, Calvin echoed Bernard's construction of union with Christ and, like the medieval doctor, spoke of a twofold grace. But unlike Bernard, who denominated the twofold grace as repentance and perseverance, Calvin identified them as justification and regeneration, or sanctification.[46]

As famous as Calvin's *Institutes* are for his language about the two-fold benefit of union with Christ, the famous Geneva Reformer did not elaborate on the doctrine of union with Christ with great specificity. There is no particular place or treatise, for example, where Calvin explained this doctrine. In many respects he simply assumed the category and employed it throughout his writings.[47] The one place, however,

---

45. John Calvin, *Institutes of the Christian Religion*, trans. John Allen (Grand Rapids, MI: Eerdmans, 1948), 3.11.1; cf. Calvin, *Institutio Christiane Religionis* (Strasbourg: Wendelinum Rihelium, 1539).

46. Many sixteenth-century Reformers wrote about the doctrine of sanctification under the term *regeneration*. Later developments in theology distinguished between the initial act of conversion (regeneration) and the transformation of the believer (sanctification). Unless otherwise noted, I employ *regeneration* and *sanctification* in their contemporary usage.

47. There is contemporary debate regarding the function of union with Christ in Calvin's theology, as well as his relationship with subsequent treatments of union in the Reformed tradition. See, e.g., the following exchange: Thomas L. Wenger, "The New Perspective on Calvin: Responding to Recent Calvin Interpretations," *JETS* 50, no. 2 (2007): 311–28; Marcus Johnson, "New or Nuanced Perspective on Calvin? A Reply to Thomas Wenger," *JETS* 51, no. 3 (2008): 543–58; Thomas L. Wenger, "Theological Spectacles and a Paradigm of Centrality: A Reply to Marcus Johnson," *JETS* 51, no. 3 (2008): 559–72. On the whole, Wenger presents a more accurate account of Calvin's view, a presentation driven by historical sensitivity rather than dogmatic claims, as with Johnson. Cf. Muller, *Calvin and the Reformed Tradition*, 202–43, 277–84, esp. 281. Also note J. Todd Billings, *Calvin, Participation, and the Gift: The Activity of Believers in Union with Christ* (Oxford: Oxford University Press, 2008); Billings, "Union with Christ and the Double Grace:

where details regarding his understanding of union with Christ appear is in several letters from Peter Martyr Vermigli to Calvin and Theodore Beza (1519–1605).

Vermigli corresponded with the two Genevan theologians in the spring of 1555, and the chief topic of discussion was union with Christ. In his letters to Beza and Calvin, Vermigli set forth a threefold doctrine of union with Christ. He began with the incarnational union: the universal union that Christ shares with all persons by virtue of his incarnation as a man. Vermigli based this union, which he denominated the *natural union*, on his understanding of Hebrews 2:14.[48]

The second union Vermigli identified he called a *spiritual union*. In his letter to Calvin, Vermigli described these two unions in the following manner: "We have then here, thus far, two communions with Christ. One is natural, which we derive through our origin from our parents: the other is effected by the Spirit of Christ by which we are from our very regeneration renewed into the fashion of His glory."[49]

Vermigli termed the third union a *mystical union*, which rests in between the natural and spiritual unions: "We grant and believe, there has to be a middle, which is secret, between the beginning and the end of this kind of communion."[50] Hence, Vermigli posited a threefold union: incarnational, mystical, and spiritual. Important to note at this point is Calvin's agreement with Vermigli on this threefold union: "In addressing you, I have glanced at it briefly, with the simple view of showing you that we entirely agree in sentiment."[51]

The threefold union that Vermigli and Calvin affirmed was very similar to the views of Zanchi, which were introduced at the beginning

Calvin's Theology and Its Early Reception," and Michael S. Horton, "Calvin's Theology of Union with Christ and the Double Grace: Modern Reception and Contemporary Possibilities," in *Calvin's Theology and Its Reception: Disputes, Developments, and New Possibilities*, ed. J. Todd Billings and I. John Hesselink (Louisville: Westminster John Knox, 2012), 49–71, 72–96.

48. Peter Martyr Vermigli, "Vermigli to Beza," in *The Peter Martyr Library*, vol. 5, *Life, Letters, and Sermons*, trans. and ed. John Patrick Donnelly, Sixteenth Century Essays and Studies 42 (Kirksville, MO: Thomas Jefferson University Press, 1999), 134–37; Vermigli, "Vermigli to Calvin," in *Gleanings of a Few Scattered Ears during the Period of the Reformation in England and of the Times Immediately Succeeding, A.D. 1533 to A.D. 1588*, ed. and trans. George C. Gorham (London: Bell and Daldy, 1857), 342.

49. Vermigli, "Vermigli to Calvin," 343.

50. Peter Martyr Vermigli, "Vermigli to Beza," in *Loci Communes D. Petri Martyris Vermigli* (London: Henry Denham and Henry Middleton, 1583), 1109.

51. John Calvin, "Calvin to Vermigli," in *Gleanings of a Few Scattered Ears During the Time of the Reformation in England and the Times Immediately Succeeding: 1533–88*, ed. and trans. George C. Gorham (London: Bell and Daldy, 1857), 352.

of this chapter. Noteworthy is the fact that Zanchi studied with both Vermigli and Calvin at different points in his life, which suggests at least two of the sources for Zanchi's views on union. This threefold union spans the incarnation through to the eschaton. Like Calvin's understanding of the twofold benefit of union, namely, justification and sanctification, Vermigli located the same two aspects of redemption in the middle, secret, mystical union that believers share with Christ. Vermigli wrote,

> In due season, faith is breathed into the elect, whereby they may believe in Christ; and thus they have not only remission of sins and reconciliation with God (wherein consists the true and solid method of justification), but, further, receive the renovating influence of the Spirit whereby our bodies also, our flesh, and blood, and nature, are made capable of immortality, and become every day more and more conformable to Christ (*Christiformia*), so to speak.[52]

Vermigli further explained the nature of this mystical union:

> But I think between these [natural and spiritual unions] there is an intermediate one [mystical union], which is the fount and origin of all the celestial and spiritual likeness which we obtain, together with Christ. It is that whereby, as soon as we believe, we obtain Christ Himself, our true head, and are made His members. Whence from the Head itself (as St. Paul says [Eph. 4:15–16]) His Spirit flows, and is derived through the joints and ligaments into us, as his true and legitimate members. This communion with our Head is prior, in nature at least, if not in time, to that later communion which is introduced through renovation.[53]

Vermigli's overall argument, one to which Calvin gave his approbation, is that the natural union leads to the mystical union, the indwelling of the believer by which he receives his justification, which segues to his spiritual union, one that finds its consummation in the believer's complete glorification—his total transformation unto the image and likeness of Christ.

---

52. Vermigli, "Vermigli to Calvin," 342–43; Vermigli, *Loci Communes*, 1095.
53. Vermigli, "Vermigli to Calvin," 343.

Like their Lutheran counterparts, Reformed theologians embraced and employed the doctrine of union with Christ, and they were equally concerned to refute the teachings of Andreas Osiander. In fact, in the definitive 1559 edition of his *Institutes*, Calvin added seven new paragraphs specifically to refute Osiander's views.[54] Calvin was concerned because Osiander had introduced his "monstrous notion of essential righteousness" and because Calvin himself was accused by several Lutherans of having a view similar to Osiander's.[55] If there was ever a time that Calvin might have been tempted to abandon the doctrine of union with Christ, it would certainly have been in the face of Osiander's doctrine. But like his Lutheran counterparts, rather than reject the doctrine, Calvin instead made careful distinctions. Calvin wrote, "He says that we are one with Christ. This we admit; but we at the same time deny that Christ's essence is blended with ours."[56] In a passage that echoes Luther's earlier 1535 statement emphasizing similar themes, namely, that we are cemented to Christ through faith and thereby become one with him in order to receive his imputed righteousness, Calvin wrote,

> I attribute, therefore, the highest importance to the connection between the head and members; to the inhabitation of Christ in our hearts; in a word, to the mystical union by which we enjoy him, so that being made ours, he makes us partakers of the blessings with which he is furnished. We do not, then, contemplate him at a distance out of ourselves, that his righteousness may be imputed to us; but because we have put him on, and are engrafted into his body, and because he has deigned to unite us to himself, therefore we glory in a participation of his righteousness.[57]

Calvin was content to continue to employ the doctrine of union with Christ but was careful, like his Lutheran counterparts, to distinguish between divine indwelling and imputed righteousness.

In fact, recent scholarship has offered close analysis of Calvin's refutation of Osiander and determined that Calvin relied on several

---

54. Calvin, *Institutes*, 3.11.5–12; Wengert, "Melanchthon and Calvin," 72.
55. Calvin, *Institutes*, 3.11.5, translation from Allen; Wengert, "Melanchthon and Calvin," 75n43.
56. Calvin, *Institutes*, 3.11.5, translation from Allen.
57. Ibid., 3.11.10, translation from Allen; cf. Luther, *Lectures on Galatians* (1535), *LW* 26:167–68.

Lutheran theologians, including Melanchthon, to construct his own formulation.[58] Calvin likely availed himself of Melanchthon's 1556 commentary on Romans, where the latter offered a number of arguments against Osiander prior to expounding the doctrine of justification. Parallels between the two Reformers appear on several fronts. They both appeal to (1) the fact that the language of justification is Hebrew terminology; (2) the inseparable but nevertheless distinct nature of justification and sanctification; (3) the believer's experience about the traces of sin that remain in justified sinners; and (4) the believer's conscience.[59] This is not to say that Melanchthon and Calvin refuted Osiander in precisely the same manner; there are certainly some differences between them. But on the whole, Reformed and Lutheran theologians equally and similarly objected to Osiander's construction of union with Christ.

As noted in the introduction, one of the fuller-orbed statements about union with Christ comes from Zanchi's confession of faith. Unlike Calvin, who treated union sporadically throughout his *Institutes*, Zanchi covered the subject as a major heading in his confession. This organizational structure is the result of Zanchi's own reflections on this doctrine, one that originated from his exegetical work on Paul's epistle to the Ephesians. Zanchi wrote a doctrinal excursus that originally appeared in his commentary on Ephesians and was later translated and published separately as a treatise in its own right.[60] Zanchi argued that the first union, the natural, is the means by which Christ entered into the human condition so that sinful people could partake of the second union and thereby gain access to his satisfaction.[61] In this second union, the redeemed were joined and incorporated into Christ by the power of the Holy Spirit.[62] But even though this union was spiritual, Zanchi was keen on arguing that it was nevertheless true and real. Even though believers remained on earth, they were nevertheless truly and really united to the body and soul of Christ, who was seated and reigning in

58. Wengert, "Melanchthon and Calvin," 71–82.
59. Ibid., 78–80; cf. Calvin, *Institutes*, 3.11.11; Philipp Melanchthon, *Commentary on Romans*, trans. Fred Kramer (St. Louis, MO: Concordia, 1992), 106–21.
60. Girolamo Zanchi, *An Excellent and Learned Treatise, of the Spiritual Marriage Betweene Christ and the Church, and Every Faithfull Man* (Cambridge: John Legate, 1592).
61. Zanchi, *De Religione*, 12.6.
62. Ibid., 12.7.

heaven.[63] Zanchi appealed to two texts to support these contentions: 2 Peter 1:4, that we are "partakers of the divine nature," and Ephesians 5:30, that we are "members of his body," bone of his bones, and flesh of his flesh. In many respects, Zanchi's confession is an outline of his understanding of union with Christ, whereas his excursus offers a full-orbed presentation of the doctrine.

In the present day, discussions about union with Christ usually deal with matters that pertain to soteriology, but during the Reformation, union encompassed a great deal more. As we have already seen, union discussions encompassed Christology, but they also embraced the doctrine of the Lord's Supper.[64] Wolfgang Musculus offers one example of a theologian connecting union and the Lord's Supper. In his major work *Loci Communes Sacrae Theologiae* (Common places of sacred theology), Musculus did not expound union with Christ in his soteriology, though he did acknowledge the category in his discussion of justification.[65] When Musculus discussed who specifically should participate in the Lord's Supper, he drew a line of demarcation with the doctrine of union with Christ. Musculus wrote, "First, we must be members in the body of Christ. For he that is not yet grafted into Christ, but is still the member of a harlot, of Antichrist, Satan, cannot be fed with this meat, wherewith Christ's body, that is to say, the church is fed."[66] Only those who are in union with Christ, therefore, may partake of the Supper and sacramentally eat his flesh and drink his blood.

For Reformed theologians, union with Christ touched on the doctrine of the sacraments because they were the means by which believers were able to strengthen and feed their communion with Christ. Union

63. Ibid., 12.8. Note that such a statement undoubtedly embodies Zanchi's teaching on union with Christ, but it was forged in the midst of the Lutheran-Reformed sacramental controversies during Zanchi's time in Strasbourg. This idea thus reflects Zanchi's Reformed understanding of the Lord's Supper in contrast with Lutheran views. See Zanchi, *De Religione*, 1.4–6; Arand, Nestingen, and Kolb, *Lutheran Confessions*, 212–14.

64. Post-Reformation Reformed formulations also encompassed the doctrine of election, where theologians posited a union of the decree, as well as legal and federal unions, to integrate the doctrines of the covenant and imputation. See Fesko, *Beyond Calvin*, 318–79.

65. Wolfgang Musculus, *Loci Communes Sacrae Theologiae* (Basel: Johannes Hervagius, 1567), 582; Musculus, *Common Places of Christian Religion* (London: R. Wolfe, 1563), fols. 227–28; Muller, *Calvin and the Reformed Tradition*, 217.

66. Musculus, *Loci Communes*, 820; Musculus, *Common Places*, fol. 324. I have followed but modified the English translation offered in the latter-cited edition.

and communion go hand in hand. In this respect, Calvin, for example, maintained that in order to effect the believer's union with Christ, the Holy Spirit employs a double instrument: Word and sacrament.[67] Calvin argued that in the preaching of the Word and the administration of the sacraments are two ministers, the external and the internal. The external minister administers the vocal Word and the sacred signs, whereas the internal minister, the Holy Spirit, freely works in the hearts of whomever he chooses to bring about their union with Christ. "This union," wrote Calvin, "is a thing internal, heavenly and indestructible."[68] Hence, Calvin explained,

> In the preaching of the Word, the external minister holds forth the vocal word, and it is received by the ears (Acts 16:14). The internal minister, the Holy Spirit, truly communicates the thing proclaimed through the Word, that is Christ, to the souls of all who will, so that it is not necessary that Christ or for that matter his Word be received through the organs of the body, but the Holy Spirit effects this union by his secret virtue, by creating faith in us, by which he makes us living members of Christ, true God and true man.[69]

This type of relationship between union with Christ, preaching, and the sacraments is common, and appears in other Reformed theologians such as Zanchi.

Zanchi, for example, described the relationship between union and the sacraments in a way similar to that of Calvin:

> We believe that his Spirit, whereby Christ both couples himself unto us and us unto him, and joins his flesh with ours and ours with his, is communicated of the same Christ unto us by his mere grace, when and where and how he please, yet ordinarily at the preaching of the gospel and administration of the sacraments. Of which thing was a visible testimony, which we read, how that they in the primitive church, which embraced the gospel by faith, and were baptized into the name of Christ or upon whomsoever the hands

---

67. John Calvin, "Summary of Doctrine concerning the Ministry of the Word and the Sacraments," in *Calvin: Theological Treatises*, trans. J. K. S. Reid, LCC 22 (London: SCM, 1960), 172.
68. Ibid., 173.
69. Ibid.

were laid, besides the invisible grace received also diverse sensible gifts of the Spirit.[70]

For Zanchi, like Calvin, union comes through Word and sacrament, but this union is nurtured through communion with Christ. Note how Zanchi joined all these ideas (union, salvation, indwelling, sacraments, and communion) in the following statement:

> Whereupon we do easily gather, which is the principal end both of preaching the gospel and administering the sacraments, namely this communion with Christ the Son of God incarnate, who suffered and died for us, but now reigns in heaven and imparts salvation and life to his chosen. Which communion was begun here, but was to be perfected in heaven, so that we by this true and real copulation of ourselves with his flesh and blood and his whole person, may also be made partakers of eternal salvation, which was purchased by him and still remains and abides in him.[71]

Zanchi did not employ the specific terms in his explanation, but his understanding of the threefold union (natural, mystical, and eschatological) lie beneath the surface. Christology, soteriology, pneumatology, ecclesiology, and eschatology all rest under the rubric of Zanchi's threefold doctrine of union with Christ. Recall once again that such formulations were part of Zanchi's confession of faith, one intended for wide acceptance. That is, such views were commonplace among Reformed theologians.[72]

Broader Context

ROMAN CATHOLICISM

In order to appreciate and grasp the nature of Protestant understandings of union with Christ, they should be set against the backdrop of other sixteenth-century formulations, most notably those from the

---

70. Zanchi, *De Religione*, 12.11.
71. Ibid., 12.12.
72. For contributions by other Reformed theologians, such as Heinrich Bullinger (1504–1575), see Fesko, *Beyond Calvin*, 173–87. The doctrine of union with Christ receives scattered treatment throughout a number of Reformed Confessions. See, e.g., the Scots Confession, art. 16; the Second Helvetic Confession, chap. 17; the Belgic Confession, arts. 14–15, 22–24, 28–29. Union also appears in post-Reformation Reformed confessions such as the Westminster Standards; see the Larger Catechism, qq. 58, 66, and WCF 25.1–2.

Roman Catholic Church, Socinians, and Jacobus Arminius. Some recent historical analysis gives the impression that one of the big differences between Calvin and the Roman Catholic Church was that the former taught union with Christ whereas the latter did not.[73] Such a characterization, however, is misleading. First, as noted earlier in this chapter, several medieval theologians, such as Aquinas, à Kempis, Bernard, and Gerson, wrote about union with Christ. These different formulations fed into the Roman Catholic understanding of union with Christ, which found its chief codification in the pronouncements of the Council of Trent. The decrees of Trent do not have a specific decree or session that treats union with Christ, but the doctrine appears in various places, such as in the decree on justification. Trent, for example, states, "For Jesus Christ himself continually imparts strength to those justified, as the head to the members and the vine to the branches, and this strength always precedes, accompanies, and follows their good works."[74] Trent employs *union with Christ* language, which is drawn from Christ's famous vine and branches discourse (John 15:1–11). Hence, Trent, like Protestant theologians, intertwines justification and union with Christ.

But how does Trent explain the origin of this union? The official catechism created by Trent explains,

> By baptism we are also united to Christ, as members to their Head. As therefore from the head proceeds the power by which the different members of the body are moved to the proper performance of their respective functions, so from the fullness of Christ the Lord are diffused divine grace and virtue through all those who are justified, qualifying them for the performance of all the duties of Christian piety.[75]

According to Trent, baptism brings people into union with Christ. Roman Catholic theologians, therefore, taught the doctrine of union with Christ. Both Roman Catholics and Protestants believed that the

---

73. Craig B. Carpenter, "A Question of Union with Christ? Calvin and Trent on Justification," *WTJ* 64 (2002): 363–86.

74. *Dogmatic Decrees of the Council of Trent (1545–63)*, sess. 6, chap. 16, in *CCFCT* 2:835.

75. *Catechism of the Council of Trent*, trans. John A. McHugh and Charles J. Callan (Rockford, IL: Tan Books, 1982), 188.

Holy Spirit regenerates sinners and brings them into union with Christ. But for Rome this occurs *ex opere operato* ("from the work worked") through the waters of baptism, while for Protestant theologians this happens *sola fide*. Protestant theologians, both Lutheran and Reformed, were united in their emphasis on *sola fide*.[76]

For example, according to Luther, faith was the means by which Christ indwelled sinners; for the German Reformer, Christ was present in faith.[77] In contrast, Trent held that baptism, apart from faith, unites sinners to Christ. In the person's baptism, the water imparts the infusion of habitual virtues—faith, hope, love—and the indwelling of Christ. The sinner's baptism constitutes his *initial* justification through union with Christ and the infusion of these virtues. By faith working through love and through these infused virtues, the baptized person then seeks to become more righteous. At the consummation and final judgment, God will judge the baptized person to determine whether he is actually righteous. Only at the final judgment will God pronounce the verdict of his *final* justification; thus, for Trent and Roman Catholic theologians justification is twofold.[78]

The different doctrines of union with Christ, informed by disparate understandings of justification, appear clearly in Luther's description of the two dissimilar views:

> Where they speak of love, we speak of faith. And while they say that faith is the mere outline but love is its living colors and completion, we say in opposition that faith takes hold of Christ and that He is the form that adorns and informs faith as color does the wall.

---

76. The general agreement between Lutheran and Reformed views on *sola fide* and justification appears in the *Harmony of the Confessions of Faith* (1581), a document assembled under the guidance of Theodore Beza. It was the Reformed counterpart to the Formula of Concord, and one of its chief purposes was to demonstrate the agreement between the Reformed and Lutheran churches on a number of doctrinal issues. See Jean-François Salvard, *The Harmony of Protestant Confessions: Exhibiting the Faith of the Churches of Christ, Reformed after the Pure and Holy Doctrine of the Gospel, throughout Europe*, ed. Peter Hall (London: John F. Shaw, 1842), 148–210; cf. Jill Raitt, "Harmony of Confessions of Faith," *OER* 2:211–12. Also noteworthy is J. Todd Billings, "The Contemporary Reception of Luther and Calvin's Doctrine of Union with Christ: Mapping a Biblical, Catholic, and Reformational Motif," in *Calvin and Luther: The Continuing Relationship*, ed. R. Ward Holder, Refo500 Academic Studies 12 (Göttingen: Vandenhoeck & Ruprecht, 2013), 165, 173–80.
77. Luther, *Lectures on Galatians* (1535), LW 26:129.
78. On twofold justification, see, e.g., Ambrosius Catharinus Politus, *Liber de Perfecta Iustificatione a Fide et Operibus*, in *Speculum Haerticorum* (Lugduni: Antonium Vicentium, 1541), 180–248; *Decrees of the Council of Trent*, sess. 6, chaps. 10–13, in CCFCT 2:831–33.

Therefore Christian faith is not an idle quality or an empty husk in the heart, which may exist in a state of mortal sin until love comes along to make it alive. But if it is true faith, it is a sure trust and firm acceptance in the heart. It takes hold of Christ in such a way that Christ is the object of faith, or rather not the object but, so to speak, the One who is present in the faith itself.[79]

The differences between the two views are palpable. Trent presented a doctrine of justification by union with Christ, which comes initially through baptism and is supplemented by the believer's good works and Christ-indwelled efforts to attain his final justification.[80] Protestant theologians, on the other hand, held that the Spirit brings sinners into union with Christ through faith alone and that in Christ they receive the twofold grace of justification and sanctification. Reformed theologians argued that the Word and sacraments play a role in bringing sinners into union with Christ but not *ex opere operato*. For Protestants, the Holy Spirit, not water, unites people to Christ by faith alone.[81]

SOCINIANISM

Socinian theologians offered their unique take on the doctrine of union with Christ. Socinian theology grew largely out of the body of writings and teachings from Faustus Socinus, though he wrote very little for the masses. Nevertheless, the spirit of his theology was eventually captured and codified in the Racovian Catechism (1605). Socinians were anti-Trinitarian theologians, which means that they did not believe in the deity of Christ or the Holy Spirit. Hence, from the outset, it is evident that Socinians' view differed significantly from Roman Catholic, Lutheran, and Reformed theologians, all of whom embraced and promoted the doctrine of the Trinity. Nevertheless, this does not mean that Socinian theology is devoid of a doctrine of union with Christ.

The Racovian Catechism, for example, states that Jesus, who is not divine, is in union with God:

79. Luther, *Lectures on Galatians* (1535), LW 26:129.

80. Hubert Jedin, *A History of the Council of Trent*, vol. 2, *The First Sessions at Trent, 1545–47*, trans. Dom Ernest Graf (London: Thomas Nelson and Sons, 1961), 185, 188–89, 247, 255–56, 308.

81. See, e.g., the Heidelberg Catechism, qq. 65–66; the Belgic Confession, arts. 33–34; the Second Helvetic Confession, 19.11; "The Augsburg Confession," art. 13, in Kolb and Wengert, *Book of Concord*, 47; "Apology of the Augsburg Confession," art. 4, in Kolb and Wengert, *Book of Concord*, 140.

Their union is discernible in this, that God, from the very beginning of the new covenant, has, through the instrumentality of Christ, performed, and hereafter will finally accomplish, all things that in any way relate to the salvation of mankind, and also, consequently, to the destruction of the wicked.[82]

The catechism contends that Christ, therefore, is in union with God through the Holy Spirit, who is not the third divine person of the Trinity but a "virtue or energy flowing from God to men, and communicated to them."[83] By extension, those who believe in Christ are also in union with him: "For no one is a member of this church who has not true faith in Christ and real piety; for by faith we are grafted into the body of Christ, and by faith and piety we remain in him."[84]

The Socinian denial of the Trinity does not mean that they lacked a doctrine of union with Christ. Believers are united to Christ by believing in him. Together, Christ and his body are united to God by the power and energy that flows from him to them both. They are not indwelt by the third person of the Trinity but rather lay hold of the impersonal power of a unitarian god. This type of construction quite obviously impacts how Socinians articulate justification and sanctification, which are denominated as the twofold blessing of union with Christ by Lutheran and Reformed theologians. In Protestant formulations, union with Christ grants the believer both the indwelling of Christ through the Holy Spirit and Christ's imputed righteousness. But in Socinian formulations, the believer does not receive the imputed righteousness of Christ. Socinus believed that Christ merited reward neither for himself nor for others.[85] This means that anyone united to Christ had to render his own obedience to secure his justification.

In contrast to classic Reformation teaching, which defines faith as trusting in Christ, Socinus believed that obedience is the substance and form of faith. Socinus made this point in no uncertain terms: "Faith

---

82. Thomas Rees, ed. and trans., *The Racovian Catechism: With Notes and Illustrations, Translated from the Latin; to Which Is Prefixed a Sketch of the History of Unitarianism in Poland and the Adjacent Countries* (London: Longman, Hurst, Orme, and Brown, 1818), 4.1.

83. Ibid., 5.6.

84. Ibid., 8.4.

85. Alan W. Gomes, "Faustus Socinus' *De Jesu Christo Servatore*, Part III: Historical Introductions, Translation, and Critical Notes" (PhD diss., Fuller Theological Seminary, 1990), 3.5. Hereafter cited as Socinus, *De Jesu Christo Servatore*.

which justifies is namely this, obedience to God."[86] Hence, believers receive the forgiveness of sins through "penitence and a changed life."[87] In the Socinian understanding, union with Christ provides the believer the opportunity to lay hold of the impersonal power of God by which he can lead a changed life of penitence and thus secure his justification and eternal life. There are some similarities between Socinian and Protestant views, but the differences are much more significant. For the Reformers, Christ saves; for the Socinians, Christ only points to a door through which believers must enter and save themselves by their own obedience. Both Protestant Reformers and Socinians nevertheless discuss their widely divergent views under the rubric of union with Christ.

Arminianism

Arminius represents another variant on the doctrine of union with Christ, one that has great similarities to Reformation views but also stands in contrast to them. Very much like Lutheran and Reformed theologians, Arminius argued that union is a key theological category: "Theology may with the utmost propriety be called, the union of God with man."[88] Humans enter into union with God through the Redeemer, through Jesus. Arminius therefore defined union with Christ in the following manner:

> That spiritual and most strict and therefore mystically essential conjunction, by which believers, being immediately connected, by God the Father and Jesus Christ through the Spirit of Christ and of God, with Christ himself, and through Christ with God, become one with him and the Father, and are made partakers of all his blessings, to their own salvation and the glory of Christ and of God.[89]

At this stage, Arminius advocated a common definition and formulation of union with Christ. He also, like Lutheran and Reformed

---

86. Faustus Socinus, *Tractatus Justificatione*, in *Opera Omnia in Duos Tomos Distincta* (Amsterdam, 1656), 1:610.

87. Socinus, *De Jesu Christo Servatore*, 3.2.

88. Jacobus Arminius, "Oration II: The Author and End of Theology," in *The Works of James Arminius*, trans. James Nichols and William Nichols (1825–1875; repr., Grand Rapids, MI: Baker, 1996), 1:362–63. All subsequent quotations from Arminius are taken from this English translation and will list the name of the treatise followed by the location in *Works*.

89. Jacobus Arminius, *Private Disputations*, 45.3, in *Works*, 2:402.

theologians, presented justification and sanctification as the twofold benefit of union with Christ.[90] But for Arminius, justification was not an indefectible judgment; a believer could lose his justified status. Arminius affirmed that "it was possible for believers finally to decline or fall away from faith and salvation."[91] In this respect, Arminius believed that "if David had died in the very moment in which he had sinned against Uriah by adultery and murder, he would have been condemned to death eternal."[92]

Arminius, therefore, held to the double benefit of union with Christ, justification and sanctification, but in his view, justification was defectible and dependent on the final perseverance of the believer. It was a process rather than a once-for-all declaration, as Luther and other Protestant theologians asserted.[93] Arminius believed that justification was twofold and therefore incomplete until the final judgment:

> But the end and completion of justification will be near the close of life, when God will grant, to those who end their days in the faith of Christ, to find his mercy absolving them from all the sins which had been perpetrated through the whole of their lives. The declaration and manifestation of justification will be in the future general judgment.[94]

Arminius's formulation was similar to later Lutheran developments regarding election, the perseverance of the saints, and a defectible justification, but it stands in contrast to Luther and the Reformed confessional tradition.[95]

Conclusion

According to theologians of the Reformation, union with Christ is a key doctrine, one that embraces a number of teachings such as the

---

90. Ibid., 48.1, in *Works*, 2:405.

91. Jacobus Arminius, *The Apology or Defense of James Arminius*, art. 2, in *Works*, 1:741.

92. Jacobus Arminius, *Certain Articles*, 20.8, in *Works*, 2:725.

93. See, e.g., Daphne Hampson, *Christian Contradictions: The Structures of Lutheran and Catholic Thought* (Cambridge: Cambridge University Press, 2001), 9–55.

94. Arminius, *Private Disputations*, 48.12, in *Works*, 2:407.

95. Cf., e.g., "Solid Declaration," art. 11, in Kolb and Wengert, *Book of Concord*, 640–56; cf. Arand, Nestingen, and Kolb, *Lutheran Confessions*, 201–16; Theodor Mahlmann, "Die Stellung der *unio cum Christo* in der lutherischen Theologie des 17 Jahrhunderts," in *Unio: Gott und Mensch in der nachreformatorischen Theologie*, ed. Matti Repo and Rainer Vinke (Helsinki: Luther-Agricola-Gesellschaft, 1996), 72–199. I am grateful to Robert Kolb for alerting me to this last-cited source.

incarnation, soteriology (justification and sanctification), ecclesiology (including the sacraments), and eschatology. But just because someone invokes the category does not mean that it automatically entails the same doctrinal commitments. Roman Catholic, Lutheran, Reformed, Arminian, and even Socinian theologians advocated doctrines of union with Christ. They all agreed that the doctrine is scriptural and therefore necessary, but they did not all agree on the specifics. They all agreed that there is a forest, but they did not all see the same trees. Depending on one's point of view, quite literally, the Devil is in the details.

Resources for Further Study

PRIMARY SOURCES

Aquinas, Thomas. *Summa Theologica*. Reprint, Allen, TX: Christian Classics, 1948.

Arminius, Jacobus. *The Works of James Arminius*. Translated by James Nichols and William Nichols. 3 vols. 1825–1875. Reprint, Grand Rapids, MI: Baker, 1996.

Calvin, John. *Institutes of the Christian Religion*. Translated by John Allen. Grand Rapids, MI: Eerdmans, 1948.

Catechism of the Council of Trent. Translated by John A. McHugh and Charles J. Callan. Rockford, IL: Tan Books, 1982.

Chemnitz, Martin. *Chemnitz's Works*. Translated by Fred Kramer, Luther Poellot, J. A. O. Preus, and Georg Williams. 8 vols. St. Louis, MO: Concordia, 2007.

Gerson, Jean. *Selections from "A Deo Exivit," "Contra Curiositatem Studentium," and "De Mystica Theologia Speculativa."* Edited and translated by Steven E. Ozment. Textus Minores 38. Leiden: Brill, 1969.

Lombard, Peter. *The Sentences*. Translated by Giulio Silano. 4 vols. Mediaeval Sources in Translation 42–43, 45, 48. Toronto: Pontifical Institute of Mediaeval Studies, 2007–2010.

Luther, Martin. *Lectures on Galatians* (1535). Vols. 26–27 in *Luther's Works*. Edited by Jaroslav Pelikan. St. Louis, MO: Concordia, 1963.

Melanchthon, Philip. "Confutation of Osiander (September 1555)." In *Documents from the History of Lutheranism 1517–1750*. Edited by Eric Lund. Minneapolis: Fortress, 2002.

Musculus, Wolfgang. *Common Places of Christian Religion*. London: R. Wolfe, 1563.

————. *Loci Communes Sacrae Theologiae*. Basel: Johannes Hervagius, 1567.

Osiander, Andreas. *Disputatio de Iustificatione (1550)*. In *Gesamtausgabe*, 9:422–47. Gütersloh: Gütersloh Verlagshaus, 1994.

Rees, Thomas, ed. and trans. *The Racovian Catechism: With Notes and Illustrations, Translated from the Latin; to Which Is Prefixed a Sketch of the History of Unitarianism in Poland and the Adjacent Countries*. London: Longman, Hurst, Rees, Orme, and Brown, 1818.

Salvard, Jean-François. *The Harmony of Protestant Confessions: Exhibiting the Faith of the Churches of Christ, Reformed after the Pure and Holy Doctrine of the Gospel, throughout Europe*. Edited by Peter Hall. London: John F. Shaw, 1842.

Staupitz, Johann von. "Eternal Predestination and Its Execution in Time." In *Forerunners of the Reformation: The Shape of Late Medieval Thought*, edited by Heiko A. Oberman and translated by Paul L. Nyhus, 175–203. Library of Ecclesiastical History. Cambridge: James Clark, 1967.

Vermigli, Peter Martyr. "Vermigli to Beza." In *The Peter Martyr Library*. Vol. 5, *Life, Letters, and Sermons*, translated and edited by John Patrick Donnelly, 134–37. Sixteenth Century Essays and Studies 42. Kirksville, MO: Thomas Jefferson University Press, 1999.

————. "Vermigli to Calvin." In *Gleanings of a Few Scattered Ears during the Period of the Reformation in England and of the Times Immediately Succeeding, A.D. 1553 to A.D. 1588*. Edited and translated by George C. Gorham. London: Bell and Daldy, 1857.

Zanchi, Girolamo. *De Religione Christiana Fides – Confession of Christian Religion*. Edited by Luca Baschera and Christian Moser. 2 vols. Studies in the History of Christian Traditions 135. Leiden: Brill, 2007.

————. *An Excellent and Learned Treatise, of the Spiritual Marriage Betweene Christ and the Church, and Every Faithfull Man*. Cambridge: John Legate, 1592.

Secondary Sources

Arand, Charles P., James A. Nestingen, and Robert Kolb, eds. *The Lutheran Confessions: History and Theology of the Book of Concord*. Minneapolis: Fortress, 2012.

Billings, J. Todd. "The Contemporary Reception of Luther and Calvin's Doctrine of Union with Christ: Mapping a Biblical, Catholic, and

Reformational Motif." In *Calvin and Luther: The Continuing Relationship*, edited by R. Ward Holder, 165–82. Refo500 Academic Studies 12. Göttingen: Vandenhoeck & Ruprecht, 2013.

Fesko, J. V. *Beyond Calvin: Union with Christ and Justification in Early Modern Reformed Theology (1517–1700)*. Reformed Historical Theology 20. Göttingen: Vandenhoeck & Ruprecht, 2012.

Hampson, Daphne. *Christian Contradictions: The Structures of Lutheran and Catholic Thought*. Cambridge: Cambridge University Press, 2001.

Jedin, Hubert. *A History of the Council of Trent*. Vol. 2. *The First Sessions at Trent, 1545–47*. Translated by Dom Ernest Graf. London: Thomas Nelson and Sons, 1961.

Mattes, Mark. "Luther on Justification as Forensic and Effective." In *The Oxford Handbook of Martin Luther's Theology*, edited by Robert Kolb, Irene Dingel, and L'ubomír Batka, 264–73. Oxford: Oxford University Press, 2014.

Muller, Richard A. *Calvin and the Reformed Tradition: On the Work of Christ and the Order of Salvation*. Grand Rapids, MI: Baker Academic, 2012.

Wengert, Timothy J. *Defending the Faith: Lutheran Responses to Andreas Osiander's Doctrine of Justification, 1551–1559*. Spätmittelalter, Humanismus, Reformation 65. Tübingen: Mohr Siebeck, 2012.

———. "Philip Melanchthon and John Calvin against Andreas Osiander: Coming to Terms with Forensic Justification." In *Calvin and Luther: The Continuing Relationship*, edited by R. Ward Holder, 63–88. Refo500 Academic Studies 12. Göttingen: Vandenhoeck & Ruprecht, 2013.

13

The Bondage and
Liberation of the Will

Matthew Barrett

ABSTRACT

First- and second-generation Reformers like Martin Luther, John Calvin, and Peter Martyr Vermigli were strong proponents of monergism, arguing that man's will is in bondage to sin and that therefore God must work alone to effectually call and regenerate his elect. The sinner is not active, cooperating in this salvific event, but is instead passive, dead in sin and enslaved to his corrupt nature. However, Philipp Melanchthon eventually introduced emphases interpreted by fellow Reformers as synergistic, suggesting that while the Spirit's enablement is necessary, even the Spirit is dependent on the will's cooperation and consent. This chapter explores the debates these Reformers entered into not only with their Catholic and humanist nemeses but also, as in Melanchthon's case, with their fellow Reformers and disciples over how to define free will, divine necessity, contingency, and the calling of God on sinners.

Introduction

It is "a wretched concoction" (*unglückliches Machwerk*). That was the assessment Albrecht Ritschl gave of Martin Luther's *De servo arbitrio*.[1] Certainly, numerous Catholics in the sixteenth century would have agreed. However, where Ritschl saw a "wretched concoction," Luther and many other Reformers saw scriptural doctrine. In other words, the Reformers affirmed the bondage of the will because they believed Scripture taught it, and Scripture was their final authority (*sola Scriptura*). Nevertheless, though their appeal was first and foremost to Scripture, they also believed their affirmation of an enslaved will was well-grounded in the tradition of Augustine, particularly in his anti-Pelagian writings. At their core, the Reformers saw themselves retrieving Augustinianism.

Nevertheless, the traditions that evolved after Augustine and led up to the Reformation era were diverse. While the *via moderna* (William of Ockham, Pierre d'Ailly, Robert Holcot, and Gabriel Biel) held an optimistic view of man's abilities, the *schola Augustiniana moderna* (Thomas Bradwardine, Gregory of Rimini, and Hugolino of Orvieto) was far more pessimistic, exposing man's inability apart from sovereign grace.

The *via moderna*, however, had an incalculable impact on the late-medieval church, particularly at the lay level, as forms of synergism took root in the context of a sacramental theology. With a covenantal tune, the *via moderna* sang, "God will not deny grace to anyone who does what lies within them" (*facienti quod in se est Deus non denegat gratiam*).[2] In contrast, the Reformers ignited a soteriologically driven Augustinian renaissance, one that once again exposed man's spiritual inability and utter reliance on God's efficacious grace and divine sovereignty in salvation.

Martin Luther's *De servo arbitrio*

Perhaps no dispute so encapsulated the essence of this debate so early in the history of the Reformation than the boxing match between Martin Luther and Erasmus.[3] In the years leading up to the Erasmus-Luther debate, the former was feeling the pressure to speak out either

---

1. Albrecht Ritschl, *Die christliche Lehre von der Rechtfertigung und Versöhnung* (Bonn: Marcus, 1870), 1:221.

2 Since the *via moderna* is addressed in Korey Maas's chapter in this book, I will not explore it here.

3. For a much fuller treatment than can be provided here, see Gerharde O. Forde, *The Captivation of the Will: Luther vs. Erasmus on Freedom and Bondage*, ed. Steven Paulson, Lutheran Quarterly Books (Grand Rapids, MI: Eerdmans, 2005).

in favor of or against Luther and his reformation. Erasmus had relatively succeeded in resisting such petitions, which pleased him, since he desired to remain neutral. Though Luther had written Erasmus in 1519 to persuade him to join his cause, Erasmus insisted that he must not take sides.

However, in time Erasmus became less and less sympathetic and all the more irritated with Luther's attacks on Rome. Eventually, Erasmus decided he must dissociate himself from Luther while simultaneously aiming not to harm the cause of reform the two of them desired.[4] Given his disagreement with Luther's views on grace and free will in *An Assertion of All the Articles of Martin Luther Condemned by the Latest Bull of Leo X* (1520), Erasmus believed that he had found the right opportunity to criticize and distance himself from Luther.[5] So in 1524, Erasmus published his diatribe, *De libero arbitrio* (*The Freedom of the Will*), which argued that Luther's denial of free will and affirmation that all things happen by necessity contradicted the beliefs of the church in ages past. Luther responded to Erasmus with *De servo arbitrio* (*The Bondage of the Will*) in 1525, arguing from both Scripture and tradition that the will is enslaved and totally dependent on God's grace for liberation. As a result of these publications, Erasmus's stance toward the Reformer and Luther's perception of the humanist no longer remained a secret. Now all knew that Erasmus would neither support Luther's reformation nor take his side against Rome but would instead oppose Luther's theology of sovereign grace.

Free Will, Contingency, and Necessity

In order to fully understand how Luther's view of the will differed from Erasmus's view, we must begin with Erasmus's definition of free choice. For example, Erasmus said, "By free choice in this place we mean a power of the human will by which a man can apply himself to the things which lead to eternal salvation, or turn away from them."[6] Erasmus undoubtedly affirmed the will's power of contrary choice, and such a definition seems to rule out divine necessity. It also makes man

---

4. See Philip S. Watson, "Introduction," *LW* 33:8.
5. Martin Luther, *Assertio omnium articulorum M. Lutheri per bullam Leonis X. novissimam damnatorum* (December 1520), WA 7:94–151.
6. As quoted in Martin Luther, *The Bondage of the Will*, *LW* 33:103.

active and cooperative (or resistive) in the conversion process, since he is able to apply himself to salvation or turn away from it.

If we are to comprehend why Erasmus's definition was untenable for Luther, we must review Luther's view of contingency and necessity when it came to human and divine choice. In Luther's mind the "thunderbolt" argument that refutes free will as Erasmus understood it was God's immutable and eternal foreknowledge. To explain, "God foreknows nothing contingently" but instead "foresees and purposes and does all things by his immutable, eternal, and infallible will."[7] It follows, therefore, that if God foreknows nothing contingently, mankind cannot possess a freedom of contrary choice. For everything man does has not only been foreseen by God but will also happen exactly as God purposed it to happen in eternity.

Another way to make such a point is to say that God "foreknows necessarily," and therefore man cannot possess the ability to choose other than that which God necessarily foreknows and wills.[8] Luther made this point bluntly: "If God foreknows a thing, that thing necessarily happens." Therefore, "there is no such thing as free choice."[9] Notice, Luther refused to divorce God's foreknowledge from God's willing of all things. The two are inseparable. "If he foreknows as he wills," said Luther, "then his will is eternal and unchanging (because his nature is so), and if he wills as he foreknows, then his knowledge is eternal and unchanging (because his nature is so)."[10] Luther anticipated the conclusion that must follow:

> From this it follows irrefutably that everything we do, everything that happens, even if it seems to us to happen mutably and contingently, happens in fact nonetheless necessarily and immutably, if you have regard to the will of God. For the will of God is effectual and cannot be hindered, since it is the power of the divine nature itself.[11]

How, then, did Luther prefer to relate man's willful choices to God's foreknowledge and decree? While Luther used the term "necessity," he

---

7. Ibid., *LW* 33:37.
8. Ibid. For Luther's extended discussion of foreknowledge and necessity, see *LW* 33:184–92.
9. Ibid., *LW* 33:195.
10. Ibid., *LW* 33:37.
11. Ibid., *LW* 33:195, 37.

lamented that it was not ideal since it might wrongly convey a "kind of compulsion," which Luther flatly denied. To be clear, Luther rejected any view that would say, fatalistically, that God or man wills under compulsion rather than out of "pleasure or desire" (two words that, for Luther, described "true freedom").[12] By denying coercion, Luther in no way intended to deny that God's will is immutable and infallible. We should not miss Luther's contrast: while God's will remains immutable, our will remains mutable, and the former governs (even controls) the latter. As Boethius poetically remarked, "Remaining fixed, Thou makest all things move." Certainly man's will is included: "Our will, especially when it is evil, cannot of itself do good."[13] In summary, God's will works by necessity but not by coercion. Luther's distinction had obvious implications for man's will: man's will is under divine necessity, though not under coercion. So he wills necessarily but not by force. As many scriptural passages confirm, "all things happen by necessity."[14]

Moreover, necessity is not only upon us from the outside (i.e., God) but is also an effect due to something within us (i.e., bondage to sin). Prior to God's converting power, man is bound and enslaved to sin and the Devil. Salvation, therefore, "is beyond our own powers and devices, and depends on the work of God alone." If God is "not present and at work in us," Luther remarked, "everything we do is evil and we necessarily do what is of no avail for salvation." "For if it is not we, but only God, who works salvation in us, then before he works we can do nothing of saving significance, whether we wish to or not."[15] Man's bondage, in other words, demands a monergistic work of God within.

Luther, however, again adding an important qualification, clarified that such necessity is not the same thing as coercion. Here we get to the meat of the nut, for Luther articulated a freedom of inclination. Necessity, in other words, does not preclude desire but actually entails

12. Ibid., *LW* 33:39.
13. Ibid.
14. Ibid., *LW* 33:39, 60. Luther further aimed to establish his argument by appealing to Rom. 9:18, 22 ("he hardens whomever he wills," and "God, desiring to show his wrath"), as well as Jesus's words in Matt. 22:14 ("many are called, but few are chosen") and John 13:18 ("I know whom I have chosen"). Additionally, Scripture says that "all things stand or fall by the choice and authority of God, and all the earth should keep silence before the Lord [Hab. 2:20]." Ibid., *LW* 33:60. How can necessity, Luther asked, be removed from these passages? (Luther also appealed to Isa. 46:10.)
15. Ibid., *LW* 33:64.

man's desire. Notice how carefully Luther worked to avoid compulsion. Luther could say man sins necessarily and not by compulsion precisely because such necessity is a necessity of inclination and desire, not coercion. Luther explained,

> When a man is without the Spirit of God he does not do evil against his will, as if he were taken by the scruff of the neck and forced to it, like a thief or robber carried off against his will to punishment, but he does it of his own accord and with a ready will. And this readiness or will to act he cannot by his own powers omit, restrain, or change, but he keeps on willing and being ready.[16]

Luther only furthered his case for a freedom of inclination that is compatible with necessity when he explained how the Spirit works within the sinner. Prior to the Spirit, the will is in bondage, and yet it is a willful, desired bondage. However, when the Spirit works within the enslaved sinner, the "will is changed" and "gently breathed upon by the Spirit of God." Does such a work by the Spirit annihilate or coerce man's will since it is irresistible? By no means. The Spirit works on the will so that the will acts from

> pure willingness and inclination and of its own accord, not from compulsion, so that it cannot be turned another way by any opposition, nor be overcome or compelled even by the gates of hell, but it goes on willing and delighting in and loving the good, just as before it willed and delighted in and loved evil.[17]

To reiterate Luther's point, the will is free not because it has a power of contrary choice but because it necessarily chooses that which it most desires, that which it finds itself inclined toward. Prior to the work of the Spirit, the will sins necessarily because it is enslaved to sin, and yet it is not a coerced bondage but one it desires more than anything else. However, when the Spirit comes upon God's elect, the will is transformed, given new desires. Again, necessity is very much at play, for the Spirit works effectually on the will.[18] Yet, such efficacy is not coercion

---

16. Ibid.
17. Ibid., *LW* 33:65.
18. When it comes to Luther's language of "absolute necessity," it should be qualified that Luther used this language, as this chapter demonstrates, in the context of his disputation with Eras-

since the sinner's new inclinations now lead him to desire Christ more than anything else. In short, whereas before it necessarily desired evil, now it necessarily desires good, finding good to be its greatest delight.

THE ENSLAVEMENT OF THE WILL

It should be apparent by now that Luther, in contrast to Rome and many late-medieval fathers, had no hesitation in affirming the will's enslavement and the spiritual inability of the sinner in matters of salvation prior to the Spirit's work of new birth and conversion.

Such bondage, however, had multiple sources. Luther identified two: the Devil and the world. Having in mind 2 Timothy 2:26, Luther demonstrated that every man is under the god of this world, captive to do his will. Does this captivity to Satan involve necessity? Absolutely. "We cannot will anything but what he wills."[19] With Luke 11:18–21 in view, Luther taught that it takes a "Stronger One" (Christ) to overcome the Devil, and Christ does just that through the Spirit. We are transferred from one slavery to another, though our slavery to Christ is actually a "royal freedom" that enables us to "readily will and do what he wills."[20]

Luther famously pictured the will situated between God and the Devil like a beast of burden: "If God rides it, it wills and goes where God wills, as the psalm says: 'I am become as a beast [before thee] and I am always with thee.'" But if Satan rides it, "it wills and goes where Satan wills." One might think, then, that the will must only run to (or choose) whichever rider he pleases. Luther countered, "Nor can it [the

---

mus. However, it does not appear that Luther leaned on such language in his writings after 1525. Later on (e.g., in his lectures on Genesis), Luther warned against misunderstanding his *De servo arbitrio*, though he never retracted what he wrote. In my personal correspondence with Luther scholar Robert Kolb, he notes that after 1525, Luther instead leaned on the promise given in the Word (oral and written) and in the sacraments in order to provide God's people with assurance, assurance that he sought to undergird by appealing to election in his *De servo arbitrio*. Perhaps this can be traced back to Luther's developing emphasis on law and gospel. While the law reveals that we are culpable for our own damnation, the gospel reveals that God receives the credit for our salvation. Luther did not try to logically sort out the tension between these twin truths; nevertheless, he believed they were each critical in pastoral care. Luther, therefore, preached law. He was aware that preaching predestination to damnation might have the unfortunate effect of either creating presumption or libertinism among those who might venture to use election as an excuse or as creating despair in those who failed to hear the promise of the gospel. For Luther, therefore, predestination was meant to undergird the promise of the gospel.

19. Luther, *Bondage*, in *LW* 33:65.
20. Ibid., *LW* 33:65.

will] choose to run to either of the two riders or to seek him out, but the riders themselves contend for the possession and control of it."[21]

LUTHER'S MONERGISM

Was Luther a monergist? As is evident already, he was indeed. But also consider Luther's appeal to 1 Peter 5:5. Luther believed that "God has assuredly promised his grace to the humble." But who are the humble? They are those "who lament and despair of themselves." Lest the reader think such repentance is not from God, Luther quickly qualified, "But no man can be thoroughly humbled until he knows that his salvation is utterly beyond his own powers, devices, endeavors, will, and works, and depends entirely on the choice, will, and work of another, namely, God alone." Luther went on to eliminate synergism, even synergism in the slightest:

> For as long as he [man] is persuaded that he himself can do even the least thing toward his salvation, he retains some self-confidence and does not altogether despair of himself, and therefore he is not humbled before God, but presumes that there is—or at least hopes or desires that there may be—some place, time, and work for him, by which he may at length attain salvation.

What, then, is the solution to man's plight? "When a man has no doubt that everything depends on the will of God, then he completely despairs of himself and chooses nothing for himself, but waits for God to work; then he has come close to grace, and can be saved."[22]

In short, the first sign that man is on the right path is when he acknowledges that nothing can come from himself but that everything must come from God. Stated otherwise, man must come to grips with

---

21. Ibid., *LW* 33:65–66. In that light, Luther wished theologians would simply avoid the phrase *free will*. It is not helpful but adds enormous confusion (and is even dangerous, said Luther). Since "we do everything by necessity, and nothing by free choice," the phrase "free will" should be abandoned lest it give people the opposite impression, namely, that free choice is a "power that can turn itself freely in either direction, without being under anyone's influence or control." Ibid., *LW* 33:68. Nonetheless, Luther was reasonable in realizing that the phrase *free will* refuses to disappear. So, he insisted, if it is to be used, then one must be sure it is used properly. If the term is used honestly, it would mean that free choice is only applied to man "with respect to what is beneath him and not what is above him," that is, matters concerning God, salvation, and damnation. Ibid., 33:70. For readers in the twenty-first century, it should be obvious that Luther rejected outright what philosophers and theologians title *libertarian freedom*.

22. Ibid., *LW* 33:61–62.

the fact that he is totally and absolutely dependent on God's grace and mercy and can do nothing, even in the slightest, to save himself: "Free choice without the grace of God is not free at all, but immutably the captive and slave of evil, since it cannot of itself turn to the good."[23] Luther recognized, however, how common it is for men to resist such a humiliating view of themselves. They condemn "this teaching of self-despair, wishing for something, however little, to be left for them to do themselves; so they remain secretly proud and enemies of the grace of God."[24]

In order to press Luther's monergism further, in contrast to Erasmus's synergism, it would be wise to revisit Erasmus's definition once more: "By free choice in this place we mean a power of the human will by which a man can apply himself to the things which lead to eternal salvation, or turn away from them."[25] Commenting on Erasmus's definition, Luther elaborated on its meaning: "On the authority of Erasmus, then, free choice is a power of the will that is able of itself to will and unwill the word and work of God, by which it is led to those things which exceed both its grasp and its perception."[26] Luther went on to point out that if, for Erasmus, man can "will or unwill," then he can also "love and hate," which also means he can "in some small degree do the works of the law and believe the gospel."[27] What was Luther's critique? If this is how we define free will, then nothing in salvation is left to the grace of God and the Holy Spirit! "This plainly means attributing divinity to free choice, since to will the law and the gospel, to unwill sin and to will death, belongs to divine power alone, as Paul says in more than one place."[28]

In contrast, Luther was convinced from Scripture that the Spirit works within us without our help (i.e., monergism): "Before man is changed into a new creature of the Kingdom of the Spirit, he does nothing and attempts nothing to prepare himself for this renewal and this Kingdom."[29] Elsewhere, Luther equally guarded his readers from

23. Ibid., *LW* 33:67.
24. Ibid., *LW* 33:62.
25. As quoted in ibid., *LW* 33:103.
26. Ibid., *LW* 33:106.
27. Ibid., *LW* 33:106–7.
28. Ibid., *LW* 33:107.
29. Ibid., *LW* 33:243.

semi-Pelagianism and semi-Augustinianism. Contrary to Erasmus, he held that it is not as if man just needs a little of God's help, and then he can "prepare himself by morally good works for the divine favor." To the contrary, "if through the law sin abounds, how is it possible that a man should be able to prepare himself by moral works for the divine favor? How can works help when the law does not help?"[30]

In summary, Luther would not grant even an inch to free will in man's new birth and conversion. To quote Luther, we must avoid the temptation to find a "middle way" that would concede even "a tiny bit" to free will.[31] It was all or nothing for Luther: "We must therefore go all out and completely deny free choice, referring everything to God; then there will be no contradictions in Scripture."[32] A stronger affirmation of divine monergism is difficult to imagine.

Law and Gospel

If Luther was right, then what is one to make of the many commands in the Bible? Do not these laws and imperatives imply ability on man's part? Does not *ought* mean *can*? Indeed, this was an argument Erasmus clung to in his defense of free will. However, Luther believed Erasmus had misunderstood the purpose of the law in reference to the unbeliever.

God's imperatives in no way are meant to imply that man has it within him to fulfill such commands. Instead, God is driving man to the law in order to reveal his impotence, as Paul asserts in Romans 3:20. "For human nature," said Luther, "is so blind that it does not know its own powers, or rather diseases, and so proud as to imagine that it knows and can do everything; and for this pride and blindness God has no readier remedy than the propounding of his law."[33] Far from proving man's freedom, biblical imperatives expose his corruption and captivity, not to mention his pride, contempt, and ignorance. Therefore, when one encounters precepts in the law, one must recognize that such precepts are not the same thing as promises. For example, God may command sinners not to have other gods or commit adultery, but

---

30. Ibid., *LW* 33:219.
31. Ibid., *LW* 33:245.
32. Ibid., *LW* 33:245.
33. Ibid., *LW* 33:121.

these commands by no means promise man that he will not sin or break God's precepts or that man even has it within his ability to fulfill such commands.

The same caution applies to divine invitations as well. For example, God says in Deuteronomy 30:15, 19, "I have set before you today life and good, death and evil. . . . Therefore choose life." Erasmus thought such verses as these proved his case. After all, God leaves it up to man, for man has the freedom to choose. But Luther disagreed. Passages like Deuteronomy 30 offer life, but God never says man has the ability to choose life, nor does God guarantee he will bestow life. Certain conditions must be met, and while God sincerely places two paths in front of man (life and death), Scripture shows that unregenerate man chooses death over life every time. So the law only shows man how impossible divine precepts are, not because there is some fault in God's commands but rather because man is corrupt and captivated by sin, the world, and the Devil. Unless God sends the Spirit, this is the state in which man will remain.[34] As Luther succinctly put it, "Man perpetually and necessarily sins and errs until he is put right by the Spirit of God."[35]

It is at precisely this point in Luther's debate with Erasmus that Luther's distinction between law and gospel played a key role. When held up against the law, man's inability is apparent; hence the gospel shines bright as man's only hope. Should we reverse this biblical order, as Luther believed Erasmus did, we would then turn law into gospel and gospel into law. Therefore, understanding the law *as* law is essential.[36]

It should not be missed that for Luther the law played a crucial role in preparing sinners for the gospel. The law makes "man's plight plain to him," breaking him down, confounding him by "self-knowledge, so as to prepare him for grace and send him to Christ that he may be saved."[37] Should the law show man his spiritual ability rather than his captivity, then the law would not lead to gospel and grace but would instead lead man right back to himself as the one who can will and achieve his own righteousness. But should the law expose man's

---

34. Ibid., *LW* 33:126.
35. Ibid., *LW* 33:177.
36. Ibid., *LW* 33:127, 132–33.
37. Ibid., *LW* 33:130–31. Luther also showed how the law and Satan differ in this respect: while Satan deceives man into thinking he is free (when really man is at Satan's mercy), Moses and the lawgiver use the law to show man that he is not free at all but bound and condemned.

captivity and depravity, man must depend entirely on what Christ has done for him and realize his reliance on the Spirit's gifts of new birth, faith, and repentance. In that light, Luther was adamant that his readers not make the mistake of Erasmus by confusing gospel with law and law with gospel.

Philipp Melanchthon and the Synergism Controversy

It has often been the case that Luther stands in the spotlight of the Reformation while Philipp Melanchthon stands in Luther's shadow. Contrary to where we might place the spotlight, at times Luther would actually shine attention on Melanchthon, even commending Melanchthon's writings over his own. Luther did exactly this in his praise of Melanchthon's *Loci Communes*. For example, in his *Table Talk* Luther gave a very clear prescription on how one might become a theologian. First, read the Bible; "afterward he should read Philip's *Loci Communes*." If one takes these two steps, then nothing can keep him from being a theologian, and not even "the devil" or a "heretic" can "shake him"![38]

Luther praised Melanchthon's *Loci Communes* not because of mere friendship but because of the book's usefulness in theology and in the church. As Luther explained,

> There's no book under the sun in which the whole of theology is so compactly presented as in the *Loci Communes*. If you read all the fathers and sententiaries [late-medieval commentators on Peter Lombard's *Four Books of Sentences*] you have nothing. No better book has been written after the Holy Scriptures than Philip's. He expresses himself more concisely than I do when he argues and instructs.[39]

Similarly, Luther reserved high praise for Melanchthon's *Loci Communes* at the start of his *Bondage of the Will*. In an effort to discredit Erasmus's arguments for free will, Luther said such arguments had been "refuted already so often by me, and beaten down and completely pulverized in Philipp Melanchthon's *Commonplaces*—an unanswer-

---

38. Luther, *Table Talk*, LW 54:439–40.
39. Ibid., *LW* 54:440.

able little book which in my judgment deserves not only to be immortalized but even canonized."[40] Higher praise is hard to come by!

These accolades for Melanchthon's *Loci Communes* are not without importance, for they show that early on Luther thought himself to be in agreement with the theology of Melanchthon as outlined in his 1521 *Loci Communes* when it came to sin, necessity, and free will.[41] However, in subsequent editions of his *Loci Communes*, Melanchthon's disagreement with Luther and sympathies for Erasmus became conspicuous.[42] For example, Melanchthon affirmed three causes (*causae*, or factors) of conversion: the Holy Spirit, the Word of God, and the will of man.[43] And in locus 4 his departure from Luther became even more transparent: "The free choice in man is the ability to apply oneself toward grace" (*facultas applicandi se ad gratiam*).[44] This sentence differs little from Erasmus's definition of free will reviewed earlier. Such an emphasis on free choice eventually resulted in the issue being addressed by the Formula of Concord. By that point, Lutherans had been debating the matter for almost fifty years. Nevertheless, as J. A. O. Preus observes, the matter was settled, and "Lutheranism no longer talks of three causes, only of the two causes of conversion."[45]

---

40. Luther, *Bondage*, LW 33:16.
41. One might wonder, then, why Luther did not rebuke Melanchthon for shifting his position toward free will later on. Some would argue that Luther's silence demonstrates that Melanchthon has been misunderstood, that Melanchthon never really became a synergist. However, this is an argument from silence (though not one without due consideration, given that Luther did not hesitate to confront even his closest friends), and it seems unwise to determine Melanchthon's position based on Luther's reaction or lack thereof. Drickamer acknowledges the peculiar silence, but he may have a better solution to this riddle: "It is puzzling that Luther did not speak out on this developing idea. Melanchthon himself may not have been aware of the implications of the direction he was following, but in this period [1530s] he was already making statements that heavily favored the error of synergism." John M. Drickamer, "Did Melanchthon Become a Synergist?," *The Springfielder* 40, no. 2 (1976): 98. Another possibility, though admittedly speculative, is that Luther's friendship with Melanchthon (which was very strong) could have kept him from seeing subtle shifts in Melanchthon's language toward an emphasis on free will.
42. Preus notes that Melanchthon kept his agreement with Erasmus private. J. A. O. Preus, "Translator's Preface," in Philipp Melanchthon, *Loci Communes 1543*, trans. J. A. O. Preus (St. Louis, MO: Concordia, 1992), 11. It should be qualified, however, that in previous decades Melanchthon did take issue with Erasmus. For an excellent history of his conflict with Erasmus, see Timothy J. Wengert, *Human Freedom, Christian Righteousness: Philip Melanchthon's Exegetical Dispute with Erasmus of Rotterdam*, Oxford Studies in Historical Theology (New York: Oxford University Press, 1998).
43. To be historically accurate, it should be qualified that *conversion* can refer to that initial conversion to Christ or to the ongoing repentance in the life of the believer. Granted, at times it is hard to decipher which of the two is in use. However, in the quotations that follow, it appears that Melanchthon often has initial conversion in view, especially since in context he refers to other indicators such as the new birth and the unregenerate.
44. Preus, "Translator's Preface," 11.
45. Ibid., 11–12.

That said, we will start with Melanchthon's 1521 edition and next move to his work in the 1530 Augsburg Confession and Apology of the Augsburg Confession, eventually transitioning to his 1543 *Loci Communes*. In the last of these we will discover that Melanchthon's view of free will underwent significant revision and at the very least left the door open for others to interpret him as advocating synergism, thus creating future controversy among Lutherans.[46]

MELANCHTHON'S 1521 *LOCI COMMUNES*

At the start of his 1521 treatment of free will, Melanchthon admitted how much he disliked the phrase because it is "completely foreign to divine Scripture and to the sense and judgment of the Spirit."[47] When Melanchthon addressed whether the will is free, he answered in the negative because he believed divine predestination entails that everything happens by necessity. Since "everything that comes about happens necessarily according to divine predestination, our will has no freedom."[48]

Melanchthon's scriptural proofs for such a stance are legion, including texts like Ephesians 1:11, which says God "works all things according the judgment of his will."[49] Melanchthon also turned to Romans 9 and 11, where Paul consigns "everything that happens to divine predestination"; Proverbs (14:12, 27; 16:4, 11–12, 33; 20:24); Ecclesiastes 9:1, where Solomon believes "that all things happen by God's will"; and Luke 12:7, where Jesus asserts with "great effect" that "all the hairs of your head are numbered."[50]

In light of these passages, Melanchthon then asked whether there is such a thing as "contingency" (chance, luck). Answer: "Scriptures teach that everything happens by necessity." What can one conclude except that "Scripture denies any freedom to our will through the

---

46. Whether Melanchthon should be called a "synergist" was not only controversial in his day but remains a controversial issue among Lutherans today as well.

47. Philipp Melanchthon, *Commonplaces: Loci Communes 1521*, trans. Christian Preus (St. Louis, MO: Concordia, 2014), 26.

48. Ibid., 29.

49. Cf. Gen. 15:16; 1 Sam. 2:25, 26; 1 Kings 12:15; Prov. 16:4, 9; 20:24; Jer. 10:23; Matt. 10:29; Rom. 11:36.

50. Melanchthon, *Commonplaces: Loci Communes 1521*, 30. Biblical translations in this paragraph are drawn from Melanchthon.

necessity of predestination." All things "come about not because of human plans or efforts, but according to the will of God."[51]

Melanchthon reacted against the "godless theology of the sophists" (i.e., scholastic theologians) who thought predestination "too harsh" and consequently "stressed upon us the contingency of things and the freedom of our will" so much so that "our tender ears now recoil from the truth of Scripture."[52] And yet, Melanchthon was careful not to ignore proper theological distinctions. For example, he acknowledged that if we are merely discussing the freedom of the will in the realm of "natural capability," then it is appropriate to affirm "freedom in external works." What Melanchthon had in mind, in other words, were the most basic human functions in society, like saying hello to someone on the road, deciding to get dressed in the morning, or sitting down to eat dinner. However, if we are referring to the "inner affections," then man does possess the power of the will.[53] Melanchthon reminded his readers that the will is the source of one's affections, so much so that the word "heart" could be used in its place. Melanchthon once again retorted against the sophists who thought that the "will naturally opposes its affections or can push aside affection, so long as the intellect advises and recommends it." No, said Melanchthon, the affections flow out of the will or heart, the latter of which Scripture calls the "highest faculty of man" and that "part of man from which affections arise."[54] Later on, Melanchthon expanded on such a point when he denied that "there is any power in man that can seriously oppose his affections."[55] In his view, the will is driven by the affections of the heart.

Such a focus on the heart transitions Melanchthon's reader to the central problem: the heart is corrupt, and therefore it follows that the will is in bondage to sin. In the "external selection of things there is a certain freedom"—that is, in civil responsibilities. However, the heart is a different matter entirely. Melanchthon proclaimed, "I completely reject

---

51. Ibid., 30–31.
52. Ibid., 31.
53. "For practical experience shows us that our will cannot of its own power push aside love, hatred, or similar affections, but one overrules another, so that, for example, you stop loving someone because he hurts you." Ibid., 32.
54. Interestingly, on this point Melanchthon is similar to Luther who, in *Bondage*, saw free will as doing that which one most desires. Melanchthon, *Commonplaces: Loci Communes 1521*, 33.
55. Melanchthon, *Commonplaces: Loci Communes 1521*, 35.

the idea that our inner affections are under our power. Nor do I grant that any will possesses the genuine power of opposing its affections."[56] And since God requires purity in heart, the natural man is in grave trouble, for his heart is corrupt, as Jeremiah 17:9 affirms. Therefore, as "soon as the affections have begun to rage and boil, they cannot be controlled and they burst forth."[57] It is such a rage and boil that brings us to Melanchthon's doctrine of sin, at least as he articulated it in 1521.

What is sin? More specifically, what is original sin? "Original sin," Melanchthon held, "is an inborn propensity and a natural impulse that actively compels us to sin, originating from Adam and extending to all his posterity." Melanchthon aimed to illustrate man's inborn power to sin by comparing it to the fire that scorches hotter because of an innate power within it or to a magnet that attracts iron to itself by an innate power. Therefore, Melanchthon concluded, sin is a "corrupt inner disposition [*affectus*] and a depraved agitation of the heart against the Law of God."[58]

In order to prove such a doctrine, Melanchthon appealed to a host of biblical texts (Gen. 6:3; Rom. 8:5, 7), as well as to Augustine's writings against the Pelagians (e.g., *On the Spirit and the Letter*, *Against Two Letters of the Pelagians*, *Against Julian*). Melanchthon did not hesitate to follow Paul, who says in Ephesians 2:3 that man is by nature a child of wrath. Lest there be any uncertainty, Melanchthon interpreted Paul to mean that "if we are children of wrath by nature, we are certainly born children of wrath. . . . For what else is Paul saying here except that we are born with all our powers subject to sin and that no good ever exists in human powers?"[59] Certainly the bondage of man's will follows from such inborn subjection of the will to sin.

Melanchthon also enlisted Romans 5, for there Paul teaches "that sin has been passed down to all men." Melanchthon denied that Paul merely has in mind one's actual, personal sins. Instead, Paul has in mind original sin. Otherwise, Paul could not say "that the many have died because of one man's transgression."[60]

---

56. Ibid.
57. Ibid., 36.
58. Ibid., 38–39.
59. Ibid.
60. Ibid., 39.

Melanchthon found further support for original sin in 1 Corinthians 15:22, where Paul writes, "For as in Adam all die, so also in Christ shall all be made alive." Melanchthon commented, "Now if we are all blessed in Christ, it follows necessarily that we are cursed in Adam." Similarly, in Psalm 51:5, David acknowledges, "Behold, I was brought forth in iniquity, and in sin did my mother conceive me." What are we to conclude but that man is "born with sin" (cf. Gen. 6:5)?[61] Melanchthon believed that Jesus captures the point precisely in John 3:6: "That which is born of the flesh is flesh." Hence, in light of original sin, each sinner is in desperate need of a new birth by the Spirit, one that counters his first birth of the flesh into guilt and corruption.[62]

Turning to passages like Romans 8, Melanchthon also showed that according to the flesh the unregenerate man cannot fulfill God's law. Why? Because "those who are of the flesh desire the things of the flesh."[63] Melanchthon, therefore, comfortably concluded with Paul that those in the flesh are at enmity with God and subject to the law. Failure to obey the law is sin, and "every motion and impulse of the soul against the Law is sin."[64] Or, to look at our state from another angle, "since we lack life, there is nothing in us except sin and death" (cf. Eph. 2:3). Apart from the Spirit, all that is within us is only "darkness, blindness, and error."[65]

In view of the depravity every man is enslaved to, Melanchthon found himself in agreement with Augustine, who denied that the beginning of repentance resides within man.[66] After all, Jesus himself said in John 6:44, "No one can come to me unless the Father who sent me draws him." But do not the commands in Scripture assume that we have the ability within us to come to Jesus? Not at all, responded Melanchthon:

---

61. Ibid.
62. Ibid., 40. Such a contrast by Melanchthon between "flesh" and "Spirit" is central to his entire argument. Melanchthon camped out in Romans and Galatians, for instance, as well as in the Gospel of John. "Flesh" designated the "old man," and "signified all the powers belonging to human nature." Melanchthon's point here was to deny the assumption that "there is something in unregenerate man, in a man not washed clean by the Spirit, that cannot be called flesh and therefore vicious." No, flesh "includes everything in us foreign to the Holy Spirit." Ibid., 46–47.
63. Ibid., 47.
64. Ibid., 48.
65. Ibid.
66. Ibid., 54.

Just because he commands us to turn to him does not mean that it is in our power to repent or turn to him. God also commands us to love him above all things. But it does not follow that we have it in our power to do it simply because he commands it. On the contrary, it is precisely because he commands it that it is not in our own power. For he commands the impossible to commend his mercy to us.[67]

As Zechariah 10:6 explains, God is the one who does the converting, not man.

At the end of his treatment of the doctrine of sin, Melanchthon helpfully pinpointed the crux of the matter. Sinful, corrupt affections "are so ingrained in man that they occupy his entire nature and hold it captive." Such depravity does not confine itself to one corner of man but pervades his entire and inmost being. Scripture teaches us that these "carnal affections cannot be overcome except by the Spirit of God, since only those whom the Son has freed are truly free (John 8:[36])."[68]

The 1530 Augsburg Confession and Its Apology

Certainly other works by Melanchthon in the 1520s could be consulted, but it is the 1530 Augsburg Confession, as well as Melanchthon's Apology of the Augsburg Confession, that must arrest our attention now.[69] The Augsburg Confession was boldly presented on June 25, 1530, by Lutheran theologians and laymen, led by Philipp Melanchthon, in response to Emperor Charles V for the purpose of defending their Lutheran beliefs and distinguishing their views from Rome, Anabaptists, and Zwinglians.[70] Afterward the Lutherans waited to see how the

---

67. Ibid., 55.

68. Ibid., 56.

69. Space does not permit exploration of Melanchthon's treatment of Colossians in 1527/28, but Kolb observes that in this work Melanchthon "averred that the will has no power to choose to turn itself to God." "The law is able to coerce some external obedience from unbelievers, but this kind of obedience apart from faith is fatally flawed by indwelling, original sin." See Robert Kolb, *Bound Choice, Election, and Wittenberg Theological Method: From Martin Luther to the Formula of Concord*, Lutheran Quarterly Books (Grand Rapids, MI: Eerdmans, 2005), 80.

70. The radical wing of the Reformation is not the focus of this chapter. Nevertheless, for their diverse views on predestination, grace, original sin, free will, see Michael W. McDill, "Balthasar Hubmaier and Free Will," in *The Anabaptists and Contemporary Baptists: Restoring New Testament Christianity: Essays in Honor of Paige Patterson*, ed. Malcolm Yarnell (Nashville: B&H Academic, 2013), 137–54; Meic Pearse, *The Great Restoration: The Religious Radicals of the 16th and 17th Centuries* (Carlisle: Paternoster, 1998), 144–45; Thor Hall, "Possibilities of Erasmian Influence on Denck and Hubmaier in Their Views on the Freedom of the Will," *MQR* 35, no. 2

emperor would reply. On August 3, he issued his response, the *Pontifical Confutation of the Augsburg Confession*, which was followed in the subsequent months with threats and demands that the Lutherans back down. But with Luther's moral support, the Lutherans did not. In reply to the emperor's *Pontifical Confutation*, Melanchthon wrote his Apology (or defense), which is a thorough refutation of Rome's views, as seen, for example, in its affirmation of *sola gratia*, *sola fide*, and *solus Christus*.

Articles 2 and 18 of the Augsburg Confession are especially relevant for our purposes. First, consider article 2 on original sin:

> Since the fall of Adam all human beings who are propagated according to nature are born with sin, that is, without fear of God, without trust in God, and with concupiscence. And they teach that this disease or original fault [*vitium originis*] is truly sin, which even now damns and brings eternal death to those who are not born again through baptism and the Holy Spirit.[71]

Here the confession teaches that the sin of Adam is inherited by his posterity. Being born in sin means that man, from the very start, is inclined to sin.

The confession's mention of concupiscence is not insignificant either, for in doing so it avoids the mistake of thinking of sin as mere action rather than as a disease within that corrupts and inclines man to evil. For this reason, Melanchthon's Apology affirms that concupiscence itself is sin.[72] Concupiscence, which all those born according to the flesh have by nature, is the "continual tendency of our nature," and because that nature finds its source in Adam, Melanchthon denied "the ability of human nature," that is, the "gift and power needed to produce fear and faith in God." To clarify, concupiscence means people not only lack this "fear and faith in God" but "are unable to produce

---

(1961): 149–70; Werner O. Packull, "An Introduction to Anabaptist Theology," in *The Cambridge Companion to Reformation Theology*, ed. David Bagchi and David C. Steinmetz (New York: Cambridge University Press, 2004), 203–7.

71. "The Augsburg Confession," art. 2, in Robert Kolb and Timothy J. Wengert, eds., *The Book of Concord: The Confessions of the Evangelical Lutheran Church*, trans. Charles P. Arand et al. (Minneapolis: Fortress, 2000), 37, 39.

72. E.g., "[Our opponents] contend that concupiscence is punishment, not sin. Luther maintains that it is sin." In support is listed Rom. 7:7, 23. "The Apology of the Augsburg Confession," art. 2, in Kolb and Wengert, *The Book of Concord*, 118.

true fear and trust in God."[73] Original sin, therefore, cannot be severed from man's spiritual inability and corrupt nature.

In the end, Melanchthon's Apology explicitly rejects any who would say that original sin is not "a fault or corruption in human nature, but only a subjection to or a condition of mortality."[74] To the contrary, original sin is the absence of original righteousness, as well as the corruption of man's nature. Naturally, then, both the confession and the Apology deny that anything in man contributes to his justification. While the "Scholastics trivialize both sin and its penalty when they teach that individuals by their own power are capable of keeping the commandments of God," the Lutherans find support in Scripture that "human nature is enslaved and held captive by the devil." Therefore, just "as the devil is not conquered without Christ's help, so we, by our own powers, are unable to free ourselves from that slavery."[75] Hence, both Christ and the Spirit are absolutely necessary. Christ must remove our sin and punishment, as well as destroy the Devil, sin, and death. The Spirit must give new birth.[76]

Second, the confession addresses "free will" in article 18 as well. Like Melanchthon's 1521 *Loci Communes*, the confession distinguishes between freedom in the realm of society and freedom in the realm of the heart. While the will may have "freedom for producing civil righteousness and for choosing things subject to reason," we do not have "power to produce the righteousness of God or spiritual righteousness without the Holy Spirit."[77] Its biblical basis for such an affirmation of the bondage of the will is 1 Corinthians 2:14: "the natural person does not accept the things of the Spirit of God."[78]

Again, the confession places blame on the "Pelagians and others" (i.e., Gabriel Biel) but really includes anyone who would teach that "without the Holy Spirit by the powers of nature alone, we are able to love God above all things and can also keep the commandments of

---

73. Ibid., 112.
74. Ibid., 112–13.
75. Ibid., 119.
76. Ibid., 118–19.
77. "The Augsburg Confession," art. 18, in Kolb and Wengert, *The Book of Concord*, 51.
78. The confession also appeals to Augustine's *Hypognosticon* (book 3) to make the same point: While man may be free "to labor in the field, to eat and drink, to have a friend, to wear clothes, to build a house, to marry, to raise cattle," and so on, this does not mean we are able "without God, to begin—much less complete—anything that pertains to God." Ibid., 51.

God 'according to the substance of the acts.'"[79] While man's nature may refrain externally from, say, murder or theft, it "cannot produce internal movements, such as fear of God, trust in God, patience, etc."[80] For the latter, God's grace must intervene. Apart from God's grace, man can do nothing spiritually good. As Melanchthon said in his Apology, we are godless, for "a bad tree cannot bear good fruit [Matt. 7:18], and 'without faith it is impossible to please God' [Heb. 11:6]." Therefore, we should not "ascribe to free will those spiritual capacities." Hence the need for the Holy Spirit in rebirth is great indeed. While civil righteousness is "ascribed to free will," spiritual righteousness is "ascribed to the operation of the Holy Spirit in the regenerate."[81]

MELANCHTHON'S 1543 *LOCI COMMUNES* AND FREE WILL

Thus far in our overview of Melanchthon's theology, as well as its wider context in the Augsburg Confession, we have seen much consistency on original sin, free will, and divine grace. However, it is fair to say that Melanchthon's theology did show substantial signs of change, so that his later theological descriptions of free will differed noticeably from his earlier statements.[82] Perhaps this is best seen if we examine his 1543 *Loci Communes*.[83]

As discovered already, Melanchthon's 1521 *Loci Communes* placed much emphasis on the bondage and captivity of the will in light of the doctrine of original sin. However, his 1543 *Loci Communes*

79. Ibid., 53.
80. Ibid., 53.
81. "The Apology of the Augsburg Confession," art. 18, in Kolb and Wengert, *The Book of Concord*, 234.
82. For a helpful chronicling of Melanchthon's shift toward synergism, see Gregory B. Graybill, *Evangelical Free Will: Philipp Melanchthon's Doctrinal Journey on the Origins of Faith*, Oxford Theological Monographs (New York: Oxford University Press, 2010).
83. However, it should be noted that already in the 1530s Melanchthon was rejecting Luther's view of necessity. Melanchthon's "repugnance toward Luther's assertion that all things happen by absolute divine necessity began to come out in the open through his treatment of contingency in human affairs within the framework of a *necessitas consequentiae*, which Melanchthon distinguished from the *necessitas consequentis*, the scholastic distinction that Luther had opposed." Additionally, "expanding his new understanding of necessity, contingency must exist and there can be no absolute necessity," which was a "repudiation of his position in 1521 as well as Luther's in 1525." Kolb, *Bound Choice*, 87, 88. See also Timothy J. Wengert, "'We Will Feast Together in Heaven Forever': The Epistolary Friendship of John Calvin and Philip Melanchthon," in *Melanchthon in Europe: His Work and Influence beyond Wittenberg*, ed. Karin Maag, Texts and Studies in Reformation and Post-Reformation Thought (Grand Rapids, MI: Baker, 1999), 26–33; Anthony N. S. Lane, "The Influence upon Calvin of His Debate with Pighius," in *Auctoritas Patrum II. Neue Beiträge zur Rezeption der Kirchenväter im 15. Um 16. Jahrhundert*, ed. Leif Grane, Alfred Schindler, and Markus Wriedt (Mainz: Zabern, 1998), 125–39.

emphasized the freedom of the will and its active participation and cooperation with divine grace. That is not to say that he eliminated all discussion of the bondage of the will. However, it does mean that a *shift* in emphasis occurred. Such a shift is noticeable and its motivation can be seen, at least in part, in Melanchthon's reaction against the fatalism and determinism of Stoicism and Manichaeism. Kolb also wonders if Melanchthon may have had in mind John Calvin's views since the two had started a correspondence, and "Calvin's doctrine of predestination and the Genevan's attempt to enlist Melanchthon in its defense troubled the Wittenberger and cast a heavy shadow over their correspondence in 1543 (and would again in 1552)."[84] As we will see, though many aspects of Melanchthon's *Loci Communes* went unchanged, it seems clear that while his 1521 *Loci Communes* appeared to affirm monergism, his 1543 edition transitioned into what could be interpreted as synergism, though it may be debated to what degree.[85]

Consider three observations. First, in locus 3 Melanchthon went to great length to argue that God is not the cause of sin, nor does he ever will sin. For example, Melanchthon quoted Exodus 7:3 ("I will harden Pharaoh's heart") but said that "in the Hebrew expression He [God] is referring to the promise of these things, not to His effectual will."[86] While Melanchthon may have emphasized necessity in his 1521 version, here he upheld contingency: "When this statement has been established that God is not the cause of sin and that He does not will sin, it follows that sin occurs by contingency, that is, that not all things which happen take place by necessity."[87] What is the "cause" of such contingency? The will of man. The "cause of the contingency of our actions is the freedom of our will."[88] Certainly such an affirmation of contingency differed from Melanchthon's previous stance for necessity.

Nevertheless, and second, Melanchthon did not believe contingency should run wild, as if it is absolute. Even contingency has limits, he said: "On the one hand, God sets limits to the things which He wills,

---

84. Kolb, *Bound Choice*, 88. See also Barbara Pitkin, "The Protestant Zeno: Calvin and the Development of Melanchthon's Anthropology," *JR* 84, no. 3 (2004): 345–78.

85. Drickamer believes Melanchthon's shift toward synergism can be traced back to as early as 1535. For his reasons, see Drickamer, "Did Melanchthon Become a Synergist?," 98.

86. Melanchthon, *Loci Communes 1543*, 36.

87. Ibid., 37.

88. Ibid.

and on the other hand, to the things which He does not will. Further, He limits the things which depend wholly on His will and the things which He Himself does in part and which the will of man does in part." In Melanchthon's subsequent argument, he sought to show that there is some degree of "freedom of choice for the human will." It does not follow, he insisted, that "all good and evil things of necessity come from God."[89]

Third, in that light the key question becomes this: Do some things happen apart from God's will? Melanchthon carefully nuanced his answer (distinguishing between absolute necessity and necessity of consequence, as well as primary and secondary causes), but he did conclude that while certain events "depend upon and arise from the will of God," others "come from some other source."[90] On the one hand, Melanchthon did not want to deny necessity. However, he was also unwilling to say that all things happen by necessity, for that would deny contingency. This much becomes clear when Melanchthon, aiming to counter Stoicism, asked critically, "For how can the man pray to God when he holds that all things happen by necessity?"[91] To demonstrate that man's will can act independently of God (thereby denying the necessity of all things), Melanchthon turned to Eve. In some sense, one must say that Eve, in turning herself away from God, did so independently: "Thus the will of Eve in turning herself away from God is a personal and independent cause of her action."[92]

Does such an abstract discussion over necessity and contingency have anything to do with free will in regard to salvation? In locus 4, "Human Powers or Free Choice," Melanchthon showed that it does. Again aiming to counter Stoicism, Melanchthon began by rejecting the necessity of all things in order to affirm contingency. Melanchthon was very concerned that we not take away man's free will. We "must not import Stoic ideas into the church or uphold the fatalistic necessity of all things; but rather we must concede that there is some place for contingency."[93]

---

89. Ibid., 38.
90. Ibid., 39.
91. Ibid.
92. Ibid., 40.
93. Ibid., 41.

Melanchthon did not give up his distinction between freedom in civil works and freedom in religious works. While man may have a freedom in the former, Melanchthon still affirmed that man is corrupted by sin, which no doubt impacts the latter. But to what degree? Melanchthon believed that if man had not been corrupted by sin, he would then have a "clearer and firmer knowledge of God," not to mention "true fear" and "trust in God." Surely man would be able to obey the law if it were not for such a corruption of his nature. So Melanchthon continued to affirm that the "nature of man is under the oppression of the disease of our origins."[94] He cannot "satisfy the law of God."[95]

But the question remains—to use Melanchthon's own words— "What and how much can the will of man do?"[96] Melanchthon confessed that "human nature is oppressed by sin," that men "do not have the freedom of overcoming this depravity which is born within us," and that the "freedom of the will is diminished." "For the will cannot cast out the depravity which is born in us, nor can it satisfy the law of God. . . . Thus this will is captive and not free to remove death and the depravity of human nature."[97] Melanchthon also affirmed the need for the Spirit: "The human will without the Holy Spirit cannot produce the spiritual desires which God demands."[98] So Pelagianism, he argued, is out of the question.

If one were to stop here, one might think Melanchthon remained a committed monergist. But it is what he said next that has raised suspicion among his interpreters. While affirming the necessity of the Spirit to deliver man from his corruption, Melanchthon did not rule out the activity of the will altogether, as if man were absolutely passive. Some activity remains in the will's power, even if it be small and accompanied by the Spirit.

Melanchthon's view, however, is nuanced. At first he appeared to affirm monergism: "We must know that the Holy Spirit is efficacious through the voice of the Gospel as it is heard and meditated on as

94. Ibid.
95. Ibid.
96. Ibid.
97. Ibid., 42.
98. Ibid.

Gal. 3:2 ff. says." Yet Melanchthon then qualified that when the Spirit comes and we are guided by the Word, there remain three causes: the Word, the Spirit, "and the human will which assents to and does not contend against the Word of God."[99] In other words, the Spirit and Word are at work, but the will of man must choose not to resist and instead to cooperate: "For the will could disregard the Word of God, as Saul did of his own free will. But when the mind, hearing and sustaining itself, does not resist or indulge in hesitation, but with the aid of the Holy Spirit tries to assent, in this contest the will is not idle."[100] In short, man is not passive but active, even if it be an activeness that is accompanied by the Spirit. Man's will must assent and refrain from resisting. Kolb keenly observes that here the "mention of the Holy Spirit is not clear enough to assure that the will's activity is actually determined by the Spirit's re-creative action." Consequently, some "students believed that their preceptor was presuming a commitment of the will *before*, and thus as a *cause* of, its regeneration by the Spirit."[101] Kolb's observation is important. While Melanchthon's three causes of good action (Word, Spirit, and human will) could possibly be interpreted as still giving the will a passive role (at least if Aristotle's categories of causation are applied), so many "other phrases in Melanchthon's writings" (like the one above about the will not being idle) give the will an "active, contributory role" as the "material cause in conversion."[102]

Such an emphasis by Melanchthon became all the more apparent when he then described how God's grace works in connection to the will of man. Melanchthon identified both a "preceding grace" and an "assenting will": "God has previously turned us, calls, warns, and helps us; but we should see to it that we do not resist Him. For it is manifest that sin arises out of us and not by the will of God. Chrysostom says, 'He who draws, draws the willing.'" And then came Melanchthon's key phrase: "But since the struggle is great and difficult, the will is not idle but assents weakly."[103]

---

99. Ibid., 43.
100. Ibid.
101. Kolb, *Bound Choice*, 94, italics added.
102. Ibid., 93.
103. Melanchthon, *Loci Communes 1543*, 43. It is hard, very hard, to tell when Melanchthon is talking about the unregenerate and when he is referring to the regenerate. While this discussion, quoted above, begins by describing conversion, one wonders at what point is he talking about

Melanchthon's preservation of free will became even more evident in how he answered the following question: "How can I hope to be received into grace, since I do not feel that new light or new virtues have been transfused into me? Besides, if free choice has nothing to do until I feel that this new birth of which you are speaking has taken place, I will continue in my rebellion and other wicked activities." In response, Melanchthon denied that we can do nothing until the new birth occurs. Instead, he argued that "free choice does do something."[104] Melanchthon's emphasis on the will's active role could not be stronger than when he concluded,

> Know that God wills that in this very manner we are to be converted, when we pray and contend against our rebelliousness and other sinful activities. Therefore, some of the ancients put it this way: The free choice in man is the ability to apply oneself toward grace, that is, our free choice hears the promise, tries to assent to it and rejects the sins which are contrary to conscience.[105]

The Formula of Concord (1577)

In the last years of his life, Melanchthon persisted in his effort to separate himself from Luther's doctrine of absolute necessity, as well as Calvin's affirmation of double predestination.[106] "There is contingency," Melanchthon stated without reservation, "and the source of contingency in our actions is the freedom of the will."[107]

However, his stance was met by opposition. Melanchthon insisted that "grace precedes" (thereby separating himself from Pelagianism and semi-Pelagianism) but that nonetheless "the will goes along with it, and God draws, but he draws the person whose will is functioning."[108] The will, in other words, is active and cooperative in the regenerative process.

---

sanctification. Since the preceding discussion concerns the "natural man," it appears that he is still talking about conversion.

104. Ibid.

105. Ibid., 44. Melanchthon often used the word "effectual" or "efficacious." However, this term did not take on the same connotation as when Luther or Calvin used such language. Instead, Melanchthon approved the efficacy of the Spirit as long as it corresponded to the assenting, nonresisting will of man. It is, therefore, a conditional efficacy.

106. On this point, see Kolb, *Bound Choice*, 99.

107. Philipp Melanchthon, *Melanchthons Werke in Auswahl* [*Studien-Ausgabe*], ed. Robert Stupperich (Gütersloh: Bertelsmann, 1955), 6:312–13.

108. *CR* 9:769. See Kolb, *Bound Choice*, 113.

Some of Melanchthon's students "could not eradicate their fears that his description of the action of the human will compromised his insistence on the exclusivity of God's grace and his gift of faith."[109] In contrast, they argued that the sinner's will is totally passive, awaiting the new birth from the Spirit who brings about the will's new inclinations. The image of new birth pictures such passivity, for as the parent births the infant, so the Spirit births the unregenerate through the power of the Word.[110]

Nevertheless, the monergism-synergism debate continued in the 1560s and 1570s with Lutherans on both sides.[111] Kolb pinpoints the hinge of the entire division between the two camps:

> In the heat of the battle . . . the Philippists remained convinced that the Gnesio-Lutherans were Stoic and Manichaean in their insistence that the human will actively opposes God until the Holy Spirit overcomes that opposition, and the Gnesio-Lutherans could not lay aside their suspicions that the Philippist insistence on human integrity led to expressions that placed a controlling role in coming to faith into the powers of the will to make some move, be it ever so tiny, in God's direction.[112]

How did the Formula of Concord fit into this heated debate? "The Formula of Concord," says Kolb, "produced a settlement that pleased most Gnesio-Lutherans, apart from Flacius's most devoted disciples, and also a majority of the Philippists."[113] Yet, at the same time, the Formula of Concord explicitly sided with Luther's stance on free will as articulated in *The Bondage of the Will*.

Consider, for example, the Formula's first two articles. Article 1 affirms that original sin is "not a slight corruption" but is "so deep that there is nothing sound or uncorrupted left in the human body or soul, in its internal or external powers."[114] Among its many denials,

---

109. "Likewise, their preceptor could not listen carefully enough to them to respond to their concerns, instead caricaturing their position so that he could dismiss it without engaging it." They believed Melanchthon to be in direct conflict with Luther's arguments against Erasmus, as well as Melanchthon's own Augsburg Confession and Apology. Kolb, *Bound Choice*, 113 (cf. 116). For an extensive treatment of the debate among those who came after Melanchthon, see 118–34, 135–69.
110. Kolb, *Bound Choice*, 117.
111. The best overview of this debate is ibid., 103–243.
112. Ibid., 287–88.
113. Ibid., 288.
114. "The Epitome of the Formula of Concord," art. 1, aff. thesis 3, in Kolb and Wengert, *Book of Concord*, 488.

the Formula rejects Pelagianism, which alleges that "even after the fall human nature has remained uncorrupted and especially in spiritual matters remains completely good and pure in its *naturalia*, that is, in its natural powers."[115] It also denies any view that would say original sin is only "a slight, insignificant smudge that has been smeared on top of the human nature, a superficial stain, underneath which human nature retains its good powers, even in spiritual matters."[116] It also rejects the teaching that original sin is "only an external obstacle for these good spiritual powers, and not a loss or lack of them."[117] Such statements rule out not only semi-Pelagianism but any view that would say that human nature and its essence are not "completely corrupted but that people still have something good about them, even in spiritual matters, such as the capability, aptitude, ability, or capacity to initiate or effect something in spiritual matters or to cooperate in such actions."[118] Such an exhaustive and detailed denial appears to remove any space for synergism, even in the slightest.

Article 2 on "Free Will" is even more important for our discussion. Given the devastating picture of man painted in the preceding article, article 2 naturally proceeds to ask this question: "What kind of powers do human beings have after the fall of our first parents, before rebirth, on their own, in spiritual matters?" And again, "Are they able, with their own powers, before they receive new birth through God's Spirit, to dispose themselves favorably toward God's grace and to prepare themselves to accept the grace offered by the Holy Spirit in the Word and the holy sacraments?"[119]

The Formula is anything but abstruse in its answer. For example, it begins by affirming, without reservation, the total depravity and spiritual inability of man from texts like 1 Corinthians 2:14. "Human reason and understanding" are "blind in spiritual matters and understand nothing on the basis of their own powers."[120] And lest anyone think man is only injured but still capable of cooperation, the Formula precludes such a notion from the start. Appealing to Genesis 8:21

---

115. Ibid., art. 1, neg. thesis 3, in Kolb and Wengert, *Book of Concord*, 489.
116. Ibid., art. 1, neg. thesis 4, in Kolb and Wengert, *Book of Concord*, 489.
117. Ibid., art. 1, neg. thesis 5, in Kolb and Wengert, *Book of Concord*, 489.
118. Ibid., art. 1, neg. thesis 6, in Kolb and Wengert, *Book of Concord*, 489–90.
119. Ibid., art. 2, Status controversiae, in Kolb and Wengert, *Book of Concord*, 491.
120. Ibid., art. 2, aff. thesis 1, in Kolb and Wengert, *Book of Concord*, 491.

and Romans 8:7, it holds that the "unregenerated human will is not only turned away from God but has also become God's enemy," and "it has only the desire and will to do evil and whatever is opposed to God."[121] The Formula's monergistic language appears even in its negative description of man: "As little as a corpse can make itself alive for bodily, earthly life, so little can people who through sin are spiritually dead raise themselves up to a spiritual life" (Eph. 2:5; 2 Cor. 3:5).[122] Certainly man is passive, therefore, and not active prior to the Spirit's regenerating work.

In light of the will's bondage and spiritual death, the Spirit, through the Word (Ps. 95:8; Rom. 1:16), opens hearts (Acts 16:14) so that sinners can "listen to it and thus be converted, solely through the grace and power of the Holy Spirit, who alone accomplishes the conversion of the human being."[123] The Spirit, and the Spirit only, is at work on the spiritually dead.

> For apart from his grace our "willing and exerting" [Rom. 9:16], our planting, sowing, and watering, amount to nothing "if he does not give the growth" [1 Cor. 3:7]. As Christ says, "Apart from me, you can do nothing" [John 15:5]. With these brief words he denies the free will its powers and ascribes everything to God's grace, so that no one has grounds for boasting before God (1 Cor. [9:16]).[124]

The Formula leaves no room at all to free will. Everything is ascribed to God's grace (*sola gratia*).

The Formula also counters synergism in its "Negative Theses." Not only does it name Pelagianism and semi-Pelagianism, but it also rejects any other type of lesser synergism that would aim to ascribe something, even the smallest cooperation, to man prior to regeneration. In other words, in the statement that follows, the Formula denies even *God-initiated* or *God-enabled* synergism, rejecting the teaching that

> although human beings are too weak to initiate conversion with their free will before rebirth, and thus convert themselves to God on

---

121. Ibid., art. 2, aff. thesis 2, in Kolb and Wengert, *Book of Concord*, 492.
122. Ibid., art. 2, aff. theses 1–2, in Kolb and Wengert, *Book of Concord*, 492.
123. Ibid., art. 2, aff. thesis 2, in Kolb and Wengert, *Book of Concord*, 492.
124. Ibid., art. 2, aff. theses 2–3, in Kolb and Wengert, *Book of Concord*, 492.

the basis of their own natural powers and be obedient to God's law with their whole hearts, nonetheless, once the Holy Spirit has made a beginning through the preaching of the Word and in it has offered his grace, *the human will is able out of his own natural powers to a certain degree, even though small and feeble, to do something, to help and cooperate, to dispose and prepare itself for grace, to grasp this grace, to accept it, and to believe the gospel.*[125]

The Formula also goes on to reject the quotation from Chrysostom that Melanchthon used in support of his view, "God draws, but he draws those who are willing" (*Deus trahit, sed volentem trahit*), as well as Melanchthon's own assertion that "the human will is not idle in conversion but also is doing something" (*hominis voluntas in conversion non est otiose, sed agit aliquid*).[126] These statements, the Formula argues, give something back to man's free will (even if it is slight) and run counter to God's grace.[127]

The Formula concludes its statement on free will by clarifying Luther's (sometimes misunderstood) statement that the will is purely passive, believing itself to be on the Reformer's side:

> When Dr. Luther wrote that the human will conducts itself *pure passive* (that is, that it does absolutely nothing at all), that must be understood *respectu divinae gratiae in accendendis novis motibus* ["Purely passively," and "in respect to divine grace in the creation of new movements"], that is, insofar as God's Spirit takes hold of the human will through the Word that is heard or through the use of the holy sacraments and effects new birth and conversion. For when the Holy Spirit has effected and accomplished new birth and conversion and has altered and renewed the human will solely through his divine power and activity, *then* the new human will is an instrument and tool

---

125. Ibid., art. 2, neg. thesis 4, in Kolb and Wengert, *Book of Concord*, 493, italics added.

126. Ibid., art. 2, neg. thesis 8, in Kolb and Wengert, *Book of Concord*, 493.

127. Does this mean, then, that the Formula sees no place for the will of man? Not at all. Rather, the issue is whether man's will is understood correctly. While man is passive prior to the new birth, in regeneration and conversion the Spirit causes the spiritually dead sinner to come alive. It is "correct to say that in conversion God changes recalcitrant, unwilling people into willing people through the drawing power of the Holy Spirit." Ibid., art. 2, neg. thesis 8, in Kolb and Wengert, *Book of Concord*, 494. Therefore, after the new birth the will, which was previously obstinate and enslaved, is free—free, that is, to follow Christ. In fact, the Formula goes on to explain that after conversion, in sanctification (the process of being conformed into the image of Christ), there is a cooperation between the regenerate believer and the Spirit toward further holiness and godliness by means of repentance.

of God the Holy Spirit, in that the will not only accepts grace but also cooperates with the Holy Spirit in the works that proceed from it.[128]

"Purely passively," "does absolutely nothing"—these are key phrases demonstrating that monergism is affirmed in this appeal to the Formula's patriarch. And yet, the Formula labors to show that by "purely passively" Luther did not intend to exclude the Spirit's work to change the will through the instrumentality of the Word. In other words, the Formula aims to avoid the fatalistic notion that God moves mechanically, as if on a mere rock or block of wood. Instead, it argues, he moves in such a way as to create faith and a personal relationship with the sinner.[129] Hence, the Formula can conclude that the sinner is left with a renewed will, and, it won't let us forget, that this work of renewal is the work of the Spirit alone.

But perhaps the statement that capitalizes on the monergistic emphasis the most can be seen in the concluding paragraph. While Melanchthon affirmed three causes of new birth and conversion (the Word, the Spirit, and the free will of man), the Formula only recognized two "efficient causes": the Holy Spirit and God's Word.[130] Free will is completely missing from the equation.

John Calvin's *The Bondage and Liberation of the Will*
JOHN CALVIN'S REACTION TO MELANCHTHON

How did Reformers (even second-generation Reformers), particularly those outside the Lutheran fold, handle Melanchthon's position? In the Reformed tradition, John Calvin's view of Melanchthon is telling.

Between 1538 and 1558, Calvin engaged Melanchthon in correspondence, and much of the time it was cordial. In the late 1530s, however, Calvin noticed Melanchthon's silence on predestination and free will, which Calvin pointed out, though graciously, in his 1539 *Commentary on Romans*.[131] However, after the publication of Melanchthon's 1543

---

128. Ibid., art. 2, neg. thesis 9, in Kolb and Wengert, *Book of Concord*, 494. Note how this mention of cooperation with the Spirit is in reference to the good works that follow new birth and conversion, not precede them.

129. I owe this insight to Robert Kolb in a personal correspondence.

130. "Epitome of the Formula," art. 2, neg. thesis 9, in Kolb and Wengert, *Book of Concord*, 494.

131. John Calvin, *Calvin's Commentaries*, vol. 19, *Commentaries on the Epistle of Paul the Apostle to the Romans*, ed. and trans. John Owen (Grand Rapids, MI: Baker, 1979), xxv, xxvi.

Loci Communes, where Melanchthon's shift away from Luther is readily apparent, it was impossible for Calvin to say nothing at all. Indeed, the timing was impeccable. As we will discuss shortly, Albert Pighius had written a book defending free will while simultaneously refuting Calvin's views. Pighius had it in for Calvin, but he also censured Melanchthon for his departure from Luther and Calvin. Wittingly, Calvin dedicated his book responding to Pighius to Melanchthon! Graybill observes how Calvin "was taking a subtle dig at Melanchthon over his newly changed formulations,"[132] though it may also be the case that Calvin was attempting to bring Melanchthon into public support of his position.

In the later correspondence between the two, it became plain that Melanchthon did not agree with Calvin's distinction between a general gospel call and a special effectual call. For Melanchthon, only the former was viable. This meant, then, that ultimately the Spirit's work was dependent on man's free-will decision. It is hard to improve on Graybill's summary of Melanchthon's view contra Calvin:

> All people, when they heard the Word of God (which was *always* illuminated by the Holy Spirit) had, at that moment, the free choice of whether or not to have faith in Christ. Predestination was not involved at all. The effectiveness of the Spirit's call was contingent upon the free response of the individual human will.[133]

Perhaps we should nuance such an assertion by recognizing that Melanchthon did believe it was the Holy Spirit who moved the human will to make such a response. Nevertheless, the success of the Spirit's call appeared to be contingent on the will—even if it was a Spirit-enabled will—and this was enough to cause consternation for Calvin, as well as for Melanchthon's Lutheran monergist colleagues.

While Calvin did not enter into open debate with Melanchthon like he did with Pighius, nevertheless, Calvin did hint at his disapproval occasionally. For example, in 1546 Calvin wrote the preface to the French edition of Melanchthon's *Loci Communes*. There Calvin noted how Melanchthon had shifted his position on free will. Even so, the

---

132. Graybill, *Evangelical Free Will*, 247.
133. Ibid., 249.

two avoided public debate since neither one of them desired to create an unnecessary barrier to further reformation.[134]

Melanchthon died in 1560. Still, even after his death his view continued to invite critique. While Calvin had been cordial in the past, at this point Calvin condemned Melanchthon's views from the pulpit, using very strong language to demonstrate how disturbed he was that Melanchthon would associate a Christian predestinarianism/determinism with Stoicism.[135] For Calvin, Melanchthon had misrepresented and compromised the biblical view Calvin himself had defended in his writings against Pighius.

THE PIGHIUS AND CALVIN DEBATE (1542–1543)

How did the Pighius-Calvin debate first lift off?[136] In 1536, the first edition of Calvin's *Institutes of the Christian Religion* hit the press. In 1539, a second edition appeared but this time three times as long. This is relevant because of two new chapters, "The Knowledge of Humanity and Free Choice" (chap. 2) and "The Predestination and Providence of God" (chap. 8). Naturally, this edition caught the attention of the Roman Catholic bishop of Aquila, Bernardus Cincius. He then passed it along to Cardinal Marcello Cervini, who shared Cincius's disgust, even agreeing that it was more dangerous than the works the Lutherans had produced. In their outrage, the two approached Albert Pighius (1490–1542), a Dutch Roman Catholic theologian, who promptly penned *Ten Books on Human Free Choice and Divine Grace* (1542).

Calvin felt that the need to respond was urgent. However, since he wanted his reply to be ready in time for the 1543 Frankfurt book fair, Calvin could only respond to Pighius's first six books on free will. His treatise was titled *Defence of the Sound and Orthodox Doctrine of the*

134. Wengert, "Epistolary Friendship of John Calvin and Philip Melanchthon," 32; Graybill, *Evangelical Free Will*, 249.

135. John Calvin, *Traité de la predestination éternelle de Dieu, par laquelle les uns sont éleuz à salut, les autres laissez en leur condemnation* (Geneva, 1560); Calvin, "An Answer to certain slanders and blasphemies, wherewith certain evil disposed persons have gone about to bring the doctrine of God's everlasting Predestination into hatred," in *Sermons on Election and Reprobation*, ed. Ernie Springer, trans. John Field (Audubon, NJ: Old Paths, 1996), 305–17.

136. The background that follows can be found in more depth in Lane's "Introduction," to which I am indebted: A. N. S. Lane, "Introduction," in John Calvin, *The Bondage and Liberation of the Will: A Defence of the Orthodox Doctrine of Human Choice against Pighius*, ed. A. N. S. Lane, trans. G. I. Davies, Texts and Studies in Reformation and Post-Reformation Thought (Grand Rapids, MI: Baker, 1996), xii–xxxiv.

Bondage and Liberation of Human Choice against the Misrepresentations of Albert Pighius of Kampen. Calvin's reply to Pighius's other four books on providence and predestination would have been released at the book fair the following year, but Pighius died and the impetus for Calvin to respond evaporated.

Everything changed when controversy erupted once again, this time with Jerome Bolsec in Geneva in 1551. Bolsec's attacks against Calvin's doctrine of predestination were met by Calvin's *Eternal Predestination of God* (1552). In this reply Calvin not only responded to Bolsec but also took the opportunity to follow up on his unfinished critique of Pighius. By 1559, Calvin had completed what would be his final edition of the *Institutes*, in which he again articulated his understanding of grace and free will but this time with all the experience of his debates with Pighius.

While the Erasmus-Luther debate is very different in many ways from the Pighius-Calvin match, nevertheless, there are similarities when one considers Pighius's aversion to divine control and his defense of free will in conversion.[137] Since our purpose here is to concentrate on the bondage and liberation of the will, we will limit ourselves to Calvin's 1543 response to Pighius and his 1559 *Institutes*.

PERVASIVE DEPRAVITY AND THE BONDAGE OF THE WILL[138]

Calvin began with the first sin of Adam and, like Paul in Romans 5, drew the connection from Adam to all humanity. When Adam sinned, he "entangled and immersed his offspring in the same miseries."[139] Calvin defined original sin as "a hereditary depravity and corruption of our nature, diffused into all parts of the soul, which first makes us liable to God's wrath, then also brings forth in us those works which

---

137. For a review of the comparisons and contrasts, see ibid., xxvii–xxix.

138. This and the following two sections on Calvin are adapted from the "John Calvin: Theologian of Sovereign Grace" section in "Monergism in the Calvinist Tradition," chap. 2 of Matthew Barrett, *Reclaiming Monergism: The Case for Sovereign Grace in Effectual Calling and Regeneration* (Phillipsburg, NJ: P&R, 2013). Used by permission of P&R Publishing.

139. Calvin, *Institutes*, 2.1.1. In 2.1.6, Calvin further explained his understanding of Romans 5, as well as his rejection of Pelagianism, which Calvin accused Pighius of adopting, calling Pighius a spiritual child of Pelagius. On the Pelagian tendencies of Pighius, see L. F. Schulze, "Calvin's Reply to Pighius—A Micro and a Macro View," in *Calvin's Opponents*, vol. 5 of *Articles on Calvin and Calvinism*, ed. Richard C. Gamble (New York: Garland, 1992), 179.

Scripture calls 'works of the flesh.'"[140] According to Calvin, the result of descending from Adam's "impure seed" and being "born infected with the contagion of sin" is the pervasive corruption of man's nature.[141] Calvin explained,

> Here I only want to suggest briefly that the whole man is overwhelmed—as by a deluge—from head to foot, so that no part is immune from sin and all that proceeds from him is to be imputed to sin. As Paul says, all turnings of the thoughts to the flesh are enmities against God [Rom. 8:7], and are therefore death [Rom. 8:6].[142]

Calvin concluded,

> Therefore if it is right to declare that man, because of his vitiated nature, is naturally abominable to God, it is also proper to say that man is naturally depraved and faulty. Hence Augustine, in view of man's corrupted nature, is not afraid to call "natural" those sins which necessarily reign in our flesh wherever God's grace is absent.[143]

Elsewhere Calvin stated, "So depraved is [man's] nature that he can be moved or impelled only to evil."[144] If man has been corrupted as by a deluge, and if sin permeates every recess so that "no part is immune from sin," then it follows that man's will is in bondage to sin. Calvin, against Pighius, wrote, "For the will is so overwhelmed by wickedness

---

140. Calvin, *Institutes*, 2.1.8. "Thus Calvin holds to original sin in the sense of both original guilt (newborn babies are not innocent before God) and original depravity." Anthony N. S. Lane, "Anthropology," in *The Calvin Handbook*, ed. Herman J. Selderhuis (Grand Rapids, MI: Eerdmans, 2008), 278.
141. Calvin, *Institutes*, 2.1.6. Cf. Eberhard Busch, "God and Humanity," in Selderhuis, *The Calvin Handbook*, 231.
142. Calvin, *Institutes*, 2.1.9 (cf. 2.3). Lane states, "The whole of human nature is corrupted—not just the sensual part but also the mind and will." Lane, "Anthropology," 278. See also Suzanne Selinger, *Calvin against Himself: An Inquiry in Intellectual History* (Hamden, CT: Archon Books, 1984), 42; Lanier Burns, "From Ordered Soul to Corrupted Nature: Calvin's View of Sin," in *John Calvin and Evangelical Theology*, ed. Sung Wook Chung (Louisville: Westminster John Knox, 2009), 90–91, 97–101.
143. Calvin, *Institutes*, 2.2.12. See also T. H. L. Parker, *Calvin: An Introduction to His Thought* (Louisville: Westminster John Knox, 1995), 51–52.
144. John Calvin, *Institutes of the Christian Religion* (1539), 2.3.5, CR 29. Lane comments, "Our nature is depraved, and it is futile to seek any good in it." Lane, "Anthropology," 278–79. See also Williston Walker, *John Calvin: The Organiser of Reformed Protestantism, 1509–1564* (New York: Schocken Books, 1969), 412.

and so pervaded by vice and corruption that it cannot in any way escape to honourable exertion or devote itself to righteousness."[145]

Calvin rejected the medieval philosophers in what is today termed libertarian freedom, or the power of contrary choice:

> They say: If to do this or that depends upon our choice, so also does not to do it. Again, if not to do it, so also to do it. Now we seem to do what we do, and to shun what we shun, by free choice. Therefore, if we do any good thing when we please, we can also not do it; if we do any evil, we can also shun it.[146]

However, the philosophers were not alone, for some of the early church fathers were even unclear in their understanding of free will, Calvin held.[147] For example, Chrysostom said,

> Since God has placed good and evil in our power, he has granted free decision of choice, and does not restrain the unwilling, but embraces the willing. Again: He who is evil, if he should wish, is often changed into a good man; and he who is good falls through sloth and becomes evil. For the Lord has made our nature free to choose.[148]

Jerome seemed to agree: "Ours is to begin, God's to fulfill; ours to offer what we can, his to supply what we cannot."[149] Nevertheless, Calvin opposed this thinking, siding instead with Augustine, who did not hesitate to title the will "unfree."[150] As Augustine argued, without the Spirit the will is not free but shackled and conquered by its desires.[151] Calvin elaborated,

---

145. Calvin, *Bondage*, 77. See also Wilhelm Niesel, *The Theology of Calvin*, trans. Harold Knight (Philadelphia: Westminster, 1956), 82; Arthur Dakin, *Calvinism* (Philadelphia: Westminster, 1946), 33–40.
146. Calvin, *Institutes*, 2.2.3.
147. Ibid., 2.2.4.
148. As quoted in ibid.
149. As quoted in ibid.
150. Calvin did observe how Augustine at one point reacted against those who say the will is "unfree" but explained that it was only because they sought to deny the decision of the will "as to wish to excuse sin." Ibid., 2.2.7.
151. Pighius would have, of course, rejected such a claim by arguing that "ought" implies "can" or "ability." In other words, God commands that his law be obeyed ("ought"); therefore, man must be able to obey it ("can")—otherwise, such a command is disingenuous. How did Calvin respond? For Calvin, "ought" did not necessitate "ability," and at the same time, God remains just to require the law. Calvin explained why this is the case: "For we ought not to measure by our own ability the duty to which we are bound nor to investigate man's capabilities with this

Likewise, when the will was conquered by the vice into which it had fallen, human nature began to lose its freedom. Again, man, using free will badly, has lost both himself and his will. Again, the free will has been so enslaved that it can have no power for righteousness. Again, what God's grace has not freed will not be free. Again, the justice of God is not fulfilled when the law so commands, and man acts as if by his own strength; but when the Spirit helps, and man's will, not free, but freed by God, obeys. And he gives a brief account of all these matters when he writes elsewhere: man, when he was created, received great powers of free will, but lost them by sinning.[152]

This does not mean, however, that man is coerced. Rather, man sins willingly—out of *necessity*, yes, but not out of *compulsion*.[153] Such a distinction was one of Calvin's chief points in his treatise against Pighius, who argued that *necessitas* ("necessity") implies *coactio* ("coercion"). However, as Paul Helm explains, for Calvin, "it does not follow from the denial of free will that what a person chooses is the result of coercion."[154] For Calvin, coercion negates responsibility, but *necessity* is "consistent with being held responsible for the action, and being praised or blamed for it."[155] Therefore, Calvin could state that

unaided power of reasoning. Rather we should maintain the following doctrine. First, even if we cannot fulfill or even begin to fulfill the righteousness of the law, yet it is rightly required of us, and we are not excused by our weakness or the failure of our strength. For as the fault for this is ours, so the blame must be imputed to us. Secondly, the function of the law is different from what people commonly suppose it to be. For it cannot make [sinners] good but can only convict them of guilt, first by removing the excuse of ignorance and then by disproving their mistaken opinion that they are righteous and their empty claims about their own strength. Thus it comes about that no excuse is left for the ungodly to prevent them from being convicted by their own conscience and, whether they like it or not, becoming aware of their guilt. . . . Therefore in issuing commands and exhortations God does not take account of our strength, since he gives that very thing which he demands and gives it for the reason that by ourselves we are helpless." Calvin, *Bondage*, 41–42 (cf. 141–42).

152. Calvin, *Institutes*, 2.2.7. With Augustine, Calvin appealed to 2 Cor. 3:17, where Paul says, "Where the Spirit of the Lord is, there is freedom." Such a passage implies that where the Spirit of the Lord is not to be found (i.e., depraved man), there is no freedom. Likewise, Jesus states in John 15:5 that "apart from me you can do nothing."

153. Ibid. Calvin's understanding of necessity is not the same as the Stoic understanding of necessity. See Charles Partee, "Calvin and Determinism," in *An Elaboration of the Theology of Calvin*, vol. 8 of Gamble, *Articles on Calvin and Calvinism*, 351–68.

154. Paul Helm, *John Calvin's Ideas* (New York: Oxford University Press, 2004), 162. See also Niesel, *Theology of Calvin*, 87.

155. Calvin, *Bondage*, 150. See also John H. Gerstner, "Augustine, Luther, Calvin, and Edwards on the Bondage of the Will," in *The Grace of God, the Bondage of the Will*, vol. 2, *Historical and Theological Perspectives on Calvinism*, ed. Thomas R. Schreiner and Bruce A. Ware (Grand Rapids, MI: Baker, 1995), 287.

man "acts wickedly by will, not by compulsion" (*male voluntate agit, non coactione*).[156]

What then is one to think of the term *free will* (*liberum arbitrium*)? Calvin, like Luther before him, would rather have done away with the term.[157] What is the purpose served by labeling such a "slight thing" with such a "proud name"? Calvin quipped, "A noble freedom, indeed—for man not to be forced to serve sin, yet to be such a willing slave [*ethelodoulos*] that his will is bound by the fetters of sin!"[158] Moreover, the term is given to misunderstanding for sinful men are prone to hear the term *free will* and think that they are their own master, having the power to turn themselves to good or evil.[159] Therefore, we are better to avoid the term. However, this does not mean that Calvin did not believe in "free will."[160] If by freedom one means, as Lombard, the Papists, and Pighius argued, that man's will in no way is determined but that man has the self-power to will good or evil toward God, so that by his own strength he can will either equally, then Calvin rejected free will. But if by free will one means, as Augustine maintained, that man wills out of *voluntary necessity* (not coercion), then willful choice can be affirmed.[161] Nevertheless, even if man wills out of necessity, such necessity is, prior to the application of effectual grace, only a necessity to sin: "For we do not say that man is dragged unwillingly into sinning, but that because his will is corrupt he is held captive under the yoke of sin and therefore of necessity wills in an evil way. For where there is bondage, there is necessity."[162] Therefore, the bondage of the will to sin remains, and yet, such slavery is voluntary and willful captivity (*voluntariae suae electioni*). As Calvin made evi-

---

156. Calvin, *Institutes*, 2.2.7; cf. 3.5. "We cannot free ourselves from our will's wrong direction. We are freed from it only through God's goodness. But this goodness liberates." Busch, "God and Humanity," 232.

157. Hugh T. Kerr, ed., *A Compend of Luther's Theology* (Philadelphia: Westminster, 1943), 88, 91.

158. Calvin, *Institutes*, 2.2.7.

159. Ibid. Calvin reaffirmed this view in *Bondage*, 68.

160. "As my *Institutes* bear witness, I have always said that I have no objection to human choice being called free, provided that a sound definition of the word is agreed between us." Calvin, *Bondage*, 311. See also Calvin, *Institutes*, 2.2.7–8.

161. Calvin, *Institutes*, 2.3.5. See also Niesel, *Theology of Calvin*, 87; John H. Leith, *John Calvin's Doctrine of the Christian Life* (Louisville: Westminster John Knox, 1989), 141–42. For a defense of Calvin as a compatibilist, see Helm, *John Calvin's Ideas*, 157–83.

162. Calvin, *Bondage*, 69. And again, "The will bereft of freedom is of necessity either drawn or led into evil." *Institutes* (1539), 2.3.5, CR 29. "Introduction," in Calvin, *Bondage*, xix–xx.

dent in his 1538 Catechism, which contains one of his clearest and most precise definitions of *free will*, man does not sin out of a "violent necessity" (*violenta necessitate*) but transgresses "out of a will utterly prone to sin" (the "necessity of sinning"):

> That man is enslaved to sin the Scriptures repeatedly testify. This means that his nature is so estranged from God's righteousness that he conceives, desires, and strives after nothing that is not impious, distorted, evil, or impure. For a heart deeply steeped in sin's poison can bring forth nothing but the fruits of sin. Yet we are not to suppose for that reason that man has been driven by violent necessity to sin. He transgresses out of a will utterly prone to sin. But because on account of the corruption of his feelings he utterly loathes all God's righteousness and is inflamed to every sort of wickedness, it is denied that he is endowed with the free capacity to choose good and evil which men call "free will."[163]

To clarify this point, Calvin distinguished between necessity and compulsion (or coercion):

> The chief point of this distinction, then, must be that man, as he was corrupted by the Fall, sinned willingly, not unwillingly or by compulsion; by the most eager inclination of his heart, not by forced compulsion; by the prompting of his own lust, not by compulsion from without. Yet so depraved is his nature that he can be moved or impelled only to evil. But if this is true, then it is clearly expressed that man is surely subject to the necessity of sinning.[164]

Calvin illustrated how an agent can be both free and under necessity using the example of the Devil. The Devil can only do evil all the time, and yet he is fully culpable for his actions and commits them voluntarily, even if out of necessity. Therefore, sin is simultaneously necessary and voluntary.[165]

---

163. "Catechism 1538," trans. Ford Lewis Battles, in I. John Hesselink, *Calvin's First Catechism: A Commentary*, Columbia Series in Reformed Theology (Louisville: Westminster John Knox, 1997), 9–10 (cf. 69).

164. Calvin, *Institutes*, 2.3.5. Lane helpfully summarizes, "The necessity to sin means that sinners cannot other than sin, but this necessity is imposed by the corruption of the will and innate human wickedness. Sinners are not coerced or forced by any external impulse but sin voluntarily." Lane, "Anthropology," 279.

165. Calvin, *Institutes*, 2.3.5; Calvin, *Bondage*, 149–50.

Although Calvin affirmed the slavery of the will (or, as Calvin called it, the "depravity of the will"), he did not reduce men to "brute beasts." Rather, he acknowledged that since the will is inseparable from human nature, it "did not perish, but was so bound to wicked desires that it cannot strive after the right."[166] Likewise with the mind: while man still possesses human understanding, he remains enslaved by the perversity of his mind.[167] It should be noted that in the 1539 edition of the *Institutes*, Calvin's language was very strong, saying that the will is abolished. However, when Pighius in 1542 set Calvin over against Augustine by misunderstanding Calvin as saying that there is no substance to the will since it is abolished, Calvin responded in *Bondage* (1543) and *Institutes* (1559) by clarifying what he meant. What takes place in man's conversion is not a destruction of the *substance* or *faculty* of our will and mind, as Pighius thought Calvin was saying, but the destruction and removal of the *habit* or *qualities* of the will, which of course is evil.[168] Therefore, Calvin made the qualification that the nature is not so much destroyed as it is repaired and made new (*nova creari*), in the sense that the corrupt nature must be radically transformed.[169] The will is "changed from an evil to a good will."[170]

How total is man's depravity according to Calvin? As stated by Calvin above, since man still "possesses human understanding" and since man's nature did not perish, it must be concluded that for Calvin depravity was not total in *intensiveness* but total in *extensiveness*.[171] Michael Horton explains,

---

166. Calvin, *Institutes*, 2.2.12. Cf. Niesel, *Theology of Calvin*, 81.
167. Calvin, *Institutes*, 2.2.12. Cf. ibid., 2.2.19–21; 2.3.1–2. See also Anthony N. S. Lane, *A Reader's Guide to Calvin's Institutes* (Grand Rapids, MI: Baker, 2009), 67–68.
168. Calvin, *Institutes*, 2.3.5. "The faculty of will is permanent in humanity, but the evil will comes from the fall and the good will from regeneration. The will remains as created, the change taking place in its habit, not its substance." Lane, "Anthropology," 284. Likewise see Euan Cameron, *The European Reformation* (Oxford: Oxford University Press, 1991), 113.
169. See Calvin, *Institutes*, 2.3.6. Cf. Lane, "Anthropology," 283. Lane notes that in the "1539 *Institutio* Calvin came dangerously close to teaching the destruction of the will." However, "Pighius's challenge on this point, so vehemently rejected by Calvin, did cause him to qualify his teaching, first in DSO [*The Bondage and Liberation of the Will*] and later in the 1559 *Institutio*. The reason why he allows himself to be moved in this direction is that the debate concerned the teaching of Augustine, for whom he had such a high regard." See also Leith, *Calvin's Doctrine*, 141.
170. Calvin, *Institutes*, 2.3.6.
171. T. F. Torrance, *Calvin's Doctrine of Man* (London: Lutterworth, 1949), 83–84. However, it is precisely on this point that several scholars seem to misinterpret Calvin and set him over against later Calvinists, as if Calvin never would have affirmed total depravity and the need for irresistible

In other words, there is no foothold of goodness anywhere in us—in our mind, will, emotions, or body—where we could rise up to God. Sin has corrupted the whole person, like a poison that works its way in greater or lesser intensity throughout the entire stream. Yet, despite ourselves, this does not eliminate the possibility of reflecting God's glory. Humanity is therefore not as bad as it could possibly be, but as badly off as it could possibly be. There is no residue of obedient piety in us, but only a *sensus divinitatis* that we exploit for idolatry, self-justification, and superstition. Thus the same remnants of original righteousness that allow even pagans to create a reasonably equitable civic order in things earthly provoke them in their corruption to false religion in things heavenly.[172]

It is evident at this point in Calvin's thought that man, apart from the Spirit, can do nothing good toward God (i.e., spiritual inability).[173] Due to man's depravity, he is willfully a slave to sin. Consequently, no willful act toward God precedes the "grace of the Spirit."[174] Therefore, man's only hope is sovereign grace.

SPECIAL CALLING AND EFFECTUAL GRACE

Thus far it is clear that for Calvin, grace is needed for the liberation of man's will.[175] Such grace comes before man's will (i.e., it is prevenient) in order to liberate him effactually from bondage rather than merely coming beside man's will to assist him (which is semi-Pelagianism).[176] As Lane explains, "The corollary is that grace is prevenient—that God's grace precedes any human good will. But Calvin wishes to say more than this. *Prevenient grace does not simply make it possible for*

---

grace. For example, see Charles Partee, *The Theology of John Calvin* (Louisville: Westminster John Knox, 2008), 133.

172. Michael Horton, "A Shattered Vase: The Tragedy of Sin in Calvin's Thought," in *A Theological Guide to Calvin's Institutes*, ed. David W. Hall and Peter A. Lillback, Calvin 500 Series (Phillipsburg, NJ: P&R, 2008), 160–61. See also Torrance, *Calvin's Doctrine of Man*, 106; James Edward McGoldrick, "Calvin and Luther: Comrades in Christ," in *Tributes to John Calvin: A Celebration of His Quincentenary*, ed. David W. Hall, Calvin 500 Series (Phillipsburg, NJ: P&R, 2010), 179.

173. "The will, because it is inseparable from man's nature, did not perish, but was so bound to wicked desires that it cannot strive after right." Calvin, *Institutes*, 2.2.12. See Leith, *Calvin's Doctrine*, 141.

174. Calvin, *Institutes*, 2.2.27.

175. "Because of the bondage of sin by which the will is held bound, it cannot move toward good, much less apply itself thereto; for a movement of this sort is the beginning of conversion to God, which in Scripture is ascribed entirely to God's grace." Ibid., 2.3.5.

176. Lane, "Introduction," in Calvin, *Bondage*, xx.

people to respond. Grace is efficacious and effects conversion."[177] In other words, unlike semi-Augustinianism and the Arminianism that would come after Calvin in the seventeenth century, grace is not prevenient in the sense that it simply makes salvation a possibility if man decides to cooperate with it. Rather, the prevenient grace Calvin spoke of is effectual, so that the conversion of the elect necessarily follows. Lane, quoting Calvin, explains,

> Prevenient grace [for Calvin] is not merely sufficient, bringing to the human will "freedom of contrary choice." Calvin is aware of and rejects what would later be known as *the Arminian view*, that God "offers light to human minds, and it is in their power to choose to accept or to refuse it, and he moves their wills in such a way that it is in their power to follow his movement or not to follow it" (DSO [*Bondage*] 204). God does not merely offer us grace and leave it up to us whether to accept or resist it. Instead conversion is "entirely the work of grace," and *God does not merely give us the ability to will the good but also brings it about that we will it* (DSO [*Bondage*] 252f).[178]

Or, as Calvin argued in his treatise against Pighius, since the human will is only evil and needs transformation and renewal to will the good, God's grace is "not merely a tool which can help someone if he is pleased to stretch out his hand to [take] it." Calvin elaborated, "That is, [God] does not merely offer it, leaving [to man] the choice between receiving it and rejecting it, but he steers the mind to choose what is right, he moves the will also effectively to obedience, he arouses and advances the endeavour until the actual completion of the work is attained."[179] Quoting Augustine, he concluded, "The human will does not obtain grace through its freedom, but rather freedom through grace."[180]

The efficacious nature of grace also reveals the particularity of God's choice. Calvin argued that free will is "not sufficient to enable man to do good works, unless he be helped by grace, indeed by special

---

177. Ibid., italics added.
178. Lane, "Anthropology," 283. DSO stands for Calvin's *Defensio sanae et orthodoxae doctrinae de servitude et liberatione humani arbitrii adversus calumnias Alberti Pighii Campensis.*
179. Calvin, *Bondage*, 114.
180. Ibid., 114, 130.

grace, which only the elect receive through regeneration."[181] Calvin explained, "For I do not tarry over those fanatics who babble that grace is equally and indiscriminately distributed."[182] Against Pighius, he asserted,

> In addition this grace is not given to all without distinction or generally, but only to those whom God wills; the rest, to whom it is not given, remain evil and have absolutely no ability to attain to the good because they belong to the mass that is lost and condemned and they are left to their condemnation. In addition, this grace is not of such a kind as to bestow on [its recipients] the power to act well on condition that they will to, so that they thereafter have the option of willing or not willing. But it effectively moves them to will it; indeed it makes their evil will good, so that they of necessity will well.[183]

Therefore, Calvin would certainly have rejected what later Arminians meant in affirming a universal prevenient grace. Rather, God's special grace is discriminate, particular, and efficacious.

Calvin's detestation for synergism becomes especially apparent not only in his arguments against Pighius but also in his opposition to Peter Lombard ("The Master of the Sentences"), who utilized the medieval distinction between "operating" and "cooperating" grace. According to Lombard, operating grace ensures that we effectively will the good, while cooperating grace follows "the good will as a help."[184] Calvin was not amused. What displeased him was that while Lombard "attributes the effective desire for good to the grace of God, yet he hints that man by his very own nature somehow seeks after the good—though ineffectively."[185] In short, this is semi-Pelagianism at its best. Parker has worded Calvin's dissatisfaction as follows:

> This distinction Calvin mislikes. Although it ascribes the efficacy of any appetite for good to grace, it implies that man has a desire for

---

181. Calvin, *Institutes*, 2.2.6.
182. Ibid. Cf. ibid., 3.22.10.
183. Calvin, *Bondage*, 136.
184. Calvin, *Institutes*, 2.2.6. "Initially (operating) grace converts the will from evil to good. The converted will then desires the good and so works together with (cooperating) grace." Lane, "Anthropology," 286.
185. Calvin, *Institutes*, 2.2.6.

good of his own nature, even if this desire is ineffectual. Nor does he like the second part any better, with its suggestion that it lies within man's own power to render the first grace vain by rejecting it or to confirm it by obedience.[186]

Calvin's frustration only escalated when Lombard "pretended" to be following Augustine in such a distinction.[187] Instead, in Calvin's assessment, whenever Augustine said something clearly, Lombard obscured it. While it is true that Augustine made the distinction, the medieval spin of it differed considerably, enabling Lombard to interpret Augustine through a semi-Pelagian lens, a common move among medieval theologians. Calvin was adamant that Augustine would never have affirmed such cooperation or synergism.[188] Calvin protested, "The ambiguity in the second part offends me, for it has given rise to a perverted interpretation. They thought we co-operate with the assisting grace of God, because it is our right either to render it ineffectual by spurning the first grace, or to confirm it by obediently following it."[189] Therefore, Calvin rejected Lombard's view because (1) cooperating grace suggests that grace is not efficacious, (2) cooperation with grace results in human merit, and (3) cooperation with grace means that perseverance is a gift only given on the basis of how we choose to cooperate with it, all of which Pighius affirmed. As Lane explains, for Calvin the consequence was that this would "make us masters of our own destiny rather than God alone."[190] Calvin sought to interpret Augustine properly, arguing that cooperating grace does not refer to our ability to determine whether God's initial grace will be accepted or resisted but instead refers to man's will *subsequent to* and *after* he has been effectually called and awakened to new life, whereby he works with God in sanctification and final perseverance.[191]

---

186. Parker, *Calvin*, 53.
187. Calvin, *Institutes*, 2.2.6.
188. Parker, *Calvin*, 56. On Calvin's interpretation of Augustine and other church fathers, see Anthony N. S. Lane, *John Calvin: Student of the Church Fathers* (Edinburgh: T&T Clark, 1999).
189. Calvin, *Institutes*, 2.2.6.
190. Concerning the first reason, Lane states, "This was just how Pighius took it, maintaining that we already cooperate at the point of conversion and that God gives initial grace only to those who cooperate with it (DSO 275f.). Against this Calvin emphasizes prevenient efficacious grace which, in Augustine's words, 'works without us to cause us to will' (DSO 195)." Lane, "Anthropology," 286.
191. Calvin, *Institutes*, 2.3.11.

Contrary to Lombard's synergism, Calvin argued for the particularity and effectual nature of grace in his exegesis of Ezekiel 36, where God removes the heart of stone and implants a heart of flesh, causing the dead sinner to walk in new life:

> If in a stone there is such plasticity that, made softer by some means, it becomes somewhat bent, I will not deny that man's heart can be molded to obey the right, provided what is imperfect in him be supplied by God's grace. But if by this comparison the Lord wished to show that nothing good can ever be wrung from our heart, unless it become wholly other, *let us not divide between him and us what he claims for himself alone.* If, therefore, a stone is transformed into flesh when God converts us to zeal for the right, whatever is of *our will is effaced. What takes its place is wholly from God. I say that the will is effaced; not in so far as it is will, for in man's conversion what belongs to his primal nature remains entire. I also say that it is created anew; not meaning that the will now begins to exist, but that it is changed from an evil to a good will. I affirm that this is wholly God's doing, for according to the testimony of the same apostle, "we are not even capable of thinking"* [II Cor. 3:5].[192]

Referencing Paul's words in Ephesians 2, Calvin went on to say that in this "second creation," which we attain in Christ, God works alone. Salvation is a free gift; therefore, "if even the least ability came from ourselves, we would also have some share of the merit."[193] With Psalm 100:3 in mind Calvin remarked, "Moreover, we see how, not simply content to have given God due praise for our salvation, he expressly excludes us from all participation in it. It is as if he were saying that not a whit remains to man to glory in, for the whole of salvation comes from God."[194] If all of salvation comes from God, including the first moment of new life, then human cooperation with God's grace is unacceptable and unbiblical.

However, Calvin anticipated an objection: "But perhaps some will concede that the will is turned away from the good by its own nature and is converted by the Lord's power alone, yet in such a way that,

---

192. Ibid., 2.3.6, italics added.
193. Ibid.
194. Ibid.

having been prepared, it then has its own part in the action."[195] Such an objection comes from the semi-Augustinian view, which argues that while God initiates grace and prepares the will for subsequent acts of grace, ultimately man must do his part for such grace to be finally successful. Contrary to such a view, Calvin answered that the very activity of the will to exercise faith is a free gift from God,[196] eliminating any possible participation of man's will.[197] As formulated in his 1538 Catechism, "If we duly ponder both how much our minds are blinded to God's heavenly mysteries and with how much unfaith our hearts labor in all things, we will have no doubt that faith far surpasses all our natural powers and is an excellent gift of God."[198] Therefore, it follows that "when we, who are by nature inclined to evil with our whole heart, begin to will good, we do so out of mere grace."[199] After expositing Ezekiel 36:26 and Jeremiah 32:39–40, Calvin explained, "For it always follows that nothing good can arise out of our will until it has been reformed; and after its reformation, in so far as it is good, it is so from God, not from ourselves."[200] He concluded,

> He [God] does not move the will in such a manner as has been taught and believed for many ages—that it is afterward in our choice *either to obey or resist the motion*—*but by disposing it efficaciously*. Therefore one must deny that oft-repeated statement

---

195. Ibid., 2.3.7.

196. Victor A. Shepherd, *The Nature and Function of Faith in the Theology of John Calvin* (Macon, GA: Mercer University Press, 1983), 80–81; Timothy George, *Theology of the Reformers* (Nashville: B&H, 1988), 223–28. On the relation of faith to intellect for Calvin, see Richard A. Muller, "*Fides* and *Cognitio* in Relation to the Problem of Intellect and Will in the Theology of John Calvin," *CTJ* 25, no. 2 (1990): 207–24.

197. Calvin had much to say about exactly how the Spirit utilizes the Word to create faith in the heart of the elect. It is the Holy Spirit who takes the Word and makes it efficacious, producing faith as a free gift. Due to man's dullness and blindness, it is absolutely necessary for the Spirit to illuminate the mind and awaken the heart to new life. Calvin quoted numerous passages in his defense, including Luke 24:27, 45; John 6:44–45; 16:13; Rom. 11:34; 1 Cor. 2:10–16. Calvin, *Institutes*, 2.2.33–34. According to Calvin, not only faith but also repentance is a gift from God. Calvin supported such a claim with passages like Isa. 63:17; Acts 11:18; 2 Cor. 7:10; Eph. 2:10; 2 Tim. 2:25–26; Heb. 6:4–6. By Calvin arguing that both faith and repentance are gifts from God, he again reaffirmed monergism and exalted the sovereign will of God instead of man's willful choice. Ibid., 2.3.21.

198. Hesselink, *Calvin's First Catechism*, 18.

199. Calvin, *Institutes*, 2.3.8. The obvious implication for Calvin is that the Spirit must change our will so that sinful man can have faith. As Muller explains, "We cannot will the good, nor can we will to have faith. Both result only from the gracious activity of the Spirit that changes the will from evil to good." Richard Muller, *The Unaccommodated Calvin: Studies in the Foundation of a Theological Tradition*, Oxford Studies in Historical Theology (New York: Oxford University Press, 2000), 166–67.

200. Calvin, *Institutes*, 2.3.8–9.

of Chrysostom: "Whom he draws he draws willing." By this he signifies that the Lord is only extending his hand to await whether we will be pleased to receive his aid.[201]

Contrary to the synergism of Chrysostom, Calvin rejected the notion that God's grace is effective only if we accept it ("Whom he draws he draws willing"). Rather, God wills to work in his elect in such a way that his special grace is always effective: "This means nothing else than that the Lord by his Spirit directs, bends, and governs, our heart and reigns in it as in his own possession."[202] Quoting Augustine, Calvin explained that while we will, it is God who causes us to will the good. Unless God first creates within us a new heart, causing us to will the good, we will remain dead in sin. Calvin appealed not only to Ezekiel 11:19–20 and 36:27 but also to the Gospel of John:

> Now can Christ's saying ("Every one who has heard . . . from the Father comes to me" [John 6:45]) be understood in any other way than that *the grace of God is efficacious of itself*. This Augustine also maintains. The Lord does not indiscriminately deem everyone worthy of this grace, as that common saying of Ockham (unless I am mistaken) boasts: grace is denied to no one who does what is in him. Men indeed ought to be taught that God's loving-kindness is set forth to all who seek it, without exception. But since it is those on whom heavenly grace has breathed who at length begin to seek after it, they should not claim for themselves the slightest part of his praise. It is obviously the privilege of the elect that, regenerated through the Spirit of God, they are moved and governed by his leading. For this reason, Augustine justly derides those who claim for themselves any part of the act of willing, just as he reprehends others who think that what is the special testimony of free election is indiscriminately given to all. "Nature," he says, "is common to all, not grace." The view that what God bestows upon whomever he wills is generally extended to all, Augustine calls a brittle glass-like subtlety of wit, which glitters with mere vanity. Elsewhere he says: "How have you come? By believing. Fear lest while you are

---

201. Ibid., 2.3.10, italics added. Cf. Calvin, *Bondage*, 174.
202. Calvin, *Institutes*, 2.3.10. Cf. Lane, "Anthropology," 284. See also Christian Link, "Election and Predestination," in *John Calvin's Impact on Church and Society, 1509–2009*, ed. Martin Ernst Hirzel and Martin Sallmann (Grand Rapids, MI: Eerdmans, 2009), 116.

claiming for yourself that you have found the just way, you perish
from the just way. I have come, you say, of my own free choice; I
have come of my own will. Why are you puffed up? Do you wish to
know that this also has been given you? Hear Him calling, 'No one
comes to me unless my Father draws him'" [John 6:44].[203]

Calvin was emphatic: unless man is drawn efficaciously by the Spirit's
special call, he is hopeless, since his will is of no avail.

Calvin again used similar biblical language in the middle of his
exposition on predestination. He viewed the Spirit's special call as the
outflow of God's unconditional election:

> Therefore, God designates as his children those whom he has cho-
> sen, and appoints himself their Father. Further, *by calling*, he re-
> ceives them into his family and unites them to him so that they may
> together be one. But when the call is coupled with election, in this
> way Scripture sufficiently suggests that in it nothing but God's free
> mercy is to be sought. For if we ask whom he calls, and the reason
> why, he answers: whom he had chosen.[204]

Calvin elaborated on this "calling" in his exegesis of Matthew 22:14:

> The statement of Christ "Many are called but few are chosen"
> [Matt. 22:14] is, in this manner, very badly understood. Nothing
> will be ambiguous if we hold fast to what ought to be clear from
> the foregoing: that there are *two kinds of call*. There is the *general
> call*, by which God invites all equally to himself through the out-
> ward preaching of the word—even those to whom he holds it out
> as a savor of death [cf. II Cor. 2:16], and as the occasion for severer
> condemnation. *The other kind of call is special*, which he deigns
> for the most part to give to the believers alone, while by the inward
> illumination of his Spirit he causes the preached Word to dwell in
> their hearts.[205]

As Muller notes, not only the *Institutes* but also Calvin's commentaries on Amos and Isaiah bear this same distinction between the gen-

---

203. Calvin, *Institutes*, 2.3.10, italics added.
204. Ibid., 3.24.1, italics added. Calvin also drew the connection from election to calling in ibid., 3.24.2.
205. Ibid., 3.24.8, italics added.

eral and special call.[206] For example, commenting on Isaiah 54:13, Calvin observed how the apostle John quotes Isaiah to demonstrate the efficacy of God's call on the elect: "The Gospel is preached indiscriminately to the elect and the reprobate; but the elect alone come to Christ, because they have been 'taught by God,' and therefore to them the Prophet undoubtedly refers."[207] Commenting on the "efficacy of the Spirit," Calvin concluded, "Besides, we are taught by this passage that the calling of God is efficacious in the elect."[208] In his commentary on the Gospel of John, Calvin returned once again to the Spirit's efficacious call. Concerning John 6:44, Calvin first explained that though the gospel is preached to all, all do not embrace it, for a "new understanding and a new perception are requisite."[209] Calvin then described what it means for the Father to draw sinners to himself:

> To come to Christ being here used metaphorically for believing, the Evangelist, in order to carry out the metaphor in the apposite clause, says that those persons are drawn whose understandings God enlightens, and whose hearts he bends and forms to the obedience of Christ. The statements amount to this, that we ought not to wonder if many refuse to embrace the Gospel; because no man will ever of himself be able to come to Christ, but God must first approach him by his Spirit; and hence it follows that all are not drawn, but that God bestows this grace on those whom he has elected. True, indeed, as to the kind of drawing, it is not violent, so as to compel men by external force; but still it is a powerful impulse of the Holy Spirit, which makes men willing who formerly were unwilling and reluctant. It is a false and profane assertion, therefore, that none are drawn but those who are willing to be drawn,

---

206. Muller, *The Unaccommodated Calvin*, 151.

207. John Calvin, *Calvin's Commentaries*, vol. 8, *Commentary on the Book of the Prophet Isaiah, Chapters 33–66*, trans. and ed. William Pringle (Grand Rapids, MI: Baker, 2005), 146.

208. Ibid., 146–47. Cameron rightly comments that for Calvin, since "faith was given and inspired, rather than attained to, God, for inscrutable reasons, chose to give faith to some people and not to others." Cameron, *The European Reformation*, 119. The same point is made by Vermigli: "We in no wise saie, that grace is common unto all men, but is given unto some; and unto others, according to the pleasure of God, it is not given." Peter Martyr Vermigli, *The common places of the most famous and renowned diuine Doctor Peter Martyr*, trans. Anthonie Marten (London: Henry Denham and Henry Middleton, 1583), 31.38. Cf. David Neelands, "Predestination and the *Thirty-Nine Articles*," in *A Companion to Peter Martyr Vermigli*, ed. Torrance Kirby, Emidio Campi, and Frank A. James III, Brill's Companions to the Christian Tradition 16 (Leiden: Brill, 2009), 364.

209. John Calvin, *Calvin's Commentaries*, vol. 17, *Commentary on the Gospel according to John*, trans. and ed. William Pringle (Grand Rapids, MI: Baker, 2005), 257.

as if man made himself obedient to God by his own efforts; for the willingness with which men follow God is what they already have from himself, who has formed their hearts to obey him.[210]

Calvin went on to explain that such a drawing does not consist in a mere external voice but is the secret operation of the Holy Spirit, whereby God inwardly teaches through the illumination of the heart.[211] Calvin revealed his monergism when he concluded by saying that man is not fit for believing until he has been drawn and that such a drawing by the grace of Christ is "efficacious, so that they necessarily believe."[212]

SOLA GRATIA AND SOLI DEO GLORIA

As seen above, God's grace, according to Calvin, does not depend on the human will, but the human will depends on God's grace. Quoting Augustine, Calvin exposed the central question of the debate: "This is the chief point on which the issue turns, 'whether this grace precedes or follows the human will, or (to speak more plainly) whether it is given to us because of the fact that we will or whether through it God also brings it about that we will.'"[213] According to Calvin, the depraved sinner does not cooperate with God's grace, but God works alone,

---

210. But what about the phrase "they shall be all taught by God"? Does this not refer to all people? Calvin disagreed: "As to the word *all*, it must be limited to the elect, who alone are the true children of the Church." Ibid., 258.

211. Calvin was not alone in such a distinction between a general call and an efficacious or special call. As David Steinmetz observes, some of Calvin's contemporaries, such as Martin Bucer, also distinguished between the *vocatio congrua* and *vocatio incongrua*. The *vocatio congrua* "is the preaching of the gospel to the elect, who are moved by God to embrace it." The *vocatio incongrua* is the preaching of the gospel to the nonelect, "who are not assisted by the mercy of God and so are left in their sins." While the *vocatio incongrua* is ineffectual or resistible, the *vocatio congrua* is effectual or irresistible. Of course, such a distinction was not original with Bucer or Calvin (as the term Calvinism might convey) but actually originated with Augustine. As Steinmetz explains, later Calvinists would utilize such a distinction between effectual and ineffectual calling. The *vocatio* to the elect is always *efficax* ("effective"), but the calling to the nonelect is designed to be *inefficax* ("ineffectual") because it is not accompanied by the Spirit. Therefore, as Muller notes, the Reformed would affirm a *vocatio specialis* ("special calling"), also titled *vocatio interna* ("internal calling") because the Spirit works within, which makes the *vocatio externa* ("external calling") *efficax*. Such distinctions among the Reformed were not novel but, as demonstrated above, are evident in the thought of Calvin in an effort both to remain faithful to the diverse *vocatio* language in Scripture and at the same time to refute those like Pighius who sought to minimize the *vocatio* to a single, universal, resistible, and ineffectual act of grace. David C. Steinmetz, *Calvin in Context* (New York: Oxford University Press, 1995), 149; cf. Richard Muller, "vocatio," in *Dictionary of Latin and Greek Theological Terms: Drawn Principally from Protestant Scholastic Theology* (Grand Rapids, MI: Baker, 2004), 329.

212. Calvin, *Commentary on John*, 256 (cf. 258–59). See also Paul Helm, *Calvin: A Guide for the Perplexed* (London: T&T Clark, 2008), 84; Edward A. Dowey Jr., *The Knowledge of God in Calvin's Theology* (New York: Columbia University Press, 1952), 150, 175–76.

213. Calvin, *Bondage*, 176. Cf. ibid., 188.

calling the sinner to himself in an efficacious manner, producing new life within through his Spirit.

Why was such a debate so crucial in Calvin's view? For him the glory of God was at stake in how one understands grace. Hesselink argues, "If that grace is undercut by some form of cooperation (synergism) between a semiautonomous 'free' human being and the sovereign Lord, the glory of God is compromised, as far as Calvin is concerned."[214] Such a compromise of God's glory was, for Calvin, not only unbiblical but also an assault against God himself. Calvin, in his controversy with Jerome Bolsec in 1551, made this apparent. When asked why some believe and others do not, Bolsec answered that it was because some exercise their free will while others do not. Calvin thought such an answer contradicted Scripture, particularly Romans 3:10–11, which says, "None is righteous, no, not one; no one understands; no one seeks for God." The unregenerate will has no ability to turn to God. Rather, it is God alone who must save depraved sinners, and in doing so, he alone receives the glory. Godfrey explains the contrast between Calvin and Bolsec well: "Bolsec's religion is man-centered. God has done all he can to save, but the ultimate decision on salvation rests with the human response. For Calvin such religion takes the glory of salvation away from God and trivializes the work of Christ."[215]

Peter Martyr Vermigli and Thomas Cranmer's Edwardian Reformation

We cannot forget that while Calvin tends to occupy central attention in many treatments of the Reformed wing of the Reformation in literature today, in the sixteenth century Calvin was one voice among

---

214. Hesselink, *Calvin's First Catechism*, 72. See also Alister E. McGrath, *A Life of John Calvin: A Study in the Shaping of Western Culture* (Cambridge, MA: Basil Blackwell, 1990), 145–73. Warfield could confidently say, "The central fact of Calvinism is the glory of God." Benjamin Breckenridge Warfield, *Calvin as a Theologian and Calvinism Today* (Grand Rapids, MI: Evangelical Press, 1969), 26. Or as Cameron puts it, "In Calvin's exposition one theme stood out: the unique unbounded sovereignty and majesty of God. God must be allowed to be God, in the fullest possible sense." Cameron, *The European Reformation*, 129.

215. W. Robert Godfrey, *John Calvin: Pilgrim and Pastor* (Wheaton, IL: Crossway, 2009), 116–17. Godfrey goes on to point out that this same issue sprouted again in 1552 with John Trolliet. On Bolsec's synergism, see Richard A. Muller, "The Use and Abuse of a Document: Beza's *Tabula Praedestinationis*, the Bolsec Controversy, and the Origins of Reformed Orthodoxy," in *Protestant Scholasticism: Essays in Reassessment*, ed. Carl R. Trueman and R. Scott Clark (Carlisle: Paternoster, 1999), 45, 49–50.

several other impressive Reformed pastors and theologians. While many examples could be given, we will focus on the biblical scholar Peter Martyr Vermigli (1499–1562), whose commentaries gave rise to his notoriety.

Our focus has gravitated toward Wittenberg and Geneva, but with Vermigli we are transported to England, at least for a time.[216] The Reformation ignited by Luther spread to England as the Reformer's books were smuggled in by German merchants. That Luther's books and pamphlets were having an influence can be seen by the fact that they were publically burnt in 1521.

However, we should not be under the impression that the only influence was German or Lutheran; actually, the Reformation in England was flavored by the Swiss and the Reformed tradition as well. For example, Archbishop Thomas Cranmer corresponded with Martin Bucer of Strasbourg,[217] and Frank James III observes how this

> relationship with the Swiss manifested itself in an abortive plan
> to form a theological alliance between the English church and the
> Swiss and South German Protestants on the continent. . . . With
> much of continental Protestantism in disarray after the victory of
> Charles V in the Schmalkald war, Cranmer believed England could
> be the rallying point for a resurgent Protestantism. He even made
> plans to compose a common doctrinal statement and to hold a
> "godly synod" of continental and English Protestants to counter
> the effects of the Council of Trent (1545–63), conferring with such
> theologians as John Calvin, Philip Melanchthon, and Heinrich Bul-
> linger about the proposal.[218]

---

216. For a far more in-depth study of Vermigli's views, see John Patrick Donnelly, *Calvinism and Scholasticism in Vermigli's Doctrine of Man and Grace*, Studies in Medieval and Reformation Thought 18 (Leiden: Brill, 1976); Neelands, "Predestination and the *Thirty-Nine Articles*," 364; Frank A. James III, *Peter Martyr Vermigli and Predestination: The Augustinian Inheritance of an Italian Reformer*, Oxford Theological Monographs (Oxford: Clarendon, 1998).

217. Bucer also contributed to the topics of predestination, election, original sin, calling, and free will. See Martin Bucer, *The Common Places of Martin Bucer*, trans. and ed. D. F. Wright, Courtenay Library of Reformation Classics 4 (Appleford: Sutton Courtenay, 1972), esp. 96–157. For Bucer's contribution to the 1549 and 1552 Books of Common Prayer, see especially 25–26 of Wright's "Introduction." For Bucer's life and theology, see Martin Greschat, *Martin Bucer: A Reformer and His Times*, trans. Stephen E. Buckwalter (Louisville: Westminster John Knox, 2004).

218. Frank A. James III, "Translator's Introduction," in Peter Martyr Vermigli, *The Peter Martyr Library*, vol. 8, *Predestination and Justification: Two Theological Loci*, trans. and ed. Frank A. James III, Sixteenth Century Essays and Studies 68 (Kirksville, MO: Truman State University Press, 2003), xvii.

With such high hopes for reformation in England in mind, Cranmer invited the Italian Vermigli, whom he most likely learned about from Bucer, to come to England in 1547, where Vermigli stayed until 1553, serving as Regius Professor of Divinity at Oxford.[219] Though his time in England was short-lived due to the sudden death of King Edward VI, nevertheless, it has been argued that of "all the continental Reformers, Martyr exerted the greatest influence."[220] Without a doubt, the "growing scholarly consensus is that Vermigli was one of the most important, if unheralded, theological influences upon Cranmer and, through Cranmer, on the Edwardian Reformation."[221] If such claims are true, then it is only right for us to give attention to the theological viewpoint of this Reformed theologian.

Vermigli was understandably celebrated for his commentary on Romans. However, we should not fail to realize that though he was first and foremost a biblical scholar, Vermigli also wrote theology, including treatments of the doctrines of predestination and justification. Charles Schmidt has argued that the Reformed doctrine of predestination owes its prominence most substantially, after Calvin, to Vermigli.[222] While we cannot occupy our attention with such historical debates, it should be noted that Vermigli defended a Reformed view of predestination in various disputes. For example, in 1553 and 1554, he encountered opposition from certain Lutherans, and Vermigli wrote to Calvin that they had "spread very foul and false reports concerning the eternal election of God, against the truth and against your name." Nevertheless, Vermigli reassured Calvin that he and Girolamo Zanchi, a convert under Vermigli, "defend your part and the truth as far as we can."[223]

---

219. Space keeps me from exploring the English Reformation in depth, as well as the debates thereafter, but see Dewey D. Wallace Jr., *Puritans and Predestination: Grace in English Protestant Theology, 1525–1695* (Chapel Hill: University of North Carolina Press, 1982); Philip E. Hughes, *Theology of the English Reformers* (London: Hodder and Stoughton, 1965), 54–76; Carl R. Trueman, *Luther's Legacy: Salvation and English Reformers, 1525–1556* (Oxford: Clarendon, 1994); Peter White, *Predestination, Policy and Polemic: Conflict and Consensus in the English Church from the Reformation to the Civil War* (New York: Cambridge University Press, 1992); Peter Newman Brooks, "The Theology of Thomas Cranmer," in Bagchi and Steinmetz, *Cambridge Companion to Reformation Theology*, 150–60; Carl R. Trueman, "The Theology of the English Reformers," in Bagchi and Steinmetz, *Cambridge Companion to Reformation Theology*, 161–73.

220. James, "Translator's Introduction," xviii.

221. Ibid., xviii–xix.

222. Cited in James, *Peter Martyr Vermigli and Predestination*, 31.

223. Peter Martyr Vermigli, *Locorum Communium Theologicorum ex ipsius scriptis sincere decerptorum* (Basel: P. Perna, 1582), 231–32. See James, "Translator's Introduction," xxiv.

Like other Reformed allies, Vermigli upheld the tradition of Augustine when it came to the matrix involving man's depravity and God's grace, as well as Gregory of Rimini's (ca. 1300–1358) late-medieval defense of Augustinianism. This may explain why the Reformers at Strasbourg in 1542 "recognized in Vermigli a kindred spirit and a ready-made Protestant."[224] As such, Vermigli and Calvin had much in common, both refuting the Dutch Catholic theologian Albert Pighius. It should not surprise us, therefore, that Vermigli had something significant to say in terms of how grace operates on the enslaved will.[225]

The Particularity of Divine Grace

In similar fashion to other Reformed theologians, Vermigli had no hesitation affirming the total depravity of man, which includes the enslavement of his will, meaning that man is utterly dependent on God's saving grace. But what kind of grace did Vermigli affirm? Was it a universal grace, given to all people equally? Vermigli acknowledged how some have imagined that God's predestination is common to all. Vermigli contended, however, that should this be the case, then "it would lie in their [man's] own power or their own hands" to be predestined, "so that they would receive grace when it is offered."[226]

In contrast, Vermigli denied that "grace is common to all" and argued instead that it "is given to some and not to others, according to the pleasure of God." He appealed to Jesus for support of such particularity in his teaching on the effectual call: "No one comes to me unless the Father who sent me draws him" (John 6:44). Vermigli asked rhetorically, "I wonder why opponents say that all are drawn to God but all will not come? . . . So they say that all are drawn by God, but besides being drawn by God, it is required that we are willing and give assent; otherwise we are not brought to Christ."[227] Vermigli demonstrated how such a view stands in contradiction to Jesus's words not

---

224. James, "Translator's Introduction," xxx, xxxi.
225. We will focus specifically on Vermigli's locus on predestination (but will zero in only on his view of effectual calling and conversion), which was located at the end of his exegesis of Romans 9 in his 1558 Romans commentary, published in Basel by Peter Perna. See James, "Translator's Introduction," xliii. However, it should be noted that though Vermigli's commentary on Romans was published in 1558, the lectures on which it was based were delivered in Oxford between 1550 and 1552. See James, *Peter Martyr Vermigli and Predestination*, 62.
226. Vermigli, *Predestination and Justification*, 53.
227. Ibid.

only in John 6:44 but also in John 3:5: "Unless one is born of water and the Spirit, he cannot enter the kingdom of God." Should we follow the logic of those who affirm universal grace, then we would have to say that "all are born again of water and Spirit." But of course this is not the case, so why would we read John 6:44 to say that all men are drawn by the Father? Vermigli, appealing to Augustine, concluded that "all are not drawn by God," for God does not give this gift to everyone but only to the elect, whom alone the Father draws irresistibly. Vermigli's concluding thought on this matter summed it up well:

> It is written in the same chapter, "All that my Father gives me will come to me" [John 6:44]. If all were drawn they would all come to Christ. In the same place it is written, "Everyone who has heard and learned from my Father comes to me" [John 6:46]. Since many do not come to Christ, it is said that many have not heard or learned. And in chapter 10, when Christ had said that he is the shepherd and has his own sheep, he says among other things, "Those whom my Father has given me no one can snatch out of my hands" [John 10:28]. We see that many fall from salvation, and so we must conclude that they are not given by the Father to Christ.[228]

The Efficacy of Divine Grace

It is paramount to note the irresistibility of this drawing and not just its particularity. Following Augustine in his writings to Simplicianus, Vermigli distinguished between two callings in Scripture. On the one hand, there is a *common, general gospel call* to all people. In this call—which goes out with the gospel proclamation—"men are called in common, but not in such a way as to be moved and converted."[229] Vermigli's qualification is key. While men everywhere receive this general gospel call, it is not the call whereby the Spirit works within to convert men. Rather, it is a call that people everywhere hear, a call to come to Christ. As Vermigli put it, "God calls all men by an outward calling, namely, through his prophets, apostles, preachers, and Scriptures. One man

---

228. Ibid., 54. Later on, Vermigli demonstrated such particularity again when he appealed to Matt. 11:25–27 and 13:11, as well as Isa. 6:9, to show that saving revelation is given not to all but only to the elect. Vermigli also appealed to Rom. 9:15 (cf. Ex. 33:19) to show that "grace is not offered equally to all." Ibid., 55, 56.

229. Ibid., 58.

is no more excluded from the promises or warnings than another, for they are set forth to all alike, although all are not predestined to attain to their fruit."[230]

Vermigli cautioned, however, against assuming that such general invitations in Scripture, rooted in this gospel call, mean that man can convert himself: "God universally invites all men, that the prophets were sent indiscriminately to all, and that the Scriptures are given to all, but this says nothing about the efficacy of grace, of which we speak."[231] While the gospel goes out, calling all to look to Jesus, there is a massive problem: man is spiritually unable to turn and believe due to his depravity and bondage of the will. Therefore, what is needed is an inward call of the Father by the power of the Spirit whereby the elect are drawn to Christ.

The second call, whereby the Spirit works within to convert, is a different calling (though not one divorced from the general call). While Vermigli did not give it a precise name, we can call it the *specific, special, or effectual call*. It is that call whereby the elect "are called as they are inclined to be moved." These two calls are significant for it is a reminder that not all men are "moved and drawn to God in the same way."[232]

When the Father draws, he does so efficaciously; that is the intent of this second call. Such efficacy is apparent in John 6:37, 44, as noted earlier, as well as in John 3:8, 27. For example, the texts in John 3 affirm that a "person cannot receive even one thing unless it is given him from heaven" (3:27) and that the Spirit "blows where it wishes" (3:8). Here is a reference to the omnipotent power of the Spirit "who regenerates" as strongly as the wind blows. Clearly, Jesus shows that the "simile is taken from the nature of the wind to show the power of the Holy Spirit."[233] As evident in the opening of Lydia's heart (Acts 16:14), the Spirit is free to work sovereignly in one and not in another.

---

230. Ibid., 60.

231. Ibid., 66. Vermigli also spent time responding to objections that appeal to texts like Matt. 23:37 ("How often would I have gathered your children together as a hen gathers her brood under her wings, and you were not willing!"). He appealed to the distinction between God's antecedent and effective wills: "Here also it is the antecedent will of the sign that is meant. God through his prophets, preachers, apostles, and Scriptures invited the Jews to fly to him by repentance time after time, but they refused, but by his effective will, which is called consequent, he always drew to himself those who were his." Ibid., 64–65.

232. Ibid., 58.

233. Ibid., 55.

Additionally, such efficacy exhibits itself not only in regeneration (John 3) but also in the conversion that follows, for even faith and repentance are gifts from God's gracious hand. When we read about repentance in Paul's second letter to Timothy (2:25), for example, we discover that "even repentance is a gift of God." We must conclude, therefore, "that it does not lie in the hands of all men to return to the right path, unless it is given to them by God."[234]

Vermigli's view sits in direct conflict with those who say not only that grace is common to all but also that it "lies in everyone's power to receive grace when it is offered them."[235] But such an assumption once again runs roughshod over Scripture, said Vermigli. For example, Paul says, "So then it depends not on human will or exertion, but on God, who has mercy" (Rom. 9:16). Vermigli concluded that this "could not be true if it lies within our will to receive grace when offered."[236] He understood Jesus to assume the same in his illustration of a tree and its fruit:

> Christ taught quite clearly that an evil tree cannot bear good fruit; therefore, so long as men are not regenerate they cannot bring forth fruit good enough to enable them to assent to God's grace when it knocks. It is first necessary that the tree be changed and evil trees turned into good. As in human generation, no one who is procreated contributes anything to it. So also is it in regeneration, for there also we are born again through Christ and in Christ.[237]

To conclude, Vermigli's appeal to Christ vividly exhibits his affirmation of monergism in regeneration. Hence, when we pray for the regeneration of the unregenerate, said Vermigli, we "do so because we believe that it lies in the hand of God to open their hearts, if he will."[238]

Conclusion: Remarkable Continuity

It is nothing short of remarkable that in an age of doctrinal controversy, most Reformers saw eye to eye in their affirmation of the bond-

---

234. Ibid., 56.
235. Ibid.
236. Ibid., 57.
237. Ibid.
238. Ibid., 58.

age of the will and the efficacy of God's grace. Melanchthon, of course, stands out as one who may have swum against this tide, though it was debated among his Lutheran successors to what extent he departed from Luther. Nevertheless, the majority of Reformers stood united in their defense of monergism. Considering how the Reformers could be worlds apart geographically, and sometimes doctrinally on other matters (e.g., the Lord's Supper), and in light of how often Rome sought to highlight the division they saw within Protestant ranks, such an accord over monergism not only strengthened the Reformation cause but also displayed that its *sola gratia* conviction was anything but tertiary; instead, it made up the very nucleus of its mission to find a gracious God.

Resources for Further Study

Primary Sources

Bucer, Martin. *The Common Places of Martin Bucer.* Translated and edited by David F. Wright. Courtenay Library of Reformation Classics 4. Appleford: Sutton Courtenay, 1972.

Calvin, John. *The Bondage and Liberation of the Will: A Defence of the Orthodox Doctrine of Human Choice against Pighius.* Edited by A. N. S. Lane. Translated by G. I. Davies. Texts and Studies in Reformation and Post-Reformation Thought 2. Grand Rapids, MI: Baker, 1996.

———. *Concerning the Eternal Predestination of God.* Translated by J. K. S. Reid. London: James Clarke, 1961.

Kolb, Robert, and Timothy J. Wengert, eds. *The Book of Concord: The Confessions of the Evangelical Lutheran Church.* Translated by Charles P. Arand et al. Minneapolis: Fortress, 2000.

Luther, Martin. *The Bondage of the Will.* In *Luther's Works.* Vol. 33, *Career of the Reformer III.* Edited by Philip S. Watson. Philadelphia: Fortress, 1972.

Melanchthon, Philipp. *Commonplaces: Loci Communes 1521.* Translated by Christian Preus. St. Louis, MO: Concordia, 2014.

———. *Loci Communes 1543.* Translated by J. A. O. Preus. St. Louis, MO: Concordia, 1992.

Rupp, E. Gordon, and Philip S. Watson, eds. *Luther and Erasmus: Free Will and Salvation.* Library of Christian Classics 17. Philadelphia: Westminster, 1969.

Vermigli, Peter Martyr. *The Peter Martyr Library*. Vol. 8, *Predestination and Justification: Two Theological Loci*. Translated and edited by Frank A. James III. Sixteenth Century Essays and Studies 68. Kirksville, MO: Truman State University Press, 2003.

Secondary Sources

Donnelly, John Patrick. *Calvinism and Scholasticism in Vermigli's Doctrine of Man and Grace*. Studies in Medieval and Reformation Thought 18. Leiden: Brill, 1976.

Forde, Gerhard O. *The Captivation of the Will: Luther vs. Erasmus on Freedom and Bondage*. Edited by Steven Paulson. Lutheran Quarterly Books. Grand Rapids, MI: Eerdmans, 2005.

Graybill, Gregory B. *Evangelical Free Will: Philipp Melanchthon's Doctrinal Journey on the Origins of Faith*. Oxford Theological Monographs. New York: Oxford University Press, 2010.

Holtrop, Philip C. *The Bolsec Controversy on Predestination from 1551–1555*. Lewiston, NY: Edwin Mellen, 1993.

Hughes, Philip E. *Theology of the English Reformers*. London: Hodder and Stoughton, 1965.

James, Frank A., III. *Peter Martyr Vermigli and Predestination: The Augustinian Inheritance of an Italian Reformer*. Oxford Theological Monographs. New York: Oxford University Press, 1998.

Kolb, Robert. *Bound Choice, Election, and Wittenberg Theological Method: From Martin Luther to the Formula of Concord*. Lutheran Quarterly Books. Grand Rapids, MI: Eerdmans, 2005.

———. "Human Nature, the Fall, and the Will." In *T&T Clark Companion to Reformation Theology*, ed. David M. Whitford, 14–31. New York: T&T Clark, 2012.

Lane, A. N. S. "Did Calvin Believe in Free Will?" *Vox Evangelica* 12 (1981): 72–90.

Slenczka, Notger. "Luther's Anthropology." In *The Oxford Handbook of Martin Luther's Theology*, edited by Robert Kolb, Irene Dingel, and L'ubomír Batka, 212–32. Oxford: Oxford University Press, 2014.

Trueman, Carl R. *Luther's Legacy: Salvation and English Reformers, 1525–1556*. Oxford: Clarendon, 1994.

Wallace, Dewey D., Jr. *Puritans and Predestination: Grace in English Protestant Theology, 1525–1695*. Chapel Hill: University of North Carolina Press, 1982.

Wengert, Timothy J. *Human Freedom, Christian Righteousness: Philip Melanchthon's Exegetical Dispute with Erasmus of Rotterdam.* Oxford Studies in Historical Theology. New York: Oxford University Press, 1998.

———. "Philip Melanchthon's Contribution to Luther's Debate with Erasmus over the Bondage of the Will." In *By Faith Alone: Essays on Justification in Honor of Gerhard O. Forde*, ed. Joseph A. Burgess and Marc Kolden, 110–24. Grand Rapids, MI: Eerdmans, 2004.

White, Peter. *Predestination, Policy and Polemic: Conflict and Consensus in the English Church from the Reformation to the Civil War.* New York: Cambridge University Press, 1992.

14

Justification by Faith Alone

Korey D. Maas

ABSTRACT

Amid doctrinal confusion, the Reformers relatively quickly reached consensus on the fundamental nature and means of justification. Justification by grace alone through faith alone on account of Christ's imputed righteousness alone came to be embraced by and enshrined in the confessions of Lutheran and Reformed alike. In subsequently clarifying its own soteriology, Rome would condemn this doctrine. Though modern scholarship attempts to narrow the divide over justification, such efforts often implicitly or explicitly abandon the Reformation doctrine. The resulting controversies and the centrality of justification to Reformation theology reveal that, even five hundred years on, the Reformation is not over.

Introduction

By way of introducing and—if the expression may be pardoned—justifying his sweeping historical survey of the Christian doctrine of justification, Alister McGrath set forth the proposition that it "constitutes the real centre of the theological system of the Christian church."[1] Exceptions and objections to such an understanding, however, are certainly not unknown.[2] Jesuit theologian Avery Dulles, for example, has observed that "justification is not a central category in contemporary Catholic dogmatics."[3] Less in the way of observation than assertion, Catholic theologian Hans Küng had already declared more bluntly that "justification is not the central dogma of Christianity."[4] Perhaps more subtly, but with even greater implications, one modern commentary on Galatians goes so far as to scrub justificatory concepts completely from the Pauline text, rendering the Greek *dikaioō* and its cognates in terms of "rectifying" rather than "justifying."[5]

As a simple description of justification's place in the history of Christian thought, then, an assertion such as McGrath's is disputable. Far less so, however, is such an assessment of justification's place in the theology of the Protestant Reformers of the sixteenth century. The most towering figure of the Reformation's first generation, Martin Luther, was quite emphatic in his exclamation that justification was "the first and chief article" of Christian theology.[6] His Wittenberg colleague Philipp Melanchthon was no less insistent that it was "the most important topic of Christian teaching."[7] Worth emphasizing also is that these statements—neither uncharacteristic of their authors—were deemed more than private opinions; the works in which each appears would be adopted as formal confessions of the Lutheran churches. Nor were such sentiments unique to the Lutheran Reformers. John Calvin, unquestionably the most influential figure of the Reformation's second generation, spoke similarly of justification being "the main hinge upon

1. Alister E. McGrath, *Iustitia Dei: A History of the Christian Doctrine of Justification*, 2nd ed. (Cambridge: Cambridge University Press, 1998), 1.
2. Indeed, McGrath himself drops this assertion from the third edition (2005) of *Iustitia Dei*.
3. Avery Dulles, "Justification in Contemporary Catholic Theology," in *Justification by Faith*, ed. H. George Anderson, T. Austin Murphy, and Joseph A. Burgess, Lutherans and Catholics in Dialogue 7 (Minneapolis: Augsburg, 1985), 256. On the same page Dulles further notes that it is "rarely discussed at length except in polemics against, or dialogue with, Protestants."
4. Hans Küng, *Justification: The Doctrine of Karl Barth and a Catholic Reflection*, trans. Thomas Collins, Edmund E. Tolk, and David Grandskou (London: Burns and Oates, 1964), 118.
5. J. Louis Martyn, *Galatians: A New Translation with Introduction and Commentary*, Anchor Bible 33A (New York: Doubleday, 1997).
6. "The Smalcald Articles," pt. 2, art. 1, in Robert Kolb and Timothy J. Wengert, eds., *The Book of Concord: The Confessions of the Evangelical Lutheran Church*, trans. Charles P. Arand et al. (Minneapolis: Fortress, 2000), 301.
7. "Apology of the Augsburg Confession," art. 4.2, in Kolb and Wengert, *Book of Concord*, 120.

which religion turns."[8] It was likewise from within the Reformed tradition that the first clear articulation of justification as "the article on which the church stands and falls" was evidenced.[9]

Much more significant than the cross-confessional agreement on the centrality of the doctrine of justification, though, is the Reformers' broad agreement on a particular understanding, explication, and confession of this central doctrine. For whatever differences sixteenth-century Catholics and Protestants might have had in their understandings of the place occupied by justification in the fuller scheme of Christian dogma, they did not mutually condemn one another's doctrines simply because they perceived them to have been granted too much or too little importance. Recognizing, though, that none deemed justification a peripheral article goes some way toward explaining not only the intensity of the Reformation debates but also the anxieties potentially provoked by the late-medieval confusions that partially precipitated these debates. In order to put into context the definition and development of the Reformers' doctrine of justification, we thus turn first to these pre-Reformation controversies.

Justification in Its Late-Medieval Context

For those accustomed to professing justification as Christianity's "main hinge" or "chief article," it might appear strange that the church of the Late Middle Ages confessed no single, dogmatically defined doctrine concerning the manner by which individuals are saved. It will perhaps seem less strange, however, when viewed in the light of similarly important doctrines that, at the time, also remained undefined. None, for example, questioned the central importance of Holy Scripture, and yet throughout the Middle Ages the precise contents of the biblical canon were never enshrined in an official decree of the church. The reason in this instance is simply that an implicit consensus on the canon rendered any dogmatic definition unnecessary. With respect to some doctrines, however, precisely the opposite was the case: the very lack of consensus precluded any clear identification of what "the church" confessed.

---

8. Calvin, *Institutes*, 3.11.1.
9. The earliest extant use of the phrase, often attributed to Luther, appears to be that of Johann Heinrich Alsted, *Theologia scholastica didactica* (Hanover: Conradi Eifridi, 1618), 711; see McGrath, *Iustitia Dei*, 448n3.

It is this second explanation for the absence of any dogmatic statement that most clearly pertains to the doctrine of justification. As Mc-
Grath has rightly noted, "In certain areas of doctrine—most notably
the doctrine of justification—there appears to have been considerable
confusion during the first decades of the sixteenth century concerning
the official teaching of the church."[10] The reason for this, he further
observes, is that "an astonishing diversity of views on the justification
of man before God were in circulation."[11] Two especially deserve brief
explication for the light they shed on the intellectual milieu out of
which the Reformation doctrine arose.

The medieval school of thought most closely approximating the
soteriology eventually defined by Rome at the Council of Trent is that
of the *via antiqua*, or "old way," most frequently associated with the
mature theology of Thomas Aquinas. Schematically, the order of salvation found in Aquinas's magisterial *Summa Theologiae* might be
summarized as a three-step process. Initiating the process by which
one is saved, God freely bestows grace on the individual. Thus gifted,
the individual is thereby empowered to cooperate with God's grace.
Finally, this meritorious cooperation, combined with and made possible by grace, is rewarded with eternal life.[12]

While largely adopting and embracing each aspect of the Thomist
order of salvation, the *via moderna*, or "new way," represented by
theologians such as William of Ockham and Gabriel Biel, radically
altered Thomas's system by introducing a fourth, and prior, step. According to the "modern" theologians, meritorious cooperation not
only followed on and flowed from divine grace but was possible even
without it. Indeed, it was such effort that was rewarded with God's
first bestowal of grace. Thus, this modern school of soteriology became
identified with its proposition that "God will not deny grace to those
who do what is in them."[13]

Even this clear contrast between the two most prominent late-

10. Alister E. McGrath, *The Intellectual Origins of the European Reformation* (Grand Rapids, MI: Baker, 1995), 16.
11. Ibid., 26.
12. Thomas Aquinas, *Summa Theologica*, trans. Fathers of the English Dominican Province (Notre Dame, IN: Christian Classics, 1981), 1a2ae.113–14.
13. See, e.g., Gabriel Biel, "Doing What Is in One," in *The European Reformations Sourcebook*, ed. Carter Lindberg (Oxford: Blackwell, 2000), 17.

medieval schools, however, underemphasizes the confusion to which such differences might lead. One of the reasons for this is found in the reference to Aquinas's "mature" theology outlined above. Earlier in his career, most importantly in his commentary on the *Sentences* of Peter Lombard, Thomas himself had embraced the "doing what is in one" typically associated with the school of Ockham and Biel. Further, despite some who argued that Thomas's later *Summa* was definitive of his thought, many late-medieval theologians continued to recognize his commentary on the *Sentences* as authoritative.[14] This is in some respects unsurprising, since Lombard's work itself remained the standard textbook for university theology into the sixteenth century.

The continuing authority of Lombard's *Sentences* likewise proved potentially confusing in one further respect. Despite the association of Aquinas with the "old way" of scholastic theology, Lombard himself represented an even older medieval soteriological tradition. For Aquinas and the *via antiqua*, the grace necessary in the process of justification was understood to be a quality created within or imparted to the individual. Lombard had previously raised but immediately dismissed this possibility. The gift that effects salvation, he concluded, is no acquired quality that an individual might then deem his own; it is the active presence of the Holy Spirit himself.[15] Especially noteworthy is not only that Aquinas would reject this view but also his reason for doing so: it would imply that the love of God made possible by grace "would cease to be voluntary and meritorious."[16]

It was also with respect to the question of grace that the *via moderna* opened the door for further confusion even within its own system. While Thomas and his followers held that grace is necessary in effecting salvation, Ockham only affirmed that this is ordinarily the case. Fearing that talk of necessity would restrict divine freedom, Ockham and his followers held that "whatever God can produce by means of secondary causes he can directly produce and preserve

---

14. See Heiko A. Oberman, "'*Iustitia Christi*' and '*Iustitia Dei*': Luther and the Scholastic Doctrines of Justification," in *The Dawn of the Reformation: Essays in Late Medieval and Early Reformation Thought* (Edinburgh: T&T Clark, 1992), 108.

15. Peter Lombard, *The Sentences, Book 1: The Mystery of the Trinity*, trans. Giulio Silano, Mediaeval Sources in Translation 42 (Toronto: Pontifical Institute of Mediaeval Studies, 2007), 17.1–6.

16. Aquinas, *Summa Theologica* 2a2ae.23.2.

without them."[17] Thus, at least in theory, God could justify sinners even without the bestowal of his grace and their subsequent cooperation. Further, and more worryingly, the opposite was also understood to be the case: being bound by no necessity, God might deny salvation even to those who cooperate with the grace he has provided. Ockham's reasoning, following that of his predecessor Duns Scotus, was that "nothing created must, for reasons intrinsic to it, be accepted by God."[18] That is, neither grace nor one's cooperation with it are deserving of salvation in and of themselves; they are accepted and rewarded only because God has voluntarily agreed to do so. Ultimately, then, one's salvation was understood to depend not only on divine grace together with human cooperation but also, and most fundamentally, on God's keeping his promise to regard these as meriting eternal life.

Even these brief summaries of only two prominent theologies of justification highlight the confusion inhering in the late-medieval context and the potential anxieties it produced. It remained unclear whether the "old" or "new" soteriology was to be deemed correct, if either was to be preferred over what remained the "textbook" theology of Peter Lombard. It remained unclear, if one followed Aquinas, whether the theology of his *Sentences* commentary or of his *Summa* was definitive. And if one embraced Ockham, it remained unclear how to determine whether one had sufficiently "done what is in one" so as to merit grace and whether a radically free God would in fact keep his promise to reward one's cooperation with grace.

Before turning to the Reformation doctrine developing in and reacting to this late-medieval milieu, however, it is necessary to highlight one soteriological aspect on which virtually all medieval theologians agreed. While the disagreements outlined above revolved around the *manner* in which justification takes place, there remained fundamental agreement on the *nature* of justification: it consisted of a real moral and ontological change in the individual. A literal and etymological reading of the Latin term *iustificare*, a compound of *iustum* ("just, righteous") and *facere* ("to make"), entailed an understanding of the sinner being made righteous in the process of justification. That is, the change understood to take place in the justified was not merely a declared change in status; sinners were accepted by God not simply because he *reckoned* them righteous. Rather, they were accepted because they had, in fact, to a sufficient degree, *become* righteous. A firm distinction between *justification* and *sanctification* remained unknown to the medieval theologians. It is this distinction especially, however, that has been called the "essential feature" of Reformation soteriology.[19] It is to the origins of this soteriology that we now turn.

The Lutheran "Breakthrough"

Just as there was no single medieval doctrine of justification, so too must one be cautious in speaking of *the* soteriology of Martin Luther. Indeed, like Aquinas, Luther would modify his theology in the course of his career and would regularly remark that his Reformation insights were not discovered all at once but developed slowly.[20] As has been rightly noted, "Luther's doctrine of justification was one thing in 1513 and became another by 1536. This development, and the failure (or refusal) to observe it carefully, has also contributed to confusion."[21] Before explicating Luther's "mature" theology of justification, then, it will be necessary to trace its evolution from the late-medieval doctrine he initially embraced.

EARLY DEVELOPMENTS IN LUTHER'S SOTERIOLOGY

Luther's own education was dominated by professors adhering to the *via moderna*.[22] It is unsurprising, then, that on his appointment to the faculty of Wittenberg University, Luther's first course of lectures (1513–1515) would reflect the opinions of his professors. The modernist tenor of such opinions is especially clear in his statement that "the teachers correctly say that to a man who does what is in him God

19. McGrath, *Iustitia Dei*, 186.

20. Cf., e.g., Martin Luther, *Table Talk*, LW 54:50 (no. 352); 54:442–43 (no. 5518); and Luther, "Preface to the Complete Edition of Luther's Latin Writings," LW 34:327–28.

21. R. Scott Clark, "*Iustitia Imputata Christi*: Alien or Proper to Luther's Doctrine of Justification?," *CTQ* 70, no. 3/4 (2006): 273.

22. Martin Brecht, *Martin Luther*, vol. 1, *His Road to Reformation, 1483–1521* (Philadelphia: Fortress, 1985), 34–38, 91–95.

gives grace without fail."[23] In keeping with medieval theology more broadly, he consistently spoke of justification as a process of renewal by which one becomes righteous.[24] That Luther remained in this period fully within the orbit of accepted medieval doctrine is made clear even by some of his harshest modern critics. The twentieth-century Jesuit Hartmann Grisar, for example, could admit not only that these lectures reveal no deviations from Roman theology but also that their content stood in stark contradiction to what he deemed Luther's later errors.[25]

Development in Luther's theology was already evident, though, in his next series of lectures. In these 1515–1516 lectures on Paul's epistle to the Romans, he already rejected the modernist's "doing what is in one" and insisted that the grace of God is received entirely passively.[26] Emphasizing his debt to Augustine, he identified the "righteousness of God" as the cause of salvation and defined this righteousness not as God's inherent righteousness but as that by which he justifies sinners by faith.[27] In light of Luther's later recollection of his theological "breakthrough," these Romans lectures have often been read as its obvious fruit. Autobiographical remarks in 1545 do indeed describe this breakthrough as entailing a new, passive understanding of the phrase "righteousness of God" and emphasize that this was the understanding found in Augustine.[28] As with his earlier Psalms lectures, however, even Luther's Catholic critics have highlighted that Luther's "new" teaching on this point is nothing other than the "old" teaching of the medieval doctors.[29] That is, while the Romans lectures evidenced Luther's break with the soteriology of the *via moderna*, this break simply brought him into line with the Augustinian emphases that had always prevailed in the *via antiqua*; it did not reveal anything like his

---

23. Martin Luther, *First Lectures on the Psalms II*, LW 11:396.
24. Ibid., *LW* 10:191–92; cf. Martin Luther, *Lectures on Romans: Glosses and Scholia*, LW 25:260.
25. Hartmann Grisar, *Luther*, trans. E. M. Lamond, ed. Luigi Cappadelta (London: Kegan Paul, Trench, Trübner, 1913), 1:74.
26. Luther, *Lectures on Romans*, LW 25:496.
27. Ibid., *LW* 25:151–52.
28. Luther, "Preface to the Complete Edition of Luther's Latin Writings," *LW* 34:337.
29. E.g., Heinrich Denifle extensively demonstrated that Luther's interpretation of the "righteousness of God" was entirely typical of his Catholic predecessors in *Luther und Luthertum. Ergänzungen*, vol. 1, *Quellenbelege: Die abendländischen Schriftausleger bis Luther über Justitia Dei (Rom. 1,17) und Justificatio* (Mainz: Kirchheim, 1905).

mature doctrine of justification. A careful reading of these lectures and the manner in which they rely on Augustine supports just such a conclusion.

Augustine had indeed defined the righteousness of God as that by which he justifies sinners[30]—as did the later theologians of the *via antiqua*. But this justification, according to Augustine, consists of being "made righteous" such that the ungodly person "may become a godly one."[31] Again, like the medievals, Augustine thus viewed justification in sanative terms. It is certainly initiated and made possible by divine grace, but it is grace understood—once again, as by Augustine's medieval heirs—as a healing substance imparted to man. With all this Luther agreed in 1515–1516. Thus he could describe the Christian as both sick and well at the same time: sick in fact but well on account of the physician's promise of health.[32] Or, more clearly, the Christian is sinful and righteous at the same time: partly sinful and partly righteous.[33]

Luther's Romans lectures did represent a significant theological development; they evidenced a clear break with the late-medieval soteriology he had imbibed as a student. But they did not yet reveal the distinctly "Protestant" doctrine that began to flower only when he moved beyond the progressive and sanative scheme formulated by Augustine and embraced by virtually all medieval theologians. That he did not do so before 1518 is evident, for example, in his Hebrews lectures of that year. Still understanding cooperation with grace to be an essential aspect of justification, he explained that Christians are called righteous "not because they are, but because they have begun to be and should become people of this kind by making constant progress."[34] It was in this year, 1518, however, that the young humanist Philipp Melanchthon joined the faculty at Wittenberg; not coincidentally, it was shortly thereafter that Luther's soteriology took dramatic turns toward what would become his mature doctrine.

---

30. Augustine, *On the Spirit and the Letter*, 15, NPNF, 1st ser., vol. 5, ed. Philip Schaff (Grand Rapids, MI: Eerdmans, 1956), 89.
31. Ibid., 45, NPNF, 1st ser., vol. 5, 102.
32. Luther, *Lectures on Romans*, LW 25:260.
33. Ibid., LW 25:434. Thus, in the same work Luther could more bluntly state that "God has not yet justified us, that is, He has not made us perfectly righteous or declared our righteousness perfect, but He has made a beginning in order that he might make us perfect." Ibid., LW 25:245.
34. Martin Luther, *Lectures on Hebrews*, LW 29:139.

MELANCHTHON'S INFLUENCE ON LUTHER'S SOTERIOLOGY

The relationship between Melanchthon's soteriology and Luther's has become a source of endless controversy.[35] Prior to the twentieth century, the predominant view held that their doctrines were essentially identical and that it was this shared doctrine that received formulation even in the last of the Lutheran confessional documents, the 1577 Formula of Concord. But beginning with the early twentieth-century "Luther Renaissance"—sparked in part by the rediscovery of the Romans lectures discussed above—many attempts have been made to drive a wedge between the two. In such cases Luther's early works have often been viewed as definitive of his soteriology, from which Melanchthon and subsequent confessional Lutherans departed. While it may be fair to describe certain soteriological articulations as Melanchthonian in origin or emphasis, the implication that such ideas were unknown—or even rejected—by Luther is entirely unwarranted. If the following is accepted as a concise statement of the mature Reformation doctrine of justification—that one is justified by grace alone through faith alone on the basis of Christ's imputed righteousness alone—it will become clear that this does not represent a Melanchthonian departure from Luther. Luther not only embraced just this confession but also did so in large part following Melanchthon's early lead.

With respect to *grace*, the first key term in the formula above, Rome had, of course, never denied its necessary role in justification. Nor did Luther. But as late as 1518, he still conceived of grace as both "old" and "new" medieval theologians had, as an inherent quality or substance by which one is prepared to become righteous. Three years later, however, he entirely abandoned this traditional view, redefining grace simply as the "favor of God."[36] Having rejected the notion of grace as a quality making possible the progressive "healing" of the sinner, he could then be so bold as to say, "Grace is a greater good than that health of righteousness. . . . Everyone would prefer—if that were pos-

---

35. Cf., e.g., Mark A. Seifrid, "Luther, Melanchthon and Paul on the Question of Imputation: Recommendations on a Current Debate," in *Justification: What's at Stake in the Current Debates*, ed. Mark A. Husbands and Daniel J. Treier (Downers Grove, IL: InterVarsity Press, 2004), 137–52; Aaron O'Kelley, "Luther and Melanchthon on Justification: Continuity or Discontinuity?," in *Since We Are Justified by Faith: Justification in the Theologies of the Protestant Reformations*, ed. Michael Parsons (Milton Keynes, UK: Paternoster, 2012), 30–43.
36. Martin Luther, *Against Latomus*, LW 32:227.

sible—to be without the health of righteousness rather than the grace of God."[37] The significance of this shift becomes clearer when it is noted that only two years earlier this definition of grace was not merely one Luther had yet to embrace but one he had explicitly rejected.[38]

The impetus for this sudden change almost certainly lay with the recently arrived Melanchthon, who from at least 1520 was making the case for understanding grace as God's favor or good will.[39] He did so perhaps most clearly in the same year that Luther first embraced this definition, in the first edition of his *Loci Communes*, where he wrote that "the word 'grace' does not mean some quality in us, but rather the very will of God, or the goodwill of God toward us."[40] This articulation in Melanchthon's *Loci* is significant not only because this work may justifiably be considered the first "systematic theology" of the Reformation but also because it profoundly influenced Luther, who regularly expressed his unreserved agreement with it, going so far as to assert hyperbolically that it deserved to be canonized.[41]

During this same period, as he developed his mature understanding of faith, Luther was even more explicit about his debt to Melanchthon. Following the Vulgate rendering of Hebrews 11:1, where faith is defined as "the substance [*substantia*] of things hoped for" (KJV),[42] Luther, in harmony with the medievals, had long understood faith to be a quality present in those being made righteous. Like grace, it played a necessary role in justification—but only as it became properly "formed." Hence, the medieval formula "faith formed by love" served to distinguish mere intellectual assent from that faith joined with love and so contributing to righteousness. Perhaps taking his cue from fellow humanist Desiderius Erasmus's annotation of Hebrews 11:1, Melanchthon, from at least 1519, began to read the Greek *pistis* ("faith") as synonymous with the Latin *fiducia* ("trust").[43] By the time he drafted the first edition of his *Loci*, he was insisting that, in accordance with ancient usage, the bibli-

---

37. Ibid., LW 32:227.
38. Martin Luther, *Lectures on Galatians* (1519), LW 27:252.
39. See Lowell C. Green, *How Melanchthon Helped Luther Discover the Gospel: The Doctrine of Justification in the Reformation* (Fallbrook, CA: Verdict: 1980), 159.
40. Philipp Melanchthon, *Loci Communes Theologici* (1521), in *Melanchthon and Bucer*, ed. Wilhelm Pauck, trans. Lowell J. Satre, LCC 19 (Philadelphia: Westminster, 1969), 87.
41. Martin Luther, *The Bondage of the Will*, LW 33:16.
42. Notice that the ESV uses "assurance" instead of "substance."
43. See Green, *How Melanchthon Helped Luther*, 144.

cal uses of *pistis* and its verbal form almost always mean "trust."[44] Not only did Luther also embrace this definition, but he credited Melanchthon with correcting his earlier traditional interpretation. Melanchthon, he explained, pointed out that the Greek term translated "substance" in Hebrews 11 is better understood as "essence" or "existence."[45] He thus came to understand justifying faith not simply as trust but as trust that the righteousness "hoped for," on account of God's favor, already existed. As such, Luther could now speak of justification in the present tense, not merely as the future result of an ongoing process.[46] Most revealing of this new emphasis was the radical repurposing of that concept of which he had made use already in his earlier Romans lectures, that of the Christian being righteous and sinful at the same time. No longer did this formula express the idea that one was partly sinful and partly righteous, or a present sinner with the future hope of being made righteous; the Christian now remained in himself completely a sinner yet, by means of faith and in the eyes of God, completely righteous.[47]

Since, Luther continued to insist, the Christian remains sinful in himself, that righteousness received by faith came to be understood as a necessarily extrinsic righteousness. Likewise, since it is not merely a partial but a complete righteousness in the present, it could only be conceived of as a righteousness imputed to the believer. Neither grace nor faith, therefore, were allowed to remain abstractions. God's favor is expressed in his unmerited imputing of Christ's righteousness to the believer, and it is in this that the believer trusts for his justification.[48]

Thus understood, Luther could starkly state that "our righteousness is nothing other than the imputation of God."[49] In doing so, he once again followed the lead of Melanchthon, who was already saying in 1519 that "all our righteousness is the gratuitous imputation of God."[50] There is some small irony in Luther's having pressed this point

---

44. Melanchthon, *Loci Communes*, 92–102.
45. Luther, *Lectures on Galatians* (1519), *LW* 27:377.
46. Martin Luther, "Two Kinds of Righteousness," *LW* 31:298–99.
47. Cf., e.g., Luther, *Against Latomus*, *LW* 32:172–73; Luther, *The Private Mass and the Consecration of Priests*, *LW* 38:158.
48. E.g., Martin Luther, *Lectures on Galatians* (1535), *LW* 26:132: "These three things are joined together: faith, Christ, and acceptance or imputation."
49. Martin Luther, *Lectures on Isaiah*, WA, vol. 31, bk. 2, 439. Cf. Luther, *Bondage*, *LW* 33:271.
50. Philipp Melanchthon, *Baccalaureatsthesen*, in *Melanchthons Werke*, ed. Robert Stupperich (Gütersloh: Bertelsmann, 1951), 1:24.

in his controversy with Erasmus, for it is likely that Melanchthon's own initial insight into imputation derived from his reading of Erasmus. In his revised Latin translation of the New Testament at Romans 4:5, Erasmus substituted *imputatum* for the Vulgate's *reputatum*, explaining that this should be understood as the remission of an unpaid debt as if it had been paid.[51] This "forensic" understanding is precisely that which Melanchthon subsequently defended at great length in his Apology of the Augsburg Confession. It was there, for example, that he gave confessional status to the forensic doctrine of justification: "'justify' is used in a judicial [*forensi*] way to mean 'to absolve a guilty man and pronounce him righteous,' and to do so on account of someone else's righteousness, namely, Christ's, which is communicated to us through faith."[52]

That Luther was in full agreement with Melanchthon on this understanding of justification becomes especially evident in light of two brief, contemporaneous controversies. In the very same year that Melanchthon penned the Apology, he perceived that fellow Reformer Johannes Brenz yet embraced the sanative view of justification by which one became inherently righteous. Not only did Melanchthon compose a letter to Brenz defending the forensic and imputative doctrine, but also Luther appended to this letter his own postscript expressing his agreement with Melanchthon.[53] Five years later, in 1536, when some suspected disagreement between the two, a formal dialogue was arranged in which Melanchthon posed to Luther the precisely worded question, "Is one righteous by renewal, as in Augustine, or by the free imputation of something outside of us, by faith, understood as trust?" Again expressing his agreement with Melanchthon, Luther affirmed the imputation of Christ's righteousness.[54]

In light of the foregoing discussion, two important emphases emerge. First, Luther's mature soteriology did not emerge instantaneously but developed gradually over the second and third decades of the sixteenth century. Second, the doctrine at which he eventually

---

51. See McGrath, *Iustitia Dei*, 211, 218.
52. "Apology of the Augsburg Confession" (quarto ed.), art. 4.305, in Theodore G. Tappert, ed. and trans., *The Book of Concord: The Confessions of the Evangelical Lutheran Church* (Philadelphia: Fortress, 1959), 154.
53. Philipp Melanchthon and Martin Luther, "Letter to Johann Brenz" (1531), WABr 6:98–101.
54. Martin Luther, "Answer to Melanchthon's Question" (1536), WABr 12:191, 194nc.

arrived—and maintained throughout the rest of his career—developed in concord with and was confessed in agreement with that of Melanchthon. That is, by the mid-1520s one could speak not only of Luther's doctrine of justification but also of a consistent "Lutheran" doctrine. The importance of this observation becomes most immediately obvious as we turn to examine the soteriology of the non-Lutheran Reformers. If even the primary architects of the Lutheran confessions fundamentally disagreed on this "chief article," as some modern scholars suggest, an even broader agreement between Lutheran and Reformed wings of the Reformation would appear highly unlikely. However, a fundamental Lutheran-Reformed agreement on justification by grace alone through faith alone on account of Christ's imputed righteousness alone is precisely what we find.

Adoption and Adaptation of Justification *Sola Fide*

Attempts to drive a wedge between Reformed and Lutheran doctrines of justification—like the attempt to separate those of Luther and Melanchthon—largely revolve around questions regarding justification's forensic nature and faith alone as its means. It is certainly correct to observe that not all sixteenth-century Reformed theologians articulated a doctrine of imputation as clearly as Melanchthon (or even Luther) and that some perhaps even retained a doctrine of progressive and intrinsic justification more closely akin to Rome's theology than Wittenberg's.[55] Yet the most substantive and representative stream of Reformed thought—that of its preeminent theologian, John Calvin, and that formulated in the various Reformed confessions—clearly and consistently defends the imputation of righteousness as the nature of justification, the extrinsic righteousness of Christ as its grounds, and faith alone as its means.

Unlike his Swiss predecessor Huldrych Zwingli, who was quick to insist, "I did not learn the teachings of Christ from Luther,"[56] Cal-

---

55. As did even some Lutheran theologians, such as Johann Brenz (noted above) and Andreas Osiander. The latter's doctrine, e.g., was concisely summarized by Calvin as professing "that to be justified is not only to be reconciled to God through free pardon but also to be made righteous, and righteousness is not a free imputation but the holiness and uprightness that the essence of God, dwelling in us, inspires." Calvin, *Institutes*, 3.11.6.

56. Huldrych Zwingli, *Exposition of the Sixty-Seven Articles*, in *Huldrych Zwingli: Writings*, vol. 1, *The Defense of the Reformed Faith*, ed. E. J. Furcha (Allison Park, PA: Pickwick, 1984), 119.

vin, coming on the scene more than a decade later, did not hesitate to acknowledge his debt to the Wittenberg Reformer. As is often noted, something of this debt is evident already in the outline of the first edition of his *Institutes*, being modeled on Luther's Small Catechism.[57] Calvin also encouraged printers to see Luther's own works through the press.[58] Calvin made such implicit endorsement more explicit on occasion, even with respect to soteriology, as when he praised Luther's "efficiency and power of doctrinal statement," especially in his attempts to "diffuse far and near the doctrine of salvation."[59] Thus, more than once Calvin entered the fray against attacks aimed specifically at Luther's theology. Most revealingly, he did so in rebuttal of certain "Articles" of the Paris theology faculty, which had objected to what was described as "Lutheran" doctrine and which defended the necessity of good works for justification. Though not himself attacked, Calvin responded in defense of justification "solely by faith in Christ."[60]

It is curious, then, that some have regarded the doctrine of justification *sola fide* to be a Lutheran doctrine not confessed by the Reformed,[61] or to assert, for example, that "for Luther, it was 'faith alone'; for the Reformed it was 'faith working by love.'"[62] By way of contrast, W. Stanford Reid has rightly remarked that "if justification by faith alone is a specifically Lutheran doctrine, we must put Calvin in the Lutheran rather than in the Reformed camp."[63] Indeed, one

57. See, e.g., Karla Wübbenhost, "Calvin's Doctrine of Justification: Variations on a Lutheran Theme," in *Justification in Perspective: Historical Developments and Contemporary Challenges*, ed. Bruce L. McCormack (Grand Rapids, MI: Baker, 2006), 99.

58. As he did with Luther's Genesis commentary. See CO 12:317 (no. 781).

59. John Calvin, "Letter to Heinrich Bullinger" (1544), in *Selected Works of John Calvin: Tracts and Letters*, ed. Henry Beveridge and Jules Bonnet (Grand Rapids, MI: Baker, 1983), 4:433. Luther likewise praised Calvin's soteriology; when he spoke of the pleasure with which he read one of Calvin's works, he almost certainly referred to the Genevan's *Reply to Sadoleto*, which had defended grace, faith, and imputed righteousness in terms virtually identical to the Lutheran theology. See Martin Luther, "Letter to Martin Bucer" (1539), WABr 8:569 (no. 3394).

60. John Calvin, *Articles Agreed upon by the Faculty of Sacred Theology of Paris, with the Antidote*, in Beveridge and Bonnet, *Selected Works*, 1:82. Calvin similarly responded to a reprinting of King Henry VIII's *Assertion of the Seven Sacraments*, which had been written against Luther's *Babylonian Captivity of the Church*. See CO 9:421–56.

61. W. Stanford Reid makes note of this curiosity specifically to challenge it. "Justification by Faith according to John Calvin," *WTJ* 42, no. 2 (1980): 290.

62. Peter A. Lillback, *The Binding of God: Calvin's Role in the Development of Covenant Theology*, Texts and Studies in Reformation and Post-Reformation Thought (Grand Rapids, MI: Baker Academic, 2001), 125.

63. Reid, "Justification by Faith," 296. Cf. Thomas Coates, "Calvin's Doctrine of Justification," *CTM* 34, no. 6 (1963): 33, who also concludes that, "by and large, it can be said that in his treatment of justification Calvin was 'Lutheran.'"

recent collection of essays on the doctrine of justification contains no distinctly Lutheran perspective because, the editor explains, the "traditional Reformed view is functionally identical in all the significant theological aspects to the traditional Lutheran view."[64] To be sure, Calvin, Luther, and their co-confessionalists revealed certain differences of nuance and emphasis, and they undoubtedly differed on important matters intimately related to the chief article—most famously those touching predestination and the place of the sacraments in justification.[65] A closer look at Calvin's soteriology, though, reveals no fundamental break with that articulated by the Wittenberg theologians.

Calvin's Articulation of Justification by Faith

Calvin expounded his doctrine of justification most systematically in the final edition of his *Institutes*, where more than once he also put forth concise definitions of the doctrine. Two such definitions, viewed together, highlight the themes and emphases consistent in Calvin's soteriology. In book 3, chapter 17, he wrote,

> We define justification as follows: the sinner, received into communion with Christ, is reconciled to God by his grace, while, cleansed by Christ's blood, he obtains forgiveness of sins, and clothed with Christ's righteousness as if it were his own, he stands confident before the heavenly judgment seat.[66]

Earlier, in chapter 11 of the same book, he had offered the following:

> We explain justification simply as the acceptance with which God receives us into his favor as righteous men. And we say that it consists in the remission of sins and the imputation of Christ's righteousness.[67]

Though each definition employs slightly different vocabulary, that of chapter 11 helpfully explicates that of chapter 17. In the latter chapter,

---

64. James K. Beilby and Paul Rhodes Eddy, eds., *Justification: Five Views* (Downers Grove, IL: IVP Academic, 2011), 10.

65. For treatment of one subtle difference, see, e.g., Phillip Cary, "*Sola Fide*: Luther and Calvin," *CTQ* 71, no. 3/4 (2007): 265–81.

66. Calvin, *Institutes*, 3.17.8.

67. Ibid., 3.11.2.

for example, Calvin said that reconciliation is effected by God's grace. The earlier definition makes clear that this grace is to be understood not as a quality but, just as it was by Luther and Melanchthon, as God's favor. Even more clearly, Calvin signaled his agreement with the Lutherans' understanding of grace vis-à-vis the medieval understanding by rejecting the Augustinian view, which "still subsumes grace under sanctification."[68]

Calvin's definition in chapter 11 similarly served as a gloss on chapter 17's mention of that righteousness with which the sinner is "clothed." The sinner may view this justifying righteousness "as if it were his own" not because it intrinsically is but, as chapter 11 clarifies, because it has been imputed as such. While acknowledging that Calvin did employ the vocabulary of imputation, some argue that he did not emphasize the concept, revealing a clear difference between his soteriology and, for example, Melanchthon's.[69] Others have gone so far as to suggest that, for Calvin, any imputation of Christ's righteousness would have been "redundant" since "justification requires no transfer or imputation of anything."[70] Such conclusions are not borne out, however, by a plain reading of Calvin's consistent explication of the doctrine of justification.

Calvin was both clear and emphatic, for example, when he wrote,

> We are justified before God solely by the intercession of Christ's righteousness. This is equivalent to saying that man is not righteous in himself but because the righteousness of Christ is communicated to him by imputation—something worth carefully noting.

It is worth "carefully noting," he continued, because the "frivolous notion" that one is justified "because by Christ's righteousness he shares the Spirit of God, by whom he is rendered righteous" is "too contrary to the above doctrine ever to be reconciled with it."[71] This being the

---

68. Ibid., 3.11.15.

69. See, e.g., Stephen Strehle, *The Catholic Roots of the Protestant Gospel: Encounter between the Middle Ages and the Reformation*, Studies in the History of Christian Thought 60 (Leiden: Brill, 1995), 66.

70. Rich Lusk, "A Response to 'The Biblical Plan of Salvation,'" in *The Auburn Avenue Theology, Pros and Cons: Debating the Federal Vision*, ed. E. Calvin Beisner (Fort Lauderdale, FL: Knox Theological Seminary, 2004), 142.

71. Calvin, *Institutes*, 3.11.23.

case, it is hardly surprising that Calvin himself "carefully noted" the forensic nature of justification not only throughout the *Institutes* but likewise in his commentaries on Scripture and in his polemical treatises.[72]

Moreover, he not only noted that this was his own doctrine but also regularly explained why this had to be recognized as the biblical doctrine. And he was neither hesitant nor ambiguous in doing so. In explaining, like Melanchthon, that the term *justification* "was taken from legal usage," he remarked that "anyone moderately versed in the Hebrew language, provided he has a sober brain, is not ignorant of the fact that the phrase arose from this source, and drew from it its tendency and implication."[73] By way of illustration, he pointed to those biblical passages in which the term could only be understood in a forensic or declarative manner, rather than denoting any transformative impartation of righteousness—most obviously in descriptions of men "justifying" God.[74] He further observed that Christ's righteousness being imputed to sinners in justification simply mirrored human sinfulness being imputed to Christ in the atonement; thus, the sinner becomes righteous before God "in the same way as Christ became a sinner."[75]

Such clear articulations, far from evidencing a lack of commitment to the forensic doctrine, support the conclusions that imputation is central to Calvin's doctrine of justification and that it is clearly and consistently so.[76] Objections to this reading of Calvin on the nature of justification are often predicated on the same concern that has led some to downplay Calvin's clear confession that faith is the sole means of justification. The concern is that a solely extrinsic righteousness appro-

72. E.g., John Calvin described justifying righteousness as existing "as a property in Christ," so "that which properly belongs to Christ is imputed to us." *The Epistles of Paul the Apostle to the Romans and to the Thessalonians*, trans. Ross Mackenzie, ed. David W. Torrance and Thomas F. Torrance (Grand Rapids, MI: Eerdmans, 1960), 118. In controversy with the Catholic Cardinal Jacopo Sadoleto, he likewise defended the proposition that there is no justification but "in the mere goodness of God, by which sin is pardoned, and righteousness imputed to us." Calvin, *Reply to Sadoleto*, in *A Reformation Debate: Sadoleto's Letter to the Genevans and Calvin's Reply*, ed. John C. Olin (Grand Rapids, MI: Baker, 1976), 67.

73. Calvin, *Institutes*, 3.11.11.

74. Ibid., 3.11.3.

75. John Calvin, *The Second Epistle of Paul the Apostle to the Corinthians and the Epistles to Timothy, Titus and Philemon*, trans. T. A. Smail, ed. David W. Torrance and Thomas F. Torrance (Grand Rapids, MI: Eerdmans, 1964), 81.

76. For a more thorough detailing of some of the issues and authors addressed in this section, see especially J. V. Fesko, "Calvin on Justification and Recent Misinterpretations of His View," *MAJT* 16 (2005): 83–114.

priated solely by faith fails adequately to account for Calvin's equally clear emphasis on regeneration—which, in the *Institutes*, he treats even before justification—and the attendant intrinsic righteousness evident in the believer's works. To be sure, Calvin did lay great stress on "the inseparable nature of 'inherent righteousness' and justification," but this is evidence neither of inherent righteousness effecting justification nor, as has been suggested, that "Luther and Calvin are in sharp disagreement" on this point.[77]

Calvin insisted that "there is in justification no place for works,"[78] and that it is "faith alone which justifies."[79] And yet he was equally clear that faith does not justify "of itself or through some intrinsic power"; rather, it is simply "a kind of vessel."[80] As such, justifying faith is not that which is formed or made effective by love but "is something merely passive."[81] Being a passive vessel or instrument, faith's value and benefit is found only in its object, Christ and his righteousness.[82]

While Calvin thus clearly embraced justification *sola fide*, it is not difficult to see how some confusion might arise on this point. Using language that is not his own, one might fairly say that, for Calvin, only faith justifies, but faith does not only justify.[83] Thus, for example, he spoke not only of "free reconciliation" but also of "newness of life" being "attained by us through faith."[84] Therefore, he could consistently maintain that "justification is not separated from regeneration," while always at the same time insisting that "they are things distinct" and that "justification must be very different from reformation into newness of life."[85] By way of clarifying his own pithy formulation of this centrally important point—"It is therefore faith alone which justifies,

---

77. Lillback, *Binding of God*, 190.
78. Calvin, *Institutes*, 3.11.6.
79. John Calvin, *Canons and Decrees of the Council of Trent, with the Antidote*, in Beveridge and Bonnet, *Selected Works*, 3:152.
80. Calvin, *Institutes*, 3.11.7.
81. Ibid., 3.13.5.
82. Cf. ibid., 3.11.7, 17. The analogy Calvin employed at 3.11.7—a vessel filled with gold—is virtually the same as that used by Martin Luther, "Sermons on John 6," *LW* 23:28.
83. Or, more precisely, only the Christ whose righteousness is received by faith justifies, but Christ does not only justify. Calvin remarked thus in his *Reply to Sadoleto*, 68, "If you would duly understand how inseparable faith and works are, look to Christ, who, as the Apostle teaches (I Cor. i.30) has been given to us for justification and for sanctification."
84. Calvin, *Institutes*, 3.3.1.
85. Ibid., 3.11.11. Cf. 3.3.1: "Man is justified by faith alone, and simple pardon; nevertheless actual holiness of life, so to speak, is not separated from free imputation of righteousness."

and yet the faith which justifies is not alone"—Calvin, paralleling Luther, offered the illustration of the sun's heat, by itself alone, warming the earth, though the sun's heat remains "constantly conjoined with light."[86]

These distinct yet inseparable effects of faith Calvin could describe as a "double grace" or twofold gift: the first of justification and the second of sanctification.[87] Elsewhere, he discussed the same under the terminology of "two kinds of righteousness," a formulation popularized by Luther already in 1519.[88] That Calvin and Luther employed the same phraseology and the same illustrations in this context indicates that there was no radical discontinuity between them on the distinctively different natures of, yet inseparable relationship between, justification and sanctification. Indeed, these shared interpretations are hardly surprising in light of both Reformers being forced to answer the charge that their doctrine of justification by faith alone could only court antinomianism. Responding, for example, to the Roman accusation that "by attributing everything to faith, we leave no room for works," Calvin clarified that "we deny that good works have any share in justification, but we claim full authority for them in the lives of the righteous"; indeed, he continued, "it is obvious that gratuitous righteousness is necessarily connected with regeneration."[89]

Calvin in Comparison with Lutheran and Reformed Positions

Precisely the same response to the same objections was offered by Luther and the Lutheran Reformers, despite continuing suggestions—even by fellow Protestants—that "Lutherans warn the Christian against sanctification."[90] In fact, the Wittenbergers adamantly insisted on it, only, like Calvin, insisting equally adamantly that justification is in no way conditioned on it. As bluntly as Calvin, if not more so, Luther

---

86. Calvin, *Canons and Decrees*, in Beveridge and Bonnet, *Selected Works*, 3:152. See also *Institutes*, 3.11.6. Cf. Martin Luther, "Preface to the Epistle of St. Paul to the Romans," *LW* 35:371: "It is impossible to separate works from faith, quite as impossible as to separate heat and light from fire."
87. Calvin, *Institutes*, 3.11.1.
88. E.g., ibid., 3.11.12. Cf. Luther, "Two Kinds of Righteousness," *LW* 31:293–306.
89. Calvin, *Reply to Sadoleto*, 66, 68. Cf. *Institutes*, 3.16.
90. P. Andrew Sandlin, "Lutheranized Calvinism: Gospel or Law, or Gospel and Law," *R&R* 11, no. 2 (2002): 124.

could even say that "works are necessary to salvation, but they do not cause salvation, because faith alone gives life."[91] Luther was well aware of the confusion that might be caused by this subtle yet crucial distinction between good works being necessary (as a consequence) *to* but not (as a condition) *for* justification. He frankly acknowledged that, given the twin errors of legalism and antinomianism, "it is difficult and dangerous to teach that we are justified by faith without works and yet to require works at the same time."[92] Yet it is precisely this that he taught consistently from the early 1520s on. Melanchthon was therefore understandably disgruntled that still a decade later "our people are falsely accused of prohibiting good works."[93] Speaking not only for himself but as a representative of Lutheran theology, he thus reiterated that "faith is bound to yield good fruits and that it ought to do good works commanded by God"—and yet "not so that we may trust in these works to merit justification."[94]

It is perhaps the case that Luther, fearing legalism more than antinomianism, laid less stress on regeneration than Calvin; nevertheless, they remained in fundamental agreement on justification and sanctification being clearly distinguished yet inseparable. It is perhaps also true that some Reformed theologians other than Calvin—as well as some sixteenth-century Lutherans—blurred this distinction in their own writings.[95] Those confessional writings that became definitive of Reformed theology, however, not only reflect Calvin's soteriology but also, like it, do not substantially deviate from that of Luther, Melanchthon, and the Lutheran confessional writings.

Though none by itself would become definitive of Reformed theology, mid-century confessional documents such as the French (1559), Belgic (1561), and Second Helvetic Confessions (1566) and the Heidelberg Catechism (1563) remain representative. Each explicitly

---

91. Martin Luther, *Disputation concerning Justification*, LW 34:165.
92. Luther, *Lectures on Galatians* (1535), LW 27:62.
93. "The Augsburg Confession," art. 20.1, in Kolb and Wengert, *Book of Concord*, 53.
94. Ibid., art. 6.1, in Kolb and Wengert, *Book of Concord*, 41.
95. McGrath suggests, e.g., that Oecolampadius subordinated justification to regeneration and that Bucer's teaching of a "double-justification" likewise confused the distinctions maintained by Calvin. *Iustitia Dei*, 220–22. These interpretations have not remained unchallenged, however. See, e.g., Jeff Fisher, "The Doctrine of Justification in the Teaching of John Oecolampadius (1482–1531)," in Parsons, *Since We Are Justified by Faith*, 44–57; Carl R. Trueman, *Luther's Legacy: Salvation and English Reformers, 1525–1556* (Oxford: Clarendon, 1994), 78–79; and the further references in each.

grounds justification in the imputation of Christ's righteousness.[96] Each professes faith alone to be the means of salvation,[97] often defining the term explicitly as "trust"[98] and clarifying its merely passive and instrumental role.[99] And while clearly distinguishing justification from regeneration and its works, each clearly emphasizes their inseparability.[100]

Roman Reactions and Responses

Partly because Luther himself had been slow to arrive at the above conclusions, initial Catholic responses to Reformation theology focused much more on issues such as ecclesiastical authority than on the specific doctrine of justification. As has been rightly noted, "The astonishing thing about the early Catholic response to the Reformation was that this doctrine simply did not figure at all prominently in the controversy."[101] Even in the 1530 Augsburg Confession, Melanchthon could thus summarize the Lutheran doctrine in a mere two sentences[102] and suggest that "there is nothing here that departs from the Scriptures or the catholic church, or from the Roman church, insofar as we can tell from its writers."[103] If he sincerely believed this, however, it quickly and finally became clear that Rome did not. The immediately forthcoming Roman Confutation of the Augsburg Confession was unambiguous: the "ascription of justification to faith alone is diametrically opposite the truth of the Gospel by which works are not excluded," and "ascription of justification to faith is not admitted since it pertains to grace and love." The Confutation

---

96. "The French Confession," 18 (147); "The Belgic Confession," 22 (437); "The Heidelberg Catechism," 60 (783); and "The Second Helvetic Confession," 15 (839–40). Each can be found in English translation in James T. Dennison Jr., ed., *Reformed Confessions of the 16th and 17th Centuries in English Translation*, vol. 2, *1552–1566* (Grand Rapids, MI: Reformation Heritage Books, 2010). Here and below, citations are by article or question number with page numbers for this edition in parentheses.

97. "The French Confession," 20 (147); "The Belgic Confession," 22 (437); "The Heidelberg Catechism," 60 (782); "The Second Helvetic Confession," 15 (839).

98. "The Heidelberg Catechism," 21 (774); "The Second Helvetic Confession," 16 (841).

99. "The Belgic Confession," 22 (437); "The Heidelberg Catechism," 61 (783); "The Second Helvetic Confession," 15 (840).

100. "The French Confession," 22 (148); "The Belgic Confession," 24 (438); "The Heidelberg Catechism," 64 (783); "The Second Helvetic Confession," 16 (842–44).

101. David Bagchi, "Luther's Catholic Opponents," in *The Reformation World*, ed. Andrew Pettegree (London: Routledge, 2000), 106.

102. "The Augsburg Confession," art. 4, in Kolb and Wengert, *Book of Concord*, 38 and 40.

103. Ibid., concl. of pt. 1, art. 1, in Kolb and Wengert, *Book of Concord*, 59.

concluded not only that "faith alone does not justify" but that "love is the chief virtue."[104]

In the following decade attempts were nonetheless made to reach a consensus on justification, and in view of the Protestant-Catholic colloquy at Regensburg in 1541, Melanchthon could yet again proclaim that "we have no doctrine different from the Roman Church."[105] Participants in the colloquy did agree on wording acceptable to all; the church bodies they represented, however, rejected the formulation as being ambiguous and thus potentially misleading.[106] Key in this regard was the confession that the sinner is justified by means of a "living and efficacious faith," which Luther, for example, feared did not preclude speaking of "faith formed by love."[107] And indeed, Melanchthon reported that some involved understood justification to occur not by faith alone but by love alone.[108] Though this was not the conclusion to be reached at the Council of Trent, the failure to reach a consensus on soteriology did mean that clarifying the Roman doctrine of justification—and condemning the Protestant doctrine—would become a central focus of the council, which opened only four years after Regensburg's failed negotiations.

That the Tridentine fathers themselves realized the seriousness of the division concerning the doctrine of justification is evident in their June 1546 report to Rome, in which they acknowledged that "the importance of the council, regarding dogma, depends principally on the article of justification."[109] This being the case, Trent's decree on

---

104. *Confutatio Pontificia*, 1.6, trans. H. E. Jacobs, in *The Augsburg Confession: A Collection of Sources*, ed. J. M. Reu (Chicago: Wartburg, 1930), 352. At Augsburg, Eck even more clearly asserted that, for justification, love is more necessary than faith. See George Spalatin, *Annales Reformationis* (Leipzig: Gleditsch, 1718), 163. Cf. the Roman Cardinal Jacopo Sadoleto, who likewise asserted that because faith includes and is formed by love, "love is essentially comprehended as the chief and primary cause of our salvation." *Letter to the Genevans*, in Olin, *A Reformation Debate*, 36. Calvin confessed to be "amazed when I read your assertion." *Reply to Sadoleto*, 69. Luther more dispassionately but not inaccurately noted that "where they speak of love, we speak of faith." *Lectures on Galatians* (1535), LW 26:129.

105. Philipp Melanchthon, "Letter to Cardinal Campeggio" (1541), CR 2:170 (no. 761).

106. For a summary of the proceedings at Regensburg, as well as a translation of the article on justification, see Anthony N. S. Lane, "A Tale of Two Cities: Justification at Regensburg and Trent (1546–1547)," in McCormack, *Justification in Perspective*, 119–45.

107. See, e.g., his correspondence in WABr 9:406–10 (no. 3616); 9:436–45 (no. 3629); 9:459–63 (no. 3637).

108. See, e.g., Melanchthon, "Opinion," CR 4:430 (no. 2279), and "Response," CR 4:485 (no. 2301).

109. *Concilium Tridentinum*, ed. Societas Goerresiana (Freiburg: Herder, 1901–2001), 10:532 (no. 444).

534 Korey D. Maas

justification—going through nearly a dozen drafts over seven months—was given more attention than any other produced by the council. One draft of the decree made especially explicit the reason for this extended attention: "At this time nothing is more vexing and disturbing to the church of God than a novel, perverse, and erroneous doctrine concerning justification."[110] Though Luther himself had died just as the council was beginning, and though Trent's canons and decrees identify no Reformers by name, it is clear that the Wittenbergers were especially in view. As one Catholic commentator concisely notes, "Luther set the agenda for the council."[111]

Despite the fact that several prominent council members were not entirely antipathetic to the "Lutheran" doctrine of justification, the views of such men, perhaps unsurprisingly, were consistently sidelined.[112] Yet the ultimate rejection of the Reformers' soteriology cannot be attributed—as it increasingly is—to a simple misunderstanding of vocabulary or to each party talking past the other. As has often been noted, by freighting the crucial terms with their own received definitions, the Tridentine theologians could very well have agreed with the confessional Lutheran definition of justification; unlike at Regensburg, however, they rejected this formulation precisely because they understood that these terms were defined very differently by the Reformers.[113]

Though Trent would distance itself from the *via moderna* by very clearly confessing that "the beginning of that justification must proceed from the predisposing grace of God,"[114] the council was equally clear in anathematizing all who would say that "the grace by which we are justified is only the good will of God."[115] Maintaining the understanding of grace as a quality within man, the decree on justification thus

---

110. Ibid., 5:420 (no. 179).

111. John W. O'Malley, *Trent: What Happened at the Council* (Cambridge: Belknap, 2013), 12.

112. See, e.g., Hubert Jedin, *A History of the Council of Trent*, vol. 2, *The First Sessions at Trent: 1545–47*, trans. Dom Ernest Graf (Edinburgh: Thomas Nelson, 1961), 172–73, 181, 190–91, 279.

113. Cf. Robert Preus, *Justification and Rome* (St. Louis, MO: Concordia, 1997), 27; Louis A. Smith, "Some Second Thoughts on the *Joint Declaration*," *Lutheran Forum* 31 (Fall 1997): 8.

114. *Canons and Decrees of the Council of Trent*, trans. H. J. Schroeder (Rockford, IL: Tan Books, 1978), sixth session, "Concerning Justification," chap. 5 (p. 31). Citations of Trent hereafter refer to the sixth session, "Concerning Justification"; decree chapters and canons are cited, with page numbers for the above translation included parenthetically.

115. Ibid., canon 11 (43).

speaks of grace being bestowed and obtained, and thus of sinners being "made" just.[116] Further, the distinction between "predisposing grace" and the "grace of justification" allows for the insistence that the former is received without any merit on man's part, while the latter is obtained by means of human cooperation.[117]

Because of this insistence on human cooperation in justification, any claims that the decrees of Trent are "not necessarily incompatible with the Lutheran doctrine of *sola fide*" remain highly questionable.[118] Again, the Tridentine fathers well understood what the Reformers meant when they spoke of justifying faith as "confidence in divine mercy," and they specifically condemned this meaning.[119] More pointedly rejected was the formula of "faith alone, meaning that nothing else is required to cooperate in order to obtain the grace of justification."[120] To be sure, Trent spoke just as highly of faith as of grace but again only in a qualified manner. Just as grace alone—without human cooperation—was deemed insufficient for justification, so too it was declared that faith cannot justify without the virtues of hope and charity.[121] Retaining the view that justification was progressively sanative, the council could thus allow only that faith constitutes "the beginning of human salvation."[122]

It was also this sanative understanding of justification that drove Trent's ultimate condemnation of any who said that "men are justified either by the sole imputation of the justice of Christ or by the sole remission of sins."[123] Certainly, Trent did not condemn the proposition that God does indeed reckon or repute men righteous; contrary to the Reformers, though, the council held that one is deemed righteous when and because one has inherently become so[124]—not only as the result of a divine infusion of righteousness but also, again, on the basis of

---

116. Cf., e.g., ibid., chap. 3 (31); canon 9 (43).
117. Cf., e.g., ibid., canons 4 (42) and 9 (43).
118. "Justification by Faith (Common Statement)," §56, in Anderson, Murphy, and Burgess, *Justification by Faith*, 35.
119. *Canons and Decrees of the Council of Trent*, canon 12 (43).
120. Ibid., canon 9 (43).
121. Ibid., chap. 7 (34).
122. Ibid., chap. 8 (35). The Lutherans rejected this view, as did Calvin. "Apology of the Augsburg Confession," art. 4.71–72, in Kolb and Wengert, *Book of Concord*, 132; Calvin, *Canons and Decrees*, in Beveridge and Bonnet, *Selected Works*, 3:114.
123. *Canons and Decrees of the Council of Trent*, canon 11 (43).
124. Cf. ibid., chaps. 7 (33) and 16 (41).

human cooperation.[125] This is perhaps made most obvious in Trent's condemnation of the Reformers' insistence that rather than being a condition of justification, good works are simply the "fruits and signs of justification obtained."[126]

Such anathemas were not pronounced on straw men; the council fathers well understood the fundamental tenets of the Protestant doctrine of justification. And if there had been some confusion about the official Roman doctrine before Trent, afterward its central features became equally clear to the Reformers. Unsurprisingly, they were not slow to respond to its formalization. Calvin himself quickly did so in his brief *Antidote* to the council's acts, where he accurately noted that "the whole dispute is as to The Cause of Justification. The Fathers of Trent," he summarized, "pretend that it is twofold, as if we were justified partly by forgiveness of sins and partly by spiritual regeneration." He could therefore concisely reject Trent's soteriological conclusions by writing that the "whole may be thus summed up—Their error consists in sharing the work between God and ourselves."[127]

Two decades later, Lutheran theologian and coauthor of the Formula of Concord Martin Chemnitz reached the same conclusion in his multivolume *Examination of the Council of Trent*. There he suggested that Trent's "one chief argument" against the Reformation doctrine was the claim that, since spiritual renewal is begun at the same time that sins are remitted, justification must be attributed to both.[128] By way of explaining the fundamental difference between Catholic and Protestant doctrines, Chemnitz observed that the Roman theologians

> understand the word "justify" according to the manner of the Latin composition as meaning "to make righteous" through a donated or infused quality of inherent righteousness, from which works of righteousness proceed. The Lutherans, however, accept the word "justify" in the Hebrew manner of speaking; therefore they define

125. See, e.g., ibid., chap. 7 (33–34). For brief commentary, see also Anthony N. S. Lane, *Justification by Faith in Catholic-Protestant Dialogue: An Evangelical Assessment* (New York: T&T Clark, 2002), 71–72, 74–75.
126. *Canons and Decrees of the Council of Trent*, canon 24 (45).
127. Calvin, *Canons and Decrees*, in Beveridge and Bonnet, *Selected Works*, 3:116, 113.
128. Martin Chemnitz, *Examination of the Council of Trent*, trans. Fred Kramer, vol. 1, *Sacred Scripture, Free Will, Original Sin, Justification, and Good Works* (St. Louis, MO: Concordia, 1971), 579–80.

justification as the absolution from sins, or the remission of sins, through imputation of the righteousness of Christ.[129]

This "Hebrew manner of speaking," Chemnitz demonstrated at length, is precisely the same manner in which the term "justify" is consistently used in both the sacred and profane literature of Greek antiquity.[130] "Among the Greek authors, therefore, the word 'justify' is not used in that sense for which alone the papalists contend," he concluded; indeed, "its forensic meaning, as we commonly say, is so manifest" that even Trent's defenders found this difficult to deny.[131]

Continuing Controversies

Given the great lengths to which both Rome and the Reformers went to articulate, explain, and defend their doctrines of justification, as well as the evidence that each party well understood the fundamentals of the doctrine it was critiquing and condemning, it bears repeating that the divisive sixteenth-century soteriological disputes were not simply the unfortunate result of unrecognized misunderstandings. This is especially so because, within the last several decades, more than one school of thought has made purported misunderstandings central to its interpretation of the Reformation theology of justification. The ecumenical dialogues culminating in the Joint Declaration on the Doctrine of Justification (1999), for example, typify the belief that Lutheran and Catholic soteriologies are essentially compatible, even if the Reformers (and their critics) did not understand this themselves. Misunderstanding of a different sort is posited by the "Finnish School" of Luther interpretation, which suggests that even Luther's immediate heirs misunderstood and so consistently distorted his doctrine of justification—which more closely resembled the soteriology of Eastern Orthodoxy than that of the Lutheran or Reformed confessions. Perhaps most closely echoing the Reformation-era debates

---

129. Ibid., 1:467.
130. See, e.g., ibid., 1:470–76.
131. Ibid., 1:471. Robert Preus also notes that "as time went on Rome did not seriously dispute that the word *dikaioō* was a forensic term. The massive evidence for this fact brought forth by Chemnitz and the later Lutherans was utterly compelling." *Justification and Rome*, 68. Elsewhere he also notes the modern philological confirmation of Chemnitz's interpretation. See Robert D. Preus, "The Doctrine of Justification in the Theology of Classical Lutheran Orthodoxy," *The Springfielder* 29, no. 1 (1965): 29.

themselves, proponents of what has come to be called the "New Perspective on Paul" posit that the Reformers fundamentally misunderstood the apostle Paul's doctrine of justification, the very doctrine they claimed to be reviving and championing. Clearly, if any of these interpretations are correct, a radical rethinking of Reformation soteriology would be warranted. Whether such revisionist readings can be substantiated is the question to be addressed in this final section.

JOINT DECLARATION ON THE DOCTRINE OF JUSTIFICATION (1999)

Though the Joint Declaration on the Doctrine of Justification is a narrowly Lutheran-Catholic statement, which no longer draws the attention it received on its signing, it deserves brief attention for a number of reasons. Not only is it the fruit of nearly two decades of ecumenical discussion specifically devoted to the most contentious of the church-dividing doctrines of the sixteenth century, but it also claims finally to have articulated a "common understanding" and "consensus on basic truths of the doctrine of justification," such that the "doctrinal condemnations of the sixteenth century do not apply" any longer to the subscribing church bodies.[132] Unsurprisingly, therefore, the document has been touted as having brought about "the end of the Reformation."[133]

While acknowledging that sixteenth-century Catholic and Lutheran soteriologies were indeed "of a different character," the Joint Declaration proclaims that "our churches have come to new insights."[134] Whether this is entirely true of both churches, however, is cast into doubt both by the text of the Joint Declaration and by other contemporary documents. Avery Dulles, for example, a Catholic participant in the dialogues leading up to the production of the Joint Declaration, admitted that in their course "the theology of justification in

---

132. The Lutheran World Federation and the Roman Catholic Church, *Joint Declaration on the Doctrine of Justification* (Grand Rapids, MI: Eerdmans, 2000), 5, 13. It must be observed, however, that the official Catholic response to the text of the Joint Declaration notes that the document's explanation of how Lutheranism understands the justified as *simul justus et peccator* ("at the same time righteous and a sinner") "is not acceptable," and thus "it remains difficult to see how [it] . . . is not touched by the anathemas of the Tridentine decree." "Response of the Catholic Church to the Joint Declaration of the Catholic Church and the Lutheran World Federation on the Doctrine of Justification," clarification 1. The text is available at the Vatican website: http://www.vatican.va /roman_curia/pontifical_councils/chrstuni/documents/rc_pc_chrstuni_doc_01081998_off-answer -catholic_en.html.

133. Matthias Gierth, "A Time to Embrace," *The Tablet*, November 20, 1999, 6.

134. *Joint Declaration*, 1, 7.

Roman Catholic teaching ha[d] undergone no dramatic changes since the Council of Trent."[135] This observation is partially borne out by the way the official *Catechism of the Catholic Church* defines *justification*: it "includes the remission of sins, sanctification, and the renewal of the inner man."[136] Within the Joint Declaration itself, justification defined as both "forgiveness of sins and being made righteous" is accurately described as the "Catholic understanding."[137] But this is also the definition the Lutheran signatories claim now to "confess together" with Rome.[138] Conversely, the document nowhere engages, much less affirms, justification as the imputation of Christ's alien righteousness. It is difficult to view the "serious omission" of this central concept of Reformation soteriology as anything but intentional.[139]

The ambiguous employment of other key words appears similarly intentional. The term *grace*, for example, is frequently invoked, but the Joint Declaration never indicates whether this is to be understood as God's favor or as a quality in the soul. Thus, the transposition of prepositions in describing justification as occurring "by faith and through grace"—rather than in the traditional Lutheran articulation, "by grace and through faith"—allows the impression that grace is the instrumental means of justification while faith is its actual cause.[140] Such a reading is further made plausible by the document's definition of justifying faith as *including* hope and love.[141]

Such formulations have led some commentators to characterize the Joint Declaration as "Regensburg Redivivus"[142] and to describe its conclusions as "much the same as at Regensburg where Protestant

135. Dulles, "Justification in Contemporary Catholic Theology," 256.
136. *Catechism of the Catholic Church* (New York: Image, 1995), 2019; cf. ibid., 2027: "Moved by the Holy Spirit, we can merit for ourselves and for others all the graces needed to attain eternal life."
137. *Joint Declaration*, 27.
138. *Joint Declaration*, "Annex to the Official Common Statement," 2A; *Joint Declaration*, 4.2. This is the case even though the official Catholic response to the document, which is "meant to complete some of the paragraphs explaining Catholic doctrine," does so by clearly stating that "eternal life is, at one and the same time, grace and the reward given by God for good works and merits." "Response of the Catholic Church," clarifications 5 and 3.
139. Lane, *Justification by Faith in Catholic-Protestant Dialogue*, 126, 158.
140. Department of Systematic Theology, Concordia Seminary, St. Louis, "A Response to the Joint Declaration on the Doctrine of Justification," in *The Joint Declaration on the Doctrine of Justification in Confessional Lutheran Perspective* (St. Louis, MO: Lutheran Church—Missouri Synod, 1999), 48n9.
141. *Joint Declaration*, 25.
142. Paul McCain, "Regensburg Redivivus?," *CTQ* 63, no. 4 (1999): 305–9.

substance was accepted in exchange for the acceptance of a measure of ambiguity."[143] Even this, though, may overstate the case since much of the "Protestant substance" of Regensburg—which frequently referred to the justified being "reckoned" righteous—is absent in the Joint Declaration, which consistently "opts to use the word 'justification' in the Catholic sense."[144] It is not entirely unwarranted, then, to believe that the Joint Declaration does speak accurately when it says that "the teaching of the Lutheran churches presented in this Declaration does not fall under the condemnations from the Council of Trent"—but only because the Lutheran teaching "presented in this Declaration" is not that of Luther himself, the Lutheran confessions, or Reformation-era Protestantism more generally.[145]

THE FINNISH SCHOOL OF LUTHER INTERPRETATION

Whatever the shortcomings of the Joint Declaration, the premise that Lutherans and Catholics have long misunderstood one another's theology is not inherently implausible. Even on its face, though, it would seem much less likely that Luther's own colleagues and immediate successors so misunderstood his soteriology that they could propound a radically different doctrine under his name. This is, however, a central claim of what has come to be known as the "Finnish" interpretation of Luther. Thus Tuomo Mannermaa, the theologian most closely associated with this interpretation, speaks dismissively of "the one-sidedly forensic doctrine of justification adopted by the Formula of Concord and by subsequent Lutheranism," and argues that "the idea of *theosis* can be found at the core of the theology of Martin Luther."[146] Others, as indicated above, argue that imputation was never emphasized in Luther (or Calvin) but only came to prominence with Melanchthon's later theology.[147] Much of the above treatment of Luther and Melanchthon serves, even in abbreviated form, to highlight the problems with

---

143. Lane, *Justification by Faith in Catholic-Protestant Dialogue*, 226.
144. Ibid., 157.
145. *Joint Declaration*, 41; see Department of Systematic Theology, "A Response to the Joint Declaration," 45.
146. Tuomo Mannermaa, "Justification and *Theosis* in Lutheran-Orthodox Perspective," in *Union with Christ: The New Finnish Interpretation of Luther*, ed. Carl E. Braaten and Robert W. Jenson (Grand Rapids, MI: Eerdmans, 1998), 28, 25.
147. Strehle, *Catholic Roots of the Protestant Gospel*, 66.

such theses. Even if it may in some sense be said that the Reformation doctrine of imputation was Melanchthonian in origin, it was not only articulated early in his career but was also subsequently and clearly embraced by Luther, Calvin, and their heirs.

In disputing this long-accepted understanding, the Finnish school claims that the central and overriding emphasis of Luther's own doctrine of justification is not the forensic notion of faith's passive reception of Christ's alien and imputed righteousness but a real ontological "participation in God's essence in Christ."[148] Thus, Luther is understood to confess that "the righteousness that stands in front of God is based on the indwelling of Christ" and that this intrinsic righteousness is "the necessary condition for God's favor."[149] The Finnish school is unquestionably correct to observe that this is not the Lutheran teaching articulated in the Formula of Concord;[150] whether the Formula can be so easily set against Luther himself is rather less clear. In addition to regularly citing Luther, for example, the Formula's authors conclude the relevant article by referring readers to "the wonderful, magnificent exposition by Dr. Luther of St. Paul's Epistle to the Galatians" for "any further, necessary explanation of this lofty and sublime article on justification."[151] It is especially in this 1535 Galatians commentary that Luther most forcefully argued that "we can obtain it [i.e., justifying righteousness] only through the free imputation and indescribable gift of God."[152]

To be sure, Luther did often explain justification in terms of a mystical or ontological union with Christ and the inherent righteousness resulting; such explanations, however, are largely concentrated in his earliest publications. In building its case especially on a foundation of these "pre-Reformation" works,[153] the Finnish school often fails

---

148. Tuomo Mannermaa, *Christ Present in Faith: Luther's View of Justification*, ed. Kirsi Stjerna (Minneapolis: Fortress, 2005), 17.

149. Simo Peura, "Christ as Favor and Gift (*donum*): The Challenge of Luther's Understanding of Justification," in Braaten and Jenson, *Union with Christ*, 66.

150. This does not at all deny a union with or indwelling of Christ but insists that "this indwelling of God is not the righteousness of faith . . . for the sake of which we are pronounced righteous before God. Rather, this indwelling is a result of the righteousness of faith which precedes it." "The Solid Declaration of the Formula of Concord," art. 3, par. 54, in Kolb and Wengert, *Book of Concord*, 572.

151. "Solid Declaration," art. 3, par. 67, in Kolb and Wengert, *Book of Concord*, 573.

152. Luther, *Lectures on Galatians* (1535), LW 26:6.

153. For some cited examples and critique, see, e.g., Carl R. Trueman, "Is the Finnish Line a New Beginning? A Critical Assessment of the Reading of Luther Offered by the Helsinki Circle," *WTJ* 65, no. 2 (2003): 235–36.

to give sufficient attention to the development of Luther's theology.[154] Perhaps partly explaining the Finnish choice of emphasis is the context in which this interpretation first arose—ecumenical dialogues between the Finnish Lutheran and Russian Orthodox churches. As Robert Jenson, himself a defender of the Finnish scholarship, admits, in the course of their dialogues the Finnish theologians "went looking . . . for some wiggle room."[155] As admirable as the ecumenical goal of doctrinal consensus on justification might be—whether with Rome or the Eastern Orthodox—such a goal cannot responsibly be reached by downplaying or ignoring important evidence of real differences.

THE NEW PERSPECTIVE ON PAUL

What would come to be called the New Perspective on Paul also arose out of reflections on a sort of ecumenism, in this case ancient rather than contemporary. Seminal works of Krister Stendahl and E. P. Sanders, for example, argued that Saint Paul's teaching on justification and the law was formulated not in view of the question of how individual sinners—whether Jew or Gentile—might be saved but in response to the question of how Gentiles might be included within the community already established by God's covenant.[156] As prominent New Perspective representative N. T. Wright has pithily summarized, justification for Paul is "not so much about salvation as about the church";[157] thus, it is "the original ecumenical doctrine."[158]

---

154. They sometimes cite passages even from Luther's 1535 Galatians commentary (and other mature works), but the tendency is often to read such passages through the lens of his earlier works and to ignore not only the clearly imputative emphases of the immediately surrounding paragraphs but also the work's paradigmatic preface. Again, see Trueman, "Is the Finnish Line a New Beginning?," 238–39.

155. Robert Jenson, "Response to Mark Seifrid, Paul Metzger, and Carl Trueman on Finnish Luther Research," *WTJ* 65, no. 2 (2003): 245. Elsewhere Jenson notes his own ecumenical motivation for appropriating the Finnish interpretation: "I can *do* very little with Luther as usually interpreted." Robert W. Jenson, "Response to Tuomo Mannermaa, 'Why Is Luther So Fascinating?,'" in Braaten and Jenson, *Union with Christ*, 21.

156. See, e.g., Krister Stendahl, "The Apostle Paul and the Introspective Conscience of the West," *HTR* 56, no. 3 (1963): 199–215; E. P. Sanders, *Paul and Palestinian Judaism: A Comparison of Patterns of Religion* (Philadelphia: Fortress, 1977).

157. N. T. Wright, *What Saint Paul Really Said: Was Paul of Tarsus the Real Founder of Christianity?* (Grand Rapids, MI: Eerdmans, 1997), 119. Even more clearly, he states that "justification is not 'how someone becomes a Christian.'" N. T. Wright, "New Perspectives on Paul," in McCormack, *Justification in Perspective*, 260.

158. Wright, "New Perspectives on Paul," 261. On the same page he further explains that this relocation of justification from the category of soteriology to ecclesiology continues to offer "a powerful incentive to work together across denominational barriers."

Understanding Paul's doctrine of justification primarily in ecclesio-logical rather than soteriological terms, Wright can then go so far as to translate the apostle's use of the word "righteousness" (*dikaiosynē*) as "covenant membership."[159]

What advocates of the New Perspective deem the radical misunder-standing of Paul's doctrine was purportedly introduced by Augustine but reasserted, and with greater consequence, by the Protestant Re-formers, especially Luther. Not only was Augustine's reading of Paul, it is suggested, colored by his own disputes with Pelagianism and its claim that one might be saved by one's own merits without the aid of divine grace, but also Luther and his successors are understood to have read Paul's disputes with Judaism through the distorting lens of their own disputes with Rome. Again, Wright concisely encapsulates this view when he speaks of interpreters who "smuggle Pelagius into Galatia."[160] The fundamental problem with such interpretations, ac-cording to the New Perspective, is that the Judaism of Paul's day did not at all embrace a legalistic "Pelagian" soteriology. Therefore, Paul could not have been attempting to refute such a theology in favor of a doctrine of salvation by grace alone through faith alone.

Just as the Finnish interpretation has helpfully refocused atten-tion on a Reformation theology of union with Christ—even if the Reformers did not understand this union to be the ground or cause of justification—so too has the New Perspective helpfully corrected sometimes inaccurate presentations of first-century Judaism as a proto-Pelagian religion of works righteousness. Emphasizing the im-portance of covenant membership, for example, Sanders has demon-strated how pervasively the rabbis emphasized that divine election was the consequence of God's free grace.[161] In doing so, however, he also stresses the distinction between what he colloquially refers to as

---

159. See, e.g., N. T. Wright, "The Letter to the Romans: Introduction, Commentary, and Reflec-tions," in *The New Interpreters Bible*, ed. Leander E. Keck (Nashville: Abingdon, 2002), 10:491; Wright, *What Saint Paul Really Said*, 124. For brief critique of this interpretation, see Simon Gathercole, "The Doctrine of Justification in Paul and Beyond," in McCormack, *Justification in Perspective*, 236–37.

160. Wright, *What Saint Paul Really Said*, 121.

161. See, e.g., Sanders, *Paul and Palestinian Judaism*, 106, where Sanders notes this point but also acknowledges that the rabbis appealed "sometimes to the concept of merit." Subsequent en-gagement with the literary sources of first-century Judaism has demonstrated that Sanders perhaps downplays the diversity of rabbinical views and that obedience was in fact often understood as a prerequisite for entrance into the covenant. See especially D. A. Carson, Peter T. O'Brien, and

"getting in" and "staying in" the covenant.[162] It is in this context that Sanders coins the label "covenantal nomism" to describe first-century Judaism. One "gets in" by grace alone (covenantal) but "stays in" by fulfilling the law (nomism). While Sanders himself shies away from describing Paul's theology as covenantal nomism,[163] other New Perspective advocates much more clearly assert that, even for Paul, "human obedience as a response to divine grace is a necessary condition for salvation."[164]

The implications of such interpretations for the Reformation doctrine of justification are clear. The New Perspective "narrows the distance between Paul and the Judaism of his day while it widens the gap between Paul and the Reformation."[165] But it does so, in part, by badly misunderstanding the actual concerns of the Reformers.[166] As above sections have highlighted, Rome had never embraced a "Pelagian" denial of the necessity of grace for salvation, nor did the Reformers understand them to have done so.[167] The Reformers instead objected to Rome's insistence—the same found in first-century Judaism—on a subsequent cooperation with divine grace being necessary for salvation. The reason, as one critic of the New Perspective concisely notes, is that, whether in the first century or the sixteenth, "covenantal nomism is still nomism."[168] As such, it stands in marked contrast to the Reformation doctrine of justification by grace alone through faith alone on account of Christ's imputed righteousness alone.[169]

Mark A. Seifrid, eds., *Justification and Variegated Nomism*, vol. 1, *The Complexities of Second Temple Judaism* (Grand Rapids, MI: Baker Academic, 2001).

162. E.g., Sanders, *Paul and Palestinian Judaism*, 17.

163. Ibid., 543.

164. Francis Watson, *Paul, Judaism and the Gentiles: A Sociological Approach*, Society for New Testament Studies Monograph Series 56 (Cambridge: Cambridge University Press, 1986), 179.

165. Richard B. Gaffin, "Paul the Theologian," *WTJ* 62 (2000): 121.

166. And, as many critics of the New Perspective argue, the theology of Paul himself. For an entrée into this debate, see, e.g., D. A. Carson, Peter T. O'Brien, and Mark A. Seifrid, eds., *Justification and Variegated Nomism*, vol. 2, *The Paradoxes of Paul* (Grand Rapids, MI: Baker Academic, 2004).

167. See, e.g., Paul F. M. Zahl, "Mistakes of the New Perspective on Paul," *Themelios* 27, no. 1 (2001): 5–11.

168. Charles A. Gieschen, "Paul and the Law: Was Luther Right?," in *The Law in Holy Scripture: Essays from the Concordia Theological Seminary, Symposium on Exegetical Theology*, ed. Charles A. Gieschen (St. Louis, MO: Concordia, 2004), 126.

169. For New Perspective critiques of a forensic soteriology of imputation, see, e.g., Sanders, *Paul and Palestinian Judaism*, 506; Wright, "New Perspectives on Paul," 252–53.

Conclusion

The Reformation doctrine of justification is neither the unique quirk of Melanchthon nor the late and reductive conclusion of a document such as the Formula of Concord. Its formulation and the specific understanding of its key terms were being clearly articulated already in the early 1520s, were adopted and embraced by Luther and Calvin alike, and were enshrined in numerous confessional documents that were and continue to be representative—and definitive—of both Lutheran and Reformed traditions. Thus, it does remain possible, with only minor qualifications, to speak of *the* Reformation doctrine of justification.

So long as objections and challenges to the confession of this doctrine continue, whether articulated in the still-normative canons and decrees of the Council of Trent or in more recent scholarly and ecumenical endeavors, the Reformation will most certainly not be "over." Nor, one might add, should it be; for as Luther himself never ceased to insist, "If we lose the doctrine of justification, we lose simply everything."[170]

Resources for Further Study

PRIMARY SOURCES

Calvin, John. *Institutes of the Christian Religion*. Edited by John T. McNeill. Translated by Ford Lewis Battles. 2 vols. Library of Christian Classics 20–21. 1559 edition. Philadelphia: Westminster, 1960.

———. *Joannis Calvini Opera Quae Supersunt Omnia*. Edited by Guilielmus Baum, Eduardus Cunitz, and Eduardus Reuss. 59 vols. *Corpus Reformatorum* 29–88. Brunswick and Berlin: Schwetschke, 1863–1900.

———. *Selected Works of John Calvin: Tracts and Letters*. Edited by Henry Beveridge and Jules Bonnet. 7 vols. 1844–1858. Reprint, Grand Rapids, MI: Baker, 1983.

Calvin, John, and Jacopo Sadoleto. *A Reformation Debate: Sadoleto's Letter to the Genevans and Calvin's Reply*. Edited by John C. Olin. Grand Rapids, MI: Baker, 1976.

Dennison, James T., Jr., ed. *Reformed Confessions of the 16th and 17th Centuries*. 4 vols. Grand Rapids, MI: Reformation Heritage Books, 2008–2014.

---

170. Luther, *Lectures on Galatians* (1535), LW 26:26.

Kolb, Robert, and Timothy J. Wengert, eds. *The Book of Concord: The Confessions of the Evangelical Lutheran Church.* Translated by Charles P. Arand et al. Minneapolis: Fortress, 2000.

Luther, Martin. *D. Martin Luthers Werke, Kritische Gesamtausgabe, Schriften.* 62 vols. Weimar: Böhlau, 1833–1986.

———. *Luther's Works.* Edited by Jaroslav Pelikan and Helmut Lehman. American ed. 75 vols. Philadelphia: Fortress; St. Louis, MO: Concordia, 1955–.

Melanchthon, Philip. *Loci Communes Theologici* (1521). In *Melanchthon and Bucer*, edited by Wilhelm Pauck, translated by Lowell J. Satre, 3–152. Library of Christian Classics 19. Philadelphia: Westminster, 1969.

———. *Philippi Melanthonis Opera Quae Supersunt Omnia.* Edited by C. G. Bretschneider and H. E. Bindseil. 28 vols. *Corpus Reformatorum* 1–28. Halle and Brunswick: Schwetschke, 1834–1860.

Schroeder, H. J., ed. and trans. *The Canons and Decrees of the Council of Trent.* Rockford, IL: Tan Books, 1978.

SECONDARY SOURCES

Anderson, H. George, T. Austin Murphy, and Joseph A. Burgess, eds. *Justification by Faith.* Lutherans and Catholics in Dialogue 7. Minneapolis: Augsburg, 1985.

Braaten, Carl E., and Robert W. Jenson, eds. *Union with Christ: The New Finnish Interpretation of Luther.* Grand Rapids, MI: Eerdmans, 1998.

Cary, Phillip. "*Sola Fide*: Luther and Calvin." *Concordia Theological Quarterly* 71, no. 3/4 (2007): 265–81.

Clark, R. Scott. "*Iustitia Imputata Christi*: Alien or Proper to Luther's Doctrine of Justification?" *Concordia Theological Quarterly* 70, no. 3/4 (2006): 269–310.

Fesko, J. V. "Calvin on Justification and Recent Misinterpretations of His View." *Mid-America Journal of Theology* 16 (2005): 83–114.

Green, Lowell C. *How Melanchthon Helped Luther Discover the Gospel: The Doctrine of Justification in the Reformation.* Fallbrook, CA: Verdict: 1980.

Hamm, Berndt. "What Was the Reformation Doctrine of Justification?" In *The German Reformation: The Essential Readings*, edited by C. Scott Dixon, 53–90. Blackwell Essential Readings in History. Oxford: Blackwell, 1999.

Husbands, Mark A., and Daniel J. Treier, eds. *Justification: What's at Stake in the Current Debates?* Downers Grove, IL: InterVarsity Press, 2004.

Lane, Anthony N. S. *Justification by Faith in Catholic-Protestant Dialogue: An Evangelical Assessment.* New York: T&T Clark, 2002.

Lehmann, Karl, ed. *Justification by Faith: Do the Sixteenth-Century Condemnations Still Apply?* Translated by Michael Root and William G. Rusch. New York: Continuum, 1997.

The Lutheran World Federation and the Roman Catholic Church. *Joint Declaration on the Doctrine of Justification.* Grand Rapids, MI: Eerdmans, 2000.

McCormack, Bruce L., ed. *Justification in Perspective: Historical Developments and Contemporary Challenges.* Grand Rapids, MI: Baker, 2006.

McGrath, Alister E. *Iustitia Dei: A History of the Christian Doctrine of Justification.* 2nd ed. Cambridge: Cambridge University Press, 1998.

Parsons, Michael, ed. *Since We Are Justified by Faith: Justification in the Theologies of the Protestant Reformations.* Milton Keynes, UK: Paternoster, 2012.

Reid, W. Stanford. "Justification by Faith according to John Calvin." *Westminster Theological Journal* 42, no. 2 (1980): 290–307.

Trueman, Carl R. "Is the Finnish Line a New Beginning? A Critical Assessment of the Reading of Luther Offered by the Helsinki Circle." *Westminster Theological Journal* 65, no. 2 (2003): 231–44.

———. "Justification." In *T&T Clark Companion to Reformation Theology*, edited by David M. Whitford, 57–71. London: T&T Clark, 2012.

Waters, Guy Prentiss. *Justification and the New Perspective on Paul: A Review and Response.* Phillipsburg, NJ: P&R, 2004.

Westerholm, Stephen. *Perspectives Old and New on Paul: The "Lutheran" Paul and His Critics.* Grand Rapids, MI: Eerdmans, 2003.

15

Sanctification, Perseverance, and Assurance

Michael Allen

ABSTRACT

Reformational theologies of sanctification in the Lutheran and Reformed traditions were neither thoroughly iconoclastic nor reactionary against the catholic tradition of discipleship. By surveying the Lutheran and Reformed approaches to sanctification, this chapter shows how they sought to reform patristic and medieval faith and practice by refocusing the doctrine Christologically, deepening the gracious character of the doctrine by going further along the Augustinian path, reprioritizing the nature of the good by emphasizing the focal role of faith (thereby going beyond the Augustinian path), limiting the definition of holiness and discipleship to that which has biblical warrant, and noting how the law of God plays a number of roles in the process of sanctification (as not only a reminder of our need for Christ but also a guide for holy living).

Introduction: Thinking Well about the Reforming of the Catholic Church

The Reformers did not deplore the tent posts of patristic and medieval faith and practice regarding Christian formation. The Creed continued to be confessed and exposited, the Lord's Prayer was still prayed and analyzed, and the Decalogue was read regularly and reflected on at length. Yet the Reformers did reconfigure some of the ways in which these foundational resources were put in play in daily life and in churchly structure. In so doing, the Reformers did not suggest an individualist or biblicistic form of piety, but they did promote a churchly form of discipleship that was always rooted in scriptural principles and beholden, therefore, to exegetical argumentation. They sought to exemplify a reformed catholicity with regard to the pursuit of holiness and the shape of the Christian life as practiced together.

Misunderstandings of the Reformation can veer in one of two directions. First, they can set the Reformers off as iconoclasts of a principled sort, running as far as possible from the religious *status quo*. Second, they can fail to note the ways in which the Reformers did press for genuine change and, in so doing, believed themselves to be calling for the catholic church to go more deeply into its own roots and catholicity. Admittedly, there are reasons these misunderstandings can arise. In many respects the Reformers have not left a simple legacy. Take Martin Luther as the most obvious example. Jaroslav Pelikan has commented,

> Martin Luther was the first Protestant, and yet he was more Catholic than many of his Roman Catholic opponents. This paradox lies at the very centre of Luther's Reformation. He claimed that his theology was derived from the Scriptures, as though the church fathers had never lived; still the theology that he claimed to derive from "Scripture alone" bore a striking family resemblance to the tradition of the church fathers. He spoke of "hating" the abstract theological terms in traditional dogmatic language about the Trinity and the person of Christ, but the traditional dogma of the Trinity was in fact basic to his entire theology. He could attack the distinction between clergy and laity as a distortion of the institution of Christ; nevertheless, he exalted the ministry of preaching as "the highest office in Christendom." He could sound utterly individualistic in his pronouncements on moral questions, asking Christians to be on their own when they made their ethical choices; at the same time he could also recognize that most Christians were not very heroic in their ethical choices and needed the moral support and discipline

of both church and state. Sometimes he sounded like an iconoclast, sometimes he sounded like a traditionalist.[1]

A judicious reading of Luther, much less of the wider Protestant Reformation, will need to do some careful synthetic work to avoid turning the Reformers into advocates of either sheer iconoclasm or blasé traditionalism. "Rebels" we understand, and "obedient" persons we can imagine. But "obedient rebels"? Such is a complex characterization, and discerning this reality is the task of Reformational historiography. Perhaps nowhere is this more difficult and yet needful than with respect to the doctrine of sanctification and the way the Reformers imagined the Christian life to unfold personally and publicly.

What becomes apparent is that historiographic concerns can be doing other work when one is ostensibly telling the story of the Reformation. Patrick Collinson has identified the tendency to tell "Whig history" or the like when addressing the generations immediately following this time period: the Elizabethan Settlement and the Puritan era.[2] Efforts at reform can easily become paradigmatic ideals, either good or bad, and one must remain disciplined to assess the data fairly, especially when it is complex. Here we must beware lest readings of Reformational reflection on sanctification become either a litany of ways in which Romanist practices and beliefs were deplorable and nothing else, or a contextualized account of localized, contingent occurrences that bore no overarching relation of opposition in any respect to the *status quo* in the catholic church of the late-medieval era. As Pelikan states in his study of Luther, the Reformers envisioned themselves as "obedient rebels," and they were equally concerned with Rome and with the Anabaptist threat. Such concerns are fluid and dynamic, varying from issue to issue, time to time, and place to place based on concrete concerns, religio-political realities, and literary interactions. While being aware of those dynamics does not guarantee that one will accurately assess their concrete appearance at any given point, it must nonetheless be a preliminary guideline to good historiography.

To reflect on the sixteenth-century Reformers and their views

---

1. Jaroslav Pelikan, *Obedient Rebels: Catholic Substance and Protestant Principle in Luther's Reformation* (New York: Harper & Row, 1964), 11.
2. Patrick Collinson, *The Reformation: A History* (London: Weidenfeld & Nicolson, 2003).

regarding the doctrine of sanctification, we will consider the two major streams of churchly reform in their historical development—the Lutheran and the Reformed—before turning to consider some synthetic judgments.

Sanctification and the Lutheran Church

Luther's Developing Thought on Sanctification

Martin Luther's reform began with concerns regarding matters of sanctification. A sober reading of the *Ninety-Five Theses* leads one to note that they say very little about justification and conversion and that they instead focus on matters of the Christian life and the ongoing process of becoming holy.[3] For example, they linger over indulgences and the role these play in the Christian's piety; we should not miss that Luther there protested what he viewed as the abuse of indulgences, not their rightful use according to church teaching of the time. Luther did not suggest that the papacy, or purgatory, was wrong; indeed, the theses are, by and large, remarkably conservative, but they were a shot across the bow of much religious culture (even if not against the scholastic theology) of the day.[4] Luther here sought a biblical reform of certain practices believed to play a pivotal role in the exercise and deepening of creaturely holiness.

Luther did not think about sanctification very long, though, without relating it to justification. And his protests quickly turned to scholastic theology as well as popular religious culture. Further, Luther did not think one could pursue holiness well without thinking first about why one should do so, and this almost always jolted him into reflecting on justification. Indeed, his thinking on this connection is clearly displayed in his "Two Kinds of Righteousness," which is believed to have been preached on Palm Sunday in 1519 and based on Philippians 2:5–6. There he distinguished between alien and proper righteousness. The first righteousness is "primary; it is the basis, the cause, the source of all our own actual righteousness." Righteousness, then, comes from the outside in, just as sin came from Adam into us: "Therefore this alien righteous-

3. Martin Luther, *Ninety-Five Theses* (1517), LW 31:17–34.
4. For an illumining account of the penitential system and lay piety at that time, see Thomas N. Tentler, *Sin and Confession on the Eve of the Reformation* (Princeton, NJ: Princeton University Press, 1977).

ness, instilled in us without our works by grace alone—while the Father, to be sure, inwardly draws us to Christ—is set opposite original sin, likewise alien, which we acquire without our works by birth alone."[5] However, the second righteousness is "our proper righteousness, not because we alone work it, but because we work with that first and alien righteousness." It is our work, but our action is a fellow partaking in the movement of Christ's righteousness that remains alien to us:

> This righteousness follows the example of Christ in this respect [1 Pet. 2:21] and is transformed into his likeness [2 Cor. 3:18]. It is precisely this that Christ requires. Just as he himself did all things for us, not seeking his own good but ours only—and in this he was the most obedient to God the Father—so he desires that we also should set the same example for our neighbors.[6]

Human righteousness is fundamentally gift, then, and only second-arily achievement by grace. Luther's theology provides a path to deep and lasting assurance, if people can look to Christ for their spiritual identity and judicial standing before God rather than to their own history of law keeping or law breaking. Luther intended directly to protest the Thomist notion of "formed faith" (*fides formata*), wherein faith's function is dependent on and inoperative until faith has been completed in the act of love. In Luther's scheme, alien righteousness is given at the very incipience of faith's exercise; it is followed by acts of love, which can be called proper righteousness, but it is not beholden to or on hold until such appear.

When it came to describing the shape of faith, Luther often turned to the first commandment. Perhaps most clearly in his *Treatise on Good Works*, he said that all failures to keep the law stem from having other gods.[7] In his Large Catechism he offered a paradigmatic sketch of the first commandment's axiomatic status:

> "You are to have no other gods." That is, you are to regard me alone as your God. What does this mean, and how is it to be under-stood? What does "to have a god" mean, or what is God?

---

5. Martin Luther, "Two Kinds of Righteousness," *LW* 31:298, 299.
6. Ibid., *LW* 31:300.
7. Martin Luther, *Treatise on Good Works*, *LW* 44:15–114.

Answer: A "god" is the term for that to which we are to look for all good and in which we are to find refuge in all need. Therefore, to have a god is nothing else than to trust and believe in that one with your whole heart. As I have often said, it is the trust and faith of the heart alone that make both God and an idol. If your faith and trust are right, then your God is the true one. Conversely, where your trust is false and wrong, there you do not have the true God. For these two belong together, faith and God. Anything on which your heart relies and depends, I say, that is really your God.[8]

Luther's account of the Decalogue in his *Treatise on Good Works* sketched out the way in which the first commandment is the pathway to keeping each of the other laws. He moved command by command, showing how they each flow from entrusting oneself to the God of the gospel. In this regard, then, Luther consistently pointed to the evangelical character of good works and of the holy life: Christian obedience must always be derived directly from faith in the triune God.

For example, Luther insisted on truth telling. He famously noted that the eighth commandment demands not only that we avoid lying but even that we render others' statements in the best possible light. Faith powers along a commitment to truth: "Where there is such faith and confidence there is also a bold, defiant, fearless heart that risks all and stands by the truth, no matter what the cost, whether it is against pope or king, as we see that the dear martyrs did." Why? "For such a heart is satisfied and serenely sure that it has a gracious, kindly-disposed God. Therefore, he despises all favors, grace, goods, and honor of men, and does not attach any value to these transitory things." And this link between faith and obedience is not unique to only this command: "For just as nobody does the work of this commandment unless he is firm and unshaken in his confidence of divine favor, so also he does no work of any of the other commandments without this same faith."[9] Luther's ethics are fixed here on the formative power of faith.

---

8. Martin Luther, "The Large Catechism," in Robert Kolb and Timothy J. Wengert, eds., *The Book of Concord: The Confessions of the Evangelical Lutheran Church*, trans. Charles P. Arand et al. (Minneapolis: Fortress, 2000), 386.

9. Luther, *Treatise on Good Works*, LW 44:112, 113.

THREE DEFINING EPISODES

Three episodes brought out clarity regarding the shape of the holy life, whose roots are in Christ and whose reception is found in this Christian faith. First, the Zwickau Prophets (three influential itinerants named Nicholas Storch, Thomas Drechsel, and Marcus Thomae) believed people were to be taught by the Spirit with no connection to the Bible, and Thomas Müntzer (ca. 1489–1525) also claimed to receive extrabiblical revelation. Sebastian Franck professed this sort of experiential and charismatic approach to the Christian life: "I believe that the outward church of Christ, including all its gifts and sacraments, because of the breaking and laying waste by Antichrist right after the death of the apostles, went up into heaven and lies concealed in the Spirit and in truth."[10] In advocating for an immediate experience of the Spirit's guidance, these enthusiasts also polemically addressed the piety of Luther and other Protestants, derisively referring to its adherence to scriptural teaching as a focus on "Bible, Babel, Bubble" (*Bibel, Babel, Babbel*). Whereas Müntzer said that Luther "knows nothing of God, even though he may have swallowed one hundred Bibles," Luther responded by noting, "I wouldn't listen to Thomas Münzer if he swallowed the Holy Ghost, feathers and all!" Thus Luther inextricably tied sanctification to Scripture.

Second, Luther spent a good deal of time in the 1520s opposing the spiritual and religious practices of the late-medieval era that focused on the *contemptus mundi* ("contempt of the world") and the religious/secular divide. During the Middle Ages, the distinction between religious men and women (priests, monks, and nuns) and secular men and women (everyone else) expanded in its significance for various reasons. Not surprisingly, an understanding that the religious exercised a holier calling came to hold significant sway among the population. One of Luther's most pointed protests, then, was to burst this bubble of dualistic spirituality. He did so by marrying a former nun and having a house full of children, scandalous choices at the time for a priest. He also preached and reflected, however, on the way worldly living related

---

10. Sebastian Franck, "A Letter to John Campanus," in *Spiritual and Anabaptist Writers*, ed. George Huntston Williams and Angel M. Mergal, LCC 25 (Philadelphia: Westminster, 1957), 149.

to the Christian faith. In *The Babylonian Captivity of the Church* in 1520, he had claimed that religious vocations were no holier than others, and throughout the 1520s and 1530s, he expanded this reflection in great detail.[11] Luther noted that marriage was a godly estate (exalting family life), that the rule of the secular kingdom was a calling from God (exalting government and civic participation), and that all men and women were given callings by God (exalting a more expansive doctrine of vocation).[12] This is illustrated by the famed story of Luther's response to the question of what he would do the next day if he knew ahead of time that Jesus would return; Luther replied that he would plant an apple tree, having already been assigned this task by his wife, Katie. Even a seemingly foolish task—who thinks an apple tree will grow within a day's time?—holds significance, because it is a part of the human vocation. It need not be measured by supposedly spiritual value or by utilitarian logic. It is valued by means of its fittingness with faith in God and the love of neighbor. Later, in his Genesis lectures in the 1530s, Luther also commented that such behavior fit with our creational nature and calling.

Third, Luther was compelled to be even more specific regarding the shape of scriptural teaching on the holy life. Whereas his engagement with the enthusiasts focused on being biblical, and his opposition to much late-medieval dualism addressed the need to be human, his encounters with antinomians required him to speak to the place of commands and laws in God's saving economy. Luther believed a false anthropology lay beneath the antinomian error:

> We are so secure, without fear and concern; the devil is far from us, and we have none of that flesh in us that was in St. Paul and of which he complains in Romans 7[:23], exclaiming that he cannot deliver himself from it as he would like, but that he is captive to it. No, we are the heroes who need not worry about our flesh and our thoughts. We are sheer spirit, we have taken captive our own flesh together with the devil, so that all our thoughts and ideas are surely and certainly inspired by the Holy Spirit, and how can he be found

11. Martin Luther, *The Babylonian Captivity of the Church* (1520), LW 36:78.
12. The most significant text regarding these issues remains Gustaf Wingren, *Luther on Vocation*, trans. Carl C. Rasmussen (Eugene, OR: Wipf & Stock, 2004).

wanting? Therefore it all has such a nice ending—namely, that both steed and rider break their necks.[13]

Luther believed that laws were needed because people lack perfect faith; the author of the famed text *The Bondage of the Will* had no time for the anthropology of the antinomians.[14] In the 1530s, he insisted that commands were given by God to shape the moral life of Christians; he typically referred to them as "commandments" rather than "laws," restricting this term for the accusatory function of scriptural imperatives.[15] Luther's moral theology is apparent in a number of his biblical expositions, ranging from sermons on the Sermon on the Mount to his lectures on Psalm 119.[16] While justification grants freedom to the Christian, the commands of God give the form for holiness.

The Lutheran tradition, largely under the influence of Philipp Melanchthon, would go still further by affirming a third use of the law, a rhetorical move that Luther never made. Luther had narrowed the biblical usage of the term "law" and focused on only one usage in a systematic way: law as accuser. He used the term "commandment" to speak of the moral imperatives given to shape the lives of those Christians freed by Christ and empowered by the Spirit. Melanchthon later led Lutherans to stick with the term "law" when referring to these exhortations and not make a distinction between "law" and "commandment" but rather a distinction between the second use of the law and the third, exclusively Christian use of the law.[17] While it was Melanchthon who pushed the Lutheran church to confess these exhortations to holiness as "law" for Christians, Luther had practiced similarly, reading biblical commands as binding imperatives for Christians (albeit not cataloging them analytically as "law").[18]

---

13. Martin Luther, *Against the Antinomians* (1539), LW 47:119.

14. Luther, *Treatise on Good Works*, LW 44:34–35.

15. See Martin Luther, *Only the Decalogue Is Eternal: Martin Luther's Complete Antinomian Theses and Disputations*, ed. Holger Sonntag (Minneapolis: Lutheran Press, 2008).

16. Martin Luther, *Commentary on the Sermon on the Mount*, LW 21:1–294, esp. 21:72–73; Luther, *Lectures on Psalm 119*, LW 11:414–534.

17. For this distinction in its discussion of the third use of the law, see "The Solid Declaration of the Formula of Concord," art. 6, in Kolb and Wengert, *Book of Concord*, 587–91. See also Timothy J. Wengert, *Law and Gospel: Philip Melanchthon's Debate with John Agricola of Eisleben over Poenitentia*, Texts and Studies in Reformation and Post-Reformation Thought (Grand Rapids, MI: Baker, 1997), esp. 177–210, where the debate and its developing terminology are traced from 1525 to 1537.

18. For instance he spoke of Psalm 119, "where the law is not anymore the law." Martin Luther, *On the Councils and the Church* (1539), WA 50:565.

In the Lutheran tradition in the sixteenth century, then, we have seen that its theology of sanctification began with consideration of its distinction from and link to justification in Christ alone, as well as its emphasis on *sola fide*. Lutherans then were compelled to reflect on the external shape of holiness, gradually developing a theology that was scriptural, embodied and engaged in the world, and alert to the specific form of God's commands (even, in Melanchthon and the "Solid Declaration," of God's law) as the moral compass for Christian living today.

Sanctification and the Reformed Churches

The second great stream of the Protestant Reformation was that of the Reformed churches. Even in their earliest forms, led by Huldrych Zwingli, they were later than the earliest protests of Martin Luther and his followers. And throughout their history, the Reformed churches viewed themselves as sharing with Luther and the Lutherans their key soteriological principles. We will not take time to mention the ways in which they agreed, but we will press on to highlight some ways in which Reformed theologians deepened Protestant reflection on sanctification and the Christian life. Because the theology and ministry of Martin Luther dominates Lutheran confessional theology, he has held sway in our account of the Lutheran view of sanctification. As we will see, while material theological concerns were very similar in the Reformed tradition, the formal shape of that tradition was quite different. While John Calvin exercised great influence, neither he nor any other significant figure (whether Zwingli, Bucer, Bullinger, Vermigli, or Ursinus) would exercise the kind of sway and hold the type of authority that Luther does in the Lutheran world. We will first consider two doctrinal links that the Reformed highlighted in talking about holiness: Christology and ecclesiology. Then we will consider how the Reformed confessions addressed the nature of good works, acts of obedience that can be called the fruit of holiness or of God's sanctification.

Holiness and Christology

The first way in which Reformed churches deepened Reformational reflection on holiness was by sketching out its relation to two doctrines: Christology and ecclesiology. First, sanctification was located within our union with Christ. As John Calvin said, "The whole substance of our salvation is not to be sought anywhere else than in Christ."[19] In trying to survey the ways that "the whole substance" is found in Christ, Calvin famously spoke of a double grace (*duplex gratia*): "By partaking of him, we . . . receive a double grace: namely, that being reconciled to God through Christ's blamelessness, we may have in heaven instead of a judge a gracious Father; and secondly, that sanctified by Christ's spirit we may cultivate blamelessness and purity of life."[20] Luther had spoken of the relationship between Christ and faith, and he had used the language of imputation to address this link, most frequently by focusing on the topic of justification. Calvin agreed, and he thought that union with Christ shaped Christian assurance. As he commented on 1 Corinthians 1:9, for example, he said,

> In short, when the Christian looks at himself he can only have grounds for anxiety, indeed despair, but because he is called into fellowship with Christ, he can think of himself, in so far as assurance of salvation is concerned, in no other way than as a member of Christ, thus making all the blessings of Christ his own.[21]

Calvin and Reformed theologians believed this "fellowship with Christ" brought assurance as one of its many blessings, because it really brought the substance of Christ to the believer.[22]

Calvin was the one who clearly addressed how sanctification was also sought in Christ as a grace, an equal even if second aspect of this "double grace" enjoyed in union with Christ. First Corinthians 1:30 was a classic text pointing in this direction. As Calvin noted, "Faith lays hold of regeneration just as much as forgiveness of sins in Christ."[23] It is worth noting, of course, that Luther spoke metaphorically in ways that pointed in this direction, and he made indirect comments along

---

19. John Calvin on John 3:16, in *CNTC* 4:73. Calvin is here extending an Augustinian approach to linking Christology and ethics: see, e.g., Augustine, *On Faith and Works*, trans. Gregory J. Lombardo, Ancient Christian Writers 48 (New York: Newman, 1988), 20.

20. Calvin, *Institutes*, 3.11.1.

21. John Calvin on 1 Cor. 1:9, in *CNTC* 9:24.

22. Calvin did not hesitate to use the language of substantial participation in Christ; see J. Todd Billings, *Calvin, Participation, and the Gift: The Activity of Believers in Union with Christ*, Changing Paradigms in Historical and Systematic Theology (New York: Oxford University Press, 2007), 61–65.

23. Calvin on 1 Cor. 1:30, in *CNTC* 9:46.

these lines. But it was Calvin and other Reformed theologians who made this a structuring principle for all the facets of the gospel, in particular for sanctification and glorification. As Paul teaches, "For all the promises of God find their Yes in him [Christ]" (2 Cor. 1:20)—union with him brings reconciliation, but it also brings renewal.

The "double grace" helps clarify the way in which Scripture speaks of faith and repentance as distinct yet related responses of the human to God's grace:

> God works in us these two things at the same time, so that we are both renewed by repentance and freed from the bondage of sin and also justified by faith and freed from their curse. These are the inseparable gifts of grace and because of the invariable bond between them repentance can rightly and fittingly be called the beginning of the way that leads to salvation, but more as an accompaniment than a cause. These are not subtle evasions but a simple explanation of the difficulty for while Scripture teaches that we never obtain the forgiveness of our sins without repentance, at the same time it teaches in many places that the only ground of our forgiveness is the mercy of God.[24]

Because both forgiveness and renewal are found in Christ, both can be characterized as gracious, both can be expected by way of God's promise, and both can be assured of "accompaniment," for they are truly "inseparable gifts of grace." Hence Reformed theologians found no conceptual hurdle to speaking of repentance and obedience as conditions for God's blessing, though they insisted that they are not (material) causes of God's blessing but are instead signs of union with Christ, who alone is the initial and perfecting cause of our salvation.[25]

A major debate erupted later in Calvin's career with Andreas Osiander. Osiander died in 1552, a controversial figure condemned by his fellow Lutherans. He taught the importance of not only union with

---

24. Ibid., 100.
25. For analysis of how union with Christ related to the application of salvation in other sixteenth-century Reformed theologians, ranging from Viret, Vermigli, and Musculus to Zanchi, Beza, and Olevianus, see Richard A. Muller, "Union with Christ and the *Ordo Salutis*: Reflections on Developments in Early Modern Reformed Thought," in *Calvin and the Reformed Tradition: On the Work of Christ and the Order of Salvation* (Grand Rapids, MI: Baker Academic, 2012), 202–43, esp. 212–26.

Christ but also participation in God through Christ. He took a strong reading of 2 Peter 1:4—"partakers of the divine nature"—to mean that Christians were infused with the divine life. For Osiander, this infusion meant that justification was on the basis of the indwelling and impartation of divine life, rather than on the forensic basis of the pardon and imputation of Christ's alien righteousness.[26] Calvin was accused by some Lutherans of being "Osiandrian," and he responded at length in his final edition of the *Institutes* (1559). Calvin noted that Reformed thinking on union with Christ did not mean that the divine life was infused into us or that the substitutionary work of the incarnate Son was moot. Instead, union with Christ involved participation in God through the incarnate mediation of Jesus (being united with the God-man and not directly with the divine as such), and union with Christ brought with it the Righteous One's benefits as just and holy. Against Osiander, Calvin upheld the Lutheran and Reformed emphasis on our need for human holiness, not for divine properties as such.[27] Union with Christ, for Calvin and the Reformed tradition, did bring the indwelling of the triune God by the Spirit's power, but it did so in tandem with bringing the justification of the ungodly. Sanctification by divine inhabitation in Christ was never juxtaposed with nor confused with a radically forensic account of justification, based on the work of Jesus Christ outside us and brought to bear on us by the glorious union we now have with him.

Holiness and Ecclesiology

Second, Reformed theologians linked holiness with the doctrine of the church. Zwingli's "Sixty-Seven Articles" of 1523 made strong use of the body metaphor from Paul's teaching to the Corinthians. Thesis 8 notes that "all who live in the Head are His members and children of God. And this is the Church or fellowship of the saints."[28] Zwingli clearly identified the church as the "saints" or holy ones in as much as

---

26. On Osiander's theology, see especially Patricia Wilson-Kastner, "Andreas Osiander's Theology of Grace in the Perspective of the Influence of Augustine of Hippo," *SCJ* 10, no. 2 (1979): 73–91.

27. For analysis of Calvin's response to Osiander, see Billings, *Calvin, Participation, and the Gift*, 53–61.

28. "Zwingli's Sixty-Seven Articles" (1523), in Arthur C. Cochrane, ed., *Reformed Confessions of the Sixteenth Century* (Louisville: Westminster John Knox, 2003), 37.

they are in Christ. At the same time, in several theses (theses 7, 9, and 10) Zwingli also insisted that identity as saints is impossible apart from the Head of that body, Jesus Christ. Indeed, the Tetrapolitan Confession of 1530 got even more specific and stated that from the church "Christ is never absent, but he sanctifies it to present it at length to himself blameless, not having spot or wrinkle."[29] Christ makes holy a church—not merely an aggregate of individuals but a congregation of saints. Election for Reformed theologians was individual, but it was personal and specific within a broader corporate purpose: men and women are elected to be in the body of Christ, wherein they enjoy that union with the incarnate Head and flourish in harmony with his guidance. As the Belgic Confession says, "All men are in duty bound to join and unite themselves with it . . . to join themselves to this congregation, wheresoever God hath established it."[30]

Reformed theologians also attested that the place of growing in grace was tied to the ongoing practice of certain means of grace: the reading and preaching of the Word and the right administration of the sacraments. Reformed theology insisted that sacraments required the lordly warrant of Christ's specific command. Other spiritual practices may be well and good (such as confession and repentance of sin), but they do not merit the title *sacrament* unless they are perpetually commanded by the Lord himself, that is, practices "which Christ our Lord hath instituted."[31]

A particularly distinctive development was the place of discipline in the Reformed vision of the Christian life. Martin Bucer was pivotal in this regard, noting that discipline was a third mark of the Christian church (alongside the preaching of the Word and the right administration of the sacraments). The church was always viewed as an eschatological project, on its way to glory but not yet there.[32] Bucer believed God had given three means of grace, to be administered by clergy, for the building up and maturing of the saints: dispensing the doctrine of Christ, administering the sacraments, and disciplining "the life and

---

29. "The Tetrapolitan Confession" (1530), in Cochrane, *Reformed Confessions*, 73.
30. "The Belgic Confession" (1561), in Cochrane, *Reformed Confessions*, 209.
31. Ibid., 213.
32. See especially Heinrich Bullinger, "Of the Holy Catholic Church," in *Zwingli and Bullinger: Selected Translations with Introductions and Notes*, ed. G. W. Bromiley, LCC 24 (Louisville: Westminster John Knox, 2006), 288–325, esp. 314–17.

manners," the penance, and the worship of the congregation.[33] Bucer's emphasis on three marks of the true church became standard among Reformed communions, whereas Lutheran churches focused more narrowly on the preaching of the Word and the administration of the sacraments.[34] While Lutheran churches maintained a seemingly loftier cadence for describing pastoral vocation (using the terminology of priests and bishops, both of which tended to be dismissed in Reformed circles—with the exception of Reformed churches in England), it was the Reformed churches who viewed the exercise of pastoral discipline (both by ordained clergy and by consistories) to be a genuine mark of the true church on par with preaching and the sacraments. The exercise of this discipline was viewed Christologically, as a way in which the body is governed by its Head.

THE CHARACTER OF GOOD WORKS

Having considered ways in which the Reformed theological approach linked sanctification to Christ's person and to his body, the church, we are now in a position to consider how Reformed theologians in the sixteenth century described the character of holy acts or good works. The Heidelberg Catechism offers a synthetic judgment regarding the shared beliefs of the Reformed churches in the Palatinate regarding the holy acts to which the Christian is called:

> Q. 91 What are good works?
> A. Only those which are done out of true faith, conform to God's law, and are done for God's glory; and not those based on our own opinion or human tradition.[35]

We will reflect on this definition by taking it in reverse order. There are four tenets found here, and they draw out a more comprehensive moral theology than was discussed when we considered the Lutheran teaching on sanctification. More important, these tenets represent wider Reformed reflection on the shape of holiness and the scope of moral theology in light of the gospel.

---

33. Martin Bucer, *De Regno Christi*, in *Melanchthon and Bucer*, ed. Wilhelm Pauck, LCC 19 (Louisville: Westminster John Knox, 2006), 232–55.
34. "The Belgic Confession," in Cochrane, *Reformed Confessions*, 210–11.
35. "The Heidelberg Catechism" (1563), in Cochrane, *Reformed Confessions*, 322.

First, good works are not merely "those based on our own opinion or human tradition." The Reformed churches shared Reformational concerns with Lutherans regarding the need to judge all faith and practice by God's Word: "The Church of Christ makes no laws or commandments without God's Word. Hence all human traditions, which are called ecclesiastical commandments, are binding upon us only in so far as they are based on and commanded by God's Word."[36] This second of the Ten Theses of Berne speaks of "human traditions" that are authoritative "only in so far as they are based on and commanded by" the Holy Scriptures.[37] "Human tradition" becomes a technical term for any practice that becomes binding without scriptural warrant. Zwingli's "Sixty-Seven Articles" of 1523 says that "in the Gospel we learn that human doctrines and traditions are of no avail to salvation"; the First Helvetic Confession of 1536 states that "we regard all other human doctrines and articles which lead us away from God and true faith as vain and ineffectual"; and the Geneva Confession of 1536 declares that "all laws and regulations made binding on conscience which oblige the faithful to things not commanded by God, or establish another service of God than that which he demands" are human traditions and "perverse doctrines of Satan."[38] "Human traditions" are juxtaposed with "divine traditions" in this technical vocabulary.[39]

The Reformed confessions were not opposing the necessity of human tradition as such, however, provided that they were not merely human traditions. Elsewhere the confessions attest to the necessary authority of the church, her synods and councils, her pastors and elders, and her confessional tradition. The Belgic Confession affirms,

> We believe, though it is useful and beneficial, that those who are rulers of the Church institute and establish certain ordinances among themselves for maintaining the body of the Church; yet they ought studiously to take care that they do not depart from those things which Christ, our only master, hath instituted. And,

---

36. "The Ten Theses of Berne" (1528), in Cochrane, *Reformed Confessions*, 49.

37. The terminology of "human traditions" or "the commandments of men" derives from Matt. 15:9.

38. "Zwingli's Sixty-Seven Articles" (1523), in Cochrane, *Reformed Confessions*, 37; "The First Helvetic Confession" (1536), in Cochrane, *Reformed Confessions*, 101; "The Geneva Confession" (1536), in Cochrane, *Reformed Confessions*, 124.

39. See "The Tetrapolitan Confession" (1530), in Cochrane, *Reformed Confessions*, 71–72.

therefore, we reject all human inventions, and all laws which man would introduce into the worship of God, thereby to bind and compel the conscience in any matter whatever.[40]

Similarly, the Scots Confession of 1560 suggests that we neither "rashly condemn" nor "receive uncritically" what is done in lawful assembly of church leaders.[41] Confessional authority is to be received with care and attentiveness—neither "rashly" nor "uncritically" because it has instrumental value as an authorized, ecclesiastical development of scriptural teaching. Thus, the Reformed confessions point to how we are to relate to the teachings of the catholic church: "Where the holy fathers and early teachers, who have explained and expounded the Scripture, have not departed from this rule, we want to recognize and consider them not only as expositors of Scripture, but as elect instruments through whom God has spoken and operated."[42] These "elect instruments" are to be gratefully and thankfully respected insofar as they minister the Word.

Second, good works are "done for God's glory." We have considered the epistemological basis of good works: how we can know that something is holy, namely, by the ultimate authority of God expressed in and through Holy Scripture—his Word—and as faithfully administered by ecclesiastical authorities. The Reformed confessions are equally insistent that the end of holiness deserves our attention. Holy acts must be done for holy reasons. The Heidelberg Catechism uses the language of "God's glory" to make this point. Obedience and loving service are meant to be done for God's sake, not merely for our own. This emphasis on the glory of God goes back still earlier, evidenced by its inclusion in the very first article of the Confession of Faith Used in the English Congregation at Geneva in 1556, where it attests that God made humanity "after His own image that in him He might be glorified."[43]

Of course, the Reformed tradition's most famous statement on

---

40. "The Belgic Confession," in Cochrane, *Reformed Confessions*, 212.
41. "The Scots Confession" (1560), in Cochrane, *Reformed Confessions*, 178.
42. "The First Helvetic Confession" (1536), in Cochrane, *Reformed Confessions*, 101. See also Huldrych Zwingli, *An Exposition of the Faith*, in Bromiley, *Zwingli and Bullinger*, 266.
43. "The Confession of Faith Used in the English Congregation at Geneva" (1556), in Cochrane, *Reformed Confessions*, 131.

God's glory would be penned nearly a century later. The Westminster Shorter Catechism begins by defining the chief end of humanity: "To glorify God and enjoy him forever." And yet this was no novelty in the Reformed churches, wherein living unto God's glory was regularly professed to be our marching order. First Corinthians 10:31 exercised signal importance in this regard, shaping Reformed thought about how all moral behavior is meant to terminate in giving glory to the triune God. Teleology matters for ethics; subjective intent (in this case the glory of God rather than the glory of the moral agent) shapes the moral value of an action. It is not enough to do something that is objectively valid; it must be done for the right purpose (to the glory of God).

Third, good works "conform to God's law." Reformed churches believed that good works must be not only scriptural (as opposed to being merely attested to by the social mores of a particular human tribe) but also specifically enjoined by the divine law found in those Holy Scriptures. Reformed thinkers typically spoke of three uses of the law (joining the later Lutheran confessional tradition, from Melanchthon onward): the law shows us our sin, the law helps maintain civic order, and the law guides the Christian life. In Christian worship, Reformed churches made use of the Decalogue both during a time of confession and also following the sermon and sacrament as a prompt or guide for the response to God's presence. In other words, Reformed liturgy emphasized both the first and third uses of the law (whereas Lutheran liturgy tended to keep Luther's own focus on the first use of the law). The reading of the law was viewed by the Reformed confessions as a great gift (as attested, for example, by their sermons on Psalm 119), because sin-plagued humans need the help of a moral recalibration, cognizant that in and of themselves sinners lack a native barometer for moral decision making that jives with God's righteous demands. God's law is a gift, then, in that it is a guide.

Fourth, good works are "only those which are done out of true faith." As Luther had emphasized the importance of the first commandment and the call to faith, so the Reformed tradition also emphasized that all true good works flow from trust in God. The phraseology of "evangelical holiness" was used to convey this very point. Righteous obedience was not merely external conformity to God's holy laws (important though that was) but external behavior that flowed from an appropriate subjective stance of faith. As with the pursuit of God's glory, this fourth point addresses the motivational and mannered nature of moral action. Our pursuit of God's glory is to take this form: dependent living before him, turning to him for our good. And this kind of dependent living takes the shape of obedience to his commands (as the one who prompts and guides us to live according to his law). There is not only a seamless but also an interpenetrating link between these various descriptions, inasmuch as, for example, respecting the command of God is a manifestation of entrusting oneself to the moral guidance of God. These are not disparate characterizations of holy action given in the Heidelberg Catechism, although they are distinct descriptions making slightly different (but complementary and yoked) points.

Reformed reflection on sanctification shared many things with Lutheran churches in the sixteenth century. Reformed theology did probe more deeply into the link between sanctification, union with Christ, and ecclesiology. In so doing, it presented an ecclesiastical or churchly form of piety, as well as one that emphasized the role of not only the proclamation of the Word and of the sacramental practices of God's people but also of pastoral discipline. These are the contexts in which holiness takes root. The Reformed tradition also gave thought to the fruits of holiness, noting its biblical shape, its purpose of giving glory to God, its accordance with the divine law, and its impulse imparted from faith itself. Having considered some of the distinctive aspects of Lutheran and Reformed doctrines of sanctification, we are now in a position to offer some synthetic judgments about the sixteenth-century Protestant movement as a whole.

Synthetic Judgments about Sanctification and the Gospel

As we have seen, the Lutheran and Reformed churches shared much regarding the doctrine of sanctification. The nature of the Christian life and the place of good works in the shape of the gospel were central issues in the sixteenth-century Protestant Reformation. In drawing our study to a close, we do well to see how their thinking on sanctification related to some of the hallmarks of wider Reformational thought and practice.

CHRIST ALONE

The single most definitive mark of Protestant thinking on sanctification in the sixteenth-century Reformation era was its focus on Christ alone as the source and sustainer of holiness: "We acknowledge that he is nevertheless present with his Church, even to the end of the world; that he renews and sanctifies it and adorns it as his only beloved bride with all sorts of ornaments of virtues."[44] Christ functions here not merely as a foundation or a bulwark but as an ongoing person of interest, one who continues to renew, sanctify, and adorn the church with grace upon grace. Christ centeredness in Reformational teaching was not merely focused on the finished work of Christ but was also cognizant of the need for his ongoing exercise of his threefold office as Prophet, Priest, and King.[45]

While Christ's work was not all finished, the very fact that sanctification was ultimately his work was a source of deep and profound assurance. The Reformers were working pastorally in a situation of deep anxiety, as historiographic accounts of the late-medieval and early-modern era have attested.[46] The Reformers not only located justification in Christ alone but also articulated an approach to sanctification that was equally Christ centered. First Corinthians 1:30 was crucial in this regard, inasmuch as Christ is attested by Paul to be not only "righteousness" but also "sanctification" for the saints who are in Christ. Christ is the sphere within which and the identity from which lived holiness flows into the daily activity of ordinary believers. Thus, sanctification was viewed not simply as a prompt (which it was, and, we might add, a stern one at that) but also as a promise from the Savior himself.

---

44. "The Tetrapolitan Confession," in Cochrane, *Reformed Confessions*, 57.

45. See, e.g., "The Heidelberg Catechism" (1563), in Cochrane, *Reformed Confessions*, 310. Three times the catechism uses the present tense in describing both the possession of his offices and the manner in which he fulfills them. In no case does this answer speak in a closed or past-tense manner.

46. On lay piety and late-medieval anxiety in German and Swiss cities, see Stephen E. Ozment, "Lay Religious Attitudes on the Eve of the Reformation," in *The Reformation in the Cities: The Appeal of Protestantism to Sixteenth-Century Germany and Switzerland* (New Haven, CT: Yale University Press, 1975), 15–46.

That sanctity is in Christ alone also reminds us of the eschatological character of our holiness. Here the Reformed tradition has emphasized the Israel-like nature of the church. While we may be tempted to view ourselves as living on some higher plane of spiritual and moral existence, the Reformed confessions call us to imagine ourselves as modern-day Israelites. Calvin addressed this when commenting on the scriptural argument ushered in by Paul in 1 Corinthians 10: "Paul says, first of all, that there is no point of difference between the Israelites and us, which would put our whole situation in a different category from theirs. . . . He begins like this: do not take pride in some special privilege, as if your standing with God is better than theirs was."[47]

GRACE ALONE

The Reformers articulated the Christ-centered nature of sanctification and the Christian life by extending the teaching of the later Augustine and the Augustinian tradition regarding grace and human action. Thus, Reformational teaching emphasized not only the importance of the agency of the Word but also the need for the Spirit's work to regenerate, illumine, and empower the saints along the path of that Word. The doctrines of election and predestination functioned to safeguard this emphasis on grace alone in the theology of Luther, Zwingli, and other early Reformers.

The Lutheran tradition did not consistently articulate this notion in the same way that Martin Luther did. Melanchthon later toned down the predestinarian teaching of the Lutheran church in such a way that Luther's emphasis on grace was no longer maintained in precisely the same form. Reformed churches, however, were more consistent in maintaining the strong Augustinian teaching of the early Reformers through the entirety of the sixteenth century. Not only second-generation Reformed thinkers like Calvin or Bullinger but also later theologians and confessions maintained the strong emphasis on God's sovereignty and grace as held by the earliest of Reformed theologians, such as Zwingli.[48]

---

47. Calvin on 1 Corinthians 10, in *CNTC* 9:200.
48. For a fuller discussion of these matters, see chap. 13, "The Bondage and Liberation of the Will," by Matthew Barrett.

Faith Alone

One area where the Reformers pushed beyond even the Augustinian heritage that they so prized was regarding the role of faith in salvation. In his treatise *On Faith and Works*, Augustine had said, "We should advise the faithful that they would endanger the salvation of their souls if they acted on the false assurance that faith alone is sufficient for salvation or that they need not perform good works in order to be saved."[49] The Reformers pushed beyond Augustine to insist that faith alone justifies. However, they agreed with their North African father that this faith that justifies cannot and will not be alone but will be matched by good works or sanctified behavior. The Reformers insisted, though, that these two responses be distinguished in terms of justification and sanctification; in this regard, they went beyond the conceptual apparatus of Augustine, who did not so distinguish them. The conceptual distinction between justification and sanctification was crucial in Reformational thought not only for providing assurance to imperfect saints but also for honoring the full breadth of God's work in Christ—outside us and inside us. Reformational churches called their believers to trust in all of Christ's work: both that he reconciles us to God and that he makes us holy.

Sanctification was also by faith, as seen above in both Luther's *Treatise on Good Works* and the Heidelberg Catechism's description of good works. Faith is not merely notional or noetic in the Reformational tradition. Calvin defined it this way: "Now we shall possess a right definition of faith if we call it a firm and certain knowledge of God's benevolence toward us, founded upon the truth of the freely given promise in Christ, both revealed to our minds and sealed upon our hearts through the Holy Spirit."[50] Calvin later noted a twofold emphasis in his definition: the Holy Spirit must make the "mind to be illumined" and the "heart . . . strengthened."[51] Faith is a matter of trust that involves heart and mind, not only knowing God to be good

49. Augustine, *On Faith and Works*, 28.
50. Calvin, *Institutes*, 3.2.7. Calvin never abandoned this definition, according to Barbara Pitkin, *What Pure Eyes Could See: Calvin's Doctrine of Faith in Its Exegetical Context*, Oxford Studies in Historical Theology (Oxford: Oxford University Press, 1999), 29.
51. Calvin, *Institutes*, 3.2.33; see also 3.2.36, where these two emphases are explicitly linked to the two faculties of the brain and the heart.

but entrusting oneself and one's good to God alone. Sanctification—the progressive transformation of the believer—was viewed as a reality dependent on God's good doings, and so it was a matter for faith or trust.

Scripture Alone

Perhaps nothing so exercised the Reformers as the issue of authority. Martin Luther's farewell sermon spoke to this theme poignantly:

> We have the idea that God could not reign if he did not have wise and understanding people to help him. . . . [The wise and understanding] are always exerting themselves; they do things in the Christian church the way they want to themselves. Everything that God does they must improve, so that there is no poorer, more insignificant and despised disciple on earth than God; he must be everybody's pupil, everybody wants to be his teacher. . . . They are not satisfied with what God has done and instituted, they cannot let things be as they were ordained to be. . . . These are the real wise-acres, of whom Christ is speaking here, who always have to have and do something special in order that the people may say, "Ah, our pastor or preacher is nothing; there's the real man, he'll get things done!" . . . Should God be so greatly pleased with these fellows who are all too smart and wise for him and are always wanting to send him back to school? . . . Things are in a fine state indeed when the egg wants to be wiser than the hen.[52]

The doctrine of *sola Scriptura* was intended not as a rebuke to all tradition but as a statement about the sort of biblical traditioning that was rightfully exercised in the communion of saints. In the realm of morals and of sanctification, Christian teaching about virtue at times ran the risk of veering into exalting certain habits and practices that were culturally valued but not biblically taught. Still further, certain sacramental and pietistic approaches to the Christian life crept into the church's life. The Reformers believed that virtues were necessary, sacraments a gift, and piety a high calling, but they insisted that each be defined biblically. It was Luther who said, "The first thing to know is

---

52. Martin Luther, "The Last Sermon, Preached in Eisleben, Matt. 11:25–30, February 15, 1546," *LW* 51:383–84.

that there are no good works except those works God has commanded, just as there is no sin except that which God has forbidden. Therefore, whoever wants to know what good works are as well as doing them needs to know nothing more than God's commandments."[53]

The rule of Scripture is not a crimp on human action, though, so much as a generative source of creaturely moral behavior: "By His Word, God alone sanctifies temples to Himself for lawful use. And if we rashly attempt anything without his command, strange inventions forthwith cling to the bad beginning and spread evil without measure."[54] Calvin and the other Reformers insisted that the Word is "living and active" as put by the anonymous author to the Hebrews (4:12). By tending to God's Word, believers and churches are living amid the life-giving power of the gospel as it addresses their persons and communities. So we do well not to think of Scripture merely as an index or rule for faith and practice; the Reformers viewed it as a means of grace and, as such, as a rule. It is a rule because it is here and only here that Christ promises to speak with perfect sway and infallible authority.

THE LAW

The previous themes all address major mantras of Reformational historiography. And it is crucial to remember that these slogans are only useful if we ask how various doctrines and practices relate to each of them, not segmenting them off from one another but treating them as a web of biblical and spiritual commitments that are mutually reinforcing. Again, though, it is important to remember that they were correctives offered amid a wider catholic heritage that was not ignored or dismissed but refined and reformed. One such aspect of this classical consensus was the role of the divine law in giving form or structure to holy living. Martin Luther did not explicitly affirm that the law shapes the Christian life. He did not do so because his way of rendering the law-gospel distinction required him to always use *law* in a negative light, casting the law religiously as a tool for convicting of sin. But if

---

53. Luther, *Treatise on Good Works*, LW 44:23. So Luther made a practice of critiquing Roman calls for priestly celibacy as early as his 1520 treatise *An Address to the German Nobility*.
54. Calvin, *Institutes*, 4.1.5.

we press a bit further and ask whether or not Luther made use of the Decalogue and of the Old Testament Torah as a way of shaping Christian ethics, the answer is a resounding *yes!*[55]

Reformed theologians were much more straightforward and consistent in noting that the law not only points to one's need for Christ but also addresses the believer as a prompt for holy living and a guide for moral behavior. Whereas Lutheran liturgies typically focused on the recitation of the Ten Commandments as a prompt to the confession of sin, Reformed churches also employed them as a responsive reading meant to guide the congregation's service to God in light of the gift of the reading and preaching of God's Word. While faith in the triune God is the manner and God's glory is the motivation for holy living, the law of God does continue to be treated as an objective shape whereby holiness is marked. This is attested by the many commentaries on the Decalogue, by the ongoing catechetical use of the Ten Commandments, and by their liturgical placement in the Reformed and Lutheran traditions.

Conclusion

So we return to the issue of reformational obedience and catholic rebellion: how do we faithfully and honestly assess the teaching of the sixteenth-century Reformers regarding the doctrine of sanctification?

---

55. For attempts to think about Luther's moral theology without being beholden solely to the law-gospel distinction as a structuring principle but reading it as a corrective to a wider classical approach to holiness, see David S. Yeago, "Gnosticism, Antinomianism, and Reformation Theology: Reflections on the Costs of a Construal," *ProEccl* 2, no. 1 (1993): 37–49; David S. Yeago, "'A Christian, Holy People': Martin Luther on Salvation and the Church," in *Spirituality and Social Embodiment*, ed. L. Gregory Jones and James J. Buckley, Directions in Modern Theology (Oxford: Blackwell, 1997), 101–20; and Reinhard Hütter, "The Twofold Center of Lutheran Ethics: Christian Freedom and God's Commandments," in *The Promise of Lutheran Ethics*, ed. Karen Bloomquist and John Stumme (Minneapolis: Fortress, 1998), 31–54.

Luther's teaching on the Christian use of the law has prompted continual debate in recent decades. In the face of twentieth-century teaching that sometimes veered close to saying that Christian freedom is equivalent to private judgment and personal interpretative autonomy, a number of "evangelical catholics" in the Lutheran world have sought to revive the twofold center of Luther's ethics: freedom and commandment. At the same time, some "Radical Lutherans" have sought to downplay this facet of Luther's teaching. It is hard to read their analysis without thinking that at times they are seeking to out-Luther Luther himself, in particular by reading the young Luther against the old Luther and by reading the most hyperbolic Luther against the confessional Lutheran tradition. Gerhard Forde and his students Stephen Paulson and Mark Mattes exemplify this trend most consistently. But the "evangelical catholic" argument surely points to legitimate practices in Luther's own ministry that are confessionally attested in the later Lutheran church and attested in the pastoral practice of Luther himself (even if not theologically articulated with clarity by the Reformer).

We would be remiss if we did not emphasize still further the ecclesial shape of holiness: guided by the pastoral discipline of the church, fed by the sacramental ministry of Christ, and ordered by the moral touch points of the Christian tradition (the Decalogue most especially but also the Apostle's Creed and the Lord's Prayer).

At the same time, there was a recalibration with regard to the way in which these catholic realities were experienced by specific men and women: God's glory was the signal calling of all, Scripture was the ultimate authority, and personal faith was necessary for acts to be truly holy. As apparent in the lives of Luther, Calvin, Bucer, Cranmer, and others, Reformational theologians believed right faith and practice regarding holiness and Christian piety were in danger of two flanks: Roman Catholicism, on the one hand, and Anabaptism or enthusiasm, on the other. Pursuit of a via media was not the result of a calculating political maneuver but the principled belief that a Christological focus required an ecclesiological commitment, for Christ promises to work through his church. Thus, these Reformers were committed to being evangelical and to being churchly. With Jaroslav Pelikan, then, we can say not only of Martin Luther or of John Calvin but also of the wider Reformational movement, its reflections on holiness and the Christian life were efforts led by "obedient rebels," and in the main they surely constituted movements toward a reformed catholicity.

Resources for Further Study

Primary Sources

Calvin, John. *Institutes of the Christian Religion*. Edited by John T. McNeill. Translated by Ford Lewis Battles. 2 vols. Library of Christian Classics 20–21. 1559 edition. Philadelphia: Westminster, 1960.

Cochrane, Arthur C., ed. *Reformed Confessions of the Sixteenth Century*. Louisville: Westminster John Knox, 2003.

Kolb, Robert, and Timothy J. Wengert, eds. *The Book of Concord: The Confessions of the Evangelical Lutheran Church*. Translated by Charles P. Arand et al. Minneapolis: Fortress, 2000.

Luther, Martin. *Treatise on Good Works*. In *Luther's Works*. Vol. 44, *The Christian in Society I*, edited by James Atkinson, 15–114. Philadelphia: Fortress, 1966.

Secondary Sources

Allen, Michael. *Sanctification*. New Studies in Dogmatics. Grand Rapids, MI: Zondervan Academic, 2017.

Barth, Karl. *The Theology of the Reformed Confessions*. Columbia Series in Reformed Theology. Translated and annotated by Darrell L. Guder and Judith J. Guder. Louisville: Westminster John Knox, 2002.

Billings, J. Todd. *Calvin, Participation, and the Gift: The Activity of Believers in Union with Christ*. Changing Paradigms in Historical and Systematic Theology. New York: Oxford University Press, 2007.

Null, Ashley. *Thomas Cranmer's Doctrine of Repentance: Renewing the Power to Love*. New York: Oxford University Press, 2000.

Yeago, David S. "Gnosticism, Antinomianism, and Reformation Theology: Reflections on the Costs of a Construal." *Pro Ecclesia* 2, no. 1 (1993): 37–49.

16

The Church

Robert Kolb

ABSTRACT

All Protestant Reformers rejected the ritual-centered, hierarchically controlled definition of Christ's church that prevailed in medieval theology and piety, instead defining the church as God's creation through his Word. They characterized the relationship of the sacraments to God's Word in varying ways, but all emphasized the place of the sacraments as marks of the church. The term *marks* was also used in varying ways among the Reformers, with the Word of God at the heart of the concept. Protestants organized the church with different forms of polity: Lutherans with some variety, Calvinists with Calvin's four offices in presbyterian form, Anglicans with an episcopal system, and Anabaptists with a congregational system. All centered worship on preaching with sacramental rites as an important part of the public life of the congregation. Each insisted on discipline of public sinners, practiced with varying degrees of seriousness. With the exception of the Anabaptists, Protestants associated their churches with secular governments, which exercised varying degrees of control over their territorial churches.

The Reformation and Medieval Doctrines of the Church

The publication of Martin Luther's *Ninety-Five Theses on Indulgences* in late 1517 provoked reactions that fed broader longings for the reform of Christendom. However, condemnations by the officials of the Western church pronounced lethal consequences on Luther and all who shared his views. The doctrine and practice surrounding indulgences to render satisfaction for the temporal punishments that the medieval church laid on sinners had not been well defined at that point,[1] and therefore, Luther's challenge of them should not have caused controversy. But Luther's theses did more than just that. They implicitly challenged the structure of authority in the Western church. "The early Catholic literary response to Luther can best be characterized by its preoccupation with authority," particularly ecclesiastical or papal authority.[2] In his defense before his Augustinian brethren at Heidelberg in April 1518, Luther quickly demonstrated that he thought reform centered around the relationship of God and sinners,[3] while his opponents had defined ecclesiology as the central question to be resolved.[4]

Practitioners of comparative religious studies suggest that six elements constitute religious systems: doctrine, narrative, ritual, ethics, community (including polity), and whatever binds these elements together (e.g., faith, submission, longing for nothingness). Each religious system constructs the relationships among these elements in a different fashion, placing one or more in a pivotal, regulating, position.[5] At the heart of the relationship between God and sinners medieval Western Christianity had placed human ritual performance of sacred rites and ceremonies—above all, the Mass—and governance of the church through the bishop of Rome and the bishops subservient to him. The

---

1. Bernhard Alfred R. Felmberg, *Die Ablasstheologie Kardinal Cajetans (1469–1534)*, Studies in Medieval and Reformation Thought 66 (Leiden: Brill, 1998).

2. David V. N. Bagchi, *Luther's Earliest Opponents: Catholic Controversialists, 1518–1525* (Minneapolis: Fortress, 1991), 265.

3. Martin Luther, "Heidelberg Disputation," WA 1:353–74; *LW* 31:35–70.

4. At this time the Western discussion of the doctrine of the church was still shaped significantly by the dispute between conciliarists and curialists. Conciliarists had promoted a powerful role for councils in the governance of the church, and under their leadership the Great Western Schism was brought to an end at the Council of Constance in 1414–1418. The reunited papal government supported the curialist position, which defended the concentration of power in the papacy and its curia. Over the course of the fifteenth century, the curialists largely silenced the conciliarists even if Luther initially attempted to further his call for reform with an appeal to a council.

5. Ninian Smart, *Worldviews: Crosscultural Explorations of Human Beliefs* (New York: Scribner, 1983), esp. 79–95.

precise form of this governing polity had aroused both critical divisions within Western Christendom in reaction to the Great Western Schism of the fourteenth and fifteenth centuries and challenges to this ecclesiology by conciliar advocates and by Jan Hus, the Bohemian Reformer burnt at the Council of Constance in 1415.[6] During the fifteenth century, forces supporting the view that the bishop of Rome held supreme power in the church triumphed over those who argued for limitations on papal power through ecumenical councils. Criticism from German humanists joined with those who were struggling to determine the proper place of authority within the church apart from total papal domination.[7]

Luther grew up within the context of this debate. His study of Scripture as a novice university instructor and his own experience convinced him that the definition of being Christian couched in terms of ritual and polity did not correspond to God's presentation of himself in Scripture. He formulated a new definition of being Christian grounded on the narrative of God's saving action, culminating in the death and resurrection of Jesus Christ, and on the doctrinal structure derived from this biblical narrative. Indeed, all sixteenth-century Reformers regarded as vital for the church's life both the adaptation of proper ritual forms to express that faith in Christ and a means of proclaiming it. Biblically faithful ritual could aid communication of the gospel. Luther believed that God exercised his authority and power in his church through his Word, given in Scripture and conveyed in a variety of oral, written, and sacramental forms, including in the liturgy.

Sixteenth-Century Lutheran Teachings on the Church

DEFINING THE CHURCH AND ITS MARKS

In the Smalcald Articles (1537), Luther's agenda for negotiating with Roman Catholic theologians at the papally called council, Luther

---

6. Matthew Spinka, *John Hus' Concept of the Church* (Princeton, NJ: Princeton University Press, 1966); Antony Black, *Council and Commune: The Conciliar Movement and the Fifteenth-Century Heritage* (London: Burns & Oates, 1979); Karl Binder, *Konzilsgedanken bei Kardinal Juan de Torquemada O.P.* (Vienna: Dom, 1976).

7. Kurt Stadtwald, *Roman Popes and German Patriots: Antipapalism in the Politics of the German Humanist Movement from Gregor Heimburg to Martin Luther* (Geneva: Droz, 1996); Götz-Rüdiger Tewes, *Die römische Kurie und die europäischen Länder am Vorabend der Reformation* (Tübingen: Niemeyer, 2001).

defined the church simply as "holy believers and the little sheep who hear the voice of their shepherd" (cf. John 10:3). Contrasting his own definition of the Word-based assembly of believers with the medieval definition that grounded itself on the performance of ritual under clerical obedience, Luther explained what the words of the Apostles' Creed "I believe in the holy Christian church" mean: "This holiness does not consist of surplices, tonsures, long albs, or other ceremonies of theirs that they have invented over and above the Holy Scriptures. Its holiness exists in the Word of God and true faith."[8]

Luther was reflecting the summary of Wittenberg ecclesiology in the Augsburg Confession, which his colleague Philipp Melanchthon had composed seven years earlier:

> [The] one holy, Christian church . . . is the assembly of all believers among whom the gospel is purely preached and the holy sacraments are administered according to the gospel. For this is enough for the true unity of the Christian church: that there the gospel is preached harmoniously according to a pure understanding and the sacraments are administered in conformity with the divine Word. It is not necessary for the true unity of the Christian church that uniform ceremonies, instituted by human beings, be observed everywhere.[9]

Both Luther and Melanchthon fervently sought Christian unity but only in conformity with God's Word and the heart of its message of justification by faith in Christ.[10]

Melanchthon's two criteria for defining the church—the proper preaching of the gospel and the proper administration of the sacraments—reflected his desire in this confession to defend the legitimacy and validity of the Wittenberg claim to be in the church catholic, for

---

8. *BSELK* 777; Robert Kolb and Timothy J. Wengert, eds., *The Book of Concord: The Confessions of the Evangelical Lutheran Church*, trans. Charles P. Arand et al. (Minneapolis: Fortress, 2000), 324–25. For an overview of Luther's ecclesiology, see David P. Daniel, "Luther on the Church," in *The Oxford Handbook of Martin Luther's Theology*, ed. Robert Kolb, Irene Dingel, and L'ubomír Batka (Oxford: Oxford University Press, 2014), 333–52.

9. *BSELK* 102–3; Kolb and Wengert, *Book of Concord*, 42–43.

10. Regarding Melanchthon's attempts at promoting Christian unity, see Irene Dingel, "Melanchthon's Paraphrases of the Augsburg Confession, 1534 and 1536, in the Service of the Smalcald League," in Irene Dingel, Robert Kolb, Nicole Kuropka, and Timothy J. Wengert, *Philip Melanchthon: Theologian in Classroom, Confession, and Controversy*, Refo500 Academic Studies 7 (Göttingen: Vandenhoeck & Ruprecht, 2012), 104–22.

they adapted the legal definition of being Christian in the Justinian Code, the prevailing legal standard of the empire.[11] Civil law and theology coincided nicely because the Wittenberg understanding of the church flowed from its Creator, the Holy Spirit, working through the Word of God in its oral, written, and sacramental forms. To avoid charges of Donatism, Melanchthon reiterated the Wittenberg insistence that within the community of believers those outside the faith remain as tares among the wheat. Only those who truly trust in Christ, however, are saved.[12]

In his *Loci Communes* of 1543, Melanchthon emphasized that the church is God's chosen people and that it is not an indefinable, spiritual entity but is rather the people gathered around the voice of the gospel. God's commitment in his promise of life and salvation through forgiveness proclaimed in the assembly of believers should be met with the believer's commitment to that assembly. The *Loci* reiterated that the Holy Spirit works through his Word in the congregation.[13]

Luther himself did not develop a full-scale ecclesiology in any one work, but in 1539, with the possibility of a papally called council in the air, he did write *On the Councils and the Church*. He embraced the creedal tradition of the ancient church, particularly the Nicene Creed, as a faithful guide to the biblical witness. This work set forth eight "marks of the church." Medieval theologians had occasionally employed the term *mark of the church*, but no single dogmatic category as such emerged under the label.[14] Luther did not attempt to create such a dogmatic category as he described how to identify the assembly of believers that was listening to Christ. His orientation to God's Word was clear in his insistence that the Holy Spirit creates the church by forgiving sin and thus bestowing trust in Christ on his chosen people, who under

---

11. Robert C. Schultz, "An Analysis of the Augsburg Confession, Article VII, 2 in Its Historical Context, May and June 1530," *SCJ* 11, no. 3 (1980): 25–35.

12. *BSELK* 102/103, 408–17; Kolb and Wengert, *Book of Concord*, 42/43, 179. In his *Loci Communes* (1543), Melanchthon dedicated a longer section to refuting the Donatist rejection of the objectivity of God's Word apart from the moral or doctrinal qualification of the minster of the Word. *Melanchthons Werke in Auswahl*, ed. Robert Stupperich, vol. 2, bk. 1 (Gütersloh: Gerd Mohn, 1951–1975), 487–92; *Loci Communes 1543*, trans. J. A. O. Preus (St. Louis, MO: Concordia, 1992), 135–37.

13. Melanchthon, *Melanchthons Werke in Auswahl*, vol. 2, bk. 1 (Gerd Mohn), 474–97, *Loci Communes 1543*, 131–38.

14. Gordon W. Lathrop and Timothy J. Wengert, *Christian Assembly: Marks of the Church in a Pluralistic Age* (Minneapolis: Fortress, 2004), 20–21.

the Spirit's guidance produce the fruits of faith. The Spirit's activities bring strength and comfort to troubled consciences, moving people to fear and love God above all else. That love for God in turn produces both a life of service and a love for fellow believers and the world.

The proclamation of God's Word is the first mark identifying the true church. From and along with proclamation of the Word, other forms of the Word mark the church: baptism, the Lord's Supper, and the public exercise of the office of the keys, or confession and absolution, which Luther regarded as the heart of the life of repentance that believers practice throughout their lives. Although Luther did not develop any detailed plans for congregational discipline, he presumed that in the exercise of the keys, personal discipline would arise from pastors and other Christians calling open sinners to repent. This life in the various forms of God's Word takes place under the care and guidance of pastors, the pastoral office being the fifth mark of the church. The response of the faithful to God's Word is expressed in the church's sixth mark, "prayer, public praise, and thanksgiving to God" and instruction in the faith. In addition, the church is identified by its suffering, the "sacred cross," as the Devil, the world, and internal sinful desires inflict "sadness, timidity, fear from within and outside, poverty, contempt, illness, and weakness" on believers corporately and individually. Persecution, Luther believed, was only one—but a significant—part of Satan's eschatological battle against God and his truth in which the church and individual believers were enmeshed. The eighth "public sign," the good works of love that the Holy Spirit produces in sanctified lives, was not a unique sign of the church's existence, for Luther believed that false believers could perform works that outwardly conform to God's law. Nonetheless, without the practice of love Luther found that the church does not become perceptible.[15] In similar presentations of the church's marks, he mentioned that the church is "people loving the Word and confessing it before others"[16] and is the place "where Christians believe in Christ, are saved by faith, and humbly give themselves to one another."[17]

---

15. Martin Luther, *On the Councils and the Church* (1539), WA 50:625.33, 643.37; *LW* 41:145–67.

16. Martin Luther, *Lectures on Psalm 90* (1534), WA, vol. 40, bk. 3, 506.7–31; *LW* 13:90.

17. Martin Luther, "Maundy Thursday Sermon" (1538), WA 46:285.7–10.

In other works Luther added to the eight marks in *On the Councils* using the Apostles' Creed as a summary of the faith, reciting the Lord's Prayer, esteeming secular rulers, honoring marriage, and not shedding the blood of other Christians—the latter three points a criticism of the papal church.[18] Melanchthon's exposition of the marks of the church focused generally on the conveying of forgiveness through God's Word in its various forms. He also rejected other signs that marked the church in medieval theology, especially "the regular succession of bishops and obedience in human traditions" and above all, the claim of bishops to interpret Scripture and establish new laws and worship practices for the church.[19]

Martin Chemnitz provided a bridge from Melanchthon and Luther to seventeenth-century teaching, especially in his commentary on Melanchthon's *Loci* but also in other works, such as his *Examination of the Council of Trent*. In this latter work he anchored the church's teaching and the authority of its councils in "the rule and norm of the sacred Scriptures," the only ultimate authority for believers.[20] Exchanges with Roman Catholic and Anabaptist definitions of the church provided orientation for Chemnitz's repetition of Luther's and Melanchthon's insights. He asserted that any definition of "church" must "apply both to particular true churches in particular places and to the truly catholic church scattered throughout the whole world, which is one body."[21] It is an assembly, and like a city set on a hill (Matt. 5:14), it shines the gospel of Christ into the world through the faithful proclamation of his Word and the proper use of the sacraments.[22] But it dare not be equated with an institution, such as the papacy; it remained, as Melanchthon put it, "the flock of such sheep, as are known by Christ and in turn knowing him, . . . never out of his hands (John 10:14, 28)."[23]

18. Martin Luther, *Against Hans Wurst*, WA 51:477.28–486.22; LW 41:194–98.

19. *Melanchthons Werke in Auswahl*, vol. 2, bk. 1 (Gerd Mohn), 492–97, *Loci Communes*, 137–38.

20. Martin Chemnitz, *Examination of the Council of Trent, Part I*, trans. Fred Kramer (St. Louis, MO: Concordia, 1971), 31.

21. Martin Chemnitz, *Loci Theologici, Parts 2–3*, trans. J. A. O. Preus, vol. 8 of *Chemnitz's Works* (St. Louis, MO: Concordia, 2008), 695.

22. The charge that sixteenth-century Lutherans had no sense of the mission of the church to other nations is not true. Cf. Robert Kolb, "Late Reformation Lutherans on Mission and Confession," *LQ* 20, no. 1 (2006): 26–43.

23. Chemnitz, *Loci Theologici*, in *Chemnitz's Works*, 8:695–98.

CHURCH POLITY AND THE STATE

Luther's distinction between the two realms or dimensions of human life, vertical and horizontal, placed the gospel proclamation of the church in the former but most of its this-worldly structures and actions in the latter, where reason informs decisions to a large extent. Thus, his views of church polity were rather open. He used the term "church" for something akin to the "invisible church," which had not yet come into technical Wittenberg terminology. Luther described the communion of saints in all the world as "the hidden church,"[24] which becomes not only visible but above all audible and perceptible as the people gather around God's Word in oral, written, and sacramental forms. His usage of "church" also embraced territorial and national churches of an institutional type, such as in Saxony or England, in his world usually associated with management by or in close cooperation with secular authorities (e.g., in France, where, since the Pragmatic Sanction of Bourges in 1438, the king had secured significantly more power in the church than the pope, parallel to similar arrangements in Iberian lands and some Italian principalities). Most specifically, however, "church" designated those gathered physically around the preached and sacramental forms of God's Word in local communities of the faithful.

Luther believed that the medieval episcopal form of church government could serve Christ's gospel effectively if it promoted biblical teaching; he approved of his colleague Nikolaus von Amsdorf assuming a bishop's office in Naumburg-Zeitz.[25] He could also, at least early in his career, promote a local congregation's exercise of responsibility for its own life.[26] While relatively open to various forms of polity, Luther sharply rejected the claims of the papacy to govern the church by divine right. Scott Hendrix has traced Luther's critique of these claims

---

24. On the development of Luther's ecclesiology in the early years of his career, see Scott H. Hendrix, *Ecclesia in Via: Ecclesiological Developments in the Medieval Psalms Exegesis and the Dictata super Psalterium (1513–1515) of Martin Luther* (London: Brill, 1974), and Carl-Axel Aurelius, *Verborgene Kirche: Luthers Kirchenverständnis in Streitschriften und Exegese, 1519–1521* (Hannover: Lutherisches Verlags-Haus, 1983).

25. Peter Brunner, *Nikolaus von Amsdorf als Bischof von Naumburg: Eine Untersuchung zur Gestalt des evangelischen Bischofamtes in der Reformationszeit* (Gütersloh: Mohn, 1961).

26. Martin Luther, *That a Christian Assembly or Congregation Has the Right and Power to Judge All Teaching and to Call, Appoint, and Dismiss Teachers . . .* (1523), WA 11:408–16; LW 39:305–14.

from "ambivalence" toward the pope and his office in Luther's early years—an attitude shared by many at the time—to "protest" following the first harsh reactions to his *Ninety-Five Theses* in late 1517 and 1518. As threats of execution for heresy became ever more frequent and finally official, the Wittenberg professor moved from "resistance" in later 1518 to "challenging" papal claims the next year to outright opposition in 1520.

By 1521, Luther's conviction that the papacy as an institution fulfilled New Testament prophecies regarding the coming of the Antichrist at the end of time began to dominate his critiques of the papacy and its supporters, answering threats, ridicule, and denunciation in kind.[27] However, if specific forms of polity did not interfere with the preaching of the gospel, Luther believed many forms could be appropriate in different situations for supporting this proclamation, which was what, in his view, forms and sustains the church. Lutherans in the Nordic kingdoms, Denmark-Norway-Iceland and Sweden-Finland, had extensive royal control for much of the early modern period. In Polish and Hungarian kingdoms, the Counter-Reformation suppressed Lutheran churches through a variety of means; there Lutheran churches preserved themselves in small groups, often lay-led, using the Bible, the catechism, and the hymnal.

In German lands Luther's Reformation was made possible in part by supportive rulers who protected leaders of the cause. Luther and Melanchthon regarded secular government as the leading member of the church and closely cooperated with and advised many German and Nordic governments,[28] although Luther was generally quicker than Melanchthon to criticize rulers and call them to repentance.[29] After the defeat of the evangelical princes and cities in the Smalcald War (1547), a divide opened within the Wittenberg circle regarding the "Leipzig Proposal" of 1548, which Melanchthon helped devise to save Lutheran pulpits for Lutheran preachers. This document offered the compro-

---

27. Scott H. Hendrix, *Luther and the Papacy: Stages in a Reformation Conflict* (Philadelphia: Fortress, 1981).

28. Eike Wolgast, "Luther's Treatment of Political and Societal Life," in Kolb, Dingel, and Batka, *Oxford Handbook of Luther's Theology*, 397–413; James M. Estes, *Peace, Order, and the Glory of God: Secular Authority and the Church in the Thought of Luther and Melanchthon, 1518–1559*, Studies in Medieval and Reformation Traditions 111 (Leiden: Brill, 2005).

29. Robert Kolb, "Luther on Peasants and Princes," *LQ* 23, no. 2 (2009): 125–46.

mise of using adiaphora to convince Emperor Charles V that electoral Saxony was conforming to the medieval customs and teachings to which he wanted to return. The settlement of the dispute avoided addressing the relationship between church and secular government, and Lutherans continued to work closely with friendly governments while repeatedly getting into trouble with their secular lords for criticizing governmental policies of several kinds.[30]

THE CHURCH GATHERED

Although Luther revolted against the domination of ritual in the medieval understanding of the way of salvation, he nonetheless held that public worship, in both its liturgy and its preaching, played a significant role in the shape of the Christian life.[31] In regular services the congregation expressed the faith of its people as that faith was fed by God's Word in oral, written, and sacramental forms. Baptism and the Lord's Supper conveyed God's promise as a part of the Holy Spirit's multimedia approach, not through any power resting in the material elements or the ritual action but because of the gospel promise conveyed with the elements. The sermon formed the center of liturgical worship. Luther insisted, "Preaching and teaching of God's Word" is "the most important part of the divine service,"[32] along with the public absolution of the sins of the worshipers, "the true voice of the gospel announcing remission of sins."[33] The Lord's Supper was also to bring the gospel of forgiveness and life to believers each week as the body and blood of Christ came in unique and mysterious form to recipients of the elements.[34] The liturgy provided the people the opportunity to join others in responding to God's Word with joy in praise and thanksgiving. Ideally, Luther believed that small groups of believers should meet for mutual consolation, study, and prayer.[35]

Although it is often suggested that Luther's views of the pastoral

30. W. D. J. Cargill Thompson, *The Political Thought of Martin Luther* (Sussex: Harvester, 1984), 119–54.

31. Vilmos Vajta, *Luther on Worship: An Interpretation* (Philadelphia: Muhlenberg, 1958); Carter Lindberg, "Piety, Prayer, and Worship in Luther's View of Daily Life," in Kolb, Dingel, and Batka, *Oxford Handbook of Luther's Theology*, 414–26.

32. Martin Luther, "The German Mass" (1526), WA 19:78.26–27; LW 53:68.

33. Martin Luther, "An Order of Mass and Communion" (1523), WA 12:213.9–11; LW 53:28.

34. Ibid., WA 12:206.15–209.10; LW 53:20–23.

35. Luther, "The German Mass" (1526), WA 19:75.3–30; LW 53:63–64.

office and its relationship to laypeople changed over time, in fact, he never ceased insisting that God had ordained that congregations have pastors in an office formally charged with the public proclamation of God's Word and the administration of the sacraments.[36] He never abandoned his belief that God has commissioned all baptized Christians as his priests to share God's Word with others, both those who do not yet believe and those who do and need to hear either its admonition or its comfort.[37] In the Augsburg Confession and in his "Treatise on the Power and Primacy of the Pope," Melanchthon defined the pastoral office in terms of the office of the keys, the power entrusted by Christ to his church to forgive or retain sins: bishops, like all other pastors have "a power and command of God to preach the gospel, to forgive or retain sin, and to administer and distribute the sacraments."[38] In the "Treatise" he added that they had the power "to excommunicate the ungodly without the use of physical force."[39] Particularly against Anabaptists and Spiritualists, who held that the Holy Spirit calls people to public preaching and ministry apart from the structures set up for orderly conduct of church life, the Wittenberg theologians argued for "rightly called" ministers of the Word.[40]

Sixteenth-century Lutheran teachers bequeathed to their successors an ecclesiology centered on the use of God's Word in Scripture that took form in various oral, written, and sacramental forms, all

---

36. Robert Kolb, "Ministry in Martin Luther and the Lutheran Confessions," in *Called and Ordained: Lutheran Perspectives on the Office of the Ministry*, ed. Todd Nichol and Marc Kolden (Minneapolis: Fortress, 1990), 49–66.

37. Martin Luther, "Sermon on Matthew 9:1–8" (1526), WA, vol. 10, bk. 1, 412–14; *Sermons of Martin Luther*, ed. John Nicholas Lenker (1905; repr., Grand Rapids, MI: Baker, 1983), 5:209; cf. WA 19:13–15; *LW* 36:359; WA 45:540.14–23; *LW* 24:87–88; WA 47:297.36–298.14; WA 44:712.33–36, 713.5–8; *LW* 8:183; WA 44:95.41–46; *LW* 6:128.

38. BSELK 186–91; Kolb and Wengert, *Book of Concord*, 92–93.

39. BSELK 489–90, 822–825; Kolb and Wengert, *Book of Concord*, 340–41.

40. See, e.g., Luther's *Against Infiltrating and Clandestine Preachers* (1532), WA, vol. 30, bk. 3, 518–27; *LW* 40:383–94; and article 14 of Melanchthon's Augsburg Confession, BSELK 108–11; Kolb and Wengert, *Book of Concord*, 46–47. Cf. also Chemnitz on the subject, *Loci Theologici, Parts 2–3*, in *Chemnitz's Works*, 8:698, cf. 8:698–719; and *Ministry, Word, and Sacraments: An Enchiridion*, trans. Luther Poellot (St. Louis, MO: Concordia, 1981). Melanchthon invented this genre with his *Examen ordinandum* (1552), *Melanchthons Werke in Auswahl* (Gerd Mohn), 6:168–259; see 6:212–21 on "The Church." Chemnitz had not abandoned the priesthood of all believers, but against those who claimed to be able to preach publicly without an orderly call from the church, he explained 1 Pet. 2:9 as follows: "All Christians are priests—not that all should carry out the function of public ministry promiscuously, without a specific call, but that they should offer up spiritual sacrifices" ("spiritual sacrifices" alluding to 1 Pet. 2:5 and described in Rom. 12:1; Heb. 13:15–16). They should speak God's Word in the home and among friends, comforting one another and confessing the gospel, but should not assume public duties of the pastoral office.

under the leadership of those called by God to the public ministry of the church.

Reformed Teachings on the Church
Martin Bucer on the Church

Luther's presentation of his "theology of the cross" to his Augustinian brothers in Heidelberg in 1518 won the mind of a young Dominican hearer, Martin Bucer. Bucer became leader of the church in Strasbourg, where circumstances of the city shaped his understanding of the church, especially its form and governance. At the Diet of Augsburg in 1530, Bucer and fellow pastors from four South German cities confessed in the Tetrapolitan Confession that the church of Christ, "frequently called the kingdom of heaven," is "the fellowship of those who have enlisted under Christ and committed themselves entirely to his faith," "with whom, nevertheless, until the end of the world those are mingled who feign faith in Christ but do not truly have it." In the strict sense, however, only those in whom "the Saviour truly reigns" are properly called the church. The Holy Spirit rules it, and it reveals itself in the fruits of faith even though it cannot be seen.[41]

The Tetrapolitan Confession emphasized the necessity of ministry within the church, of ministers who proclaim no error. Christ's sheep follow no stranger's voice.[42] Ministers have no power apart from edifying hearers with God's Word. They serve the church in answer to the call of the Holy Spirit, who provides the wisdom and willingness to preach God's Word properly and to care for the people. The Spirit acts through the church's ministers to accomplish his goal of saving his people. They are charged with exercising discipline in Christ's stead so that souls may be renewed.[43] As a minister responsible for the spiritual welfare of the entire population of Strasbourg, Bucer recognized that those who reject the Holy Spirit remain in the outward fellowship of believers and that believers also still struggle against their sinful desires. These themes permeate Bucer's understanding of the church

41. "Confession Tetrapolitana," in James T. Dennison Jr., ed., *Reformed Confessions of the 16th and 17th Centuries in English Translation*, vol. 1, *1523–1552* (Grand Rapids, MI: Reformation Heritage Books, 2008), 154–58.
42. Ibid., 1:156–58.
43. Ibid., 1:154–56.

as centered in God's Word, through which the Holy Spirit brings it into being, with Christ as its Head. The Spirit gathers Christ's people around his Word and sacrament so that they may receive forgiveness of sins. Thus, the church serves as the instrument of the Spirit in creating and maintaining the people of God. Word, sacrament, and discipline mark the church.[44]

Bucer's efforts in behalf of restoring the unity of the Western church demonstrate both his commitment to that unity and his insistence that unity was possible only with massive reform of medieval doctrine and practice.[45] For him, the unity of the church rested on a Word-based definition of the church. Luther's reformulation of the doctrine of the church helped shape Bucer's commitment to restoring the church's oneness in its proclamation and life.

HULDRYCH ZWINGLI AND HEINRICH BULLINGER ON THE CHURCH

Huldrych Zwingli formulated his doctrine of the church in a municipal setting as well, in Zurich. He had worked for reform before he acclaimed Luther as the third Elijah in 1520, and his doctrine of the church reflected both the common concerns of the two Reformers and his own understanding of its nature. Zwingli established the origins of the church on the basis of God's covenant with the elect.[46] Local assemblies taken together constitute the universal church.[47] His mature theology finds expression in his *Exposition of the Faith*, composed in 1530 but published posthumously in 1536, which is an appeal to King Francis I of France for the reform of the church, and in his *Account of the Faith* presented to Emperor Charles V in 1530 at the Diet of Augsburg.

The *Exposition* began its treatment of the church by focusing on the invisible church, "which knows and embraces God by the enlightenment of the Holy Spirit," and is universal; its members are not invisible,

44. W. P. Stephens, *The Holy Spirit in the Theology of Martin Bucer* (Cambridge: Cambridge University Press, 1970), 156–66.

45. Volkmar Ortmann, *Reformation und Einheit der Kirche: Martin Bucers Einigungsbemühungen bei den Religionsgesprächen in Leipzig, Hagenau, Worms und Regensburg, 1539–1541* (Mainz: Zabern, 2001).

46. J. Wayne Baker, *Heinrich Bullinger and the Covenant: The Other Reformed Tradition* (Athens: Ohio University Press, 1980), 1–19.

47. W. P. Stephens, *The Theology of Huldrych Zwingli* (Oxford: Clarendon, 1986), 260–70.

but human perception cannot reliably identify them as believers. The visible church, Zwingli insisted, is not the church subject to the Roman pontiff and other bishops, but those who openly profess the faith, although among them, may be some who have no inward faith.[48] The *Account* repeated the themes of the *Exposition*, defining the church more clearly as the gathering of the elect, who have the Holy Spirit as the pledge of salvation, to whom God gives faith and thus creates the church.[49] Christ alone is the Head of the church; he bestows on it his purity and holiness. His are those who adhere to God's Word and live for Christ. However, within the assembly of the faithful, hypocrites and unfaithful people remain; this became a point of contention between Zwingli and local Anabaptists.

Although like other Reformers he rejected medieval views of ordination as a sacrament, Zwingli insisted on called, trained pastors as a necessary part of the church; their chief task he regarded as the preaching of God's Word.[50] Zwingli's goal of purifying the church of superstitious usages required the simplification of Sunday morning worship to basic elements of the hearing of God's Word, prayer, and praise.[51]

Zwingli limited discipline of sinners to those who committed public offenses, prescribed a series of admonitions in accord with Matthew 18:15–17, and then placed the execution of excommunication in the hands of the secular government. Zurich's system of church government earns it the designation of "the birthplace of Erastianism," named after the Heidelberg professor Thomas Erastus, a disciple of Zwingli, who in 1558 advanced the argument that secular governments have the right and duty to exercise jurisdiction in ecclesiastical affairs, including church discipline. In 1530, Zwingli posited the "Erastian" position in his *Exposition*: the presence of the insolent and hostile within the external fellowship creates "the need of government for the punishment of flagrant sinners, whether it be the government of princes or of the nobility. . . . There are shepherds in the church, and amongst these we may number princes. . . . Without civil government a church is maimed

48. Huldrych Zwingli, *An Exposition of the Faith*, in *Zwingli and Bullinger: Selected Translations with Introductions and Notes*, ed. G. W. Bromiley, LCC 24 (Philadelphia: Westminster, 1953), 265–66.

49. *BSRK*, 84–86.

50. Stephens, *Theology of Zwingli*, 274–81.

51. Charles Garside, *Zwingli and the Arts* (New Haven, CT: Yale University Press, 1966).

and impotent."[52] Robert Walton attributes Zwingli's assignment of significant power for secular rulers in the church to his "desire to insure the Gospel its rightful place in the life of the community," as well as to his despair "of the church's ability to reform itself."[53]

Zwingli's successor as leader of Zurich's church, Heinrich Bullinger, treated the topic of "the holy catholic church" in his catechetical sermons, published between 1549 and 1552. The sermon on the church defined it as "the whole company and multitude of the faithful . . . partly in heaven and partly . . . upon earth . . . in unity of faith or true doctrine and in the lawful partaking of the sacraments."[54] God's gift of a covenant relationship with his chosen, predestined people establishes the church; the covenant is given to God's people as a whole.[55] Its universality or catholicity extends over the church triumphant in heaven and the church militant on earth, which remains locked in the battle against sinful desires, the world, and Satan. This church militant contains both the "faithful and elect of God, lively members, knit unto Christ . . . in spirit and faith" as the chosen bride of Christ; these are known only to God. In the wider sense, the church militant also includes wicked people and hypocrites.[56]

Bullinger emphasized the essential role of God's Word, which creates and preserves the church. Its ministers must be faithful to the Word; they possess no authority apart from it. The invisible church does not err, but the visible church may fall into false teaching at times.[57] These positions were affirmed in his Second Helvetic Confession (1562, 1566). There Bullinger distinguished the universal church from the particular churches of specific times and places. This confession collected biblical designations for the church: the home of the living God, Christ's virgin and bride, his flock of sheep, and the body of Christ, of which he is the Head. Bullinger shared the conviction of all Reformers that outside the church there is no salvation, while within

---

52. Zwingli, *Exposition of the Faith*, in *Zwingli and Bullinger*, 266; cf. Stephens, *Theology of Zwingli*, 270–74.
53. Robert C. Walton, *Zwingli's Theocracy* (Toronto: University of Toronto Press, 1967), 291, and passim.
54. Bullinger, "Of the Holy Catholic Church," in *Zwingli and Bullinger*, 289.
55. Baker, *Bullinger and the Covenant*, 27–106.
56. Bullinger, "Holy Catholic Church," in *Zwingli and Bullinger*, 288–99. See Peter Opitz, *Heinrich Bullinger als Theologe: Eine Studie zu den "Dekaden"* (Zurich: TVZ, 2004), 417–61.
57. Bullinger, "Holy Catholic Church," in *Zwingli and Bullinger*, 314–25.

the visible church are many hypocrites who are not among the saved. External rites do not determine the legitimacy of the church.[58]

Bullinger regarded the civil magistrate as exercising a "pivotal role as the supreme governing power in the ordering of religion in the realm." His views not only continued the model developed under Zwingli in Zurich but also influenced the development of the exercise of royal power within the Anglican church.[59]

Although Zwingli and Bullinger did advise municipal authorities in exercising church discipline, including excommunication, Bullinger did not include discipline among the outward marks of the church. He posited only two in his *Decades*: "sincere preaching of God's Word and the lawful partaking of Christ's sacraments." He observed that some would add "the study of godliness and unity, patience in affliction, and calling on the name of God by Christ."[60] Those who trust in Christ but are deprived of participation in preaching and the sacraments do remain, however, in the company of the church. Bullinger also taught that believers possess inward marks, "the fellowship of God's Spirit, a sincere faith, and twofold charity," which link them with Christ their Head and all the members of his body.[61] Bullinger's Second Helvetic Confession treated the pastoral ministry in detail, grounding it in Christ's institution and focusing its work on conveying God's Word and exercising the office of the keys, while rejecting papal teaching on the office of priest and monk.[62]

John Calvin on the Church

The parallel Reformation that developed in Geneva shaped its own understanding of the church, undoubtedly with influence from both Zurich and Wittenberg. John Calvin's teaching on the church grew out of his study of Scripture and his understanding of the covenant that God makes with human creatures.[63] Taking distinct forms in the Old and

58. *BSRK*, 195–99.
59. W. J. Torrance Kirby, *The Zurich Connection and Tudor Political Theology*, Studies in the History of Christian Traditions 131 (Leiden: Brill, 2007), 25–57, 203–33. Kirby shows continuing influence from the Zurich circle in the works of Peter Martyr Vermigli as well. Ibid., 59–202.
60. Bullinger, "Holy Catholic Church," in *Zwingli and Bullinger*, 299–304.
61. Ibid., 304–7.
62. *BSRK*, 200–205.
63. See Georg Plasger, "Kirche," and Robert M. Kingdon, "Kirche und Obrigkeit," in *Calvin Handbuch*, ed. Herman J. Selderhuis (Tübingen: Mohr Siebeck, 2008), 317–25, 349–55.

New Testaments, this covenant was grounded in Christ and executed through God's election of his chosen people. The covenant established the people of God, his church, from the beginning, but the renewal of God's promise both to Abraham and at the exodus constituted special developments in his dealings with his people.[64]

Defining Marks of the Church

As Guillaume Farel was introducing the Reformation, his doctrinal manifesto, probably prepared with Calvin's help, confessed that

> while there is only one church of Jesus Christ . . . necessity requires companies of the faithful be distributed in different places. . . . The proper mark by which rightly to discern the church of Jesus Christ is that his holy gospel be purely and faithfully preached, proclaimed, heard, and kept, that his sacraments be properly administered, even if there be some imperfections and faults, as there will always be among human beings.[65]

Nine years later, Calvin wrote in his Catechism of the Church of Geneva that it is necessary to believe this teaching to avoid rendering Christ's death ineffective. The church's holiness consists in the justification God gives on the basis of Christ's redeeming sacrifice. Its holiness is not yet perfect, for it is "never wholly purged of the vestiges of vice." Visible signs mark the church, but the invisible church actually consists of "the company of those whom, by secret election, he has adopted for salvation."[66]

Calvin tied the New Testament church closely to Old Testament Israel, continuing the covenant relationship of those whom God chooses as his own.[67] He bound the church closely to God's Word and the ministry

---

64. Benjamin Charles Milner Jr., *Calvin's Doctrine of the Church*, Studies in the History of Christian Thought 5 (Leiden: Brill, 1970), 71–98. See the overview of the debates over Calvin's concept of the covenant in Baker, *Bullinger and the Covenant*, 193–215.

65. *BSRK*, 115; *Calvin: Theological Treatises*, trans. J. K. S. Reid, LCC 22 (Philadelphia: Westminster, 1961), 31. Cf. Milner, *Calvin's Doctrine*, 99–133.

66. *BSRK*, 125–26; *Calvin: Theological Treatises*, 102–3. Cf. David Foxgrover, ed., *Calvin and the Church: Papers Presented at the 13th Colloquium of the Calvin Studies Society, May 24–26, 2001* (Grand Rapids, MI: CRC, 2002); Richard C. Gamble, ed., *Calvin's Ecclesiology: Sacraments and Deacons*, vol. 10 of *Articles on Calvin and Calvinism* (New York: Garland, 1992). Cf. also Jan Rohls, *Theologie reformierter Bekenntnisschriften: Von Zürich bis Barmen* (Göttingen: Vandenhoeck & Ruprecht, 1987), 198–210.

67. Hermann J. Selderhuis, "Church on Stage: Calvin's Dynamic Ecclesiology," in Foxgrover, *Calvin and the Church*, 46–64.

of the means of grace. "Church" referred to both the visible and the invisible church, the latter being God's elect. Calvin accentuated the invisible nature of the assembly of God's saints by placing it in the context of its struggle against the Devil. Within this context Satan attacks not only with false teaching and deceptive, idolatrous practices but also with physical persecution, which Christ's followers had experienced and were experiencing in France, the Low Countries, the British Isles, Italy, and central Europe.[68] Thus, martyrologies, a genre far less important to Lutherans (who indeed faced persecution in some areas but had relatively secure refuge in many parts of the German lands and the Nordic realms), played a significant role in shaping the consciousness and faithfulness to their churches of Reformed believers.[69] Calvin did not include this persecution in his marks of the church, however; Word and the sacraments identified the church, and he warned against the deceit of those who claimed to be the church apart from these two marks.[70] Where they are present in the visible church, believers should remain, even if they recognize wicked people within the outward fellowship, for the church does not in a sinful world become totally pure. Instead, it exists to bring the message of forgiveness to sinners in that world.[71]

Although not a mark of the church in Calvin's view, discipline, or the exercise of the power of the keys, did play a necessary role in the church's life, for it provided a bond that holds the congregation together and preserves people in the faith. It begins with privately admonishing fellow believers practicing sin. When such admonitions are rejected, witnesses should be called, and if that fails, the assembly

---

68. Calvin, *Institutes*, 4.1.1–4.

69. Above all, Jean Crespin's *Actiones et Monumenta Martyrum* . . . (Geneva: Crespin, 1560); John Foxe, *Commentarii rerum ecclesia gestarum* . . . (Strasbourg: Rihel, 1554); Foxe, *Rerum in ecclesia gestarum* . . . (Basel: Brylinger and Oporinus, 1559); Foxe, *Acts and Monuments of these Latter and perilous days* . . . (London: John Daye, 1563); and Adrian van Haemstede, *De Geschiedenesse ende de doot der vromer Martelanen* . . . (Emden?, 1559). Cf. Jean François Gilmont, *Jean Crespin, un éditeur réformé du XVIe siècle* (Geneva: Droz, 1981), J. F. Mozley, *John Foxe and His Book* (London: SPCK, 1940); William Haller, *The Elect Nation: The Meaning and Relevance of Foxe's Book of Martyrs* (New York: Harper & Row, 1963); Fredrik Pijper, *Martelaarsboek* ('s Gravenhage: Nijhoff, 1924). For Anabaptists, martyrology was a most significant form of pious expression; see Brad S. Gregory, "Anabaptist Martyrdom: Imperatives, Experience, and Memorialization," in *A Companion to Anabaptism and Spiritualism, 1521–1700*, ed. John D. Roth and James M. Stayer, Brill's Companion to the Christian Tradition 6 (Leiden: Brill, 2007), 467–506. For a thorough overview, see Brad Gregory, *Salvation at Stake: Christian Martyrdom in Early Modern Europe* (Cambridge, MA: Harvard University Press, 1999).

70. Calvin, *Institutes*, 4.1.7–13.

71. Ibid., 4.1.14–25.

of the elders should attempt to bring the sinner to repentance. If that also fails, Christ's command to remove despisers of the church from the congregation must be obeyed, according to Matthew 18:15–17.[72] Three concerns govern the practice of this discipline: first, the honor of God and his church and the integrity of the Lord's Supper, which may be profaned by administering it indiscriminately; second, prevention of the good people in the church becoming corrupted; and third, the repentance of even stubborn sinners.[73]

Calvin's context demanded that Roman Catholic critics accuse him of establishing a false church. Jacopo Sadoleto, cardinal and bishop of Carpentras in southern France, addressed an invitation to the Genevan city council to return to the Roman obedience as the Reformation was being introduced there (1539); Calvin's reply laid out his critique of the papal church,[74] a theme that arises often in his writings, including the *Institutes*. In detail he explained why the Roman obedience had departed from true doctrine and proper worship, using these two marks of the church as fundamental criteria for what constitutes the true church. Rome had replaced the faithful ministry of God's Word with a compound of lies,

> which partly extinguishes the pure light, partly chokes it. The foulest sacrilege has been introduced in place of the Lord's Supper. The worship of God has been deformed by a diverse and unbearable mass of superstitions. Doctrine, apart from which Christianity cannot stand, has been entirely buried and driven out.

This resulted in "idolatry, ungodliness, ignorance of God and other sorts of evils."[75] Calvin specifically criticized the practices associated with clerical celibacy and monastic vows.[76]

Church Polity and the State

The biblical teaching on the order that God had woven into his entire creation formed a vital framework for Calvin's understanding of the

---

72. Ibid., 4.1.4–6.
73. Ibid., 4.12.5; 4.12.10–11.
74. CR 33:385–416; *Calvin: Theological Treatises*, 221–56.
75. Calvin, *Institutes*, 4.2.2; cf. 4.2.1–11.16. Calvin expanded on his critique of the Roman church and above all the papacy in *Institutes*, 4.5.1–11.16.
76. Ibid., 4.12.22–13.21.

church and its ministry.[77] He emphasized the importance of the public ministry for the church's life. The ministers' dispensation of the
means of grace, disciplined by God's Word in Scripture, stood at the
center of all that the church is and does.[78] Conciliar authority rested
alone on Scripture; when councils taught contrary to Scripture, their
decrees were to be ignored.[79] Christ is indeed Head of the church, but
he appoints his ambassadors to serve as a bond for the congregation.
As the chief sinew of Christ's body and the principal servants in his
kingdom,[80] the ministers hold the church together by dispensing and
distributing God's gifts to the church and thus preserving its unity in
God's Word.[81]

The Genevan church created a specific form of church government that characterized many (though not all) Reformed churches,
a form that flowed from its missionary activity. God called pastors
"to proclaim God's Word, to instruct, admonish, exhort and censure,
both in public and private, to administer the sacraments and to enjoin
brotherly corrections along with the elders and colleagues." The second order of governance was the teachers, who were to instruct the
faithful "in true doctrine, in order that the purity of the gospel may
not be corrupted either by ignorance or by evil opinions." This office
embraced lecturers in theology (particularly biblical studies) and those
who "teach the little children." "Oversight of the life of all," admonition, and fraternal correction were the duties of the elders, the third
order of church governance. Deacons, the fourth order, were "to receive, dispense, and hold goods for the poor, not only daily alms, but
also possessions, rents, and pensions," and "to tend and care for the
sick and administer allowances to the poor."[82]

The Genevan form of governing the church encountered a challenge
in 1562 when Jean Morély, sire de Villiers, a French layman, began to
argue that authority to exercise true discipline rests in the entire body

---

77. Milner, *Calvin's Doctrine*, 7–70, 134–63; Alexandre Ganoczy, *Ecclesia Ministrans: Die-
nende Kirche und Kirchlicher Dienst bei Calvin* (Freiburg: Herder, 1968).
78. Calvin, *Institutes*, 4.1.4–6.
79. Ibid., 4.9.1–14.
80. Milner, *Calvin's Doctrine*, 168–75, 179–89.
81. Calvin, *Institutes*, 4.3.1–3.
82. As specified in the draft of the *Ecclesiastical Ordinances* of Geneva, 1541, in *Calvin: Theological Treatises*, 58–66. Cf. Calvin, *Institutes*, 4.3.4–15.

of believers instead of the elders and the consistory. The debate raged for a decade within French Calvinism,[83] and although most Calvinist churches adopted the Genevan model with modifications suitable to their specific situations, some disciples of Genevan theology did live within other systems, such as the Church of England's episcopal hierarchy. In lands beyond Germany, Calvinist churches developed larger structures, organizing into presbyteries and synods.[84]

In contrast to Zurich, which placed power to execute discipline and manage church affairs in the hands of the municipal government, Geneva, under Calvin's guidance, reserved power over teaching and discipline for the consistory of the church, although he sought to maintain a consensual relationship between church and secular government,[85] which, Calvin believed, God had ordained. God had established two kingdoms or governments, one for the administration of the affairs of this world, the other for proclaiming God's Word and serving his chosen people's spiritual needs.[86] While he sharply criticized tyrannous exercise of political power, he insisted that subjects obey legitimately established authority, even when rulers abused their power,[87] sharing the concern for public order common to his time.

As Reformed churches were established beyond Zurich and Geneva, they revealed different combinations of the emphases of Bullinger and Calvin, but the influence of the doctrines of the church held by each did shape the confession regarding this article of faith, with various emphases taken from the Swiss traditions. The Word of God produced the one universal church; Christ and the Holy Spirit govern and preserve it, even when it appears as though only a remnant persists in faithfulness, for unfaithful members of the church and its outright opponents battle against its truth. God appoints servants of his Word,

83. Robert M. Kingdon, *Geneva and the Consolidation of the French Protestant Movement, 1564–1572* (Madison: University of Wisconsin Press, 1967), 37–137.

84. Calvin conceded the freedom to preach the Genevan theology in other forms. Cf. Kingdon, "Kirche und Obrigkeit," 350.

85. See *Registers of the Consistory of Geneva in the Time of Calvin*, ed. Robert M. Kingdon, Thomas A. Lambert, Isabella M. Watt, and Jeffrey R. Watt, trans. M. Wallace McDonald (Grand Rapids, MI: Eerdmans, 2000–).

86. David VanDrunen, *Natural Law and the Two Kingdoms: A Study in the Development of Reformed Social Thought* (Grand Rapids, MI: Eerdmans, 2010), esp. 67–99.

87. Calvin, *Institutes*, 4.20.1–32; cf. William G. Naphy, "Calvin and State in Calvin's Geneva," in Foxgrover, *Calvin and the Church*, 13–28.

though confessions differed on whether to prescribe the full order of four offices.[88]

The Reformed churches paid special attention to forms of polity, but they all anchored their ecclesiologies in the proper proclamation of God's Word and the right use of the sacraments. Therefore, the public ministry of the church and its worship life won careful attention in their public teaching as necessary elements of the common life of God's people.

Anglican Teachings on the Church

When King Henry VIII declared the independence of the English church from Rome in 1532, his action resembled moves shielding national churches from papal power at various points in the Middle Ages in England, France, and other lands. In the context of the Protestant Reformation on the Continent, however, his move eventually took on more radical and permanent form, even though that future direction was not immediately apparent and even went contrary to the king's intentions. Henry sought as little substantial change in the church's teaching and life as possible, satisfied as he was, by and large, with the piety and doctrine with which he had been raised.[89] Royal appointments of bishops in the wake of Henry VIII's declaration of the independence assured that the crown played a strong role in English ecclesiastical life, although the so-called Puritans ensured that lively pious activities went on at the edge of episcopal control or just beyond it in the latter decades of the sixteenth century.[90] With the ascension of Edward VI in 1547, the public definition of the Christian faith and teaching changed dramatically, although the episcopal form of church government and royal control of the church, as well as many elements in the church's liturgy and ritual, did not. The Forty-Two Articles of 1552–1553 defined the church as "a congregation of faithful men in which the pure Word of God is preached and the sacraments be duly

---

88. *BSRK* 229 (*Confessio gallicana*, 1559), 243 (*Confessio belgica*), 256–58 (*Confessio Scotiae*, 1561), 426–44 (*Confessio ungarica*, 1562), 936–37 (*Corte Belydinghe des Gheloofs*, 1566).

89. G. W. Bernard, *The King's Reformation: Henry VIII and the Remaking of the English Church* (New Haven, CT: Yale University Press, 2005).

90. Leo F. Solt, *Church and State in Early Modern England, 1509–1640* (New York: Oxford University Press, 1990).

administered according to Christ's ordinance."[91] The Book of Common Prayer, which quickly became the defining document of the Church of England, did reform the liturgy but left its structure in place.[92] After Elizabeth's accession to the throne, her redesign of church life bequeathed the official English church a moderate, inclusive tone, set by bishops, centered on the Book of Common Prayer, and aimed at the proclamation of the gospel of Jesus Christ and an orderly Christian life for the good of the entire nation.

Perhaps nowhere did tensions between maintaining the doctrinal integrity of the church and retaining its close connections to society and especially its political establishment play a more important role in shaping reform than in England. There defenders of the unity and establishment of the Church of England clashed with "Puritans," as they were dubbed by their opponents.[93] The Puritans represented a wide spectrum of those who pushed for further reforms beyond the Elizabethan Settlement, generally encouraging a more stringent practice of the faith, a more strictly Calvinist doctrinal system, and the abolition of various elements of medieval practice, including episcopal governance and a host of liturgical usages.[94]

In the Admonition Controversy begun in 1572, John Whitgift, then master of Trinity College, Cambridge, defended the moderate settlement that had reestablished the Church of England under Elizabeth against Puritan calls for a return to strict adherence to Old Testament laws, while discarding all traces of medieval practice that seemed superstitious. Thomas Cartwright led the Puritan critique, assisted especially by Walter Travers; both were friends of Theodore Beza. They proposed that control of church life be placed in the hands of ordained

---

91. Gerald L. Bray, ed., *Documents of the English Reformation* (Cambridge: Clarke, 1994), 296.

92. Brian Cummings, ed., *The Book of Common Prayer, The Texts of 1549, 1559, and 1562* (Oxford: Oxford University Press, 2011); Charles Hefling and Cynthia Shattuck, eds., *The Oxford Guide to the Book of Common Prayer: A Worldwide Survey* (Oxford: Oxford University Press, 2006); Francis Procter and Walter Howard Frere, *A New History of the Book of Common Prayer* (London: Macmillan, 1949).

93. Patrick Collinson, *Richard Bancroft and Elizabethan Anti-Puritanism*, Cambridge Studies in Early Modern British History (Cambridge: Cambridge University Press, 2013), 1–5.

94. See, e.g., Patrick Collinson, *The Elizabethan Puritan Movement* (New York: Methuen, 1982); Collinson, *The Religion of Protestants: The Church in English Society, 1559–1625* (Oxford: Clarendon, 1982); Collinson, *Godly People: Essays on English Protestantism and Puritanism* (London: Hambledon, 1983).

ministers who formed a regional presbytery. Through excommunication of evildoers, a pure church would develop. Faithful disciples
of Calvin, Cartwright, and Travers remained within the established
church, though other Puritans formed independent groups. Among
the most devastating of the incessant critiques of the establishment
were the "Marprelate Tracts" (1588–1589), anonymous satires on
the extravagance and foibles of high-Anglican clergy, which called for
strict reform of doctrine and life in a purified church.[95] Though most
Puritans remained within the Church of England and there agitated for
further purification and reform of life, Puritanism contained within it
the seeds of separatism and independent churches.[96]

Puritans objected in different degrees to the Book of Common
Prayer. All found in it certain medieval accretions to pure worship
of God, but many accepted its general form and at least in principle
its prescribed prayers. Others argued for free prayer and the right of
individual ministers to shape worship form for their congregations, rejecting anything that might feed the superstitious dependence on ritual
performance of medieval practice. The organization of small groups
for prayer and Bible study, a form of house church, also aroused fierce
opposition from the establishment.[97]

Puritans held intensely to the general Anglican belief that

> the Church was constituted, not by the Christians of whom it was
> composed, nor by the sincerity of their profession, but by the purity
> of the doctrine publicly preached and upheld by authority, and by
> the sincere administration and reception of the sacraments, safe-
> guarded by the exercise of church discipline. . . . The gospel was
> good news of salvation; but it was also to be obeyed, and obeyed
> universally.

The Puritans sought not merely toleration of their own consciences but
the purity of the entire church and the completion of its reformation.[98]
Associated with that purity was the governance of the church not by
bishops but by a presbyterial system that showed significant influence

---

95. Collinson, *Elizabethan Puritan Movement*, 391–418.
96. Collinson, *Religion of Protestants*, 242–83.
97. Collinson, *Elizabethan Puritan Movement*, 356–82.
98. Ibid., 25–26.

from Geneva.[99] In 1645, a *Book of Discipline* appeared in print, a work allegedly found in manuscript in Thomas Cartwright's library. The book's program had circulated already in the 1570s and 1580s in the circle around Travers and Cartwright. It proposed, in contrast to the episcopal system, a synodical form of church government, independent of the throne, managing church affairs through a presbyterian organization on the congregational level, with meetings of representative pastors and elders in classes for dealing with the affairs of the entire national church.[100] The establishment reacted vigorously with its critique.

In the 1580s and 1590s, Richard Hooker arose as the defender of episcopal polity, the Book of Common Prayer, and a close working relationship between church and state. He distinguished the visible dimensions of the church from its mystical dimensions. The mystical body of Christ, he said, cannot be identified through speculation regarding election. God knows the elect, but Christians must regard those who participate in worship and the sacraments as true brothers and sisters in Christ.[101]

Unresolved, festering tensions mounted into confrontations between Puritans and other Anglicans under Archbishop Laud and culminated in civil war in the mid-seventeenth century. These developments gradually led to the opening of toleration and societal acceptance for a range of free churches alongside the established church, thus altering the public face of the church in the modern age.

Anabaptist and Spiritualist Teachings on the Church

Anabaptists held a wide range of positions on many issues, but most affirmed that the church was but a remnant and consisted of those who had committed themselves to God and remained faithful to him in obedience to his law in daily life.[102] Dennis Bollinger concludes that "the Ecclesial Anabaptists gave priority to their developing implicit

99. Collinson, *Religion of Protestants*, 81–91, 177–88.

100. Collinson, *Elizabethan Puritan Movement*, 291–316; on details of congregational organization and life, see 333–55.

101. Paul Avis, *Anglicanism and the Christian Church: Theological Resources in Historical Perspective*, 2nd ed. (New York: T&T Clark, 2002).

102. See the essays in *A Companion to Anabaptism*, 39, 47, 61, 66–67, 71, 78, 90, 96, 352, 359, and George Huntston Williams, *The Radical Reformation*, 3rd ed., Sixteenth Century Essays and Studies 15 (Kirksville, MO: Sixteenth Century Journal Publishers, 1992), 92–93, 147–48, 575–82, 687–90, 913, 1017–23, 1076–78, 1178–83, 1262–63.

ecclesiology. . . . They concentrated, to the virtual exclusion of most other doctrines, on the discussion of the nature, function, and structure of the local church."[103] While using much of the terminology of the ancient creeds and of Lutheran and Reformed ecclesiology, Anabaptists tolerated tares among the wheat much less gladly; stricter exercise of discipline marked their communities. Michael Sattler's Schleitheim Articles, composed in February 1527, summarizes early South German and Swiss beliefs of those who were continuing a tradition of protests based on a biblicistic, moralistic, antisacramental, anticlerical, and millenarian definition of Christianity. His seven articles did not treat the doctrine of the church as such but did teach that those who have been called by God to a common faith, baptism, Spirit, and body (Eph. 4:3–6) must separate themselves from evil and wickedness. The unfaithful are "a great abomination before God," and so Christ must be separated from Belial, including "all popish and anti-popish works and worship, meetings and services, drinking houses, civic affairs, commitments made in unbelief . . . all the unrighteousness in the world." God's children should also withdraw from Babylon and Egypt "that we may not be partakers of the pain and suffering which the Lord will bring upon them." Pastors should "read, admonish and teach, warn, discipline, excommunicate, lead out in prayer for the promotion of all brothers and sisters, lift up the bread when it is to be broken, and in all things care for Christ's body." This teaching established the local congregation as a "hermeneutic community, in which the scriptures were to be read and interpreted"—and lived.[104] The revolutionary ecclesiology of the Münsterite kingdom, which presumed to embrace the entire society of the city, was a singular exception to Anabaptist organization of the church.[105]

Discipline of these true believers formed an important part of the life of the community. Those who "have given themselves to the Lord, to walk in his commandments, and who are baptized into the body of

---

103. Dennis E. Bollinger, *First-Generation Anabaptist Ecclesiology, 1525–1561: A Study of Swiss, German, and Dutch Sources* (Lewiston, NY: Mellen, 2008), 241.

104. Werner O. Packull, "An Introduction to Anabaptist Theology," in *The Cambridge Companion to Reformation Theology,* ed. David Bagchi and David C. Steinmetz (Cambridge: Cambridge University Press, 2004), 196.

105. James M. Stayer, *Anabaptists and the Sword* (Lawrence, KA: Coronado, 1967); Williams, *Radical Reformation,* 553–88.

Christ and are called brothers or sisters," must be admonished twice in secret if they are inadvertently overtaken by sin. If they do not repent, they should be openly disciplined and then banned according to Christ's command in Matthew 18. This is to be done "so that we may break and eat one bread, with one mind and in one love."[106]

The *Account of the Faith* (1528) by Sattler's contemporary Balthasar Hubmaier also emphasized discipline at the core of congregational life. Without using the terms "visible" and "invisible," he distinguished "all people who are gathered and united in one God, one Lord, one faith, one baptism, and who confess this faith, . . . the universal bodily Christian church and community of saints gathered in the Spirit of God alone" from the "particular and outward gathering, group, or parish, which belongs to a pastor or bishop, which comes together bodily for teaching, baptism, and the supper." Both are called to bind and loose sins. But the particular church can err, as the papal church had. The verbal confession that Jesus is Christ is the foundation of the church. In the community of believers, all are to exercise "the power of brotherly correction," admonishing fellow believers who have fallen into sin.[107] Those who refuse to repent should be excluded, cut off from the community, and Christians should have no association with those set against reconciling with the church or renouncing sin. Those who repent are to be received back into fellowship with joy.[108] Those who remain faithful look to their water baptism as the church's confirmation of their faith, and the church therefore has the obligation to call believers to repentance when the vows of faith are broken.[109]

Another expression of the emphasis on setting the church apart from society and especially secular governments because such association would corrupt believers (even though God had ordained such coercive power to preserve a sinful world) is found in the work of Peter Riedemann, who synthesized the theology of the Hutterites. Riedemann composed a strict, incisive argument and program for separating

106. Mark Noll, ed., *Confessions and Catechisms of the Reformation* (Grand Rapids, MI: Baker, 1991), 52–54.
107. Balthasar Hubmaier, *Schriften*, ed. Gunnar Westin and Torsten Bergsten (Gütersloh: Mohn, 1962), 478–79; cf. Denis Janz, trans., *Three Reformation Catechisms: Catholic, Anabaptist, Lutheran*, Texts and Studies in Religion 13 (New York: Mellen, 1982), 151–56.
108. Hubmaier, *Schriften*, 485–86.
109. Ibid., 315–16.

the members of the church from society's evil influences and aiding their practice of the devout Christian life.[110]

For the most part, Anabaptists did not form larger ecclesiastical organizations easily, although Hutterites and Mennonites, for example, formed communities connecting the like-minded that have maintained substantial membership over the centuries.

Conclusion

While sixteenth-century Reformers differed on significant ecclesiological issues, all agreed that God's Word stood at the center of the church's life, determined its nature, and prescribed its activities. They agreed on the significance of the sacraments, even though they had radically different understandings of the relationship of baptism and the Lord's Supper to the faith of believers and the Word of God. Their differences regarding polity sparked sharp debates, and they viewed the relationship between church and society, particularly secular government, in considerably divergent ways, especially concerning the latter's assistance to the church in matters such as discipline. Nonetheless, they all defined the nature of the church as the assembly of believers who hearken to Christ and trust in him, living in obedience to his plan for human life. They all professed that God's Word governs the community of Christ's faithful. These convictions governed Protestant reactions against the medieval definition of the church in terms of ritual, centered on the Mass, and in terms of hierarchy, governance by the pope and bishops loyal to him. From that criticism of medieval belief and practice and from the complementary conviction of the centrality of proclaiming the gospel of Christ arose the doctrines of the church that shaped modern perceptions of the church and the Christian life.

Resources for Further Study

Primary Sources

Bray, Gerald L., ed. *Documents of the English Reformation.* Cambridge: Clarke, 1994.

. Andrea Chudaska, *Peter Riedemann: Konfessionsbildendes Täufertum im 16. Jahrhundert* (Gütersloh: Gütersloher Verlagshaus, 2003), 273–330.

Bromiley, G. W., ed. *Zwingli and Bullinger: Selected Translations with Introductions and Notes*. Library of Christian Classics 24. Philadelphia: Westminster, 1953.

Chemnitz, Martin. *Examination of the Council of Trent, Part I*. Translated by Fred Kramer. St. Louis, MO: Concordia, 1971.

Cummings, Brian, ed. *The Book of Common Prayer, The Texts of 1549, 1559, and 1562*. Oxford: Oxford University Press, 2011.

Hubmaier, Balthasar. *Schriften*. Edited by Gunnar Westin and Torsten Bergsten. Gütersloh: Mohn, 1962.

Janz, Denis, trans. *Three Reformation Catechisms: Catholic, Anabaptist, Lutheran*. Texts and Studies in Religion 13. New York: Mellen, 1982.

Melanchthon, Philipp. *Loci theologici*. Translated by J. A. O. Preus. St. Louis, MO: Concordia, 1989.

Noll, Mark A., ed. *Confessions and Catechisms of the Reformation*. Grand Rapids, MI: Baker, 1991.

SECONDARY SOURCES

Avis, Paul. *Anglicanism and the Christian Church: Theological Resources in Historical Perspective*. 2nd ed. New York: T&T Clark, 2002.

Bagchi, David V. N. *Luther's Earliest Opponents: Catholic Controversialists, 1518–1525*. Minneapolis: Fortress, 1991.

Bernard, G. W. *The King's Reformation: Henry VIII and the Remaking of the English Church*. New Haven, CT: Yale University Press, 2005.

Black, Antony. *Council and Commune: The Conciliar Movement and the Fifteenth-Century Heritage*. London: Burns & Oates, 1979.

Bollinger, Dennis E. *First-Generation Anabaptist Ecclesiology, 1525–1561: A Study of Swiss, German, and Dutch Sources*. Lewiston, NY: Mellen, 2008.

Collinson, Patrick. *The Religion of Protestants: The Church in English Society, 1559–1625*. Oxford: Clarendon, 1982.

Daniel, David P. "Luther on the Church." In *The Oxford Handbook of Martin Luther's Theology*, edited by Robert Kolb, Irene Dingel, and L'ubomír Batka, 333–52. Oxford: Oxford University Press, 2014.

Estes, James M. *Peace, Order, and the Glory of God: Secular Authority and the Church in the Thought of Luther and Melanchthon, 1518–1559*. Studies in Medieval and Reformation Traditions 111. Leiden: Brill, 2005.

Foxgrover, David, ed. *Calvin and the Church: Papers Presented at the 13th Colloquium of the Calvin Studies Society, May 24–26, 2001.* Grand Rapids, MI: CRC, 2002.

Gamble, Richard C., ed. *Calvin's Ecclesiology: Sacraments and Deacons.* Vol. 10 of *Articles on Calvin and Calvinism.* New York: Garland, 1992.

Hendrix, Scott H. *Ecclesia in Via. Ecclesiological Developments in the Medieval Psalms Exegesis and the* Dictata super Psalterium *(1513–1515) of Martin Luther.* London: Brill, 1974.

———. *Luther and the Papacy: Stages in a Reformation Conflict.* Philadelphia: Fortress, 1981.

Kingdon, Robert M. *Geneva and the Consolidation of the French Protestant Movement, 1564–1572.* Madison: University of Wisconsin Press, 1967.

Kirby, W. J. Torrance. *The Zurich Connection and Tudor Political Theology.* Studies in the History of Christian Traditions 131. Leiden: Brill, 2007.

Kolb, Robert. "Luther on Peasants and Princes." *Lutheran Quarterly* 23, no. 2 (2009): 125–46.

———. "Ministry in Martin Luther and the Lutheran Confessions." In *Called and Ordained: Lutheran Perspectives on the Office of the Ministry,* ed. Todd Nichol and Marc Kolden, 49–66. Minneapolis: Fortress, 1990.

Lathrop, Gordon W., and Timothy J. Wengert. *Christian Assembly: Marks of the Church in a Pluralistic Age.* Minneapolis: Fortress, 2004.

Lindberg, Carter. "Piety, Prayer, and Worship in Luther's View of Daily Life." *The Oxford Handbook of Martin Luther's Theology,* edited by Robert Kolb, Irene Dingel, and L'ubomír Batka, 414–26. Oxford: Oxford University Press, 2014.

Procter, Francis, and Walter Howard Frere. *A New History of the Book of Common Prayer.* London: Macmillan, 1949.

Solt, Leo F. *Church and State in Early Modern England, 1509–1640.* New York: Oxford University Press, 1990.

Spinka, Matthew. *John Hus' Concept of the Church.* Princeton, NJ: Princeton University Press, 1966.

Stadtwald, Kurt. *Roman Popes and German Patriots: Antipapalism in the Politics of the German Humanist Movement from Gregor Heimburg to Martin Luther.* Geneva: Droz, 1996.

Thompson, W. D. J. Cargill. *The Political Thought of Martin Luther*. Sussex: Harvester, 1984.

Vajta, Vilmos. *Luther on Worship: An Interpretation*. Philadelphia: Muhlenberg, 1958.

VanDrunen, David. *Natural Law and the Two Kingdoms: A Study in the Development of Reformed Social Thought*. Grand Rapids, MI: Eerdmans, 2010.

Walton, Robert C. *Zwingli's Theocracy*. Toronto: University of Toronto Press, 1967.

Wolgast, Eike. "Luther's Treatment of Political and Societal Life." In *The Oxford Handbook of Martin Luther's Theology*, edited by Robert Kolb, Irene Dingel, and L'ubomír Batka, 397–413. Oxford: Oxford University Press, 2014.

17

Baptism

Aaron Clay Denlinger

ABSTRACT

This chapter explores differences over baptism—its nature, its efficacy, and its proper recipients—which came to define Roman Catholic, Protestant, and Anabaptist identities over against one another in the Reformation period. Attention is given first to Martin Luther and Huldrych Zwingli, first-generation Reformers who jointly criticized Rome's particular understanding of baptismal efficacy but expressed very different understandings of the sacrament. While Luther maintained that baptism is principally a divine word of promise that, when coupled with faith, communicates the spiritual realities it signifies, Zwingli recognized baptism as principally a human word of commitment that strictly signifies the saving benefits of Christ's work. The Anabaptist insistence that baptism be administered only to mature individuals on profession of their intention to follow Christ, as well as Luther and Zwingli's respective responses to such teaching, is then explored. The efforts of second-generation Reformers such as John Calvin and Heinrich Bullinger to achieve a Protestant consensus on baptism and to stem the tide of Anabaptism are subsequently noted. Despite similarities in these Reformed thinkers' arguments in favor of paedobaptism, fundamental disagreement persisted between Calvin, who—like Luther—recognized baptism as an instrument of the realities it signifies, and Bullinger, who maintained that baptism signifies and seals God's saving promises to believers without communicating saving realities to them. A final section of this chapter explores early-modern confessional statements that both clarified various baptismal perspectives and solidified disagreement between Roman Catholic, Lutheran, Reformed, and Baptistic identities on the sacrament.

Introduction

Few subjects fostered as much controversy in the sixteenth century as that of the sacraments. Disagreement regarding their number, efficacy, and proper recipients figured critically in the gradual emergence of distinctly Protestant, Roman Catholic, and radical (Anabaptist) identities. Disagreement regarding the precise relationship of the sacraments to the salvific realities they purportedly signified extended to the magisterial Reformers themselves and so proved instrumental in the development of distinctly Lutheran and Reformed Protestant identities. Sacramentology emerged as the singular bane of a unified Protestantism, much to the delight of Roman apologists, who championed unity as a mark of the genuine church and cheerfully broadcasted the failure of the Reformers to reach consensus on a matter of such significance.

It is the task of this chapter and the next to explore contending doctrines of the sacraments in the Reformation era, treating not only differing Protestant views but also Tridentine Roman Catholic and Anabaptist perspectives, and to trace the major conflicts as well as the occasionally successful attempts at rapprochement that occurred between persons of various persuasions. As background, some general consideration of late-medieval sacramental teaching and brief attention to the main features of Luther's initial salvo against medieval sacramentology are in order.

The Sacraments in Late-Medieval Perspective

The amount of space devoted to the sacraments in Peter Lombard's *Sentences*—forty-two of fifty distinctions in the fourth and final book—indicates how significant sacramental theology had become to Western divines by the mid-twelfth century.[1] Lombard defined a sacrament as "a sign of God's grace [*gratia*] and a form of invisible grace"; that is, a ritual that "bears [the] image" of grace and "is its cause."[2] With this definition Lombard identified two constitutive features of a sacrament: first, a sacrament signifies some grace; second, a sacrament communicates the grace that it signifies.

Subsequent medieval theologians quibbled about the precise nature of the relationship between sacramental cause (ritual) and effect (grace), but they were unanimous in affirming the twofold character of a *sacramentum* as both symbol and, in one way or another, source of saving grace. "A sacrament," wrote Duns Scotus, "is a sensible sign, ordered to the salvation of the wayfaring human being, *efficaciously signifying*—by divine institution—the grace of God."[3] Similarly, Thomas Aquinas defined "a sacrament" as "the sign of a holy thing [*res sacra*]" or "a sign of grace" that "makes men holy" by serving as "an instrumental cause of grace."[4]

Medieval divines were also agreed, recalling Augustine's writings against the Donatists, that sacraments communicate grace by virtue of their enactment as such (*ex opere operato*), as opposed to any virtue of the priest administering them or persons receiving them (*ex opere operantis*). They qualified this point, however, by acknowledging that the recipient of a sacrament must at least possess, in Thomas's words, the "intention of receiving the sacrament" in order to receive grace from it.[5] That is, the recipient of a sacrament cannot, according to the medieval view, make the sacrament effectual by personal faith or any other virtue, but he can render the sacrament *in*effectual by a lack of real intention to receive the same.

Lombard identified seven rituals that meet the criteria for sacramental status: baptism, confirmation, the Eucharist, penance, extreme unction, ordination, and marriage. The disproportionate attention

1. Peter Lombard, *The Sentences*, trans. Giulio Silano, Mediaeval Sources in Translation 42–43, 45, 48 (Toronto: Pontifical Institute of Mediaeval Studies, 2007–2010). The final eight distinctions of book 4, by way of comparison, deal with the resurrection and the final judgment.
2. Lombard, *The Sentences, Book 4: On the Doctrine of Signs*, 1.4.2.
3. John Duns Scotus, *Ordinatio* 4.1.2n9, quoted in Richard Cross, *Duns Scotus*, Great Medieval Thinkers (New York: Oxford University Press, 1999), 136, italics added.
4. Thomas Aquinas, *Summa Theologiae* 3a.60.2, 4.
5. Ibid., 3a.68.7. See also 3a.68.8.

Lombard paid specifically to penance and marriage in his *Sentences* reflects the need he felt to shore up the sacramental credentials of those particular rites in his day.[6] Only baptism and the Eucharist had been universally acknowledged as sacraments since the earliest days of Latin theological reflection, and quite a few rituals beyond Lombard's seven had been proffered as candidates for the sacramental fold in preceding centuries. Nevertheless, by the thirteenth century Lombard's list had become definitive. Thomas offered a variety of arguments in defense of acknowledging Lombard's exact list. His most compelling if implicit argument was his recognition, bordering on further definition of a sacrament as such, that proper sacraments "are instituted by Christ Himself," whether we know such from Scripture or from extrascriptural tradition.[7]

These basic aspects of late-medieval sacramental teaching were sanctioned by the Council of Trent in March 1547. In its seventh session, the council affirmed that sacraments "contain the grace which they signify" and "confer that grace on those who do not place an obstacle thereunto." Persons denying "any one of the seven" sacraments to have been "instituted by Jesus Christ" or to be "truly and properly a sacrament" were anathematized.[8]

Luther's Attack on Medieval Sacramentology

Late in 1520, Martin Luther, largely resigned to his looming excommunication, launched a full-scale attack on late-medieval sacramental teaching with his *Babylonian Captivity of the Church*.[9] Luther's polemic rested on a redefinition of the term *sacramentum* per se. His redefinition of *sacramentum* rested, in turn, on convictions regarding the authority and content of sacred Scripture that had recently reached maturity in his thought.

"Everything in Scripture," Luther observed, "is either a command or a promise."[10] Divine commands serve to make sinners aware of their

---

6. See Thomas M. Finn, "The Sacramental World in the *Sentences* of Peter Lombard," *Theological Studies* 69 (2008): 557–82.
7. Aquinas, *Summa Theologiae* 3a.64.2; see also 3a.65.1.
8. CCFCT 2:840.
9. Martin Luther, *The Babylonian Captivity of the Church*, LW 36:3–126.
10. Ibid., *LW* 36:124.

failure to meet God's righteous standard and their inability to make amends for their misdeeds. Divine promises point sinners to Christ's sacrificial death and resurrection on their behalf, extending forgiveness and eternal life on the basis of Christ's work. The proper response, on the part of sinners, to God's offer of gratuitous forgiveness is faith that God genuinely delivers what he promises. Faith "unites the soul with Christ as a bride is united with her bridegroom." This union serves as the basis for the soul's happy exchange of her "sins, death, and damnation" for Christ's "righteousness, life, and salvation."[11] It is because faith thus serves as the instrumental means of justification that "the whole of Scripture is concerned with provoking us to faith."[12] The promises of God, however, perform a peculiar role in eliciting faith from those in need of reconciliation with God.

With immediate reference to the role that commands and promises thus play in the process of salvation, Luther ascribed "the name of sacrament to those promises which have signs attached to them," differentiating such thereby from "bare promises."[13] Medieval definitions of *sacramentum* as a sign and cause of "grace" (*gratia*) or a holy "thing" (*res*) are nebulous in comparison to Luther's definition; for him, the sign must specifically point to God's *promissio* of forgiveness, or even more precisely to the work of Christ (his death and resurrection) and the incorporation of a sinner into Christ and his work through which the *promissio* is realized.[14] Signs qualifying as sacraments must, moreover, have been personally instituted by Christ as recorded in Scripture.[15]

Brandishing this definition, Luther made short work of the late-medieval catalog of sacraments. The rituals of confirmation and ordination fail the sacramental test because they lack the ingredient of a divine promise of forgiveness.[16] Marriage and private confession (an element of penance) are good and proper practices as such, but neither include the ingredient of a sign necessary to a sacrament.[17] Extreme

---

11. Martin Luther, *The Freedom of a Christian*, LW 31:351–52.
12. Luther, *Babylonian Captivity*, LW 36:124.
13. Ibid., LW 36:124.
14. Ibid., LW 36:124.
15. Ibid., LW 36:118.
16. Ibid., LW 36:91, 106–7.
17. Ibid., LW 36:92, 124. Note that Luther included penance among the true sacraments earlier in this work; see LW 36:18, 81–90.

unction—that is, the anointing with oil described in James 5, which the church had, much "to the detriment of all other sick persons," increasingly "administered to none but the dying"—was not personally instituted by Christ.[18]

Luther's redefinition of a sacrament as a "promise of forgiveness" accompanied by a "divinely instituted sign" also had profound implications for his understanding of those rites that he acknowledged as genuine sacraments—baptism and the Lord's Supper. His teaching required that the instituted signs be accompanied by a clear and comprehensible declaration of the promises that they embody. It also required critical qualification of the medieval doctrine of sacramental efficacy *ex opere operato*. Just as "the whole Scripture" is generally concerned "with provoking us to faith," so "the sacraments" were peculiarly "instituted to nourish faith." Indeed, "their whole efficacy . . . consists in faith."[19] Luther rejected, then, the notion that the sacraments might communicate salvific grace irrespective of faith, where a bare intention to receive the sacrament pertains. A sacrament remains *valid*—that is, it remains a legitimate promise—even when it encounters unbelief in the recipient, but at the same time, it remains entirely *ineffective*. Where "faith is unmistakably present," however, the sacraments "certainly and effectively impart grace."[20]

Luther's treatment of the sacraments held further, more specific implications for the doctrines of baptism and the Eucharist respectively. I turn now to a consideration of the first of those sacraments in Reformation thought. My treatment of various theologies of baptism in the Reformation era will proceed in four stages. First, I will examine the teaching of the first-generation magisterial Reformers, specifically noting points of agreement and divergence in the doctrines of Luther and Huldrych Zwingli. Second, I will consider the emergence of radical (Anabaptist) teachings on baptism and the response of the magisterial Reformers to the issues they raised. Third, I will survey attempts by second-generation Reformers to navigate differences among first-generation Reformers and create Protestant consensus concerning the

18. Ibid., *LW* 36:117–19, quotation on 119.
19. Ibid., *LW* 36:124, 61, 65.
20. Ibid., *LW* 36:67.

sacrament of baptism. Fourth, I will examine the consolidation of baptismal views that occurred in the process of confessionalization peculiar to the later years of the Reformation.

Early Reformation Teaching on Baptism

MARTIN LUTHER

"The *first* thing to be considered about baptism is the divine promise."[21] Thus, in the *Babylonian Captivity*, Luther brought his understanding of sacraments as "promises which have signs attached to them" to bear on the doctrine of baptism. In time he would define baptism as "water used according to God's command and connected with God's word," emphasizing both the promissory nature of the ritualistic application of water to believers and the divine words of institution establishing such a practice (Matt. 28:19).[22] Luther advocated full immersion, even for infants, as the proper mode of baptism on the basis both of the meaning of the Greek term *baptismos* and of the proper correspondence between the ritual and that which it chiefly signifies.[23] He identified God as the ultimate agent of this ritual; the recipient of baptism should "look upon the person administering it as simply the vicarious instrument of God, by which the Lord sitting in heaven thrusts [him] under the water with his own hands, and promises [him] forgiveness of [his] sins."[24] By recognizing that God was the proper agent of baptism, Luther, following Augustine, was able to acknowledge the validity of baptisms administered by profane or even apostate or heretical persons.[25]

The promise embodied in baptism—broadly denoted "forgiveness of sins" or "full and complete justification"—is brought into sharper relief by considering the twofold significance of the ritual, which, joined to the promissory word, constitutes baptism.[26] Baptism signifies, first of all, the "washing away of sins," that is, the divine forgiveness that renders "truly pure, without sin, and wholly guiltless" those who

---

21. Ibid., *LW* 36:58. For a fuller treatment of Luther on baptism, see Jonathan D. Trigg, *Baptism in the Theology of Martin Luther* (Leiden: Brill, 2001).

22. CCFCT 2:40.

23. Martin Luther, *The Holy Sacrament of Baptism* (1519), *LW* 35:29; Luther, *Babylonian Captivity*, *LW* 36:64, 68.

24. Luther, *Babylonian Captivity*, *LW* 36:62.

25. Martin Luther, *Concerning Rebaptism* (1528), *LW* 40:250.

26. Luther, *Babylonian Captivity*, *LW* 36:58–64 passim.

embrace with faith the promise embodied in baptism.[27] The reality and power of sin persist in baptized believers, but God "pledges himself not to impute to [them] the sins which remain in [their] nature after baptism."[28]

Second, though of first importance, baptism signifies "a blessed dying unto sin and a resurrection in the grace of God, so that the old man, conceived and born in sin, is there drowned, and a new man, born in grace, comes forth and rises."[29] The consequences of one's union with Christ extend beyond mere forgiveness: "The sinner does not so much need to be washed as he needs to die, in order to be wholly renewed and made another creature, and to be conformed to the death and resurrection of Christ, with whom he dies and rises again through baptism."[30] Luther named this "death and resurrection" in and with Christ "the new creation, regeneration, and spiritual birth." It comprises not only the beginning but the entire course of the Christian life: "For as long as we live we are continually doing that which baptism signifies." Indeed, "our whole life should be baptism, and the fulfilling of the sign or sacrament of baptism, since we have been set free from all else and given over to baptism alone, that is, to death and resurrection."[31]

Based on this understanding, Luther advanced two fundamental criticisms of late-medieval teaching on baptism. He faulted the scholastics, first, for reducing "the power of baptism to such small and slender dimensions that, while they say grace is indeed inpoured by it, they maintain that afterwards it is poured out again through sin."[32] Medieval divines had taught that "every sin" is "taken away" when baptism is received but that sins committed subsequent to baptism require subsequent (sacramental) grace, obtained especially through penance.[33] In Luther's judgment, no sin but that of final unbelief could eradicate the abiding promise and effect of one's baptism, and thus believers were to look constantly to their baptisms, rather than to ad-

---

27. Ibid., *LW* 36:68; Luther, *Holy Sacrament*, *LW* 35:32.
28. Luther, *Holy Sacrament*, *LW* 35:34.
29. Ibid., *LW* 35:30.
30. Luther, *Babylonian Captivity*, *LW* 36:68.
31. Ibid., *LW* 36:70.
32. Ibid., *LW* 36:69.
33. Aquinas, *Summa Theologiae* 3a.69.1.

ditional means of grace, for both comfort and inspiration to fulfill the dying and rising again that baptism signifies.

Luther faulted the scholastics, second, for teaching that baptism communicates that which it signifies irrespective of faith. In his judgment, the sacraments as a whole "have attached to them a word of promise which requires faith, and they cannot be fulfilled by any other work"; thus, in the final analysis, "we owe everything to faith alone and nothing to rituals."[34] Only where God's promise and human faith "meet" does baptism possess "a real and most certain efficacy."[35] Luther directly criticized, in this connection, the medieval definition of sacraments as "'effective signs' of grace"—"all such things are said to the detriment of faith," which alone serves as the proper instrument by which sinners lay hold of God's saving grace.[36]

Luther's emphasis on the necessity of faith to the proper realization (or fulfillment) of baptism requires careful attention, especially given his comments that seemingly ascribed regenerative power to baptism: "Baptism truly saves in whatever way it is administered"; baptism "effects forgiveness of sins, delivers from death and the devil, and grants eternal salvation."[37] Because Luther viewed the sacraments wholly as *divine* words of promises (rather than *human* words or works), his statement that "baptism truly saves" was merely an affirmation that God's word of promise truly saves. And this received further qualification: properly speaking, it is the faith that responds to God's promise in the sacrament that lays hold of those realities signified in baptism. Thus, ultimately, "it is not baptism that justifies or benefits anyone, but it is faith in that word of promise to which baptism is added."[38] And again, "It is not the water that produces these effects, but the word of God connected with the water, and our faith which relies on the word of God connected with the water."[39]

The baptismal virtue thus ultimately attributed to faith in God's promise establishes the possibility that baptism might become effective at some point in time subsequent to its administration, or even—in

---

34. Luther, *Babylonian Captivity*, LW 36:64–65.
35. Ibid., LW 36:67.
36. Ibid., LW 36:66.
37. Ibid., LW 36:63; CCFCT 2:40.
38. Luther, *Babylonian Captivity*, LW 36:66.
39. CCFCT 2:41.

the case of one who falsely believes herself baptized—entirely apart from its administration.[40] In the case of infants, whom some might claim "cannot have the faith of baptism," Luther suggested that "the faith of others, namely, those who bring them for baptism," renders their baptisms effective, appealing by way of analogy to "the paralytic in the Gospel, who was healed through the faith of others" (Mark 2:3–12). Luther hinted, moreover, at the possibility that faith itself, which is ultimately a divine gift, might be communicated to infants *through* baptism, thus rendering effective their baptisms and leaving them "changed, cleansed, and renewed."[41]

In later years Luther demonstrated increasing zeal to clarify his baptismal views vis-à-vis Anabaptist teaching and so placed greater emphasis on the objective *promissio* in baptism and less on the subjective response of *fides*. But the main features of his doctrine remained constant, with the exception, noted below, of his rationale for infant baptism.

Huldrych Zwingli

In 1525, the Zurich Reformer Huldrych Zwingli advanced his own rather different convictions regarding baptism in two works, his *Commentary on True and False Religion* and *On Baptism, Rebaptism, and Infant Baptism*.[42] Zwingli's baptismal theology as expressed in these works can, perhaps, be understood most readily by highlighting two fundamental points of contrast between his doctrine and Luther's teaching.

First, in distinction to Luther's recognition of baptism as a *divine* word of promise, Zwingli initially viewed baptism—that is, "immersion in water"[43]—as a *human* word of promise: "Baptism is an initiatory sacrament by which those who [are] going to change their life and

---

40. Luther, *Concerning Rebaptism*, LW 40:246, 260.
41. Luther, *Babylonian Captivity*, LW 36:73.
42. Huldrych Zwingli, *Commentary on True and False Religion*, ed. Samuel Macauley Jackson and Clarence Nevin Heller (1929; repr., Durham, NC: Labyrinth, 1981). A partial English translation of *On Baptism, Rebaptism, and Infant Baptism* exists in *Zwingli and Bullinger: Selected Translations with Introductions and Notes*, ed. G. W. Bromiley, LCC 24 (Philadelphia: Westminster, 1953), 129–75. For a fuller treatment of Zwingli's baptismal theology, see W. P. Stephens, *The Theology of Huldrych Zwingli* (Oxford: Clarendon, 1986), 194–217.
43. Zwingli, *On Baptism, Rebaptism, and Infant Baptism*, 132.

ways [mark] themselves out and [are] enrolled among the repentant."[44] Recognition of baptism as a human pledge to "repent" of one's "old life" and to "begin a new one" followed from Zwingli's broader definition of sacraments as "signs or ceremonials . . . by which a man proves to the Church that he either aims to be, or is, a soldier of Christ."[45] As essentially a human word, baptism cannot properly serve as a prop to that saving faith that "looks unwaveringly"—and without the assistance of rituals—"to the death of Christ and finds rest there."[46]

Second, in distinction to Luther's admission that baptism—when received in faith as the promise that it is—communicates the "washing away of sins" and "spiritual birth" that it signifies, Zwingli firmly maintained that "dipping effects nothing."[47] While, in Zwingli's judgment, the scholastic notion of *ex opere operato* crassly attributed "cleansing power" to water, Luther's doctrine offered little improvement with its supposition that "the thing signified by the sacraments" is "at once" applied "within" to the person who receives the sacrament in faith.[48] This too close association of *signum* ("sign") with *res significata* ("the thing signified")—even when faith in God's promise is assumed—can only serve, Zwingli believed, to supplant faith with superstitious "awe of the water" and to prejudice "the liberty of the divine Spirit," rendering God "absolutely bound by the signs."[49] Zwingli urged his readers to "let the sacraments be real sacraments" and not to "describe them as signs which actually are the things which they signify."[50]

Zwingli's baptismal views proved less static than Luther's, perhaps as a result of more extensive engagement with Anabaptist doctrine. In particular, his increasing employment of covenantal motifs in defense of paedobaptism specifically prejudiced his identification of baptism as exclusively a human word. Zwingli eventually named baptism "the sign of the covenant God struck with us through his Son," and saw reflected in that sign the divine initiative proper to the covenant. He thus increasingly acknowledged baptism to be, at

---

44. Zwingli, *True and False Religion*, 186.
45. Ibid., 184, 186.
46. Ibid., 182.
47. Ibid., 189.
48. Ibid., 182–83.
49. Ibid.
50. Zwingli, *On Baptism, Rebaptism, and Infant Baptism*, 131.

least at one level, a *divine* word of promise—a ritual that symbolizes, without ever effecting or communicating, spiritual benefits that God imparts in salvation.[51] From this followed increasing admission that baptism might at least buttress the faith of believers, a development reflected in Zwingli's willingness to subscribe at Marburg (1529) to the statement that baptism is "a sign and work of God by which our faith grows."[52]

The agreement expressed by Luther and Zwingli regarding baptism at Marburg is nevertheless remarkable given the very real differences that persisted between them. In part, the agreement they expressed may reflect the simple truth that concord on any front is easier when two parties face a common adversary. By 1529, the magisterial Reformers possessed a common foe on the issue of baptism in those persons typically labeled Anabaptists.

Anabaptist Teaching and the Response of the Reformers

Questions about the legitimacy of baptizing infants, stimulated at least in part by the Reformation impulse to test traditional beliefs and practices by the light of Scripture, surfaced in the early 1520s in both Luther's Saxony and Zwingli's Zurich. In Saxony the long-established practice of paedobaptism was criticized by the Zwickau Prophets, Thomas Müntzer, and Andreas Karlstadt. In Zurich persons eventually known as the "Swiss brethren" parted ways with Zwingli over the propriety of paedobaptism, despite the fact that Zwingli himself had briefly waffled on the issue in the early 1520s.[53]

As George Huntston Williams remarks, "There is," in fact, "a great gap between antipedobaptism and anabaptism"—that is, actual *re*-baptism of persons baptized in infancy.[54] Given that truth, we should be careful not to label the earliest critics of infant baptism as proper Anabaptists. They did, to be sure, withhold baptism from infants within their ecclesiastical reach, having become persuaded that the sacrament rightly belongs to persons who have committed themselves to Christ and his church by their *own* informed choice. But they did not

---

51. Stephens, *Theology of Zwingli*, 206, 215.
52. CCFCT 2:794.
53. See Stephens, *Theology of Zwingli*, 194–95.
54. George Huntston Williams, *The Radical Reformation* (Philadelphia: Westminster, 1975), 126.

immediately declare the baptisms that they themselves and others had received as infants invalid, nor did they seek to receive or administer second (valid) baptisms.

The "gap between antipedobaptism and anabaptism" was bridged in Zurich on January 21, 1525, when the layman Conrad Grebel rebaptized by affusion the former priest George Blaurock in the home of Felix Mantz. All three men became leaders of the Swiss Anabaptist movement; all three were incarcerated for their doctrine, and Mantz was executed by city officials in 1527, thus inaugurating widespread and prolonged persecution of Anabaptist Christians in the Swiss Cantons and beyond by Protestant and Roman Catholic civil authorities alike. Multiple factors informed the maltreatment of Anabaptists, but their practice of rebaptism provided the justification for their persecution; ancient Roman law embodied in the Justinian Code prescribed capital punishment for both rebaptizers and rebaptized.

As the Anabaptist movement grew and spread, it assumed divergent forms, making it difficult if not impossible to identify consistent convictions regarding the nature and efficacy of baptism among those traditionally given the Anabaptist label.[55] Swiss and South German Anabaptists typically viewed baptism, much like Zwingli in his writings of the mid-1520s, as a *human* word of testimony and commitment to God or other believers. So, for example, Balthasar Hubmaier, in a catechism completed one year before he was burnt at the stake in Vienna for his Anabaptist views, named "water baptism" an "outward and public testimony of the inner baptism in the Spirit"—a "commitment made to God publically and orally . . . in which the baptized person renounces Satan" and a vow made to "the church" to "dutifully accept brotherly discipline from it and its members."[56] As intimated in Hubmaier's words, baptism might be considered "ecclesiologically constitutive" by those stressing its testimonial function, but in no way was it considered a vehicle of salvific grace.[57]

By way of contrast, Michael Servetus—the rather notorious anti-Trinitarian Spaniard executed in Geneva in 1553, whose views on

55. See the overview of radical views on baptism in ibid., 300–319.
56. CCFCT 2:678–79.
57. Williams, *Radical Reformation*, 302.

baptism were apparently forged in dialogue with Strasbourg Anabaptists in the early 1530s—relegated the testimonial aspect of baptism to negligible status and ascribed regenerative and even deifying efficacy to the sacrament.[58] Servetus defended his doctrine of baptismal regeneration by appeals to Old Testament parallels such as Namaan's cleansing from leprosy by washing in the Jordan; he defended his doctrine of baptismal deification by appeals to certain church fathers, for example, Clement of Alexandria, who reportedly taught that "being baptized, we are . . . made gods."[59]

What these rather disparate examples of Anabaptist teaching—and, for that matter, all other species of Anabaptist teaching—had in common was the rejection of paedobaptism in favor of administering the sacrament to more mature persons. Hubmaier's doctrine assumed that recipients of baptism would possess the requisite level of cognitive and spiritual development to render public testimony and pledge themselves to God and others. Servetus, similarly though not entirely obviously, believed that infants lacked the maturity necessary to appropriate the regenerative or deifying benefits of baptism and that Jesus Christ, in any case, had "set forth as the proper age for baptism that of thirty years" by his own example.[60]

The Reformers, accordingly, applied their energies vis-à-vis Anabaptist teaching to defending the practice of baptizing infants. Luther, in his 1528 *Concerning Rebaptism*, defended paedobaptism on the basis of its divine institution, which he deduced from several lines of evidence: the antiquity and apparent success of the practice (innumerable persons baptized as infants who clearly possessed the Spirit in adulthood), the unlikelihood that the church had withheld *valid* baptism from her members for over a millennium (thereby effectively rendering her no true church), and biblical texts either mandating baptism without explicit respect to age (Matt. 28:19) or positively evidencing Christ's concern for children (Matt. 18:10).[61] The bulk of Luther's argument, however, was directed toward questioning the Anabaptist

---

58. See ibid., 311–18.
59. Michael Servetus, *Restitutio Christianismi* (1553; repr., Nuremberg: Christoph Gottlieb von Murr, 1790), 209–12; see Williams, *Radical Reformation*, 312.
60. Servetus, *Restitutio*, 90, quoted in Williams, *Radical Reformation*, 313.
61. Martin Luther, *Concerning Rebaptism*, LW 40:254–58.

assumption that infants lack faith. He placed on his opponents the onus of producing "a single Scripture verse which proves that children cannot believe."[62] He observed, moreover, that if *certainty* regarding the presence of faith were a prerequisite to administering or receiving baptism, not even adults could be baptized.[63]

Luther's engagement with Anabaptism marked some development in his doctrine. Previously he had embraced the medieval teaching that justified paedobaptism on the basis of the faith of those who brought a child to baptism (*fides aliena*). From 1528 onward he justified paedobaptism—to whatever extent it required justification in light of its divine institution—on the basis of a faith presumed present in, or imparted to, the infant baptized (*fides infantium*). Both positions were consistent with his emphasis on the efficacy that faith imparts to the sacrament, while the latter position was arguably more consistent with his doctrine of justification by (personal) faith alone.[64]

Zwingli addressed the issue of paedobaptism more extensively than Luther, particularly in response to Anabaptist writings from Hubmaier and Caspar Schwenkfeld. His earliest defense of paedobaptism was informed by his characteristic perception of sacraments as human words of commitment: "Baptism is the initiation both of those who have already believed and those who are going to believe."[65] Infants are pledged to follow Christ prior to any personal experience of faith much as the recipients of John's baptism—which Zwingli refused to distinguish from Christian baptism—pledged themselves to follow Christ before they had any certain knowledge of the Savior. When pressed for biblical warrant to baptize infants, Zwingli appealed, citing Colossians 2:11–12, to the analogy between circumcision and baptism, noting that circumcision testified to an existing faith for Abraham but preceded actual faith for Abraham's children (cf. Rom. 4:11–12).[66]

In Zwingli's later writings, his emphasis on the analogy between circumcision and baptism was buttressed by discussion of the essen-

---

62. Ibid., *LW* 40:243.
63. Ibid., *LW* 40:239–41.
64. See, for example, ibid., *LW* 40:241–45.
65. Quoted in Stephens, *Theology of Zwingli*, 196.
66. Stephens, *Theology of Zwingli*, 196.

tial unity between the old and new covenants. Believers of every age, he insisted, belong to one and the same covenant of grace. Baptism is increasingly acknowledged as the "sign" of this divinely initiated covenant—and thus a promise of forgiveness to those who fulfill their covenantal obligation to believe—more than a human word of testimony or commitment. The essential singularity of God's gracious covenant suggests the continued practice of applying the covenant sign to the children of covenant members; in baptism, then, infants become heirs of God's covenantal promises, to be realized by a future faith. His refusal to acknowledge baptism as in any sense an instrument or cause of that which it signifies remained intact throughout Zwingli's writings on paedobaptism.[67]

Later Reformation Teaching on Baptism

The second-generation Reformers inherited two problems related to the doctrine of baptism: first, disagreement among their predecessors regarding the proper efficacy, if any, of baptism; second, the rising tide of Anabaptism, unsuccessfully stemmed by the first-generation Reformers. In exploring their efforts to navigate these problems, our focus here will be on theologians in what would eventually be recognized as the Reformed Protestant tradition, especially Heinrich Bullinger and John Calvin. These Reformers evidenced greater interest than their Lutheran counterparts both in achieving a united Protestantism and in developing the doctrinal argument against Anabaptism (perhaps due to greater exposure to Anabaptists). Second-generation Lutheran thinkers generally evidenced every intention of remaining true, first and foremost, to Luther's baptismal teaching.[68]

Heinrich Bullinger

Though committed in principle to pursuing Protestant unity on the sacraments (and so greater consensus on baptism), Heinrich Bullinger, who succeeded Zwingli as *antistes* (or head of the church) in Zurich, was also dedicated to defending his predecessor's much-maligned repu-

---

67. Ibid., 203–11.
68. See Robert Kolb, "The Lutheran Theology of Baptism," in *Baptism: Historical, Theological, and Pastoral Perspectives*, ed. Gordon L. Heath and James D. Dvorak, McMaster Theological Study Series 4 (Eugene, OR: Pickwick, 2011), 53–75.

tation and maintaining at least some of his sacramental distinctives. Bullinger took a small step toward his Protestant peers by acknowledging that baptism was *principally* a divine word to sinners. While Christians "by baptism" do "profess and witness [themselves] to be under Christ [their] captain's banner," baptism is chiefly a "heavenly and public witness . . . whereby the Lord testifieth, that [he] . . . maketh us partakers and heirs of all his goodness."[69] As a word of divine testimony, baptism—a "holy action instituted of God . . . whereby the people of God are dipped in the water in the name of the Lord"—serves two fundamental purposes. First, it symbolically represents salvific realities to humankind—namely, cleansing from sin, regeneration, and the ongoing "mortification and vivification of Christians."[70] Second, it serves to "seal" or "confirm" God's promises of forgiveness and renewal to those who believe and consequently functions to reinforce human faith in God's promises.

Bullinger proved less flexible on the question of whether the ritual of baptism in any way causes the realities it signifies. His baptismal theology, like his Eucharistic theology, was informed by the principle that *signum* ("sign") and *res significata* ("the thing signified") "retain their natures distinguished, not communicating properties." Sacraments, then, do not confer the realities they signify, a truth made apparent by the fact that "many be partakers of the sign, and yet are barred from the thing signified."[71] In response to charges that he thus robbed baptism of any real force or efficacy, Bullinger responded that baptism was, according to his doctrine, thoroughly "effectual, and not without force," producing that very "effect and end" intended for it by God— the confirmation of faith and the recollection of duty in the baptized.[72]

Bullinger's defense of paedobaptism, like Zwingli's, rested on the recognition of the essential unity of God's covenant with sinners throughout salvation history and the essential correspondence between baptism and circumcision. The children of covenant members belong to the covenant themselves in every age; thus baptism—having succeeded

---

69. Henry Bullinger, *The Decades of Henry Bullinger*, ed. Thomas Harding (1849–1852; repr., Grand Rapids, MI: Reformation Heritage Books, 2004), 2:236, 316 (second set of pagination).
70. Ibid., 2:352, 329.
71. Ibid., 2:279, 270.
72. Ibid., 2:314.

circumcision as "a seal" of God's promise to be the God of (and for) his people—"is due unto them."[73]

Bullinger felt no qualms about acknowledging that the "infants of Christians" brought for baptism "believe not."[74] Insofar as baptism remains distinct from the saving realities it signifies, baptism is valid regardless of the presence of faith. Baptism merely establishes an infant's standing in God's covenant and right to lay claim to God's promises if he exercises faith as he matures.[75]

Martin Bucer and John Calvin

While Bullinger tread largely in Zwingli's footsteps in his theology of baptism, Calvin—at least from his time in Strasbourg (1538–1541) onward—pursued a path blazed especially by the first-generation Reformer Martin Bucer, who had from early on attempted to occupy middle ground between Zurich and Wittenberg on the sacraments.[76] In 1536, Bucer had made significant progress in his efforts to achieve Protestant unity by convincing the Wittenberg Reformers and South German evangelicals—though not the German-speaking church leaders of Zurich—to subscribe to a joint statement on the sacraments (the Wittenberg Concord).[77] The Wittenberg Concord's section on baptism dealt exclusively with the issue of the proper recipients of the sacrament (perhaps assuming agreement on the *nature* of baptism in light of the involved parties' joint subscription to the Marburg Articles). It defended paedobaptism on the grounds that infants are susceptible to God's regenerating work and, by virtue of that work, possess at the very least "inclinations to believe Christ and love God," which "inclinations" justify the statement that "infants have faith."[78] This doctrine of *fides infantium*, of course, ran counter to both Zwingli and Bullinger's teaching. But it found expression in Calvin's doctrine, as did

---

73. Ibid., 2:344. Bullinger developed this theme especially in his 1534 *De testament seu foedere Dei unico et aeterno*, a significant work in the evolution of Reformed covenant theology. See the English translation, *A Brief Exposition of the One and Eternal Testament or Covenant of God*, in Charles S. McCoy and J. Wayne Baker, *Fountainhead of Federalism: Heinrich Bullinger and the Covenantal Tradition* (Louisville: Westminster John Knox, 1991), 99–138.
74. Bullinger, *Decades*, 2:323.
75. Ibid., 2:323.
76. On Bucer's doctrine of baptism, see David F. Wright, *Martin Bucer: Reforming Church and Community* (Cambridge: Cambridge University Press, 1994), 95–106 (cf. 97–100).
77. See the text with introduction in CCFCT 2:796–801.
78. CCFCT 2:801.

Bucer's more general effort to distinguish without entirely disjoining sacramental signs from the realities they signify.[79]

Calvin's Doctrine of Baptism

Calvin defined "a sacrament" as "a visible word, or sculpture and image of that grace of God, which the word more fully illustrates."[80] Baptism, in Calvin's understanding, is principally a "word" from God to believing sinners: God "promises us in baptism and shows us by a sign given that . . . we have been led out and delivered . . . from the bondage of sin."[81] But, like Bullinger (and, presumably, in partial deference to Zwingli), Calvin was happy to acknowledge that baptism might serve secondarily as a human word of testimony to God and the church: "Baptism . . . is the mark by which we . . . openly affirm our faith."[82]

As an "image" of salvific grace, baptism pictures, first, the "cleansing" that properly occurs when believers are washed in "Christ's blood" and thus forgiven of their sins. Like Luther, Calvin emphasized the continuing assurance that baptism provides in this regard: "As often as we fall away, we ought to recall the memory of our baptism and fortify our mind with it, that we may always be sure and confident of the forgiveness of sins."[83] Baptism signifies, second, one's engrafting into Christ, and especially one's participation in Christ's death and resurrection, on which both the justifying and sanctifying benefits of Christ's work to believers are based: in baptism "the free pardon of sins and the imputation of righteousness are first promised us, and then the grace of the Holy Spirit to reform us to newness of life."[84]

In examining the relationship between *signum* and *res significata* in Calvin's baptismal theology, and thus the degree to which baptism might constitute a vehicle of saving grace, differences with Bullinger emerge. Both Reformers, to be sure, labored to *distinguish* the ritual

---

79. On Calvin's baptismal theology see J. V. Fesko, *Word, Water, and Spirit: A Reformed Perspective on Baptism* (Grand Rapids, MI: Reformation Heritage Books, 2010), 79–94; and Wim Janse, "The Sacraments," in *The Calvin Handbook*, ed. Herman J. Selderhuis (Grand Rapids, MI: Eerdmans, 2009), 348–51.
80. Quoted in Fesko, *Word, Water, and Spirit*, 80.
81. Calvin, *Institutes*, 4.15.9.
82. Ibid., 4.15.6.
83. Ibid., 4.15.3.
84. Ibid., 4.15.5.

of baptism from that which it signifies, noting in that process that unbelieving recipients of baptism possess none of the saving realities signified by their baptisms. But Calvin proved equally concerned not to entirely *separate* baptism from the realities it signifies and so was willing to acknowledge baptism as an instrument, given certain terms, of those realities. For Calvin, preserving a real (sacramental) union between *signum* and *res significata* was a matter of maintaining God's integrity: "[God] washes away sins . . . as truly and surely as we see our body outwardly cleansed, submerged, and surrounded with water. . . . He does not feed our eyes with a mere appearance only, but leads us to the present reality and effectively performs what it symbolizes."[85]

This stronger bond between sacramental sign and things signified in Calvin's doctrine (vis-à-vis Bullinger's) informs statements that, as was observed regarding similar declarations from Luther, might appear tantamount to a doctrine of baptismal regeneration: "At whatever time we are baptized, we are once for all washed and purged for our whole life"; "through baptism Christ makes us sharers in his death, that we may be engrafted in it."[86] Yet, like Luther, Calvin himself qualified such statements. He insisted, for instance, that God is the proper agent of this sacrament; baptism "is to be received as from the hand of the Author himself." Thus, "it is *he* who purifies and washes away sins, and wipes out the remembrance of them; . . . it is *he* who makes us sharers in his death."[87] Moreover, Calvin noted that, properly speaking, it is not water but "Christ's blood" (the former related to the latter as *signum* to *res significata*) that purifies those baptized.[88] Recognition of "Christ's blood" as the "true and only laver" in which believers are savingly washed should, in Calvin's judgment, serve to prevent superstitious or idolatrous opinions regarding the baptismal water.

Calvin also went to considerable lengths to highlight the indispensability of true faith to the reception of any real benefit from baptism: "It is not my intention to weaken the force of baptism by not joining reality and truth to the sign, in so far as God works through outward means. But from this sacrament, as from all others, we obtain only

---

85. Ibid., 4.15.14.
86. Ibid., 4.15.3, 5.
87. Ibid., 4.15.14, italics added.
88. Ibid., 4.15.2

as much as we receive in faith." Reception of baptism without faith, Calvin added, is a failure to believe the promise specifically embodied *in* baptism.[89]

This emphasis on the necessity of faith to receive any benefit from baptism establishes the possibility that baptism might be received at some interval of time from the reception of those salvific realities signified by the sacrament.[90] Thus there are some who finally grasp God's promise and exercise saving faith in that promise sometime after their baptisms. Calvin pointed to himself and others who were baptized in the late-medieval Roman church to illustrate this possibility. The baptism—that is, the promise of God of "forgiveness of sins"—administered to those who subsequently broke with Rome was entirely valid when delivered, but it "lay long buried" and "neglected" and was only appropriated when true faith in God's promise was born.[91]

While some receive the realities signified sometime after the sign, others—and here, perhaps, a significant difference with Luther emerges—receive the realities signified *before* they receive the sign. There are, in other words, persons who believe, and so obtain all the benefits that faith properly bestows, sometime prior to their baptisms. According to Calvin, such was the case with Cornelius, the centurion in Acts 10 who had "already received forgiveness of sins and the visible graces of the Holy Spirit" before he was baptized.[92] Calvin emphasized that no "ampler forgiveness of sins" is offered those baptized at a point subsequent to their believing; the forgiveness of sins that follows immediately from faith in Christ's finished work is perfect, and so impervious to improvement. For such persons, then, baptism chiefly communicates an "increase of assurance" regarding the pardon they have already received through faith in God's promises.[93]

In responding to "certain frantic spirits [who] have grievously disturbed the church over infant baptism," Calvin, like Luther, defended the propriety of paedobaptism on the basis, first and foremost, of that

89. Ibid., 4.15.14.
90. See ibid., 4.15.15, 17.
91. Ibid., 4.15.17.
92. Ibid., 4.15.15.
93. Ibid.

practice's divine institution.[94] "In baptizing infants we are obeying the Lord's will."[95] Calvin kept closer step with Zwingli and Bullinger, however, in providing a theological rationale for paedobaptism. Thus he emphasized the singularity of the gracious covenant made with believers in every age: "If the covenant . . . remains firm and steadfast, it applies no less today to the children of Christians than . . . it pertained to the infants of the Jews."[96] And in connection with his insistence on the unity of God's covenant with believers of every age, he emphasized the correspondence between circumcision and baptism: "Apart from the difference in the visible ceremony, whatever belongs to circumcision pertains likewise to baptism."[97]

Calvin freely admitted that infants, unlike "grown men," are initiated into God's covenant before they possess any real "understanding" of the "provisions of the covenant."[98] Absence of "understanding" does not, however, translate necessarily into absence of faith. In the earliest edition of his *Institutes of the Christian Religion*, Calvin spoke confidently about the presence of faith in (some) baptized newborns: "Baptism . . . rightly applies to infants, who possess faith in common with adults."[99] In later editions of that work, he spoke more circumspectly about the "seed" of faith (or, analogously, the "tiny spark" of the "knowledge of God") that "lies hidden within them by the secret working of the Spirit."[100] At the same time, he speculated more freely in later writings about the regeneration of (some) children of believers in infancy: "It is perfectly clear that those infants who are to be saved (as some are surely saved from that early age) are previously regenerated by the Lord."[101] Calvin reasoned to this position from the conviction that persons must be regenerated "before they can be admitted into God's kingdom" (cf. John 3:5), in conjunction with Christ's affirmation that children have, in fact, been admitted to that kingdom (Matt. 19:14). He discovered a biblical-historical example of infant regenera-

---

94. Ibid., 4.16.1.
95. Quoted in Fesko, *Word, Water, and Spirit*, 92.
96. Calvin, *Institutes*, 4.16.5
97. Ibid., 4.16.4.
98. Ibid., 4.16.24.
99. Quoted in Fesko, *Word, Water, and Spirit*, 91.
100. Calvin, *Institutes*, 4.16.19–20.
101. The term "regeneration" in Calvin comprises both what later Reformed divines intended by the term as well as that which they typically referred to as "sanctification."

tion in the case of John the Baptist, who was "filled with the Holy Spirit" while yet in his mother's womb (Luke 1:15).[102]

Lutheran and Reformed Engagement with Calvin's Sacramental Doctrine

It is necessary, before we conclude our consideration of Calvin's doctrine, to highlight a certain tension that existed in Calvin's theology of baptism—a tension that his Lutheran antagonists of the 1550s readily perceived and exploited. Calvin, as noted, was eager to maintain— more so than Bullinger—a sacramental union between the ritual of baptism and the salvific realities signified by that ritual. For Calvin, *signum* and *res significata* are *distinctio sed non separatio* ("distinct but not separated").[103] Thus he affirmed that baptism, where faith is present, communicates the spiritual realities it signifies. Yet, as becomes apparent in his defense of paedobaptism, Calvin believed that, at least in most instances, elect infants, much like the centurion Cornelius, have already received the realities signified by baptism when they are baptized. If the forgiveness of sins appropriated through (the seed of) faith cannot be increased, and if regeneration and the engrafting of an elect infant into Christ occur, at least potentially, prior to baptism, there would seem to be nothing left for baptism to actually communicate to recipients beyond confirmation of that which is already theirs by faith. Thus Calvin's Lutheran antagonists of the 1550s charged him—like they charged Bullinger (and ultimately Zwingli)—with reducing baptism to the status of a sign of salvific grace, and, at least by implication, denying it to be a genuine *instrument* of the same.[104]

In responding to his critics on this score, Calvin refused, on the one hand, to back down from affirming a genuine (sacramental) connection between baptism and those realities signified by baptism, and so an instrumental role for baptism in communicating those salvific realities. Thus he insisted, in defending his sacramental teaching against the

---

102. Calvin, *Institutes*, 4.16.17.
103. See Fesko, *Word, Water, and Spirit*, 85; Jill Raitt, "Three Inter-Related Principles in Calvin's Unique Doctrine of Infant Baptism," *SCJ* 11, no. 1 (1980): 51–62.
104. See especially Calvin's reply to Westphal's criticism of his baptismal theology in *Selected Works of John Calvin: Tracts and Letters*, ed. Henry Beveridge and Jules Bonnet, trans. Henry Beveridge (1849; repr., Grand Rapids, MI: Baker, 1983), 2:336–45.

Hamburg Lutheran Joachim Westphal, that "God truly performs and effects by baptism what he figures," that "the proper office of baptism is to [engraft] us into the body of Christ," and that (believing) persons "are regenerated by baptism."[105] On the other hand, Calvin insisted that baptism does not necessarily "work effectually at the same moment at which it is performed" (or, for that matter, necessarily "work" at all where faith is not present). "It is erroneous," he observed, "to infer that the free course of Divine grace is tied down to instants of time." Calvin apparently saw nothing problematic in affirming both that baptism represents *and* presents (to use sacramental language he employed elsewhere) the realities signified by baptism and that it does so at some point in time removed, to one degree or another, from the actual reception of the sacrament.[106] His opponents may, perhaps, be forgiven for having felt like Calvin was attempting to have his sacramental cake and eat it too.

Calvin's admission that the things signified by baptism might be—indeed, typically are—appropriated at some time other than the reception of baptism per se did at least bring his doctrine closer to Bullinger's. It thus facilitated the agreement that Calvin and Bullinger formally expressed on the sacraments with the Zurich Consensus of 1549.[107] Article 20 of that document affirmed that "the benefit which we receive from the sacraments ought not to be restricted to the time at which they are administered to us. . . . For those who [are] baptized in first infancy God regenerates in childhood or at the start of adolescence or even sometimes in old age."[108] This language could be stretched to accommodate both Calvin's assumption that regeneration typically precedes infant baptism and Bullinger's assumption that regeneration (like faith) follows infant baptism.[109]

The Zurich Consensus more generally stopped short of explicitly crediting sacramental signs with an instrumental role in communicat-

---

105. Calvin, *Selected Works*, 2:337, 339, 340.
106. "God, whenever he sees meet, fulfills and exhibits in immediate effect that which he figures in the sacrament. But no necessity must be imagined so as to prevent his grace from sometimes preceding, sometimes following, the use of the sign. The dispensation of [grace], its Author so tempers as not to separate the virtue of his Spirit from the sacred symbol." Calvin, *Selected Works*, 2:342.
107. CCFCT 2:802–15.
108. CCFCT 2:811.
109. It arguably also implies that "regeneration" is properly the "benefit" of baptism, which would reflect Calvin's position more than Bullinger's.

ing salvific realities, even while it insisted that "we do not disjoin the truth from the signs."[110] The closest it came to expressing Calvin's own understanding of the sacramental union between *signa* and *res significata* was in its definition of sacraments as "organs [*organa*] by which God acts efficaciously." Even this affirmation, however, remains vague because it fails to detail what exactly God "efficaciously" *does* through the "organs" of baptism and the Lord's Supper. Does God, as Calvin believed, "efficaciously" communicate the realities signified by the sacraments, or does God, as Bullinger insisted, "efficaciously" confirm the faith of believers by symbolically illustrating and sealing his promise of saving realities (which realities are properly communicated entirely apart from the sacraments)?[111]

Whatever the ambiguities of the sacramentology articulated in the Zurich Consensus, the document achieved its purpose of bringing Geneva and Zurich into lasting theological alliance and ultimately established the boundaries of "Reformed" (as opposed to Roman Catholic, Lutheran, or radical) teaching on both baptism and the Lord's Supper. Lutheran polemicists found opportunity in the publication of the Consensus (in 1551) to renew criticism of the evangelical leaders of Zurich, who, in their judgment, remained committed to Zwingli's reduction of both sacraments to mere symbols of saving realities. They also found opportunity to cry "foul" on church leaders of other cities who were in theory committed to the Wittenberg Concord but now subscribed to the Consensus, interpreting their alliance with Zurich and commitment to a statement that—in their judgment—denied salvific efficacy to the sacraments as a violation of their previous allegiances.

Baptism played second fiddle to the Lord's Supper in the renewed conflicts between Reformed and Lutheran thinkers in the 1550s. The central point at issue between Reformed and Lutheran parties on baptism in this later period was whether or not baptism really serves as an instrument of the realities it signifies.[112] Without denying Luther's

---

110. CCFCT 2:808.

111. See further Paul E. Rorem, "The Consensus Tigurinus (1549): Did Calvin Compromise?," in *Calvinus Sacrae Scripturae Professor: Calvin as Confessor of Holy Scripture; Die Referate Des Congrès International Des Recherches Calviniennes Vom 20. Bis 23. August 1990 in Grand Rapids*, ed. Wilhelm H. Neuser (Grand Rapids, MI: Eerdmans, 1994), 72–90.

112. See especially Wim Janse, "The Controversy between Westphal and Calvin on Infant Baptism, 1555–1556," *Perichoresis* 6, no. 1 (2008): 1–43.

634   *Aaron Clay Denlinger*

emphasis on the efficacy that faith imparts to baptism, Lutherans were keen to make it clear that baptism *does* communicate the realities it signifies and so remains indispensable to salvation. Westphal's insistence that dying infants *must* be baptized in order to be regenerated and gain entrance to God's eternal kingdom well illustrates the Lutheran stance. Calvin's response that elect persons dying in infancy are regenerated and admitted into God's kingdom regardless of whether or not they receive baptism hardly captures the nuances of his baptismal theology *in toto*. But Lutherans discovered in that response proof that Reformed thinkers, when push came to shove, dispensed with the necessity of baptism for salvation as a general principle.[113] Calvin's further admission that *surviving* infants were typically regenerated *before* baptism, even while he simultaneously insisted that they were regenerated *by* baptism, struck Westphal and company as doublespeak and failed to reassure them that Reformed thinkers did grant baptism a genuine instrumental role in communicating saving grace.

Confessional Positions on Baptism

Controversies between Lutheran and Reformed thinkers of the 1550s provided impetus for clarifying and solidifying various sacramental views in official statements of faith. Rome had already defined its position on the sacraments vis-à-vis Protestant and Anabaptist doctrines in the seventh session of the Council of Trent (1547). In the late 1550s and early 1560s, the Reformed churches, in a significant number of confessions, defined their doctrine vis-à-vis not only Roman and Anabaptist but also Lutheran Protestant teaching. And in the following decade, Lutheran divines reciprocated in kind by adding the Formula of Concord to their existing catechisms and confessions as an authoritative statement of their faith, thereby clarifying Lutheran sacramental theology vis-à-vis Roman, Anabaptist, and Reformed Protestant doctrines. As a summary and conclusion to this chapter, various confessional positions on baptism will be outlined. Very brief attention will also be given to certain seventeenth-century developments related to confessional statements on baptism.

---

113. Ibid., 13, 20–21.

TRIDENTINE ROMAN CATHOLIC DOCTRINE

The Council of Trent, which dealt with sacramentology in its seventh session, formalized late-medieval teaching on baptism and issued anathemas against both evangelical and Anabaptist baptismal theologies. Baptism was declared to "contain the grace" it signifies and to "confer that grace"—"through the sacramental action itself" (*ex opere operato*)—"on those who do not place an obstacle thereunto."[114] Persons claiming that "the grace of justification" is properly appropriated by "faith alone" or that baptism "is not necessary for salvation" were anathematized.[115] Trent also insisted that the grace that baptism properly confers *can* be lost through mortal sin, and it condemned those who extended the grace of baptism—or rather, faith in the promise embodied in baptism—to cover all future sins.[116] By insisting that the benefit of baptism could be lost, Trent reinforced the sacramental (and thus indispensable) character of penance and likewise established penance's proper function of recovering the "grace of justification" in cases where such was forfeited through mortal sin. Trent's final canons on baptism dealt with the sacrament's proper recipients, anathematizing persons who withheld baptism from infants or rebaptized those who had been baptized as infants in later years.[117]

THE REFORMED CONFESSIONS

The French Reformed Confession (1559), Scots Confession (1560), and Belgic Confession (1561) advanced very similar statements on sacramentology in general and on baptism in particular. All three confessions reveal a debt to Calvin in the use of language that—more so than that discovered in the Zurich Consensus—emphasized the sacramental union between baptism and the realities signified by baptism and thus the instrumental role that baptism performs in communicating salvific grace to believers. The French Confession states, "By [baptism] we are grafted into the body of Christ, so as to be washed and cleansed by his blood, and then renewed in purity of life by his Holy Spirit,"

---

114. *CCFCT* 2:840.
115. Ibid.
116. Ibid., 2:841.
117. Ibid., 2:842.

while the Scots Confession affirms, "By baptism we are engrafted in Christ Jesus, to be made partakes of his justice, by the which our sins are covered and remitted."[118] Such statements are premised on a carefully defined relationship between sacramental *signa* and *res significata*. Signs and things signified cannot be disjoined from one another; thus the French Confession asserts, "With these signs is given the true possession and enjoyment of that which they present to us."[119] Nevertheless, as the Scots Confession states, signs and things signified must not be confused: "We will [not] worship the signs in place of that which is signified by them."[120]

Contra Rome, the necessity of faith to receive any benefit from baptism is emphasized in these confessions. So also is the permanency of the spiritual benefit that baptism communicates to believing recipients, as captured in the Belgic Confession: "This baptism is profitable not only when the water is on us and when we receive it, but throughout our entire lives."[121] The propriety of baptizing infants of believers is established on the basis of their membership in church and covenant and of—at least in the Belgic Confession—their participation in those spiritual benefits that baptism signifies and communicates: "Christ has shed his blood no less for washing the little children of believers than he did for adults."[122]

In 1566, the Second Helvetic Confession, written entirely by Bullinger though subsequently endorsed by several national churches, was published. Though similar in content to the Reformed confessions just noted, Bullinger's confession was characterized by more extensive discussion of the relationship between *signa* and *res significata* in the sacraments, and it arguably reduced that relationship to one of mere signification.[123] Bullinger studiously avoided language suggesting that baptism might communicate the spiritual blessings it signifies, and he emphasized the *assurance* of spiritual blessings that baptism—as a sign and seal of God's covenant—delivers to believers: "Inwardly we are regenerated, purified, and renewed by God through the Holy Spirit;

118. Ibid., 2:384, 400.
119. Ibid., 2:385.
120. Ibid., 2:401.
121. Ibid., 2:422.
122. Ibid., 2:423.
123. Ibid., 2:504–8.

and outwardly we receive the assurance of [these] gifts in the water, by which also [these] great benefits are represented, and, as it were, set before our eyes to be beheld."[124]

Although our treatment of baptism in this chapter has largely been limited to the sixteenth century, it is necessary—before taking leave of the Reformed confessions—to take notice of two seventeenth-century texts and their doctrines of baptism. The first of these is the Westminster Confession of Faith, completed in 1646, which deserves attention simply because of the position it has come to occupy as the theological standard for so many Presbyterian denominations throughout the world today. The Westminster Confession begins its treatment of baptism by detailing the significance of the ritual and proceeds to outline the proper form and mode ("pouring or sprinkling water upon the person") of the same. It asserts the propriety of baptizing those "that do actually profess faith" as well as "the infants of one, or both, believing parents."[125] While condemning contempt for baptism, the confession acknowledges that "grace and salvation are not so inseparably annexed unto it . . . that no person can be regenerated, or saved, without it," and it observes that unbelieving recipients of baptism receive no saving benefit from the sacrament.[126] Regarding the critical question of whether baptism, given certain terms (particularly the presence of faith), communicates the blessings it signifies, the Westminster Confession concludes,

> The efficacy of baptism is not tied to that moment of time wherein it is administered; yet, notwithstanding, by the right use of this ordinance, the grace promised is not only offered, but really exhibited, and conferred, by the Holy Ghost, to such (whether of age or infants) as that grace belongeth unto, according to the counsel of God's own will, in his appointed time.[127]

One finds reflected in this statement the tension in Calvin's doctrine noted above: it admits some space of time between the application of baptism and the appropriation of the spiritual realities signified

---

124. Ibid., 2:509.
125. Ibid., 2:641.
126. Ibid., 2:641–42.
127. Ibid., 2:642.

by baptism, but it nevertheless identifies baptism as an instrument of salvific grace.

The seventeenth century witnessed the emergence of groups that, for the first time, married the rejection of paedobaptism to Protestantism's Scripture principle and soteriological emphasis on justification *sola fide*.[128] Baptistic Protestants in London produced a series of doctrinal confessions consistent with this development. The second of these, published in 1677 and adopted by an assembly of Particular Baptist Churches in 1689, was largely modeled on the Westminster Confession but parted ways—naturally—with that Confession's teaching on the subject of baptism. Three points of contrast between the Westminster Confession and the Second London Baptist Confession should be noted. First, the latter confession insisted that "those who do actually profess repentance towards God, faith in, and obedience, to our Lord Jesus Christ, are the only proper subjects of this ordinance," thereby precluding infants from the sacrament of baptism. Second, it affirmed that "immersion, or dipping" was the proper mode of baptism. And third, it strictly identified baptism as "a sign" of union with Christ, of the "remission of sins," and of "newness of life," thus avoiding (without explicitly denying) any suggestion that baptism—by virtue of a sacramental union between *signum* and *res significata*—might serve in some way to communicate the salvific realities it signifies.[129]

THE LUTHERAN CONFESSIONS

The Formula of Concord (1577) resolved differences between Lutherans that had emerged after Luther's death in 1546. With regard to sacramentology, the Formula was focused principally on the Supper. Its significance for this survey lies chiefly in the authority it imputed

---

128. I would argue that Anabaptist groups of the sixteenth century largely rejected *sola Scriptura* and *sola fide* as those principles were understood by the magisterial Reformers. Such a claim has a bearing upon the question of present-day Baptists' origins, regarding which see David W. Bebbington, *Baptists through the Centuries: A History of a Global People* (Waco, TX: Baylor University Press, 2010).
129. William J. McGlothlin, ed., *Baptist Confessions of Faith* (Philadelphia: American Baptist Publication Society, 1911), 269–70. The 1689 London Baptist Confession's failure to explicitly attribute efficacy to baptism did not prevent some seventeenth-century (or later) Baptists from acknowledging such. See the argument of Stanley K. Fowler in *More than a Symbol: The British Recovery of Baptismal Sacramentalism*, Studies in Baptist History and Thought 2 (Eugene, OR: Wipf and Stock, 1997).

to earlier statements of Lutheran faith that contain more thorough accounts of baptism, including the Augsburg Confession, Melanchthon's Apology of the same, Luther's catechisms, and the Smalcald Articles.

Among these earlier Lutheran statements of faith, Luther's Large Catechism contains the fullest treatment of baptism. The Large Catechism identifies baptism as a divinely instituted practice and thus as "God's work," the "power, effect, benefit, fruit, and purpose" of which is "to save."[130] The "power" of baptism to deliver sinners from "sin, death, and the devil" and bring them into the "Kingdom of Christ" does not, according to the catechism, jeopardize the truth that sinners are justified by faith alone. Faith alone apprehends the benefit that baptism communicates—Rome's doctrine of baptismal efficacy is thereby rejected. But faith must have an object. Insofar as God has added his promise to the water of baptism, faith rightly "clings to the water, . . . in which there is sheer salvation and life."[131] The nervousness one discovers in Reformed confessions over idolatry of the sacramental elements is lacking here. Sinners properly exercise (saving) faith in God's commitment to save them *through* "the water comprehended in God's word"—that is, in God's promise that "whoever believes and is baptized will be saved" (Mark 16:16).[132] The Large Catechism concludes its treatment of baptism by defending the legitimacy of paedobaptism and stressing the durability of the grace that baptism grants to believers.[133]

The Formula of Concord includes no discrete section on baptism. It does, however, address issues related to baptism in its remarks on "factions and sects." In harmony with the earlier Lutheran confessional standards, the Formula condemns what it perceives to be the Anabaptist error of withholding the sacrament from children of believers. The Formula also, interestingly, condemns (among "heretical" doctrines of Anabaptists) the opinion that "the children of Christians, since they are born of Christian and believing parents, are holy and children of God even without and *prior to Baptism*."[134]

---

130. Theodore G. Tappert, ed. and trans., *The Book of Concord: The Confessions of the Evangelical Lutheran Church* (Philadelphia: Muhlenberg, 1959), 439.
131. Ibid., 440.
132. Ibid., 437–38.
133. Ibid., 442–46.
134. Ibid., 634, italics added.

This could be seen to strike at Calvin's teaching as much, if not more than, Anabaptist doctrine. If, in fact, Calvin's doctrine was in view, this would merely reflect the tendency among late sixteenth-century Lutherans to lump Reformed Protestants in with radical sectarians, even while Reformed Protestants persisted in recognizing Lutherans as Christian brethren and promoting intercommunion between their respective fellowships.

Conclusion

"Make every effort to keep the unity of the Spirit through the bond of peace. There is one body and one Spirit, just as you were called to one hope when you were called; one Lord, one faith, one baptism; one God and Father of all" (Eph. 4:3–6 NIV). Commenting on this text in the late 1540s, Calvin discovered in Scripture's recognition of "one baptism" not an argument against rebaptism (as tempting as that interpretation must have been in his historical context) but the doctrine that there is "one baptism . . . common to all, . . . by means of [which] we begin to form one body and one soul." The Reformer could hardly have written these words without an acute awareness that baptism had become, in his day, something that—to all appearances—divided rather than united the body of Christ. Yet the subsequent identification of "one God and Father" of all true believers apparently gave Calvin hope, even in the midst of an age defined by theological conflict. "How comes it," he wrote, "that we are united by faith, by baptism, or even by the government of Christ, but because God the Father, extending to each of us his gracious presence, employs these means for gathering us to himself?"[135] Contrary to all appearances, Calvin concluded, baptism unites rather than divides true Christians—regardless of their disagreements over it—because it is, quite simply, the one true God's tool for doing just that. Given the reality that the differences over baptism that emerged in the sixteenth century remain very much with us today, Calvin's perspective seems like a conclusion worth stealing and repeating in service to this chapter.

---

135. John Calvin, *Commentaries on the Epistles of Paul to the Galatians and Ephesians*, trans. William Pringle (Edinburgh: Thomas Clark, 1841), 251.

Resources for Further Study

PRIMARY SOURCES

Aquinas, Thomas. *Summa Theologiae*. Vols. 13–20 of *The Latin/English Edition of the Works of St. Thomas Aquinas*. Translated by Laurence Shapcote. Edited by John Mortensen and Enrique Alarcón. Lander, WY: Aquinas Institute for the Study of Sacred Doctrine, 2012.

Bromiley, G. W., ed. *Zwingli and Bullinger: Selected Translations with Introductions and Notes*. Library of Christian Classics 24. Philadelphia: Westminster, 1953.

Bullinger, Heinrich. *A Brief Exposition of the One and Eternal Testament or Covenant of God*. Translated by Charles S. McCoy and J. Wayne Baker. In McCoy and Baker, *Fountainhead of Federalism: Heinrich Bullinger and the Covenantal Tradition*, 99–138. Louisville: Westminster John Knox, 1991.

———. *The Decades of Heinrich Bullinger*. Edited by Thomas Harding. 2 vols. 1849–1852. Reprint, Grand Rapids, MI: Reformation Heritage Books, 2004.

Calvin, John. *Institutes of the Christian Religion*. Edited by John T. McNeill. Translated by Ford Lewis Battles. 2 vols. Library of Christian Classics 20–21. 1559 edition. Philadelphia: Westminster, 1960.

———. *Second Defence of the Pious and Orthodox Faith concerning the Sacraments*. In *Selected Works of John Calvin: Tracts and Letters*, edited by Henry Beveridge and Jules Bonnet, translated by Henry Beveridge, 2:245–345. 1849. Reprint, Grand Rapids, MI: Baker, 1983.

Lombard, Peter. *The Sentences*. Translated by Giulio Silano. 4 vols. Mediaeval Sources in Translation 42–43, 45, 48. Toronto: Pontifical Institute of Mediaeval Studies, 2007–2010.

Luther, Martin. *The Babylonian Captivity of the Church*. In *Luther's Works*. Vol. 35, *Word and Sacrament I*, edited by Abdel Ross Wentz, 3–126. Philadelphia: Fortress, 1959.

———. *Concerning Rebaptism*. In *Luther's Works*. Vol. 40, *Church and Ministry II*, edited by Conrad Bergendoff, 225–62. Philadelphia: Fortress, 1959.

McGlothlin, William J., ed. *Baptist Confessions of Faith*. Philadelphia: American Baptist Publication Society, 1911.

Melanchthon, Philip. *Commonplaces: Loci Communes 1521*. Translated by Christian Preus. St. Louis, MO: Concordia, 2014.

Pelikan, Jaroslav, and Valerie Hotchkiss, eds. *Creeds and Confessions of Faith in the Christian Tradition.* Vol. 2, part 4, *Creeds and Confessions of the Reformation Era.* New Haven, CT: Yale University Press, 2003.

Tappert, Theodore G., ed. and trans. *The Book of Concord: The Confessions of the Evangelical Lutheran Church.* Philadelphia: Fortress, 1959.

Zwingli, Huldrych. *Commentary on True and False Religion.* Edited by Samuel Macaulay Jackson and Clarence Nevin Heller. 1929. Reprint, Durham, NC: Labyrinth, 1981.

SECONDARY SOURCES

Fesko, J. V. *Word, Water, and Spirit: A Reformed Perspective on Baptism.* Grand Rapids, MI: Reformation Heritage Books, 2010.

Heath, Gordon L., and James D. Dvorak, eds. *Baptism: Historical, Theological, and Pastoral Perspectives.* McMaster Theological Study Series 4. Eugene, OR: Pickwick, 2011.

Janse, Wim. "The Controversy between Westphal and Calvin on Infant Baptism, 1555–1556." *Perichoresis* 6, no. 1 (2008): 1–43.

Raitt, Jill. "Three Inter-Related Principles in Calvin's Unique Doctrine of Infant Baptism." *Sixteenth Century Journal* 11, no. 1 (1980): 51–62.

Riggs, John W. *Baptism in the Reformed Tradition.* Columbia Series in Reformed Theology. Louisville: Westminster John Knox, 2002.

Stephens, W. P. *The Theology of Huldrych Zwingli.* Oxford: Clarendon, 1986.

Trigg, Jonathan D. *Baptism in the Theology of Martin Luther.* Leiden: Brill, 2001.

Williams, George Huntston. *The Radical Reformation.* 3rd ed. Sixteenth Century Essays and Studies 15. Kirksville, MO: Truman State University Press, 1992.

Wright, David F. *Martin Bucer: Reforming Church and Community.* Cambridge: Cambridge University Press, 1994.

18

The Lord's Supper

Keith A. Mathison

ABSTRACT

The sixteenth-century debates over the nature of the Lord's Supper resulted in divisions that exist to this day. The Reformers agreed that the Roman Catholic doctrine, which understood the Supper as a representation or repetition of Christ's sacrifice, was unbiblical. They also agreed in their rejection of the Roman Catholic doctrine of transubstantiation. When pressed to provide their own explanation of the presence of Christ in the Supper, however, they were unable to come to agreement. Martin Luther insisted that Christ's words "This is my body" mean that the bread is his body. Andreas Karlstadt, Huldrych Zwingli, Johannes Oecolampadius, and others disagreed, arguing that Christ's words must be understood symbolically. The disagreement resulted in a lengthy and bitter controversy. Through the efforts of Martin Bucer, who eventually took a somewhat mediating position, a modicum of peace was achieved with the Wittenberg Concord of 1536. When Bucer's protégé John Calvin and Zwingli's younger colleague Heinrich Bullinger hammered out the Zurich Consensus in 1549, a second controversy began because some Lutherans saw it as a capitulation to a wholly symbolic doctrine of the Supper. The written debates between the

Reformed and the Lutherans, particularly John Calvin and Joachim Westphal, further cemented the divisions between these branches of the church. By the end of the sixteenth century, the Reformed and Lutheran confessions, as well as the Council of Trent, had drawn the doctrinal lines that exist to this day.

Introduction

By the end of the sixteenth century, the body of Christ had been broken by disagreements and debates over the Lord's Supper. Various theologians had already begun to systematize the arguments for and against the different views, and the confessions of the Roman Catholic, Lutheran, and Reformed churches had established the boundaries. The battle lines were drawn for a conflict that has yet to end. In order to understand where we are today, we must understand the various Eucharistic views of those who were involved in the great debates of the sixteenth century, and in order to understand those views, we must first take a step back and look at their medieval historical context.

The Medieval Context

The Reformation-era conflicts about the Lord's Supper did not occur in a historical vacuum.[1] Their roots can be found in the teaching and practices of the early and medieval Latin church. For the first eight hundred years of the church's existence, most writers spoke of the sacramental elements of bread and wine as the body and blood of Christ but without further explanation. In this, they were simply following the example of Jesus when he said of the Passover bread, "This is my body" (Matt. 26:26). However, as is the case with Christ's words of institution, the verbal identification of those in the early church was capable of more than one interpretation.

Some church fathers (e.g., Gregory of Nyssa, Cyril of Alexandria) appear to have been using such language in a more literal sense, while others (e.g., Origen, Augustine) appear to have had a more figurative intent. Making matters more difficult, very few of the church fathers at-

---

1. For a broader discussion of the sacraments in medieval perspective, see Aaron Denlinger's introduction to chap. 17, "Baptism," in the present volume.

tempted to provide any kind of doctrinal explanation of their language. Some historians have attempted to categorize the views of the church fathers as either "realist" or "symbolic," but those terms are simply inadequate given the nature of much of the patristic commentary on the sacrament.[2]

In spite of the different emphases found in the writings of the early church fathers, there were no known Eucharistic controversies for the first eight hundred years of the church's history. The first Eucharistic discussion that came anywhere near being an actual debate did not occur until the ninth century when Paschasius Radbertus and Ratramnus, two monks at the abbey of Corbie, each wrote treatises outlining different concepts of Christ's presence in the Supper.[3]

Radbertus presented a view emphasizing that the consecrated bread and wine became the very same body that was born of the Virgin Mary. The visible bread and wine point to this inward, invisible reality. His view was a forerunner to the later developed Roman Catholic doctrine of transubstantiation. Ratramnus, on the other hand, argued that the bread and wine are the "spiritual" body and blood of Christ. There is a difference, therefore, between the body born of the Virgin Mary and the body present in the Supper.[4] In the immediately following centuries, Radbertus's view won the day.[5]

In the eleventh century, the theologian Berengar of Tours raised objections to the Radbertian view that had become dominant in the church by that time. These objections were met with resistance. The thirty-year controversy that followed eventually resulted in Rome's dogmatic declaration "Ego Berengarius" (1079).[6] According to this

---

2. J. N. D. Kelly, *Early Christian Doctrines*, rev. ed. (San Francisco: Harper Collins, 1978), 440–49. Kelly uses the word "realist" here to refer to the way some speak of the bread and wine as the body and blood of Christ without necessarily specifying how or why this identification is made. He uses "symbolic" to refer to the way in which others sometimes indicate specifically that the elements are symbols or signs. The terms are inadequate because, among other reasons, many early Christian fathers simultaneously used both language that can be described as "realist" and language that can be described as "symbolic."

3. For an English translation of both works, see George E. McCracken, trans. and ed., *Early Medieval Theology*, LCC 9 (Philadelphia: Westminster, 1957), 90–147.

4. For a good overview of the controversy and the teachings of both Radbertus and Ratramnus, see John F. Fahey, *The Eucharistic Teaching of Ratramn of Corbie* (Mundelein, IL: Saint Mary of the Lake Seminary, 1951).

5. Patricia McCormick Zirkel, "The Ninth-Century Eucharistic Controversy: A Context for the Beginnings of Eucharistic Doctrine in the West," *Worship* 68 (1994): 2–23.

6. Giulio D'Onofrio, *History of Theology*, vol. 2, *The Middle Ages*, trans. Matthew J. O'Connell (Collegeville, MN: Liturgical Press, 2008), 132–35.

declaration, the bread and wine are "substantially changed" (*substan-tialiter converti*) into the true and proper body and blood of Christ.[7] The twelfth-century theologian Peter Lombard (ca. 1090–1160) maintained this tradition: "When these words [of institution] are pro-nounced, the change of the bread and wine into the substance of the body and blood of Christ occurs."[8] In 1215, the Fourth Lateran Coun-cil declared, "His Body and Blood are truly contained in the sacrament of the altar under the appearances of bread and wine, the bread being transubstantiated into the body by the divine power and the wine into the blood."[9] The mere use of the word "transubstantiation," however, did not completely settle matters. Theologians continued to debate what transubstantiation actually entailed.[10]

It fell to Thomas Aquinas (1225–1274) to provide the Roman church with a comprehensive doctrine of transubstantiation.[11] He did so by using Aristotelian metaphysical categories.[12] Briefly, in Aristotle's metaphysics, the word "substance" (Gk. *ousia*) describes the funda-mental reality or nature of a thing—that which makes something what it is. The word "accidents," on the other hand, refers to nonessential attributes such as height, weight, and color.[13] According to Thomas, the miracle of transubstantiation involves a change in the substance of the bread and wine without a change to the accidents.[14]

While the doctrine of Christ's bodily presence in the Supper was developing, the Roman church, in connection with that idea, was also

---

7. For the full text, see DH §700.

8. Peter Lombard, *The Sentences, Book 4: On the Doctrine of Signs*, trans. Giulio Silano, Me-diaeval Sources in Translation 48 (Toronto: Pontifical Institute of Mediaeval Studies, 2010), 8.4.

9. DH §802.

10. Gary Macy, "The Dogma of Transubstantiation in the Middle Ages," *JEH* 45, no. 1 (1994): 11–41; Macy, "The Medieval Inheritance," in *A Companion to the Eucharist in the Reformation*, ed. Lee Palmer Wandel, Brill's Companions to the Christian Tradition 46 (Leiden: Brill, 2014), 15–38.

11. I am tempted to say that Thomas was the first to "flesh out" the meaning of the word *transubstantiation*.

12. See Brian Davies, *The Thought of Thomas Aquinas* (Oxford: Clarendon, 1992), 364–76.

13. The metaphysical definition of "substance" should not be confused with the definition found in modern scientific textbooks, where "substance" is generally understood as "matter with specific properties." In Aristotle and Thomas, "substance" does not equal "matter."

14. Thomas Aquinas, *Summa Theologiae*, vols. 13–20 of *The Latin/English Edition of the Works of St. Thomas Aquinas*, trans. Laurence Shapcote, ed. John Mortensen and Enrique Alar-cón (Lander, WY: Aquinas Institute for the Study of Sacred Doctrine, 2012), 3a.75.1–8; see also 3a.77.1. Not all medieval theologians agreed with Thomas's interpretation; see, e.g., James F. McCue, "The Doctrine of Transubstantiation from Berengar through Trent: The Point at Issue," *HTR* 61, no. 3 (1968): 393–402.

elaborating its doctrine of the Lord's Supper as a repetition or representation of Christ's sacrifice. The roots of this idea can also be found in the early church.[15] But by the beginning of the sixteenth century, the Mass had come to be understood by many influential Roman theologians as a propitiatory sacrifice offered by priests through which the repentant could obtain mercy.[16]

Forerunners of the Reformation

Not all medieval Christians were content with the Roman Catholic doctrine of transubstantiation or the idea of the sacrifice of the Mass. One of the most significant opponents of the Roman doctrine was John Wyclif (ca. 1328–1384). In his treatise *On the Eucharist*, he expressed many ideas that different Reformers would later borrow. Wyclif argued, for example, that Christ's words "This is my body" should be taken figuratively.[17] The bread is not literally the body of Christ, he held. Instead, the bread is the "efficacious sign" of the body of Christ.[18] Furthermore, we do not physically eat the body of Christ; instead, our souls feed on Christ by faith.[19] Ultimately, Wyclif's views were condemned at the Council of Constance in 1415.[20]

A late-medieval figure who indirectly influenced the sixteenth-century debates was the Dutch theologian Wessel Gansfort (1419–1489). His treatise *The Sacrament of the Eucharist* is a beautifully written work of devotional theology. Unlike Wyclif, Gansfort accepted transubstantiation, but Gansfort's emphasis on spiritual communion was to be the catalyst in a chain reaction of events with repercussions

---

15. Bengt Hägglund, *History of Theology*, trans. Gene J. Lund (St. Louis, MO: Concordia, 1968), 155; Kelly, *Early Christian Doctrines*, 449–55.

16. Cardinal Thomas Cajetan (1469–1534), e.g., presented this view, a view that would later be declared dogma by the Council of Trent. For a summary of Cajetan's doctrine, see Edward J. Kilmartin, *The Eucharist in the West: History and Theology*, ed. Robert J. Daly (Collegeville, MN: Liturgical Press, 2004), 163–64.

17. John Wyclif, *On the Eucharist*, in *Advocates of Reform: From Wyclif to Erasmus*, ed. Matthew Spinka, LCC 14 (Philadelphia: Westminster, 1953), 82.

18. Ibid., 70.

19. Ibid., 62–66.

20. DH §1151–95. This council also condemned and executed Jan Hus (ca. 1369–1415) for a number of alleged heresies. One of the demands Hus and his followers had made was that the Supper be administered "under both kinds." In other words, Hus insisted that the laity receive both the bread and the wine, rather than the bread alone, as had become the custom. His demands were rejected. See Steven Ozment, *The Age of Reform, 1250–1550: An Intellectual and Religious History of Late Medieval and Reformation Europe* (New Haven, CT: Yale University Press, 1980), 166.

he could not have foreseen.[21] For Gansfort, "the remembrance of what our Lord did and suffered for our salvation" was the true Eucharist.[22] Since we can remember Christ at any time, we can have the benefit of his Supper at any time. However, if a man eats the visible elements but has no faith, he does not eat spiritually. In order to eat spiritually, he must remember Christ and all he did. In other words, he must believe.[23]

Prelude to the First Eucharistic Controversy (1520–1524)

One of the most significant difficulties faced by any student of the doctrine of the Lord's Supper at the time of the Reformation is the fact that the views of almost every major player underwent development to one degree or another. For some, the development involved little more than a clarification of their thinking and a strengthening of their arguments. For others, the development of their views involved wholesale changes of mind. It is insufficient, therefore, to speak merely of Luther's view or of Zwingli's view, for example. It is necessary to look at each theologian's view in the context of its own progressive development. In the years leading up to the outbreak of the controversies among the Reformers, the writings of four such figures are of particular importance: Martin Luther, Philipp Melanchthon, Andreas Karlstadt, and Cornelius Hoen.

Turning first to Martin Luther, we note that several key themes dominated his three earliest writings on the Lord's Supper.[24] First and foremost was the idea that the sacrament is a testament in which Christ promises forgiveness of sins and eternal life to his people.[25] The greatest part of the sacraments are "the words and promises of God, without

21. George Huntston Williams, *The Radical Reformation* (Philadelphia: Westminster, 1975), 30–31.

22. Wessel Gansfort, "The Sacrament of the Eucharist," in Edward W. Miller, *Wessel Gansfort: Life and Writings*, trans. Jared W. Scudder (New York: G. P. Putnam's Sons, 1917), 2:4.

23. Ibid., 17, 24–25, 31.

24. Martin Luther, *The Blessed Sacrament of the Holy and True Body of Christ* (1519), LW 35:45–73; Luther, *A Treatise on the New Testament, That Is, the Holy Mass* (1520), LW 35:75–111; Luther, *The Babylonian Captivity of the Church* (1520), LW 36:3–126. Even among Luther's earliest writings, there is a discernible shift in emphasis between the writing of *The Blessed Sacrament* and the *Treatise on the New Testament*. The first strongly emphasizes the horizontal dimension of the Eucharist, namely, fellowship and bearing one another's burdens. The second emphasizes the vertical dimension, the promise of forgiveness made by God to man.

25. Luther, *Holy Mass*, LW 35:86–87; Luther, *Babylonian Captivity*, LW 36:37–40; Luther, *The Misuse of the Mass* (1521), LW 36:179. See Carter Lindberg, *The European Reformations* (Malden, MA: Blackwell, 1996), 188; cf. also David C. Steinmetz, "Scripture and the Lord's Supper in Luther's Theology," *Int* 37, no. 3 (1983): 258.

which the sacraments are dead and are nothing at all."[26] Because the Supper is a promise or testament, it cannot possibly be a sacrifice as Rome teaches. If it is a sacrifice or work, we lose the gospel.[27] In addition, the promissory nature of the Supper means that the proper and necessary response is faith, not works.[28]

The second major theme dominating Luther's earliest writings on the Supper was the doctrine of Christ's true presence in the bread and wine. Luther argued that this belief is demanded by Christ's words "This is my body." He believed that the church should not require anyone to accept the doctrine of transubstantiation as the only orthodox explanation of the manner of Christ's bodily presence.[29] Luther never rejected, however, Christ's true bodily presence in the elements of the Supper.[30]

A third key theme in Luther's earliest writings on the Supper was the relationship between the word and the sign. Luther explained that "in every promise of God two things are presented to us, the word and the sign, so that we are to understand the word to be the testament, but the sign to be the sacrament."[31] In other words, the testament is the promise of Christ, and the sacrament is the bread and wine, in which are the body and blood of Christ. Understanding this aspect of Luther's thought will help us to better grasp the reasons for some of the later disagreements between him and the other Reformers.[32] While Luther's primary distinction was between the word and the sign (the promise and the sign of the promise), the primary distinction emphasized by many of the other Reformers was between the sign (the bread and wine) and the thing signified (the body and blood of Christ). In other words, for Luther, the body and blood of Christ in the bread and wine

26. Luther, *Holy Mass*, LW 35:91.

27. Ibid., LW 35:97.

28. Luther, *Blessed Sacrament*, LW 35:63; Luther, *Misuse of the Mass*, LW 36:169. Because of the necessity of faith in the promise, the sacrament also does not justify *ex opere operato*. See Gordon A. Jensen, "Luther and the Lord's Supper," in *The Oxford Handbook of Martin Luther's Theology*, ed. Robert Kolb, Irene Dingel, and L'ubomír Batka (Oxford: Oxford University Press, 2014), 323.

29. Luther, *Holy Mass*, LW 35:86–87; Luther, *Babylonian Captivity*, LW 36:29–34.

30. Luther, *Blessed Sacrament*, LW 35:60–61; Luther, *Holy Mass*, LW 35:86–87; Luther, *Babylonian Captivity*, LW 36:29, 33–34. See Hermann Sasse, *This Is My Body: Luther's Contention for the Real Presence in the Sacrament of the Altar* (Minneapolis: Augsburg, 1959), 100.

31. Luther, *Babylonian Captivity*, LW 36:44.

32. I must thank my colleague Aaron Denlinger for this insight.

are the signs of the promise. For many others, the bread and wine are the signs of the body and blood of Christ.

In December 1521, Philipp Melanchthon, Luther's most devoted disciple and colleague, published the first edition of his *Loci Communes*.[33] This work is a basic summary of Luther's theology. Luther himself praised the book as "worthy not only of immortality but also of the Church's canon."[34] Like Luther, Melanchthon emphasized the promissory nature of the sacraments. In Scripture, "signs are added to the promises as seals, both to remind us of the promises and to serve as sure testimonies of God's goodwill toward us, confirming that we will certainly receive what God has promised."[35] The Supper is certainly not a sacrifice, as Rome teaches. Instead, it is a "testimony of the promised Gospel."[36] Regarding the true presence of Christ's body and blood, Melanchthon assumed Luther's doctrine without elaboration.[37] Finally, Melanchthon noted that the purpose of this sacrament is "to strengthen us whenever our consciences waver and we doubt God's goodwill toward us."[38]

Andreas Karlstadt was another of Luther's colleagues at Wittenberg. His doctrine of the Supper, like that of many of the other Reformers, developed over time.[39] In his earliest writings, he expressed views that were virtually indistinguishable from those of Luther.[40] He too emphasized the nature of the sacrament as a testament or promise. He too affirmed the true presence of the body and blood of Christ in the bread and wine. He too affirmed that the key distinction in the sacrament is between the word/promise of God and the sign (the body and blood of Christ in the bread and wine).[41] Karlstadt's doctrine of the Supper, however, soon underwent a radical transformation.

By 1521, at the latest, the Wittenberg Reformers were already

---

33. Philip Melanchthon, *Commonplaces: Loci Communes 1521*, trans. Christian Preus (St. Louis, MO: Concordia, 2014).

34. Martin Luther, *The Bondage of the Will*, LW 33:16.

35. Melanchthon, *Commonplaces*, 167.

36. Ibid., 182.

37. Ibid.

38. Ibid., 183.

39. Karlstadt's Eucharistic works have been translated into English in *The Eucharistic Pamphlets of Andreas Bodenstein von Karlstadt*, trans. and ed. Amy Nelson Burnett, Early Modern Studies 6 (Kirksville, MO: Truman State University Press, 2011).

40. Amy Nelson Burnett, *Karlstadt and the Origins of the Eucharistic Controversy: A Study in the Circulation of Ideas*, Oxford Studies in Historical Theology (Oxford: Oxford University Press, 2011), 23.

41. Karlstadt, *Eucharistic Pamphlets*, 24, 30, 43, 45, 52, 62–63.

aware of interpretations of the Supper that entailed the rejection of the corporeal presence of Christ in the bread and wine.[42] The Dutchman Hinne Rode had carried the writings of Wessel Gansfort and a letter by a lawyer named Cornelius Hoen to Wittenberg sometime in the latter part of 1521.[43] The Wittenberg theologians likely read Hoen's letter at this time. Because of its importance to the subsequent development of the Eucharistic debates, we must briefly examine the background and contents of Hoen's letter.[44]

An encounter with Wessel Gansfort's *The Sacrament of the Eucharist* seems to have inspired Hoen's reinterpretation of the Supper more than any other single event.[45] Hoen made Gansfort's emphasis on spiritual communion central to his own view. Hoen's key exegetical insight was his insistence that Christ's words of institution, "This is my body," should be interpreted as "This *signifies* my body."[46] There is, therefore, no corporeal presence of the body and blood of Christ in the elements of bread and wine. Hinne Rode carried Hoen's letter to Wittenberg in 1521. In January 1523, he traveled to Basel and met with Johannes Oecolampadius, who urged him to share the letter with Huldrych Zwingli. Rode complied. In 1524, he met with Martin Bucer in Strasbourg.[47] Reactions to the letter varied. Luther rejected Hoen's views.[48] Zwingli, on the other hand, was persuaded, and in 1525, he published the letter. Hoen's letter also influenced Karlstadt, and many of Hoen's arguments found their way into his writings, in spite of the fact that Karlstadt rejected Hoen's specific interpretation of the words of institution.

The First Eucharistic Controversy (1524–1536)

If any single event can be considered the starting point of the first Eucharistic controversy, it would be the heated exchange between Luther

---

42. Burnett, *Karlstadt and the Origins*, 56.

43. Ibid., 16, 56. Hoen's letter was probably written early in 1521, but it was not published until 1525.

44. See Bart Jan Spruyt, *Cornelius Henrici Hoen (Honius) and His Epistle on the Eucharist (1525): Medieval Heresy, Erasmian Humanism, and Reform in the Early Sixteenth-Century Low Countries*, Studies in Medieval and Reformation Traditions 119 (Leiden: Brill, 2006).

45. Williams, *Radical Reformation*, 35–36.

46. Cornelisz Hoen, "A Most Christian Letter," in *Forerunners of the Reformation: The Shape of Late Medieval Thought*, ed. Heiko A. Oberman, trans. Paul L. Nyhus, Library of Ecclesiastical History (Cambridge: James Clarke, 1967), 269.

47. Williams, *Radical Reformation*, 86–89.

48. Martin Luther, *The Adoration of the Sacrament* (1523), LW 36:279–80.

and Karlstadt at the Black Bear Inn in Jena on August 22, 1524.[49] Luther had preached in Jena earlier in the day against some of the radical reforms in which Karlstadt was involved. Karlstadt asked to meet with Luther, and at the meeting, on hearing Karlstadt's response to his sermon, Luther threw down the gauntlet and challenged Karlstadt to put his arguments in writing. Karlstadt was more than willing to oblige, and in October he published five separate tracts expressing his new view of the Lord's Supper.[50] Karlstadt was the first of those associated with the Reformation movement to go public with a view of the Lord's Supper that differed significantly from Luther.[51] He would not be the last.

THE POLEMICAL PHASE

In four of his five pamphlets, Karlstadt presented his case for rejecting the corporeal presence of Christ. In the tract *Whether One Can Prove from Holy Scripture That Christ Is in the Sacrament with Body, Blood, and Soul*, he responded to and rejected seven arguments for the corporeal presence of Christ.[52] For example, even if Christ used the words of consecration to change the elements, Karlstadt argued, this does not mean that the priests can do the same by repeating those words. If so, he said, let them read these words: "'God spoke, let there be earth, and it was' [Gen. 1:9]. And see whether through the power of such powerful and holy words they can create heaven and earth, water and fire, fish and animals."[53]

In his next tract, he looked at the words of institution and argued that they nowhere state that the bread *is* the body of Christ.[54] In fact, according to Karlstadt, Greek grammar prohibits such an interpretation. In his *Dialogue*, he put in the mouth of an imaginary layman the idea that Christ was pointing to his own body when he said, "*This is my body.*"[55] This is the idea with which Karlstadt is most com-

---

49. Burnett, *Karlstadt and the Origins*, 3.
50. Ibid. See also Lindberg, *The European Reformations*, 137–38.
51. Bernhard Lohse, *The Theology of Martin Luther: Its Historical and Systematic Development*, trans. Roy A. Harrisville (Minneapolis: Fortress, 1999), 170. Again, Hoen's letter was not published until 1525.
52. Karlstadt, *Eucharistic Pamphlets*, 116–43.
53. Ibid., 123.
54. Ibid., 144–62.
55. Ibid., 175.

monly associated, but it was not his central concern. Karlstadt's central conviction was "that the sacrament was instituted so that Christians would remember Christ's suffering and death as the fulfillment of Old Testament prophecy."[56] Karlstadt's public defense of a symbolic view encouraged others such as Huldrych Zwingli to write.

Early in Zwingli's career as a Reformer, his view had undergone development. He briefly held a view similar to that of Luther. Sometime in 1523 or 1524, however, Zwingli adopted a radically symbolic view.[57] His change of mind seems to have resulted, at least in part, from reading Hoen's letter. The publication of Karlstadt's violently anti-Lutheran pamphlets forced Zwingli to state his own view clearly, distinguishing it from that of Karlstadt. Zwingli wrote his *Letter to Matthew Alber concerning the Lord's Supper* in November 1524. His theological and exegetical starting point in this letter was John 6, and this would remain his starting point in all his subsequent writings on the doctrine of the Eucharist.

Zwingli argued that John 6 provides the theological context in which Christ's words of institution should be interpreted. Jesus presents himself there as the "bread of life" and distinguishes "spiritual food" from bodily food.[58] Christ's words in John 6, therefore, clearly indicate that when Jesus explains to those listening to him the necessity of "eating His flesh," he is really speaking of the necessity of faith. To *eat* Christ is to *believe* in him.[59] If we keep in mind Jesus's words in John 6, interpreting his words of institution becomes much less difficult. Agreeing with Hoen's view instead of Karlstadt's, Zwingli argued that "This is my body" should be interpreted to mean "This signifies my body."[60] The word "is" has to be interpreted as "signifies," or else the sign *is* the thing it signifies and is no longer a sign.[61] Although he would add more arguments to his case in later writings, these basic ideas would characterize Zwingli's teaching until his death.

---

56. Ibid., 3.
57. Carrie Euler, "Huldrych Zwingli and Heinrich Bullinger," in Wandel, *Companion to the Eucharist in the Reformation*, 58–59.
58. Huldrych Zwingli, *Letter to Alber*, in Zwingli, *Writings*, vol. 2, *In Search of True Religion: Reformation, Pastoral, and Eucharistic Writings*, trans. H. Wayne Pipkin (Allison Park, PA: Pickwick, 1984), 132–33.
59. Ibid., 136.
60. Ibid., 138–39.
61. W. P. Stephens, *The Theology of Huldrych Zwingli* (Oxford: Clarendon, 1986), 185.

As he had promised he would, Luther responded to Karlstadt, addressing the issue in his two-part treatise *Against the Heavenly Prophets*, completed in early 1525.[62] In this work, he took aim at Karlstadt's exegesis of the words of institution. He argued that Karlstadt's interpretation had Jesus talking about the bread ("Take, eat"), then suddenly changing the subject to discuss his own body ("This is my body"), and then returning to the subject of the bread again ("Do this in remembrance of me"). This interpretation, according to Luther, was absurd: "How would it sound if I gave someone a piece of bread and said, 'Take and eat,' and as I offered and asked him to eat it, I immediately went on to say, 'This is a pound of gold in my pocket'?"[63] According to Luther, we should not try to explain away Christ's words. We should believe that the bread is Christ's body simply because that is what Jesus says it is. For Luther, the starting point was always the clear declaration of Christ: "This is my body."[64]

Throughout the remainder of 1525, several responses to Luther were written. Zwingli published his *Commentary on True and False Religion* in March. In this work, Zwingli expanded on the basic themes he introduced in his *Letter to Matthew Alber*. The sacraments are nothing more than initiatory ceremonies by which a man pledges himself to be a soldier of Christ.[65] In the Lord's Supper, he argued, "we give proof that we trust in the death of Christ."[66] The starting point for Zwingli was again John 6.[67] He appealed repeatedly to the words of John 6:63 in particular: "The flesh profiteth nothing."[68] These words help us understand what Christ means when he says, "This is my body." According to Zwingli, "This expression ['The flesh profiteth nothing'] is strong enough to prove that 'is' in this passage is used for 'signifies' or 'is a symbol of.'"[69] Karlstadt responded to Luther in two tracts. Appealing to 1 Corinthians 10:3, he again asserted

---

62. Martin Luther, *Against the Heavenly Prophets in the Matter of Images and Sacraments* (1525), *LW* 40:75–143, 144–223.

63. Ibid., *LW* 40:169.

64. Ibid., *LW* 40:216.

65. Huldrych Zwingli, *Commentary on True and False Religion*, ed. Samuel Macauley Jackson and Clarence Nevin Heller (1929; repr., Durham, NC: Labyrinth, 1981), 181, 184.

66. Ibid., 184.

67. Ibid., 200.

68. Ibid., 212, 219, 220, 248. The translation of John 6:63 comes from Zwingli's *Commentary*.

69. Ibid., 231.

that the only way we eat and drink the body and blood of Christ is through faith.[70]

In September 1525, Oecolampadius added his voice with the publication of *On the Genuine Exposition of the Lord's Words*. His work differed from the others in that he focused largely on patristic evidence in order to demonstrate that a symbolic understanding of the Supper should not be considered a heresy. Although his view was, in many ways, similar to Zwingli's, a few of his most significant emphases should be mentioned.[71] Regarding the words of institution, Oecolampadius believed that the figure of speech was found in the predicate ("body") rather than in the verb ("is"). He argued that the phrase should be read, "This is a sign of my body."[72] Second, Oecolampadius suggested that for those who partake of the Supper in faith, they participate in a spiritual eating of Christ that occurs parallel to the eating of the bread. A third important emphasis was his claim that the goal of the Supper is to lift our hearts to Christ, who is seated at the right hand of God.[73] We will encounter these ideas again in the writings of later Reformers.

In August 1525, Zwingli published his *Subsidiary Essay on the Eucharist* in order to flesh out more fully the arguments he had presented in his *Commentary*. The most significant new exegetical argument that Zwingli added was the appeal to Exodus 12:11 to help clarify the words of institution. He explained the parallels between the two passages:

> A commemoration is instituted in the one case and in the other. In the one it is of deliverance in the flesh, in the other of reconciliation unto the Most High God. In the first case the symbol of commemoration was instituted before the thing had been accomplished of which it was to be the symbol in the fleeting ages. So in the other was instituted the symbol of the killing of Christ for us before he was killed, which was yet to be in ensuing time the symbol of his

---

70. Karlstadt, *Eucharistic Pamphlets*, 222–23.
71. For a helpful summary of Oecolampadius's doctrine, see Ian Hazlett, "The Development of Martin Bucer's Thinking on the Sacrament of the Lord's Supper in Its Historical and Theological Context, 1523–1534" (Dr. theol. diss., Universität Münster, 1975), 112–13.
72. Nicholas Piotrowski, "Johannes Oecolampadius: Christology and the Supper," *MAJT* 23 (2012): 134.
73. Hazlett, "Development of Martin Bucer's Thinking," 112–13.

having been killed. There was instituted in the evening the figure of the deliverance which followed on the morrow.[74]

These parallels indicate that the words of Jesus should be interpreted in the same symbolic manner. Zwingli argued that the word "is" in the statement "It is the Lord's Passover" is exactly parallel to the word "is" in the statement "This is my body." In both cases "is" means "signifies."[75]

In March 1526, the Strasbourg pastor and theologian Martin Bucer made his first significant written contribution to the debate with his *Apologia*. Although Bucer held views very similar to those of Luther in the early years of the Reformation, by 1526 he had adopted a view heavily influenced by Hoen, Zwingli, and Oecolampadius, which is represented in the *Apologia*. There he argued that the Supper is a memorial, nothing more than a commemoration of Christ's death.[76] Bucer also introduced an idea in this work that he maintained consistently throughout his career, namely the denial that unbelievers partake of the body and blood of Christ in any sense.[77]

Luther's next contribution sparked a bitter phase of the debate. In his *The Sacrament of the Body and Blood of Christ—Against the Fanatics*, he responded to several arguments made by Karlstadt, Zwingli, and Oecolampadius and advanced several new arguments for his own view. He again asserted that the words of institution are clear: "These are the words on which we take our stand."[78] He then responded to several objections, including the claim that it is unnecessary for Christ's body and blood to be in the bread and wine. He reminded his readers that we do not decide what is necessary; God does.[79]

Luther also provided several analogies to prove that it is possible for Christ to be present in the bread and wine. He argued, for example, that if his own small voice could be present in the ears of many people, then surely Christ's body could be present in many different places.

---

74. Huldrych Zwingli, *Subsidiary Essay*, in *Writings*, 2:212.

75. Ibid., 209–12.

76. Martin Bucer, *Apologia*, in *Common Places of Martin Bucer*, trans. and ed. David F. Wright, Courtenay Library of Reformation Classics 4 (Appleford: Sutton Courtenay, 1972), 319–21.

77. Ibid., 331.

78. Martin Luther, *The Sacrament of the Body and Blood of Christ—Against the Fanatics*, LW 36:335–37.

79. Ibid., LW 36:338–44.

Also, by means of the preaching of the Word, many separate individuals have Christ in their hearts. If Christ can do this through the preaching of the Word, Luther asked, why not also in the promise associated with the bread?[80] Finally, Luther introduced the idea that Christ's body can be present in so many different places because his human nature "is present everywhere."[81] This notion of the ubiquity of Christ would later become a source of controversy between the Lutherans and the Reformed.[82]

Two major works on the Supper, by Zwingli and Luther, appeared simultaneously in February 1527. Zwingli's *Friendly Exegesis, That Is, Exposition of the Matter of the Eucharist to Martin Luther* was his most important book on the subject. He began by answering Luther's arguments and then proceeded to outline all the arguments for his own understanding of Christ's words. His interpretation of the words of institution remained the same as it had been, and he continued to interpret these words in light of John 6. He argued that Luther begged the question by appealing to the words of Christ when it was the meaning of those very words that was under consideration.[83] Luther said that the words of institution are as clear as if one handed another person a roll and said, "Take, eat. This is a roll." Zwingli replied that the analogy would be more relevant to the current debate if Luther gave another person a roll and said, "Take, eat. This is a watermelon."[84]

Zwingli also introduced a Christological argument in favor of his view. The human body of Christ, he argued, is a true human body and therefore finite. The finite human body of Christ is at the right hand of God in heaven until the second coming, according to the ancient creeds. It cannot, therefore, be present in the bread and wine.[85] To claim, as Luther did, that the human body of Christ can be everywhere, leads inevitably to a docetic view of Christ, according to Zwingli.

Luther's book *That These Words of Christ, "This Is My Body,"*

---

80. Ibid., *LW* 36:339–340.
81. Ibid., *LW* 36:342.
82. For Luther's Christological reasoning (i.e., *communicatio idiomatum*), see chap. 9, "The Person of Christ," by Robert Letham.
83. Huldrych Zwingli, *Friendly Exegesis*, in *Writings*, 2:282–83.
84. Ibid., 2:309–10.
85. Ibid., 2:319–36.

Still Stand Firm against the Fanatics was a restatement and defense of his views.[86] He insisted that the whole debate concerned the proper understanding of Christ's words of institution. On this issue, there is no middle ground: "One side must be of the devil, and God's enemy."[87] His opponents, he argued, cannot prove that "body" means "sign of the body" or that "is" means "signifies" in Christ's words of institution.[88] He also rejected Zwingli's Christological argument, claiming that the right hand of God is not a place but the power of God. The right hand of God is everywhere, and where the right hand of God is, there is Christ's body as well.[89]

Luther's last major work on the Supper was his *Confession concerning Christ's Supper*, published in February 1528. In it, Luther restated all the arguments for his view again, emphasizing the words of institution. He also attempted to clarify his view in light of the criticisms he had received. One of the most significant points he made was to state that Christ is not present in the Lord's Supper "in a visible, mortal, and earthly mode."[90] In order to explain what he meant, he introduced the scholastic distinction between local, definitive, and repletive presence. Something is present locally if it can be measured spatially. Christ's body can be present in this way as it has been in the past and will be on the last day. Definitive presence is not measurable spatially. Angels and human souls are present definitively. This is also the manner in which Christ's body was present during the brief period of time during which he passed through the stone covering his tomb. This, according to Luther, is the manner in which Christ is substantially present in the bread and wine. Repletive presence is a kind of presence that is true only of God. It is omnipresence. According to Luther, it is possible for the body of Christ to be present in this way by virtue of the unity of the two natures in the one person.[91]

In order to explain how the substance of bread and the substance of the body of Christ can be spoken of as one object, Luther also

86. Martin Luther, *That These Words of Christ, "This Is My Body," Still Stand Firm against the Fanatics*, LW 37:3–150.
87. Ibid., LW 37:26.
88. Ibid., LW 37:35.
89. Ibid., LW 37:57, 63–64.
90. Martin Luther, *Confession concerning Christ's Supper*, LW 37:197.
91. Ibid., LW 37:207–16.

elaborated on his idea of sacramental union (*unio sacramentalis*).[92] Although two different substances cannot be one substance, Christ's words "This is my body" speak of the two as one.[93] The bread is present and the body is present in this one sacrament, and this is rightly termed a sacramental union. Because of the sacramental union, what is done to the bread is rightly attributed to the body of Christ. If one eats the bread, he eats Christ's body but not in the same way he would eat any other kind of flesh.[94]

Although the *Confession concerning Christ's Supper* was Luther's last major contribution to the polemical phase of the controversy, it was not the last thing he wrote on the subject. In 1529, he wrote his Small Catechism and his Large Catechism. Both discuss the "Sacrament of the Altar," which he defined in the Small Catechism as "the true body and blood of our Lord Jesus Christ, under the bread and wine, given to us Christians to eat and to drink."[95] The benefit of the sacrament is found in the words "for you" and "for the forgiveness of sins."[96] The words of promise when accompanied by eating and drinking "are the chief things in the sacrament, and he who believes these words has what they say and declare: the forgiveness of sins."[97]

THE (MOSTLY) CONCILIATORY PHASE

A turning point in the first Eucharistic controversy was reached in 1529 at the Colloquy of Marburg. Martin Bucer had become convinced after reading Luther's *Confession concerning Christ's Supper* that some type of accord was possible. He spent the next several years working toward this goal.[98] Because of his efforts, Luther and Melanchthon met with Zwingli, Oecolampadius, and Bucer himself at Marburg in October 1529. Discussions took place over four days, and while they reached consensus on a number of issues, the participants could not

---

92. According to Bernhard Lohse, this idea describes Luther's view better than the word *consubstantiation*. See Lohse, *Theology of Martin Luther*, 309.
93. Luther, *Confession concerning Christ's Supper*, LW 37:295.
94. Ibid., LW 37:300.
95. "The Small Catechism," art. 6.2, in Theodore G. Tappert, ed. and trans., *The Book of Concord: The Confessions of the Evangelical Lutheran Church* (Philadelphia: Fortress, 1959), 351.
96. Ibid., 6.6, in Tappert, *Book of Concord*, 352.
97. Ibid., 6.8, in Tappert, *Book of Concord*, 352.
98. David F. Wright, "Martin Bucer (1491–1551): Ecumenical Theologian," in Wright, *Common Places of Martin Bucer*, 33–34.

agree on the manner of Christ's presence in the Lord's Supper.[99] Luther composed fifteen articles. Both sides were able to agree on fourteen of them, but article fifteen indicated that there were still areas of deep disagreement:

> We all believe and hold concerning the supper of our dear Lord Jesus Christ . . . that the sacrament of the altar is a sacrament of the true body and blood of Jesus Christ, and that the spiritual partaking of this body and blood is especially necessary for every true Christian. . . . And although at present we are not agreed as to whether the true body and blood are bodily present in the bread and wine, nevertheless each party should show Christian love to the other, so far as conscience can permit, and both should fervently pray Almighty God that he, by his Spirit, would confirm us in the right understanding. Amen.[100]

These fifteen articles were signed by all present, including Luther and Zwingli. The failure to reach a complete accord at Marburg was a setback, but it did not prevent Bucer from continuing to work toward that goal.

In 1530, the Holy Roman emperor, Charles V, announced the Diet of Augsburg. He demanded that the Reformers explain themselves, which generated a flurry of activity among the various Protestant cities. On June 25, Melanchthon submitted the Augsburg Confession on behalf of the Lutherans. On July 8, Zwingli submitted his *Fidei Ratio* in defense of his view. And on July 11, those South German cities aligned with Strasbourg submitted the Tetrapolitan Confession, written by Bucer and Wolfgang Capito.

Article 10 of the Augsburg Confession on the Lord's Supper is very brief. It presents the heart of Luther's view of Christ's presence in the Supper: "It is taught among us that the true body and blood of Christ are really present in the Supper of our Lord under the form of bread and wine and are there distributed and received." The confession does not attempt to explain how Christ is present. The article on the Sup-

---

99. On the history of the Marburg Colloquy, see Sasse, *This Is My Body*, 187–294.
100. Jaroslav Pelikan, *Credo: Historical and Theological Guide to Creeds and Confessions of Faith in the Christian Tradition* (New Haven, CT: Yale University Press, 2003), 213.

per in Bucer's Tetrapolitan Confession is longer but not much more detailed, simply affirming that

> to all those who sincerely have given their names among His disciples and receive this Supper according to His institution, He deigns to give His true body and true blood to be truly eaten and drunk for the food and drink of souls, for their nourishment unto life eternal, so that now He may live and abide in them, and they in Him, to be raised up by Him at the last day to new and immortal life.

The confession also rejects the idea "that nothing save mere bread and mere wine is administered in our Supper."[101] Zwingli's *Fidei Ratio* reaffirmed the doctrine that he had taught in all his previous writings: the body of Christ is present only "by the contemplation of faith"—there is no real presence.[102]

Although the emperor refused to present the latter two confessions to the Diet, he did ask the Catholic theologians to refute all of them. The Roman Catholic emperor was not persuaded to accommodate the Protestants, and on September 22, he ordered them to return to the Catholic faith by April 15, 1531. The Reformation had reached a critical stage. Many now considered an agreement on the Supper to be necessary for survival. Bucer intensified his attempts at reaching concord, meeting with many, including Melanchthon, Luther, and Zwingli. By this point in time, because Bucer had moved away from Zwingli's view, Melanchthon and Luther were becoming much more receptive to his proposals.[103]

In February 1531, a Protestant defensive league was formed. Membership in the Schmalkaldic League originally required subscription to the Augsburg Confession, although for a brief period of time subscription to the Tetrapolitan Confession was allowed as well. Bucer's own city of Strasbourg, therefore, was able to join this defensive League, which was composed largely of Lutheran cities, but he was unable to convince the Swiss to join. By this time, Zwingli had become frustrated

---

101. This translation is found in James T. Dennison Jr., ed., *Reformed Confessions of the 16th and 17th Centuries in English Translation* (Grand Rapids, MI: Reformation Heritage Books, 2008), 1:159.

102. Ibid., 1:126.

103. Martin Greschat, *Martin Bucer: A Reformer and His Times*, trans. Stephen E. Buckwalter (Louisville: Westminster John Knox, 2004), 96–97.

with Bucer, believing him to have made too many concessions to Luther. At the second meeting of the Schmalkaldic League in March and April 1531, many of the Lutherans demanded that membership be conditioned on acceptance of the Augsburg Confession alone. Those Swiss loyal to Zwingli were becoming more isolated. On October 11, at the second Battle of Kappel, Swiss Catholics attacked and defeated Zurich's armies. Zwingli was killed in the battle.[104] One month later, on November 24, Oecolampadius died of the plague. The two most powerful representatives of the symbolic view of the Supper were now silenced.

Political events moved rapidly, and Bucer continued to work tirelessly in his attempts to reach an agreement among the Protestants. His encounters with Anabaptist views of the Supper had awakened him to the dangers of an overly symbolic view, and his doctrine of the Lord's Supper had developed in a direction closer to that of Luther and Melanchthon.[105] Bucer wrote three of his most important works on the Supper during this period. In 1532, he penned his Schweinfurt Confession, which Ian Hazlett calls "one of the finest and most coherent summary-accounts that Bucer ever wrote on the subject."[106] In 1534, he wrote his *Report from Holy Scripture* and his *Defense against the Catholic Axiom*. These works gained him a hearing among the Lutherans.

Because of Bucer's ongoing attempts to reach some type of consensus among the Protestants, he has sometimes been accused of duplicity. However, as Nicholas Thompson observes, "We have to remember that he worked and wrote as confessional boundaries were *beginning* to harden."[107] He did not take Protestant division for granted as we do today. His unique theology of the Supper, occupying a mediating position between Luther and Zwingli, is significant in its own right and is characterized by several features. First, Bucer

---

104. Ibid., 97–98.
105. Hazlett, "Development of Martin Bucer's Thinking," 197–98. There is no single "Anabaptist" doctrine of the Eucharist. Instead, there are as many Anabaptist doctrines of the Eucharist as there are Anabaptists. See John D. Rempel, *The Lord's Supper in Anabaptism: A Study in the Christology of Balthasar Hubmaier, Pilgram Marpeck, and Dirk Philips*, Studies in Anabaptist and Mennonite History 33 (Waterloo, ON: Herald, 1993); Rempel, "Anabaptist Theologies of the Eucharist," in Wandel, *A Companion to the Eucharist*, 115–37.
106. Hazlett, "Development of Martin Bucer's Thinking," 366.
107. Nicholas Thompson, "Martin Bucer," in Wandel, *A Companion to the Eucharist*, 95.

borrowed Luther's concept of sacramental union without adopting Luther's full explanation of it. This concept allowed Bucer to focus on the relationship between the Supper and union with Christ.[108] Bucer also spoke repeatedly of the "presentation" (*exhibitio*) of the body and blood of Christ with the bread and wine. With his use of this word, he intended "the actual delivery of Christ to the believing communicant, and not merely the representative value of the bread and wine."[109]

Of central importance to Bucer's doctrine of the Supper was the idea that there is a "temporal conjunction" between the earthly signs and actions and the heavenly realities they signified. At the same time that the believer eats the bread and wine, he partakes of the body and blood of Christ in the heavenly dimension.[110] It is possible that Bucer may have been influenced by Oecolampadius, who had also spoken of a parallelism between physical eating and spiritual eating in the sacrament. Regardless of his source, this idea helps us understand what he meant when he asserted that the body and blood of Christ are together "with" the bread and wine. Bucer insisted on using the word "with" because it allowed him to assert that when the bread is eaten, the body of Christ is eaten without affirming the local inclusion of the body of Christ in the bread itself.[111] This dualistic parallelism and resultant "double eating" was central to Bucer's Eucharistic theology.[112]

Bucer's tireless efforts to reach an agreement paid off in October 1535 when Luther finally suggested that all sides meet in the city of Eisenach to discuss their doctrinal differences, particularly in regard to the Lord's Supper.[113] However, despite Bucer's best efforts to convince them to come, the Swiss chose not to attend. Bucer had hoped for more from them given that the First Helvetic Confession—published in February 1536 and heavily influenced by his own involvement in its composition—had affirmed in article 21 that the sacraments are "not bare signs." This Swiss confession even went so far as to say that "as

---

108. Wright, "Martin Bucer (1491–1551)," 35.
109. Ibid.
110. Ibid.
111. Jensen, "Luther and the Lord's Supper," 328–29.
112. Hazlett, "Development of Martin Bucer's Thinking," 187–88.
113. Greschat, *Martin Bucer*, 135–36.

the signs are received through the mouth of the body, so the spiritual things [are received] by faith."[114] In spite of what Bucer saw as a real opportunity, the Swiss could not be persuaded.

Because Luther was ill at the time the meeting was to take place, the South German delegates traveled to Wittenberg, arriving on May 21, 1536.[115] Luther opened the meeting by interrogating his guests about their doctrine. When the meeting continued the next day, the discussion centered on the question of whether unbelievers receive the body of Christ in the Supper. Luther affirmed this, and Bucer denied it. One of the Lutheran delegates found a solution by suggesting a distinction Bucer himself had used in the past. The participants were able to agree that the "unworthy" (imperfect Christians) partake of Christ, but they left unanswered the question of unbelievers.[116] Finally, an agreement was reached. Luther publicly acknowledged their fellowship as Christian brothers, and Melanchthon put the agreement into writing.

The Wittenberg Concord of 1536 was a remarkable achievement given the vitriolic nature of the debate in the preceding years. It was a testimony to Bucer's perseverance. The Lutherans based the accord on the understanding that the South Germans believed that "with the bread and wine the body and blood of Christ are truly and substantially present, offered and received."[117] Furthermore, the Concord stated that although the South Germans did not believe that the body of Christ was locally included in the bread, they affirmed that "by the sacramental union, the bread is the body of Christ; that is, they hold that when the bread is held out the body of Christ is at the same time present and truly tendered."[118] After the Concord was signed, Luther encouraged Bucer to continue his attempts to reach accord with the Swiss and to do so on the basis of the Wittenberg Concord, but the Swiss never formally accepted or rejected it.[119]

---

114. Dennison, *Reformed Confessions*, 1:349.
115. Greschat, *Martin Bucer*, 137.
116. Ibid., 137–38.
117. CCFCT 2:799.
118. Ibid.
119. Greschat, *Martin Bucer*, 139–42; see also Gordon A. Jensen, "Luther and Bucer on the Lord's Supper," *LQ* 27 (2013): 167–87. I would like to thank Robert Kolb for bringing this article to my attention.

Cease-Fire on the Lord's Supper (1536–1549)

The Wittenberg Concord marked the end of the first Eucharistic controversy. Representatives of the various views continued to write on the subject, but compared to the previous decade, the next thirteen years were marked by relative calm. The most important development related to the doctrine of the Lord's Supper to occur during these years was the arrival on the scene of the young French theologian John Calvin. As is true with almost every other Protestant during this period, Calvin's understanding of the Lord's Supper showed a degree of development. His works dating from his first stay in Geneva (1536–1538), including the first edition of his *Institutes*, reveal a distinctively symbolic emphasis. His older colleague, the Genevan Reformer William Farel, had also adopted a more symbolic view of the Supper, but it appears that the two reached a similar point of view separately.[120]

In the spring of 1538, Calvin and Farel were driven out of Geneva. Calvin eventually settled in Strasbourg, where he worked alongside Martin Bucer. As Bruce Gordon observes, "The Zwinglian influences detectable in the 1536 *Institutes* evaporated during Calvin's stay in Strasbourg between 1538 and 1541."[121] This was largely the result of Bucer's influence on his younger colleague.[122] With regard to the doctrine of the Supper, Calvin followed largely in Bucer's footsteps.[123]

---

120. See Farel's *Summary* (1529), in Dennison, *Reformed Confessions*, 1:51–111; cf. also Bruce Gordon, *Calvin* (New Haven, CT: Yale University Press, 2009), 70.

121. Gordon, *Calvin*, 167.

122. Bucer not only influenced Calvin's theological understanding but also inspired Calvin with his ongoing efforts to unite the German and the Swiss Protestants. See David C. Steinmetz, *Calvin in Context* (New York: Oxford University Press, 1995), 172; see also Joseph N. Tylenda, "The Ecumenical Intention of Calvin's Early Eucharistic Teaching," in *Reformatio Perennis: Essays on Calvin and the Reformation in Honor of Ford Lewis Battles*, ed. B. A. Gerrish (Pittsburgh: Pickwick, 1981), 27–28.

123. Melanchthon's influence is also detectible, and some even suggest that he was a stronger influence than Bucer. See Richard A. Muller, "From Zurich or from Wittenberg? An Examination of Calvin's Early Eucharistic Thought," *CTJ* 45, no. 2 (2010): 255. Muller argues that Calvin often used the language of Melanchthon's 1531 Apology of the Augsburg Confession and the Wittenberg Concord. Melanchthon and Bucer had been involved in numerous theological discussions in the years leading up to the Wittenberg Concord and had mutually influenced each other's thought. It is no surprise, therefore, to find Melanchthon's influence in Calvin's work on the Lord's Supper, whether we consider that influence to be direct or indirect. It is worth noting, however, that Calvin also influenced Melanchthon's views. See, for example, Wim Janse, "Calvin's Doctrine of the Lord's Supper," *Perichoresis* 10, no. 2 (2012): 146–47. For more on the Calvin-Melanchthon relationship, see Timothy Wengert, "'We Will Feast Together in Heaven Forever': The Epistolary Friendship of John Calvin and Philip Melanchthon," in *Melanchthon in Europe: His Work and Influence beyond Wittenberg*, ed. Karin Maag, Texts and Studies in Reformation and Post-Reformation Thought (Grand Rapids, MI: Baker, 1999), 19–44.

By 1541, when Calvin returned to Geneva, his doctrine of the Supper was basically settled. He continued to clarify and explain it for the remainder of his life, but the doctrine remained substantially the same.[124]

Like Bucer, Calvin directly associated his doctrine of the Supper with his doctrine of union with Christ.[125] Calvin, however, conceived of three types of union with Christ. This threefold union can be inferred in many of his writings, but it is most clearly explained in his 1555 correspondence with Peter Martyr Vermigli.[126] In this correspondence, Calvin described what Duncan Rankin terms an incarnational union, a mystical union, and a spiritual union.[127] The incarnational union is the unique union between the divine nature and the human nature in the one person of Jesus Christ. The mystical union is the once-for-all union with Christ that occurs when believers are regenerated and engrafted into his body. The spiritual union is the effect and fruit of the mystical union. It is an ongoing and progressive union. It can grow and be strengthened throughout the believer's life.[128] Calvin explicitly associated this third type of union with the Lord's Supper, which is given to nourish us and strengthen our mystical union with Christ.

Regarding Christ's words of institution, Calvin argued that the words "This is my body" should be understood figuratively. The name of the reality is here given to the sign.[129] Therefore, Christians must *distinguish* the sign from the reality. But the sign, although distinguished from the reality, must never be separated from it. The sign and the reality are connected. Calvin wrote, "It is regarded by me as beyond all controversy, that the reality is here conjoined with the sign."[130] Calvin,

---

124. To suggest that his view continued to undergo substantive change, as some have argued, seems to be overstating the case. The strongest argument for substantive development and change has been made by Thomas J. Davis in *The Clearest Promises of God: The Development of Calvin's Eucharistic Teaching*, AMS Studies in Religious Tradition 1 (New York: AMS, 1995); cf. also Wim Janse, "Calvin's Eucharistic Theology: Three Dogma-Historical Observations," in *Calvinus Sacrarum Literarum Interpres: Papers of the International Congress on Calvin Research*, ed. Herman J. Selderhuis (Göttingen: Vandenhoeck & Ruprecht, 2008), 39.

125. See B. A. Gerrish, *Grace and Gratitude: The Eucharistic Theology of John Calvin* (Minneapolis: Augsburg Fortress, 1993), 133.

126. An English translation of the relevant portion of Calvin's letter is found in Theodore Beza, *The Life of John Calvin*, trans. Francis Sibson (Philadelphia: J. Whetham, 1836), 309–11.

127. W. Duncan Rankin, "Calvin's Correspondence on Our Threefold Union with Christ," in *The Hope Fulfilled: Essays in Honor of O. Palmer Robertson*, ed. Robert L. Penny (Phillipsburg, NJ: P&R, 2008), 250.

128. "Letter to Peter Martyr," in Beza, *Life of John Calvin*, 311.

129. Calvin, *Institutes*, 4.17.20–25.

130. Calvin, *Calvin's Commentaries*, vol. 20, *Commentary on the Epistles of Paul the Apostle to the Corinthians*, ed. John Pringle (Grand Rapids, MI: Baker, 2003), 378 (1 Cor. 11:24).

following Bucer, also saw a parallelism between the earthly sacramental action and the corresponding heavenly action. As he explained, "Now if it is true that the visible sign is offered to us to seal the gift of the invisible thing, we must have this indubitable confidence that, in taking the sign of the body, we likewise receive the body."[131]

What this means, according to Calvin, is that believers actually partake of Christ's body: "To have our life in Christ our souls should be fed on his body and his blood, as their proper food."[132] Christ is the One to whom we are united and thus the object of our partaking. But what does it actually mean to partake of Christ's body? According to Calvin, "We eat [Christ's] flesh, when, by means of it, we receive life."[133] The Supper, then, is associated with our spiritual union with Christ because by means of it, believers who are already engrafted into Christ "grow more and more together with him, until he perfectly joins us with him in the heavenly life."[134] Thus, according to Calvin, we partake of (i.e., are united to and receive life from) the true body of Christ. Calvin's view, like Bucer's, must therefore be distinguished from both Luther's view and Zwingli's view.[135]

During these same years of relative peace, Zwingli's younger colleague Heinrich Bullinger continued to defend his deceased mentor's

---

131. John Calvin, *Institutes of the Christian Religion: 1541 French Edition*, trans. Elsie Anne McKee (Grand Rapids, MI: Eerdmans, 2009), 557.

132. John Calvin, "Short Treatise on the Supper of Our Lord," in *Calvin: Theological Treatises*, ed. J. K. S. Reid, LCC 22 (Louisville: Westminster John Knox, 2006), 2:147.

133. Calvin, *Calvin's Commentaries*, vol. 17, *Commentary on a Harmony of the Evangelists, Matthew, Mark, and Luke*, ed. William Pringle (Grand Rapids, MI: Baker, 1996), 210 (Matt. 26:26).

134. Calvin, *Institutes*, 4.17.33.

135. For a more complete discussion of Calvin's view of the sacraments in general and the Lord's Supper in particular, see my chapter in *John Calvin: For a New Reformation*, ed. Derek Thomas and John Tweeddale (Wheaton, IL: Crossway, forthcoming). Calvin's doctrine of the Lord's Supper has occasionally been the source of controversy within the Reformed churches. A significant debate between Charles Hodge and John Williamson Nevin occurred in the middle of the nineteenth century. Nevin had written a book titled *The Mystical Presence*, in which he lamented the fact that most Reformed churches of his day had adopted a view of the Supper that was more Zwinglian than Calvinist. Hodge responded by arguing that aspects of Calvin's doctrine were foreign elements in the system of Reformed theology. I have discussed this debate at some length in my book *Given for You: Reclaiming Calvin's Doctrine of the Lord's Supper* (Phillipsburg, NJ: P&R, 2002), 136–56. I believe that Nevin had a better grasp of Calvin's doctrine, but it should be observed that he read Calvin through German idealist lenses and that that affected his interpretation. Hodge appears to have misunderstood Calvin almost completely. All the primary sources in this debate have recently been republished in the Mercersburg Theology Study Series, edited by W. Bradford Littlejohn. See John Williamson Nevin, *The Mystical Presence and the Doctrine of the Reformed Church on the Lord's Supper*, ed. Linden J. DeBie, Mercersburg Theology Study Series 1 (Eugene, OR: Wipf & Stock, 2012), and John Williamson Nevin and Charles Hodge, *Coena Mystica: Debating Reformed Eucharistic Theology*, ed. Linden J. DeBie, Mercersburg Theology Study Series 2 (Eugene, OR: Wipf & Stock, 2013).

doctrine, but he also moved beyond it. One of the most extensive presentations of his views is found in his *Decades*, sermons published between 1549 and 1551 as the second Eucharistic controversy was heating up. In the *Decades*, Bullinger held forth a modified Zwinglian understanding of the Supper. He defined sacraments as "witnesses and seals of the preaching of the Gospel."[136] Echoing Zwingli, Bullinger argued that the sign and the thing signified are joined together "by faithful contemplation." This meant that "the faithful have *in themselves* both twain coupled together, which otherwise in the sign or with the sign are *knit together with no bond*."[137] The signs direct our eyes to spiritual things, but the signs are not connected with those things. His explanation of the Lord's Supper therefore echoed Zwingli's in many of its essential features.[138]

The Second Eucharistic Controversy (1549–1561)

The second Eucharistic controversy was ignited in 1549 when Calvin and Bullinger worked out a consensus statement on the Lord's Supper known as the Zurich Consensus (or Consensus Tigurinus).[139] After the signing of the Wittenberg Concord in 1536, Luther had encouraged Bucer to continue his attempts to reach agreement with the Swiss. Calvin shared Bucer's desire to reach agreement, and after much correspondence and often heated debate, he and Bullinger were able to agree on the Zurich Consensus.[140]

The Zurich Consensus represents the theology of neither Bullinger nor Calvin completely. Each made concessions in order to produce a formulation both sides could sign.[141] Calvin was apparently willing to omit certain phrases that he used everywhere else, but he was not entirely pleased with the result. In a letter to Bucer about the Consensus, he said, "Indeed it was not my fault that these items were not fuller.

136. Heinrich Bullinger, *The Decades of Heinrich Bullinger*, ed. Thomas Harding (1849–1852; repr., Grand Rapids, MI: Reformation Heritage Books, 2004), 2:234.

137. Ibid., 2:279, italics added.

138. Ibid., 2:401–78.

139. For the text, see CCFCT 2:802–15.

140. Paul Rorem, *Calvin and Bullinger on the Lord's Supper* (Nottingham: Grove Books, 1989).

141. Paul Rorem, "The Consensus Tigurinus (1549): Did Calvin Compromise?," in *Calvinus Sacrae Scripturae Professor: Calvin as Confessor of Holy Scripture; Die Referate Des Congrès International Des Recherches Calviniennes Vom 20. Bis 23. August 1990 in Grand Rapids*, ed. Wilhelm H. Neuser (Grand Rapids, MI: Eerdmans, 1994), 90.

Let us therefore bear with a sigh that which cannot be corrected."[142] Despite his disappointment with its final form, Calvin would defend the Consensus in the coming years by interpreting it along the lines of his own doctrine of the Supper. He was forced to defend it because its publication ignited a second Eucharistic controversy. Calvin's willingness to omit certain phrases enabled the Swiss to sign it, but the Lutherans interpreted the agreement as a wholesale capitulation to Zwinglianism.

Joachim Westphal, the Lutheran pastor at Hamburg, fired the first shots with three books published between 1552 and 1555. In these books, he defended a hard-line version of Luther's doctrine. Lutherans such as Melanchthon who had adopted a modified version of Luther's doctrine were not always pleased with Westphal's language. Calvin finally responded with his *Defense of the Sound and Orthodox Doctrine of the Sacraments* (1555).[143] Westphal and Calvin continued to exchange fire over the next few years. Other Lutheran and Reformed theologians contributed to the debate as well. Calvin contributed his final work on the subject when he responded to the criticisms of the Lutheran Tileman Heshusius in 1561.[144] By the time this controversy settled down, any hope for reconciliation between the Lutherans and the Reformed on the doctrine of the Supper had all but vanished.

Consolidation and Confessions

The confessions of the churches helped to consolidate the various Eucharistic doctrines that had been developed in the first half of the sixteenth century. At the Council of Trent (1545–1563), the Roman Catholic Church responded to the criticisms of the Protestants and restated its own position, defending transubstantiation, the adoration

---

142. Cited in Rorem, *Calvin and Bullinger on the Lord's Supper*, 49.

143. See Joseph N. Tylenda, "The Calvin-Westphal Exchange: The Genesis of Calvin's Treatises against Westphal," *CTJ* 9, no. 2 (1974): 182–209; Steinmetz, *Calvin in Context*, 172–83; Wim Janse, "Joachim Westphal's Sacramentology," *LQ* 22, no. 2 (2008): 137–60; Esther Chung-Kim, "Use of the Fathers in the Eucharistic Debates between John Calvin and Joachim Westphal," *Reformation* 14, no. 1 (2009): 101–25.

144. Calvin's contributions to this debate are found in *Tracts, Part 2*, vol. 2 of *John Calvin: Tracts and Letters*, ed. Henry Beveridge and Jules Bonnet, trans. Henry Beveridge (1849; repr., Edinburgh: Banner of Truth, 2009).

of the host, and the doctrine of the sacrifice of the Mass.[145] Solemn anathemas were declared against those who denied the Roman Catholic doctrine of the Supper.

The sixteenth-century Reformed confessions reflect the range of views found among theologians of that time. As B. A. Gerrish observes, some reflect Bullinger's modified Zwinglian views. Still others teach a view consistent with the teachings of Bucer and Calvin.[146] For example, the 1559 French Confession, the 1560 Scots Confession, and the 1561 Belgic Confession are Bucerian and Calvinistic in their language about the Supper. The 1566 Second Helvetic Confession, on the other hand, reflects the Eucharistic doctrine of its author, Heinrich Bullinger. However, by the time Bullinger completed this confession, a Calvinistic influence had become detectible. We see hints of this influence when we read the following words in chapter 21 of the confession: "Therefore, the faithful receive that which is given by the minister of the Lord and eat the bread of the Lord, and drink of the Lord's cup. But yet, by the working of Christ, through the Holy Ghost, they receive also the flesh and blood of the Lord and feed on them to life everlasting."[147]

The confessional standards of the Lutheran churches are contained in the Book of Concord (1580). This work was compiled in order to end internal debates that were troubling the Lutheran churches. In addition to the Apostles' Creed, the Nicene Creed, and the Athanasian Creed, the Book of Concord also contains the Augsburg Confession as well as Melanchthon's Apology of the Augsburg Confession (a defense against condemnations made by Rome) and his *Treatise on the Power and Primacy of the Pope*. It contains Luther's Small and Large Catechisms as well as his Smalcald Articles (1536). Finally, it contains the Formula of Concord (1577), a restatement and explanation of certain doctrines that had become a source of disagreement among Lutherans. The Book of Concord adopts Luther's doctrine of the Supper and takes a strong stand against both the Eucharistic doctrine of Rome and the various views held by those in the Reformed churches.

---

145. The thirteenth session (1551) dealt with the sacrament of the Eucharist, and the twenty-second session (1562) dealt with the sacrifice of the Mass. See H. J. Schroeder, ed. and trans., *The Canons and Decrees of the Council of Trent* (Charlotte, NC: Tan Books, 1978), 72–80, 146–54.

146. B. A. Gerrish, *The Old Protestantism and the New: Essays on the Reformation Heritage* (Edinburgh: T&T Clark, 1982), 118–30.

147. This translation is found in Dennison, *Reformed Confessions*, 2:866.

Conclusion

There is something inherently tragic about the fact that the sacrament Calvin spoke of as a "bond of love" became the source of so much strife and division in the church.[148] There was a reason that Bucer, Melanchthon, Calvin, and others worked so hard in an attempt to reach consensus. That they failed does not mean that their efforts were misguided. It does not seem likely today that the disagreements will be resolved until Christ returns and all who trust him sit down at one table and feast together. However, even if resolution is not humanly possible, perhaps a better understanding of the factors that led to the division is possible, and my hope is that this discussion has contributed in some small way toward that goal.

Resources for Further Study

PRIMARY SOURCES

Bucer, Martin. *Apologia*. In *Common Places of Martin Bucer*, translated and edited by David F. Wright, 313–53. Courtenay Library of Reformation Classics 4. Appleford: Sutton Courtenay, 1972.[149]

Calvin, John. *Institutes of the Christian Religion*. Edited by John T. McNeill. Translated by Ford Lewis Battles. 2 vols. Library of Christian Classics 20–21. 1559 edition. Philadelphia: Westminster, 1960.

———. "Short Treatise on the Supper of Our Lord." In *Calvin: Theological Treatises*, edited by J. K. S. Reid, 142–66. Library of Christian Classics 22. Louisville: Westminster John Knox, 2006.

Hoen, Cornelisz. "A Most Christian Letter." In *Forerunners of the Reformation: The Shape of Late Medieval Thought*, edited by Heiko Oberman and translated by Paul L. Nyhus, 268–78. Library of Ecclesiastical History. Cambridge: James Clarke, 1967.

Karlstadt, Andreas Bodenstein von. *The Eucharistic Pamphlets of Andreas Bodenstein von Karlstadt*. Translated and edited by Amy Nelson Burnett. Early Modern Studies 6. Kirksville, MO: Truman State University Press, 2011.

---

148. Calvin, *Institutes*, 4.17.38.
149. Many of Bucer's Eucharistic works are in the process of being translated into English for the first time as part of the forthcoming Bucer in English Translation series by Truman State University Press.

Luther, Martin. "Confession concerning Christ's Supper." In *Luther's Works*. Vol. 37, *Word and Sacrament III*, edited by Robert H. Fischer, 151–372. Philadelphia: Fortress, 1961.

Schroeder, H. J., ed. and trans. *The Canons and Decrees of the Council of Trent*. Charlotte, NC: Tan Books, 1978.

Tappert, Theodore G., ed. and trans. *The Book of Concord: The Confessions of the Evangelical Lutheran Church*. Philadelphia: Fortress, 1959.

Zwingli, Huldrych. *Commentary on True and False Religion*. Edited by Samuel Macauley Jackson and Clarence Nevin Heller. 1929. Reprint, Durham, NC: Labyrinth, 1981.

———. *Writings*. Vol. 2, *In Search of True Religion: Reformation, Pastoral, and Eucharistic Writings*. Translated by H. Wayne Pipkin. Allison Park, PA: Pickwick, 1984.

SECONDARY SOURCES

Burnett, Amy Nelson. *Karlstadt and the Origins of the Eucharistic Controversy: A Study in the Circulation of Ideas*. Oxford Studies in Historical Theology. Oxford: Oxford University Press, 2011.

Davis, Thomas J. *The Clearest Promises of God: The Development of Calvin's Eucharistic Teaching*. AMS Studies in Religious Tradition 1. New York: AMS, 1995.

———. *This Is My Body: The Presence of Christ in Reformation Thought*. Grand Rapids, MI: Baker Academic, 2008.

Gerrish, B. A. *Grace and Gratitude: The Eucharistic Theology of John Calvin*. Minneapolis: Augsburg Fortress, 1993.

Janse, Wim. "Calvin's Eucharistic Theology: Three Dogma-Historical Observations." In *Calvinus Sacrarum Literarum Interpres: Papers of the International Congress on Calvin Research*, edited by Herman J. Selderhuis, 37–69. Göttingen: Vandenhoeck & Ruprecht, 2008.

Jensen, Gordon A. "Luther and the Lord's Supper." In *The Oxford Handbook of Martin Luther's Theology*, ed. by Robert Kolb, Irene Dingel, and L'ubomír Batka, 322–32. Oxford: Oxford University Press, 2014.

McDonnell, Kilian. *John Calvin, the Church, and the Eucharist*. Princeton, NJ: Princeton University Press, 1967.

Sasse, Hermann. *This Is My Body: Luther's Contention for the Real Presence in the Sacrament of the Altar*. Minneapolis: Augsburg, 1959.

Thompson, Nicholas. *Eucharistic Sacrifice and Patristic Tradition in the Theology of Martin Bucer, 1534–1546*. Studies in the History of Christian Traditions 119. Leiden: Brill, 2005.

Wandel, Lee Palmer, ed. *A Companion to the Eucharist in the Reformation*. Brill's Companions to the Christian Tradition 46. Leiden: Brill, 2014.

———. *The Eucharist in the Reformation: Incarnation and Liturgy*. Cambridge: Cambridge University Press, 2006.

19

The Relationship of
Church and State

Peter A. Lillback

ABSTRACT

Church and state in the Reformation were shaped by caesaro-papism and papal primacy. The medieval era bequeathed concili-arism, populists, and social movements, while Luther's theology weakened church power. Erastianism, sphere sovereignty, and total separation theories developed, as Reformers appealed to Scripture, classical political theories, and experience. Impelled by persecution, Protestants appropriated covenantal thinking to help forge theories of resistance to tyranny. Resistance by the lesser magistrate led to theories of popular resistance to tyranny. Lutherans, Calvinists, Huguenots, and Catholics contributed to this process. Rutherford, Althusius, and Grotius expressed a mature theory of popular re-sistance, and the melding of natural and biblical law yielded a permanent impact on Western thought.

Introduction

In the sixteenth century, the struggles between earthly powers, po-tentates, popes, and Protestant peoples created significant political

problems, proposals, and promises. Indeed, the Reformation era manifests that Christian beliefs can greatly influence government and politics.[1] John T. McNeill observes,

> The names that throng the histories of political theory are not the
> names of politicians or statesmen, but of philosophers, law schol-
> ars, and theologians. . . . Contributors to it, in fact included virtu-
> ally all the eminent figures among the church fathers, Scholastics,
> and Reformers.[2]

The institutions of church and state are different but have at times
shared common goals.[3] Still, human government is concerned with the
exercise of power, while the church is concerned with eternal destinies
when the seventh trumpet sounds and the voices in heaven proclaim,
"The kingdom of the world has become the kingdom of our Lord and
of his Christ, and he shall reign forever and ever" (Rev. 11:15).

There is an inherent tension between the two, evident at the birth of
Christianity when Jesus distinguished the legitimate rights of God and
of Caesar in Matthew 22:21 without demarcating their boundaries.[4]
The apostles taught subordination to government (Rom. 13:1–7; 1 Pet.
2:13–25), but the New Testament also displays the tension between
earthly kingdoms and the coming kingdom (Matt. 6:10). Christian
submission to the state has limits. Peter declared in Acts 5:29 that man
must obey God rather than man. Paul insisted that the magistrate is to
administer justice (Rom. 13:3–4). But does this not forbid a magistrate
from pursuing a political program that leads to tyranny?

If God is obeyed over man, then questions confront the Christian
and earthly kings, producing controversy. And the Reformation era

---

1. J. H. Burns, ed., *The Cambridge History of Political Thought, 1450–1700*, with the assistance of Mark Goldie (Cambridge: Cambridge University Press, 1991), 159–253; Quentin Skinner, *The Foundations of Modern Political Thought*, 2 vols. (Cambridge: Cambridge University Press, 1978); Jean Touchard et al., *Histoire des idées politiques* (Paris: Presses Universitaires de France, 1959).
2. John T. McNeill, "Calvinism and European Politics in Historical Perspective," in *Calvinism and the Political Order*, ed. George L. Hunt (Philadelphia: Westminster, 1965), 11.
3. For helpful surveys of Reformed understandings of church and state issues, see Paul Wells, "Le Dieu créateur et la politique (Romans 13.1–7)," "L'État et l'Église dans la perspective de la théologie réformée," and "Le calvinisme et la liberté politique," in *En toute occasion, favorable ou non: Positions et propositions évangéliques* (Aix-en-Provence: Kerygma, 2014), 56–66, 247–67, 450–64.
4. Robert D. Linder, "Church and State," in *Evangelical Dictionary of Theology*, ed. Walter A. Elwell (Grand Rapids, MI: Baker, 1984), 233–38.

was no exception.[5] To the questions of politics and religion in the public square,[6] the Reformation debate offered diverse answers that continue to influence Western civilization.[7] The concerns of church and state remain[8] and have led to research called political theology.[9] This field is vast.[10] The issues addressed span the spectrum of governmental concerns, religion, and the Christian faith.[11]

Some of the abiding questions asked include the following: (1) Which form of government is best? (2) Does the church follow the state, or does the state follow the church, or are they separate bodies that must vie unceasingly for authority and control? (3) How can tyrannical rulers, whether in the state or in the church, be stopped? (4) And if church and state both cherish the kingdom of God, can there be room for heretics, dissidents, or unbelievers? How the Reformation answered such questions is the burden of this chapter.

The Legacy of Church and State Bequeathed to the Reformation

The Reformers drank from the traditions they inherited.[12] In the early church, Christianity grew in spite of persecutions. In 313, with the

---

5. John Eidsmoe, *Historical and Theological Foundation of Law*, 3 vols. (Powder Springs, GA: Tolle Lege, 2011).

6. John Frame, "Toward a Theology of the State," *WTJ* 51, no. 2 (1989): 199–226; Richard John Neuhaus, *The Naked Public Square: Religion and Democracy in America* (Grand Rapids, MI: Eerdmans, 1984).

7. Jacques Ellul, *Histoire des institutions* (Paris: Presses Universitaires de France, 1956); Gary Scott Smith, ed., *God and Politics: Four Views on the Reformation of Civil Government: Theonomy, Principled Pluralism, Christian America, National Confessionalism* (Phillipsburg, NJ: Presbyterian and Reformed, 1989); Derek H. Davis, ed., *The Oxford Handbook of Church and State in the United States* (New York: Oxford University Press, 2010).

8. Robert L. Cord, *Separation of Church and State: Historical Fact and Current Fiction* (New York: Lambeth, 1982); Linder, "Church and State," 233–38; John Witte Jr., *The Reformation of Rights: Law, Religion, and Human Rights in Early Modern Calvinism* (Cambridge: Cambridge University Press, 2007).

9. Peter J. Leithart, review of *The Desire of the Nations: Rediscovering the Roots of Political Theology*, by Oliver O'Donovan, *WTJ* 63, no. 1 (2001): 209–11.

10. P. C. Kemeny, ed., *Church, State, and Public Justice: Five Views* (Downers Grove, IL: IVP Academic, 2007); Oliver O'Donovan and Joan Lockwood O'Donovan, eds., *From Irenaeus to Grotius: Sourcebook in Christian Political Thought, 100–1625* (Grand Rapids, MI: Eerdmans, 1999); James W. Skillen, "Government," in Elwell, *Evangelical Dictionary of Theology*, 477–79.

11. Richard Bauckham, *The Bible in Politics: How to Read the Bible Politically* (Louisville: Westminster John Knox, 1989); John Eidsmoe, *Christianity and the Constitution: The Faith of Our Founding Fathers* (Grand Rapids, MI: Baker, 1987); Eidsmoe, *God and Caesar: Biblical Faith and Political Action* (Westchester, IL: Crossway, 1984).

12. John N. Figgis, *Studies of Political Thought from Gerson to Grotius, 1414–1625*, 2nd ed. (Cambridge: Cambridge University Press, 1931); R. W. Carlyle and A. J. Carlyle, *History of Medieval Political Theory in the West*, 6 vols. (Edinburgh: William Blackwood and Sons, 1962).

Edict of Milan, persecution ended. Until then, the church had no direct role in civil government.

WHO SHOULD LEAD CHURCH AND STATE?
CAESAROPAPISM AND THE PRIMACY OF THE POPE

With Constantine I's conversion, the church became the official religion of Rome. This raised questions of how much power the church could exercise and how much power Caesar was to wield over the church. In the East, this introduced *caesaropapism*, meaning that Caesar was the pope, or head of the church. This view was held in the Eastern sphere of the empire but not in the West, where the church had greater freedom. There the fall of Rome forced a new land-based social pattern called feudalism.[13] In this economy the renter became the vassal of his lord, who owned the land. This relationship developed theological overtones as the word *sacramentum* was used to describe it.[14]

Gradually, the struggle between the spheres of spiritual and earthly power became pronounced. The absence of Roman hegemony increased the power of the church in medieval Europe.[15] With the church's ascendancy, "Christendom" appeared—a single society with two expressions of power. The coronation of Charlemagne by Pope Leo III in 800 made the question of who governed Christendom less clear.

Thus, a conflict erupted between church and state known as the investiture controversy. The issues at stake were the right of the papacy to depose monarchs and the powers of secular kings to appoint bishops and church leaders of their liking. The controversy saw the demise of both popes[16] and kings.[17] The nadir of kingly power was penitent Henry IV humbled before Pope Gregory VII at Canossa (1077). Because of papal interdict, Henry's kingdom could no longer celebrate Mass. Gregory forgave the king, but later, Henry's army defeated the pope's troops, and the secular crown again held sway. The rule of pope over secular power has been called *the primacy of the pope*,

---

13. *Encyclopedia Britannica*, 11th ed., 10:297–302, s.v., "Feudalism."
14. Ibid., s.v., "Sacrament."
15. Carlyle and Carlyle, *Medieval Political Theory*.
16. Heinrich Geffcken, *Church and State: Their Relations Historically Developed*, trans. Edward F. Taylor (London: Longmans, 1877), 1:177.
17. Figgis, *Studies of Political Thought*, 6.

papal supremacy, and *the power of the keys* (based on Matt. 16:19). It is a form of *theocracy*, the rule of God over the state through his representatives.

THE PRE-REFORMATION DEVELOPMENT OF THE POLITICAL COVENANT

The political aspects of medieval covenantal thought began with Augustine. He saw society built on a pact of obedience to the king—a social contract.[18] While Augustine never precisely defined his conception of the city of God with respect to the political order, it is clear that the relationship between the two was intimate.[19] Further, this pact of men and king, brought about in part by the sacraments, carried mutual responsibilities,[20] because both were subject to the church.[21] Augustine forbade resistance, teaching that tyrants must be obeyed, for they are divinely ordained to rule.[22]

Medieval society utilized covenantal ideas in many contexts.[23] Within eleventh-century papal absolutism, ecclesiastical political thinkers identified a baptismal covenant of Christians to the pope. Failure to obey the pope resulted in a breach of covenant. This thinking entitled the pope to resist even kings and to require subjects to do the same.

Thus, covenant breaking was a ground for resisting political authority. When leaders were declared unfaithful to their baptismal covenant, they were viewed as covenant breakers and excommunicated sinners. Consequently, they could be resisted or deposed. The covenantal character of medieval resistance theory is illustrated in Charles the Bald of Italy in 876[24] and in the clash between Pope Gregory VII and King

---

18. Cf. Otto Gierke, *Political Theories of the Middle Ages*, trans. Frederic W. Maitland (Cambridge: Cambridge University Press, 1958), 187n306.
19. Cf. Augustine, *Reply to Faustus* 19.11, NPNF, 1st ser., vol. 4, ed. Philip Schaff (Grand Rapids, MI: Eerdmans, 1979), 243; *PL* 42:355.
20. Cf. Augustine, "Letter 138 (AD 412): To Marcellinus," 2.15, NPNF, 1st ser., vol. 1, 486; *PL* 33:531–32; and Augustine, *De civitate Dei* 2.19, NPNF, 1st ser., vol. 2, 33–34; *PL* 41:64–65.
21. Norman Hepburn Baynes, *The Political Ideas of St. Augustine's "De civitate Dei"* (London: Bell, 1936), 12–13.
22. Cf. Fritz Kern, *Gottesgnadentum und Widerstandsrecht im früheren Mittelalter*, ed. Rudolf Buchner (Darmstadt: Wissenschaftliche Gesellschaft, 1967), 334n399.
23. Derk Visser, "Discourse and Doctrine: The Covenant Concept in the Middle Ages," in *Calvin and the State: Papers and Responses Presented at the Seventh and Eighth Colloquia on Calvin and Calvin Studies, Sponsored by the Calvin Studies Society*, ed. Peter De Klerk (Grand Rapids, MI: Calvin Studies Society, 1993), 1–14.
24. Carlyle and Carlyle, *Medieval Political Theory*, 1:242–43. Cf. Figgis, *Studies of Political Thought*, 197n12.

Henry IV from 1075 to 1077.[25] Thus, tyranny was a basis for dissolving the feudal covenant between kings and their subjects, permitting both resistance and deposition.

THE RISE OF CONCILIARISM

Rising nationalism, due in part to the Crusades, caused the diminishing of papal power. This was exacerbated by the "Babylonian captivity of the church" in Avignon between 1309 and 1377 and by the Great Western Schism from 1378 to 1417. During this time three popes were claiming legitimacy and excommunicating each other. This evoked the conciliar movement, wherein the united leaders of the church determined that they had power to depose popes for the good of the church.[26]

The conciliar movement was advised by canonists, or ecclesiastical lawyers, who discussed the problem of a pope turned tyrant and whether he could be resisted.[27] The conciliarists concluded that a council could force a heretical pope from power by resistance. Conciliarism contrasted with curialism, which defended the absolute power and primacy of the pope and would later prevail. The conciliarists asserted that the greatest power on earth—the pope—could be judged by those who were normally viewed as inferior in power. By means of collective strength under dire circumstances, they could assume authority over the occupant of Christ's earthly throne, forcing a recalcitrant, heretical pope to step down. Thus the reforming councils ended the schism.

Upon resolution, the efforts at creating a constitutional papacy under a general council failed. The decree of the Council of Constance (1414–1418) declared that a council should be held every ten years, but this was defeated by papal intrigue and refuted by the 1459 bull

---

25. Carlyle and Carlyle, *Medieval Political Theory,* 3:164–67; 4:188–210, 232–33; 5:99–101.

26. A. J. Black, "The Political Ideas of Conciliarism and Papalism, 1430–1450," *JEH* 20, no. 1 (1969): 45–65; John T. McNeill, "The Emergence of Conciliarism," in *Medieval and Historiographical Essays in Honor of James Westfall Thompson,* ed. James L. Cate and Eugene N. Anderson (Chicago: University of Chicago Press, 1938), 269–301; Brian Tierney, "A Conciliar Theory of the Thirteenth Century," *CHR* 36, no. 4 (1951): 415–40; Michael J. Wilks, *The Problem of Sovereignty in the Later Middle Ages: The Papal Monarchy with Augustus Triumphus and the Publicists,* Cambridge Studies in Medieval Life and Thought, n.s., 9 (Cambridge: Cambridge University Press, 1963).

27. Cf. Brian Tierney, *Origins of Papal Infallibility, 1150–1350: A Study on the Concepts of Infallibility, Sovereignty, and Tradition in the Middle Ages,* Studies in the History of Christian Thought 6 (Leiden: Brill, 1972), 50. See also Tierney, "Pope and Council: Some New Decretist Texts," *Mediaeval Studies* 19 (1957): 204; cf. Carlyle and Carlyle, *Medieval Political Theory,* 4:352; and Wilks, *Sovereignty,* 499–506.

of Pope Pius II titled *Execrabilis*, which condemned all appeals to a future general council.[28]

The ramifications of conciliarism's failure were profound. In essence, there was no longer any possibility of reform in the church if the pope did not approve, unless one assumed the stance of a heretic.[29] This guaranteed that a successful reform movement would have to occur outside the church by support from the laity and the temporal magistrates. When a legitimate pope finally came to power, he had no interest in calling church councils to evaluate his rule, so conciliarism faltered. But calls for a reforming council would again be heard from Luther and early Protestants.[30]

MEDIEVAL EXPERIENCE OF POPULAR SOVEREIGNTY

The Publicists

Another approach to resisting the pope came from political thinkers called *publicists*, so named because they saw all power, including the church's, to be derived from the people. The most famous was Marsilius of Padua. He asserted that not only a heretical pope was to be resisted and deposed but that *every* pope should be resisted and deposed, because the papacy had usurped the rightful role of the temporal government. The pope was a usurper occupying a tyrant's office. Consequently, both pope and papacy had to be abolished.[31] If there was a divine origin of power, and hence a divine-right theory of government, this divine right resided in the people, not the papacy.

Social Covenantal Movements

The covenant idea also appeared in the medieval period and gave force to ideas of popular rule. Imperial cities in southern Germany developed

---

28. Oliver J. Thatcher and Edgar H. McNeal, *A Source Book for Mediaeval History: Selected Documents Illustrating the History of Europe in the Middle Ages* (New York: Scribner, 1905), 331–32.

29. Cf. Earle E. Cairns, *Christianity through the Centuries: A History of the Christian Church*, rev. ed. (Grand Rapids, MI: Zondervan, 1977), 281–82.

30. Hans Margull, ed., *The Councils of the Church: History and Analysis*, trans. Walter F. Bense (Philadelphia: Fortress, 1966); John Dillenberger, ed., *Martin Luther* (New York: Anchor, 1961), 43–44.

31. Marsilius of Padua, *The Defender of Peace*, vol. 2, *The Defensor Pacis*, ed. and trans. Alan Gewirth, Records of Civilization, Sources, and Studies 46 (New York: Columbia University Press, 1951–1956), 2:27–28, 87–89, 113–52; Thatcher and McNeal, *Source Book for Medieval History*, 318–24.

the concept of a "sacral society."[32] Thus, community life was permeated with a common religious binding and may explain why southern Germany accepted Zwingli's reformation over Luther's. Swiss theology stressed the social dimension of faith, while Luther emphasized individual justification. The covenant appeared in medieval German radical political movements,[33] such as the apocalypticism of Thomas Müntzer.[34] The conciliarist struggle,[35] Scottish banding practices,[36] and the recovery of Roman contract law[37] appear to have played a role in conceptions of the people's role in government. Medieval social movements affected Reformed thinking in terms of political resistance.[38] Other examples of medieval social covenants include the Swiss *Gemeinde*,[39] the German *Bundshuh* and *Bundesgenossen*,[40] and religious orders such as the Franciscans.[41]

RENAISSANCE FORERUNNERS ON VIEWS OF CHURCH AND STATE

A byproduct of renewed interest in biblical studies during the Renaissance was a reassessment of medieval political realities. Thus Reformational forerunners addressed biblical texts, bringing political issues forward as they called for ecclesiastical reforms. This was evident in Wyclif,[42] Hus,[43]

32. Bernd Moeller, *Imperial Cities and the Reformation: Three Essays*, ed. and trans. H. C. Erik Midelfort and Mark U. Edwards Jr. (Philadelphia: Fortress, 1972), 90–103.

33. George Huntston Williams, *The Radical Reformation*, Sixteenth Century Essays and Studies 15 (Kirksville, MO: Sixteenth Century Journal Publishers, 1992), 50–77.

34. Jürgen Moltmann, "Föderaltheologie," in *Lexikon für Theologie und Kirche* (Freiburg: Herder, 1995), 4:190.

35. Leonard J. Trinterud, "The Origins of Puritanism," *CH* 20, no. 1 (1951): 41.

36. S. A. Burrell, "The Covenant Idea as a Revolutionary Symbol: Scotland, 1596–1637," *CH* 29 (1958): 338–50; J. F. Maclear, "Samuel Rutherford: The Law and the King," in Hunt, *Calvinism and the Political Order*, 69–70.

37. Gottlob Schrenk, *Gottesreich und Bund im älteren Protestantismus vornehmlich bei Johannes Cocceius* (Gutersloh: Bertelsmann, 1923), 49n1, 62n4, 78n2.

38. Lowell H. Zuck, "Anabaptist Revolution through the Covenant in Sixteenth-Century Continental Protestantism" (PhD diss., Yale University, 1954).

39. George R. Potter, *Zwingli* (Cambridge: Cambridge University Press, 1976), 58.

40. Williams, *Radical Reformation*, 60–63, 74, 77.

41. Martin Greschat, "Der Bundesgedanke in der Theologie des späten Mittelalters," *Zeitschrift für Kirchengeschichte* 81 (1970): 46–48.

42. Takashi Shogimen, "Wyclif's Ecclesiology and Political Thought," in *A Companion to John Wyclif: Late Medieval Theologian*, ed. Ian Christopher Levy, Brill's Companions to the Christian Tradition 4 (Leiden: Brill, 2006), 199–240; Lowrie John Daly, *The Political Theory of John Wyclif* (Chicago: Loyola University Press, 1962).

43. Jan Hus, *The Church*, trans. David S. Schaff (1915; repr., Westport, CT: Greenwood, 1974); Latin original in Harrison S. Thomson, ed. *Tractatus de ecclesia*, Studies and Texts in Medieval Thought (Boulder: University of Colorado Press, 1956). See also H. B. Workman and R. M. Pope, eds., *The Letters of John Hus* (London: Hodder and Stoughton, 1904); Thomas A. Fudge, "Hussite Theology and the Law of God," in *The Cambridge Companion to Reformation Theology*, ed. David Bagchi and David C. Steinmetz (New York: Cambridge University Press, 2004), 22–27;

and Savonarola.[44] However, the Renaissance also gave expression to the political theory of the ends justifying the means.[45] For Machiavelli, victory alone justified politics.[46] McNeill explains,

> Machiavelli exonerates and applauds the founders and defenders of states who have secured their power by fratricide or massacre. A conqueror should "either caress or extinguish" a conquered people. Machiavelli's one positive aim was the unification of Italy. No action tending to this end, however base or cruel, was to be condemned.[47]

The Reformation witnessed both principled commitment and unbridled force. The Catholic powers were ruthless in their efforts to preserve power, employing persecution, war, and even massacres.

The Tensions in the Medieval Legacy of Church and State

As the Reformers engaged their task to reform Christendom, they had a medieval millennium of statecraft at their disposal. As "magisterial" Reformers, they drew on concepts like the covenantal relationship in feudalism and the legitimate power of kings. But the Reformers inherited political theories favoring monarchy. The medieval epoch believed that absolute governmental power was essential, whether wielded by the state or by the church. Figgis explains,

> From 1450 onwards it seemed to most practical statesmen, and to all sovereigns, that "the tendency of advancing civilization is a tendency towards pure monarchy"; and popular movements in every land were deemed . . . as not merely wrong but stupid—inefficient clogs upon the wheels of government, which would retard the

Fudge, *Jan Hus: Religious and Social Revolution in Bohemia*, International Library of Historical Studies 73 (New York: I. B. Tauris, 2010).

44. Girolamo Savonarola, *Liberty and Tyranny in the Goverment* [sic] *of Men*, trans. C. M. Flumiani (Albuquerque, NM: American Classical College Press, 1982); Savonarola, *Selected Writings of Girolamo Savonarola: Religion and Politics, 1490–1498*, trans. and ed. Anne Borelli and Maria Pastore Passaro (New Haven, CT: Yale University Press, 2006); Stefano Dall'Aglio, *Savonarola and Savonarolism*, trans. John Gagné (Toronto: Center for Reformation and Renaissance Studies, 2010); Donald Weinstein, *Savonarola: The Rise and Fall of a Renaissance Prophet* (New Haven, CT: Yale University Press, 2011).

45. F. J. C. Hearnshaw, *The Social and Political Ideas of Some Great Thinkers of the Renaissance and the Reformation* (New York: Barnes & Noble, 1942); Paul Oskar Kristeller, *Renaissance Thought: The Classic, Scholastic, and Humanistic Strains* (New York: Harper & Row, 1961).

46. Niccolò Machiavelli, *The Prince and the Discourses* (New York: Modern Library, 1940).

47. McNeill, "Calvinism and European Politics," 12.

progress of intelligence and enlightenment. Pure monarchy was
the only gentlemanly form of government.[48]

The Impact of Luther's Reformation
on the Authority of the Church[49]

Luther's reformation began with a return to the Augustinian view of
man's fallen nature, leaving behind the more optimistic assessment of
Thomism. God's grace had to overcome mankind's bondage to sin if
the sinner was to be saved.[50]

LUTHER'S THEOLOGY REDUCED THE
POWER OF THE VISIBLE CHURCH

Salvation was only possible through justification by faith alone, and
such a belief radically altered Luther's view of the church. Instead of
being the mediating authority between God and the Christian, the
church became the community of believers. The priesthood of the believer—that all Christians, not only members of the clergy, have direct
access to God—meant that priestly authority was diminished and the
absolute authority of the church was rejected.[51] This reduced ecclesiastical power in relationship to the state. Skinner reasons that Luther

> continues to speak of the Two Kingdoms (*Zwei Reiche*) through
> which God exercises His complete dominion over the world. . . . It
> is generally clear, however, that what he has in mind when discuss-
> ing the rule of the spiritual kingdom is a purely inward form of

---

48. Figgis, *Studies of Political Thought*, 46. Cf. Carlyle and Carlyle, *Medieval Political Theory*;
J. H. Burns, ed., *The Cambridge History of Medieval Political Thought, c. 350–c. 1450* (New York:
Cambridge University Press, 1988), 46.

49. For resources on Luther's and Lutheranism's views on church and state, see Jonathon David
Beeke, "Martin Luther's Two Kingdoms, Law and Gospel, and the Created Order: Was There a
Time When the Two Kingdoms Were Not?," *WTJ* 73, no. 2 (2011): 191–214; Frédéric Hartweg,
"Autorité temporelle et droit de résistance: permanence et évolution chez Martin Luther," and Luise
Schorne-Schütte (trans. Jean Clédière), "Luther et la politique," in *Luther et la Réforme, 1525–
1555: Le temps de la consolidation religieuse et politique*, ed. Jean-Paul Cahn and Gérard Schneilin
(Paris: Éditions du temps, 2001), 133–50, 162–70; Nicolaus von Amsdorff, *Bekentnis Unterricht
vnd vermanung der Pfarrhern vnd Prediger der Christlichen Kirchen zu Magdeburgk: Anno 1550.
Den 13. Aprilis.* Magdeburgk: Lotther, [1550]; John W. Allen, *A History of Political Thought in
the Sixteenth Century* (1928; repr., London: Methuen, 1977), 15–34; James M. Estes, "The Role of
Godly Magistrates in the Church: Melanchthon as Luther's Interpreter and Collaborator," *CH* 67,
no. 3 (1998): 463–83; Lewis W. Spitz and Wenzel Lohff, eds., *Discord, Dialogue, and Concord:
Studies in the Lutheran Reformation's Formula of Concord* (Philadelphia: Fortress, 1977).

50. Skinner, *Foundations*, 2:3–4.

51. Ibid., 2:10–11.

government, "a government of the soul," which has no connection with temporal affairs, and is entirely dedicated to helping the faithful to attain their salvation.[52]

Thus Luther advocated a system where secular rulers supervised the church, reflecting the early tradition of the church under Constantine. It also enabled the reformation of the Roman church, which had no desire to reform or to call a council to consider claims of papal abuses.

Luther was thus influenced by political ideas growing out of medieval Europe. He was sympathetic to a tenet of conciliarism in that he called the pope to submit to a council's review. At the same time, Luther's rejection of the covenant of the papacy with all Christians was so decisive that some opponents sought to refute Marsilius, thinking that they thereby refuted Luther.[53]

With respect to resistance, Luther, until 1530, was committed to the Augustinian prohibition of any resistance to the king. He accepted a conditional oath to a secular leader but without lawful personal resistance. Thus Luther occupied the medieval covenant tradition in terms of the relationship of Christian kings and subjects. The Peasants' War in Germany (1524–1525) manifested the potent social impacts of the Protestant Reformation unleashed by Luther's reforms. Luther's emphasis on liberty, seen especially in his early writings of 1520 (*To the Christian Nobility of the German Nation*, *The Babylonian Captivity of the Church*, and *The Freedom of the Christian*), was misapplied by the peasants to the political and social order—to Luther's horror.[54] He condemned the uprising and supported its suppression by the army of the Swabian League. This further galvanized his conservative stance regarding resistance to the civil magistrates.[55] Luther later concluded that lesser powers resisting the higher power was consonant with the gospel if the prince was in error.[56]

---

52. Ibid., 2:14.
53. Gewirth, *The Defender of Peace*, vol. 1, *Marsilius of Padua and Medieval Political Philosophy*, 303.
54. Cf. Martin Luther, *Three Treatises*, 2nd ed. (Philadelphia: Fortress, 1970).
55. See Skinner, *Foundations*, 2:9–18, and Witte, *Reformation of Rights*, 218. After the Peasants' War, Luther wrote the following work with the telling title of *Against the Robbing and Murdering Hordes of Peasants* (1525), LW 46:45–55.
56. Cf. Carlyle and Carlyle, *Medieval Political Theory*, 6:272–87; Ernst Troeltsch, *The Social Teaching of the Christian Churches*, trans. Olive Wyon (London: Allen and Unwin, 1961), 2:352n252.

The Reformation's New Views of the Relationship of Church and State

The oft-used distinctions between the radical, magisterial, and Counter- or Catholic Reformations[57] suggest that the issues of church and state are especially the concerns of the magisterial and Catholic Reformations.[58] The Reformed tradition in general has been called "the magisterial Reformation" since its leaders worked with the state to reform the church.

The reforming nations often declared their faith through confessions that included articles on church and state.[59] For example, the first official document of the Genevan reforms was written by Farel and Calvin during November 1536 and had an article on "Magistrates."[60]

The radical reformation was "radical" because it abandoned the history and traditions of Christianity and went back to the Scriptures for a fresh beginning of Christianity.[61] It was also radical because it rejected any role of the state to restore the apostolic church. The Anabaptist view of total separation did not play a dominant role in the Reformation but would greatly impact the development of religious liberty in the New World.[62]

The Identification or Separation of Church and State in Reformation Europe

Thus, the views of church and state in the Reformation divide between those who sought to identify the church and state and those who sought to separate them.[63] Luther's position rejected the primacy of the pope

57. Williams, *Radical Reformation*; Allen, *History of Political Thought*.

58. Allen, *History of Political Thought*; William A. Mueller, *Church and State in Luther and Calvin: A Comparative Study* (Nashville: Broadman, 1954).

59. Philip Schaff, *The Creeds of Christendom: With a History and Critical Notes*, 3 vols. (1877; repr., Grand Rapids, MI: Baker, 1990).

60. John T. McNeill, "John Calvin on Civil Government," in Hunt, *Calvinism and the Political Order*, 31.

61. Allen, *History of Political Thought*, 49–72; "The Schleitheim Confession (1527)," and "The Dordrecht Confession (1632)," in *The Doctrines of the Mennonites*, ed. John Christian Wenger (Scottdale, PA: Mennonite Publishing House, 1950), 69–74, 75–85; Arnold Snyder, *Anabaptist History and Theology: An Introduction* (Kitchener, ON: Pandora, 1995); James M. Stayer, *Anabaptists and the Sword* (Lawrence, KS: Coronado, 1972); John D. Roth and James M. Stayer, eds., *A Companion to Anabaptism and Spiritualism, 1521–1700*, Brill's Companions to the Christian Tradition 6 (Leiden: Brill, 2007).

62. William R. Estep, *Revolution within the Revolution: The First Amendment in Historical Context, 1612–1789* (Grand Rapids, MI: Eerdmans, 1990).

63. Allen, *History of Political Thought*, 11.

over the church and state. Instead, he advocated that the state governs the church, which was later called *Erastianism* and was especially identified with Zwingli's Zurich reforms.[64] England took the Erastian route, where King Henry VIII became the "pope" of the Church of England.

John Calvin in Geneva,[65] however, advocated the independence of the two institutions. This has been identified as *sphere sovereignty*. While he separated church and state, he insisted on their reciprocal cooperation and mutual support.[66] Calvin's views of the church were influenced by Martin Bucer during Calvin's three-year sojourn in Strasbourg, and Bucer would also later have a substantial impact on English Puritan thought.[67] In 1538, during Calvin's first stay in Geneva, the city council demanded that the Genevan ministers follow the council's guidelines for the Lord's Supper, but in reaction to the state's meddling in church affairs, Calvin and Guillaume Farel refused to celebrate the Lord's Supper on Easter. This led the council to expel them from Geneva. Already then, their concern was to preserve the church from the state's interference. When Calvin was recalled to Geneva after his stay in Strasbourg (1541), he was eager not only to establish a program of Christian instruction with his Geneva Catechism (1542) but also to rightly establish the order of the church through his *Ecclesiastical Ordinances* (1541). This document sought to compromise church and

---

64. William Cunningham, *Discussions on Church Principles: Popish, Erastian, and Presbyterian* (Edinburgh: T. & T. Clark, 1863); Robert C. Walton, *Zwingli's Theocracy* (Toronto: Toronto University Press, 1967).

65. André Biéler, *The Social Humanism of Calvin*, trans. Paul T. Fuhrmann (Richmond, VA: John Knox, 1964); Quirinus Breen, *John Calvin: A Study in French Humanism* (Grand Rapids, MI: Eerdmans, 1931); David W. Hall, "Calvin on Human Government and the State," in *A Theological Guide to Calvin's Institutes: Essays and Analysis*, ed. David W. Hall and Peter A. Lillback, Calvin 500 Series (Phillipsburg, NJ: P&R, 2008), 411–40; Peter A. Lillback, *The Binding of God: Calvin's Role in the Development of Covenant Theology*, Texts and Studies in Reformation and Post-Reformation Thought (Grand Rapids, MI: Baker, 2001); John T. McNeill, *John Calvin on God and Political Duty*, 2nd ed., The Library of Liberal Arts 23 (New York: Liberal Arts Press, 1956); Willem Nijenhuis, "The Limits of Civil Disobedience in Calvin's Last-Known Sermons: Development of His Ideas on the Right of Civil Resistance," in *Ecclesia Reformata: Studies on the Reformation* (New York: Brill, 1994), 2:73–97; W. Stanford Reid, ed., *John Calvin: His Influence in the Western World* (Grand Rapids, MI: Zondervan, 1982); Sheldon S. Wolin, "Calvin and the Reformation: The Political Education of Protestantism," *APSR* 51, no. 2 (1957): 428–53.

66. McNeill, "John Calvin on Civil Government," 41–42.

67. *Melanchthon and Bucer*, ed. Wilhelm Pauck, LCC 19 (Philadelphia: Westminster, 1969); Willem van 't Spijker, "The Kingdom of Christ according to Bucer and Calvin," in De Klerk, *Calvin and the State*, 109–32; Martin Greschat, "The Relation between Church and Civil Community in Bucer's Reforming Work," and Willem van 't Spijker, "Bucer's Influence on Calvin: Church and Community," in *Martin Bucer: Reforming Church and Community*, ed. David F. Wright (New York: Cambridge University Press, 1970), 17–31, 32–44; Hans Baron, "Calvinist Republicanism and Its Historical Roots," *CH* 8, no. 1 (1939): 30–42.

state by preserving the independence of the church and advocating that ministers ought not to be involved in politics.[68]

The Anabaptists and others in England promoted a *total separation* of the church from the state, believing religious liberty required such separation. The Anabaptist commitment to total separation was solidified after the failed military attempt to conquer Münster, Germany, and make it the Anabaptist New Jerusalem on earth.[69] A less violent expression of Anabaptist theology is found in the Schleitheim Confession (1527) by Michael Sattler.[70] The sixth article deals with government and the use of the sword, making a sharp distinction between civil punishment, instituted for unbelievers, and discipline administered in the church. Further, Christians ought not to be magistrates, after Christ's example (e.g., John 6:15), or soldiers. This dichotomy was based on the following principle: "The authorities' governance is according to the flesh, but the Christian's is according to the spirit. . . . Their citizenship is of this world, but the Christian's is in heaven."[71] The distinction between carnal and spiritual warfare (cf. Eph. 6:12) was used to argue against military service for Christians. The seventh article, based on the Sermon on the Mount (Matt. 5:34–35), forbade oaths for Christians; Williams, however, notes that under Martin Bucer in Strasbourg, the Anabaptists were persuaded "to take the civic oath."[72] Thus, Anabaptists held to a variety of views and anticipated modern concepts of nonviolent resistance and separation of church and state. This was done, however, by a dualism that few Christians today would embrace.

The Reformers' Use of Classical Political Philosophy

The Reformers possessed ancient political sources. Ancient Greek political philosophy,[73] the Augustinian understanding of Roman law,[74]

---

68. For these aspects of Calvin's ministry and life in relation to Geneva, see, for instance, T. H. L. Parker, *John Calvin: A Biography* (1975; repr., Louisville: Westminster John Knox, 2006), 90, 108–11.

69. Williams, *Radical Reformation*, 553–74.

70. Ibid., 288–313. This confession gave rise to responses by both Zwingli and Calvin. For the text of the confession, see Michael G. Baylor, ed., *The Radical Reformation*, Cambridge Texts in the History of Political Thought (New York: Cambridge University Press, 1991), 172–80.

71. Baylor, *The Radical Reformation*, 178.

72. Williams, *Radical Reformation*, 294.

73. Aristotle, *Politics* 4.6.3; Plato, *Republic* 8.2; cf. Calvin, *Institutes*, 4.20.8; McNeill, "John Calvin on Civil Government," 37.

74. F. Edward Cranz, "The Development of Augustine's Ideas on Society before the Donatist Controversy," *HTR* 47, no. 4 (1954): 255–316; Thomas M. Garrett, "St. Augustine and the

and biblical sources from the Old and New Testament eras[75] were at hand for Reformation scholars. Erasmus, the early humanist reformer, wrote in part to enable the proper education of the prince.[76]

POLITICAL THEORY IN ZURICH: ZWINGLI AND BULLINGER

Zwingli's interest in the covenant idea was far stronger than that of Luther or Erasmus.[77] The social structure of Switzerland and its confederacy served as an example for his conception of the Christian's baptismal pledge.[78] The beginning of what would become a staple in the Reformed understanding of resistance theory, however, appears in Zwingli's sermon *Der Hirt*. Zwingli, referring to political evil in the church, stated that just as the Spartans had their ephors, the Romans their tribunes, and the German towns their guild masters, with their authority to check the higher rulers, so God has provided pastors as officers to stand on guard for the people.[79] This was congruent to the conclusion conciliarists reached with respect to heretical popes. Zwingli, however, did not apply this reasoning to civil politics. He died prematurely in the battle of Kappel (1531) defending the reforms in Zurich against the neighboring Catholic cantons. However, his appeal to the ephors would be applied to resistance of magisterial tyranny by Vermigli and Calvin.

Bullinger's view of the magistrate was based on the Old Testament, where kings are magistrates and prophets are pastors.[80] And so this produced tension in Bullinger's thought: while he preferred republicanism, the Old Testament foundation of his thought compelled him toward

---

Nature of Society," *The New Scholasticism* 30, no. 1 (1956): 16–36; Baynes, *Political Ideas of St. Augustine*.

75. F. F. Bruce, "Render to Caesar," in *Jesus and the Politics of His Day*, ed. Ernst Bammel and C. F. D. Moule (Cambridge: Cambridge University Press, 1984), 249–63; C. E. B. Cranfield, "The Christian's Political Responsibility according to the New Testament," *SJT* 15, no. 2 (1962): 176–92; Oscar Cullmann, *The State in the New Testament* (New York: Scribner, 1956).

76. Desiderius Erasmus, *The Education of a Christian Prince* (New York: Columbia University Press, 1936).

77. See Lillback, *Binding of God*, 81–109.

78. Huldrych Zwingli, "Of Baptism," in *Zwingli and Bullinger: Selected Translations with Introductions and Notes*, ed. G. W. Bromiley, LCC 24 (Philadelphia: Westminster, 1953), 131; *ZSW* 4:218.

79. Huldrych Zwingli, "The Shepherd," in Zwingli, *Writings*, vol. 2, *In Search of True Religion*, trans. H. Wayne Pipkin (Allison Park, PA: Pickwick, 1984), 102; *Der Hirt*, in *ZSW* 3:36.

80. J. Wayne Baker, "Covenant and Community in the Thought of Heinrich Bullinger," in *The Covenant Connection: From Federal Theology to Modern Federalism*, ed. Daniel J. Elazar and John Kincaid (Lanham, MD: Lexington Books, 2000), 18–20.

certain authoritarian tendencies, since Israel had a monarchy.[81] Baker explains, "Bullinger's praise for republicanism has a hollow sound. . . . While he lauded republicanism and wrote of the divine limits to political power, his removal of effective checks on magisterial power and his denial of a right of resistance tended to reinforce a certain authoritarianism."[82]

PETER MARTYR VERMIGLI AND
CLASSIC GREEK POLITICAL PHILOSOPHY

Peter Martyr Vermigli,[83] an early Italian Reformer who influenced Calvin as well as the English Reformation, was well versed in classical political thought. Robert Kingdon writes,

> Another obvious set of sources for Vermigli's political ideas is to be found in the writings of classical antiquity. He depends particularly heavily as one might expect, on Aristotle's *Politics*. His most striking use of that work is his adoption of Aristotle's analysis of the types of government into six categories, according to the locus of sovereignty in each: three good types—monarchy, aristocracy, and polity—matched by the three bad types into which they tend to degenerate—tyranny, oligarchy, and democracy.[84]

Vermigli applied these insights in his discussion of the church. The church ideally should reflect the classical value of mixed government:

> It is monarchic in that Christ is its King and remains its supreme legislator, even though He is in Heaven. It is aristocratic in that it is ruled by "bishops, elders, doctors" and others, chosen by merit rather than by wealth, favor or birth. It is popular in that some of its most important decisions, for example as to whether to excommunicate a notorious sinner, should be "referred unto the people."[85]

---

81. Baker, "Covenant and Community," 22–23.
82. Ibid., 23.
83. John Patrick Donnelly, "Peter Martyr Vermigli's Political Ethics," Robert M. Kingdon, "Peter Martyr Vermigli on Church Discipline," and Giulio Orazio Bravi, "Über Die Intellektuellen Wurzeln Des Republikanismus von Petrus Martyr Vermigli," in *Peter Martyr Vermigli: Humanism, Republicanism, Reformation*, ed. Emidio Campi, Frank A. James III, and Peter Opitz, Travaux d'humanisme et Renaissance 365 (Geneva: Droz, 2002), 60–65, 67–76, 119–41. These essays provide valuable insights into Vermigli's ideas of war, church discipline, and republican thought.
84. Robert M. Kingdon, *The Political Thought of Peter Martyr Vermigli: Selected Texts and Commentary*, Travaux d'humanisme et Renaissance 178 (Geneva: Droz, 1980), VII.
85. Ibid., VII.

Vermigli also wrestled with biblical teachings such as Gideon in Judges 8 to establish what should be the best form of political government and to critique the papal abuse of political power.[86]

Calvin's Republicanism

Calvin's biblical scholarship and pastoral duties did not remove his concern for political matters,[87] as "his writings are strewn with penetrating comments on the policies of rulers and illuminating passages on the principles of government."[88]

Calvin knew covenantal thought from the social dimension of medieval Europe, such as legal history and its sundry examples of mutual political covenants.[89] He studied in Paris, the conciliarist stronghold.[90] And he presented his view of the general purposes of government in his *Institutes*.[91] After distinguishing spiritual and civil government, Calvin explained that good civil government also has religious duties.

Calvin found his work in the Republic of Geneva[92] agreeable, as evidenced by a remark that first appeared in his 1543 edition of the *Institutes*:

---

86. Torrance Kirby, "Political Theology: The Godly Prince," in *A Companion to Peter Martyr Vermigli*, ed. Torrance Kirby, Emidio Campi, and Frank A. James III, Brill's Companions to the Christian Tradition 16 (Leiden: Brill, 2009), 409–10.

87. Hunt, *Calvinism and Political Order*; David W. Hall, *The Genevan Reformation and the American Founding* (Lanham, MD: Lexington Books, 2003); Douglas F. Kelly, *The Emergence of Liberty in the Modern World: The Influence of Calvin on Five Governments from the 16th through 18th Centuries* (Phillipsburg, NJ: P&R, 1992); Dominique A. Troilo, "L'œuvre de Pierre Viret: Le problème des sources," *BSHPF* 144 (1998): 759–90.

88. McNeill, "John Calvin on Civil Government," 24.

89. Cf. Calvin on Ezek. 17:9, in *Calvin's Commentaries* (1844–1856; repr., Grand Rapids, MI: Baker, 1979), 12:202–3; *CO* 40:413.

90. Cf. John Major, "A Disputation of the Authority of a Council: Is the Pope Subject to Brotherly Correction by a General Council? (1529)," in *Advocates of Reform: From Wyclif to Erasmus*, ed. Matthew Spinka, LCC 14 (London: SCM, 1953), 175. In this passage, Major asserted that the University of Paris had held to the conciliarist position since the Council of Constance.

91. "Civil government has as its appointed end, so long as we live among men, to cherish and protect the outward worship of God, to defend sound doctrine of piety and the position of the church, to adjust our life to the society of men, to form our social behavior to civil righteousness, to reconcile us with one another, and to promote general peace and tranquility." Calvin, *Institutes*, 4.20.2.

92. Jeong Koo Jeon, "Calvin and the Two Kingdoms: Calvin's Political Philosophy in Light of Contemporary Discussion," *WTJ* 72, no. 2 (2010): 299–320; John T. McNeill, *The History and Character of Calvinism* (New York: Oxford University Press, 1954); Reid, *John Calvin: His Influence*; McNeill, *John Calvin on God and Political Duty*; Jean-Marc Berthoud, *Pierre Viret: A Forgotten Giant of the Reformation: The Apologetics, Ethics, and Economics of the Bible* (Tallahassee, FL: Zurich, 2010); Robert D. Linder, "John Calvin, Pierre Viret, and the State," in De Klerk, *Calvin and the State*, 171–85; Menna Prestwich, ed., *International Calvinism: 1541–1715* (Oxford: Clarendon, 1985).

For if the three forms of government which the philosophers discuss be considered in themselves, I will not deny that aristocracy, or a system compounded of aristocracy and democracy [*vel aristocratian vel temperatum ex ipsa et politia statum*] far excels all others.[93]

Calvin's republican program in Geneva was assisted by Pierre Viret, who believed that godly government preserved humanity and prevented man's descent into living like "brute beasts." "The maintenance of the state was as necessary for a public form of religion and an ordered human society as was food, water and air."[94]

Church Discipline: An Indicator of Political Theory in the Reformation

Political views influenced Reformation practices of discipline. Specifically, the Reformers developed varied approaches to Jesus's words of discipline in Matthew 18:17, "Tell it to the church."[95] For example, the Erastianism of Zwingli shaped church discipline in Zurich.[96] Zwingli insisted that Jesus intended that we must report the sinner to a community, not to an individual like a bishop. He thought that ever since Christianity was established, "Tell it to the church" meant "Tell it to the Christian government." In Zurich, the government could excommunicate, but ministers could not.

After Zwingli's death, Heinrich Bullinger replaced him as leader of the Zurich church. He secured the requirement that pastors take an annual oath of loyalty to Zurich and its council. The relationship between Zurich's church and government was clear: the state possessed all pow-

93. Quoted in McNeill, "John Calvin on Civil Government," 37. Cf. McNeill, "The Democratic Element in Calvin's Thought," *CH* 18, no. 3 (1949): 153–71.
94. Robert Dean Linder, *The Political Ideas of Pierre Viret*, Travaux d'humanisme et Renaissance 64 (Geneva: Droz, 1964), 83–84.
95. Robert M. Kingdon, "Ecclesiology: Exegesis and Discipline," in Kirby, Campi, and James, *A Companion to Peter Martyr Vermigli*, 382–85.
96. Huldrych Zwingli, *An Exposition of the Faith*, in *Zwingli and Bullinger*, 239–79; Pamela Biel, *Doorkeepers at the House of Righteousness: Heinrich Bullinger and the Zurich Clergy, 1535–1575*, Zürcher Beiträge zur Reformationsgeschichte 15 (Bern: Peter Lang, 1991); Charles S. McCoy and J. Wayne Baker, *Fountainhead of Federalism: Heinrich Bullinger and the Covenantal Tradition* (Louisville: Westminster John Knox, 1991); Jan Rohls, *Reformed Confessions: Theology from Zurich to Barmen*, trans. John Hoffmeyer, Columbia Series in Reformed Theology (Louisville: Westminster John Knox, 1998), 254–64; Andries Raath and Shaun de Freitas, "Theologico-Political Federalism: The Office of Magistracy and the Legacy of Heinrich Bullinger (1504–1575)," *WTJ* 63, no. 2 (2001): 285–304; Heinrich Bullinger, *The Decades of Henry Bullinger*, ed. Thomas Harding (1849–1852; repr., Grand Rapids, MI: Reformation Heritage Books, 2004); Baker, "Covenant and Community," 15–29.

ers of coercion, and the pastors were under the city council's final control.[97] For Bullinger, then, excommunication belonged not to the church but to the magistrates; the circumstances found in the New Testament were temporary.[98] Bullinger reasoned that if Jesus at the Last Supper offered the elements to Judas, the disciple who was to betray him, then how could a clergyman refuse to serve anyone, no matter how sinful?

But many, such as Oecolampadius, the Reformer of Basel, disagreed with Zurich's approach. He said that in Matthew 18 Jesus was not intending a secular government but a church organization. For Anabaptists, Jesus's words meant placing someone under a "ban" and urging everyone in the community to "shun" that individual, even within a family. For Catholics, "Tell it to the church" meant "Tell it to a bishop."

Calvin explained that there was no Christian church in existence when Jesus said these words. And so as a Jew, he meant a Jewish institution, probably the Sanhedrin, a body he called "the Jewish Consistory."[99] He interpreted the phrase to mean "Tell it to the consistory." Thus Bullinger disagreed with Calvin over the nature of the Christian community. Bullinger insisted that the Christian community was under the Christian magistracy. Bullinger's emphasis on the magistrate having the final word on church discipline was distinct from Calvin's separation of the responsibilities of the two spheres.[100] Beza did not want Geneva to emulate Zurich's Erastian government, and he strove to maintain a balance between ecclesiastical and civic authorities.[101]

But Bullinger and Calvin agreed that heretics should face the discipline of the church and the state. Bullinger declared that the magistrate should punish and if necessary execute incorrigible heretics, such as Anabaptists and false teachers. He supported Geneva's execution of Michael Servetus in 1553 and Calvin's opposition to Sebastian Castellio, an advocate of religious liberty.[102] This tragic event deserves a

---

97. J. Wayne Baker, "Bullinger, Heinrich," *OER* 1:228.

98. Baker, "Covenant and Community," 20.

99. Calvin, *Institutes*, 4.8.15. The French version reads, "au consistoire qui estoit establi entre les Iuifs." *CO* 4:740.

100. Baker, "Bullinger," *OER* 1:229.

101. Jill Raitt, "Bèze, Théodore de," *OER* 1:149–50.

102. Baker, "Bullinger," *OER* 1:229. Theodore Beza, not Calvin, responded in writing to Castellio. While Castellio defended religious freedom, Beza in his *Treatises on the Authority of the Magistrates in the Punishment of Heretics* (1554) anticipated his later views about resistance to magistrates;

few comments as it relates to church discipline and the relationship of church and state. When Servetus arrived in Geneva, he was fleeing Catholic France, where he was already condemned to death for his denial of the Trinity. Servetus's trial was conducted by the civil authorities, who were at the time somewhat at odds with Calvin. Calvin's role in the trial was as an expert witness on theological matters, but he did not have the final say. In fact, he objected to Servetus's execution by burning, proposing a more humane form of capital punishment, but the council rejected his recommendation. Moreover, the strife over Servetus was part of a larger conflict between the Reformers and the libertines in Geneva. While heirs of Calvin condemn the execution of Servetus, most reject his heterodox theology. This event illustrates both the distinct roles of the church and state in Geneva and at the same time the then-prevailing notion that the state ought to combat heresy.[103]

Early Reformation Thought on Political Resistance to Tyranny

As Reformation leadership faced opposition from Catholic leaders, questions of civil disobedience and resistance surfaced, raising an ethical dilemma. Jesus had not advocated military resistance. Apostolic teaching insisted on submission to authority, even if magistrates dealt harshly with Christians. Thus early Reformers, following Augustine's lead, were reticent to advocate resistance.

HULDRYCH ZWINGLI

Zwingli's sermon *Der Hirt* applied the ephors allusion only to pastors. But as leader of the Zurich reformation, he participated in resistance to Catholicism by fighting and dying in battle against the Catholic cantons at Kappel in 1531.

HEINRICH BULLINGER

Bullinger asserted that the magistrate was obliged to rule justly in covenant fidelity to God but was not accountable to the people and could

---

see Robert M. Kingdon, "Les idées politiques de Bèze d'après son *Traitté de l'authorité du magistrat en la punition des hérétiques*," *Bibliothèque d'Humanisme et Renaissance* 22, no. 3 (1960): 566–69.

103. This function of the state did not imply for Calvin that the state was in charge of church discipline. For a more detailed account of the events surrounding Servetus's death, see Parker, *John Calvin*, 146–57.

not be checked by his subjects. Bullinger taught that tyranny was often God's chastisement on his unfaithful people. The only just response to a tyrant was to return to God's covenant through repentance and wait on God's providence to raise up judges to deliver them, as Israel had. God permitted only passive opposition to unjust rulers.[104]

PETER MARTYR VERMIGLI

In a biblical scholium, Vermigli asked, "Whether it be lawfull for subjectes to rise against their Prince?" His answer denied private resistance, but he affirmed the examples of the *ephoroi* and others as grounds for resistance to a tyrant by those who are "inferior" powers. He was concerned for the safety of all royalty, given the difficulty of satisfying subjects.[105] Whether influenced by Zwingli or not, Vermigli applied his ecclesiastical reliance on the ephors to the magisterial context, as did Calvin.

JOHN CALVIN

Calvin first wrote on the ethics of politics in his 1532 commentary on Seneca's *De Clementia*, which has been characterized as "a muzzle for Machiavellianism."[106] His defense of the Reformation addressed to King Francis I began every version of his *Institutes* to prevent his movement from being branded anarchist like the Anabaptists.

Calvin knew that Roman law allowed even private citizens to resist force with force. He was cognizant of the scholastic theologians' covenantal arguments developed during the conciliar crisis to limit the powers claimed by kings and popes.[107] Thus, his conception of resistance was congruent to the conciliarist approach to a tyrannical pontiff—the lesser magistrate corrects the covenant-breaking tyrant.[108] But his followers' development from passive disobedience to justified *popular* resistance to tyranny was not embraced by Calvin.[109]

---

104. Baker, "Covenant and Community," 23.

105. Kingdon, *Political Thought of Vermigli*, 99–100.

106. McNeill, "Calvinism and European Politics," 13.

107. See Lillback, *Binding of God*, 27–28, 34–35.

108. Cf. Calvin, *Institutes*, 4.20.31; CO 2:1116. McNeill points out the similarity of Calvin's position with Zwingli's comment in *Der Hirt* and suggests Calvin's dependence on him. "Democratic Element," 163.

109. Robert M. Kingdon, "Resistance Theory," OER 3:423–25.

His views of resistance to the Catholic clergy, however, laid the groundwork for later political resistance theories. Calvin observed that Malachi 2:1–9 taught that God's covenant with Levi required the priest to speak as God's interpreter. When Levi's descendants failed to speak God's Word, they violated the covenant and lost their right to be respected as servants of God. Similarly, the Roman priests were covenant breakers,[110] and covenant breaking was warrant for Reformational resistance.

The revolutionary character of Calvin's reforms became explicit in the ecclesiastical setting. Calvin insisted that the covenant breaking of the priesthood allows the Christian to "resist" the priests and to "subvert the whole of the Papacy." This is warranted by God's covenant demands for a pure clergy.[111] Calvin did not apply this doctrine to popular resistance in the political sphere.[112] Following Augustine, he rejected revolutionary action. Yet Calvin once almost implied popular rather than representative resistance, stating that a tyrant should rather be spit at than be obeyed![113]

Calvin extended Zwingli's appeal to the ephors of Sparta from the ecclesiastical context to the magistrates. Thus he, as with Vermigli, recognized appeal to lesser magistrates for resistance to tyrannical government:

> I am speaking all the while of private individuals. For if there are now any magistrates of the people, appointed to restrain the willfulness of kings (as in ancient times the ephors were set against the Spartan kings, or the tribunes of the people against the Roman consuls, or the demarchs against the senate of the Athenians; and perhaps, as things now are, such power as the three estates exercise in every realm when they hold their chief assemblies), I am so far from forbidding them to withstand, in accordance with their duty, the fierce licentiousness of kings, that, if they wink at kings who

110. Calvin, *Institutes*, 4.2.3; cf. CO 2:770. See also Calvin's discussion of the following references on the covenant and the priest: Deut. 33:9 (*Calvin's Commentaries*, vol. 3, bk. 4, 389; CO 25:388–89); Heb. 7:11 (*Calvin's Commentaries*, 22:166; CO 40:88–89); Heb. 7:20 (*Calvin's Commentaries*, 22:173; CO 40:93); and Heb. 8:6 (*Calvin's Commentaries*, 22:184–85; CO 40:99–100).
111. Calvin on Mal. 2:4, in *Calvin's Commentaries*, 15:520–21; CO 44:433.
112. Calvin, *Institutes*, 4.20.31.
113. Calvin on Dan. 6:22, in *Calvin's Commentaries*, 12:382; CO 41:26; cf. Calvin, *Institutes*, 1519n54.

violently fall upon and assault the lowly common folk I declare
that their dissimulation involves nefarious perfidy, because they
dishonestly betray the freedom of the people, of which they know
that they have been appointed protectors by God's ordinance.[114]

Here Calvin warranted resistance to tyranny through the "lesser magistrate." His disjunction between "private individuals" and "magistrates of the people" would be reconsidered in the Wars of Religion.

JOHN KNOX AND SCOTTISH PRESBYTERIANISM[115]

John Knox studied under Calvin. The notions of resistance and the
lesser magistrate[116] appear in Knox's reforming efforts in Scotland. The
Scottish reformation succeeded precisely because of its "bold disobedience by nobles, ministers, and people to Mary of Guise and Mary
Stuart."[117] George Buchanan, author of *The Law of Scottish Kingship*
(1579), sought to limit royal power by employing Calvin's appeal to
the ancient ephors.[118]

Knox played an initiating role in expressing the Reformed view
of popular resistance to tyranny. He was a link with the Lutheran
beginnings of popular resistance to tyranny. Knox stepped beyond
Calvin and developed a doctrine of resistance in his *On the Monstrous
Regiment of Women* (1558). England's Elizabeth I ascended the throne
when his fiery pamphlet appeared, causing an English breech with Geneva and thereby distressing Calvin.[119] Knox also related in his *History
of the Reformation in Scotland* that in a debate in 1564, he appealed
to the Lutheran Magdeburg Confession, which "affirms the duty of
armed resistance to a ruler who violates the law of God."[120]

---

114. Calvin, *Institutes*, 4.20.31.
115. J. H. Burns, "John Knox and Revolution, 1558," *History Today* 8, no. 8 (1958): 565–73; Burrell, "Covenant Idea as a Revolutionary Symbol," 338–50; Richard C. Gamble, "The Clash of King and Kirk: The 1690 Revolution Settlement in Presbyterian Scotland," in *The Practical Calvinist: An Introduction to the Presbyterian and Reformed Heritage in Honor of Dr. D. Clair Davis*, ed. Peter A. Lillback (Fearn, Ross-shire, Scotland: Christian Focus, 2002), 215–31; Richard L. Greaves, *Theology and Revolution in the Scottish Reformation: Studies in the Thought of John Knox* (Grand Rapids, MI: Christian University Press, 1980); W. Stanford Reid, "John Knox: The First of the Monarchomachs?," in Elazar and Kincaid, *The Covenant Connection*, 119–41.
116. McNeill, "Calvinism and European Politics," 14–15.
117. Ibid., 15.
118. Ibid.
119. Calvin, *Institutes*, 4.20.31.
120. Ibid.

Explicit Protestant Support for Popular Resistance to Tyranny

The maturation of magisterial resistance theory occurred in the heated conflicts of Reformation Europe that provoked riots, wars, assassinations, and massacres. These crises evoked popular political resistance to the manifold tyranny of religious persecution.[121]

Magdeburg

Lutherans resisted decrees that their worship was illegal from the time of Luther's being placed under the ban of the Holy Roman Empire in 1521 until the Peace of Augsburg in 1555.[122] In 1550, there appeared the first manifesto to legitimate Christian popular resistance, titled the Confession of Magdeburg, signed by Nikolaus von Amsdorf and eight clergymen.[123] The confession "seems to be the first formal enunciation of a theory of rightful forcible resistance by any Protestants who can be called orthodox."[124]

The clergymen argued that "passive resistance to a ruler seeking to destroy true religion is not sufficient to satisfy God. In that case the subject is bound to defend it 'mit Leib und Leben.' For a ruler who attempts such a thing represents not God, but the devil." It is impossible, they argued, to believe that God commands nonresistance in all cases. To believe that is to believe that in some cases God wills the maintenance of evil and commands disobedience to himself. It can only be the Devil who inspires men with such a belief.[125]

The Schmalkald League of Protestants argued that the emperor could be resisted due to the Holy Roman Empire's constitution. The emperor was not given absolute power, as he was checked by seven other royal electors who voted him into office. There were also other "inferior magistrates" who held the rights to other powers on a local basis, including the provision of "true" religious worship. If the emperor sought to change this by the power of the sword, these other

---

121. Kingdon, "Resistance Theory," *OER* 3:423–25.
122. Ibid., 424.
123. Allen, *History of Political Thought*, 103–6; David M. Whitford, *Tyranny and Resistance: The Magdeburg Confession and the Lutheran Tradition* (St. Louis, MO: Concordia, 2001); Amsdorff, *Bekentnis Unterricht*; Ludwig Cardauns, *Die Lehre vom Widerstandsrecht des Volks gegen die rechtmässige Obrigkeit im Luthertum und Calvinismus des 16. Jahrhunderts* (1903; repr., Darmstadt: Wissenschaftliche Buchgesellschaft, 1973).
124. Allen, *History of Political Thought*, 104.
125. Ibid., 104–5.

leaders had the right to resist him by force. These notions were put into practice in the Schmalkald Wars. After a decisive Catholic victory in the first war of 1546–1547, the emperor made efforts to enforce Roman Catholic worship. However, committed Lutherans in Magdeburg refused to cooperate, catalyzing the second war of 1552–1555. As a result, the Peace of Augsburg was signed in 1555, enabling Catholic and Lutheran princes to establish whichever form of worship they preferred for their domains. Thus, resistance theory was no longer a primary concern for Lutherans.[126]

The Huguenots in France

News of the successful Lutheran theory of resistance soon spread to Calvinist lands. Vermigli and Calvin's view justifying resistance if the opposition to the magistrate was led by lawfully authorized "inferior magistrates" was generally embraced. However, as noted, John Knox had begun his own views of popular resistance and openly cited the Confession of Magdeburg. Generally, Calvin's more subdued conservative perspective prevailed.[127]

The French Protestants, popularly called Huguenots, were followers of Calvin's theology.[128] In 1562, the Wars of Religion between the Roman Catholics and the Huguenots exploded in France. The Huguenot leaders justified their resistance by explaining that they were actually seeking to deliver the royal family from malevolent political advisors. However, such justifications could not be made "after the Saint Bartholomew's Day Massacre . . . (1572), for which

---

126. Kingdon, "Resistance Theory," *OER* 3:424.
127. Myriam Yardeni, "French Calvinist Political Thought, 1534–1715," in Prestwich, *International Calvinism, 1541–1715*, 315.
128. Philip Benedict, "Prophets in Arms? Ministers in War, Ministers on War: France, 1562–74," *Past and Present* 214, supplement 7 (2012): 163–96; Guy Howard Dodge, *The Political Theory of the Huguenots of the Dispersion with Special Reference to the Thought and Influence of Pierre Jurieu* (New York: Columbia University Press, 1947); William Farr Church, *Constitutional Thought in Sixteenth-Century France: A Study in the Evolution of Ideas*, Harvard Historical Studies 47 (1941; repr., New York: Octagon Books, 1969); Julian H. Franklin, ed. and trans., *Constitutionalism and Resistance in the Sixteenth Century: Three Treatises by Hotman, Beza, and Mornay* (New York: Pegasus, 1969); Paul F.-M. Méaly, *Les Publicistes de la Réforme sous François II et Charles IX: Origines des idées politiques libérales en France* (Paris: Librairie Fischbacher, 1903); J. H. M. Salmon, *The French Religious Wars in English Political Thought* (Oxford: Clarendon, 1959); Salmon, *Society in Crisis: France in the Sixteenth Century* (New York: St. Martin's, 1975); Salmon, "Wars of Religion," *OER* 4:258–63; Georges Weill, *Les théories sur le pouvoir royal en France pendant les guerres de religion* (1892; repr., Geneva: Slatkine Reprint, 1971).

the royal family openly claimed responsibility."[129] Accordingly, Huguenot resistance theories were born, inspired in part by the Magdeburg Confession, as they regrouped to defend themselves against the onslaught of royal power aimed at the annihilation of Calvinism in France.[130]

Shortly after Calvin's death, French authors and followers of Calvin extended his covenantal perspective to its logical end of organized popular resistance to tyranny. He had taught that the papacy, a political power of immense strength, was to be resisted, even subverted, due to its covenant breaking. How could this ecclesiastical notion fail to penetrate the sphere of the state in the milieu of political tyranny, especially since he had legitimated appeal to the royal lesser magistrates? After the Saint Bartholomew's Day Massacre, this logic was irresistible.[131]

THE LEADING MONARCHOMACHS

The French resistance theorists of the time have been dubbed the "monarchomachs," meaning "enemies of the monarch" or "fighters against the king." They united on the medieval conception that magistrates were created for the people and not people for their rulers. Three great monarchomach classics were produced. The first, *Franco-Gallia*, appeared in 1573 and was written by Francois Hotman. The following year, Theodore Beza's *Du droit des Magistrats sur leurs sujets* was published. Finally, in 1579, the *Vindicae contra Tyrannos* was written by Philippe Du Plessis-Mornay.[132]

Francois Hotman

Hotman based his theory in *Franco-Gallia* on a history of the French constitution. He asserted that royal power in France had depended on a council of elite advisors, forerunners of the States General, who invested power in the king and thus had the authority to remove it in the event he became a tyrant.

---

129. Kingdon, "Resistance Theory," *OER* 3:424.
130. McNeill, "Calvinism and European Politics," 14.
131. See Calvin's comments on 1 Pet. 2:15 in *Calvin's Commentaries*, 22:83; CO 55:246; and on Ezek. 17:19 in *Calvin's Commentaries*, 12:203; CO 40:414.
132. Yardeni, "French Calvinist Political Thought, 1534–1715," 320–24.

Theodore Beza[133]

Beza, the successor of Calvin, was committed to Calvin's theology but developed it in distinctive ways. Subtle differences of exegesis are evident in their understandings of Romans 13:1–7, the *locus classicus* of the relationship of church and state in the New Testament.[134] But their differing views became obvious in Beza's *Du droit des Magistrats sur leurs sujets*. Under the pressure of the Saint Bartholomew's Day Massacre, Beza's position moved beyond Calvin's position of passive resistance and reluctance to appeal to the magistrate.

Du droit des Magistrats was originally a course Beza gave in Geneva. He asserted that all authority of every king is God given but is imparted through the election of the people. Magistrates could require submission from their subjects only to the extent that they kept the law of God. Thus, royalty is always responsible under God to the people, and should kings become tyrants, the people possess the right to resist them, under the lead of their elected magistrates. He argued that open tyrants should be punished and that the States General possessed the right to depose a tyrant.

Beza declared that resistance did not demand a leader of royal blood;[135] a legitimate magistrate of the people could organize resistance.[136] He differentiated two types of "inferior magistrates," those entitled to advise the king because of their social rank and those

---

133. Theodore Beza, *Du droit des Magistrats*, ed. Robert M. Kingdon, Les Classiques de la pensée politique 7 (Geneva: Droz, 1970); Alfred Cartier, *Les idées politiques de Théodore de Bèze d'après le traité Du droit des Magistrats sur leurs sujets* (Geneva: Jullien, 1900); Robert M. Kingdon, "Calvinism and Resistance Theory, 1550–1580," in Burns, *Cambridge History of Political Thought, 1450–1700*, 193–218; Paul-Alexis Mellet, ed., *Et de sa bouche sortait un glaive: Les Monarchomaques au XVIe siècle: Actes de la Journée d'étude tenue à Tours en mai 2003* (Geneva: Droz, 2006); Richard C. Gamble, "The Christian and the Tyrant: Beza and Knox on Political Resistance Theory," *WTJ* 46, no. 1 (1984): 125–39; Robert M. Kingdon, "The First Expression of Theodore Beza's Political Ideas," *Archiv für Reformationsgeschichte* 46, no. 1 (1955): 88–100; Kingdon, "Les idées politiques de Bèze," 566–69; John F. Southworth Jr., "Theodore Beza, Covenantalism, and Resistance to Political Authority in the Sixteenth Century" (PhD diss., Westminster Theological Seminary, 2003).

134. Richard A. Muller, "Calvin, Beza, and the Exegetical History of Romans 13:1–7," in *The Identity of Geneva: The Christian Commonwealth, 1564–1864*, ed. John B. Roney, Martin I. Klauber, Contributions to the Study of World History 59 (Westport, CT: Greenwood, 1998), 39–56.

135. Raitt, "Bèze," *OER* 1:149–50.

136. Beza discussed the question, "Si, estant persecuté pour la Religion, on se peut defendre par armes en bonne conscience," in *Du droit des Magistrats*, 63–68. His answer permitted resistance to a tyrant. Cf. also, du Plessis-Mornay or Hubert Languet, *A Defence of Liberty against Tyrants: A Translation of the "Vindiciae contra Tyrannos,"* ed. Harold J. Laski (1924; repr., Gloucester, MA: Peter Smith, 1963).

charged with administering local governments. Both had the right to disobey and resist a monarch turned tyrant.[137] Thus Beza denied the accepted view that a legitimate revolt had to be led by princes with royal pedigree.[138]

Du Plessis-Mornay[139]

Mornay composed the *Vindiciae contra Tyrannos*, the fullest treatment of the three works. He answered four critical questions of the time:

1. whether subjects were obliged to obey a prince who commanded them to transgress the law of God;
2. whether they could resist him and in what way;
3. whether they could resist a prince who violated the laws of the state; and
4. whether in these two last cases neighboring princes had the right or duty to intervene.

His first two questions were answered in that God is superior to the king and had to be obeyed first. Further, the right to resist comes from earthly considerations such as constitutions but belongs only to communities, not to individuals. Communities and their magistrates had a right of self-defense, especially against the king, since he was supposed to protect his subjects.

The last two questions he explained in terms of a dual covenant between God, the king, the lesser magistrates, and the people. God was in covenant with the king, but he was also in covenant with the lesser magistrates and the people. In light of this, the king was in covenant with his subjects. It was the covenantal obligation of magistrates in their shared covenant with God to see to it that the king kept his covenant duties for his subjects. "Seen in the context of the realities of the Wars of Religion, this is a coherent and brand-new political system

137. Kingdon, "Resistance Theory," *OER* 3:424.
138. Raitt, "Bèze," *OER* 1:149–50. Paul T. Fuhrmann, "Philip Mornay and the Huguenot Challenge to Absolutism," in Hunt, *Calvinism and the Political Order*, 47–48.
139. Philippe Du Plessis-Mornay or Hubert Languet, *A Defence of Liberty against Tyrants*; Du Plessis-Mornay or Languet, *Vindiciae contra Tyrannos: Traduction française de 1581*, Les classiques de la pensée politique 11 (Geneva: Droz, 1979); Joachim Ambert, *Duplessis Mornay ou Études historiques et politiques sur la situation de la France de 1549 à 1623*, 2nd ed. (Paris: Comptoir des Imprimeurs-Unis, 1848); Raoul Patry, *Philippe du Plessis-Mornay: Un Huguenot homme d'État (1549–1623)* (Paris: Fischbacher, 1933).

which links the feudal past with a democracy that was to be born some centuries later."[140]

THE MAIN ARGUMENTS OF THE MONARCHOMACHS' THEORIES OF POPULAR RESISTANCE TO TYRANNY

Huguenot theories of popular resistance to a tyrannical prince were supported by several key arguments. What follows are the leading examples.

The Constitutional Argument[141]

The writers sought to operate within the expressed terms and structure of the constitution that governed them.

Theory of Sovereignty: The People Create the King[142]

Political sovereignty emerges from the people. Even in hereditary monarchies, magistrates are created by the people. The *Vindiciae* declares, "Never was a man born with a crown on his head and the scepter in his hand."[143]

Appeal to Inferior Magistrates[144]

The resistance was not the fruit of anarchy but of ordered governmental structure. Part of the duty of the inferior magistrates was to correct the king: "Only the subordinate magistrates could act in the name of the people and even appeal to foreign powers for help against a tyrant."[145]

Dual-Covenant View

McNeill states, "The covenant principle of limited monarchy was further advanced by the *Vindiciae contra tyrannos* (1579), written in part by Philip du Plessis-Mornay. More explicitly than in earlier treatises the sacred covenant of ruler and people here involves a covenant of both with God."[146] The delegation of the people's power to the monarch by

---

140. Yardeni, "French Calvinist Political Thought, 1534–1715," 324.
141. Kingdon, "Resistance Theory," *OER* 3:423–25.
142. Fuhrmann, "Mornay and the Huguenot Challenge," 48–49.
143. Ibid., 48.
144. Kingdon, "Resistance Theory," *OER* 3:423–25.
145. Yardeni, "French Calvinist Political Thought, 1534–1715," 323.
146. McNeill, "Calvinism and European Politics," 16–17.

their consent is conditional because it is a covenant or contract. "Inferior magistrates," if necessary, could lead resistance. This is because all government involves two covenants, one between God and the general population inclusive of both the king and his subjects and a second between the monarch and his subjects. A king who broke these contracts lost God's support and the legitimate expectation of human obedience.[147]

Corporate-Resistance View

While the king was a lesser universe than the people, he was still a greater individual than any solitary person. Thus, resistance to a monarch had to be the work of the people, not of a mere individual, who would thus be a seditious person.[148] In this view, resistance was not anarchical because it did not legitimate individual subjects' resistance to the king or permit assassination or tyrannicide. This follows from popular consent, which brings a government into existence. The formation of a government is accomplished by the people considered collectively. Mornay argued that the ruler is a *minor universis* ("a lesser universe") when compared to all the people who create the monarchy, but the king is a *maior singulis* ("a greater individual"), as every other individual, inclusive of magistrates, is lesser than the king as an individual. So no private citizen on his own can ever have the right to resist a legitimately enthroned monarch. Thus, "the people 'create the prince not as individuals but all together,'" and "their rights against him are the rights of a corporation, not the rights" of a single member. Accordingly, "private individuals who 'draw the sword' against their kings are thus 'seditious, no matter how just the cause may be.'"[149]

Universal Human Dignity

In the aftermath of the Saint Bartholomew's Day Massacre,[150] a lesser known work, the *Reveille-matin*, asked that "all our Catho-

147. Kingdon, "Resistance Theory," *OER* 3:423–25; Fuhrmann, "Mornay and the Huguenot Challenge," 47–49.
148. Skinner, *Foundations*, 2:334.
149. Ibid.
150. The Saint Bartholomew's Day Massacre is a key event in French history, which influenced the Huguenots' political views. On the eve of Saint Bartholomew's Day, August 24, 1572, the Huguenot leader Gaspard de Coligny was murdered in Paris, and thousands of other Huguenots were killed throughout France. Yardeni asserts, "What characterized French Calvinist political thought

lics, our patriots, our good neighbours and all the rest of the French, who are treated worse than beasts, should wake up this time so as to perceive their misery and take counsel together how to remedy their misfortunes."[151] This was a cry for all to see necessary limits on the king's authority. By the king's denial of the humanity of his subjects, he himself was no longer a public person. Thus, he was no longer a person worthy of respect and of protection from revolt but a tyrant who usurped the attributes of God, who alone can take life.

Separation of Powers

Paul Fuhrmann offers us a concise summary of Mornay and monarchomachists' views on the separation of powers:

> Mornay caught sight of the fact that if the legislative power is the same as the executive, there are then no bounds to the executive power. The only safeguard of the liberty and security of persons is to be found in the separation of political powers. With imposing gravity, Mornay and the Monarchomachists set forth the four great principles: sovereignty of the nation, political contract, representative government, and the separation of powers that really makes up all our modern constitutions.[152]

This assessment underlines the often overlooked substantive contribution of Huguenot thinkers to the development of modern political theories.

THE ENGLISH CIVIL WAR: SCOTTISH COVENANTERS AND ENGLISH PURITANS RESIST THE ANGLICAN KING

The Covenanters[153] have long been identified with the Presbyterian resistance to the British crown in Scotland.[154] The king of the United Kingdom was not a king in the Scottish Kirk but a mere member:

---

between the Conspiracy of Amboise and the massacre of St Bartholomew was a slide from the *right* to resist to the *duty* to resist." Yardeni, "French Calvinist Political Thought, 1534–1715," 319.

151. Ibid., 321.

152. Fuhrmann, "Mornay and the Huguenot Challenge," 64.

153. Burns, "John Knox and Revolution, 1558," 565–73; Greaves, *Theology and Revolution in the Scottish Reformation*; John R. Gray, "The Political Theory of John Knox," *CH* 8, no. 2 (1939): 132–47; Richard L. Greaves, "John Knox and the Covenant Tradition," *JEH* 24, no. 1 (1973): 23–32.

154. Burrell, "Covenant Idea as a Revolutionary Symbol," 338–50.

Presbyterian partisans adopted the two kingdom theory of church-state relations. . . . Although this doctrine also taught the Christian magistrate's freedom from clerical dictation, its practical effect in Scotland was to promote the exclusion of the king as king from ecclesiastical decision. "Thair is twa Kings and twa Kingdomes in Scotland," went Melville's famous rebuke. "Thair is Chryst Jesus the King, and his kingdome the Kirk, whase subject King James the Saxt is, and of whase kingdome nocht a king, nor a lord, nor a heid, bot a member!"[155]

The English context also produced Puritan independency[156] and the Westminster Standards[157] in the context of a civil war against the British king who was the head of the Church of England. Charles I had continued the policy of his father, James I, in persecuting the Puritans in England and the Presbyterians in Scotland. But when the Church of England attempted to impose its worship on the Scottish Calvinists, they responded by signing, in 1637, the Scottish National Covenant, which abolished the Anglican episcopal form of church government. Charles met such strong opposition in Knox's Scotland that he had to call for the election of a Parliament to raise men and resources to carry on the war.

But to the king's surprise and anger, the people elected a Parliament with a majority of Puritans, which the king then dissolved, calling for another election. The second Parliament, however, had an even greater number of Puritans. When Charles ordered it to dissolve, Parliament refused, forcing Charles to field an army to force the members to obey him. Soon Parliament called on the Scottish Presbyterians to join them. Their army, led by Oliver Cromwell, defeated Charles, who was be-

---

155. Maclear, "Samuel Rutherford," 72–73.

156. Allen, *History of Political Thought*, 210–30; Patrick Collinson, *The Elizabethan Puritan Movement* (Berkeley: University of California Press, 1967); William Haller, *Liberty and Reformation in the Puritan Revolution* (New York: Columbia University Press, 1955); Perry Miller and Thomas H. Johnson, eds., *The Puritans* (New York: American Book Company, 1938); Richard Schlatter, ed., *Richard Baxter and Puritan Politics* (New Brunswick, NJ: Rutgers University Press, 1957); A. Craig Troxel and Peter J. Wallace, "Men in Combat over the Civil Law: 'General Equity' in WCF 19.4," *WTJ* 64, no. 2 (2002): 307–18; L. John Van Til, *Liberty of Conscience: The History of a Puritan Idea* (Nutley, NJ: Craig, 1972).

157. John W. Allen, *English Political Thought, 1603–1660*, 2 vols. (London: Methuen, 1938); Robley J. Johnston, "A Study in the Westminster Doctrine of the Relation of the Civil Magistrate to the Church," *WTJ* 12, no. 1 (1949): 13–29; Johnston, "A Study in the Westminster Doctrine of the Relation of the Civil Magistrate to the Church (Continued)," *WTJ* 12, no. 2 (1950): 121–35.

headed in 1649. The Commonwealth was established, and eventually, Cromwell became the Lord Protector of England and Scotland. Cromwell ruled from 1653 until 1658. But with Cromwell's death, there was no one of his stature to lead Parliament, and in 1660, Charles II was restored to his father's throne.

During the more than five years of civil war, the Westminster Assembly sought to reform the Church of England. The delegates to the Assembly included 121 ministers; all except for two had been ordained by a bishop in the Church of England. They began their work at the Westminster Abbey in London on July 1, 1643. After abandoning the attempt to revise the Thirty-Nine Articles of Religion, they produced a new confession, the Westminster Confession of Faith, completed in 1646. The confession itself acknowledges the right of Christian magistrates to convene a religious assembly like the Westminster Assembly: "Magistrates may lawfully call a synod of ministers and other fit persons to consult and advise with about religion."[158] The American revision of the Westminster Confession, however, specifies that church leaders ought "to appoint such assemblies."

Regarding the separation of church and state, the American revision of the Westminster Confession moved toward greater separation than the original position of the Westminster Confession. Yet the original confession stated that "the Lord Jesus, as king and head of his Church, hath therein appointed a government in the hand of Church officers, distinct from the civil magistrate."[159] Thus, the government of the church is separate from that of the state. Moreover, church discipline belongs to ministers: "To these officers the keys of the kingdom of heaven are committed."[160] Nevertheless, the original text of the confession asserted that "the civil magistrate" had to insure "that unity and peace be preserved in the Church, that the truth of God be kept pure and entire, that all blasphemies and heresies be suppressed."[161] American Presbyterians revised the confession at this point as follows: "It is the duty of civil magistrates to protect the Church of our common

---

158. WCF 31.2.
159. WCF 30.1.
160. WCF 30.2. Cf. WCF 23.3: "The civil magistrate may not assume to himself the administration of the Word and Sacraments, or the power of the keys of the kingdom of heaven."
161. WCF 23.3.

Lord, without giving the preference to any denomination of Christians above the rest." The Westminster Confession was composed in the context of the magisterial Reformation, while the American revisions reflect the the context of a young nation that had disestablished religion at the federal level.

REFORMATIONAL RESISTANCE IN THE NETHERLANDS AND OTHER EUROPEAN COUNTRIES

Many efforts at religiously based resistance in the Reformation era occurred across Europe in England,[162] the Palatinate and German Reformed churches,[163] Hungary, and Poland.[164] Dutch Calvinism had a long struggle with Spanish domination and Roman Catholic persecution.[165] And the legacy of Calvin was heard in William of Orange's Apology in 1581 during the Netherlands' revolt against Spanish rule.[166]

Roman Catholic Resistance Theories

The Roman Catholic tradition is deeply committed to an authoritarian structure.[167] However, when the Catholic princes realized they would

---

162. Allen, *English Political Thought, 1603–1660*; Allen, *History of Political Thought*, 121–33; J. Wayne Baker, "John Owen, John Locke, and Calvin's Heirs in England," in De Klerk, *Calvin and the State*, 83–102.

163. Zacharias Ursinus, *The Commentary of Dr. Zacharias Ursinus on the Heidelberg Catechism*, trans. G. W. Williard (1852; repr., Phillipsburg, NJ: Presbyterian and Reformed, n.d.), 285–303, 440–63; Charles D. Gunnoe, *Thomas Erastus and the Palatinate: A Renaissance Physician in the Second Reformation*, Brill's Series in Church History 48 (Leiden: Brill, 2011); Ruth Wesel-Roth, *Thomas Erastus: Ein Beitrag zur Geschichte der reformierten Kirche und zur Lehre von der Staatssouveränität* (Lahr: Schauenburg, 1954); Bard Thompson, "Historical Background of the Catechism," in *Essays on the Heidelberg Catechism* (Philadelphia: United Church Press, 1963), 8–30.

164. Thomas Rees, ed. and trans., *The Racovian Catechism: With Notes and Illustrations, Translated from the Latin; to Which Is Prefixed a Sketch of the History of Unitarianism in Poland and the Adjacent Countries* (London: Longman, Hurst, Orme, and Brown, 1818); Dariusz M. Bryćko, *The Irenic Calvinism of Daniel Kalaj (d. 1681): A Study in the History and Theology of the Polish-Lithuanian Reformation*, Refo500 Academic Studies 4 (Göttingen: Vandenhoeck & Ruprecht, 2012).

165. P. S. Gerbrandy, *National and International Stability: Althusius, Grotius, van Vollenhoven* (London: Oxford University Press, 1944); W. Robert Godfrey, "Church and State in Dutch Calvinism," in *Through Christ's Word: A Festschrift for Dr. Philip E. Hughes*, ed. W. Robert Godfrey and Jesse L. Boyd III (Phillipsburg, NJ: Presbyterian and Reformed, 1985), 223–43; Nicolaas H. Gootjes, *The Belgic Confession: Its History and Sources*, Texts and Studies in Reformation and Post-Reformation Thought (Grand Rapids, MI: Baker, 2007), 127–31, 185–87; James W. Skillen, "From Covenant of Grace to Tolerant Public Pluralism: The Dutch Calvinist Contribution," in Elazar and Kincaid, *The Covenant Connection*, 71–99; John Christian Laursen and Cary J. Nederman, eds., *Beyond the Persecuting Society: Religious Toleration before the Enlightenment* (Philadelphia: University of Pennsylvania Press, 1988).

166. McNeill, "Calvinism and European Politics," 17.

167. Allen, *History of Political Thought*, 199–209; 445–501; Frederic J. Baumgartner, *Radical Reactionaries: The Political Thought of the French Catholic League*, Étude de philologie

be under Protestant kings, as in Huguenot France and Protestant England, they too wrestled with arguments for resistance. The Catholics mirrored the Huguenots' theories when the tables were turned.[168]

But their arguments had a distinctively Catholic character to them, as they wrestled with the pope's role in legitimate resistance to royalty. The pope could be a supranational, neutral arbiter in international conflicts.[169] Further, on what basis could the pope depose a ruler? Cardinal Bellarmine reasoned that as the pope was a religious leader and not a magistrate, he had to use indirect power to remove a leader by licensing Catholic "inferior magistrates" or bordering Catholic rulers to topple a tyrant.[170] Other arguments included the monarchs' violations of their coronation oaths to protect the Catholic faith[171] or violation of sworn promises.[172]

The Law of Nature and the Law of God in Reformational Political Theory

Several Reformation-era writers composed substantial treatises on political themes that grew out of the fires of Reformation controversies. These works elevated and integrated notions of the law of nature in conjunction with the law of God. Thereby they laid the foundation for Western political thought, providing a blueprint for government that shaped the Protestant colonies in the New World.

SAMUEL RUTHERFORD: THE RULE OF LAW

The main theme of *Lex, Rex* is that all rightful authority lies in law.[173] The king is truly king only when he identifies himself with the law. "*Rex*

---

et d'histoire 29 (Geneva: Droz, 1975); A. Lynn Martin, *Henry III and the Jesuit Politicians*, Travaux d'humanisme et Renaissance 134 (Geneva: Droz, 1973); Victor Martin, *Le Gallicanisme et la Réforme catholique: Essai historique sur l'introduction en France des décrets du Concile de Trente (1563–1615)* (1919; repr., Geneva: Slatkine-Megariotis Reprints, 1975); J. H. M. Salmon, "Catholic Resistance Theory, Ultramontanism, and the Royalist Response, 1580–1620," in Burns, *Cambridge History of Political Thought, 1450–1700*, 219–53.

168. Salmon, "Catholic Resistance Theory," 219–20.
169. Kingdon, "Resistance Theory," *OER* 3:424.
170. Ibid.
171. Ibid.
172. Ironically, the Catholic resistance arguments began to parallel aspects of Calvin's view; compare Calvin, *Institutes*, 4.20.31.
173. Samuel Rutherford, *A Free Disputation against Pretended Liberty of Conscience* (London: R. I. for Andrew Crook, 1649); Rutherford, *Lex, Rex, or the Law and the Prince* (1644; repr., Harrisonburg, VA: Sprinkle Publications, 1982); Crawford Gribben, "Samuel Rutherford and Liberty of Conscience," *WTJ* 71, no. 2 (2009): 355–73; John L. Marshall, "Natural Law and the

est lex viva, animata, loquens lex: The king is a living, breathing, and speaking Law." He is necessary because human nature avoids submission to law. The more the king personifies the law, the more of a king he is; "in his remotest distance from Law and Reason, he is a Tyrant."[174]

Rutherford saw the origin of government in God and in the people's initiation of political systems, regardless of form. He accepted Mornay's dual-covenant scheme from the *Vindiciae*: three parties in the covenants—God, the ruler, and the people—and two compacts, one between God and everyone and the other between the ruler and the people.[175] Rutherford wrote,

> The Lord and the people giveth a crown by one and the same action . . . seeing the people maketh him a king covenant-wise, and conditionally so he rule according to God's law, and the people resigning their power to him for their safety. . . . It is certain God giveth a king that same way by that same very act of the people.[176]

If the king breaks the covenant with God, the political covenant is shattered, and the ruler is no longer a lawful king. Then the people "are presumed to have no king . . . and . . . to have the power in themselves, as if they had not appointed any king at all."[177] According to Rutherford, the Bible's written covenant rules over natural law if there is no formal written covenant for the king and the people:

> Where there is no vocal or written covenant . . . then those things which are just and right according to the law of God, and the rule of God in moulding the first king, are understood to regulate both king and people, as if they had been written; and here we produce our written covenant, Deut. 17.15; Josh. 1.8, 9; 2 Chron. 32.32 [*sic*; 2 Chron. 31:21].[178]

Covenant: The Place of Natural Law in the Covenantal Framework of Samuel Rutherford's *Lex, Rex*" (PhD diss., Westminster Theological Seminary, 1995); Andries Raath and Shaun de Freitas, "Theologically United and Divided: The Political Covenantalism of Samuel Rutherford and John Milton," *WTJ* 67, no. 2 (2005): 301–21; John Coffey, *Politics, Religion and the British Revolutions: The Mind of Samuel Rutherford*, Cambridge Studies in Early Modern British History (New York: Cambridge University Press, 1997); Christopher Hill, *Intellectual Origins of the English Revolution* (Oxford: Clarendon, 1965).
174. Maclear, "Samuel Rutherford," 77–78.
175. Ibid., 75.
176. Rutherford, *Lex, Rex*, 57; cf. Maclear, "Samuel Rutherford," 75.
177. Rutherford, *Lex, Rex*, 56; cf. Maclear, "Samuel Rutherford," 76.
178. Rutherford, *Lex, Rex*, 59; cf. Maclear, "Samuel Rutherford," 76, 202n26.

Rutherford recognized legitimate popular resistance, since by injustice the magistrate abandons his office and forfeits claim on the obedience of religious men. Rutherford rejected the notion that people would revolt for minor infractions, arguing that tyranny is obvious: "The people have a natural throne of policy in their conscience to give warning . . . against the king as a Tyrant. . . . Where tyranny is more obscure . . . the king keepeth possession; but I deny that tyranny can be obscure long." Still both people and king are bound in covenant, and the king's duty is to compel them to observe its terms: "Each may compel the other to mutual performance."[179]

THE MUTUAL CONSENT IN THE POLITICAL PACT BETWEEN PEOPLE AND MAGISTRATE: JOHN ALTHUSIUS

John Althusius, a Geneva-trained German and author of *Politics Methodically Set Forth* (*Politica methodice digesta*, 1603), lived in the Netherlands.[180] His study proposed a plan of government in which there would be the fullest cooperation between magistrates and people.[181] It has been called "the first full-bodied political theory of the modern age."[182] Althusius began with a community in covenant with one another:

> Politics is the art of *consociating* men for the purpose of establishing, cultivating, and conserving social life among them. Whence it is called "symbiotics." The subject matter of politics is therefore consociation, in which the symbiotes pledge themselves each to the other, by an explicit or tacit pact, to *mutual communication* of whatever is useful and necessary for the harmonious exercise of social life.[183]

---

179. Rutherford, *Lex, Rex*, 117, 190; cf. Maclear, "Samuel Rutherford," 77.
180. Johannes Althusius, *Politica Methodice Digesta of Johannes Althusius*, ed. Carl J. Friedrich, 3rd ed. (1614; repr., Cambridge, MA: Harvard University Press, 1932); Carl J. Friedrich, *Johannes Althusius und sein Werk im Rahmen der Entwicklung der Theorie von der Politik* (Berlin: Duncker und Humblot, 1975); Otto von Gierke, *The Development of Political Theory*, trans. Bernard Freyd (New York: Fertig, 1966); Thomas O. Hueglin, *Early Modern Concepts for a Late Modern World: Althusius on Community and Federalism* (Waterloo, ON: Wilfrid Laurier University Press, 1999); Hueglin, "Covenant and Federalism in the Politics of Althusius," in Elazar and Kincaid, *The Covenant Connection*, 31–54; James Skillen, "The Political Theory of Johannes Althusius," *Philosophia Reformata* 39, nos. 3–4 (1974): 170–90.
181. McNeill, "Calvinism and European Politics," 17–18.
182. Hueglin, "Covenant and Federalism," 31.
183. Quoted in ibid., 31–32.

The law that was to govern this community was the Scriptures. Introducing the second edition, he wrote,

> I more frequently use examples from sacred scripture because it has God or pious men as its author, and because I consider that no polity from the beginning of the world has been more wisely and perfectly constructed than the polity of the Jews. We err, I believe, whenever in similar circumstances we depart from it.[184]

Althusius carried forward the Reformers' concern that the law of the state be grounded in the law of God:

> This rule, which is solely God's will for men manifested in his law, is called law in the general sense that it is a precept for doing those things that pertain to living a pious, holy, just, and suitable life. That is to say, it pertains to the duties that are to be performed toward God and one's neighbour, and to the love of God and one's neighbour.[185]

THE AUTHORITY AND RIGHTS OF THE LAW OF NATURE: JOHN BODIN, HUGO GROTIUS, JOHN PONET

Other important political theorists include John Bodin,[186] Hugo Grotius,[187] and John Ponet.[188] John Bodin wrote *De la république* (1576). Having lived in Geneva and in France, his thought moved in the direction of absolutism while insisting on the foundational importance of the law of nature and the law of God. He believed that the

---

184. Quoted in ibid., 34.
185. Quoted in Skillen, "From Covenant of Grace to Tolerant Public Pluralism," 77.
186. Jean Bodin, *The Six Bookes of a Commonweale. A Facsimile Reprint of the English Translation of 1606, Corrected and Supplemented in the Light of a New Comparison with the French and Latin Texts*, ed. Kenneth Douglas McRae, Harvard Political Classics (Cambridge, MA: Harvard University Press, 1962); Allen, *History of Political Thought*, 394–444; Julian H. Franklin, *Jean Bodin and the Sixteenth-Century Revolution in the Methodology of Law and History* (New York: Columbia University Press, 1963); Beatrice Reynolds, *Proponents of Limited Monarchy in Sixteenth-Century France: Francis Hotman and Jean Bodin* (New York: Columbia University Press, 1931); Henri Chevreul, *Étude sur le XVIe siècle: Hubert Languet, 1518–1581* (Paris: L. Potier, 1852).
187. Hugo Grotius, *The Rights of War and Peace*, ed. Richard Tuck from the edition by Jean Barbeyrac, 3 vols. (Indianapolis, IN: Liberty Fund, 2005), originally published as *De jure belli ac pacis libri tres* (1625); E. Dumbauld, *The Life and Legal Writings of Hugo Grotius* (Norman, OK: University of Oklahoma Press, 1969); W. S. M. Knight, *The Life and Works of Hugo Grotius* (1925; repr., New York: Oceana Publications, 1962).
188. John Ponet, *A Short Treatise of Politic Power* (1556; repr., Menston, Yorkshire: Scolar, 1970); Allen, *History of Political Thought*, 118–20; Winthrop S. Hudson, *John Ponet (1516?–1556): Advocate of Limited Monarchy* (Chicago: University of Chicago Press, 1942).

various forms of government reflected the character and circumstances of various populations in differing nations.[189]

Hugo Grotius's chief work was *Right of War and Peace* (*De jure belli et pacis*, 1625). He is considered by many to be the founder of modern international law. Generally Arminian in theology rather than Calvinistic, his basic conception was that natural law is essentially the law of God and so divinely established that not even God can change it. It is inborn and inseparable from human nature. Magisterial violation of the law of nature requires disobedience and can lead to the ruler's deposition or execution.[190]

John Ponet, the Bishop of Winchester, was the most radical. His *Shorte Treatise of Politike Power* (1556) sought to establish the right for tyrannicide. He wrote in the context of his flight for safety from "Bloody Mary"—Mary Tudor of England.[191] He reasoned from the law of nature and Scripture that persecuted peoples have the authority to remove and to judge their persecutors.[192]

American Theology and Politics in the Aftermath of the Reformation

As we conclude our survey of the relationship between church and state in the Reformation age, we should recognize that theological concepts from this era remain a part of our theological discourse. One hears echoes of the Reformation in discussions of sphere sovereignty,[193] two kingdoms,[194]

---

189. McNeill, "Calvinism and European Politics," 15–16.
190. Ibid., 18.
191. Kingdon, "Resistance Theory," *OER* 3:423–25.
192. McNeill, "Calvinism and European Politics," 14.
193. William Edgar, review of *Creating a Christian Worldview: Abraham Kuyper's Lectures on Calvinism*, by Peter S. Heslam, *WTJ* 60, no. 2 (1998): 355–58; McKendree R. Langley, "Emancipation and Apologetics: The Formation of Abraham Kuyper's Anti-Revolutionary Party in the Netherlands, 1872–1880" (PhD diss., Westminster Theological Seminary, 1995); Paul Woolley, *Family, State, and Church: God's Institutions* (Grand Rapids, MI: Baker, 1965).
194. Robert G. Clouse, Richard V. Pierard, and Edwin M. Yamauchi, *Two Kingdoms: The Church and Culture through the Ages* (Chicago: Moody Press, 1993); Edmund P. Clowney, "The Politics of the Kingdom," *WTJ* 41, no. 2 (1979): 291–310; Charles W. Colson, *Kingdoms in Conflict* (Grand Rapids, MI: Zondervan, 1987); Jacques Ellul, *The False Presence of the Kingdom* (New York: Seabury, 1972); John H. Frame, *The Escondido Theology: A Reformed Response to Two Kingdom Theology* (Lakeland, FL: Whitefield Media Productions, 2011); Ryan C. McIlhenny, ed., *Kingdoms Apart: Engaging the Two Kingdoms Perspective* (Phillipsburg, NJ: P&R, 2012); J. Marcellus Kik, *Church and State: The Story of Two Kingdoms* (New York: Nelson, 1963); David VanDrunen, "The Two Kingdoms and the *Ordo Salutis*: Life Beyond Judgment and the Question of a Dual Ethic," *WTJ* 70, no. 2 (2008): 207–24; VanDrunen, *Living in God's Two Kingdoms: A Biblical Vision for Christianity and Culture* (Wheaton, IL: Crossway, 2010); VanDrunen, "The

and the appropriate balance between political and social activism in the church.[195]

Following the Reformation and building on its contributions and struggles, political theorists, philosophers, and theologians made advances in the important areas of religious liberty and freedom of conscience.[196] Thus it has been debated, is American liberty the fruit of the Reformation?[197] This has generated discussions of principled pluralism,[198] theonomy,[199] national confessionalism,[200] and the "Christian America" thesis.[201] Catholic historian E. Jarry emphasizes that "in the *political* domain, Calvinist ideas are at the origin of the revolution which from the 18th to the 19th centuries gave birth and growth

Two Kingdoms Doctrine and the Relationship of Church and State in Early Reformed Tradition," *JChSt* 49, no. 4 (2007): 743–63.

195. D. A. Carson, *Christ and Culture Revisited* (Grand Rapids, MI: Eerdmans, 2008).

196. Charles James Butler, "Covenant Theology and the Development of Religious Liberty," in Elazar and Kincaid, *The Covenant Connection*, 101–17; Estep, *Revolution within the Revolution*; Paul T. Fuhrmann, *Extraordinary Christianity: The Life and Thought of Alexander Vinet* (Philadelphia: Westminster, 1964); Peter Lillback, *Proclaim Liberty: A Broken Bell Rings Freedom to the World* (Bryn Mawr, PA: Providence Forum, 2001); Perry Miller, Robert L. Calhoun, Nathan M. Pusey, and Reinhold Niebuhr, *Religion and Freedom of Thought* (New York: Doubleday, 1954); Otto Erich Strasser, *Alexandre Vinet: Sein Kampf um ein Leben der Freiheit* (Erlenbach-Zurich: Rotapfel, 1946).

197. Eidsmoe, *Christianity and the Constitution*; Hall, *Genevan Reformation*; H. Wayne House, ed., *The Christian and American Law: Christianity's Impact on America's Founding Documents and Future Direction* (Grand Rapids, MI: Kregel, 1998); Martyn P. Thompson, "The History of Fundamental Law in Political Thought from the French Wars of Religion to the American Revolution," *AHR* 91, no. 5 (1986): 1103–28.

198. Phillip E. Hammond, "Pluralism and Law in the Formation of American Civil Religion," in *America, Christian or Secular? Readings in American Christian History and Civil Religion*, ed. Jerry S. Herbert (Portland, OR: Multnomah, 1984), 205–29; Robert T. Handy, ed., *Religion in the American Experience: The Pluralistic Style* (Columbia: University of South Carolina Press, 1972); Franklin H. Littell, *From State Church to Pluralism: A Protestant Interpretation of Religion in American History* (New York: Macmillan, 1971); James W. Skillen and Rockne M. McCarthy, eds., *Political Order and the Plural Structure of Society*, Emory University Studies in Law and Religion 2 (Atlanta, GA: Scholars Press, 1991); James W. Skillen, *Recharging the American Experiment: Principled Pluralism for Genuine Civic Community* (Grand Rapids, MI: Baker, 1994); Kathryn J. Pulley, "The Constitution and Religious Pluralism Today," in *Liberty and Law: Reflections on the Constitution in American Life and Thought*, ed. Ronald A. Wells and Thomas A. Askew (Grand Rapids, MI: Eerdmans, 1987), 143–55.

199. Greg L. Bahnsen, *Theonomy in Christian Ethics* (Nutley, NJ: Craig, 1977); T. David Gordon, "Critique of Theonomy: A Taxonomy," *WTJ* 56, no. 1 (1994): 23–43; John H. Frame, "*The Institutes of Biblical Law*: A Review Article," *WTJ* 38, no. 2 (1976): 195–217; Meredith G. Kline, "Comments on an Old-New Error," *WTJ* 41, no. 1 (1978): 172–89; William S. Barker and W. Robert Godfrey, eds., *Theonomy: A Reformed Critique* (Grand Rapids, MI: Academie Books, 1990); Douglas A. Oss, "The Influence of Hermeneutical Frameworks in the Theonomy Debate," *WTJ* 51, no. 2 (1989): 227–58; Vern S. Poythress, *The Shadow of Christ in the Law of Moses* (Phillipsburg, NJ: P&R, 1991); Rousas John Rushdoony, *The Institutes of Biblical Law*, vol. 1 (Nutley, NJ: Craig, 1973).

200. Smith, *God and Politics*.

201. Richard John Neuhaus and Michael Cromartie, eds., *Piety and Politics: Evangelicals and Fundamentalists Confront the World* (Washington, DC: Ethics and Public Policy Center, 1987); Gary S. Smith, "Tracing the Roots of Modern Morality: Calvinists and Ethical Foundations," *WTJ* 44, no. 2 (1982): 327–51.

to the parliamentary democracies of Anglo-Saxon type."[202] Kingdon observes,

> The constitutional resistance theories of the Reformation period persisted for centuries. They were adapted for important use in seventeenth-century Germany (e.g., Althusius) and England (e.g., John Locke). Versions of them helped support the American and French Revolutions of the eighteenth century. Traces of them linger to the present.[203]

Whether one agrees with them or not, eminent scholars, as J. Marcellus Kik has observed, have attributed America's founding to the Reformer of Geneva:

> German historian Leopold von Ranke: "John Calvin was the virtual founder of America."

> American historian George Bancroft: "He that will not honor the memory, and respect the influence of Calvin, knows but little of the origin of American liberty. . . . The genius of Calvin infused enduring elements into the institutions of Geneva, and made it for the modern world the impregnable fortress of popular liberty, the fertile seed plot of democracy."

> Church historian Philip Schaff: "The principles of the Republic of the United States can be traced thro' the intervening link of Puritanism to Calvinism, which, with all its theological rigor, has been the chief educator of manly character and promoter of constitutional freedom in modern times."[204]

More recently, John Witte Jr. has shown how the Calvinist Reformation's wrestling with human rights in terms of law and religion influenced Europe and eventually America.[205] It is not insignificant

202. Fuhrmann, "Mornay and the Huguenot Challenge," 50.
203. Kingdon, "Resistance Theory," *OER* 3:425.
204. Kik, *Church and State*, 71. D. G. Hart, in his book on Calvinism, is more reserved about Calvinism's influence. He acknowledges that modern political theories were affected by Geneva's Calvinism but also leaves room for other influences. He asserts too that "Calvinism was as much an agent of authoritarianism and intolerance as it was of liberty and popular sovereignty." D. G. Hart, *Calvinism: A History* (New Haven, CT: Yale University Press, 2013), 304.
205. Witte, *Reformation of Rights*.

that the only clergyman to sign the Declaration of Independence, John Witherspoon, was a Presbyterian clergyman and a lineal descendant of John Knox.[206]

Conclusion

The Reformation deeply and permanently shaped the debate over the relationship of church and state. By building on an ancient Christian legacy of how the two institutions interact, in a volatile age of change, the Reformation bequeathed insights and theories to subsequent generations in the West that continue throughout the world even today.

Moreover, there is an enduring value to Calvin's political insights.[207] An important example of a reformational thinker who influenced European and American government was the Calvinist theologian-statesman Abraham Kuyper.[208] Yet one can lament the contemporary lack of appreciation for the historical foundations of human rights, including the contributions made by the Protestant tradition:

> Today, modern human rights thought . . . largely stands devoid of critical grounding. . . . The grand theological narratives of the Protestant Reformation are also invisible in human rights declarations and conventions of the last several decades. . . . A new critical grounding for human rights is required if the entire tradition is not to explode into scores of conflicting subjective wants that have no real authority and, in reality, can never be implemented.[209]

In fact, Witte makes the controversial claim,

> Human rights norms need religious narratives to ground them critically. . . . Religion is an ineradicable condition of human lives and human communities. . . . Religions must thus be seen as indispens-

---

206. On Witherspoon, see Martha L. L. Stohlman, *John Witherspoon: Parson, Politician, Patriot* (Philadelphia: Westminster, 1976), and James Hastings Nichols, "John Witherspoon on Church and State," in Hunt, *Calvinism and the Political Order*, 130–39.
207. McNeill, *John Calvin on God and Political Duty.*
208. Abraham Kuyper, *Christianity and the Class Struggle*, trans. Dirk Jellema (Grand Rapids, MI: Piet Hein, 1950); Kuyper, *Lectures on Calvinism* (Grand Rapids, MI: Eerdmans, 1953); Edgar, review of *Creating a Christian Worldview*, 355–58; and Mark J. Larson, *Abraham Kuyper, Conservatism and Church and State* (Eugene, OR: Wipf & Stock, 2015).
209. Don S. Browning, "The United Nations Convention on the Rights of the Child: Should It Be Ratified and Why?," *EILR* 20, no. 1 (2006): 172–73.

able allies in the modern struggle for human rights. To exclude them from the struggle is impossible, indeed catastrophic.[210]

With appropriate historical allowances, the Reformers would have agreed.

Resources for Further Study

PRIMARY SOURCES

Althusius, Johannes. *Politica Methodice Digesta of Johannes Althusius*. Edited by Carl J. Friedrich. 3rd ed. 1614. Reprint, Cambridge, MA: Harvard University Press, 1932.

Baylor, Michael G., ed. *The Radical Reformation*. Cambridge Texts in the History of Political Thought. New York: Cambridge University Press, 1991.

Bromiley, G. W., ed. *Zwingli and Bullinger: Selected Translations with Introductions and Notes*. Library of Christian Classics 24. Philadelphia: Westminster, 1953.

Bullinger, Henry. "Of the One and Eternal Testament or Covenant of God: A Brief Exposition." In *Thy Word Is Still Truth: Essential Writings on the Doctrine of Scripture from the Reformation to Today*. Translated by Peter A. Lillback. Edited by Peter A. Lillback and Richard B. Gaffin Jr. Phillipsburg, NJ: P&R, 2013.

Calvin, John. *Calvin's Commentary on Seneca's "De Clementia."* Translated and edited by Ford Lewis Battles and André Malan Hugo. Renaissance Text Series 3. Leiden: Brill, 1969.

———. *Institutes of the Christian Religion*. Edited by John T. McNeill. Translated by Ford Lewis Battles. 2 vols. Library of Christian Classics 20–21. 1559 edition. Philadelphia: Westminster, 1960.

Du Plessis-Mornay, Philippe, or Hubert Languet. *A Defence of Liberty against Tyrants: A Translation of the "Vindiciae contra Tyrannos."* Edited by Harold J. Laski. 1924. Reprint, Gloucester, MA: Peter Smith, 1963.

Grotius, Hugo. *The Rights of War and Peace*. Edited by Richard Tuck from the edition by Jean Barbeyrac. 3 vols. Indianapolis, IN: Liberty Fund, 2005. Originally published as *De jure belli ac pacis libri tres* (1625).

---

210. Witte, *Reformation of Rights*, 334–36.

Kingdon, Robert M. *The Political Thought of Peter Martyr Vermigli: Selected Texts and Commentary.* Travaux d'humanisme et Renaissance 178. Geneva: Droz, 1980.

O'Donovan, Oliver, and Joan Lockwood O'Donovan, eds. *From Irenaeus to Grotius: Sourcebook in Christian Political Thought, 100–1625.* Grand Rapids, MI: Eerdmans, 1999.

Pauck, Wilhelm, ed. *Melanchthon and Bucer.* Library of Christian Classics 19. Philadelphia: Westminster, 1969.

Rutherford, Samuel. *Lex, Rex, or the Law and the Prince.* 1644. Reprint, Harrisonburg, VA: Sprinkle Publications, 1982.

Schaff, Philip, ed. *The Creeds of Christendom.* Revised by David S. Schaff. 3 vols. 1931. Reprint, Grand Rapids, MI: Baker, 1990.

Spinka, Matthew, ed. *Advocates of Reform: From Wyclif to Erasmus.* Library of Christian Classics 14. London: SCM, 1953.

Zwingli, Huldrych. "The Shepherd." In Huldrych Zwingli. *Writings.* Vol. 2, *In Search of True Religion.* Translated by H. Wayne Pipkin. Allison Park, PA: Pickwick, 1984.

SECONDARY SOURCES

Allen, John William. *A History of Political Thought in the Sixteenth Century.* 1928. Reprint, London: Methuen, 1977.

Burns, J. H., ed. *The Cambridge History of Political Thought, 1450–1700.* With the assistance of Mark Goldie. Cambridge: Cambridge University Press, 1991.

Carlyle, R. W., and A. J. Carlyle. *History of Medieval Political Theory in the West.* 6 vols. Edinburgh: William Blackwood and Sons, 1962.

Elazar, Daniel J., and John Kincaid, eds. *The Covenant Connection: From Federal Theology to Modern Federalism.* Lanham, MD: Lexington Books, 2000.

Figgis, John N. *Studies of Political Thought from Gerson to Grotius, 1414–1625.* 2nd ed. Cambridge: Cambridge University Press, 1931.

Hunt, George L., ed. *Calvinism and the Political Order.* Philadelphia: Westminster, 1965.

Kik, J. Marcellus. *Church and State: The Story of Two Kingdoms.* New York: Nelson, 1963.

Kingdon, Robert M. "Resistance Theory." In *The Oxford Encyclopedia of the Reformation,* edited by Hans J. Hillerbrand, 3:423–25. Oxford: Oxford University Press, 1996.

McNeill, John T. "Calvinism and European Politics in Historical Perspective." In *Calvinism and the Political Order*, edited by George L. Hunt, 11–22. Philadelphia: Westminster, 1965.

Raitt, Jill. "Bèze, Théodore de." In *The Oxford Encyclopedia of the Reformation*, edited by Hans J. Hillerbrand, 1:149–51. Oxford: Oxford University Press, 1996.

Skinner, Quentin. *The Foundations of Modern Political Thought*. 2 vols. Cambridge: Cambridge University Press, 1978.

Williams, George Huntston. *The Radical Reformation*. Sixteenth Century Essays and Studies 15. Kirksville, MO: Sixteenth Century Journal Publishers, 1992.

Witte, John, Jr. *The Reformation of Rights: Law, Religion, and Human Rights in Early Modern Calvinism*. Cambridge: Cambridge University Press, 2007.

———. *Religion and the American Constitutional Experiment: Essential Rights and Liberties*. Boulder, CO: Westview, 2000.

20

Eschatology

Kim Riddlebarger

ABSTRACT

Martin Luther and John Calvin affirmed the traditional teaching of the church regarding the last things—Jesus Christ ascended into heaven and promised to physically return on the last day in order to raise the dead, judge the world, and then create a new heaven and new earth. Focusing on the unfolding drama of redemptive history, both were thoroughly eschatological in their thinking. Although neither Luther nor Calvin sought to make major adjustments to the received eschatological categories of the Christian church, both believed that the death and resurrection of Jesus were the central events in biblical revelation and provided the framework to understand the unfolding course of human history until the Lord returns. This enabled them to discuss the second coming of Jesus Christ in the nonapocalyptic terms of a semirealized (already/not-yet) eschatology. The two Reformers vehemently opposed the radical Anabaptists and all forms of speculative date setting and millenarianism associated with them. Both men were also convinced that the papacy had become the Antichrist—a clear biblical sign of the end—and both believed that God would have mercy on his people and hasten the return of Christ to preserve his persecuted elect on the earth.

Introduction

When we consider the scope of the Protestant Reformation in terms
of theological debate, the formal and the material principles of the
Reformation quickly come to mind—the authority of Scripture and
the doctrine of justification *sola fide* (i.e., the way in which sinners are
reckoned righteous before the holy God). One may add to the formal
and material principles the important debates over church government
and authority, as well as the extensive debate regarding the nature and
efficacy of the sacraments. But as Richard Muller points out, "It is
worth recognizing from the outset that the Reformation altered comparatively few of the major loci of theology."[1] The Reformers held
much in common with the Roman church, and eschatology is one of
the relatively unaltered loci to which Muller refers.

At first glance, eschatology was not a significant point of contention between the burgeoning Protestant movement and the Roman
church because the Reformers' views on the central matters with
which eschatology is concerned are substantially those of catholic
Christianity: doctrines such as the second advent of Jesus Christ, the
resurrection of the dead, and the final judgment. That said, the Reformers did take issue with Rome on certain aspects of the intermediate state (especially Rome's doctrine of purgatory), and they rejected
Rome's emphasis on Christ returning as a stern and menacing judge,
not as the gracious Savior of God's elect.[2] Both Luther and Calvin
identified the papacy with Antichrist, and Luther even went so far as
to identify his own era as "the end times." Although the Reformers
left the locus of eschatology largely intact, it would be a mistake to
assume that eschatology was completely overlooked, especially in the
context of the Reformers' desire to return the teaching of the church
to a more biblical footing.

Historians suggest a number of reasons as to why the Reformers did
not much concern themselves with eschatology. One reason is that none
of the magisterial Reformers produced a commentary on the book of

---

1. Richard A. Muller, *The Unaccommodated Calvin: Studies in the Foundation of a Theological Tradition*, Oxford Studies in Historical Theology (New York: Oxford University Press, 2000), 39.
2. Heinrich Quistorp, *Calvin's Doctrine of the Last Things*, trans. Harold Knight (1955; repr., Eugene, OR: Wipf & Stock, 2009), 12.

Revelation or preached extensively from it.[3] However, Martin Luther produced two prefaces to the Revelation of Saint John (1522, 1542), in the first questioning the canonicity of Revelation, while in the second affirming it.[4] Luther also applied apocalyptic images from Revelation—those of the beast and the dragon—to the papacy.[5] John Calvin appealed twice to John's vision at critical points in his 1534 polemic against "soul sleep," *Psychopannychia*,[6] and cited Revelation more than twenty times in his *Institutes of the Christian Religion*, including in his discussion of the resurrection.[7] Although no source is ever produced, Calvin is often quoted as saying he did not produce a commentary on Revelation because he did not understand it well enough to comment on it. The more likely reason Calvin did not write a commentary on Revelation or preach from it may be that he did not live long enough to take up a detailed study of Revelation, something he may have intended after completing studies of two Old Testament prophetical/apocalyptic books, Daniel and Ezekiel.[8]

Late-Medieval Apocalypticism and the Radical Reformers

Another reason given as to why the Reformers did not focus extensively on eschatology is that the Reformers were so put off by the extreme apocalypticism of the late-medieval period,[9] as well as that found among their Anabaptist contemporaries, that they avoided the subject.[10] While the eschatological views of the radical Anabaptists were indeed highly

---

3. T. H. L. Parker, *Calvin's New Testament Commentaries*, 2nd ed. (Louisville: Westminster John Knox, 1993), 116–19.

4. Martin Luther, "Preface to the Revelation of Saint John," in *Works of Martin Luther with Introductions and Notes*, ed. Adolph Spaeth, Philadelphia ed. (1932; repr., Grand Rapids, MI: Baker, 1982), 6:479–91. In his first preface, Luther dismissed John's Revelation as canonical because he thought it was preoccupied with prophecy, unlike the canonical writings of Peter and Paul and the sayings of Jesus. Luther greatly moderated his views in the second preface of 1545.

5. Martin Luther, *Lectures on Galatians* (1535), LW 26:219–26.

6. John Calvin, *Psychopannychia*, in *Selected Works of John Calvin: Tracts and Letters*, ed. Henry Beveridge and Jules Bonnet, trans. Henry Beveridge (1851; repr., Grand Rapids, MI: Baker, 1983), 3:413–90.

7. Calvin, *Institutes*, 3.25.5.

8. For a discussion of this issue, see Cornelis P. Venema, "Calvin's Doctrine of the Last Things: The Resurrection of the Body and the Life Everlasting," in *A Theological Guide to Calvin's Institutes: Essays and Analysis*, ed. David W. Hall and Peter A. Lillback, Calvin 500 Series (Phillipsburg, NJ: P&R, 2008), 454–55.

9. *Apocalypticism* is defined as the belief that God has revealed that the end of human history is imminent, entailing a number of catastrophic events foretold in Scripture, all leading to the Lord's return. See Bernard J. McGinn, John J. Collins, and Stephen J. Stein, eds., *The Continuum History of Apocalypticism* (New York: Continuum, 2003), ix.

10. Parker, *Calvin's New Testament Commentaries*, 119. As Oberman notes, this assumption may be incorrect: "Jaroslav Pelikan has traced 'some uses of Apocalypse in the magisterial reformers.' Bernd Moeller has gathered further evidence for the eschatological orientation in early

speculative, the Reformers did not ignore them. Luther was certainly influenced by late-medieval prophetic ideas and assumptions, including the sense that the final judgment was at hand as the culmination of the ages-long struggle between God and the Devil. As Luther fleshed out this expectation over the course of his career, he came to see the recovery of the gospel as the critical turning point in this all-encompassing cosmic war.[11]

The conception that history was entering a third and final phase— the age of the Holy Spirit—was also widespread in the Late Middle Ages, in which eschatological expectations were heightened and speculative prophetic calculations were common. The "pursuit of the millennium" (typical of apocalypticism) lived on into the Reformation era but especially among the so-called "radical Reformers" who were influenced to varying degrees by Joachim of Fiore (ca. 1135–1202) and the Spiritual Franciscans.[12] Although increasingly convinced that the end was at hand, Luther rejected the speculative elements in these movements, including Joachim's "third dispensation."[13] Nevertheless, in 1541, Luther published his *Suppatio annorum mundi* (*Chronology of the World*), in which he argued that the year 1540 was the 5,500th year after creation, and although he reckoned that another five hundred years remained until the eternal Sabbath would begin, marking the 6,000th year of creation, he reasoned that the Lord promised to shorten the days for the sake of the elect and could return sooner.[14]

Although Luther rejected the radical elements of medieval apocalypticism, he was thoroughly eschatological in his theological outlook, seeing eschatology as intertwined with the unfolding of human history. Luther's focus on *solus Christus* in the doctrine of justification by faith provided the orientation for his entire theology, including his view of the end times.[15] Because the justified sinner is delivered from the wrath

Reformation preaching." See Heiko A. Oberman, *The Impact of the Reformation: Essays* (Grand Rapids, MI: Eerdmans, 1994), 57.

11. Robin Barnes, "Images of Hope and Despair: Western Apocalypticism ca. 1500–1800," in McGinn, Collins, and Stein, *The Continuum History of Apocalypticism*, 329.

12. Timothy George, *Theology of the Reformers* (Nashville: Broadman, 1988), 38.

13. Barnes, "Images of Hope and Despair," 330.

14. T. F. Torrance, "The Eschatology of the Reformation," in *Eschatology: Four Papers Read to the Society for the Study of Theology*, ed. T. F. Torrance and J. K. S. Reid, Scottish Journal of Theology Occasional Papers 2 (Edinburgh: Oliver and Boyd, 1957), 43.

15. Jane E. Strohl, "Luther's Eschatology: The Last Times and the Last Things" (PhD diss., University of Chicago Divinity School, 1989), 9–10.

of God and eternal punishment, the doctrine of justification, which was at the heart of the newly recovered gospel, drives all history toward its final goal. It is the continual preaching of law and gospel—inimical to those blind to the truth—that provokes much of the upheaval and conflict that God's people will face until the end of history from the Devil and those whom he has blinded. Only then will Jesus Christ's victory over sin, death, the Devil, the law, and the wrath of God be gloriously manifest.[16]

The "Last Days" and Church Reform

In contrast, therefore, to the widespread assumption that the Reformers did not preoccupy themselves with eschatology, their work of reform was profoundly influenced by their understanding of the age in which they lived. According to Timothy George,

> For all of its stress on returning to the pristine church of the New Testament and patristic age, the Reformation was essentially a forward-looking movement. It was a movement of the "last days" which lived out of an intense eschatological tension between the "no longer" of the old dispensation and the "not yet" of the consummated kingdom of God. None of the reformers . . . was much taken with the radical apocalyptic eschatologies which flourished in the sixteenth century. . . . Each of them was convinced that the kingdom of God was breaking into history in the events in which he was led to play a part. Imbued with this sense of eschatological urgency, Calvin wrote in 1543 to the Holy Roman Emperor Charles V: "The Reformation of the Church is God's work, and is as independent of human life and thought as the resurrection of the dead, or any such work is."[17]

The Reformers saw themselves as participants in a vital work of God: reforming the church. Because they believed they were mere instruments in the sovereign purposes of God, they understood the end times as "now," unfolding before their very eyes. Luther complained that the Roman church and its leaders were content to wait for the final

---

16. Philip S. Watson, *Let God Be God! An Interpretation of the Theology of Martin Luther* (London: Epworth, 1947), 116–17.
17. George, *Theology of the Reformers*, 323.

judgment for reform of the church. Luther put the matter as only he could: "In Rome it takes two men for a reformation, 'one to milk the billy goat, the other to hold the strainer.'"[18]

In a comment on Galatians 4:6, Luther described his sense of focus in the work God had given him: "We have begun to demolish the kingdom of Antichrist. But they will provoke Christ to hasten the day of his glorious coming, when he will abolish all principalities, powers, and might, and will put all His enemies under his feet."[19] In Luther's estimation, "These last days have already started, and . . . therefore the 'last things' have commenced *in* our historical time, so that the eschatological clock has started to tick."[20] Eschatology is not something to be pushed off into the distant future, as God's ongoing work of redemption places us within the end times, which unfold until the Lord's return.

If the Reformers did not rewrite the church's established dogma regarding the end times—that Jesus would return at the end of the age to judge the world, raise the dead, and establish a new heaven and new earth—they certainly tweaked it a bit, and incorporated their eschatological framework into their polemics and pastoral theology, as well as their dogmatic writings.

Luther and Calvin as Key Figureheads

Before we consider the respective eschatological views of Martin Luther and John Calvin, it is important to offer an explanation for limiting the scope of this chapter to Luther and Calvin as representative of "the eschatology of the Reformers."[21] There are three reasons for doing so. First, Martin Luther (b. Nov. 10, 1483) and John Calvin (b. July 10, 1509) are representative of the first two generations of Reformers. Luther was twenty-six years older than Calvin and represents the first generation of those involved in the work of reform (including Philipp Melanchthon, Huldrych Zwingli, and Martin Bucer), while

---

18. Martin Luther, "Borrede, Rachwort, und Marginalglossen," WA 50:362.7, quoted in Heiko A. Oberman, *Luther: Man between God and the Devil* (New York: Image Books, 1992), 64.
19. Luther, *Lectures on Galatians* (1535), LW 26:383.
20. Quoted in Oberman, *Impact of the Reformation*, 196.
21. This chapter will not neglect to interact with the views of Rome and the radical Reformers, but it will do so through the polemical lens of Luther and Calvin.

Calvin's life and work were conducted in the huge shadow of Luther's evangelical breakthrough of October 1517.

Second, the two men had completely different temperaments and labored under different circumstances. Luther was a Reformer in the truest sense of the term, devoting his life to preaching, teaching, and writing.[22] Luther famously struggled with a deep inner conflict (*Anfechtungen*) in a life caught between the existential fear of the eternal wrath of God and the blessed good news of the gospel through which the Holy Spirit united believers to Jesus Christ, whose victory over sin and the grave in his cross and resurrection was the only true hope in both this life and the next.[23] Luther wrote,

> The longer the world stands, the worse it becomes. . . . The more we preach, the less attention people pay, . . . bent on increasing wickedness and wantonness at an overwhelming speed. We cry out and preach against this. . . . But what good does it do? It does, however, do good in that we may expect the Last Day sooner. Then the godless will be hurled into hell, but we shall obtain eternal salvation on that Day. . . . So we may confidently expect that the Last Day is not far away.[24]

Calvin the pastor also struggled with a deep despair he felt in this life, expressed in a remarkable section in his *Institutes* devoted to "meditation on the future life."[25] He exhorted Christians to give up all undue attachments to the things of this world, which pale in light of the next. At the same time, the struggles associated with life in a fallen world must also be considered in light of the unshakable hope given by God to struggling believers through the resurrection of Jesus Christ from the dead and his ascension to the Father's right hand.[26]

---

22. As Oberman points out, "Luther never styled himself a 'reformer.' He did, however, not shrink from being seen as a prophet; he wanted to spread the Gospel as an 'evangelist.' He called himself preacher, doctor, or professor and was all of these. Yet he never presumed to be a reformer, nor did he ever claim his movement to be the 'Reformation.'" Oberman, *Luther: Man between God and the Devil*, 79.

23. Fred P. Hall, "Martin Luther's Theology of Last Things," in *Looking into the Future: Evangelical Studies in Eschatology*, ed. David W. Baker (Grand Rapids, MI: Baker Academic, 2001), 141.

24. From Luther's 1532 sermon on Luke 21:25–33 in WA 47:623, quoted in Ewald M. Plass, *What Luther Says: An Anthology* (St. Louis, MO: Concordia, 1959), 689.

25. Calvin, *Institutes*, 3.9.1–6.

26. Ibid., 3.25.1–12.

Calvin said, "When, therefore, with our eyes fast fixed on Christ we wait upon heaven, and nothing on earth hinders them from bearing us to the promised blessedness, the statement is truly fulfilled 'that where our treasure is, our heart is' [Matt. 6:21]."[27] Calvin wrote that believers are to await patiently the final restoration of all things at Christ's return just as a sentry faithfully guards his post until recalled by his commander.[28] He described this struggle as that of a life lived in exile far away from one's beloved homeland:

> Let the aim of believers in judging mortal life, then, be that while they understand it to be of itself nothing but misery, they may with greater eagerness and dispatch betake themselves wholly to meditate upon that eternal life to come. When it comes to a comparison with the life to come, the present life can not only be safely neglected but, compared to the former, must be utterly despised and loathed. For, if heaven is our homeland, what else is the earth but our place of exile?[29]

In his commentary on Paul's first letter to Timothy, Calvin added, "The only remedy for all these difficulties is to look forward to Christ's appearing and always to put our trust in it."[30] Exiles endure their pilgrimage by keeping the joy of returning home ever before their eyes.

Third, these two Reformers are the seminal figures in the two largest Reformation traditions—Lutheran and Reformed. While there certainly have been theological developments in both traditions, such as the Lutheran tradition modifying Luther's view of the intermediate state as one of "sleep,"[31] both Reformers stand at (or in the case of Calvin, near) the headwaters of the nearly five-hundred-year-old dogmatic, confessional, and ecclesiastical traditions identified with them. Luther and Calvin serve as apt representatives of the eschatology of the Reformers.

---

27. Ibid., 3.25.1.
28. Ibid., 3.9.4.
29. Ibid.
30. Calvin on 1 Tim. 6:14, in *CNTC* 10:279.
31. Francis Pieper, *Christian Dogmatics* (St. Louis, MO: Concordia, 1953), 3:511–15; Paul Althaus, *The Theology of Martin Luther*, trans. Robert C. Schultz (Philadelphia: Fortress, 1966), 417.

Eschatology according to Huldrych Zwingli and Martin Bucer

Although eventually overshadowed within the Reformed tradition by Calvin, first-generation Reformers Huldrych Zwingli of Zurich (1484–1531) and Martin Bucer of Strasbourg (1491–1551) merit brief mention. Like the early Luther, Zwingli doubted the canonicity of Revelation,[32] and with Luther and Calvin, he adamantly rejected the Roman doctrine of purgatory, calling it a "baseless invention."[33] With Calvin, Zwingli affirmed that the Anabaptist doctrine of soul sleep was contrary to Scripture and "contradicts all reason."[34] And in article 12 of his *Fidei Ratio* (1530), Zwingli affirmed the existence of hell as a place of eternal punishment, against both the Roman view of purgatory and the teaching of several Anabaptist groups that God would grant universal forgiveness at the time of the end.[35]

Martin Bucer published the most important Reformation-era text on political theology, yet one with important eschatological implications, his 1550 *De Regno Christi* (*The Kingdom of Christ*). In this volume Bucer defined the kingdom of Christ as follows:

> The Kingdom of our Savior Jesus Christ is that administration and care of the eternal life of God's elect, by which this very Lord and King of Heaven by his doctrine and discipline, administered by suitable ministers chosen for this very purpose, gathers to himself his elect, those dispersed throughout the world who are his but whom he nonetheless wills to be subject to the powers of this world. He incorporates them into himself and his church and so governs them in it that purged more fully day by day from sins, they live well and happy both here and in the time to come.[36]

Bucer's distinction between the kingdom of Christ and the powers of the world bears a strong formal resemblance to Luther's "two

---

32. W. P. Stephens, *The Theology of Huldrych Zwingli* (Oxford: Clarendon, 1986), 56, citing *ZSW* 2:208.33–209.5.

33. Zwingli, *Fides Expositio* (1531), in James T. Dennison Jr., ed., *Reformed Confessions of the 16th and 17th Centuries in English Translation*, vol. 1, *1523–1552* (Grand Rapids, MI: Reformation Heritage Books, 2008), 185–86.

34. Zwingli, *Fides Expositio*, 205–7.

35. Zwingli, *Fides Ratio* (1530), in Dennison, *Reformed Confessions of the 16th and 17th Centuries*, 133–36.

36. Martin Bucer, *De Regno Christi*, in *Melanchthon and Bucer*, ed. Wilhelm Pauck, LCC 19 (Philadelphia: Westminster, 1969), 225.

kingdoms" distinction between the kingdom of grace (Christ's kingdom) and the kingdom of power (the civil kingdom). Yet, according
to Bucer, these two kingdoms are united as the body of Christ through
the Word and the Spirit. As such, the kingdom of Christ is "visibly and
actually realized in the Church on earth, and through obedience to the
church's witness, also in the state."[37] As God's elect are incorporated
into the body of Christ, their election unto salvation will be evident in
the ongoing unfolding of history in the midst of the worldly powers as
they "live well and happy" until that time when Jesus Christ returns
to consummate his ever-unfolding kingdom. For Luther, on the other
hand, this kingdom comes through the act of proclaiming the gospel,
not through its effects.[38]

Bucer was in exile in England at the time—he had become Regius
Professor of Divinity at Cambridge in 1549 at the invitation of Thomas
Cranmer (1489–1556) when the former was exiled from Strasbourg—
and his *De Regno* was intended as a blueprint for reform in England.
Bucer's book was presented to the young King Edward VI on publica-
tion in 1551, but both men died shortly thereafter—Bucer in 1551 and
Edward in 1553. No doubt, Edward's early death negatively affected
Bucer's earlier intent of providing a theological foundation for the
ongoing work of civic reform in England.

Although not a work of eschatology per se, Bucer's *De Regno* illustrates the antiapocalyptic thinking of much of the early Reformed
tradition, as the coming kingdom of Jesus Christ is realized in God's
continuous activity through the church and its divinely appointed mission of preaching, administering the sacraments, and disciplining its
members. Such faithfulness, in turn, leads to the consequential transformation of that society where the church is faithful to its mission.
When the kingdom of Christ is defined in these (or similar) terms,
eschatology becomes a present concern in addition to a future hope.[39]

---

37. Torrance, "Eschatology of the Reformation," 54.
38. Ibid.
39. According to Oberman, Calvin's "difference with Luther can be noticed at many points
but none so fundamentally as Calvin's view of God as 'leislatuer et roy,' whereas one of the most
perceptive Counter-Reformers, Ambrosius Catharinus Politus O.P., had indicated that the heart of
the 'Lutheran error' was the denial that Christ is both 'redemptor' *et* 'legislator.' Calvin's theme
throughout [his 1564 sermons on the second book of Samuel] is the rule of God who appointed
Christ as King, his faithful Viceroy. Reformation is the re-ordering of the lives of the faithful. Confusion and dispersal is the undermining of the God-intended order by Satan and his evil instruments.

This sentiment was echoed by Calvin who noted, "His Kingdom's first effect is to tame the desires of our flesh. And now, as the Kingdom of God increases, stage upon stage, to the end of the world, we must every day pray for its coming."[40]

As we now turn to the distinctive eschatological views of Luther and Calvin, we should not lose sight of the fact that the two Reformers' views on these matters are substantially the same. Both fit within the modern designation *amillennial* (i.e., that the thousand years of Revelation 20 are a description of the present age until the Lord returns, not a future eschatological hope, as in *pre-* and *postmillennialism*), and both looked to the second advent of Jesus Christ, the bodily resurrection at the end of the age, and deliverance of believers from God's final eschatological judgment as the Christian's only sure and certain hope in the midst of the struggles of this life. It is in light of such large measure of agreement that we can discuss their eschatological distinctives.

While acknowledging that the "line [between them] should not be drawn too sharply," Torrance observes that their differences arise in part because of historical circumstances and because they draw on different sources within the Christian tradition. Luther's eschatological focus, Torrance says, centered on the final judgment while drawing on certain Latin church fathers such as Cyprian, who were concerned with "the decay and collapse of the world." Calvin's emphasis fell more on the resurrection of the body and the reordering of the world as he drew on the Greek fathers' emphasis on the incarnation as the basis for the renewal of all things.[41] While Torrance's claim of discernible Latin-Greek intellectual pedigrees for Luther and Calvin is debatable, I take Torrance's sense of the difference in emphasis between the two Reformers to be generally correct.

By the grace and power of God this new order is here and there restored in local churches as well as in public life of some cities and regions. The true restoration, re-assembling and final establishment of law and order, however, is to be awaited in patience by the faithful as the eschatological act of God." This theme is given thorough articulation by Bucer in his *De Regno Christi*. Heiko A. Oberman, *The Dawn of the Reformation: Essays in Late Medieval and Early Reformation Thought* (Edinburgh: T&T Clark, 1986), 237.

40. Calvin on Matt. 6:10, in *CNTC* 1:208.

41. Torrance, "Eschatology of the Reformation," 40. Quistorp disagrees: "Luther's eschatology is governed more strongly than that of Calvin by the thought of the resurrection of the dead." Quistorp, *Calvin's Doctrine of the Last Things*, 97.

Luther's Eschatological Distinctives

REDEMPTIVE HISTORY, JUSTIFICATION, AND A NEARING END

The church that Luther sought to reform was in many ways dominated by the medieval view that grace perfects nature and that the kingdom of God was essentially manifest in the institutions of the Roman church. The manifestation of God's kingdom, in effect, was to be found in church dogma and in the ongoing work of God in the offices and councils of the church. Such a church necessarily stood above and beyond all need of radical reform. If the church and its infallible *magisterium* possessed the sole power to bind and loose, then any historical development of the church in the future had to be tied to the dogma and conciliar decisions of the past. On this understanding, eschatology was chiefly concerned with the future of Christ's relationship to his church, and the very idea that eschatology was tied to history was "totally alien."[42]

The conception that God's kingdom is manifest in his church explains the negative reaction to those such as Joachim of Fiore who sought to focus on last things in the light of history, not ecclesiology. To counter such troubling aberrations, Thomas Aquinas (1225–1274) not only criticized the speculative eschatology of Joachim but even went so far as to argue that when grace perfects nature at the time of the end, those plants and animals incapable of such perfection will cease to exist.[43] Even human nature will be radically transformed.[44] In the estimation of Torrance, "In the last resort nature is transformed into supernature, the earthly into a heavenly reality."[45]

In large measure, then, the eschatological thought of the Reformers is to be found in their return to an emphasis on redemptive history as read through the lens of the sufficiency of Scripture as the final court of appeal on all matters of doctrine. The revelation of the redemptive work of Christ in the Word is essentially historical in nature. This renewed interest in redemptive history pushed the Reformers to look beyond Aquinas's synthesis for prior theological antecedents in the

---

42. Ernest Lee Tuveson, *Millennium and Utopia: A Study in the Background of the Idea of Progress* (New York: Harper Torchbooks, 1964), 19.
43. Aquinas, *Summa Theologiae Supplementum* 91.5.
44. Aquinas, *Scriptum super Sententiis* 4.48.11.1.
45. Torrance, "Eschatology of the Reformation," 38.

early church so as to help them recover and frame their understanding of the church's missionary mandate. In contrast to Rome's view, the Reformers believed that the kingdom of God was manifest through the preaching of the gospel, with the ministers focusing on the death of Jesus as its center and the resurrection of the body as the Christian hope. This approach also stood over against those speculative approaches to eschatology of the period that were preoccupied with the signs of the end and with fanciful interpretations of prophetic and apocalyptic biblical texts.

Both Luther and Calvin held that in the person and work of Christ, the new creation had already dawned and would be progressively revealed until the last day, when a new heaven and earth would become the everlasting home of righteousness. In the words of Torrance, against Rome's "docetic interpretation of redemption and eschatology the Reformers were in full revolt."[46] The implication of this "reformed" conception of the church's mission and its gospel message was that God works in and through history in the present until Christ returns. The Word rightly preached and the sacraments properly administered were the Holy Spirit's means of bringing about the new creation, which even now breaks in on the present. As a consequence, the kingdom of God was seen as dynamic and brought about by the Spirit through the Word, not static and tied to the councils, traditions, and institutions of the Roman church.

As Luther's thought developed against this backdrop, we see a crystallization of his distinction between heaven and earth, along with the corresponding antithesis between two divinely ordained kingdoms—that of "grace" (Christ's kingdom) and that of "power" (the civil kingdom)—over which Jesus rules. Luther's antithesis between law and gospel, as well as that of sin and grace, were thoroughly eschatological. Grace does not transform nature in this life, something Luther knew full well from his own struggles with the sinful passions of the flesh. The necessary transformation of his soul would not happen soon enough—Luther understood that he would die before it was completed—and even then, whatever transformation had been accomplished could not

---

46. Ibid., 39.

help him become sufficiently righteous before God to withstand God's judgment—something Luther greatly feared.

The solution to the latter problem is revealed by God in the gospel when the sinner is declared righteous before God through faith in the merits of Christ, so that he or she will be delivered from the eschatological wrath of God on the last day. Justification amounts to a "not guilty" verdict in the heavenly court, proclaimed to the sinner through the Word long before the return of Jesus Christ on the day of judgment (assuming the Lord's return is delayed long past the sinner's death), when the "not guilty" verdict will finally be realized in the resurrection of the body and eternal life of the justified. This is no mere legal fiction, as Rome had accused Luther of fabricating. The righteousness that justifies sinners in the present is that of Jesus himself, imputed to the sinner through the instrument of faith but done so in anticipation of the final "not guilty" verdict given on the day of judgment.

Luther's dictum that a sinner is simultaneously sinful yet counted as righteous through faith in Jesus Christ is inseparable from a proper understanding of redemptive history. The antithesis between law and gospel means that the justified sinner lives in two "times" or "ages":

> Therefore the Christian is divided this way into two times. To the extent he is flesh, he is under the law; to the extent he is spirit, he is under the Gospel. To his flesh there always cling lust, greed, ambition, pride, etc. So do ignorance of God, impatience, grumbling, and wrath against God because he obstructs our plans and efforts, and because he does not immediately punish the wicked who despise him. These sins cling to the flesh of the saints. Therefore if you do not look at anything beyond the flesh, you will permanently remain under the time of the Law. But those days have been shortened, for otherwise no human being would be saved (Matt. 24:22). An end has to be set for the Law, where it will come to a stop. Therefore the time of the Law is not forever; but it has an end, which is Christ. But the time of grace is forever; for Christ having died once for all, will never die again (Rom. 6:9–10). He is eternal, therefore the time of grace is eternal also.[47]

---

47. Luther, *Lectures on Galatians* (1535), LW 26:342.

On the one hand, Luther could point out that the coming of Jesus Christ marks a fundamental break with the old covenant. Yet, on the other hand, the believer still remains in the flesh, subject to the law's constant demands, exposing the fact that even those who embrace Christ and are presently justified still remain sinners. It is because the justified remain "flesh," Luther believed, that God will graciously shorten the days of struggle until Jesus Christ returns to put an end to fleshly human existence by ushering in the eternal age of grace. It is in this sense, then, that Luther's understanding of salvation was thoroughly eschatological and was the ground of his expectation that Christ's return was near.

Luther's eschatological framing of the doctrine of justification also militated against the popular apocalypticism of his day. Although Luther anticipated the return of Jesus Christ to be near in time, he was well aware of the date setting of his Anabaptist contemporaries, many of whom eventually renounced Luther because they did not think him radical enough. Luther was uninterested in exterminating the ungodly from the land in order to bring about reform. Many of those who grew disenchanted with Luther turned to the more radical Thomas Müntzer (ca. 1489–1525), who, along with his company of "prophets," was banned from Zwickau and was eventually arrested for denouncing the landed aristocracy and leading his followers into battle at the conclusion of the so-called Peasant's revolt. Müntzer was subsequently beheaded.[48]

A former disciple of Müntzer, Hans Hut, predicted that Jesus would return to earth on Pentecost Sunday in 1528. Hut sought to gather together 144,000 elect saints "whom he 'sealed' by baptizing them on the forehead with the sign of the cross." Hut was dead by 1528 and his "charred body (he had set fire to his prison cell in a futile effort to escape) was condemned posthumously." Melchior Hoffman similarly set a location and date for the Lord's return (Strasbourg in 1534), and this too failed to come to pass.[49]

Accepting Augustine's interpretation of Revelation 20, Luther believed that shortly before the time of the end, Satan would be loosed for a brief period before the Lord returned to destroy him and cast him

---

48. Oberman, *Luther: Man between God and the Devil*, 61.
49. George, *Theology of the Reformers*, 256.

into the lake of fire (Rev. 20:7–10). When, in 1523, Luther learned that the first two martyrs of the Reformation were burnt in Brussels, he was not surprised and understood this as a manifestation of the final loosing of Satan. Luther even expressed sadness that such martyrdom was not granted to him because he opposed the Devil so passionately.[50]

ANTICHRIST, SOUL SLEEP, AND RESURRECTION

In light of Luther's overall view of redemptive history, the recovery of the gospel, and the sense of the end's nearness, we can note three additional points of emphasis in Luther's eschatological thinking. First, we will consider Luther's identification of the papacy as Antichrist. Second, we will examine his view that after death the soul "sleeps" until the resurrection. Third, we will discuss Luther's unique framing of the resurrection and second advent of Jesus Christ as the Christian's hope for escaping God's eschatological wrath on the day of judgment.

Although many in the medieval period had identified individual popes as Antichrist, one of Luther's most significant contributions to subsequent Protestant eschatological thought was the identification of the *office* of the papacy as the seat of Antichrist, ensuring that the sitting pope is the chief henchman of the Devil and the source of many of the countless ills plaguing the faithful. In making this identification, Luther claimed that what had been hidden in the age-old conflict between God and the Devil was now brought out into the open with the rise of Antichrist, whose eventual defeat would mark the final stage in human history. In the Smalcald Articles of 1537, Luther made his view crystal clear:

> The pope is not the head of all Christendom by divine right or according to God's word. . . . [Rather] the pope is the real Antichrist who has raised himself over and set himself against Christ, for the pope will not permit people to be saved except by his own power, which amounts to nothing since it is neither established nor commanded by God. This is actually what St. Paul calls exalting oneself over and against God.[51]

---

50. Oberman, *Impact of the Reformation*, 196.
51. Theodore G. Tappert, ed. and trans., *The Book of Concord: The Confessions of the Evangelical Lutheran Church* (Philadelphia: Fortress, 1959), 298–301.

Elsewhere Luther added, "Why is it that the pope is so full of here-sies and has introduced one after the other into the world? . . . He is and remains the greatest enemy of Christ. He is and remains the true Antichrist."[52] Again, Luther stated, "Christ says yes, but the pope says no. Since they are so opposed to each other, one of them must certainly be lying. But Christ does not lie. Therefore I conclude that the pope is a liar and the real Antichrist besides."[53] As Paul Althaus points out, for Luther, "Eschatological events are taking place in the midst of the pres-ent. Because the antichrist is already present, Luther expects and hopes that the end will come in the near future." What is more, Luther "de-sires it," because the coming of Jesus will "bring an end to antichrist and bring about redemption. Luther can call it 'the most happy day.'"[54]

No doubt, Luther's most innovative eschatological emphasis was the "sleep of death." Countless folk of Luther's age were preoccupied with death and with related questions about the nature of the inter-mediate state and paradise—questions raised by the Roman doctrine of purgatory. Who went to purgatory rather than to hell? How long would people remain there before becoming sufficiently purified? How could the living faithful shorten the time their loved ones spent in purgatory? There were even topographical maps available to provide answers, and these were known to Luther.[55]

Luther's answer to this troubling fear and doubt was to counter with the certainty that those who die in Christ are assured of eternal life and of future deliverance from God's wrath. But should a believer die before the Lord's return, Luther taught, they "rest in the bosom of Christ," not in a state of limbo.[56] Using the death of Abraham as an illustration, Luther wrote,

> The death of the saints is most peaceful and precious in the sight of God (Ps. 116:15) and . . . the saints do not taste death but most pleasantly fall asleep (cf. Isa. 57:1–2; 26:20). . . . In the eyes of the world the righteous are despised, spurned, and thrust aside. Their

52. Quoted in Plass, *What Luther Says*, 631.
53. Quoted in ibid., 1071.
54. Althaus, *Theology of Martin Luther*, 420–21. Althaus quotes from a 1540 letter Luther wrote to his wife in WABr 9:175.
55. Althaus, *Theology of Martin Luther*, 412.
56. Martin Luther, *Lectures on Genesis 21–25*, LW 4:314.

death seems exceedingly sad. But they are sleeping a most pleasant sleep. When they lie down on their beds and breathe their last, they die just as if sleep were gradually falling on their limbs and senses.[57]

According to Köstlin, "The matter of chief importance is, and always remains for [Luther], that the souls of the pious certainly yet live, are free from all distress and temptation, and have, in the presence of God and in the hand of Christ, secure and blessed rest."[58]

But what of those who sleep in Christ? What happens to them on the last day? This leads to the third eschatological distinctive in Luther, his teaching regarding the resurrection and second advent of Jesus Christ as the Christian's hope for escaping God's wrath on the day of judgment.

As for those who sleep in Christ, Luther said, "Just as a man who falls asleep and sleeps soundly until morning does not know what has happened to him when he wakes up, so shall we suddenly rise on the Last Day; and we shall know neither what death has been like or how we have come through it."[59] The last day, as Luther saw it, had to come soon because Antichrist had been revealed and the gospel had been preached to most of the earth. Yet wickedness would also increase, in spite of the fact that the world's "dissolution is standing at the door."[60] Those in Christ will awake when their bodies are raised, and they will enter into eternal life and the blessedness that the Lord has prepared for them, while evil men and angels, along with the Devil and his angels, will enter into eternal death.[61]

The basis for the believer's awakening from sleep when Jesus returns is to be found in baptism: "The spiritual birth takes its rise in Baptism, proceeds and increases, but only in the last days is its significance fulfilled. Only in death are we rightly lifted out of Baptism by the angels into eternal life."[62] Since Luther understood water baptism as a baptism into the death of Jesus and into burial with Jesus, the act

57. Ibid., *LW* 4:309.
58. Julius Köstlin, *The Theology of Luther*, trans. Charles E. Hay (Philadelphia: Lutheran Publication Society, 1897), 2:578.
59. Martin Luther, "Luthers Faftenpoftille: Begonnen von G. Theile, vollendet von G. Buchwald," WA 17:11.235.
60. Plass, *What Luther Says*, 696–97.
61. Althaus, *Theology of Martin Luther*, 417.
62. Martin Luther, "Sermon on the Sacrament of Baptism" (1518), quoted in Torrance, "Eschatology of the Reformation," 49.

of new creation given in baptism is therefore progressively realized until the Lord's return. The new creation has dawned in Christ's tomb and, through faith, in the font, and will be consummated on the last day. United to Christ in his death and resurrection implies full participation in Christ and eternal life in the form of the resurrection of the body on the last day. "Christ waits for us in death and at the end of the world."[63]

For Luther, then, the day of judgment was that day when "there will be great destruction. Then the elements will be reduced to ashes, and the whole world return to its primordial chaos. Then a new heaven and earth will be fashioned and we will be changed."[64] Because Luther understood that a recreated heaven and earth are tied to Christ's return, this left no place for a future thousand-year reign of Christ on the earth at some time after he returns yet before a day of final judgment when the so-called millennial reign ended (i.e., premillennialism).

On the last day, "Christ will appear and reveal himself in such a way that all creatures will know and see that He had power over His enemies. . . . But He intended to hide Himself in this way in order to reveal himself at the time of His choosing." This is why believers must "cling to the Word and strengthen ourselves in faith, patience, and hope until the hour of His glory and power and of our Redemption comes."[65] So, said Luther, quoting from Revelation 22:20, "may our Lord Jesus Christ come to perfect His work which He has begun in us, and may he hasten the day of our redemption for which by the grace of God, we long with uplifted hands and for which we sigh and wait with pure faith and with a good conscience."[66]

As Christians struggle under the *Anfechtungen* of this life and dread the horrors of the coming wrath of God on the day of judgment, the gospel reminds us that we are simultaneously justified even while remaining sinners. We have been joined to Christ's death and resurrection in our baptism and through our faith in his promise that he has already defeated the world, the flesh, and the Devil. If Christ be our Judge, then we live with the knowledge that he has taken our judgment on himself.

63. Quoted in Althaus, *Theology of Martin Luther*, 413.
64. Luther on Titus 2:13 in a 1531 sermon, quoted in Plass, *What Luther Says*, 700.
65. Quoted in ibid., 700–701.
66. Quoted in ibid., 701.

Calvin's Eschatological Distinctives

According to David Holwerda, Calvin has never been well known for his eschatological views, but he has drawn significant interest from political and economic historians. For example, one historian considers Calvin and Karl Marx to be the two most influential revolutionaries of the modern world![67] I am sure Calvin would be surprised to be considered a "revolutionary" on the scale of Marx. More to the point is Holwerda's astute observation that a Christian theologian of the stature of Calvin cannot possibly have such a robust (if not revolutionary) view of history without at the same time possessing a significant eschatological framework underlying it.[68]

GOD'S ETERNAL DECREE:
THE FRAMEWORK FOR REDEMPTIVE HISTORY

Many of Calvin's interpreters locate the center of Calvin's thought in his views on divine providence and predestination. While there is some justification for doing so, Calvin's stress on God's sovereignty does not eliminate eschatology from his thought, nor does it render eschatology incidental. Rather, Calvin's stress on divine sovereignty ensures that eschatology plays a significant role in his theology.

Like Luther, Calvin's theology is thoroughly eschatological because of the way he conceived of God's redemption of sinners. While Luther emphasized the dialectic of the hidden God versus the revealed will within the context of the justification of the sinner (who is declared just before the final judgment), Calvin emphasized God's eternal decree and its execution in time. In his *Commentary on a Harmony of the Gospels Matthew, Mark, and Luke*, Calvin contended that "God's will, as far as it concerns Himself, is one and simple but it is set before us in the Scriptures as twofold. God's pleasure is said to be done, when He executes the hidden decrees of His providence."[69] God's decree is simple and therefore one, but Christians must distinguish between that decree (which remains hidden) and the execution of that decree in time

---

67. David E. Holwerda, "Eschatology and History: A Look at Calvin's Eschatological Vision," in *Exploring the Heritage of John Calvin: Essays in Honor of John Bratt*, ed. David E. Holwerda (Grand Rapids, MI: Baker, 1976), 110.
68. Ibid., 110.
69. Calvin on Matt. 6:10, in *CNTC* 1:208.

(in which God's will is revealed). This is the theological lens through which we must interpret Calvin's teaching regarding the return of Jesus Christ, the resurrection, the final judgment, and the restoration of all things.

Because Calvin viewed redemptive history as the progressive unfolding of God's eternal decree, redemptive history therefore has a divinely ordained *telos*. It is precisely because there is a divinely ordained outcome to human history that biblical revelation is eschatological in both its proximate and ultimate orientation. When seen in this light, Calvin's semirealized eschatology becomes apparent. For Calvin, Jesus Christ's incarnation and first advent must culminate in the final restoration of all things and in the resurrection of the dead on the day of our Lord's return, because this is the divinely decreed *telos*. Reflecting on God's sovereignty in Romans 8, Calvin connected God's decree to the final outcome—the resurrection:

> The eternal decree of God would have been void unless the promised resurrection, which is the effect of that decree, were also certain. By this decree God has chosen us as His sons before the foundation of the world, He bears witness to us concerning it by the Gospel, and he seals the Faith of it in our hearts by the Holy Spirit.[70]

God's decree not only ensures a final resurrection, it also ensures that the saving work of Jesus is applied to elect believers by the Holy Spirit.

CALVIN'S "ALREADY BUT NOT YET" ESCHATOLOGY

We can see this tension between the "already" and the "not yet" (to use a contemporary expression) where Calvin mapped out the broad course of redemptive history in the *Institutes*:

> For, as Christ our Redeemer once appeared, so in his final coming he will show the fruit of the salvation brought forth by him. In this way he scatters all the allurements that becloud us and prevent us from aspiring as we ought to heavenly glory. Nay, he teaches us to travel as pilgrims in this world that our celestial heritage may not perish or pass away.[71]

70. Calvin on Rom. 8:23, in *CNTC* 8:175.
71. Calvin, *Institutes*, 3.7.3.

Calvin grounded this pilgrim journey in the certain hope of the Lord's return because Jesus has already accomplished our salvation and ensured our celestial (heavenly) heritage. In light of the certain *telos* (the restoration of all things and the bodily resurrection at the end of the age), Calvin contended that the restoration of all things began when Jesus died on the cross, triumphing over sin and securing the salvation of his people. In his commentary on John's Gospel, Calvin stated,

> For in the cross of Christ, as in a splendid theater, the incomparable goodness of God is set before the whole world. The glory of God shines, indeed, in all creatures on high and below, but never more brightly than in the cross, in which there is a wonderful change of things—the condemnation of all men was manifested, sin blotted out, salvation restored to man; in short the whole world was renewed and all things restored to order.[72]

Earlier in the same commentary, Calvin had written, "Although Christ had already begun to set up the kingdom of God, it was His death that was the true beginning of a properly-ordered state and the complete restoration of the world."[73] When Jesus Christ ushers in his kingdom and defeats sin and the grave, he is thereby beginning the process of restoration that will be completed at his return.

In his *Commentary on the Epistle of Paul the Apostle to the Hebrews*, Calvin likewise connected the progressive advance of God's kingdom to the eventual renewal of all things:

> What the apostle refers to expressly as "the world to come" has relevance here; for he takes in it the sense of the renewed world. To make it clearer, let us imagine a twofold world—first the old one, which was corrupted by the sin of Adam; secondly the one later in time as it is renewed through Christ. The state of the first creation has decayed, and has fallen with man as far as man himself. Until there is a new restoration through Christ, this psalm [110] has no place. Hence it is now clear that the world to come is so described not only as that which we hope for after the resurrection, but as

---

72. Calvin on John 13:31, in *CNTC* 5:68.
73. Calvin on John 12:31, in *CNTC* 5:42.

that which begins from the rise of the kingdom of Christ, and it will find its fulfillment in the final redemption.[74]

As pilgrims living between the time of Christ's death, resurrection, and ascension and the time of his second advent, Christians must strive, Calvin believed, to keep a proper perspective on things earthly and heavenly. As mentioned earlier, in his "meditation on the future life,"[75] Calvin could write of the misery of this life (in the old world), while at the same time exhorting his reader to live in the hope of the Lord's return (when the world is renewed). In his discussion of the resurrection of Jesus in the *Institutes*, Calvin encouraged Christians to keep their eyes fixed on the final outcome of God's hidden decree, because the end—the resurrection—is the *telos*.[76]

> To the huge mass of miseries that almost overwhelms us are added the jests of profane men, which assail our innocence when we, willingly renouncing the allurements of present benefits, seem to strive after a blessedness hidden from us as if it were a fleeting shadow. Finally, above and below us, before us and behind, violent temptations besiege us, which our minds would be quite unable to sustain, were they not freed of earthly things and bound to the heavenly life, which appears to be far away. Accordingly, he alone has fully profited in the gospel who has accustomed himself to continual meditation upon the blessed resurrection.[77]

The final goal may seem far away to pilgrims, which is why they must realize that the goal is partially realized in the present through the ongoing expansion of the kingdom of God. Calvin's understanding of the nature of redemptive history, then, became the basis for his aversion to the apocalypticism and speculative eschatology typical of his age. What is hidden now will be revealed in God's perfect time—not before. What is revealed, however, is certain. There is nothing to be gained by attempting to discern God's hidden decree. Focusing on the *telos* of history, rather than being preoccupied with "signs of the end,"

---

74. Calvin on Heb. 2:5, in *CNTC* 12:22.
75. Calvin, *Institutes*, 3.9.1–6.
76. Ibid., 3.25.
77. Ibid., 3.25.1.

will keep God's people from being overwhelmed by the struggles of life in a fallen world.

Keeping this big picture in mind, believers should strive to live in the light of the cross and empty tomb while groping their way through the darkness of the present age. To Christian pilgrims struggling in this life, Calvin held out this promise: "[Jesus] reigns, I say, even now, when we pray that his kingdom may come. He reigns, indeed, while he performs miracles in his servants, and gives the law. . . . But his kingdom will properly come when it will be completed." The kingdom "will be completed when he will plainly manifest the glory of his majesty to his elect for salvation, and to the reprobate for confusion."[78] The final consummation comes only when God's eternal decree to save his elect has been accomplished in time. It is enough, said Calvin, for us to know *that* the Lord will return, not *when* he will return.

Therefore, Calvin's understanding of the course of the interadvental age derived from his belief that God's sovereign and gracious decree to save his elect cannot be divorced from the ends for which God predestined those whom he intends to save. If predestination deals with the former (God's decree), then eschatology deals with the latter (the end to which the elect have been predestined, the resurrection of the dead). In this sense, predestination and eschatology function as promise and fulfillment.[79] Because of his conception of redemption as an unfolding drama with a divinely appointed goal, Calvin was unflinching in his belief that Christ would return to raise the dead and restore this fallen world.

Calvin was adamant that Christians not speculate about the end times. When commenting on Jesus's words in the Olivet Discourse, Calvin wrote, "The glory and majesty of Christ's kingdom will only appear at His final coming, . . . the completion of those things that started at the resurrection, of which God gave his people only a taste, to lead them further along the road of hope and patience."[80] Calvin said, "[The Lord] wants his disciples to walk in the light of faith and, without knowing times with certainty, to expect the revelation with

78. Calvin, *Psychopannychia*, 465.
79. Torrance, "Eschatology of the Reformation," 49.
80. Calvin on Matt. 24:29, in *CNTC* 3:93.

patience. Beware then not to worry more than the Lord allows over details of time."[81] God does not want us to know when Christ returns, so that we will walk in faith.

We can see that, in making this point, Calvin used a tone in discussing eschatological hope that differed from Luther's in his stress on the imminency of the Lord's return. The variance between the two men is likely due to their different temperaments. Holwerda's assessment of Calvin's refusal to speculate is no doubt correct:

> There is nothing speculative about Calvin's eschatology. "He was no conjurer in numerical calculations." Specific numbers in Daniel and Revelation had to be interpreted figuratively. Through them God promises his elect some moderation, some shortening of the days; but the precise point of termination remains hidden in the secret counsel of God.[82]

While Luther spoke openly about living in the end times and was quite willing to affirm the nearness of the end, Calvin refused to do so because God's hidden decree cannot be known until God reveals it.

CALVIN'S REJECTION OF SOUL SLEEP

There are two additional emphases in Calvin's eschatology that merit discussion. The first is Calvin's opposition to the doctrine of "soul sleep" held by radical Anabaptists of his day, who believed that the soul does not have consciousness apart from the body. They held that at death the soul "sleeps" until the general resurrection at the end of the age, when the person awakens unto eternal life. Calvin disagreed vehemently with the Roman doctrine of purgatory and addressed it pointedly,[83] but he devoted considerable effort over the course of his career to refuting soul sleep, even summarizing his arguments against it in his chapter on the resurrection in the *Institutes*.[84]

Calvin's first published work of theology was the *Psychopannychia* (On the sleep of the soul), published in 1542, although the first draft

---

81. Calvin on Matt. 24:36, in *CNTC* 3:98.
82. Holwerda, "Eschatology and History," 133, quoting from Calvin's commentary on Dan. 7:25.
83. Calvin, *Institutes*, 3.5.6–10.
84. Ibid., 3.25.

of the manuscript was written as early as 1534, and Calvin revised it several times before publication.[85] Ironically, even as Calvin took issue with those Anabaptists who held that the soul is deprived of consciousness after death, this view was quite similar to Luther's "soul sleep." Calvin never mentioned Luther's view, and both Martin Bucer and Wolfgang Capito (1478–1541) urged Calvin not to publish the *Psychopannychia* so as to avoid exposing any differences between the Reformed and Lutherans and thus keep Roman or Anabaptist critics from pouncing.[86]

In his critique of the doctrine of soul sleep, Calvin began with philology. He pointed out that Scripture uses the words "spirit" and "soul" in different ways, while the creation account in Genesis 1 clearly affirms that the image of God in man must be identified with the human spirit. Furthermore, if one follows the course set out by the church fathers, Calvin argued, the interpreter of Scripture must distinguish between the soul and the body, something Anabaptist writers were apt to confuse.[87] Calvin contended, "We, following the whole doctrine of God, will hold for certain that man is composed and consisteth of two parts, that is to say, body and soul." He continued, adding, "What is the estate of the souls after the separation from their bodies? The Anabaptists do think that they be asleep like dead. We say they have life and feeling."[88]

The great irony is that the doctrine of soul sleep affirms the very thing Paul disparages: "For the Apostle [Paul] himself says that we are miserable if we have Christ in this life only." Calvin added, "True, there is the declaration of Paul, that we are more miserable than all men if there is no Resurrection; and there is no repugnance in these words to the dogma, that the spirits of the just are blessed before the Resurrection, since it is because of the Resurrection."[89]

85. For a discussion of Calvin's early contact with Anabaptists and a literary history of the *Psychopannychia*, see Willem Balke, *Calvin and the Anabaptist Radicals*, trans. William J. Heynen (Grand Rapids, MI: Eerdmans, 1981), 17–38; see also Quistorp, *Calvin's Doctrine of the Last Things*, 55–107.

86. Balke, *Calvin and the Anabaptist Radicals*, 31.

87. Ibid., 304.

88. John Calvin, *A Short Instruction for to Arm All Good Christian People against the Pestiferous Errors of the Common Sect of Anabaptists* (London, 1549), 113–14, quoted in Balke, *Calvin and the Anabaptist Radicals*, 305.

89. Calvin, *Psychopannychia*, 471, 472.

The soul is created immortal and lives on after death, but the body is mortal and must be raised imperishable to undo the consequences of the curse.

For Calvin, the very idea that the soul "sleeps" until the resurrection made no sense, given the unique properties of the human soul. As a creationist, Calvin affirmed that the human soul is not eternal but is uniquely created by God at the moment of conception and possesses independent and immortal existence apart from the body. Although the soul is the primary location of the divine image in humanity, nevertheless, "the state of man was not perfected in the person of Adam; but it is a peculiar benefit conferred by Christ, that we may be renewed to a life which is celestial, whereas before the fall of Adam, man's life was only earthly."[90] Even though created innocent, human nature must be perfected. This made perfect sense in light of the fact that redemptive history culminates in the resurrection of the body and the renewal of the heavens and the earth, for this is what God had decreed and had then revealed in the person and work of Christ.

Redemption from sin and the overturning of the consequences of the fall on human nature (death) are therefore necessarily eschatological in their orientation. The redeemed soul has been given eternal life through the work of Christ, by the Holy Spirit, who is the "earnest of our inheritance, that is, of eternal life, unto redemption, that is, until the day of this redemption comes. . . . And we who have received the firstfruits of the Spirit . . . shall enjoy it in reality, when Christ shall appear in judgment."[91] The nature of the soul and the divine purpose in the resurrection mean that "earthly life from the beginning is destined to eternity" and that "the delivered soul that is conscious after death awaits its consummation of the day of judgment."[92] According to Balke, in contrast to the Anabaptists,

> Calvin held that the soul in its essence is immortal. The rest after death consists of complete fellowship with God. . . . The Bible assures us that we already have eternal life here on earth and that

---

90. Calvin on Gen. 2:7, in Calvin, *Commentary on the First Book of Moses Called Genesis*, trans. John King (Edinburgh: Banner of Truth, 1984), 112–13.
91. Calvin on Eph. 1:14, in *CNTC* 11:132.
92. Quistorp, *Calvin's Doctrine of the Last Things*, 67, 87.

cannot be interrupted. To say that the soul sleeps is tantamount to saying that God forsakes his work.[93]

While Calvin comforted Christians with the reminder that "whatever hardships distress us, let this 'redemption' sustain us until its completion,"[94] he also warned his readers at the conclusion of the *Psychopannychia* that the radical Anabaptists of his day had built "a forge which has already fabricated, and is daily fabricating, so many monsters."[95]

CALVIN'S REJECTION OF CHILIASM (MILLENNIALISM)

It is also necessary to consider Calvin's vehement rejection of chiliasm (millennialism), a doctrine associated with the apocalypticism of the age and a doctrine that Calvin considered "childish" and "horrible." Calvin followed Luther in rejecting millennialism as when the latter rejected the Anabaptist millennial "dream" in no uncertain terms:

> That before the Last Day all the enemies of the Church will be physically exterminated and a Church assembled which shall consist of pious Christians only; they will govern in peace, without any opposition or attack. But this text [Psalm 110] clearly and powerfully says there are to be enemies continuously as long as this Christ reigns on earth. And certain it is, too, that death will not be abolished until the Last Day, when all his enemies shall be exterminated with one blow.[96]

Calvin too was appalled by the Anabaptist radicals who declared the city of Münster to be the new Zion—especially when connected to the revival of chiliasm tied to messianic expectations and radical social reform.[97] The Genevan pastor thought this doctrine highly problematic on several accounts. It secularized the reign of Christ and justified all sorts of fanciful speculation. People embrace this error, Calvin contended: "When we apply to [the kingdom of God] the measure of our own understanding, what can we conceive that is not gross

---

93. Balke, *Calvin and the Anabaptist Radicals*, 307.
94. Calvin, *Institutes*, 3.25.2.
95. Calvin, *Psychopannychia*, 490.
96. Martin Luther, "Sermon on Psalm 110" (1535), LW 13:263–64.
97. Balke, *Calvin and the Anabaptist Radicals*, 295.

and earthly? So it happens that like the beasts our senses attract us to what appeals to our flesh." Calvin concluded, "We see that the Chiliasts [i.e., those who believe that Christ would reign on earth for a thousand years] fell into like error and so took all the prophecies which describe the Kingdom of Christ figuratively on the pattern of earthly kingdoms."[98]

Arising from the misguided hermeneutic of interpreting heavenly things through carnal eyes, Calvin concluded that such forms of chiliasm are a childish fiction:

> But Satan has not only befuddled men's senses to make them bury with the corpses the memory of resurrection; he has also attempted to corrupt this part of the doctrine with various falsifications that he might at length destroy it. I pass over the fact that in Paul's day he began to overthrow it [1 Cor. 15:12 ff.]. But a little later there followed the chiliasts, who limited the reign of Christ to a thousand years. Now their fiction is too childish either to need or to be worth a refutation. And the Apocalypse, from which they undoubtedly drew a pretext for their error, does not support them. For the number "one thousand" [Rev. 20:4] does not apply to the eternal blessedness of the church but only to the various disturbances that awaited the church, while still toiling on earth. On the contrary, all Scripture proclaims that there will be no end to the blessedness of the elect or the punishment of the wicked [Matt. 25:41, 46].[99]

Furthermore, when commenting on Paul's words in 1 Thessalonians 4:17 ("so we will always be with the Lord"), Calvin described the consequence of millennialism—Christ's reign limited to a thousand years—as something too horrible to utter:

> These words [from Paul] more than sufficiently disprove the aberrations of . . . the Chiliasts. When believers have once been gathered together into one kingdom, their life will have no end any more than Christ's. To allot Christ a thousand years, so that afterwards he would cease to reign, is too horrible to speak of.[100]

98. Calvin on Acts 1:7, in *CNTC* 6:32.
99. Calvin, *Institutes*, 3.25.5.
100. Calvin on 1 Thess. 4:17, in *CNTC* 8:366.

Taking Augustine's view that the thousand years of Revelation 20 refer to the church age, not a period of time after the Lord's return, Calvin added,

> Accordingly, in the same book John has described a twofold Resurrection as well as a twofold death; namely, one of the soul before judgment, and another when the body will be raised up, and when the soul also will be raised up to glory. "Blessed," says he, "are those who have part in the first Resurrection; on them the second death takes no effect." (Rev. 20:6.) Well, then, may you be afraid who refuse to acknowledge that first Resurrection, which, however, is the only entrance to beatific glory.[101]

Along with Luther, Calvin stood firmly in the Augustinian tradition. He was thoroughly familiar with the writings of contemporary millenarians such as Müntzer and Hofmann, and Calvin "wanted no part of this."[102]

THE PAPACY AS ANTICHRIST AND THE LAST DAYS

In connection with Calvin's disdain of the chiliasm of his day and the eschatological speculations that went with it, it is important to consider that when Luther identified the papacy as the seat of Antichrist, he considered the presence of this foe as a sign that Christians were living in the last days. As we have seen, Luther believed that God might shorten the time until the Lord's return to spare his people from their sufferings at Antichrist's hand. This meant the Lord's coming was imminent.

Calvin took a different track. He followed Luther in identifying the papacy with Antichrist when he affirmed, "Daniel [Dan. 9:27] and Paul [II Thess. 2:4] foretold that Antichrist would sit in the Temple of God. With us, it is the Roman pontiff we make the leader and standard bearer of that wicked and abominable kingdom."[103] Calvin also agreed with Luther that "the name Antichrist does not designate a single individual, but a single kingdom which extends throughout many generations."[104]

---

101. Calvin, *Psychopannychia*, 446.
102. Balke, *Calvin and the Anabaptist Radicals*, 295.
103. Calvin, *Institutes*, 4.2.12.
104. Calvin on 2 Thess. 2:7, in *CNTC* 8:404.

But in his most detailed discussion of Antichrist in his commentary on 2 Thessalonians, it became evident that Calvin was much more reticent than Luther to affirm that Antichrist's presence is an indication that Christ's return is imminent. According to Calvin, the last days of Christ cannot come until a great apostasy occurs and the Antichrist—who is diametrically opposed to the kingdom of Christ and takes to himself those things that rightly belong to our Lord—has been revealed. Antichrist has already appeared in the form of the papacy. Yet, Calvin noted, the reign of Antichrist will be temporary, and the timing of his end will be determined by God. Antichrist will be destroyed by the Word of Christ at our Lord's appearing when the final restoration of all things comes to pass.

Calvin was largely in agreement with Luther but was content to interpret the words of Paul while saying nothing about when this would come to pass.[105] In doing so, Calvin was attempting to follow his own theological methodology set forth elsewhere: "In all religious doctrine . . . we ought to hold to the rule of modesty and sobriety; not to speak or guess, or even seek to know, concerning obscure matters anything except what has been imparted to us by God's word."[106] Would that all Christian theologians and pastors sought to follow Calvin's wise dictum, especially those who write in the field of eschatology.

Conclusion

With a good deal of historical justification, we can say that neither Martin Luther nor John Calvin were eschatological innovators. Both Reformers believed the traditional teaching of the church regarding the last things—when Jesus Christ ascended into heaven, he promised to physically return on the last day in order to raise the dead, judge the world, and then create a new heaven and new earth—was biblical. Both men easily fit within the modern designation *amillennial* because both followed Augustine in believing that the events depicted in Revelation 20 are symbolic of the church age, not a period of time *after* Christ's return.

---

105. Calvin on 2 Thess. 2:2–12, in CNTC 8:397–408.
106. Calvin, *Institutes*, 1.14.4.

Yet it is a mistake to conclude that because neither Luther nor Calvin were innovators, they were uninterested in eschatology. On the contrary, by placing the person and work of Jesus Christ at the center of their theology, both Reformers focused on the unfolding drama of redemptive history, unlike Roman Catholic theologians, who tended to see the progress of redemption through the lens of ecclesiology. The consequence of this intellectual move was that although neither Luther nor Calvin sought to make major adjustments to the received eschatological categories of the Christian church, they were thoroughly eschatological in their thinking. Heinrich Quistorp frames the matter correctly when he writes,

> The theology of the reformers is not primarily concerned with questions of eschatology (we are thinking especially of Luther and Calvin). Their chief concern is with the problem of justification and the matters immediately relevant to it. . . . Yet their whole theology is eschatologically oriented in so far as it is, in the Biblical-Pauline sense, a *theologia crucis* demanding sheer faith in the hidden glory of Christ and His kingdom and also at the same time a lively hope of its future manifestation.[107]

Both Luther and Calvin believed that the death and resurrection of Jesus were the central events in biblical revelation—foretold throughout the Old Testament and, in turn, providing the framework to understand the unfolding course of human history until the Lord returns. This enabled them to discuss the second coming of Jesus Christ in the nonapocalyptic terms of a semirealized (already/not yet) eschatology.

Because Christ's merits were sufficient to save sinners (when received through faith alone), Jesus himself provided Christians with the sure and certain hope of the resurrection of the body on the last day when he returns. While Luther and Calvin disagreed about the nature of the intermediate state, both anchored the Christian's hope and assurance in Jesus Christ's once-for-all victory over sin, death, and the grave. This life may be a constant struggle—as both men described it—but there is no reason for God's people to live in despair. As surely as Jesus

---

107. Quistorp, *Calvin's Doctrine of the Last Things*, 11.

died for our sins and was raised for our justification (Rom. 4:25), so too he will come again in his own appointed time to mete out judgment to the enemies of the gospel and to ensure that God's people will stand secure on the day of judgment. The day of judgment is a day of terror to those who know not Christ but good news to those who die in the Lord and await the Lord's return in faith.

While rejecting Rome's notion that eschatology was to be understood in light of the eventual perfection of the Roman church, neither man was willing to embrace the radical apocalypticism of the age. In fact, both Luther and Calvin vehemently opposed the radical Anabaptists and all forms of speculative date setting and millenarianism with as much vigor as they opposed the Roman doctrine of purgatory. Luther and Calvin were convinced that the papacy had become the Antichrist—a clear biblical sign of the end—and both believed that God would have mercy on his people and hasten the return of Christ to preserve his persecuted elect on the earth. Luther spoke openly about his belief that the Lord's return was near, while Calvin was content to quote Scripture and say no more. It is here, perhaps, that we see most clearly the temperamental differences between the two men.

Both Luther and Calvin—were they to counsel us today—would scold those who use eschatology as a springboard to fanciful predictions and who offer unfounded interpretations of the eschatological language in Scripture. Both would exhort us to look for comfort in the second coming of Jesus Christ as Paul reminds us to do:

> For all the promises of God find their Yes in him. That is why it is through him that we utter our Amen to God for his glory. And it is God who establishes us with you in Christ, and has anointed us, and who has also put his seal on us and given us his Spirit in our hearts as a guarantee. (2 Cor. 1:20–22)

Resources for Further Study

PRIMARY SOURCES

Bucer, Martin. *De Regno Christi*. In *Melanchthon and Bucer*, edited by Wilhelm Pauck, 174–394. Library of Christian Classics 19. Philadelphia: Westminster, 1969.

Calvin, John. *Institutes of the Christian Religion*. Edited by John T. Mc-
Neill. Translated by Ford Lewis Battles. 2 vols. Library of Christian
Classics 20–21. 1559 edition. Philadelphia: Westminster, 1960.

———. *Psychopannychia*. In *Selected Works of John Calvin: Tracts and
Letters*, edited by Henry Beveridge and Jules Bonnet, translated by
Henry Beveridge, 3:413–90. 1851. Reprint, Grand Rapids, MI: Baker,
1983.

———. *A Short Instruction for to Arm All Good Christian People against
the Pestiferous Errors of the Common Sect of Anabaptists*. London,
1549.

Luther, Martin. "Preface to the Revelation of Saint John." In *Works of
Martin Luther with Introductions and Notes*, edited by Adolph Spaeth,
6:479–91. Philadelphia ed. 1932. Reprint, Grand Rapids, MI: Baker,
1982.

———. "Sermon on Psalm 110" (1535). In *Luther's Works*. Vol. 13, *Selected Psalms II*, edited by Jaroslav Pelikan, 263–64. Philadelphia:
Fortress, 1972.

Zwingli, Huldrych. *Fides Expositio* (1531). In *Reformed Confessions of
the 16th and 17th Centuries in English Translation*. Vol. 1, *1523–
1552*, edited by James T. Dennison Jr., 176–225. Grand Rapids, MI:
Reformation Heritage Books, 2008.

———. *Fides Ratio* (1530). In *Reformed Confessions of the 16th and
17th Centuries in English Translation*. Vol. 1, *1523–1552*, edited by
James T. Dennison Jr., 112–36. Grand Rapids, MI: Reformation Heritage Books, 2008.

Secondary Sources

Balke, Willem. *Calvin and the Anabaptist Radicals*. Translated by William J. Heynen. Grand Rapids, MI: Eerdmans, 1981.

Hall, Fred P. "Martin Luther's Theology of Last Things." In *Looking into
the Future: Evangelical Studies in Eschatology*, edited by David W.
Baker, 124–43. Grand Rapids, MI: Baker Academic, 2001.

Holwerda, David E. "Eschatology and History: A Look at Calvin's Escha-
tological Vision." In *Exploring the Heritage of John Calvin: Essays in
Honor of John Bratt*, edited by David E. Holwerda, 110–39. Grand
Rapids, MI: Baker, 1976.

Quistorp, Heinrich. *Calvin's Doctrine of the Last Things*. Translated by
Harold Knight. 1955. Reprint, Eugene, OR: Wipf & Stock, 2009.

Strohl, Jane E. "Luther's Eschatology: The Last Times and the Last Things." PhD diss., University of Chicago Divinity School, 1989.

Torrance, T. F. "The Eschatology of the Reformation." In *Eschatology: Four Papers Read to the Society for the Study of Theology*, edited by T. F. Torrance and J. K. S. Reid, 36–62. Scottish Journal of Theology Occasional Papers 2. Edinburgh: Oliver and Boyd, 1957.

Contributors

Michael Allen (PhD, Wheaton College) is professor of systematic and historical theology at Reformed Theological Seminary in Orlando, Florida. He is the author of *Justification and the Gospel: Understanding the Contexts and Controversies*; *Reformed Theology*; *Christ's Faith: A Dogmatic Account*; and *Reformed Catholicity: The Promise of Retrieval for Theology and Biblical Interpretation* (with Scott Swain). He is also the editor of *Theological Commentary: Evangelical Perspectives*; *Reformation Readings of Paul: Explorations in History and Exegesis* (with Jonathan A. Linebaugh); and *Christian Dogmatics: Reformed Theology for the Church Catholic* (with Scott Swain).

Matthew Barrett (PhD, The Southern Baptist Theological Seminary) is tutor of systematic theology and church history at Oak Hill Theological College in London. The executive editor of *Credo Magazine*, he is also the editor of the 5 Solas Series and the author of *God's Word Alone: The Authority of Scripture*; *Owen on the Christian Life: Living for the Glory of God in Christ* (with Michael A. G. Haykin); *Salvation by Grace: The Case for Effectual Calling and Regeneration*; *The Grace of Godliness: An Introduction to Doctrine and Piety in the Canons of Dort*.

Gerald Bray (DLitt, University of Paris-Sorbonne) is research professor of divinity at Beeson Divinity School, Samford University, in Birmingham, Alabama. He is the editor of *Galatians, Ephesians* in the Reformation Commentary on Scripture series and the author of *Biblical Interpretation: Past & Present*; *The Doctrine of God*; *God is Love: A Biblical and Systematic Theology*; *God Has Spoken: A History of Chris-*

tian Theology; *Augustine on the Christian Life: Transformed by the Power of God*; and *The Church: A Theological and Historical Account*.

Graham A. Cole (ThD, Australian College of Theology) is dean and professor of biblical and systematic theology at Trinity Evangelical Divinity School in Deerfield, Illinois. He is the author of *He Who Gives Life: The Doctrine of the Holy Spirit*; *Engaging With the Holy Spirit: Real Questions, Practical Answers*; *God the Peacemaker: How Atonement Brings Shalom*; and *The God Who Became Human: A Biblical Theology of Incarnation*.

Aaron Clay Denlinger (PhD, University of Aberdeen) is professor of church history and historical theology at Reformation Bible College in Sanford, Florida. He is the editor of *Reformed Orthodoxy in Scotland: Essays on Scottish Theology, 1560–1775*, and the author of *Omnes in Adam ex pacto Dei: Ambrogio Catarino's Doctrine of Covenantal Solidarity and Its Influence on Post-Reformation Reformed Theologians*.

J. V. Fesko (PhD, King's College, University of Aberdeen, Scotland) is academic dean and professor of systematic theology and historical theology at Westminster Seminary California in Escondido, California. He is the author of *Justification: Understanding the Classic Reformed Doctrine*; *Beyond Calvin: Union with Christ and Justification in Early Modern Reformed Theology (1517–1700)*; and *The Theology of the Westminster Standards: Historical Context and Theological Insights*.

Douglas F. Kelly (PhD, University of Edinburgh) is professor of theology emeritus at Reformed Theological Seminary in Charlotte, North Carolina. He is the author of the multivolume *Systematic Theology: Grounded in Holy Scripture and Understood in the Light of the Church*, and of *Creation and Change: Genesis 1:1–2:4 in the Light of Changing Scientific Paradigms*; *The Emergence of Liberty in the Modern World: The Influence of Calvin on Five Governments from the 16th through 18th Centuries*; *If God Already Knows, Why Pray?* (with Caroline S. Kelly); and *Revelation: A Mentor Expository Commentary*.

Eunjin Kim is a PhD candidate in church history at Westminster Theological Seminary in Glenside, Pennsylvania. She holds an MDiv from

Hapdong Theological Seminary in South Korea and a ThM from Duke Divinity School. Her interests include sixteenth- and seventeenth-century Reformed theology and the history of biblical interpretation in the Reformation era.

Robert Kolb (PhD, University of Wisconsin–Madison) is professor emeritus of systematic theology at Concordia Seminary in St. Louis, Missouri. He is the author of *The Genius of Luther's Theology: A Wittenberg Way of Thinking for the Contemporary Church*; *Luther and the Stories of God: Biblical Narratives as a Foundation for Christian Living*; *Martin Luther: Confessor of the Faith*; *Bound Choice, Election, and Wittenberg Theological Method: From Martin Luther to the Formula of Concord*; *Martin Luther as Prophet, Teacher, and Hero: Images of the Reformer, 1520–1620*; and *Martin Luther and the Enduring Word of God: The Wittenberg School and Its Scripture-Centered Proclamation*.

Robert Letham (PhD, University of Aberdeen) is professor of systematic and historical theology and oversees research degrees at Union School of Theology, based in Oxford, England. He is the author of *Union with Christ: In Scripture, History, and Theology*; *The Westminster Assembly: Reading Its Theology in Historical Context*; *The Holy Trinity: In Scripture, History, Theology, and Worship*; and *The Work of Christ*.

Peter A. Lillback (PhD, Westminster Theological Seminary) is president and professor of historical theology and church history at Westminster Theological Seminary in Glenside, Pennsylvania. He is the author of *George Washington's Sacred Fire* and *The Binding of God: Calvin's Role in the Development of Covenant Theology*. He is the editor of *Thy Word Is Still Truth: Essential Writings on the Doctrine of Scripture from the Reformation to Today* (with Richard B. Gaffin Jr.), and *A Theological Guide to Calvin's Institutes: Essays and Analysis* (with David W. Hall).

Korey D. Maas (DPhil, University of Oxford) is assistant professor of history at Hillsdale College in Hillsdale, Michigan. He is the author of *The Reformation and Robert Barnes: History, Theology, and Polemic in Early Modern England* and is a contributor to volume 60 of *Luther's Works*.

Donald Macleod (DD, Westminster Theological Seminary) was professor of systematic theology at the Free Church of Scotland College in Edinburgh and was also the school's principal from 1999–2011. He is the author of *Christ Crucified: Understanding the Atonement*; *The Person of Christ*; *A Faith to Live By: Understanding Christian Doctrine*; *From Glory to Golgotha: Controversial Issues in the Life of Christ*; *Jesus Is Lord: Christology Yesterday and Today.*

Keith A. Mathison (PhD, Whitefield Theological Seminary) is professor of systematic theology at Reformation Bible College in Sanford, Florida. He is the author of *Given For You: Reclaiming Calvin's Doctrine of the Lord's Supper*; *From Age to Age: The Unfolding of Biblical Eschatology*; and *The Shape of Sola Scriptura*. He also served as an associate editor of *The Reformation Study Bible*.

Michael Reeves (PhD, King's College, London) is president and professor of theology at Union School of Theology, based in Oxford, England. Previously he served as head of theology for the Universities and Colleges Christian Fellowship. He is the author of *The Unquenchable Flame: Discovering the Heart of the Reformation*; *Delighting in the Trinity: An Introduction to the Christian Faith*; *Rejoicing in Christ*; and *Why the Reformation Still Matters* (with Tim Chester). He is also the coeditor of *Adam, the Fall, and Original Sin: Theological, Biblical, and Scientific Perspectives* (with Hans Madueme).

Kim Riddlebarger (PhD, Fuller Theological Seminary) is senior pastor of Christ Reformed Church in Anaheim, California, and is cohost of the White Horse Inn radio program. He is the author of *A Case for Amillennialism: Understanding the End Times*; *The Man of Sin: Uncovering the Truth about the Antichrist*; *First Corinthians*; and *The Lion of Princeton: B. B. Warfield as Apologist and Theologian.*

Scott R. Swain (PhD, Trinity Evangelical Divinity School) is academic dean and professor of systematic theology at Reformed Theological

Seminary in Orlando, Florida. He is the coeditor of *Christian Dogmatics: Reformed Theology for the Church Catholic* (with Michael Allen), and the author of *Reformed Catholicity: The Promise of Retrieval for Theology and Biblical Interpretation* (with Michael Allen); *The God of the Gospel: Robert Jenson's Trinitarian Theology*; *Trinity, Revelation, and Reading: A Theological Introduction to the Bible and Its Interpretation*; and *Father, Son and Spirit: The Trinity and John's Gospel* (with Andreas Köstenberger).

Mark D. Thompson (DPhil, University of Oxford) is the principal and the head of the department of theology, philosophy, and ethics at Moore Theological College in Sydney, Australia. He is the author of *A Clear and Present Word: The Clarity of Scripture*, and *A Sure Ground on Which to Stand: The Relation of Authority and Interpretive Method in Luther's Approach to Scripture*.

Carl R. Trueman (PhD, University of Aberdeen) is the Paul Woolley Chair of Church History at Westminster Theological Seminary in Glenside, Pennsylvania. He is the author of *Luther on the Christian Life: Cross and Freedom*; *The Creedal Imperative*; *Histories and Fallacies: Problems Faced in the Writing of History*; *Reformation: Yesterday, Today, and Tomorrow*; *John Owen: Reformed Catholic, Renaissance Man*; and *Luther's Legacy: Salvation and English Reformers, 1525–1556*.

Cornelis P. Venema (PhD, Princeton Theological Seminary) is president and professor of doctrinal studies at Mid-America Reformed Seminary in Dyer, Indiana. He is the author of *The Promise of the Future*; *Heinrich Bullinger and the Doctrine of Predestination: Author of "the Other Reformed Tradition"?*; *The Gospel of Free Acceptance in Christ: An Assessment of the Reformation and New Perspectives on Paul*; *Accepted and Renewed in Christ: The "Twofold Grace of God" and the Interpretation of Calvin's Theology*; and *Christ and the Future: The Bible's Teaching about the Last Things*.

Name Index

Albert the Great, 82, 87
Alexander of Hales, 79–80, 87, 305
Alsted, Johann Heinrich, 21, 396
Althaus, Paul, 190, 316, 386, 737
Althusius, John, 675, 711–12, 715
Ambrose, 69n4, 324, 336
Amsdorf, Nikolaus von, 584, 698
Amyraut, Moïse, 375
Andraeus, Jacob, 274, 338, 339
Anselm, 192, 377, 380
Aristotle, 229, 475, 646
Arminius, Jacobus, 423, 425, 442, 446–47
Athanasius, 285, 308, 324, 402
Atkinson, James, 315, 321
Augustine, 69n4, 229, 283, 452, 486
    Christology of, 336
    on church and Scripture, 148, 182
    on conversion, 253
    on creation, 286
    on free will, 487, 492, 494, 497, 504, 505
    on image of God, 293–94, 295–96
    interpretation of Revelation chap. 20,
        735, 750, 751
    on justification, 84–85, 570
    on Lord's Supper, 644
    on Pelagius, 306, 466
    on predestination, 244–45, 265, 277
    on purgatory, 75–76
    reading of Paul, 543
    on revolutionary action, 696
    on righteousness of God, 518–19
    on Scripture, 147–48
    on the sacraments, 611
    on the Trinity, 192
    on union with Christ, 427
Aulén, Gustav, 347, 380
Aus der Au, Christina, 13
Averroës, 229

Baker, J. Wayne, 261n48, 690
Baldwin of Forde, 69–70
Balke, Willem, 403, 744–48
Bancroft, George, 715
Baro, Peter, 133
Barth, Karl, 148, 157, 227n50
Basil of Caesarea, 152
Bavinck, Herman, 354
Beaton, David, 134
Beckwith, Carl L., 395
Beda, Noel, 124
Bellah, Robert, 30
Bellarmine, Robert, 314, 709
Berengar of Tours, 645
Berkhof, Louis, 354
Bernardino of Siena, 49
Bernard of Clairvaux, 77, 192, 423, 426,
    429, 434, 442
Beza, Theodore, 127, 128–30, 273, 274–75,
    338, 339, 375, 376, 435, 443n76, 599,
    700, 701–2
Bibliander, Theodor, 122
Biel, Gabriel, 90–93, 105–6, 152, 306, 452,
    470, 514–15
Blaurock, George, 621
Bodin, John, 712
Boethius, 229, 455
Boice, James Montgomery, 60–61
Bollinger, Dennis, 601–2
Bolsec, Jerome, 127, 261, 263n52, 267n67,
    484, 501
Bonaventure, 82, 87
Bonhoeffer, Dietrich, 18–19
Boniface, Saint, 76
Boniface VIII, Pope, 100
Bora, Katharina von (wife of Luther), 114
Bownde, Nicholas, 133
Bradwardine, Thomas, 244n3, 452

Bray, Gerald, 191–92, 203, 410
Brenz, Johannes, 322, 325, 336, 523
Bromiley, Geoffrey, 320–21, 414, 415
Bruce, A. B., 324–25, 327, 328
Brunner Emil, 354
Bruno of Cologne, 86
Bucer, Martin, 125, 195, 228, 268n72,
    500n211, 562, 660, 687, 746
  on baptism, 626–27
  on the church, 588–89
  eschatology of, 729–30
  influence on Calvin, 665
  on Lord's Supper, 643, 656, 659–64, 665,
    667, 670, 671
Buchanan, George, 136
Bullinger, Heinrich, 54, 120, 121–23, 128,
    183, 196, 244n4, 384, 424
  on baptism, 609, 624–26, 636–37
  on biblical authority, 168–73, 178
  on the church, 591–92
  on church and state, 689–90, 692–93
  on creation and redemption, 286
  on image of God, 297–98, 304, 309–10
  on incomprehensibility of God, 222
  on infant baptism, 625–26, 632
  on knowledge of God, 226
  on life after death, 307
  on Lord's Supper, 667–68, 670
  on names of God, 232–33, 234–35, 288
  on predestination, 260–66, 267, 269
  on resistance to tyranny, 694–95
  on threefold office of Christ, 353

Cajetan, Cardinal Thomas, 153, 647n16
Calvin, John, 43, 123–30, 337
  on accommodation, 177–78, 225, 349,
    365, 369, 372
  on the atonement, 375–80
  on baptism, 609, 626–34, 639
  on biblical authority, 173–79
  on Christ as Prophet, 363–65, 367–68
  on the church, 592–97
  on church and state, 686, 687, 691–92
  on church discipline, 693–94
  commentary on Genesis, 291, 292
  concern for pure worship, 51n33
  on creation, 287
  on creation, fall, and redemption, 285–87
  on descent into hell, 373–75
  eschatology of, 721, 722–23, 750–51
  and *extra Calvinisticum*, 328–34
  on free will, 481–501
  on the Holy Spirit, 394

  on image of God, 295–97, 304–5, 308–9
  on infant baptism, 629–30, 632
  on justification, 512–13, 524–31, 545
  on kingship of Christ, 382–84
  on Lord's Supper, 644, 665–69, 670, 671
  on mediatorial work of Christ, 349–50
  on meditation on the future life, 727–728,
    743
  on *munus triplex*, 347, 352–55
  on names of God, 233–34, 289
  as Nestorian, 330, 331n80
  on power of God, 218, 220, 237
  on preaching, 51, 54–55, 57–58, 369–70
  on predestination, 241, 255–60, 261, 279,
    498
  on priesthood of Christ, 370–72
  on the Reformation, 725
  on resistance to tyranny, 695–97
  on the sacraments, 404–6
  on sanctification, 570–71
  as second-generation Reformer, 726
  and the Spirit, 403–9
  theocentric perspective of, 221
  on the Trinity, 200–209, 287n8
  on two natures of Christ, 355–56, 361–62
  on union with Christ, 425, 426, 433–38,
    666
  on Word and Sacrament, 440
  on Word as controlling principle of wor-
    ship, 59
Capito, Wolfgang, 291, 660, 746
Cameron, Euan, 43, 499n208, 501n214
Cameron, John, 375
Cameron, Nigel, 291
Caroli, Pierre, 125
Carson, D. A., 15
Cartwright, Thomas, 133, 599–601
Castellio, Sebastian, 127
Catherine of Aragon, 130
Cervini, Marcello, 483
Chandieu, Antoine de, 301
Charlemagne, 97, 105, 678
Charles I, King, 706–7
Charles V, Emperor, 107, 321, 468, 502,
    586, 589, 660
Charles Emmanuel I, Duke, 129
Charles the Bald, 679
Chemnitz, Martin, 322–25, 339, 425,
    432–34, 536–37, 583, 587n40
Chrysostom, John, 352, 475, 480, 486, 497
Cicero, 227
Cincius, Bernardus, 483

Clement V, Pope, 100
Clement VII, Pope, 107
Clement of Alexandria, 622
Cochlaeus, Johann, 172
Collinson, Patrick, 551
Columbus, Christopher, 107
Comestor, Peter, 78, 86
Constantine, 678, 685
Cop, Nicholas, 124
Cordier, Mathurin, 124
Craig, John, 364
Cranmer, Thomas, 50, 131, 146, 502–3, 730
   on the Apocrypha, 416n93
   on biblical authority, 180–85
   on the Holy Spirit, 394, 409–15
Cromwell, Oliver, 706–7
Cunningham, William, 375
Cyprian, 731
Cyril of Alexandria, 321, 324, 336, 644

d'Ailly, Pierre, 104, 452
Daniell, David, 294
Darwin, Charles, 291
Dean, Jonathan, 409
de Bure, Idelette (wife of Calvin), 125
de Coligny, Gaspard, 704n150
Democritus, 290
Donnelly, John Patrick, 268n72, 270n78
Dragas, George, 308
Drechsel, Thomas, 555
Drickamer, John M., 463n41
Dulles, Avery, 22–23, 512, 538–39
Duns Scotus, John, 89–90, 268n72, 516, 611

Eck, Johann, 113, 161
Edward VI, King, 131, 503, 598, 730
Einstein, Albert, 290n14
Elert, Werner, 247n7
Elizabeth I, Queen, 132, 135, 599, 697
Entfelder, Christian, 211
Erasmus, 105, 114–15, 159, 247–48,
   452–62, 463, 521
Erastus, Thomas, 590
Eugenius IV, Pope, 104
Eusebius, 324
Eutyches, 335
Evans, Gillian, 147

Farel, Guillaume, 124–25, 593, 665, 686,
   687
Ferguson, Sinclair, 206
Figgis, John N., 683–84
Finney, Charles G., 19

Forde, Gerhard, 223n26, 573n55
Fowler, Stanley K., 638n129
Foxe, John, 131
Francis, Pope, 13
Francis I, King of France, 124, 589
Franck, Sebastian, 555
Frederick III, Elector Palatine, 123, 136
Fuhrman, Paul, 705

Gansfort, Wessel, 647–48, 651
Gentile, Valentine, 314
George, Timothy, 45n6, 57–58, 59n67,
   396n9, 402, 725
Gerrish, B. A., 670
Gerson, Jean, 104, 426–28, 442
Göbel, Max, 417n99
Godfrey, W. Robert, 60, 501
Gordon, Bruce, 123, 665
Gratian, 76–77, 98
Graybill, Gregory B., 482
Grebel, Konrad, 120, 621
Gregory, Brad, 230n62
Gregory II, Pope, 76
Gregory VII, Pope, 98, 678, 679
Gregory of Nazianzus, 203, 374
Gregory of Nyssa, 381, 644
Gregory of Rimini, 244n3, 268n72, 452,
   504
Gregory Palamas, 323
Grenz, Stanley, 32–34
Grisar, Hartmann, 518
Grotius, Hugo, 675, 712–13
Grudem, Wayne, 354

Haimo of Auxerre, 86
Hall, Christopher, 395–96
Hamilton, Patrick, 134
Harding, Thomas, 298n46
Hart, D. G., 715n204
Hätzer, Ludwig, 211
Hazlett, Ian, 662
Helm, Paul, 372, 487
Hendrix, Scott, 584
Henry IV, King, 103, 678, 680
Henry VII, King, 130
Henry VIII, King, 130–31, 598, 687
Henry of Ghent, 151
Hervé de Bourg-Dieu, 86
Hess, John, 162
Hesselink, I. John, 501
Hildebert of Tours, 69
Hildebrand. *See* Gregory VII, Pope
Hodge, Charles, 354, 667n135

Hoen, Cornelius, 651, 653, 656
Hofmann, Melchior, 340, 342, 735, 750
Holcot, Robert, 452
Holwerda, David, 740, 745
Hooker, Richard, 146, 601
Hooper, John, 131
Horton, Michael, 490–91
Hotman, Francois, 700
Hubmaier, Balthasar, 120, 220, 341, 603, 621, 623
Hughes, Philip E., 50
Hugh of St. Victor, 69, 77, 149, 183
Hugolino of Orvieto, 452
Hus, Jan, 44n3, 90, 103, 104, 108, 579, 647n20, 682
Hut, Hans, 735
Hutchinson, Roger, 213

Ignatius of Loyola, 137, 214
Illyricus, Matthias Flacius, 116–17
Innocent III, Pope, 100
Irenaeus, 204, 295, 360, 365
Ivo of Chartres, 80

James, Frank A., III, 268n72, 502
James V, King, 134
James VI, King of Scotland, 135–36
Jansen, John Frederick, 363–64, 383
Jarry, E., 714–15
Jenson, Robert, 542
Jerome, 486
Joachim of Fiore, 724, 732
John of Antioch, 336
John of Damascus, 218
John of the Cross, 214
Jud, Leo, 120

Kant, Immanuel, 30, 31
Karlstadt, Andreas, 161, 341, 620, 643, 648, 650–54, 656
Keller, Tim, 15
Kelly, J. N. D., 645n2
Kendall, R. T., 376
Kik, J. Marcellus, 715
Kim, Nam-Joon, 19
Kingdon, Robert, 690, 715
Knox, John, 134–35, 138, 271n81, 300–301, 384, 687, 699, 706
Kolb, Robert, 457n18, 475, 477
Koop, Karl, 340
Köstlin, Julius, 738
Küng, Hans, 512
Kuyper, Abraham, 716

Lane, Anthony N. S., 203, 485n142, 485n144, 490n169, 491–92, 494
Latimer, Hugh, 57, 131
Laud, William, 601
Le Goff, Jacques, 77, 81
Leo I, Pope, 324, 336
Leo III, Pope, 678
Leo IX, Pope, 97–98
Leo X, Pope, 154
Letham, Robert, 203
Lever, Thomas, 56
Lidgett, J. S., 204
Lindbeck, George, 25–26
Lindberg, Carter, 44n3, 45, 47n16, 112
Locke, John, 715
Lombard, Peter, 67, 90, 98, 150, 218, 230n64, 307n86, 426, 515, 646
  on grace, 493–95
  on image of God, 283
  on justification, 428
  on sacraments, 68–72
  on the Trinity, 192–93
Lucretius, 290
Luther, Martin, 112–16, 550–51
  on accommodation, 223
  as antispeculative, 224
  on the atonement, 347
  on baptism, 609, 615–18, 738–39
  on the bondage of the will, 452–62
  on the church, 578–80, 581–83
  on church and state, 686–87
  on church polity, 584
  commentary of Genesis, 291, 292
  on communication of attributes, 314–18
  on corruption of the gospel, 46
  debate with Zwingli, 138, 154
  on the Devil, 381–86, 457, 724, 736
  on doctrine of God, 218
  eschatology of, 721, 722–23, 732–39
  as Eutychian, 321
  as first-generation Reformer, 726
  on forerunners of the Reformation, 44n3
  on free will, 477
  on God as "clothed in his Word," 223–24
  on grace, 93
  on Holy Spirit, 199, 394, 396–400
  on image of God, 293–94, 303–4, 309
  on incomprehensibility of God, 222
  on infant baptism, 622–23
  on the Jews, 116
  on justification, 46, 512, 517–24, 545
  on the law, 566, 572–73

on law and gospel, 366, 460–62, 733–34
on Lord's Supper, 643, 648–50, 654–59,
    661, 664, 667, 669
on Melanchthon, 462–63
on names of God, 232–33, 235–36
on papal reform, 107
on Pelagianism, 45n10
on preaching, 55, 114, 157, 369
on purgatory, 53, 83
on resistance to tyrants, 685
on sacraments, 398, 612–14
on sanctification, 552–57
on Scripture, 56, 146, 153–61
on *sola Scriptura*, 571
temperament of, 727
on theology of the cross, 347, 386–89,
    588
on the Trinity, 194–99
on two kingdoms, 684–85
on two natures of Christ, 355–56, 362
on union with Christ, 425, 427, 428–29
on worship, 586

MacCulloch, Diarmaid, 415
MacGregor, Kirk R., 341
Machen, J. Gresham, 17
Machiavelli, 683
Manetsch, Scott, 48, 51n33, 52, 55
Mani, 147
Mannermaa, Tuomo, 540
Mantz, Felix, 621
Marpeck, Pilgram, 342
Marsilius of Padua, 101, 102, 108, 681, 685
Martin V, Pope, 104
Marx, Karl, 740
Mary, Queen of Scots, 135
Mary I, Queen, 57, 131–32, 134–35, 713
Mary of Guise, 134, 135
Masson, Robert, 268
Matheson, Peter, 397n17
Mattes, Mark, 573n55
McGrath, Alister, 44n3, 44n5, 45, 190,
    511–12, 514, 531n95
McLoughlin, William, 31
McNeill, John T., 676, 683, 703
Melanchthon, Philipp, 47n17, 62n75,
    115–16, 134, 337, 376, 438
on atonement, 380
on Christ as Prophet, 366–67
Christology of, 357–58, 360
on the church, 580–81, 583
on *communicatio idiomatum*, 327
on creation, 286

on free will, 451, 462–83, 508
on image of God, 306, 310
on imputed righteousness, 540–41
influence on Calvin, 665n123
influence on Luther, 519, 520–24
on justification, 512, 545
on Lord's Supper, 650, 661, 669
on original sin, 466–67
on philosophical speculation, 196, 218
on predestination, 250–54, 464, 569
on Scripture, 154, 161–65
on third use of the law, 566
on threefold office of Christ, 353
on the Trinity, 194–95
on two natures of Christ, 355
on union with Christ, 425, 429–32
Mergel, Angel, 419
Molnar, Paul, 24
Moltmann, Jürgen, 386
Morély, Jean, 596
Mornay, Philippe de, 700, 702–3, 704, 705,
    710
Muller, Richard, 190–91, 212, 259n40,
    263n52, 266n63, 270n78, 273n86,
    275n88, 277, 496n199, 498–99, 722
Müntzer, Thomas, 27, 397–98, 555, 620,
    682, 735, 750
Musculus, Wolfgang, 122, 222, 232,
    266n63, 272n84, 425, 439
Myconius, Oswald, 122

Neill, Stephen, 410
Nestorius, 321
Nevin, John Williamson, 667n135
Newman, Cardinal John Henry, 20, 354
Newton, Isaac, 290n14
Null, Ashley, 413

Oberman, Heiko, 92, 727n22, 730n39
O'Carroll, Michael, 201
Oecolampadius, Johannes, 121, 122, 531n95,
    643, 655, 656, 659, 662, 663, 693
Olevian, Caspar, 210, 338
Olson, Roger, 394n3, 395–96, 418
Origen, 644
Orombi, Henry Luke, 19
Osiander, Andreas, 353, 370, 425, 430–31,
    437–38, 560–61
Othobon, 99–100
Owen, John, 351

Parker, T. H. L., 493–94
Paschasius Radbertus, 645

Paul III, Pope, 137
Paulson, Stephen, 573n55
Pelagius, 484n139, 543–44
Pelikan, Jaroslav, 550–51, 574
Perkins, William, 131, 273, 354, 357, 358, 365, 380
Philip, Landgrave of Hesse, 115, 321
Philip II, 132
Philips, Dietrich, 342
Pighius, Albert, 482–84, 486n151, 487, 490, 492–94, 500n211, 504
Pius II, Pope, 681
Placher, William, 28
Plato, 229
Pole, Reginald, 132
Politus, Ambrosius Catharinus, 730n39
Ponet, John, 712–13
Prenter, Regin, 396
Preus, J. A. O., 463
Prierias, Sylvestro, 152

Quistorp, Heinrich, 731n41, 752

Raitt, Jill, 338
Ranke, Leopold von, 715
Rankin, Duncan, 666
Ratramnus, 645
Reardon, Bernard, 31
Reid, W. Stanford, 525
Reinhart, Anna (wife of Zwingli), 119
Richard II, King, 103
Richard of St. Victor, 149–50
Ridley, Nicholas, 131
Riedemann, Peter, 603–4
Ritschl, Albrecht, 451–52
Rode, Hinne, 651
Rutherford, Samuel, 675, 709–11

Sadoleto, Cardinal Jacopo, 126, 175, 201, 528n72, 595
Sanders, E. P., 542, 543–44
Sattler, Michael, 602, 688
Savonarola, Girolamo, 49, 683
Schaff, Philip, 715
Schleiermacher, Friedrich, 33, 354
Schmidt, Charles, 503
Schwenkfeld, Caspar, 341–42, 420, 623
Selderhuis, Herman, 221
Servetus, Michael, 127, 202, 212, 420, 621–22, 693–94
Simons, Menno, 342, 394, 396, 415–19
Simplicianus, 505
Skinner, Quentin, 684–85

Smalley, Beryl, 147
Smeeton, Donald Dean, 294
Socinus, Faustus, 211, 220, 423, 425, 444
Staupitz, Johann von, 427, 429
Steinmetz, David, 250n16, 500n211
Stendahl, Krister, 542
Storch, Nicholas, 555
Stott, John, 20
Sulzer, Simon, 122
Swarup, Paul, 19

Teresa of Avila, 214
Tetzel, John, 53, 113
Theodoret, 324, 336
Thiselton, Anthony, 394n2
Thomae, Marcus, 555
Thomas à Kempis, 426, 442
Thomas Aquinas, 198, 268n72, 442, 732
    commentaries of, 147
    on image of God, 283, 305–6
    on infused grace, 87–88
    on justification, 428, 514–16
    on predestination, 263
    on purgatory, 82–83
    on sacraments, 611, 612
    on Scripture, 150–51
    on threefold office of Christ, 353
    on transubstantiation, 646
    on the Trinity, 192–94, 202
    on union with Christ, 426
Thomas of Chobham, 78, 81
Thompson, Nicholas, 662
Tillich, Paul, 33
Tocqueville, Alexis de, 30
Tong, Stephen, 19
Torrance, T. F., 203, 290n14, 296, 308, 731, 732–33
Travers, Walter, 599–601
Trolliet, John, 501n215
Turretin, Francis, 358
Twisse, William, 375
Tyndale, William, 199–200, 288, 294–95

Urban II, Pope, 98
Ursinus, Zacharias, 354, 356–57, 358, 359, 374, 376, 380
Ussher, James, 354

Valla, Lorenzo, 105, 106
Vermigli, Peter Martyr, 122, 225, 370, 373, 376, 378, 380, 499n208, 666
    on bondage of the will, 501–7
    Christology of, 334–37, 356

on church and state, 690–91
on divine simplicity, 229–30
on general revelation, 227
on predestination, 267–70, 272n84
on resistance to tyranny, 695, 696
on union with Christ, 425, 435–36
Viret, Pierre, 298–300, 692

Walton, Robert, 591
Warfield, B. B., 16–17, 20, 234n84, 245n5,
    364, 403
Webster, John, 191
Weinandy, Thomas, 331n80
Wenger, Thomas L., 434n47
Westphal, Joachim, 331, 632, 634, 644, 669
Whitford, David M., 44n5
Whitgift, John, 133, 298n46, 599
Wilbur, E. M., 212
William of Auvergne, 78–79
William of Auxerre, 87
William of Ockham, 90, 93, 102, 106, 108,
    194, 452, 514–16
William of Orange, 708
Williams, George Huntston, 211–12, 342,
    419, 620, 688
Willis, David, 333, 338
Wishart, George, 134
Witherspoon, John, 716
Witte, John, Jr., 715, 716–17
Wright, N. T., 542–43

Wyclif, John, 44n3, 90, 102, 103, 104, 108,
    130, 294, 647, 682

Younan, Munib, 13

Zanchi, Girolamo, 210, 267, 272n84,
    424–25, 435–36, 438–41, 503
Zeigler, Clement, 342
Zwingli, Huldrych, 58n65, 115, 117–21,
    524
    on *alloiosis*, 317, 318–21
    on baptism, 609
    on biblical authority, 165–68
    Christology of, 341, 358, 359, 361
    on the church, 589–91
    on church and state, 689
    death of, 662, 689
    differences with Luther, 138
    on divine impassibility, 230–31
    ecclesiology of, 561–62
    Erastianism of, 687
    eschatology of, 729
    on the Holy Spirit, 394, 400–402
    on image of God, 294, 309
    on infant baptism, 623
    on Lord's Supper, 402, 643, 651, 653–61,
        667–68, 670
    as Nestorian, 321
    on predestination, 266–67
    on resistance to tyranny, 694, 696
    on veneration of saints, 228

Subject Index

absolute creation, 287
absolute necessity, 456n18, 473, 476
absolute power, 218, 220
accommodation
    Calvin on, 177–78, 225, 349, 365, 369,
       372
    Luther on, 223
Acts and Monuments (Foxe), 131
Adam, sin of, 292, 484–85
ad fontes, 47
adiaphora, 586
adoption, 207–9
affair of the placards, 124
affair of the sausages, 118–19
alien righteousness, 428–29, 432, 539,
    552–53, 561
allegorical interpretation, 292
alloiosis, 317, 318–21
already/not-yet, 721, 741–45
amillennialism, 731, 751
Anabaptists, 27, 120, 121, 175, 212, 398,
    468, 551, 574, 587
    apocalypticism of, 723–24
    on the ban, 419, 693
    on baptism, 609, 619, 620–24, 639
    Christology of, 340–43
    on the church, 601–4
    eschatology of, 729, 748, 753
    on Lord's Supper, 662
    martyrology of, 594n69
    rejection of *sola Scriptura* and *sola fide*,
      638n128
    on separation of church and state, 686,
      688
    on soul sleep, 745–48
analogy of Scripture, 159
anarchy, 703, 704
Anfechtungen, 727, 739
Anglicanism, 14, 414, 598–601

anhypostasia, 315, 321
anointing of the sick, 70
anthropomorphism, 225
Anthropomorphites, 225
Antichrist, 585, 721, 722, 726, 736–37,
    750–51
antinomianism, 202, 531, 556–57
anti-Trinitarianism, 190, 192, 200, 211–13
apocalypticism, 682, 723–24, 735, 748
apocryphal writings, 416
Apollinarianism, 374
Apology of the Augsburg Confession, 350,
    464, 470–71, 523, 639
Apostles' Creed, 197, 202, 370, 373, 399,
    549, 574, 580, 583, 670
Arianism, 95, 125, 189, 200, 212, 213
Arians, 194
Aristotelianism, 193, 194, 218, 646
Arminianism, 133, 446–47
assurance, 93, 260n44
    and baptism, 636–37
    and election, 279
    and penance, 90
Athanasian Creed, 200, 670
atonement, 370–72
    extent of, 274–76, 375–77
    as "fortunate"/"happy" exchange, 385,
      613
    necessity of, 377–78
    sufficiency of, 377, 378–80
    as victory, 380–84
Augsburg Confession, 115–16, 219, 252,
    306, 338, 350, 429, 464, 468–71, 532,
    580, 639, 660–62, 670
Augustinian renaissance, 452
autonomy, 29–30, 34
autopistos, 172, 173
autotheos, 203, 314

"Babylonian captivity" of the papacy, 101, 680
ban, Anabaptist practice of, 419, 693
baptism, 68, 398, 402, 408, 609–40
  as death and resurrection, 616
  as divine word of promise, 609, 617–18, 625, 627
  as human word of testimony, 609, 621, 627
  and Trinity, 208
baptismal deification, 622
baptismal regeneration, 617, 622, 628
beatific vision, 225–26
Belgic Confession, 270, 271, 302, 531, 562, 564–65, 635, 636, 670
Bible. *See* Scripture
biblicism, of anti-Trinitarianism, 212
bishop of Rome, 578
bondage of the will, 451–508
Bondage of the Will (Luther), 159, 247–50, 251, 253, 452–62
Book of Common Prayer, 131, 132, 135, 138, 180, 183, 410, 599, 600, 601
Book of Concord, 15, 123, 670
Books of Homilies, 50, 132, 180, 182

caesaropapism, 675, 678
calling, faithfulness to, 388
"Calvin against the Calvinists," 275–76
Calvin's First Catechism (1538), 489, 496
canon law, 99–100, 106
Canons of Dort, 274, 275
Cappadocians, 203, 323
carnal vs. spiritual warfare, 688
Catechism of the Council of Trent, 352
Catholic Reformation, 44n3, 137, 214, 394n4, 686. *See also* Counter-Reformation
"central dogma" thesis, 255, 276–78
chiliasm, 748–50
Christendom, 678
"Christian America" thesis, 714
Christian life
  discipline in, 562–63
  as pilgrimage, 741–43
Christology, 313, 328, 428. *See also* Jesus Christ
  and holiness, 558–61
church
  authority of, 179
  catholicity of, 550
  as community of believers, 400, 418–19, 684

  as community of faith, 400
  and Holy Spirit, 399–400
  as keeper of Scripture, 182
  as mixed body, 418–19
  as modern-day Israelites, 569
  no salvation outside, 591
  and Trinity, 208
  unity of, 589
  as visible and invisible, 408
church and state, 133, 138, 420, 585, 675–717
church architecture, 48
church councils, 95
church discipline, 125, 574, 582, 590, 592, 594, 597, 688, 692–94
church fathers
  on authority of the church, 93–96
  Cranmer on, 185
  on Lord's Supper, 644–45
  Luther's appeal to, 155
  Melanchthon on, 162
church government, 133
church militant, 591
Church of England, 14, 600, 706
church polity, 595–98
church triumphant, 591
civil government, 138
  Anabaptists on, 603–4
  Bullinger on, 592
  Zwingli on, 590–91
clerical celibacy, 114, 119, 595
clerical vestments, 132–33
Clericis laicos, 100
Clunia reformers, 97–98
coercion, 455, 488–89
comfort, from election, 259–60, 279
common grace, 407–8
communicatio idiomatum (communication of attributes), 313, 314–18, 321
  Beza on, 339
  Calvin on, 329–30
  Cranmer on, 415
  In Lutheranism, 322–28
  Zwingli on, 319
communion of saints, as "hidden church," 584
community, 33
Company of Pastors (Geneva), 126, 130
compulsion, 456–57
Concept of Cologne, 340
conciliarism, 108, 578n4, 682, 685
conciliar movement, 104–5

concupiscence, 306, 469

condemnation, 246n6

condign merit, 89–90, 92

Confession of Faith Used in the English Congregation at Geneva, 565

confessions and catechisms, 17, 35

confirmation, 68, 69

Confutation of the Augsburg Confession, 532–33

congruent merit, 89–90

Consensus Tigurinus, 122, 128, 337, 384, 632–33, 635, 643, 668

consequent hypothetical necessity (atonement), 377

consilia, 80

consistory, 597

Constantinople, 96–97, 105

constitutional argument (popular resistance), 703

contingency, 454–57, 464, 471n83, 472–73

conversion, 463n43

corporate-resistance view (political resistance), 704

Council for Promoting Christian Unity, 23

Council of Basel, 104

Council of Chalcedon, 95, 321, 359

Council of Constance, 104, 578n4, 579, 647, 680

Council of Constantinople, First (381), 95n72, 96

Council of Constantinople, Second (553), 315n13, 321, 329

Council of Constantinople, Third (680–681), 324

Council of Nicaea, 95n72

Council of Trent, 19, 22–23, 26, 46n10, 107n89, 112, 123, 137, 179, 243n1, 260n44, 306, 348, 378, 425, 442, 502, 533–36, 545, 612, 634, 635, 669

Counter-Reformation, 21, 44n3, 213–14, 585. *See also* Catholic Reformation

covenant, 120, 123, 163

  Calvin on, 691–92

  and resistance to tyranny, 675, 679–80, 702

  unity of, 624, 625

  Zwingli on, 689

covenantal nomism, 544

covenanters, 705–6

covenant membership, righteousness as, 543

covenant of redemption, 210

creation, 284

  and attributes of God, 287–89

  goodness of, 286

  and redemption, 284–85

  restoration of, 742

creationism (soul), 747

creation scientists, 293n20

Creator-creature distinction, 228–30, 402

creeds, Luther's appeal to, 155

cross, 386–89

Crusades, 98, 103, 680

curialism, 578n4, 680

"curious questions," 263n52

day of judgment, 738–39

deacons, 126, 596

Decades (Bullinger), 122, 168–69, 173, 298n46, 592, 668

Decalogue, 550, 554, 566, 573, 574

decree, 259, 276

  as hidden, 743–45

  order of distinct elements of, 273, 278

  and redemptive history, 740–41

"degrees of election," 257

deism, 289–90

depravity

  Calvin on, 484–91

  Melanchthon on, 465–68

descent into hell, 373–75, 382

desire, 455–56

determinism, 472, 483

Deus absconditus, 249

Deus revelatus, 249

Devil, 381–86, 457, 489, 736

dicta probanta, 154

Diet of Augsburg (1518), 113, 153

Diet of Augsburg (1530), 588, 589, 660

Diet of Worms, 114, 155–56

discipleship, 549, 550

disposition. See *habitus*

divine goodness, 230–31

divine impassibility, 218, 220, 230–31

divine names, 231–36

divine simplicity, 228–31

docetism, 657

doctrinal indifference, 14, 16, 18, 20

domestication of transcendence, 28

Donatism, 95, 148, 581, 611

"double eating" (Lord's Supper), 663

double grace. *See* twofold benefit of union with Christ

"double justification," 531n95

double predestination, 122, 246, 278, 476

dual-covenant theory (political resistance), 702, 703, 710
dualist spirituality (sacred and secular callings), 555–56
Dutch Calvinism, 708

early church. *See* church fathers
Eastern Empire, 96
Eastern Orthodoxy, 401, 537
East-West schism (1054), 98
ecclesia reformata, semper reformanda, 47, 48
Ecclesiastical Ordinances (Calvin, 1541), 126
ecclesiology
    and holiness, 561–63
    and sanctification, 567
Edict of Milan, 678
effectual call, 482, 491–500, 506
elders, 126, 596
election, 207, 243–45, 246, 498, 562
    comfort from, 259–60, 279
    and person and work of Christ, 263–64
election and reprobation, asymmetry between, 258, 259n40, 272, 278–79
Elizabethan Settlement, 551
Elohim, 210, 288
El Shaddai, 232–35
emotionalism, 31
English Civil War, 705–8
English Reformation, 130–34
enhypostasia, 315, 321
Enlightenment, 14, 28, 289–91
enthusiasm, 27–32, 555, 574
episcopal polity, 584, 601
Erastianism, 136, 138, 590, 675, 687
eschatology, 721–55
Eucharist, 72–73. *See also* Lord's Supper
Eutychianism, 321
"evangelical holiness," 566–67
evangelicalism, minimalism of, 14–16, 20, 26
evangelical rationalists, 420
Evangelical Reformed Churches of Christ (Nigeria), 14
"Evangelicals and Catholics Together," 22
evolution, 290–92
excessive curiosity, in doctrine of election, 256
excommunication, 592, 693
ex opere operantis, 89, 611
ex opere operato, 89, 443–44, 611, 614, 635
expiation, 384, 386

external penance, 91
extra Calvinisticum, 328–34, 338, 361–62
extreme unction, 68, 70, 73, 613–14

faith
    and baptism, 617, 629, 636
    of infants, 623, 626, 630
    and justification, 528–32, 613. See also *sola fide*
    and sacraments, 612–13
    and sanctification, 570
"faith formed by love," 85, 428, 521, 533, 553
"faith working by love," 525
fall of mankind, 285, 286
fatalism, 268, 472
fellowship, 16–17
fellowship with Christ, 433
filioque, 396, 409
final judgment, 722
final justification (Roman Catholicism), 443
"Finnish School" of Luther interpretation, 537, 540–42
First Blast of the Trumpet against the Monstrous Regiment of Women (Knox), 134–35
First Book of Discipline (Church of Scotland, 1560), 135
first-century Judaism, 543
First Helvetic Confession, 121, 134, 219, 663
flesh, 735
"flesh" and "Spirit," 467n62
forerunners, on church and state, 682–83
formal principle of the Reformation, 145, 185, 242, 722
Formula of Concord, 116–17, 251, 252–54, 301, 325–27, 432, 443n76, 463, 476–81, 541, 638–69, 670
Forty-Two Articles of Religion, 180, 410–15
fourfold exegesis, 152
Fourth Lateran Council, 70, 78, 81, 646
Franciscans, 682, 724
Frankish power, 97
free will
    Calvin on, 481–501
    in Formula of Concord, 476–81
    Luther and Erasmus debate on, 452–62
    Melanchthon on, 462–83
French Confession, 219, 270, 271, 301–2, 531, 635
fundamentalism, 15, 29

general gospel call, 482, 505–6
general revelation, 227
Geneva, 123–30, 138
    as center of Reformed faith, 129
    church government of, 596
Geneva Academy, 127, 128, 129
Geneva Catechism, 353–54, 363, 593, 687
Genevan Confession, 350n9
genus majestaticum, 316
genus tapeinoticon, 316
German Reformed churches, 708
"Gift of Salvation, The," 22
Global South, 14, 20
glorification, 560
glory of God, 565–66
Gnesio-Lutherans, 116–17, 337, 477
Gnostics, 28
God
    accommodation of, 223, 225, 231–32
    aseity of, 287–89
    essence of, 204, 323
    fatherhood of, 204–5, 206
    foreknowledge of, 454
    free mercy in eternal election, 256–57
    as gracious, 53
    incomprehensibility of, 222–23
    not a tyrant, 258
    not the cause of sin, 472
    persons of, 203–5
    sovereignty of, 118, 242, 411
godliness, 51, 171–72
good works, 92–93, 413, 563–67, 582
    and faith, 570
    and justification, 530, 531, 536
gospel
    at center of Reformation, 45
    vs. other gospels, 24
    as treasure of the church, 46
Gospel Coalition, 15
grace, 520–21, 527, 534–35, 539
    as sacramentally dispensed, 115
    "operating" and "cooperating," 493–94
Great Awakening, 31
"Great Commonplaces" (Cranmer), 184–85
Great Western Schism, 100–101, 103–5,
    578n4, 579, 680

habitus, 88, 91–92, 432
Habsburgs, 107
Heidelberg Catechism, 136, 138, 209, 270,
    271, 302–3, 354, 363–64, 367, 374,
    376, 531, 563, 565, 567, 570
Heidelberg Disputation, 113, 224n27, 386

hell, 373
heresy, 103, 693–94
hidden God, 740
historical faith, 402
historico-literal interpretation of Scripture,
    291–92, 293n20
holiness, 202, 549, 552, 557, 563, 566–67,
    568–69
    and Christology, 558–61
    and church discipline, 574
    and ecclesiology, 561–63
holy orders. *See* ordination: as sacrament
Holy Roman Empire, 97, 107, 136
Holy Spirit, 393–420
    and the church, 399–400
    as Giver of life, 198–99
    illumination of, 500
    indwelling of, 561
    as the Love of God, 192–93
    personhood and deity of, 420
    and sacraments, 398, 402, 404–6, 408–9,
    417
    and salvation, 398–99, 401–2, 411–14,
    417–18
    testimony of, 178–79, 404
    and the Word, 397, 400–401, 403–4,
    410–11, 416–17
Huguenots, 49n22, 136, 699–700, 705, 709
human immortality, 307–8
human rights, 715, 716–17
human tradition, 564–65
Hungary, 708
Hutterites, 603–4
hypostatic union, 313, 316, 321, 322, 336,
    338–39, 343, 428
    in Lutheranism, 322–25
    Reformed on, 328–34

iconoclasm, 49, 119
idolatry, 52, 135
ignis purgatorius, 78
image, and likeness, 283, 295–96
image of God, 291, 292, 293–302
    deforming of, 302–6
    and immortality, 307–8
    restoration of, 308–10
images and relics in the church, 119–20
immortality of the soul, 307–8
imperatives of God, 460–61
imputed righteousness, 429, 432, 522, 524,
    527–28, 535, 539, 540–41
incarnation, 432–34
incarnational union, 666

"in Christ," 424
individual election, 257
individualism, 156
indulgences, 80–85, 113, 552, 578
indulgentiae, 80
infant baptism, 120, 420, 620, 622–24,
    625–26, 629–30, 632
    rejection of, 415, 417, 638
inferior magistrates. *See* lesser magistrates
infralapsarianism, 246n6, 262, 270, 272,
    273–74
infused righteousness, 85–88, 432
inherent righteousness, 529
initial justification (Roman Catholicism),
    443
inner penance, 70
Institutes of the Christian Religion (Calvin),
    62n75, 173
    1536 edition (first), 124, 200, 202, 353,
        379, 382, 433–34, 483, 525, 630, 665
    1539 edition (second), 125, 352, 434, 483
    1559 edition (final), 127, 176, 178–79,
        202–9, 256, 354, 379, 382, 484, 490,
        526
intermediate state, 75–77, 722, 728
internal penance, 91
intrinsic righteousness, 541
invisible church, 584, 589, 591, 593, 603
invitations of God, 461
Islam, 96
Israel, general election of, 257

Jesuits, 129, 132, 137
Jesus Christ
    ascension of, 313, 320, 322, 325, 327,
        328, 334, 337, 415
    death and resurrection of, 25
    deity of, 16
    descent into hell, 373–75, 382
    as Head of the church, 590
    humiliation of, 326
    as King, 380–86
    as Mediator, 348–52
    obedience of, 25, 360–61, 406
    as Preacher, 369–70
    as Priest, 347, 370–80
    as Prophet, 363–70
    return of, 722, 726, 738–39, 744–45
    as second Adam, 292
    as Teacher, 365–68
    two natures of, 355–62
Joint Declaration on the Doctrine of Justifi-
    cation, 21–24, 537, 538–40

justification, 511–45
    Arminius on, 447
    as article of standing or falling church, 21,
        242, 395n5, 512
    consensus among Reformers on, 511–13
    distinct from sanctification, 423, 429,
        517, 530, 558, 570
    drives history to final goal, 725
    and ecclesiology, 543
    Finney on, 19
    as forensic, 523, 524, 541
    by love expressed through faith (Augus-
        tine), 85
    as "main hinge on which religion turns,"
        512–13
    and merit of grace, 88–89
    missing from NAE doctrinal statement,
        17–18
    Protestant–Roman Catholic dialogue on,
        21–24
    and redemptive history, 734
    and union with Christ, 428–29
justification by faith, 16, 115
    not a peculiarly Lutheran doctrine,
        241–42, 276
Justinian Code, 581, 621

Kampen Confession, 340
kenosis, 360, 361
keys of the kingdom, 582, 587, 594
kingdom of God, 733, 742–44
knowledge of God, 198, 226–27
    unmediated in beatific vision, 225–26

Lambeth Articles, 133
Large Catechism (Luther), 381, 399, 639,
    659
last days, 725–26
late-medieval period, biblical authority in,
    147–53
Lausanne Congress (Cape Town, 2010), 20
law
    first use of, 566
    and sanctification, 572
    third use of, 557, 566
law and gospel, 366, 460–62, 572–73,
    733–34
law-gospel dialectic, 163
lectio continua, 52, 57–58
legalism, 531
Leipzig Disputation, 146, 161
"Leipzig Proposal," 585
lesser magistrates, 675, 696–97, 701–2,
    703–4

letter vs. spirit, 28
liberal theology, 33
libertarian freedom, 458n21, 486
limbo, 82
limbus patrum, 373
limited atonement, 375, 376
literal interpretation, 152
Loci Communes (Melanchthon), 134, 163,
    462–64
    1521 edition, 194–95, 251, 327, 464–68,
        470, 472, 521, 650
    1543 edition, 196, 471–76, 481–82, 581
    1555 edition, 327
locus purgatorius, 78
Lollards, 294
Lord's Prayer, 550, 574
Lord's Supper, 68, 138, 402, 408, 643–71
    administered "under both kinds," 647n20
    frequency of, 126
    and union with Christ, 439–40
"lucid brevity" of Calvin, 125
Lutheran Reformation, 112–17
Lutherans
    on baptism, 638–40
    Christology of, 322–27
    on justification, 530–31
    on predestination, 247–54
    resistance theory of, 698–700
    on sanctification, 552–58
    on union with Christ, 428–33
Lutheran World Federation, 13, 21

Magdeburg Confession, 697, 698, 699–700
magisterial Reformation, 138, 419–20, 686
mainline Protestantism, 15
Malbronn Colloquy, 314, 337–38
Manichaeans, 147, 407, 472, 477
Marburg Colloquy, 115, 120, 314, 318, 320,
    321, 620, 626, 659–60
marks of the church, 562–63, 577, 580, 583,
    593–95
"Marprelate Tracts," 600
marriage
    Luther on, 556
    as a sacrament, 68, 72, 612, 613
martyrologies, 594
Mass, 48, 73, 378–80, 578
    as propitiatory sacrifice, 647
material principle of the Reformation, 185,
    722
means of grace, 562
mediator, 348–49

medieval theology
    on authority of Scripture, 147–53
    on the church, 604
    on justification, 513–17
    on Lord's Supper, 644–47
    on sacraments, 610–12, 613
    semi-Pelagianism of, 244
    on Trinity, 192–94
    on union with Christ, 426–28
meditation on the future life, 727–728, 743
Mennonites, 604
merit, and justification, 88–89
method of correlation (Tillich), 33
missionary activity of the church, 128, 596
Missouri Synod Lutheran Church, 14
modernism, 15
modern science, 290
monarchomachs, 700–705
monasticism, 137
monastic vows, 595
monergism, 246, 254, 262, 263n52, 451,
    474, 481, 508
    of Luther, 458–60
    of Vermigli, 507
Montbéliard Colloquy, 314, 338, 339
Münster, 602, 748
munus duplex, 363
munus triplex, 348, 351, 352–55, 357, 363
Muslims, 29, 98, 100
mystical union, 435, 436, 666
mystics, 28

National Association of Evangelicals, doctri-
    nal statement of, 17–18
national confessionalism, 714
nationalism, 680
National Presbyterian Church of Mexico, 14
naturalism, 289
natural law, 709–13
natural union, 435, 436
necessity, 454–57, 471n83, 472–73, 488–89
Nestorianism, 321, 326, 329
    of Beza, 339
    in Calvin, 330, 331n80
new birth, 18, 19
new creation, 495, 733
new heaven and new earth, 733
New Perspective on Paul, 538, 542–44
New World, 107
Nicene Creed, 219, 395, 581, 670
Niceno-Constantinopolitan Creed, 203
Ninety-Five Theses (Luther), 83, 107, 113,
    152, 578–79, 585

Nominalists, 305–6
norma normans, 411, 416
norma normata, 411

oaths, 688
offices in the church, 126, 596
oral confession, 71
orality, of the Word, 157n25
oral tradition, 171–72
ordained power, 218, 220
ordination, as sacrament, 68, 72, 73
original sin, 74, 466–67, 470
outer penance, 70–71

Palatinate, 708
papacy
    as the Antichrist, 721, 722, 736–37,
        750–51
    emergence of, 96–100
    infallibility, 108
    medieval challenges to, 100–103
    in need of reform, 107
    primacy of, 675, 678–79
Papal States, 97
"partakers of the divine nature," 439, 561
Particular Baptist Churches, 638
pastoral care, 237
pastors, 126, 587, 596
patriarchates, 96
Peace of Augsburg, 116, 136, 337, 699
Peasants' War, 114, 685, 735
Pelagianism, 19, 45n10, 241, 243, 244, 252,
        277, 306, 413, 466, 470, 474, 478,
        479, 484n139
penance, 48, 53–54, 68, 70–73, 612, 613
Pentecostalism, on continuing revelations, 34
permissive will of God, 268–70
persecution, 582, 594, 677
Philippists, 116, 337, 477
philosophical speculation, 194–95
Pietism, 14, 15, 28, 31
Poland, 708
political sovereignty, 703
political theology, 677
polity, 577
postmillennialism, 731
potentia absoluta, 218
potentia ordinata, 218
praecepta, 80
prayer
    for the dead, 74
    to saints, 74–75, 198, 350

preaching, 48–49
    Calvin on, 51, 54–55, 57–58, 369–70
    decline in England, 50
    Luther on, 55, 114, 157, 369
    as mark of the church, 580, 582
    as means of grace, 52, 54
predestination, 122, 127, 241–46, 411, 503,
        569
    and eschatology, 744
    in Lutheranism, 247, 254
    not a peculiarly Reformed doctrine,
        241–42, 276, 278
    among Reformed, 254–77
    in Reformed confessions, 270–72
premillennialism, 731
Presbyterian Church in America, 14
Presbyterian Church in Nigeria, 14
Presbyterians, 14, 135–36, 705–6
preterition, 246n6
prevenient grace, 491–92
priesthood of all believers, 587
principled pluralism, 714
printing press, 120–21
private masses, 73
promise and fulfillment, 744
proof texts, 154
proper righteousness, 552–53
Prophezei (school of the prophets), 168
propitiation, 372, 384
"Protestantism without the Reformation," 18
providence, 118, 245, 263, 266–67, 740
Psalms, singing of, 52
publicists, 681
punishment for sin, 91
purgatory, 53, 67, 75–80, 106, 722, 729,
        737
Puritans, 132–33, 135, 551, 598–99, 601,
        706

Quadriga, 152

Racovian Catechism, 212–13, 425, 444–45
radical Reformation, 175, 420, 468n70
    and doctrine of God, 220
    eschatology of, 723–25
    on the Trinity, 211–12
rationalism, of anti-Trinitarians, 212–13
reason, 198
reconciliation, 371
Redeemer, 348, 349, 364, 371
redemption, 210, 284–85
redemptive history, 732–33, 740–41

Reformation
    in the churches, 35
    as "obedient rebels," 551, 574
    opposition to speculation, 194–95
    recovery of the sermon, 48–51
    as rediscovery, 47
    as renaissance of Paulinism, 424
    as theological movement, 44–45
    variety within, 44n3, 112, 138
Reformed
    Christology of, 328–39
    on predestination and election, 254–77
    on sanctification, 558–67
    on union with Christ, 433–47
reformed catholicity, 550
Reformed confessions
    on baptism, 635–38
    on image of God, 301–2
    on justification, 531–32
    on Lord's Supper, 670
    on predestination, 270–72
    on union with Christ, 441n72
    unity and diversity of, 138–39
regeneration, 434n46, 529–30, 531
Regensburg, 533, 534, 539–40
regulative principle of worship, 59–60, 135
religious disestablishment, 708
reprobation, 246, 263, 274, 278
    Bullinger on, 264–65
    and justice of God, 258
    in Reformed confessions, 272
    Vermigli on, 269–70
republicanism, 689–90, 691–92
resistance to tyranny, 675, 679–80, 685,
    689, 694–709
resurrection, 722, 738–39, 741, 743
Revelation, canonicity of, 723, 729
revival movements, 14
righteousness, as covenant membership, 543
righteousness of God, 342, 518–19. *See also*
    alien righteousness; imputed righteous-
    ness
Roman Catholic Church
    on church authority, 67
    on church government, 578–79
    on justification, 431–32, 443–44, 532–37
    resistance theories, 708–9
    on union with Christ, 441–44
Romanticism, 31

Sabbatarianism, 133
Sabellianism, 189, 200
sacramental system, 73

sacramental union, 628, 631, 659, 663
sacraments, 562
    Calvin on, 208
    and Holy Spirit, 398, 402, 404–6, 408–9,
    417
    in late-medieval theology, 67
    as mark of the church, 580, 582
    missing from NAE doctrinal statement, 17
    numbering seven, 67, 68
    Protestant disagreement over, 610
sacra pagina, 147
Saint Bartholomew's Day Massacre, 136,
    699, 701, 704
Saint Pierre's (Geneva), 51–52
saints, prayer to, 74–75, 198, 350
salvation, and Holy Spirit, 398–99, 401–2,
    411–14, 417–18
sanctification, 434n46, 549–74
Satan, loosing of, 736
sausages. *See* affair of the sausages
saving faith, 402
Schleitheim Articles, 340, 602, 688
schola Augustiniana moderna, 452
scholasticism, of Vermigli, 268–69
Schweinfurt Confession, 662
Scots Confession, 135, 219–20, 270, 271,
    300–301, 307, 565, 635–36, 670
Scottish National Covenant, 706
Scottish Reformation, 134–36
Scripture. See also *sola Scriptura*
    authority of, 145–55, 164–65, 171–72,
    174–76, 180, 184–85
    as center and content of worship, 58–60
    clarity of, 160, 162, 166, 173, 174
    as own interpreter, 159
    self-authentication of, 172, 178–79, 404
    as spectacles, 54
    sufficiency of, 19, 32, 171
    and tradition, 34, 107, 109
    as Word of God, 157, 167, 169–70,
    182–85
secondary creation, 287
Second Book of Discipline (Church of Scot-
    land, 1578), 135
second creation. *See* new creation
Second Helvetic Confession, 54, 123,
    261–66, 270, 424, 531, 591, 592,
    636–37, 670
Second London Baptist Confession, 638
secularism, 289
"seed of religion," 176–77
semi-Augustinianism, 460, 496

semi-Pelagianism, 241, 243, 244, 277, 460, 476, 478, 479, 491, 493–94
semirealized eschatology, 721, 741
sermon, as center of worship, 586
sign and thing signified, 625, 627–29, 631–33, 636, 638, 666
simul justus et peccator, 522, 538n132
sin. *See also* depravity
　guilt and punishment of, 91
　mortal and venial, 73, 79, 81
"Sixty-Seven Articles" (Zwingli), 561–62
Smalcald Articles, 303–4, 397, 579, 670, 736
Smalcald League, 116, 661–62, 698
Smalcald War, 585
Small Catechism (Luther), 199, 381, 399, 525, 639, 659
social contract, 679
social covenantal movements, 681–82
Socinianism, 212–13, 444–46
Socinians, 425, 442
sola fide, 25–26, 29, 46, 48, 53, 56, 185, 348, 413, 469, 525, 722
　and baptism, 638
　and sanctification, 558, 570
　and union with Christ, 443–44
sola gratia, 29, 46, 53, 56, 243–44, 469, 479, 500–501, 508
　and sanctification, 569
sola Scriptura, 27–34, 47n16, 48, 55–56, 68, 104, 113, 119, 145, 185–86
　and bondage of the will, 452
　Cranmer on, 181
　and doctrine of God, 195–96
　Luther on, 154–61
　and sanctification, 571–72
　Zwingli on, 168
solas of the Reformation, 20–21
soli Deo gloria, 500–501
solus Christus, 24–25, 29, 33, 34, 53, 56, 348, 469, 724
　and sanctification, 568–69
Son
　accomplishes redemption, 205
　emptying of, 328
　as "true God of true God," 203
sonship, 205, 206
soul, 298, 747
soul sleep, 729, 737–38, 745–48
special providence, predestination as, 245, 263
sphere sovereignty, 675, 687, 713

Spirit, application of redemption, 205–6
Spirituali, 214
Spiritualists, 420, 587
spirituality, from within, 32–33
spiritual union, 435, 436, 666–67
state churches, 108
"statements of faith," 17
Stoicism, 472, 473, 477
Strasbourg, 124, 125, 588
substance and accidents, 646
substitutionary atonement, 19, 384
suffering, 388–89, 582
"superadded gift," 305–6
supralapsarianism, 246n6, 273–74, 375
Swabian League, 685
Swiss Brethren Confession of Hesse, 340
Swiss Reformation, 117–23
synergism, 246, 451, 458–60, 479, 493, 495, 497, 501
　of Melanchthon, 251–52, 254
Synod of Dort, 146, 273
systematic theologies, of the Reformers, 62n75

teachers (office in the church), 126, 596
telos, of redemptive history, 741, 743
Temple de Paradis (painting), 50–51
Tetrapolitan Confession, 228, 562, 588, 660–61
theistic evolution, 292
theocracy, 679
theodidacti (taught by God), 167
theological education, Calvin on, 127
theology of glory, 113, 224n27, 386–88
theology of the cross, 113, 224n27, 347, 386–89, 588
theonomy, 714
third use of the law, 557
Thirty-Nine Articles of Religion, 15, 132, 133, 180, 302–3, 707
"This is my body," 154, 402, 643, 644, 652–59, 666
threefold office. See *munus triplex*
Three Forms of Unity, 15
tradition, and Scripture, 34, 107, 109
transcendence, domestication of, 28
transubstantiation, 69–70, 120, 213, 326, 415, 645–47, 649
Trinity, 16, 189–215, 395, 420
　Calvin on, 200–209, 287n8
　Counter-Reformation on, 213–14
　Luther on, 194–99
　in Reformed tradition, 209–10

Socinian denial of, 212–13, 445
Tyndale on, 199–200
trust, 521
truth, 554
two ages, 734–35
twofold benefit of union with Christ, 434, 436, 447, 530, 559–60
two kinds of righteousness, 530
two kingdoms, 597, 684–85, 713, 729–30, 733
tyrannicide, 704, 713. *See also* resistance to tyranny

ubiquity of Christ's humanity, 319, 325, 336–37, 338, 362, 398, 415, 657–58
Unam sanctam, 100
union with Christ, 198, 332, 409, 423–48, 666
   Finnish school on, 541
   and Lord's Supper, 439–40
   and proclamation of God's Word, 55
universal church, 597
universal human dignity (political resistance), 704
universe, as dazzling theatre of God's glory, 177

Variata of the Augsburg Confession, 116, 128, 138
Vatican II, 21
veneration of saints, 228
vertical and horizontal realms (Luther), 584
vestments, 132–33
via antiqua, 514–15, 518–19
via moderna, 452, 514, 517–18, 534
Victorines, 149–50, 192
violent necessity, 489
visible church, 590, 591–92, 593–94, 603
vocation, 500n211, 555–56
voluntary necessity, 489
voluntas beneplaciti, 224
voluntas signi, 224
votive mass, 73

Waldensians, 83
Wars of Religion, 697, 699, 702

Waterlander Confession, 340–41
Wesleyan quadrangle, 33
Western Christendom, 97
Westminster Assembly, 273, 707
   Scottish delegates to, 136
Westminster Confession of Faith, 354, 372, 637, 707–8
Westminster Larger Catechism, 354, 364
Westminster Shorter Catechism, 354, 364, 566
Westminster Standards, 15, 274
"Whig history," 551
will of good pleasure, 224
will of the sign, 224
Wisconsin Synod Lutheran Church, 14
Wittenberg Concord, 643, 664–65, 668
Word
   at center of church's life, 604
   as incarnate, 158
   as inscripturated, 158
   internal vs. external, 420
   as living and active, 572
   as preached, 158
Word and sacrament, 440–41
word and sign, 649
Word and Spirit, 52, 175, 397, 400–401, 403–4, 410–11, 416–17, 730
works of supererogation, 83–84
works righteousness, 543
World Council of Churches, 13
worship
   centrality of the Word in, 59–60
   in English Reformation, 132
   Luther on, 586
   in Scottish Reformation, 135
wrath of God, 372, 386, 727, 737, 739

Yahweh, 234–35, 288

Zurich, 118, 168, 261, 589, 692
Zurich Consensus. *See* Consensus Tigurinus
Zwickau Prophets, 555, 620, 735
Zwinglians, 128, 468

Scripture Index

Genesis
book of..............283, 284, 291n17,
292, 305, 457n18
1.....................746
1–11 ....284, 291
1:1 284
1:26 ....287, 287n8, 295, 297,
299
1:28 72
2:7 ....298, 747n90
3 285
3:7 304
3:15 285
6 225
6:3 466
6:5 467
6:5–6 222
6:6 225
8:21 478
14:18 ....380n143
15:16 ....464n49
17:1 232
19 158
27:27 207

Exodus
3:14 ....232, 233, 234
3:15 235
6:3 234
7:3 472
12:11 655
29:7 355
31:2 408
33:3 304
33:19 ....505n228
35:30 408

Numbers
6:24–26 59

Deuteronomy
5:5 348
17:15 710
18:18 363
29:29 366
30 461
30:15 461
30:19 461

Joshua
1:8 710
1:9 710

Judges
8 691

1 Samuel
2:25 ....464n49
2:26 ....464n49
3:9 293
10:1 355
16:13 355

1 Kings
12:15 ....464n49

2 Chronicles
31:21 710
32:32 710

Job
book of.............291n17
4:19 307
10:8 301

Psalms
book of.............183, 235, 291n17
2:1–6 382
2:7 351
8 283

21:5 223
23 . . . . .232, 236
45 156
48:15 . . . . .307n86
51:5 . . . . .304, 467
89:3 351
94:9 . . . . .227, 227n50
95:8 479
100:3 495
102:18 163
110 . . . . .742, 748
111:4 235
116:15 737
119 . . . . .557, 557n18, 566
124:8 59
139 . . . . .300, 317

Proverbs
14:12 464
14:27 464
16:4 . . . . .464, 464n49
16:9 . . . . .464n49
16:11–12 464
16:33 464
20:24 . . . . .464, 464n49

Ecclesiastes
9:1 464

Isaiah
book of 498
6:9 . . . . .505n228
7:14 329
26:20 737
42:1 361
46:10 . . . . .455n14
52:13–15 383
53:12 383
53:13 . . . . .368n93
54:13 499
57:1–2 737
61:1 355
63:17 . . . . .496n197

Jeremiah
10:23 . . . . .464n49
17:9 466
32:39–40 496

Ezekiel
book of 723
11:19–20 497
17:19 . . . . .700n131

36 495
36:26 496
36:27 497

Daniel
book of 723, 745
7:25 . . . . .745n82
9:27 750

Amos
book of 498

Jonah
book of 372

Habakkuk
2:4 93
2:20 . . . . .455n14

Zechariah
10:6 468

Malachi
2:1–9 696

Matthew
book of 295
1:23 329
5–7 364
5:9–10 205
5:34–35 688
6:10 676
6:21 728
7:18 471
8:19 364
10:29 . . . . .464n49
11:25–27 . . . . .505n228
11:27 365
12:28 361
13:11 . . . . .505n228
16:18 35
16:19 . . . . .71, 679
17 149
18 . . . . .603, 693
18:10 622
18:11 371
18:15–17 . . . . .590, 595
18:15–18 419
18:17 692
19:14 630
21:11 364
22:14 . . . . .455n14, 498
22:21 676

23:8 364
23:37. . . . . .506n231
24:22. 734
24:29. . . . . .744n80
24:36. . . . . .745n81
25:1–13 74
25:41. 749
25:46. 749
26:26. . . . . .154–55, 644, 667n133
26:28. 352
27:46. 359
28:19. . . . . .615, 622

Mark
2:3–12. 618
4:38 364
9:35 316
10:38 10 74
13:32. 366
14:36. 361
16:16. 639

Luke
1:15 631
2:1 . . . . .95n73
4:18 364
4:18–19 355
10:16. 369
11:18–21 457
12:7 464
12:32. 35
13:24. 264
22:20. 356
23:34. 359
24:27. . . . . .159, 496n197
24:45. . . . . .496n197

John
book of. 467, 497
1:1 56
1:1–3 284
1:29 330
3 . . . . .506, 507
3:2 364
3:5 . . . . .505, 630
3:6 467
3:8 506
3:16 . . . . .559n19
3:27 506
4:24 52
4:25 363
5 159

5:21–23 330
5:39 159
6 . . . . .319, 653, 654, 657
6:14 364
6:37 506
6:44 . . . . .467, 498, 499, 504, 505, 506
6:44–45 . . . . .496n197
6:45 497
6:46 505
6:56 429
6:63 . . . . .320, 654, 654n68
8:12 330
8:36 468
9:5 330
10 505
10:3 580
10:11. 330
10:14. 583
10:28. . . . . .505, 583
10:28–29 248
11:28. 364
12:31. . . . . .742n73
13–17 364
13:13. 364
13:18. . . . . .455n14
13:31. . . . . .742n72
14:8 387
14:9 . . . . .226, 387
15:1 330
15:1–11 442
15:5 479
15:13. . . . . .378n133
16:13. . . . . .496n197
16:33. 35
17:4 352
17:21. 309
19:30. 380
20:30–31 171

Acts
1:7 . . . . .749n98
2:22 361
3:22 364
5:29 676
10 629
10:38. 361
11:18. . . . . .496n197
15 94
16:14. . . . . .479, 506
17:2 155
20:28. 357

Romans
book of.............154, 206, 291n17,
                 292, 467
1:3–4..............355
1:16...............479
1:17...............93
1:19...............227, 227n50
1:20...............387
1:21...............195
3:10–11............501
3:20...............460
3:24...............86n43, 207
3:31...............86n45
4..................237
4:5................523
4:11–12............623
4:17...............237
4:25...............360, 753
5..................283, 466
5:5................192
5:11...............303
5:12...............304
5:20...............86n44
6:9................360
6:9–10.............734
6:12...............310
7:23...............556
8..................467, 741
8:5................466
8:6................485
8:7................466, 479, 485
8:11...............359
8:15...............206
8:17...............206n51, 208n58
8:23...............741n70
8:29...............406
8:34...............350
9..................250, 250n16, 251n18,
                 464, 504
9–11...............257, 258
9:15...............505n228
9:16...............479, 507
9:18...............455n14
9:22...............455n14
10:17..............29
11.................464
11:17..............406
11:34..............496n197
11:36..............464n49
12:1...............587n40
13:1–7.............676, 701
13:3–4.............676

1 Corinthians
book of............75
1:9................559n21
1:20...............387
1:21...............195
1:23...............389
1:30...............201, 559, 559n23, 568
2:10–16............496n197
2:12–13............167
2:14...............252, 470, 478
3:7................479
3:11–15............75
7:1–2..............72
7:6................72
9:16...............479
10.................569
10:3...............654
10:31..............566
11:23..............367
15.................283
15:3–8.............367
15:12ff............749
15:22..............467
15:25–28...........94
15:27..............331

2 Corinthians
1:20...............560
1:20–22............753
2:16...............498
3..................27
3:5................479, 495
3:17...............487n152
3:18...............297, 308, 553
7:10...............496n197

Galatians
book of............467, 541
1:11–12............367
2:20...............375
3:2ff..............475
3:13...............356, 382, 384
3:27...............406
4:6................206, 726
5:6................85
6:14...............388

Ephesians
1..................250
1:4................206n52
1:5–6..............207
1:11...............464
1:14...............747n91

2 495
2:3 . . . . .372, 466, 467
2:5 479
2:10 . . . . .496n197
4:3–6 . . . . .602, 640
4:15 406
4:15–16 436
4:22–28 309
4:24 . . . . .297, 305
5:30 439
5:31–32 72
6:12 688

Philippians
2:5–6 552
2:6 . . . . .315, 360
2:6–7 316
2:7 . . . . .360n59

Colossians
2:11–12 623
2:15 383
3:10 . . . . .297, 305
3:16 163

1 Thessalonians
4:17 . . . . .749, 749n100

2 Thessalonians
book of 751
2:2–12 . . . . .751n105
2:4 750
2:7 . . . . .750n104

1 Timothy
2 376
2:4 376
2:5 . . . . .349, 350, 350n9
4:13 163
6:4 20
6:15–16 308

2 Timothy
2:25 507
2:25–26 . . . . .496n197
2:26 457
3:16–17 170

Titus
3:5 208

Hebrews
1:2 365

2:14 435
2:14–18 385
3:1–2 363
3:2 . . . . .351, 351n14, 351n18
4:12 572
4:14 . . . . .354n29
4:15 359
5:4 . . . . .351, 351n14
6:4–6 . . . . .496n197
8:6 349
9–10 380
9:15 349
10:10 379
11 522
11:1 521
11:3 284
11:6 471
12:24 349
13:15–16 . . . . .587n40

James
5:14–15 70
5:16 71

1 Peter
2:5 . . . . .587n40
2:9 . . . . .587n40
2:13–25 676
2:15 . . . . .700n131
2:21 553
3:19 373
5:5 458

2 Peter
1:4 . . . . .424, 433, 439, 561

1 John
2 376
2:2 . . . . .376, 376n128
2:27 167
3:2 . . . . .208n57

Revelation
book of 723, 745
5:6 359
11:15 676
20 . . . . .415n87, 731, 735,
750, 751
20:4 749
20:6 750
20:7–10 736
22:20 739